MW00813824

TEUTONIC MYTHOLOGY.

JACOB GRIMM.

TEUTONIC MYTHOLOGY

BY

JACOB GRIMM.

TRANSLATED FROM THE FOURTH EDITION.

WITH

NOTES AND APPENDIX

BY

JAMES STEVEN STALLYBRASS.

VOL. II.

LONDON: GEORGE BELL & SONS, YORK STREET,
COVENT GARDEN.
1883.

KF14796

Butler & Tanner,
The Selwood Printing Works,
Frome, and London.

CONTENTS.

VOL. II.

CHAPTER XVII.

WIGHTS AND ELVES.

Apart from deified and semi-divine natures there stands a whole order of other beings distinguished mainly by the fact that, while those have issued from men or seek human fellowship, these form a separate community, one might say a kingdom of their own, and are only induced by accident or stress of circumstances to have dealings with men. They have in them some admixture of the superhuman, which approximates them to gods; they have power to hurt man and to help him, at the same time they stand in awe of him, being no match for him in bodily strength. Their figure is much below the stature of man, or else mis-shapen. They almost all have the faculty of making themselves invisible.[1] And here again the females are of a broader and nobler cast, with attributes resembling those of goddesses and wise-women; the male spirits are more distinctly marked off, both from gods and from heroes.[2]

The two most general designations for them form the title of this chapter; they are what we should call *spirits* nowadays. But the word *spirit* (geist, ghost),[3] like the Greek δαίμων, is too comprehensive; it would include, for instance, the half-goddesses discussed in the preceding chapter. The Lat. *genius* would more nearly hit the mark (see Suppl.).

The term *wiht* seems remarkable in more than one respect, for its variable gender and for the abstract meanings developed from

---

[1] But so have the gods (p. 325), goddesses (p. 268) and wise-women (p. 419).

[2] Celtic tradition, which runs particularly rich on this subject, I draw from the following works: Fairy Legends and Traditions of the South of Ireland, by Crofton Croker, Lond. 1825; 2nd ed., parts 1, 2, 3, Lond. 1828. The Fairy Mythology, by Th. Keightley, vols. 1, 2, Lond. 1828. Barzas-Breiz, chants populaires de la Bretagne, par Th. de la Villemarqué, 2e éd., 2 vol., Paris 1840.

[3] OHG. *keist*, AS. *gâst*, OS. *gêst* (see root in Gramm. 2, 46); Goth. *ahma*, OHG. *âtum* for ahadum, conn. with Goth. aha (mens), ahjan (meminisse, cogitare), as *man* (homo), *manniska*, and *manni*, *minni* belong to munan, minnen (pp. 59. 344. 433).

it. The Gothic *vaíhts*, gen. *vaíhtáis*, is feminine, and Ulphilas hardly ever uses it in a concrete sense ; in Luke 1, 1 he translates by it πρᾶγμα, and much oftener, when combined with a negative, οὐδέν (Gramm. 3, 8. 734). This, however, does not exclude the possibility of *vaíhts* having at other times denoted to the Goths a spirit regarded as female; and in 1 Thess. 5, 22 the sentence ἀπὸ παντὸς εἴδους πονηροῦ ἀπέχεσθε is rendered: af allamma vaíhtê ubiláizô afhabáiþ izvis, where the Vulg. has : ab omni specie mala abstinete vos ; the use of the pl. ' vaíhteis ubilôs ' of itself suggests the notion of spirits. The other Teutonic tongues equally use the word to intensify and make a substantive of the negative, and even let it swallow up at last the proper particle of negation ;[1] but in all of them it retains its personal meaning too. The OHG. writers waver between the neut. and masc.; the Gothic fem. is unknown to them. Otfried has a neut. *wiht*, with the collective pl. *wihtir*,[2] and likewise a neut. pl. *wihti*, which implies a sing. wihti; thus, armu wihtir, iv. 6, 23 ; armu wihti, ii. 16, 117; krumbu wihti, iii. 9, 5 ; meaning ' poor, crooked creatures,' so that *wiht* (derivable from wîhan facere, creare) seems altogether synonymous with being, creature, person, and can be used of men or spirits : ' in demo mere sint wunderlîchin wihtir, diu heizent sirenae,' Hoffm. Fundgr. 19, 17. In MHG. sometimes neut. : unreinez *wiht*, Diut. 1, 13 ; Athis H. 28 ; trügehaftez *wiht*, Barl. 367, 11 ; vil tumbez *wiht*, 11, 21; sometimes masc. : bœser *wiht*, Barl. 220, 15 ; unrehter *bœsewiht*, MS. 2, 147ᵃ, Geo. 3508 ; kleiner *wiht*, Altd. bl. 1, 254; der *wiht*, Geo. 3513-36; der tumbe *wiht*, Fragm. 42ᵃ; and often of indeterminable gender: bœse *wiht*, Trist. 8417 ; helle *wiht*, Geo. 3531 ; but either way as much applicable to men as to spirits. Ghostly wights are the ' minuti dii ' of the Romans (Plaut. Casina, ii. 5, 24). In Mod. Germ. we make *wicht* masc., and use it slightingly of a pitiful hapless being, fellow, often with a qualifying epithet : ' elender wicht, bösewicht (villain).' If the diminutive form be added, which intensifies the notion of littleness, it can only be used of spirits : *wichtlein, wichtelmann* ;[3]

---

[1] Aught = â-wiht, any wight or whit ; naught = n'â-wiht, no wight, no whit.—TRANS.

[2] So : thiu diufilir, iii. 14, 58, by the side of ther diufal, iii. 14, 108.

[3] In Hesse *wichtelmänner* is the expression in vogue, except on the Diemel in Saxon Hesse, where they say ' gute holden.'

MHG. diu *wihtel*,[1] MS. 1, 157ᵃ; bœsez *wihtel*, Elfenm. cxviii.; kleinez *wihtelin*, Ls. 1, 378, 380, Wolfdietr. 788, 799; OHG. *wihtelin* penates; *wihtelen* vel helbe (*i.e.* elbe), lemures, dæmones, Gl. Florian. The *dernea wihti*, occulti genii, in Hel. 31, 20. 92, 2 are deceitful demonic beings, as 'thie derno' 164, 19 means the devil himself; *lêtha wihti*, 76, 15; *wrêda wihti* 76, 1. In Lower Saxony *wicht* is said, quite in a good sense, of little children: in the Münster country 'dat *wicht*' holds especially of girls, about Osnabrück the sing. *wicht* only of girls, the pl. *wichter* of girls and boys; 'innocent *wichte*' are spoken of in Sastrow, 1, 351. The Mid. Nethl. has a neut. *wicht* like the H. German: quade *wicht*, clene *wicht* (child). Huyd. op St. 3, 6. 370; arem *wiht*, Reinh. 1027; so the Mod. Dutch *wicht*, pl. *wichteren*: arm wicht, aardig wicht, in a kindly sense. The AS. language agrees with the Gothic as to the fem. gender: *wiht*, gen. wihte, nom. pl. wihta; later *wuht*, wuhte, wuhta; *seo wiht*, Cod. Exon. 418, 8. 419, 3. 5. 420, 4. 10. The meaning can be either concrete: yfel *wiht* (phantasma), leás *wiht* (diabolus), Cædm. 310, 16; *sæwiht* (animal marinum), Beda, 1, 1; or entirely abstract=thing, affair. The Engl. *wight* has the sense of our wicht. The ON. *vætt* and *vættr*, which are likewise fem., have preserved in its integrity the notion of a demonic spiritual being (Sæm. 145ᵃ): allar *vættir*, genii quicunque, Sæm. 93ᵇ; hollar *vættir*, genii benigni, Sæm. 240ᵇ; *ragvættir* or *meinvættir*, genii noxii,[2] *landvættir*, genii tutelares, Forum. sög. 3, 105. Isl. sög. 1, 198, etc. In the Färöes they say: 'feår tû têar til *mainvittis* (go to the devil)!' Lyngbye, p. 548. The Danish *vette* is a female spirit, a wood-nymph, *meinvette* an evil spirit,

---

[1] Swer weiz und doch niht wizzen wil, Whoso knows, yet will not know,
der slæt sich mit sin selbes hant; Smites himself with his own hand;
des wisheit aht ich zeime *spil*, His wisdom I value no more than a play
daz man *diu wihtel* hât genannt: That they call 'the little wights':
er lât uns schouwen wunders vil, He lets us witness much of wonder,
der ir dâ waltet. Who governs them.

The passage shows that in the 13th cent. there was a kind of *puppet-show* in which ghostly beings were set before the eyes of spectators. 'Der ir waltet,' he that wields them, means the showman who puts the figures in motion. A full confirmation in the Wachtelmäre, line 40: 'rihtet zu *mit den snüeren* (strings) die tatermanne!' Another passage on the *wihtel-spil* in Haupt's Zeitschr. 2, 60: 'spilt mit dem *wihtelin* ûf dem tisch umb guoten win.'

[2] Biörn supposes a masc. (fem.?) *meinvattr* and a neut. *meinvætti*; no doubt *mein* is noxa, malum; nevertheless I call attention to the Zendic *mainyus*, dæmon, and agramainyus, dæmon malus.

Thiele 3, 98. The Swedish tongue, in addition to *vätt* (genius) and a synonymous neut. *vättr*, has a *wikt* formed after the German, Ihre, p. 1075. Neither is the abstract sense wanting in any of these dialects.

This transition of the meaning of *wight* into that of thing on the one hand, and of devil on the other, agrees with some other phenomena of language. We also address little children as 'thing,' and the child in the märchen (No. 105) cries to the lizard: '*ding*, eat the crumbs too!' Wicht, ding, wint, teufel, vâlant (Gramm. 3, 734. 736) all help to clinch a denial. O. French *males choses*, mali genii, Ren. 30085. Mid. Latin *bonæ res* = boni genii, Vinc. Bellov. iii. 3, 27 (see Suppl.).

We at once perceive a more decided colouring in the OHG. and MHG. *alp* (genius), AS. *œlf*, ON. *âlfr*; a Goth. *albs* may safely be conjectured. Together with this masc., the OHG. may also have had a neut. *alp*, pl. elpir, as we know the MHG. had a pl. *elber*; and from the MHG. dat. fem. *elbe* (MS. 1, 50ᵇ) we must certainly infer a nom. diu *elbe*, OHG. *alpia*, elpia, Goth. *albi*, gen. albjôs, for otherwise such a derivative could not occur. Formed by a still commoner suffix, there was no doubt an OHG. *elpinna*, MHG. *elbinne*, the form selected by Albrecht of Halberstadt, and still appearing in his poem as remodelled by Wikram;[1] AS. *elfen*, gen. elfenne. Of the nom. pl. masc. I can only feel sure in the ON., where it is *âlfar*, and would imply a Goth. albôs, OHG. alpâ, MHG. albe, AS. ælfas; on the other hand an OHG. *elpi* (Goth. albeis) is suggested by the MHG. pl. *elbe* (Amgb. 2ᵇ, unless this comes from the fem. elbe above) and by the AS. pl. *ylfe*, gen. pl. *ylfa* (Beow. 223).[2] The Engl. forms

---

[1] Wikram 1, 9. 6, 9 (ed. 1631, p. 11ᵃ 199ᵇ). The first passage, in all the editions I have compared (ed. 1545, p. 8ᵃ), has a faulty reading: 'auch viel *ewinnen* und *freyen*,' rhyming with '*zweyen*.' Albrecht surely wrote 'vil *elbinnen* und *feien*.' I can make nothing of 'freien' but at best a very daring allusion to Frigg and Frea (p. 301); and 'froie' = fräulein, as the weasel is called in Reinh. clxxii., can have nothing to say here.

[2] Taking AS. *y* [as a modified *a*, *æ*, *ea*,] as in yldra, ylfet, yrfe, OHG. eldiro, elpiz, erpi. At the same time, as *y* can also be a modified *o* (orf, yrfe = pecus), or a modified *u* (wulf, wylfen), I will not pass over a MHG. *ulf*, pl. *ülve*, which seems to mean much the same as *alp*, and may be akin to an AS. *ylf*: 'von den *ülven* entbunden werden,' MS. 1, 81ᵃ; '*ülfheit* ein suht ob allen sühten,' MS. 2, 135ᵃ; 'der *sich ülfet* in der jugent,' Helbl. 2, 426; and conf. the *ôlp* quoted from H. Sachs. Shakspeare occasionally couples elves and goblins with similar beings called *ouphes* (Nares sub v.). It speaks for the identity of the two forms, that one Swedish folk-song (Arwidsson 2, 278) has *Ulfver* where another (2, 276) has *Elfver*.

elf, elves, the Swed. *elf,* pl. masc. *elfvar* (fem. elfvor), the Dan. *elv,* pl. *elve,* are quite in rule; the Dan. compounds *ellefolk, ellekoner, elleskudt, ellevild* have undergone assimilation. With us the word *alp* still survives in the sense of night-hag, night-mare, in addition to which our writers of the last century introduced the Engl. *elf,* a form untrue to our dialect; before that, we find everywhere the correct pl. *elbe* or *elben.*[1] H. Sachs uses *ölp*: ' du ölp! du dölp!' (i. 5, 525ᵇ), and ölperisch (iv. 3, 95ᶜ); conf. *ölpern* and *ölpetrütsch,* alberdrütsch, drelpetrütsch (Schm. 1, 48); *elpentrötsch* and tölpentrötsch, trilpentrisch (Schmid's Swab. dict. 162); and in Hersfeld, hilpentrisch. The words mean an awkward silly fellow, one whom the elves have been at, and the same thing is expressed by the simple *elbisch,* Fundgr. 365. In Gloss. Jun. 340 we read *elvesce wehte,* elvish wights.

On the nature of Elves I resort for advice to the ON. authorities, before all others. It has been remarked already (p. 25), that the Elder Edda several times couples *œsir* and *âlfar* together, as though they were a compendium of all higher beings, and that the AS. *ês* and *ylfe* stand together in exactly the same way. This apparently concedes more of divinity to elves than to men. Sometimes there come in, as a third member, the *vanir* (Sæm. 83ᵇ), a race distinct from the æsir, but admitted to certain relations with them by marriage and by covenants. The Hrafnagaldr opens with the words: Alföðr orkar (works), *âlfar* skilja, *vanir* vita," Sæm. 88ᵃ; Allfather, *i.e.* the âs, has power, âlfar have skill (understanding), and vanir knowledge. The Alvîsmâl enumerates the dissimilar names given to heavenly bodies, elements and plants by various languages (supra, p. 332); in doing so, it mentions *œsir, âlfar, vanir,* and in addition also *goð, menn, ginregin, iötnar, dvergar* and denizens of *hel* (hades). Here the most remarkable point for us is, that *âlfar* and *dvergar* (dwarfs) are two different things. The same distinction is made between *âlfar* and *dvergar,* Sæm. 8ᵇ; between *dvergar* and *döckâlfar,* Sæm. 92ᵇ; between three kinds of norns, the âs-kungar, âlf-kungar and dœtr Dvalins, Sæm. 188ᵃ, namely, those descended from âses, from elves and from dwarfs; and our MHG. poets, as we see by Wikram's Albrecht, 6, 9, continued to separate *elbe*

---

[1] Besold. sub v. *elbe*; Ettner's Hebamme, p. 910, *alpen* or *elben.*

·from *getwerc*.[1] Some kinship however seems to exist between them, if only because among proper names of dwarfs we find an *Alfr* and a *Vindâlfr*, Sæm. 2. 3. Loki, elsewhere called an *âs*, and reckoned among *âses*, but really of iötun origin, is nevertheless addressed as *âlfr*, Sæm. 110[b]; nay, Völundr, a godlike hero, is called '*âlfa* lioði,' alforum socius, and '*vîsi âlfa*,' alforum princeps, Sæm. 135ᵃ ᵇ. I explain this not historically (by a Finnish descent), but mythically: German legend likewise makes Wielant king Elberich's companion and fellow smith in Mount Gloggensachsen (otherwise Göugelsahs, Caucasus?). Thus we see the word *âlfr* shrink and stretch by turns.

Now what is the true meaning of the word *albs, alp* = genius? One is tempted indeed to compare the Lat. *albus,* which according to Festus the Sabines called *alpus*; ἀλφός (vitiligo, leprosy) agrees still better with the law of consonant-change. Probably then *albs* meant first of all a light-coloured, white, good spirit,[2] so that, when *âlfar* and *dvergar* are contrasted, the one signifies the white spirits, the other the black. This exactly agrees with the great beauty and brightness of *âlfar*. But the two classes of creatures getting, as we shall see, a good deal mixed up and confounded, recourse was had to composition, and the elves proper were named *liosâlfar*.[3]

The above-named *döckâlfar* (genii obscuri) require a counterpart, which is not found in the Eddic songs, but it is in Snorri's prose. He says, p. 21: 'In Alfheim dwells the nation of the *liosâlfar* (light elves), down in the earth dwell the *döckâlfar* (dark elves), the two unlike one another in their look and their powers, *liosâlfar* brighter than the sun, *döckâlfar* blacker than pitch.' The *liosâlfar* occupy the third space of heaven, Sn. 22. Another name which never occurs in the lays, and which at first sight seems synonymous with döckâlfar, is *svartâlfar* (black

---

[1] In Norway popular belief keeps *alfer* and *dverge* apart, Faye p. 49.
[2] The word appears in the name of the snowclad mountains (*alpes*, see Suppl.), and that of the clear river (*Albis*, Elbe), while the ON. *elf* elfa, Swed. *elf*, Dan. *elv* = fluvius, is still merely appellative; the ghostly elvish swan (OHG. alpiz, MHG. elbez, AS. ælfet, ON. alpt, p. 429) can be explained both by its colour and its watery abode; likewise the Slav. labud, lebed, from Labe.
[3] *Vanir* also may contain the notion of white, bright; consider the ON. *vænn* (pulcher), the Ir. *ban* (albus), *ben, bean* (femina), Lat. *Venus*, Goth. *qinð*, AS. *cwen*. To this add, that the Ir. *banshi, ban-sighe* denotes an elvish being usually regarded as female, a fay. The same is expressed by *sia, sighe* alone, which is said to mean properly the twilight, the hour of spirits (see Suppl.).

elves);[1] and these Snorri evidently takes to be the same as
dvergar, for his dvergar dwell in Svartâlfaheim, (Sn. 34. 130.
136). This is, for one thing, at variance with the separation
of *âlfar* and *dvergar* in the lays, and more particularly with
the difference implied between *döckâlfar* and *dvergar* in Sæm.
92[b] 188[a]. That language of poetry, which everywhere else imparts such precise information about the old faith, I am not
inclined to set aside here as vague and general. Nor, in connexion with this, ought we to overlook the *nâir*, the deadly pale
or dead ghosts named by the side of the dvergar, Sæm. 92[b],
though again among the dvergar themselves occur the proper
names Nâr and Nâinn.

Some have seen, in this antithesis of light and black elves, the
same Dualism that other mythologies set up between spirits good
and bad, friendly and hostile, heavenly and hellish, between angels
of light and of darkness. But ought we not rather to assume
three kinds of Norse genii, *liosâlfar*, *döckâlfar*, *svartâlfar*? No
doubt I am thereby pronouncing Snorri's statement fallacious:
‘ döckâlfar eru svartari en bik (pitch).’ *Döckr*[2] seems to me not so
much downright black, as dim, dingy; not niger, but obscurus,
fuscus, aquilus. In ON. the adj. *iarpr*, AS. *eorp*, fuscus, seems to
be used of dwarfs, Haupt's Zeitschr. 3, 152; and the female name
Irpa (p. 98) is akin to it. In that case the identity of dwarfs
and *black* elves would hold good, and at the same time the Old
Eddic distinction between dwarfs and *dark* elves be justified.

Such a Trilogy still wants decisive proof; but some facts can
be brought in support of it. Pomeranian legend, to begin with,
seems positively to divide subterraneans into *white*, *brown*, and
black;[3] elsewhere popular belief contents itself with picturing
dwarfs in *gray* clothing, in *gray* or *brown* cap-of-darkness;
Scotch tradition in particular has its *brownies*, spirits of brown
hue, *i.e.* döckâlfar rather than svartâlfar (see Suppl.). But here
I have yet another name to bring in, which, as applied to such
spirits, is not in extensive use. I have not met with it outside

---

[1] Thorlac. spec. 7, p. 160, gives the liosâlfar another name *hvîtâlfar* (white
elves); I have not found the word in the old writings.
[2] Conf. OHG. tunchal, MHG. tunkel (our dunkel), Nethl. donker.
[3] E. M. Arndt's Märchen und Jugenderinnerungen, Berl. 1818, p. 159. In Phil.
von Steinau's Volkssagen, Zeitz 1838, pp. 291-3, the same traditions are given,
but only white and black (not brown) dwarfs are distinguished.

of the Vogtland and a part of East Thuringia. There the small elvish beings that travel especially in the train of Berchta, are called the *heimchen* (supra, p. 276); and the name is considered finer and nobler than querx or erdmännchen (Börner p. 52). It is hardly to be explained by any resemblance to chirping crickets, which are also called heimchen, OHG. heimili (Graff 4, 953); still less by heim (domus), for these wights are not home-sprites (domestici); besides, the correct spelling seems to be *heinchen* (Variscia 2, 101), so that one may connect it with 'Friend Hein,' the name for death, and the Low Sax. *heinen*kleed (winding-sheet, Strodtmann p. 84).[1] This notion of departed spirits, who appear in the 'furious host' in the retinue of former gods, and continue to lead a life of their own, may go to support those *nâir* of the Edda; the *pale* hue may belong to them, and the gray, brown, black to the coarser but otherwise similar dwarfs. Such is my conjecture. In a hero-lay founded on thoroughly German legend, that of Morolt, there appear precisely three troops of spirits, who take charge of the fallen in battle and of their souls: a *white*, a *pale*, and a *black* troop (p. 28[b]), which is explained to mean 'angels, kinsmen of the combatants coming up from hades, and devils.' No such warlike part is ever played by the Norse âlfar, not they, but the valkyrs have to do with battles; but the traditions may long have become tangled together, and the offices confounded.[2] The *liosâlfar* and *svartâlfar* are in themselves sufficiently like the christian *angels* and *devils*; the pale troop '*uz der helle*' are the *döckâlfar* that dwell '*niðri í iörðu*,' nay, the very same that in the Alvîsmâl are not expressly named, but designated by the words '*i heljo*.' Or I can put it in this way: liosâlfar live in *heaven*, döckâlfar (and nâir?) in *hel*, the heathen hades, svartâlfar in *Svartâlfaheim*, which is never used in the same sense as hel (see Suppl.). The dusky elves are souls of dead men, as the younger poet supposed, or are we to separate döckâlfar and nâir? Both have their abode in the realms of hades, as the light ones have in those of heaven. Of no other elves has the Edda so much to tell as of the black,

---

[1] '*Heinen*kleed is *not* conn. with Friend Hein, but means a *hünen*kleed (ch. XVIII.); conf. also the hünnerskes, and perhaps the haunken, or aunken in the Westph. sgönaunken.'—Extr. from Suppl.
[2] The different races of elves contending for a corpse (Ir. Elfenm. 68).

who have more dealings with mankind; svartálfar are named in abundance, liosálfar and döckálfar but fitfully.

One thing we must not let go: the identity of *svartálfar* and *dvergar*.

Dvergr, Goth. *dvaírgs?* AS. *dweorg*, OHG. *tuerc*, MHG. *tverc*, our *zwerg*,[1] answer to the Lat. nanus, Gr. νάννος (dwarf, puppet), Ital. nano, Span. enano, Portug. anão, Prov. nan, nant, Fr. nain, Mid. Nethl. also naen, Ferg. 2243-46-53-82. 3146-50, and nane, 3086-97; or Gr. πυγμαῖος. Beside the masc. forms just given, OHG. and MHG. frequently use the neut. form *gituerc, getwerc*, Nib. 98, 1. 335, 3. MS. 2, 15ᵃ. Wigal. 6080. 6591. Trist. 14242. 14515. daz *wilde getwerc*, Ecke 81. 82. Wh. 57, 25. *Getwerc* is used as a masc. in Eilhart 2881-7. Altd. bl. 1, 253-6-8; *der twerk* in Hoffm. fundgr. 237. Can θεουργός (performing miraculous deeds, what the MHG. would call *wundersære*) have anything to do with it? As to meaning, the dwarfs resemble the Idæan Dactyls of the ancients, the Cabeiri and πάταικοι: all or most of the dvergar in the Edda are cunning *smiths* (Sn. 34. 48. 130. 354). This seems the simplest explanation of their *black sooty* appearance, like that of the cyclopes. Their forges are placed in caves and mountains: *Svartálfaheimr* must therefore lie in a mountainous region, not in the abyss of hell. And our German folk-tales everywhere speak of the dwarfs as *forging* in the mountains: 'von golde wirkent si diu *spæhen werc*' says the Wartburg War of the getwerc Sinnels in Palakers, whereas elves and elfins have rather the business of *weaving* attributed to them. Thus, while dwarfs border on the smith-heroes and smith-gods (Wielant, Vulcan), the functions of elves approach those of fays and good-wives (see Suppl.).[2]

If there be any truth in this view of the matter, one can easily conceive how it might get altered and confused in the popular belief of a later time, when the new christian notions of angel and devil had been introduced. At bottom all elves, even the light ones, have some devil-like qualities, *e.g.* their loving to

---

[1] In Lausitz and E. Thuringia *querx*, in Thüringerwald *querlich*. Jac. von Königshofen, p. 89, has *querch*. In Lower Saxony sometimes *twärm*, for twarg.

[2] In Bretagne the *korr*, pl. *korred* answers to our elf, the *korrigan* to our elfin; and she too is described like a fay: she sits by the fountain, combing her hair, and whoever catches her doing so, must marry her at once, or die in three days (Ville-marqué 1, 17). The Welsh *cawr* means a giant.

teaze men; but they are not therefore devils, not even the black
ones, but often good-natured beings. It appears even that to these
black elves in particular, *i.e.* mountain spirits, who in various
ways came into contact with man, a distinct *reverence* was paid,
a species of *worship*, traces of which lasted down to recent
times. The clearest evidence of this is found in the Kormakssaga pp. 216–8. The hill of the elves, like the altar of a god,
is to be reddened with the blood of a slaughtered bull, and of
the animal's flesh a feast prepared for the elves: ' Höll einn er
heðan skamt í brott, *er álfar búa í* (cave that elves dwell in);
gráðúng þann, er Kormakr drap (bull that K. slew), skaltû fâ, ok
rióða blóð gráðúngsins á hólinn ûtan, en *gera álfum veizlu* (make
the elves a feast) af slâtrinu, ok mun þer batna.' An actual
álfablót. With this I connect the superstitious custom of cooking
food for angels, and *setting* it for them (Superst. no. 896). So
there is a *table covered* and a pot of *food placed* for home-smiths
and kobolds (Deut. sagen, no. 37. 38. 71); meat and drink for
domina Abundia (supra, p. 286); *money* or *bread* deposited in
the caves of subterraneans, in going past (Neocorus 1, 262. 560).[1]
There are plants named after elves as well as after gods: *alpranke*,
alpfranke, alfsranke, alpkraut (lonicera periclymen., solanum dul-
cam.), otherwise called geissblatt, in Denmark troldbär, in Sweden
trullbär; *dweorges dwosle*, pulegium (Lye), Mone's authorities
spell dwostle, 322[a]; *dvergeriis*, acc. to Molbech's Dial. Lex. p. 86,
the spartium scoparium. A latrina was called *álfrek*, lit. genios
fugans, Eyrb. saga, cap. 4 (see Suppl.).

Whereas man grows but slowly, not attaining his full stature
till after his fifteenth year, and then living seventy years, and a
giant can be as old as the hills; the dwarf is already grown up
in the third year of his life, and a greybeard in the seventh;[2]
the Elf-king is commonly described as old and white-bearded.

---

[1] The Old Pruss. and Lith. *parstuk* (thumbkin) also has food placed for him,
conf. Lasicz 54. The Lett. *behrstuhki* is said to mean a child's doll, Bergm. 145.
[2] Emp. Ludwig the Bavarian (1847) writes contemptuously to Markgraf Carl of
Moravia: ' Recollige, quia nondum venit hora, ut pigmei de Judea (l. India) statura
cubica evolantes fortitudine gnauica (l. gnanica, *i.e.* nanica) terras gygantium de-
trahere debeant in ruinas, et ut pigmei, id est homines bicubitales, qui in anno
tercio crescunt ad perfectam quantitatem et in septimo anno senescunt et moriun-
tur, imperent gygantibus.' Pelzel's Carl IV. 1 urk. p. 40. Conf. Böhmer's Font.
1, 227. 2, 570. Yet this description does not look to me quite German; the more
the dwarfs are regarded as elves, there is accorded to them, and especially to elfins
(as to the Greek oreads), a *higher* and semi-divine age; conf. the stories of changelings quoted further on. Laurin, acc. to the poems, was more than 400 years old.

Accounts of the creation of dwarfs will be presented in chap. XIX.; but they only seem to refer to the earthly form of the black elves, not of the light.

The leading features of elvish nature seem to be the following :—

Man's body holds a medium between those of the giant and the elf; an elf comes as much short of human size as a giant towers above it. All elves are imagined as small and tiny, but the *light* ones as well-formed and symmetrical, the *black* as ugly and misshapen. The former are radiant with exquisite beauty, and wear shining garments: the AS. *œlfsciene*, Cædm. 109, 23. 165, 11, sheen as an elf, bright as angels, the ON. ' fríð sem *álfkona*,' fair as elfin, express the height of female loveliness. In Rudlieb xvii. 27 a dwarf, on being caught, calls his wife out of the cave, she immediately appears, ' parva, *nimis pulchra*, sed et auro vesteque compta.' Fornald. sög. 1, 387 has : ' þat er kunnigt í öllum fornum frásögnum um þat fólk, er *álfar* hêtu, at þat var miklu fríðara enn önnur mankind.' The Engl. *elves* are slender and puny: Falstaff (1 Henry IV. i. 4) calls Prince Henry ' you starveling, you *elfskin* !' [1] The dwarf adds to his repulsive hue an ill-shaped body, a humped back, and coarse clothing; when elves and dwarfs came to be mixed up together, the graceful figure of the one was transferred to the other, yet sometimes the dwarfs expressly retain the *black* or *grey* complexion: ' *svart* i synen,' p. 457; ' a little *black* mannikin,' Kinderm. no. 92 ; ' *grey* mannikin,' Büsching's Wöch. nachr. 1, 98. Their very height is occasionally specified : now they attain the stature of a four years' child,[2] now they appear a great deal smaller, to be measured by the span or thumb: ' kûme *drîer spannen* lanc, gar *eislich getân*,' Elfenm. cxvi.; *two spans* high, Deut. sag. no. 42 ; a little wight, ' reht als ein *dûmelle* lanc,' a thumb long, Altd. bl. 2, 151 ; ' ein kleinez weglin (l. wiht*lin*)

---

[1] In Denmark popular belief pictures the *ellekone* as young and captivating to look at in front, but hollow at the back like a kneading-trough (Thiele 1, 118); which reminds one of Dame Werlt in MHG. poems.

[2] Whether the OHG. *pusilln* is said of a dwarf as Graff supposes (3, 352 ; conf. Swed. *pyssling*), or merely of a child, like the Lat. pusus, pusio, is a question. The Mid. Age gave to its *angels* these small dimensions of elves and dwarfs : ' Ein iegelich *engel* schînet alsô gestalter als ein kint in *jâren vieren* (years 4) in der jugende,' Tit. 5895 (Hahn) ; ' junclîche gemalet als ein kint daz dâ *vünf jâr* (5 year) alt ist,' Berth. 184. Laurîn is taken for the *angel* Michael ; Elberich (Otnit, Ettm. 24) and Antilois (Ulr. Alex.) are compared to a child of four.

·*dûmeln* lanc,' Ls. 1, 378.   In one Danish lay, the smallest trold
is no bigger than an ant, D.V. 1, 176.   Hence in fairy tales
däumling (thumbling, petit poucet) indicates a dwarfish figure;
the δάκτυλος Ἰδαῖος is to be derived from δάκτυλος (finger);
πυγμαῖος pigmæus from πυγμή (fist); the O. Pruss. *parstuck,*
perstuck, a dwarf, from Lith. pirsztas, Slav. perst, prst (finger);
and a Bohem. name for a dwarf, *pjdimuzjk* = span-mannikin, from
pjd' (span).[1]   In Sansk. *bâlakhilya* = geniorum genus, pollicis
magnitudinem aequans, sixty thousand of them sprang out of
Brahma's hair, Bopp's Gloss. Skr. p. 122ᵃ (ed. 2, p. 238ᵇ); bâla,
bâlaka = puer, parvulus, the ' ilya ' I do not understand.   There
are curious stories told about the deformity of dwarfs' *feet,* which
are said to be like those of *geese* or *ducks;*[2] conf. queen Berhta,

[1] When we read in a passage quoted by Jungmann 4, 652: 'mezi pjdimužjky
kraluge trpasljk' (among thumblings a dwarf is king), it is plain that a *trpasljk* is
more than a pjdimužjk.   Can this trp- (Slovak. krpec, krpatec) be conn. with our
knirps, knips, krips, gribs (v. infra), which means one of small stature, not quite a
dwarf?   Finn. *peukalo,* a thumbling, Kalew. 13, 67 ; *mies peni, pikku mies,* little
man three fingers high 13, 63-8. 24, 144.——For dwarf the MHG. has also ' der
kurze man,' Wigal. 6593. 6685. 6710; 'der *wénige man,*' Er. 7442.   Ulr. Alex. (in
Wackern.'s Bas. Ms., p. 29ᵇ), in contrast with the ' michel man ' or giant.   One
old name for a dwarf was *churzibolt,* Pertz 2, 104, which otherwise means a short
coat, Hoff. Gl. 36, 13.   Roth. 4576.   Conf. *urkinde* (nanus), Gramm. 2, 789.
[2] Deutsche Sagen, no. 149; I here give a more faithful version, for which I am
indebted to Hr. Hieron. Hagebuch of Aarau.——Vo de *härdmändlene* uf der Ramsflue.   Hinder der Ärlisbacher egg, zwüschenem dörfle Hard und dem alte Lorenze-
kapällele, stoht im ene thäle so ganz eleigge e grüsle verträite flue.   se sägere
dRamsflue.   uf der hindere site isch se hohl, und dhöle het numme e chline igang.
Do sind denn emol, me weiss nid äxact i wele johrgängs, so rarige *mändle* gsi, die
sind i die höhle us und i gange, händ ganz e so es eiges läbe geführt, und en
apartige hushaltig, und sind ganz bsunderig derhär cho, so wärklich gestaltet, und
mit eim wort, es isch halt kei mönsch usene cho, wer se denn au seige, wohär se
cho seige, und was se tribe.   ämel gekochet händ se nüt, und würsle und beeri
ggässe.   unde a der flue lauft es bächle, und i dem bächle händ die *mändle* im summer badet, *wie tüble,* aber eis vonene het immer wacht gha, und het pfiffe, wenn
öpper derhär cho isch, uf dem fuesswäg: denn sind se ame gsprunge, was gisch
was hesch, der bärg uf, dass ene kei haas noh cho wer, und wie der schwick *in*
ehre höhle gschloffe.   dernäbe händ se kem mönsch nüt zleid tho, im gägetheil,
gfälligkäite, wenn se händ chönne.   Einisch het der Hardpur es füederle riswälle
glade, und wil er elei gsi isch, het ers au fast nid möge.   E sones *mändle* gsehts vo
der flue obenabe, und chunt der durab zhöpperle über driese, und hilft dem pur,
was es het möge.   wo se do der bindbaum wänd ufe thue, so isch das *mändle* ufem
wage gsi, und het grichtet, und der pur het überunde azoge a de bindchneble.   do
het das *mändle* sseil nid rächt ume gliret, und wo der pur azieht, schnellt der baum
los und trift s*mändle* ane finger und hets würst blessiert; do foht der pur a jom-
mere und seit ' o heie, o heie, wenns numenan mer begegnet wer ! '   do seit das
mändle ' abba, das macht nüt, sälben tho, sälben gha.'*   mit dene worte springts
vom wage nabe, het es chrütle abbroche, hets verschafiet und uf das bluetig fin-

* Swab. ' sell thaun, sell haun,' Schmid p. 628.   More neatly in MHG., ' selbe
tæte, selbe habe,' MS. 1, 10ᵇ. 89ᵃ.

p. 280, and the swan-maidens, p. 429. One is also reminded
of the *blatevüeze*, Rother 1871. Ernst 3828; conf. Haupt's
Zeitschr. 7, 289.

The Mid. Nethl. poem of Brandaen, but no other version of the
same legend, contains a very remarkable feature.[1] Brandan met
a man on the sea, who was *a thumb long*, and *floated on a leaf*,
holding a little bowl in his right hand and a pointer in his left:
the pointer he kept dipping into the sea and letting water drip
from it into the bowl; when the bowl was full, he emptied it out,
and began filling again: it was his doom to be measuring the
sea until the Judgment-day (see Suppl.). This liliputian floating
on the leaf reminds us of ancient, especially Indian myths.[2]

The âlfar are a *people*, as the Edda expressly says (Sn. 21), and

gerle gleit, und das het alles ewäg puzt. do springts wider ufe wage, und het zum
pur gseit, er soll aseil nume wider ume ge. Mängisoh, wenn rächtschafne lüt durn
tag ghenet oder bunde händ und se sind nit fertig worde bis zobe, und ahet öppe
welle oho rägne, so sind die *hârdmândle* oho, und händ geschaffet und gewärnet
druf ine, bis alles im schärme gai isoh. oder wenns durt dnacht isoh oho wättere,
händ se sheu und schorn, wo dusse gläge isoh, de lüte zum tenn zue träit, und am
morge het halt alles gross auge gmacht, und se händ nid gwüsst, wers tho het. den
händ erst no die *mândle* kei dank begehrt, numensu dass me se gern hät. Amenim
winter, wenn alles stei und bei gfrore gai isoh, sind die *mândle* is oberst hus oho
zArlispach: se händ shalt gar guet chönnen mit dene lüte, wo dert gwohnt händ,
und sind ame durt dnacht ufem ofe gläge, und am morge vortag händ se se wieder
drus gmacht. was aber gar gspässig gai isoh, *si händ ehre flüessle nie vüre glo, händ
es charlachrothe mântele träit, vom hals bis ufe bode nabe*. jetzt hets im dorf so
gwunderige meitle und buebe gha, die sind einisch znacht vor das hus go gen äsche
streue, dass se gsäche, was die *hârdmândle* für flüessle hebe. und was händse
gfunde? sisch frile wunderle: *ânte und geissfüess* sind in der äsche abdrückt gai.
Aber vo sälber stund a isoh keis *mandle* meh oho, und se sind au ntimme uf der
Ramsflue bliebe, i dkräche händ se se *verschloffe*, tief id geissflue hindere, und händ
keis zeiche me von ene ge, und chömme nümme, so lang dlüt eso boshaft sind
(see Suppl.). — [Substance of the above. *Earth-mannikins* on the Ramsflue:
lived in a cave with a narrow entrance; cooked nothing, ate roots and berries;
bathed in a brook *like doves*, set one to watch, and if he whistled, were up the hills
faster than hares, and *slipt into their cave*. Never hurt men, often helped: the
farmer at Hard was alone loading, a dwarf came down, helped to finish, got on the
waggon, did not properly run the rope over the bind-pole, it slipped off, the pole
flew up and hurt him badly. Farmer: 'I wish it had happened to me.' Dwarf:
'Not so; self do, self have.' Got down, picked a herb, and cured the wound instantly. Often, when honest folk cut hay or tied corn, dwarfs helped them to
finish and get it under shelter; or in the night, if rain came on, they brought in
what was lying out, and didn't the people stare in the morning! One severe winter
they came every night to a house at Arlisbach, slept on the oven, departed before
dawn; *wore scarlet cloaks reaching to the ground, so that their feet were never seen;*
but some prying people sprinkled ashes before the house, on which were seen the
next morning marks of *duck's* and *goose's feet*. They never showed themselves
again, and never will, while men are so spiteful.]

[1] Blommaert's Oudvlaemsche gedichten 1, 118ᵇ. 2, 26ᵃ.

[2] Brahma, sitting on a lotus, floats musing across the abysses of the sea. Vishnu,
when after Brahma's death the waters have covered all the worlds, sits in the shape
of *a tiny infant on a leaf* of the pipala (fig-tree), and floats on the sea of milk,
sucking the toe of his right foot. (Asiat. Res. 1, 345.)

as the Alvîsmâl implies by putting âlfar, dvergar, and helbûar (if
I may use the word), by the side of men, giants, gods, âses and
vanir, each as a separate class of beings, with a language of its
own.   Hence too the expressions 'das stille *volk;* the good
people (p. 456); huldu-*fôlk ;* ' in Lausitz *ludki,* little folk (Wend.
volksl. 2, 268), from lud, liud (nation), OHG. liut, Boh. lid ; and
in Welsh *y teulu* (the family), *y tylwyth têg* (the fair family, the
pretty little folk, conf. Owen sub v. tylwyth, and Diefenbach's
Celtica ii. 102.   Whether we are to understand by this a historical realm situate in a particular region, I leave undecided here.
Dvergmâl (sermo nanorum) is the ON. term for the echo: a very
expressive one, as their calls and cries resound in the hills, and
when man speaks loud, the dwarf replies, as it were, from the
mountain. Herrauŏssaga, cap. 11, p. 50: ' Sigurŏr stilti svâ
hâtt hörpuna, at *dvergmâl* qvaŏ î höllunni,' he played so loud
on the harp, that dwarf's voice spoke in the hall.   When heroes
dealt loud blows, '*dvörgamâl* sang uj qvörjun hamri,' echo
sang in every rock (Lyngbye, p. 464, 470) ; when hard they
hewed, '*dvörgamâl* sang uj fiödlun,' echo sang in the mountains
(ibid. 468).   ON. '*qveŏr viŏ* î klettunum,' reboant rupes.   Can
græti âlfa (ploratus nanorum) in the obscure Introduction to
the Hamdismâl (Sæm. 269ᵃ) mean something similar ?   Even our
German heroic poetry seems to have retained the same image :

Dem fehten allez nâch erhal,	To the fighting everything resounded,
dô beide berg und ouch diu tal	then both hill and also dale
gâben ir slegen *stimme.*	gave voice to their blows.

(Ecke, ed. Hagen, 161.)

Daz dâ beide berg und tal
vor ir slegen wilde wider einander allez hal.   (ibid. 171.)

The hills not only rang again with the sword-strokes of the
heroes, but uttered voice and answer, *i.e.* the dwarfs residing in
them did.[1]

This nation of elves or dwarfs has over it a *king.* In Norse
legend, it is true, I remember no instance of it among âlfar
or dvergar; yet Huldra is *queen* of the huldrefôlk (p. 272), as

---

[1] The Irish for echo is similar, though less beautiful: *muc alla,* swine of the rock.

Berchta is of the heinchen (p. 276), and English tradition tells of an *elf-queen*, Chaucer's C. T. 6442 (the fairy queen, Percy 3, 207 seq.); I suppose, because Gallic tradition likewise made female fairies (fées) the more prominent. The OFr. fable of Huon of Bordeaux knows of a *roi* Oberon, *i.e.* Auberon for Alberon, an *alb* by his very name: the kingdom of the fays (royaume de la féerie) is his. Our poem of Orendel cites a dwarf *Alban* by name. In Otnit a leading part is played by *künec Alberich, Elberich*, to whom are subject "manec berg und tal;" the Nib. lied makes him not a king, but a vassal of the kings Schilbung and Nibelung; a nameless *king of dwarfs* appears in the poem of Ecke 80; and elsewhere *king Goldemâr* (Deut. held-ensage p. 174. Haupt's Zeitschr. 6, 522-3), *king Sinnels* and *Laurin* (MS. 2, 15ᵃ); 'der getwerge künec Bilei,' Er. 2086. The German folk-tales also give the dwarf nation a king (no. 152); *king* of erdmännchen (Kinderm. 3, 167). *Gübich* (Gibika, p. 137) is in the Harz legends a dwarf-king. *Heiling* is *prince* of the dwarfs (no. 151).[1] These are all kings of black elves, except Oberon, whom I take to be a light alb. It appears that human heroes, by subduing the sovereign of the elves, at once obtain dominion over the spirits; it may be in this sense that Völundr is called *vísi álfa* (p. 444), and Siegfried after conquering Elbe-rich would have the like pretensions (see Suppl.).

The ON. writings have preserved plenty of dwarfs' names which are of importance to the study of mythology (loc. princ. Sæm. 2ᵇ 3ᵃ). I pick out the rhyming forms *Vitr* and *Litr*, *Fili* and *Kili*, *Fialarr* and *Galarr*, *Skirvir* and *Virvir*, *Anar* and *Onar*, *Finnr* and *Ginnr*, as well as the absonant *Bivor* and *Bavor*. *Nâr* and *Nâinn* are manifestly synonymous (mortuus), and so are *Thrâr* and *Thrâinn* (contumax, or rancidus?). With *Nâinn* agrees *Dâinn* (mortuus again); with *Oinn* (timidus) *Moinn*; *Dvalinn, Durinn, Thorinn, Fundinn*, shew at least the same

---

[1] A curious cry of grief keeps recurring in several dwarf-stories: 'the *king* is dead! *Urban* is dead! old *mother Pumpe* is dead!' (Büsching's Wöch. nachr. 1, 99. 101); the *old schumpe* is dead! (Legend of Bonikau), MHG. schumpfe, Fragm. 36ᵉ; conf. Bange's Thür. chron. 49ᵃ, where again they say '*king* Knoblauch (garlic) is dead!' Taking into account the saying in Saxony, 'de *gaue fru* ist nu al dot!' with evident allusion to the motherly goddess (p. 258), and the similar phrase in Scandinavia, 'nu eru dauðar *allar dîsir!*' (p. 402); all these exclama-tions seem to give vent to a grief, dating from the oldest times, for the death of some superior being (see Suppl.).

participial ending. *Alfr, Gandálfr,* and *Vindálfr* place the connexion of elves and dwarfs beyond doubt. *Ai* occurs twice,
and seems to mean avus, as in Sæm. 100ᵃ; *Finnr* and *Billíngr*
are like the heroes' names discussed on pp. 373, 380. *Nýr,* and
Niði, Nýr and *Nýráðr* have reference to phases of the moon's
light; a few other names will be touched upon later. In Sæm.
45ᵇ and Sn. 48. 130 all dwarfs are said to be '*Ivalda* synir,'
sons of *Ivaldi,* and he seems identical with the elvish *Ivaldr,*
father of Iðunn, Sæm. 89ᵃ, just as Folkvaldr and Folkvaldi (AS.
Folcwealda), Dômvaldr and Dômvaldi=Domaldi, are used indifferently. *Ivaldr* answers to the Dan. Evald and our Ewald,
a rare name in the older documents: we know the two *St.
Ewalds* (niger et albus) who were martyred in the elder Pipin's
time (695) and buried at Cologne, but were of English origin.
Beda 5, 10 spells it *Hewald,* and the AS. transl. *Heáwold* (see
Suppl.).

Of the dwellings of light elves in heaven the folk-tales have
no longer anything to tell; the more frequently do they describe those of dwarfs in the rifts and caves of the mountains.
Hence the AS. names *bergælfen, dunælfen, muntælfen.* ON. 'bý
ec *for iörð* neðan, â ec *undr steini* stað,' I dwell underneath
the earth, I have under stone my stead, Sæm. 48ᵃ. 'dvergr sat
undir steininum,' Yngl. saga, cap. 15. 'dvergar búa *í iörðu oc
í steinum,*' Sn. 15. *Elbenstein, Elphinstone,* are names of noble
families, see *Elwenstein,* Weisth. 1, 4. In the Netherlands
the hills containing sepulchral urns are vulgarly denominated
alfenbergen (Belg. mus. 5, 64). Treasures lie hidden in graves
as they do in the abodes of elves, and the dead are subterraneans
as these are. And that is why dwarfs are called *erdmännlein,
erdmanneken,* in Switzerland *härdmändle,* sometimes even *unter-
irdische,* Dan. *underjordiske.*[1] They scamper over moss and fell,
and are not exhausted by climbing steep precipices: '*den wilden*

---

[1] I cannot yet make out the name *arweggers,* by which the earth-men are called
up in Kinderm. 2, 163–4. [erd-wihte? v. ar- for erd-, p. 467, l. 3; and *weglin,* p. 449].
The ON. *ârvakr* is hardly the same (see Suppl.). In Pruss. Samogitia 'de *under-
hördschkes*'; the tales about them carefully collected by Reusch, no. 48–59. The
Wends of Lüneburg called subterranean spirits *gôrzoni* (hill-mannikins, fr. gora,
hill), and the hills they haunted are still shown. When they wished to borrow
baking utensils of men, they gave a sign without being seen, and people placed
them outside the door for them. In the evening they brought them back, knocking
at the window and adding a loaf by way of thanks (Jugler's Wörterb.). The Esthonian mythology also has its subterraneans (*ma allused,* under ground).

getwergen wære ze stîgen dâ genuoc,' enough climbing for wild dwarfs, says Wh. 57, 25, speaking of a rocky region.[1] The popular beliefs in Denmark about the *biergmand, biergfolk, biergtrold,* are collected in Molbech's Dial. lex. p. 35-6. The biergmand's wife is a *biergekone.* These traditions about earth-men and mountain-sprites all agree together. Slipping[2] into cracks and crevices of the hills, they seem to vanish suddenly, 'like the schwick,' as the Swiss tale has it, and as suddenly they come up from the ground; in all the places they haunt, there are shown such *dwarf's holes, querlich's holes.* So the *ludki* in Lausitz make their appearance out of underground passages like mouseholes; a Breton folk-song speaks of the *korred's grotto* (Villemarqué 1, 36). In such caves they pursue their occupations, collecting treasures, forging weapons curiously wrought; their kings fashion for themselves magnificent chambers underground, Elberich, Laurîn dwell in these wonderful mountains, men and heroes at times are tempted down, loaded with gifts, and let go, or held fast (see Suppl.). Dietrich von Bern at the close of his life is fetched away by a dwarf, Deut. heldens. p. 300; of Etzel, says the Nibelungs' Lament 2167, one knows not 'ob er sich *ver-slüffe in löcher der steinwende,*' whether he have slipped away into holes of the rocks[3]: meaning probably, that, like Tannhäuser and faithful Eckart, he has got into the mount wherein *Dame Venus* dwells. Of this Dame Venus's mount we have no accounts before the 15-16th centuries; one would like to know what earlier notions lie at the bottom of it: has *Dame Venus* been put in the place of a subterranean elf-queen, or of a goddess, such as Dame Holda or Frikka? Heinrich von Morunge sings of his beloved, MS. 1, 55ᵃ:

> Und dunket mich, wie si gê zuo mir *dur ganze mûren,*
> ir trôst und ir helfe lâzent mich niht trûren;
> swenne si wil, so *vüeret sie mich hinnen*
> mit ir wîzen hant *hôhe über die zinnen.*
> ich wæne sie ist ein *Vênus* hêre.

---

[1] Other instances are collected in Ir. Elfenm. lxxvi. 'den *bere* bûten *wildiu getwerc,*' wild dwarfs inhabited the hill, Sigenot 118.
[2] *Sliefen* is said of them as of the fox in Reinh. xxxi.; our subst. schlucht stands for *sluft* (beschwichtigen, lucht, kracht, for swiften, luft, kraft), hence a hole to slip into.
[3] Conf. Deutsche sagen, no. 383, on Theoderic's soul, how it is conveyed into Vulcan's abyss.

(Methinks she comes to me through solid walls, Her help, her comfort lets me nothing fear; And when she will she wafteth me from here With her white hand high o'er the pinnacles. I ween she is a Venus high.) He compares her then to a Venus or Holda, with the elvish power to penetrate through walls and carry you away over roof and tower (see chap. XXXI., Tannhäuser; and Suppl.). Accordingly, when a Hessian nursery-tale (no. 13) makes three *haule-männerchen* appear, these are henchmen of Holle, elves in her retinue, and what seems especially worthy of notice is their being *three*, and *endowing with gifts*: it is a rare thing to see male beings occupy the place of the fortune-telling wives. Elsewhere it is rather the little earth-wives that appear; in Hebel (ed. 5, p. 268) Eveli says to the wood-wife: 'God bless you, and if you're the *earth-mannikin's wife*, I won't be afraid of you.'[1]

There is another point of connexion with Holda: the expressions 'die *guten holden*' (p. 266), '*guedeholden*' penates (Teutonista), or *holdichen, holdeken, holderchen* seem perfectly synonymous with 'the good elves;' *holdo* is literally a kind, favourably disposed being, and in Iceland *liuflingar* (darlings) and *huldufölk, huldumenn* (p. 272) are used for âlfar. The form of the Dan. *hyldemänd* is misleading, it suggests the extraneous notion of hyld (sambucus, elder-tree), and makes Dame Holda come out as a *hyldemoer* or *hyldeqvind*, viz., a dryad incorporated with that tree (Thiele 1, 132); but its real connexion with the huldre is none the less evident. Thus far, then, the elves are good-natured helpful beings; they are called, as quoted on p. 452, the *stille volk* (Deut. sagen, No. 30-1), the *good people, good neighbours, peaceful folk* (Gael. daoine shi, Ir. daoine maith, Wel. dynion mad). When left undisturbed in their quiet goings on, they maintain peace with men, and do them services when they can, in the way of smith-work, weaving and baking. Many a time have they given to people of their *new-baked bread* or *cakes* (Mone's Anz. 7, 475). They too in their turn require man's advice and assistance in certain predicaments, among which are

---

[1] One winter Hadding was eating his supper, when suddenly an earth-wife pushed her *head up through the floor by the fireside*, and offered him green vegetables. Saxo, p. 16, calls her *cicutarum gerula*, and makes her take Hadding into the subterranean land, where are meadows covered with grass, as in our nursery-tales which describe Dame Holla's underground realm. This grass-wife resembles a little earth-wife.

to be reckoned three cases in particular. In the first place, they
fetch goodwives, midwives, to assist *she-dwarfs in labour ;* [1] next,
men of understanding to *divide a treasure*, to settle a dispute ; [2]
thirdly, they borrow a hall to hold their weddings in ; [3] but they
requite every favour by bestowing jewels which bring luck to the
man's house and to his descendants. They themselves, however,
have much knowledge of occult healing virtues in plants and
stones. [4] In Rudlieb xvii. 18, the captured dwarf retorts the
taunt of treachery in the following speech :

[1] Ranzan, Alvensleben, Hahn. (Deut. sag. no. 41, 68-9) ; Müllenh. Schlesw.
holst. sag. no. 443-4. Asbiörn Norw. s. 1, 18.   Irish legends and fairy tales 1,
245-250.   Mone's Anz. 7, 475 ; conf. Thiele 1, 36.—Hülpher's Samlingen om
Jämtland (Westeras 1775, p. 210) has the following Swedish story :——'år 1660, då
jag tillika med min hustru var gången til fäboderne, som ligga ¼ mil ifrån Ragunda
prästegård, och der sent om qvällen suttit och talt en stund, kom *en liten man*
ingående genom dören, och bad min hustru, det ville hon hjelpa hans *hustru*, som
då låg och *qvaldes med barn*.   karlen var eljest liten til växten, *svart i synen*, och
med gamla grå kläder försedd.   Jag och min hustru sutto en stund och undrade
på denne mannen, emedan vi understodo, at han var et *troll*, och hört berättas, at
sådane, af bondfolk *vettar* kallade, sig altid i fäboderne uppehålla, sedan folket om
hösten sig derifrån begifvit.   Men som han 4 à 5 gånger sin begäran påyrkade, och
man derhos betänkte, hvad skada bondfolket berätta sig ibland af *vettarne* lidit,
då de antingen svarit på dem, eller eljest vist dem med vränga ord til helvetet ;
ty fattade jag då til det rådet, at jag läste öfver min hustru några böner, välsignade
henne, och bad henne i Guds namn följa med honom.   Hon tog så i hastighet någre
gamla linkläder med sig, och följde honom åt, men jag blef qvar sittande.   Sedan
har hon mig vid återkomsten berättat, at då hon gått med mannen utom porten,
tykte hon sig liksom föras udi vädret en stund, och kom så uti en stuga, hvarest
bredevid var en liten mörk kammare, das hans hustru låg och våndades med barn
i en säng, min hustru har så stigit til henne, och efter en liten stund hjelpt henne,
då hon födde barnet, och det med lika åtbörder, som andra menniskor pläga hafva.
Karlen har sedan tilbudit henne mat, men som hon dertil nekade, ty tackade han
henne och följde henne åt, hvarefter hon åter likasom farit i vädret, och kom efter
en stund til porten igen vid passklockan 10.   Emedlertid voro en hoper *gamla
silfverskedar* lagde på en hylla i stugan, och fann min hustru dem, då hon andra
dagen stökade i vråarne : kunnandes förstå, at de af *vettret* voro dit lagde.   At så
i sanning är skedt, vitnar jag med mitt namns undersättande.   Ragunda, d. 12
april, 1671.   Pet. Rahm.'   [Substance of the foregoing :——I, the undersigned, and
my wife were accosted by a *little man* with *black face* and old gray clothes, who
begged my wife to come and aid his wife then *in labour*.   Seeing he was a *troll*,
such as the peasantry call *vettar* (wights), I prayed over my wife, blessed her, and
bade her go.   She seemed for a time to be borne along by the wind, found his wife
in a little dark room, and helped, etc.   Refused food, was carried home in the
same way ; found next day a heap of *old silver vessels* brought by the *vettr.*]
    In Finland the vulgar opinion holds, that under the altars of churches there live
small mis-shapen beings called *kirkonwäki* (church-folk) ; that when their women
have difficult labour, they can be relieved by a Christian woman visiting them and
laying her hand on them.   Such service they reward liberally with gold and silver.
Mnemosyne, Abo 1821, p. 313.
    [2] Pref. p. xxx.   Neocorus 1, 542.   Kinderm. 2, 43.   3, 172. 225.   Nib. 92, 3.
Bit. 7819.   Conf. Deutsche heldensagen, p. 78.
    [3] Hoia (Deut. sagen, no. 35).   Bonikau (Elisabeth von Orleans, Strassb. 1789,
p. 133 ; Leipzig 1820, p. 450-1).   Büsching's Wöchentl. nachr. 1, 98 ; conf. 101.
    [4] The wounded *hårdmändle*, p. 450-1.   Here are two Swedish stories given in
Ödman's Bahuslän pp. 191, 224 :——Biörn Mårtensson, accompanied by an archer,

Absit ut inter nos unquam regnaverit haec fraus!
non tam *longaevi* tunc essemus neque *sani*.
Inter vos nemo loquitur nisi corde doloso,
hinc neque ad aetatem maturam pervenietis :
pro cujusque fide sunt ejus tempora vitae.
Non aliter loquimur nisi sicut corde tenemus,
neque cibos varios edimus morbos generantes,
longius incolumes hinc nos durabimus ac vos.

Thus already in the 10th century the dwarf complains of the
faithlessness of mankind, and partly accounts thereby for the
shortness of human life, while dwarfs, because they are honest
and feed on simple viands, have long and healthy lives.   More
intimately acquainted with the secret powers of nature, they can
with greater certainty avoid unwholesome food.   This remarkable passage justifies the opinion of the longevity of dwarfs ; and
their avoidance of human food, which hastens death, agrees
with the distinction drawn out on p. 318 between men and gods
(see Suppl.).

went hunting in the high woods of Örnekulla ; there they found a *bergsmed*
(mountain-smith) asleep, and the huntsman ordered the archer to seize him, but
he declined : 'Pray God shield you ! the bergsmith will fling you down the hill.'
But the huntsman was so daring, he went up and laid hands on the sleeper ; the
bergsmith cried out, and begged they would let him go, he had a wife and seven
little ones, and he would forge them anything they liked, they had only to put the
iron and steel on the cliff, and they'd presently find the work lying finished in the
same place. Biörn asked him, whom he worked for ? 'For my fellows,' he
replied. As Biörn would not release him, he said : 'Had I my cap-of-darkness
(*uddehat*, p. 463), you should not carry me away ; but if you don't let me go, none
of your posterity will attain the greatness you enjoy, but will go from bad to worse.'
Which afterwards came true. Biörn secured the bergsmith, and had him put in
prison at Bohus, but on the third day he had disappeared.
   At Mykleby lived Swen, who went out hunting one Sunday morning, and on the
hill near Tyfweholan he spied a fine buck with a ring about his neck ; at the same
instant a cry came out of the hill : 'Look, the man is shooting our ring-buck !'
'Nay,' cried another voice, 'he had better not, he has not washed this morning'
(*i.e.*, been sprinkled with holy water in church).   When Swen heard that, he
immediately —— ——, washed himself in haste, and shot the ring-buck.   Then
arose a great screaming and noise in the hill, and one said : 'See, the man has
taken his belt-flask and washed himself, but I will pay him out.'   Another
answered : 'You had better let it be, the *white buck* will stand by him.'   A tremendous uproar followed, and a host of trolls filled the wood all round.   Swen
threw himself on the ground, and crept under a mass of roots ; then came into his
mind what the troll had said, that the white buck, as he contemptuously called the
church, would stand by him.   So he made a vow, that if God would help him out
of the danger, he would hand over the buck's ring to Mykleby church, the horns to
Torp, and the hide to Langeland.   Having got home uninjured, he performed all
this : the ring, down to the year 1732, has been the knocker on Mykleby church
door, and is of some unknown metal, like iron ore ; the buck's horn was preserved
in Torp church, and the skin in Langeland church.

Whilst in this and other ways the dwarfs do at times have dealings with mankind, yet on the whole they seem to shrink from man; they give the impression of a downtrodden afflicted race, which is on the point of abandoning its ancient home to new and more powerful invaders. There is stamped on their character something *shy* and something *heathenish*, which estranges them from intercourse with christians. They chafe at human faithlessness, which no doubt would primarily mean the apostacy from heathenism. In the poems of the Mid. Ages, Laurîn is expressly set before us as a *heathen*. It goes sorely against the dwarfs to see churches built, *bell-ringing* (supra, p. 5) disturbs their ancient privacy; they also hate the clearing of forests, agriculture, new fangled pounding-machinery for ore.[1]

---

[1] More fully treated of in Ir. Elfenm. xciv. xcv.; conf. Thiele 1, 42. 2, 2. Faye p. 17, 18. *Heinchen* driven away by grazing herds and *tinkling sheepbells*, Variscia 2, 101. Hessian tales of *wichtelmännerchen*, Kinderm. no. 39, to which I add the following one:——On the Schwalm near Uttershausen stands the Dosenberg; close to the river's bank are two apertures, once the exit and entrance holes of the *wichtelmänner*. The grandfather of farmer Tobi of Singlis often had a little wichtelmann come to him in a friendly manner in his field. One day, when the farmer was cutting corn, the *wichtel* asked him if he would undertake a carting job across the river that night for a handsome price in gold. The farmer said yes, and in the evening the *wichtel* brought a sack of wheat to the farmhouse as earnest; so four horses were harnessed, and the farmer drove to the foot of the Dosenberg. Out of the holes the *wichtel* brought heavy invisible loads to the waggon, which the farmer took through the water to the other side. So he went backwards and forwards from ten in the evening till four in the morning, and his horses at last got tired. Then said the wichtel: 'That will do, now you shall see what you have been carrying.' He bid the farmer *look over his right shoulder*, who then saw *the whole wide field full of little wichtelmen*. Said the *wichtel*: 'For a thousand years we have dwelt in the Dosenberg, our time is up now, we must away to another country; but there is money enough left in the mountain to content the whole neighbourhood.' He then loaded Tobi's waggon full of money, and went his way. The farmer with much trouble got his treasure home, and was now a rich man; his descendants are still well-to-do people, but the *wichtelmen* have vanished from the land for ever. On the top of the Dosenberg is a bare place where nothing will grow, it was bewitched by the *wichtel holding their trysts upon it*. Every seven years, generally on a Friday, you may see a *high blue flame* over it, covering a larger space of ground than a big caldron. People call it the *geldfeuer*, they have brushed it away with their feet (for it holds no heat), in hopes of finding treasure, but in vain: the devil had always some new hocuspocus to make some little word pop out of their mouths.

Then, lastly, a Low Saxon story of the Aller country:——Tau Offensen bin Kloster Wienhusen was en groten buern, Hövermann nenne he sick, die harre ok en schip up der Aller. Eins dages komt 2 lüe tau jüm un segget, he schölle se over da? water schippen. Tweimal fäuert hei over de Aller, jedesmal na den groten rume, den se Allerô heiten dauet, dat is ne grote unminschliche wische lang un breit, dat man se kums afkiken kann. Ans de buer taun tweitenmale over efäuert is, segt ein von den *twarmen* to öme: 'Wut du nu ne summe geldes hebben, oder wut du na koptal betalt sin?' 'Ick will leiver ne summe geld nemen' sä de buer. Do nimt de eine von den *lütjen lüen* sinen haut af, un settet den dem schipper up: 'Du herrst dik doch beter estan, wenn du na koptal efodert herrst' segt de *twarm ;*

Breton legend informs us : A man had dug a treasure out of a
dwarf's hole, and then cautiously covered his floor with ashes and
glowing embers ; so when the dwarfs came at midnight to get
their property back, they burnt their feet so badly, that they set
up a loud wail (supra, p. 413) and fled in haste, but they smashed
all his crockery.   Villemarqué 1, 42 (see Suppl.).

From this dependence of the elves on man in some things,
and their mental superiority in others, there naturally follows
a *hostile* relation between the two.   Men disregard elves, elves
do mischief to men and *teaze* them.   It was a very old belief,
that dangerous *arrows* were shot down from the air by elves ;
this evidently means light elves, it is never mentioned in stories
of dwarfs, and the AS. formula couples together ' ésagescot and
ylfagescot,' these elves being apparently armed with weapons
like those of the gods themselves ; [1] the divine thunderbot is even
called an *albschoss* (pp. 179, 187), and in Scotland the *elf-arrow*,
elf-flint, *elf-bolt* is a hard pointed wedge believed to have been
discharged by spirits ; the turf cut out of the ground by lightning is supposed to be thrown up by them.[2]   On p. 187 I have
already inferred, that there must have been some closer connexion, now lost to us, between elves and the Thundergod : if it
be that his bolts were *forged* for him by elves, that points rather
to the black elves.

Their *touch*, their *breath* may bring sickness or death on man
and beast ; [3] one whom their *stroke* has fallen on, is lost or in-
capable (Danske viser 1, 328) : lamed cattle, bewitched by them,

un de buer, de vorher nichts nich seien harre, un den et so lichte in schipp vorko-
men was, ans of he nichts inne herre, stüt de ganze *Allerô von luter lütjen minschen
krimmeln un wimmeln.*   Dat sind de *twarme* west, dei wier trökken sind.   Von der
tit heft Hövermanns noch immer vull geld ehat, dat se nich kennen dêen, averst nu
sind se sau ein nan annern ut estorven, un de hof is verkoft.   'Wann ist denn das
gewesen ? '   Vor olen tien, ans de twarme noch sau in der welt wesen sind, nu
gift et er wol keine mehr, vor drüttig, virzig jaren.   [Substance of the foregoing :
——Hövermann, a large farmer at Offensen, had also a ship on the R. Aller.   Two
little men asked him to ferry them over.   He did so twice, each time to a large
open space called Allerô.   Dwarf : ' Will you have a lump sum, or be paid so much
a head ? '   Farmer : ' A lump sum.'   Dwarf : ' You'd better have asked so much
a head.'   He put his own hat on the farmer's head, who then saw the whole *Allerô
swarming with little men*, who had been ferried across.   The Hövermanns grew rich,
have now all died out, farm sold.   ' When did that happen ? '   Ages ago, in the
olden time, when dwarfs were in the world, 30 or 40 years ago.]

[1] *Arrows* of the Servian *vila*, p. 436.   The Norw. *äli-skudt*, elf-shotten, is said
of sick cattle, Sommerfelt Saltdalens prästegield, p. 119.   Scot. *elfshot*.

[2] Irish Elf-stories xlv. xlvi. cii.

[3] Ibid. ciii.

are said in Norway to be *dverg-slagen* (Hallager p. 20) ; the term
elbentrötsch for silly halfwitted men, whom their avenging hand
has touched, was mentioned on p. 443. One who is seduced by
elves is called in Danish *ellevild*, and this *ellevildelse* in reference
to women is thus described : ' at elven legede med dem.'
Blowing puffing beings language itself shews them to be from
of old : as *spiritus* comes from spirare, so does *geist, ghost* from
the old verb gîsan (flari, cum impetu ferri) ; the ON. gustr,
Engl. gust, is flatus, and there is a dwarf named Gustr (Sæm.
181^b) ;[1] other dwarfs, *Austri, Vestri, Norðri, Suðri* (Sæm. 2^b. Sn.
9. 15. 16) betoken the four winds, while *Vindâlfr*, still a dwarf's
name, explains itself.[2] Beside the breathing, the mere *look* of
an elf has magic power : this our ancient idiom denominates
intsehan (torve intueri, Gramm. 2, 810), MHG. *entsehen* : ' ich
hân in gesegent (blessed), er was *entsehen*,' Eracl. 3239 ; ' von
der *elbe* wirt *entsehen* vil maneger man,' MS. 1, 50^b (see Suppl.).

The *knot-holes in wood* are popularly ascribed to elves. In
Småland a tale is told about the ancestress of a family whose
name is given, that she was an elfmaid, that she came into the
house *through a knot-hole* in the wall *with the sunbeams ;* she was
married to the son, bore him four children, then *vanished* the
same way as she had come. Afzelius 2, 145. Thiele 2, 18.
And not only is it believed that they themselves can creep
through, but that whoever looks through can see things otherwise hidden from him ; the same thing happens if you look
through the hole made in the skin of a beast by an elf's arrow.
In Scotland a knot-hole is called *elfbore*, says Jamieson : ' a hole
in a piece of wood, out of which a knot has dropped or been
driven : viewed as the operation of the fairies.' They also say
auwisbore, Jutish *ausbor* (Molbech's Dial. lex. p. 22. 94). If on
the hill inhabited by elves the following rhyme be uttered 15
times :

> ällkuon, ällkuon, est du her inn,
> saa ska du herud paa 15 iegepinn !

(elf-woman, art thou in here, so shalt thou come out through 15

---

[1] Norweg. *alvgust*, an illness caused by having been breathed upon by elves,
Hallager 4^b.
[2] Old French legend has an elf called *Zephyr ;* there is a German home-sprite
Blaserle, Mone's Anzeiger 1834, p. 260.

oak knot-holes, egepind), the elfin is bound to make her appearance, Molb. Dial. 99 (see Suppl.).

In name, and still more in idea, the elf is connected with the ghostlike butterfly, the product of repeated changes of form. An OHG. gloss (Graff 1, 243) says : brucus, locusta quae nondum volavit, quam vulgo *albam* vocant. The *alp* is supposed often to assume the shape of a butterfly, and in the witch-trials the name of *elb* is given by turns to the caterpillar, to the chrysalis, and to the insect that issues from it. And these share even the names of *gute holden* and *böse dinger* (evil things) with the spirits themselves.

These light airy sprites have an advantage over slow unwieldy man in their godlike power (p. 325) of *vanishing* or making themselves *invisible*.[1] No sooner do they appear, than they are snatched away from our eyes. Only he that wears the ring can get a sight of Elberich, Ortn. 2, 68. 70. 86. 3, 27. With the light elves it is a matter of course, but neither have the black ones forfeited the privilege. The invisibility of dwarfs is usually lodged in a particular part of their dress, a *hat* or a *cloak*, and when that is accidentally dropt or cast aside, they suddenly become visible. The dwarf-tales tell of *nebelkappen* (Deut. sag. nos. 152-3-5), of *gray coats* and *red caps* (Thiele 1, 122. 135), of *scarlet cloaks* (supra, p. 451n.).[2] Earlier centuries used the words *helkappe, helkeplein, helkleit* (Altd. bl. 1, 256), *nebelkappe* (MS. 2, 156ª. 258ᵇ; Morolt 2922. 3932) and *tarnkappe*. By Alberích's and afterwards Sigfrit's *tarnkappe* (Nib. 98, 3. 336, 1. 442, 2. 1060, 2) or simply *kappe* (335, 1) we must understand not a mere covering for the head, but an entire cloak; for in 337, 1 we have also *tarnhût*, the protecting skin, and the

---

[1] 'Hujus tempore principis (Heinrici ducis Karinthiae) in montanis suae ditionis *gens gnana* in cavernis montium habitavit, cum hominibus vescebantur, ludebant, bibebant, choreas ducebant, sed *invisibiliter*. Literas scribebant, rempublicam inter se gerebant, legem habentes et principem, fidem catholicam profitentes, domicilia hominum *latenter* intrantes, hominibus consedentes et arridentes. . . . Principe subducto, nihil de eis amplius est auditum. Dicitur quod *gemmas gestant*, quae *eos reddunt invisibiles*, quia *deformitatem et parvitatem* corporum erubescunt.' Anon. Leobiens. ad ann. 1335 (Pez 1, 940ª).

[2] Ol. Wormius's pref. to Claussön's Dan. transl. of Snorre, Copenh. 1633 : 'der-for sigis de (dverger) at hafve *hätte* paa, huormid kunde giöre sig usynlig.' Other proofs are collected in Ir. Elfenm. lxxiv. lxxv. A schretel wears a *rötes keppel* on him (not on his head), ibid. cxvi. Rollenhagen's 'bergmännlein' wear little white shirts and *pointed caps*, Froschmeuseler xx. vᵇ. Maugis, the Carolingian sorcerer, is called 'lerres (latro) o le *noir chaperon*.'

schretel's 'rôtez *keppel*' becomes in H. Sachs 1, 280[b] a '*mantel scharlach rot des zwergleins.*' Beside invisibility, this cloak imparts superior strength, and likewise control over the dwarf nation and their hoard. In other instances the cap alone is meant: a Norwegian folk-tale in Faye p. 30 calls it *uddehat* (pointed hat ?), and a home-sprite at Hildesheim bears the name of *Hôdeken* from the felt hat he wore. Probably the OHG. *helot-helm* (latibulum), Gl. Hrab. 969[a], the OS. *helith-helm*, Hel. 164, 29, AS. *heolðhelm*, Cod. Exon. 362, 31, *hælðhelm*, Cædm. 29, 2, ON. *hialmr hulis* (an Eddic word for cloud), Sæm. 50[a],[1] and the AS. *grimhelm*, Cædm. 188, 27. 198, 20. Beow. 666, all have a similar meaning, though the simple helm and grîme (p. 238) already contain the notion of a covering and a mask; for *helm* is from helan (celare) as huot, hood, or hat, from huotan (tegere). No doubt other superior beings, beside elves and dwarfs, wore the invisible-making garment; I need only mention Oðin's *hat* with turned-up brim (p. 146), Mercury's *petasus*, Wish's hat, which our fairy-tales still call *wishing-hat*,[2] and Pluto's or Orcus's *helmet* (Ἄϊδος κυνέη, Il. 5, 845. Hesiod, Scut. 227). The dwarfs may have stood in some peculiar, though now obscured, relation to Oðinn, as the hat-wearing pataeci, cabiri and Dioscuri did to Jupiter (see Suppl.).

From such ability to conceal their form, and from their teazing character in general, there will arise all manner of deception and disappointment (conf. Suppl. to p. 331), to which man is exposed in dealing with elves and dwarfs. We read: der *alp triuget* (cheats), Fundgr. 327, 18; den *triuget*, weiz Got, nicht der *alp*, not even the elf can trick him, Diut. 2, 34; Silvester 5199; die mag *triegen* wol der *alp*, Suchenwirt xxxi. 12; ein *getroc* daz mich in dem slâfe *triuget*, Ben. 429; dich *triegen* die *elbin* (l. elbe, rhyme selbe), Altd. bl. 1, 261; *elbe triegent*, Amgb. 2[b]; diu *elber triegent*, Herbort 5[b]; in bedûhte daz in *trüge* ein *alp*, Ir. elfenm. lvii.; *alfs ghedroch*, Elegast 51, 775. Reinh. 5367, conf. Horae Belg. 6, 218-9; *alfsche droch*, Reinaert (prose lxxii.[a]). In our

---

[1] Fornm. sög. 2, 141 says of Eyvindr the sorcerer: 'giörði þeim *hulidshialm*,' made for them a mist, darkness. *hulinhialmr*, Fornald. sög. 3, 219; *kuflshöttr* 1, 9. 2, 20. See Rafn's Index sub v. dulgerfi.
[2] A weighty addition to the arguments for the identity of Wuotan and Mercury; conf. p. 419 on the wishing-rod.

elder speech *gitroc, getroc, âgetroc, abegetroc,* denotes trickery especially diabolic, proceeding from evil spirits (Gramm. 2, 709. 740–1).[1] To the same effect are some other disparaging epithets applied to elves: *elbischez getwâs, elbischez âs, elbischez ungehiure,* as the devil himself is called a getwâs (fantasma) and a monster. So, of the morbid oppression felt in sleep and dreaming, it is said quite indifferently, either: 'the devil has shaken thee, *ridden* thee,' 'hînaht *ritert* dich satanas (Satan shakes thee to-night),' Fundgr. 1, 170; or else the *elf,* the *nightmare*[2]: 'dich hat *geriten* der *mar,*' 'ein *alp zoumet* dich (bridles thee).' And as Dame Holle *entangles* one's spinning or hair (p. 269), as she herself has *tangled* hair,[3] and as stubbly hair is called *Hollenzopf;*[4] so the nightelf, the nightmare, rolls up the hair of men or the manes and tails of horses, in knots, or chews them through: *alpzopf, druten-zopf, wichtelzopf, weichselzopf* (of which more hereafter), in Lower Saxony *mahrenlocke, elfklatte* (Brem. wörtb. 1, 302), Dan. *mare-lok,* Engl. *elflocks* (Nares sub v.), *elvish knots,* and in Shakspeare to *elf* means to mat: 'elf all my hair in knots,' K. Lear ii. 3. Here will come in those '*comae* equorum diligenter *tricatae,*' when the white women make their midnight rounds (supra, p. 287). The Lithuanian elf named *aitwaras* likewise mats the hair: *aitwars* yo plaukus suzindo, suwele (has drawn his hair to-gether). Lasicz 51 has: *aitwaros,* incubus qui post sepes habitat (from twora sepes, and ais pone). Some parts of Lower Saxony give to the wichtelzopf (plica polonica) the name of *selkensteert,* selkin's tail (Brem. wörtb. 4, 749), *sellentost* (Hufeland's Journal 11. 43), which I take to mean tuft of the goodfellow, homesprite

---

[1] Daz analutte des sih pergenten *trugetieveles,* N. Bth. 44; *gidrog* phantasma, O. iii. 8, 24; *gedrog,* Hel. 89, 22; tievels *getroc,* Karl 62ª; 'ne dragu io ênic drugi thing,' Hel. 8, 10. The dwarf Elberich (Ortn. 3, 27. 5, 105) is called 'ein *trüge-wiz*'; conf. infra, bilwiz.

[2] Our *nachtmar* I cannot produce either in OHG. or MHG. Lye gives AS. '*mære·fæcce*' incubus, ephialtes, but I do not understand fæcce. Nearly akin is the Pol. *mora,* Boh. *mûra,* elf and evening butterfly, sphinx. In the Mark they say both *alb* and *mahre,* Adalb. Kuhn, p. 374. French *cauchemare, cochemar,* also *chaucheville, chauchi vieilli* (Mém. des Antiq. 4. 399; J. J. Champollion Figeac patois, p. 125); Ital. *pesaruole,* Span. *pesadilla,* O. Fr. *appesart;* these from *caucher* (calcare), and *pesar* (to weigh down).

[3] In Kinderm. 3, 44, Holle gets her terrible hair combed out, which had not been combed for a year. A girl, whom she has gifted, combs pearls and precious stones out of her own hair.

[4] Hess. *Hollezaul* (for -zagel, tail), *Hollezopp,* Schmidt's Westerw. idiot. 341. Adelung has: '*höllenzopf,* plica polonica, Pol. koltun, Boh. koltaun.'

(gesellchen).[1] In Thuringia *saellocke*, Prætorius's Weltbeschr. 1, 40. 293 (see Suppl.).

The Edda nowhere represents either âlfar or dvergar as mounted, whilst our poems of the Mid. Ages make both Elberich and Laurín come *riding*. Heinrich von Ofterdingen bestows on them a steed 'als ein *geiz* (goat),' and Ulrich's Alexander gives the dwarf king Antilois a pony the *size of a roe*,[2] while Altd. bl. 2, 151 without more ado mounts the wihtel on a *white roe*. Antilois is richly dressed, bells tinkle on his bridle-reins; he is angry with Alexander for spoiling his flower-garden, as Laurín is with Dietrich and Wittich. The Welsh stories also in Crofton Croker 3, 306 say : 'they were very diminutive persons riding four abreast, and mounted on *small white horses no bigger than dogs*' (see Suppl.).

All dwarfs and elves are *thievish*. Among Eddic names of dwarfs is an *Alþiofr*, Sæm. 2[b]; *Alpris*, more correctly Alfríkr dvergr, in Vilk. saga cap. 16, 40. is called 'hinn mikli stelari'; and in the Titurel 27, 288 (Hahn 4105), a notorious thief, who can steal the eggs from under birds, is *Elbegast* (corrupted into Elegast, Algast). In our Low German legends they lay their plans especially against the *pea-fields*.[3] Other thefts of dwarfs

---

[1] Ogonczyk Zakrzewaki, in his Hist. of plica polonica (Vienna, 1830), observes, that its cure also is accomplished with superstitious ceremonies. In Podlachia the elftuft is solemnly cut off at Easter time and buried. In the Skawina district about Cracow, it is partially cropped with redhot shears, a piece of copper money tied up in it, and thrown into the ruins of an old castle in which evil spirits lodge ; but whoever does this must not look round, but hasten home as fast as he can. Superstitious formulas for the cure of plica are given by Zakrzewaki, p. 20, out of an Old Boh. MS. of 1325.

[2] Wackernagel's Basel MSS. p. 28.

[3] Deut. sagen, nos 152, 155 ; to which I will here add two communicated by Hr. Schambach. The first is from Jühnde, near Göttingen :——Vor nich langer tid gaf et to Jüne noch twarge. Düse plegten up et feld to gan, un den lüen de arften (leuten die erbsen) weg to stelen, wat se üm sau lichter konnen, da se unsichtbar wören dor (durch) ene kappe, dei se uppen koppe harren (hatten). Sau wören nu ok de twarge enen manne ümmer up sin grat arftenstücke egan, un richteden öne velen schäen darup an. Düt duerde sau lange, bet hei up den infal kam, de twarge to fengen. Hei tog alsau an hellen middage en sel (seil) rings üm dat feld. As nu de twarge unner den sel dorkrupen wollen, fellen önen de kappen af, se seiten nu alle in blaten köppen, un wören sichtbar. De twarge, dei sau esfongen wören, geiwen öne vele gaue wore, dat he dat sel wegnömen mögde, un versproken ene mette (miethe) geld davor to gewen, hei solle mant *vor sunnenupgange* weer (wieder) an düse stëe komen. En ander man segde öne awer, hei mögde nich gegen sunnenupgang, sundern schon üm twölwe hengan, denn da wöre de dag ok schon anegan. Düt dê he, und richtig wören de twarge da met ener mette geld. Davon heiten de lüe, dei dei mette geld ekregen harren, Mettens. [Epitome :—Dwarfs at Jühnde preyed on the pea-fields ; wore caps which made them invisible. One man at high noon stretched a cord round his field. Dwarfs, creeping under it, brushed

are collected in Elfenm. xcii. xciii., and their longing for children
and blooming maids is treated of, p. civ. cv. Dwarf-kings *run
away with* maidens to their mountains : Laurîn with the fair
Similt (Sindhilt ?), Goldemar or Volmar with a king's daughter
(Deut. heldensag. 174, Haupt's Zeitschr. 6, 522-3) ; the Swed.
folk-lay ' Den *bergtagna* ' (-taken) tells of a virgin, who spends
eight years with a *mountain-king*, and brings him seven sons and
a daughter, before she sees her home again.[1] The following

their caps off, became visible and were caught ; promised him money, if he came
there again *before sunrise*. A friend advised him to go as early as 12, for even
then the day (of the dwarfs?) was begun. He did so, and got his meed.]

The second story is from Dorste in Osterode bailiwick :——En buere harre arften
buten stan, dei wören öne ümmer utefreten. Da word den bueren esegt, hei solle
hengan un slaen met wêenrauen (weidenruten) drupe rüm, sau sleugde gewis einen
de kappe af. Da geng he ok hen met sinnen ganzen lüen, un funk ok enen twarg,
dei sie (sagte) tau öne, wenn he öne wier las lan (wieder los lassen) wolle, sau wolle
öne enn wagen vul geld gewen, hei möste awer *vor sunnenupgange* komen. Da leit
ne de buere las, un de twarg sie öne, wo sine hülle wöre. Do ging de buere henn
un frang enn, wunnir dat denn die sunne upginge? Dei sie tau öne, dei ginge
glocke twölwe up. Da spanne ok sinen wagen an, un tug hen. Asse (as he) vor
de hülen kam, do juchen se drinne un sungen :

> Dat ist gaut, dat de büerken dat nich weit,
> dat de sunne üm twölwe up geit !

Asse sek awer melle, wesden se öne en afgefillet perd, dat solle mêe (mit) nömen,
wier (weiter) können se öne nits gewen. Da was de buere argerlich, awer hei wolle
doch fleisch vor sine hunne mêe nömen, da haude en grat stücke af, un laud et
upen wagen. Asser mêe na hus kam, da was alles schire gold. Da wollet andere
noch nae langen, awer da was hülle un perd verswunnen. [Epitome :—A farmer,
finding his peas eaten, was advised to beat all round with willow twigs, sure to
knock a dwarf's cap off. Caught a dwarf, who promised a waggon full of money if
he'd come to his cave *before sunrise*. Asked a man when sunrise was? 'At
twelve.' Went to the cave, heard shouting and singing: ' 'Tis well the poor
peasant but little knows that twelve is the time when the sun up goes !' Is shown
a skinned horse, he may take that ! Gets angry, yet cuts a great piece off for his
dogs. When he got home, it was all sheer gold. Went for the rest ; cave and
horse were gone.]

The remarkable trysting-time *before sunrise* seems to be explained by the dwarf-
kind's shyness of daylight, which appears even in the Edda, Sæm. 51ᵇ : they *avoid
the sun*, they have in their caves a different light and different time from those of
men. In Norse legends re-appears the trick of engaging a trold in conversation till
the sun is risen : when he looks round and sees the sun, he splits in two ; Asbiörnsen
and Moe, p. 186. [The märchen of Rumpelstilzchen includes the dwarfs' song,
' 'Tis well,' etc., the splitting in two, and the kidnapping presently to be mentioned.]

[1] But she-dwarfs also marry men ; Ödman (Bahuslän, p. 78-9, conf. Afzelius 2,
157) relates quite seriously, and specifying the people's names :——Reors föräldrar i
Hogen i Lurssockn, some bodde i Fuglekärr i Svarteborgssockn ; hvars farfar var
en skött, ok bodde vid et berg, ther fick han se mitt på dagen *sitjande en vacker
piga på en sten*, ther med at fänga henne, *kastade han stål emellan berget ok henne*,
hvarpå hennes far gasmade eller log in i berget, ok öpnade bergets dörr, tilfrågandes
honom, om han vill ha hans dotter? Hvilket han med ja besvarade, ok efter *hon
var helt naken*, tog han sina kläder ok hölgde ofver henne, ok lät christna henne.
Vid afträdet sade hennes far til honom : ' när tu skalt ha bröllup, skalt tu laga til
12 tunnor öl ok baka en hop bröd ok kiött efter 4 stutar, ok kiöra til *jordhögen* eller
berget, ther jag håller til, ok när brudskänken skall utdelas, skall jag väl ge min ' ;

legend from Dorste near Osterode, it will be seen, transfers to
dwarfs what the Kindermärchen No. 46 relates of a sorcerer :—
Et was enmal en mäken int holt nan arberen egan, da keimen de
twarge un neiment môe.   Da se na örer hülen keimen, da verleifde
sek de eine *twarg* in se, un da solle se öne ok frien, awer iest
(erst) wollen de *twarge* de andern twarge taur hochtit bidden,
underdes solle dat mäken in huse alles reine maken un taur hochtit
anreien.   Awer dat mäken, dat wolle den *twarg* nich frien, da
wollet weglopen, awer dat se't nich glik merken, tug et sin teug
ut un tug dat ne strawisch an, un da sach et ne tunne vul hunig,
da krup et rinder (hinein), un da sach et ok ne tunne vul feddern,
un da krup et ok rinder, un da et wedder ruter kam, was et gans
vul feddern, un da leip et weg un steig upn hoagen boam.   Da
keimen de *twarge* derbunder (darunter) vorbi, un da se't seichen,
meinen se, et wöre en vugel, da reipen se't an un sêen :

     ' Wohen, woher du schöäne feddervugel ? '
     ' Ek kome ut der *twarges hüle.*'
     ' Wat maket de schöäne junge brût ? '
     ' Dei steit metn bessen un keret dat hus.'
     ' Juchhei ! sau wil wie ok hen.'

Und da se hen keimen, sêen se taur brut ' gûen morgen,' un
sêen noch mehr dertau ; awer da se nich antwure, sleuchten se'r
hinder de aren, un da fell se hen [1] (see Suppl.).

<hr/>

hvilket ok skedde.   Ty när de andre gåfvo, *lyfte han up tacket ok kastade en så stor*
penningeposse ther igenom, at bänken så när gådt af, ok sade thervid : ' ther är min
skänk ! ' ok sade ytterligare : ' när tu skal ha tin hemmagifta, skaltu kiöra med 4
hästar hit til berget ok få tin andel.'   Tå han sedermera efter hans begäran kom
tit, fik han *kopparkittlar,* then ene större än then andre, tils then yttersta störste
kättelen blef upfyld med andra mindre ; item brandcreatur, som voro hielmeta, af
hvilken färg ok creaturslag, som äro stora ok frodiga, the än ha qvar på rik, i
Tanums gäll beläget.   Thenne mannen Reors far i Foglekärsten benämd, aflade en
hop barn med thenna sin således från berget afhämtade hustru, bland hvilka var
nämnemannen Reor på Hogen ; so har Ola Stenson i stora Rijk varit Reors syster-
son, hvilken i förledit år med döden afgik.   [Epitome :—Reor's fathers dwelt, etc.
One, an archer, lived near a hill, saw one day at noon a *fine girl sitting on a stone ;*
to get her, he *threw steel between her and the hill.*   Her father opened the door of
the hill, asked him if he wanted his daughter.   He answered yes, and as she was
naked, threw some of his clothes over her ; had her christened.   Father : ' At thy
wedding bring ale, bread and horseflesh to my *hill,* and I will give thee a wedding
gift.'   This being done, he lifted their roof and threw in a great sum of money.
' Now for house-furniture, come here with four horses.'   The man did so, and received *copper kettles* of all sizes, one inside the other, etc., etc.   By this wife, thus
fetched from the hill, he had many children ; one was Reor, whose nephew O. S.
died only last year.]
  [1] Translation :—Once a girl had gone into the wood after strawberries, when the

They *abstract* well-shaped children from the cradle, and substitute their own ugly ones, or even themselves. These sup-
posititious creatures are called changelings, *cambiones* (App.,
Superst. E.); OHG. *wihselinga* (N. Ps. 17, 46. Cant. Deuteron.
5), our *wechselbälge;* Swed. *bytingar,* Dan. bittinger; also our
kielkröpfe, dickköpfe from their thick necks and heads. (Stories
about them in Thiele 1, 47. 3, 1. Faye p. 20. Ir. Elfenm.
xli.-xlv. cv. Deut. sag. nos. 81-2, 87-90.)[1] So early as in the
poem 'Zeno' (Bruns p. 27 seq.) it is the *devil* that fills the
place of a stolen child. The motive of the exchange seems to be,
that elves are anxious to improve their breed by means of the
human child, which they design to keep among them, and for
which they give up one of their own. A safeguard against such
substitution is, to place a key, or one of the father's clothes, or

dwarfs came and carried her off. When they got to their cave, one dwarf fell in
love with her, and she was to marry him; but first the dwarfs were going to bid the
other dwarfs to the wedding, in the meantime the girl was to make the house clean
and prepare it for the wedding. But the girl, she did not want to marry the dwarf,
so she would run away; but that they might not notice it at once, she pulled her
dress off and put it round a bundle of straw; then she saw a tub full of honey and
crept into it, and then she saw a tub full of feathers and crept into that also, and
when she came out again, she was all over feathers; then she ran away, and climbed
up a high tree. Then the dwarfs came past under it, and when they saw her, they
thought she was a bird, and called to her and said: 'Whither and whence, thou
pretty feathered bird?'——'I come out of the dwarf's hole '——'What does the
pretty young bride?'——'She stands with a besom and sweeps the house.'——
'Hurra! then we'll go there too.'——And when they got there, they said to the
bride 'good morning,' and said other things too; but as she never answered, they
boxed her ears, and down she fell.

Assuredly the dwarfs in this story are genuine and of old date. Besides, it can
be supplemented from Kinderm. 3, 75, where the returning dwarfs are preceded by
foxes and bears, who also go past and question the 'Fitcher's fowl.' There the
tub of *honey* in the dwarf's house is a cask of *blood,* but both together agree wonderfully with the vessels which the dwarfs Fialar and Galar keep filled with Kvâsi's
precious blood and with honey. Sn. 83. 84.

[1] Dresd. saml. no. 15, of the ' müllers sun.' A foolish miller begs a girl to teach
him the sweetness of love. She makes him lick honey all night, he empties a big
jar, gets a stomach-ache, and fancies himself about to become a parent. She sends
for a number of old women to assist him: ' da fragt er, war sein kind wer komen
(what's come of the baby)? sie sprachen: hastu nit vernommen? ez was ain rehter
wislonbalk (regular changeling), und tett als ein *guoter schalk:* da er erst von
deinem leib kam (as soon as born), da fuer ez pald hin und entran hin uff zuo dem
fürst empor. Der müller sprach: pald hin uff das spor! vachent ez (catch him)!
pringent ez mir herab!' They bring him a swallow in a covered pot.——Again a
Hessian folk-tale: A woman was cutting corn on the Dosenberg, and her infant lay
beside her. A *wichtel-wife* crept up, took the human child, and put her own in its
place. When the woman looked for her darling babe, there was a frightful thick-
head staring in her face. She screamed, and raised such a hue and cry, that at last
the thief came back with the child; but she would not give it up till the woman
had put the *wichtelbalg* to her breast, and nourished it for once with the generous
milk of human kind.

steel and needles in the cradle (App., Superst. Germ. 484. 744. Swed. 118).[1]

One of the most striking instances of agreement that I know of anywhere occurs in connection with prescriptions for *getting rid of your changeling.*

In Hesse, when the wichtelmann sees water boiled over the fire in eggshells, he cries out: 'Well, I am as *old as the Wester-wald,* but I never saw anything boiled in eggshells;' Km. no. 39. In Denmark a pig stuffed with skin and hair is set before the changeling: 'Now, I have seen the *wood* in Tisö *young three times over,* but never the like of this': Thiele 1, 48. Before an Irish changeling they also boil eggshells, till he says: 'I've been *in the world* 1500 *years,* and never seen that'; Elfenm. p. 38. Before a Scotch one the mother puts twenty-four eggshells on the hearth, and listens for what he will say; he says: 'I was *seven* before I came to my nurse, I have lived *four years* since, and never did I see so many milkpans;' Scott's Mintrelsy 2, 174. In the Breton folksong (Villemarqué 1, 29) he sees the mother cooking for ten servantmen in one eggshell, and breaks out into the words: 'I have seen the *egg before* [it became] *the white hen,* and the *acorn before the oak,* seen it acorn and sapling and oak in Brezal wood, but never aught like this.' This story about the changeling is also applied to Dame Gauden's little dog, chap. XXXI. Villemarqué 1, 32, quotes in addition a Welsh legend and a passage from Geoffrey of Monmouth, in which the Breton and Welsh formula for great age is already put into the mouth of Merlin the wild; in each case an ancient forest is named. In all these stories the point was, by some out-of-the-way proceeding, to get the changeling himself to confess his age, and consequently the exchange. Such traditions must have been widely spread in Europe from the earliest times; and it was evidently assumed, that elves and korred had a very different term of life assigned them from that of the human race (see Suppl.).

All elves have an irresistible fondness for *music* and *dancing.* By night you see them tread their round on the moonlit meadows,

---

[1] The Finns call a changeling *luoti*: monstrum nec non infans matre dormiente a magis suppositus, quales putant esse infantem rachitide laborantem (Renvall). A Breton story of the *korrigan* changing a child is in Villemarqué 1, 25.

and at dawn perceive their track in the dew: Dan. *älledands*, Swed. *älfdands*, Engl. *fairy rings*, *fairy green*. The sight of mountain-spirits *dancing* on the meadows betokens to men a fruitful year (Deut. sag. no. 298). An Austrian folk-song in Schottky, p. 102, has: 'und duärt drobn afm beargl, da *dânzn* zwoa zweargl, de dânzn so rar.' In Laurin's mountain, in Venus's mountain, there murmurs a gay seductive music, dances are trod in them (Laurin, 24); in the Ortnit (Ettm. 2, 17) there is 'ein *smalez* pfat getreten mit *kleinen* füezen,' a small path trod by little feet. Songs of *elfins* allure young men up the mountain, and all is over with them (Svenska fornsånger 2, 305. Danske viser 1, 235–240).[1] This performance is called *elffrus lek*, *elfvelek*. The ordinary fornyrðalag[2] bears among Icelandic poets the name *liuflingslag* (carmen genii), Olafsen p. 56; in Norway that kind of sweet music is called *huldreslât* (supra, p. 271). One unprinted poem in MHG. (Cod. pal. 341. 357ᵃ) contains the remarkable passage: 'there sat fiddlers, and all fiddled the *albleich* (elf-lay)'; and another (Altd. bl. 2, 93) speaks of 'seiten spil und *des wihtels schal*': it must have been a sweet enchanting strain, whose invention was ascribed to the elves.[3] Finn Magnusen derives the name of the dwarf Haugspori (Sæm. 2ᵇ) from the footmarks printed on grass by an elf roaming over the hills at night. And a song in Villemarqué 1, 39 makes the dwarfs dance themselves out of breath (see Suppl.).

This fondness of elves for melody and dance links them with higher beings, notably with half-goddesses and goddesses. In the ship (of Isis) songs of joy resound in the night, and a dancing multitude circles round it (p. 258). In Dame Holda's dwelling, in Dame Venus's mountain, are the song and the dance. Celtic traditions picture the fays as *dancing* (Mém. de l'acad. celt. 5, 108); these fays stand midway between elfins and wise women.[4] The Hymn to Aphrodite 260 says of the mountain-nymphs:

δηρὸν μὲν ζώουσι καὶ ἄμβροτον εἶδαρ ἔδουσι,
καί τε μετ' ἀθανάτοισι καλὸν χορὸν ἐρρώσαντο.

---

[1] Folk-tale of the Hanebierg in the Antiqvariske Annaler 1, 331–2.
[2] Forn-yrða-lag, ancient word-lay, the alliterative metre of narrative verse, in which the poems of the Elder Edda are written.—TRANS.
[3] Conf. Ir. Elfenm. lxxxi.-lxxxiii., and the wihtel-show above, p. 441 note; Ihre sub v. älfdans; Arndt's Journey to Sweden 3, 16.
[4] Like the Servian *vily*, who hold their dance on mountain and mead, p. 436.

(On deathless food they feed, and live full long, And whirl with gods through graceful dance and song.) No wonder our sage elves and dwarfs are equally credited with having the gift of *divination*. As such the dwarf Andvari appears in the Edda (Sæm. 181ª), and still more Alvís (all-wise); dwarf Eugel (L. Germ. Ögel) prophesies to Siegfried (Hürn. Sifr. 46, 4. 162, 1), so does Grípir in the Edda, whose father's name is Eylimi; in the OFr. Tristran, the nains (nanus) Frocin is a *devins* (divinator), he interprets the stars at the birth of children (ll. 318-326. 632). When, in legends and fairy tales, dwarfs appear singly among men, they are *sage counsellors* and helpful, but also apt to fire up and take offence. Such is the character of Elberich and Oberon; in a Swiss nursery-tale (no. 165), '*e chlis isigs mandle*' (a little ice-grey mannikin), '*e chlis mutzigs mandle*' (stumpy m.), appears in an '*isige chläidle*' (grey coat), and guides the course of events; elves forewarn men of impending calamity or death (Ir. Elfenm. lxxxvi.). And in this point of view it is not without significance, that elves and dwarfs ply the *spinning* and *weaving* so much patronized by Dame Holda and Frikka. The flying gossamer in autumn is in vulgar opinion the thread spun by elves and dwarfs; the Christians named it Marienfaden (-thread), Mariensommer, because Mary too was imagined spinning and weaving. The Swed. *dverg* signifies araneus as well as nanus, and *dvergs-nät* a cobweb.[1] The ON. saga of Samson hinn fagri mentions in cap. 17 a marvellous '*skickja, sem álfkonurnar höfðu ofit,*' mantle that elfins had woven. On a hill inhabited by spirits you hear at night the *elfin* .(which 'troldkone' here must mean) *spinning*, and her wheel humming, says Thiele 3, 25. Melusina the fay is called *alvinne* in a Mid. Nethl. poem (Mone's Niederl. Volkslit. p. 75).——On the other hand, the male dwarfs *forge* jewels and arms (supra, p.444-7, and in fuller detail in Ir. Elfenm. lxxxviii.).[2]

---

[1] So the Breton *korr* is both dwarf and spider.

[2] Here is one more legend from Ödman's Bahuslän, p. 79 :——Thessutan har man åtskillige berättelser ok sagor om *smedar*, så i högar som bärg, såsom här i Fossumstorp högar, hvarest man hördt, at the smidt *liksom i en annan smidja* om aftonen *efter solenes nedergång*, ok eljest midt på höga middagen. För 80 år sedan gik Olas fadar i Surtung, benämd Ola Simunsson, här i församlingen från Slängevald hafvandes med sig en hund, hvilken tå han blef varse mitt på dagen *bärgsmannen*, som tå *smidde på en stor sten*, skiälde han på honom, hvar på *bärgsmeden*, som hade en *liusgrå råk* ok *bldvulen hatt*, begynte at snarka åt hunden, som tillika med husbonden funno rådeligast, at lemna honom i fred. Thet gifvas ok ännu ibland gemene man små crucifixer af metall, som gemenligen halles före vara i fordna

To bring pig-iron to dwarfs, and find it the next morning outside
the cave, ready worked for a slight remuneration, is a feature of
very ancient date; the scholiast on Apollon. Rhod. (Argon. 4,
761) illustrates the ἄκμονες Ἡφαίστοιο (anvils of H.) by a story
of the volcanic isles about Sicily taken from Pytheas's Travels:
τὸ δὲ παλαιὸν ἐλέγετο τὸν βουλόμενον ἀργὸν σίδηρον ἀποφέρειν
καὶ ἐπὶ τὴν αὔριον ἐλθόντα λαμβάνειν ἢ ξίφος ἢ εἴ τι ἄλλο ἤθελε
κατασκευάσαι, καταβαλόντα μισθόν (see Suppl.).

What I have thus put together on the nature and attributes of
elves in general, will be confirmed by an examination of particular
elvish beings, who come forward under names of their own.

Among these I will allot the first place to a genius, who is
nowhere to be found in the Norse myths, and yet seems to be
of ancient date. He is mentioned in several MHG. poems:

> Sie wolten daz kein *pilwiz*
> si dâ schützze durch diu knie.   Wh. 324, 8.
> Er solde sîn ein *guoter*
> und ein *pilewis* geheizen,
> davon ist daz in reizen
> die übeln ungehiure.   Rüediger von zwein gesellen (Cod.
> regimont.) 15[b].
>
> Dâ kom ich an *bulwechsperg* gangen,
> dâ schôz mich der *bulwechs*,
> dâ schôz mich die *bulwechsin*,
> dâ schôz mich als ir ingesind.   Cod. vindob. 2817.   71[a].
> Von schrabaz *pilwihten*.   Titur. 27, 299 (Hahn 4116).
> Sein part het manchen *pilbiszoten*.   Casp. von der Rön.
> heldenb. 156[b].

Out of all these it is hard to pick out the true name.   Wolfram

tider *smidde i bärg*, hvilka the oförståndige bruka at hänga på boskap, som hastigt
fådt ondt ute på marken, eller som säges blifvit *väderslagne*, hvarigenom tro them
bli helbregda. Af sådana *bärgsmiden* har jag ok nyligen kommit öfver ett, som
ännu är i förvar, ok på ofvannämde sätt gik i lån at bota siukdommar.   [Epitome:
——Many stories of *smiths* in the mountains, who worked *as at any other smithy*,
after sunset or else at high noon. Eighty years ago Ola Simunsson was coming,
etc. ; had with him a dog, which, on seeing a *hill-man forging on a great stone*,
barked at him ; but the *hill-smith*, who wore a *light-grey coat* and *blue woollen cap*,
snarled at the dog, etc.   There are small metal crucifixes held to have been *forged
in the hills* in former times, which simple folk still hang on cattle hurt in the field
or *weather-stricken*, whereby they trow them to get healed.   Of such *hill-wrought*
things I have lately met with one, that used to be lent out to cure sicknesses.]

makes pilwiz (var. pilbiz, bilwiz, bilwitz) rhyme with biz (morsus),
where the short vowel in the last syllable seems to point to
pilwiht; the same with bilbis in another poem, which would have
spelt it bilbeis if it had been long; so that we cannot connect it
with the OS. balowîs, nor immediately with the bilwîs and balwîs
contrasted on p. 374. The varying form is a sign that in the
13-14th century the word was no longer understood; and later
on, it gets further distorted, till bulwechs makes us think of a
totally unconnected word balwahs (hebes).[1] A confession-book
of the first half of the 15th century (Hoffmann's Monatschr. 753)
has *pelewysen* synonymous with witches, and Colerus's Hausbuch
(Mainz 1656), p. 403, uses *bihlweisen* in the same sense; several
authorities for the form *pilbis* are given in Schm. 4, 188. We
welcome the present Westph. Nethl. *belewitten* in the Teutonista,
where Schuiren considers it equivalent to *guede holden* and *witte
vrouwen* (penates). Kilian has *belewitte* (lamia); and here comes
in fitly a passage from Gisb. Vœtius de miraculis (Disput., tom.
2, 1018): 'De illis quos nostrates appellant *beeldwit* et *blinde
belien*, a quibus nocturna visa videri atque ex iis arcana revelari
putant.' *Belwit* then is penas, a kindly disposed home-sprite,
a *guote holde* (supra, p. 266), what Rüediger calls 'ein *guoter*
und ein *pilewiz*.' Peculiar to AS. is an adj. *bilwit, bilewit*,
Cædm. 53, 4. 279, 23, which is rendered mansuetus, simplex, but
might more exactly mean aequus, justus. God is called '*bilewit*
fæder' (Andr. 1996), Boeth. metr. 20, 510. 538; and is also
addressed as such in Cod. exon. 259, 6; again, '*bilwitra* breoste'
(bonorum, aequorum pectus), Cod. exon. 343, 23. The spelling
bilehwit (Beda 5, 2, 13, where it translates simplex) would lead
to hwît (albus), but then what can *bil* mean? I prefer the better
authorized *bilewit*, taking 'wit' to mean scius, and *bilwit*, OHG.
pilawiz, pilwiz? to mean aequum[2] sciens, aequus, bonus, although

---

[1] Fundgr. 1, 343, where palwasse rhymes with vahse, as MHG. often has 'wahs
for acutus, when it should be 'was,' OHG. huas, AS. hwæs, ON. hvass; thus the
OHG. palohuas = badly sharp, *i.e.* blunt, ON. bôlhvass? just as palotât = baleful
deed. A later form bülwächs in Schm. 4, 15.

[2] The simple *bil* seems of itself to be aequitas, jus, and mythic enough (p. 376).
MHG. *billich* (aequus), Dint. 3, 38. Fundgr. ii. 56, 27. 61, 28. 66, 19. Reinh.
354. Iw. 1630. 5244. 5730. 6842. Ls. 2, 329. *billichen* (jure), Nib. 450, 2. der
billich (aequitas), Trist. 6429. 9374. 10062. 13772. 18027. An OHG. *billih* I only
know from W. lxv. 27, where the Leyden MS. has *bilithlich*. As the notions
'aequus, aequalis, similis' lie next door to each other, piladi, bilidi (our bild) is
really aequalitas, similitudo, the ON. likneski (imago). The Celtic *bil* also means
good, mild; and Leo (Malb. Gl. 38) tries to explain bilwiz from bilbheith, bilbhith.

an adj. 'vit, wiz' occurs nowhere else that I know of, the ON.
vitr (gen. vitrs) being provided with a suffix -r. If this etymology
is tenable, *bilwiz* is a good genius, but of elvish nature; he haunts
mountains, his *shot* is dreaded like that of the elf (p. 460), hair
is tangled and matted by him as by the alp (p. 464). One
passage cited by Schm. 4, 188, deserves particular notice: 'so
man ain kind oder ain gewand opfert zu aim *pilbispawm*,' if one
sacrifice a child or garment to a pilbis-tree, *i.e.* a tree supposed
to be inhabited by the pilwiz, as trees do contain wood-sprites
and elves. Börner's Legends of the Orlagau, p. 59. 62, name a
witch *Bilbze*. The change of *bilwiz, bilwis* into *bilwiht* was a step
easily taken, as in other words also *s* and *h*, or *s* and *ht* inter-
change (lios, lioht, Gramm. 1, 138), also *st* and *ht* (forest, foreht,
Gramm. 4, 416); and the more, as the compound *bilwiht* gave
a not unsuitable meaning, 'good wight.' The Gl. blas. 87ᵃ offer
a *wihsilstein* (penas), nay, the varying form of our present names
for the plica (p. 464), *weichselzopf, wichselzopf, wichtelzopf (bich-
telzopf)* makes the similar shading off of *bilweichs, bilwechs, bil-
wicht* probable: I have no doubt there is even a *bilweichszopf,
bilwizzopf* to be found.[1]

Popular belief in the last few centuries, having lost the old and
higher meaning of this spiritual being, has retained, as in the case
of the alb, of Holla and Berhta, only the hateful side of its nature:
a tormenting terrifying spectre, tangling your hair and beard,
cutting up your corn, it appears mostly in a female form, as a
sorceress and witch. Martin von Amberg's Mirror of Confession
already interprets *pilbis* by devil, as Kilian does *belewitte* by
lamia, strix. The tradition lingers chiefly in Eastern Germany,

---

[1] Another Polish name for plica, beside koltun, is *wieszcsyce* (Linde 6, 227), and
vulgar opinion ascribes it to the magic of a *wieszczka* wise woman, witch. This
wieszczyce agrees with our *weichsel*-zopf, and also with the *-wis, -weis* in bilwis.
If we could point to a compound bialowieszczka (white witch, white fay; but I
nowhere find it, not even among other Slavs), there would arise a strong suspicion
of the Slavic origin of our *bilwis*; for the present its German character seems to
me assured both by the absence of such Slavic compound, and by the AS. bilwit
and Nethl. belwitte: besides, our *wis* comes from wizan, and the Pol. *wieszcz* from
wiedzieć [O.Sl. védeti, to wit], and the kinship of the two words can be explained
without any thought of borrowing. Of different origin seem to me the Slovèn.
paglawits, dwarf, and the Lith. Pilvitus (Lasicz 54) or Pilwite (Narbutt 1, 52), god
or goddess of wealth. [The Russ. *vèshch* (shch pron. as in parish-church) has the
same sound as *wieszcz*, but means thing, Goth. vafht-s; for kt, ht becomes shch,
as in noshch, night. I am not sure therefore that even *wieszczka* may not be
"little wiht."—TRANS.]

in Bavaria, Franconia, Vogtland and Silesia. H. Sachs uses *bilbitzen* of matting the hair in knots, *pilmitz* of tangled locks : ' ir har *verbilbitzt*, zapfet und stroblet, als ob sie hab der rab gezoblet,' i. 5, 309[b]. ii. 2, 100[d] ; '*pilmitzen*, zoten und fasen,' iii. 3, 12[a]. In the Ackermann von Böhmen, cap. 6, *pilwis* means the same as witch; '*pielweiser*, magician, soothsayer,' Böhme's Beitr. zum schles. recht 6, 69. 'an. 1529 (at Schweidnitz), a *pielweiss* buried alive,' Hoffmann's Monatschr. p. 247. '1582 (at Sagan), two women of honest carriage rated for *pilweissen* and ——,' ibid. 702. 'du *pilweissin !*' A. Gryphius, p. 828. ' Las de deine *bilbezzodn* auskampln' says the angry mother to her child, 'i den *bilmezschedl* get nix nei,' get your *b.* clots combed out, you don't come in in that shaggy scalp, Schm. 1, 168. *pilmeskind*, a curse like devil's child, Delling's Bair. idiot. 1, 78. On the Saale in Thuringia, *bulmuz* is said of unwashed or uncombed children; while *bilbezschnitt, bilwezschnitt, bilfezschnitt, pilmasschnid* (Jos. Rank. Böhmerwald, p. 274) denotes a cutting through a field of corn, which is regarded as the work of a spirit, a witch, or the devil.

This last-mentioned belief is also one of long standing. Thus the Lex Bajuvar. 12 (13), 8 : 'si quis messes alterius initiaverit maleficis artibus, et inventus fuerit, cum duodecim solidis componat, quod *aranscarti*[1] dicunt.' I dare say such a delinquent was then called a *piliwiz, pilawis ?* On this passage Mederer remarks, p. 202-3 : An honest countryman told me about the so-called *bilmerschnitt, bilberschnitt*, as follows : ' The spiteful creature, that wants to do his neighbour a rascally mischief, goes at midnight, stark naked, with a *sickle tied to his foot*, and repeating magic spells, through the middle of a field of corn just ripe. From that part of the field that he has passed his sickle through, all the grains fly into his barn, into his bin.' Here everything is attributed to a charm practised by man.[2]

---

[1] Goth. *asans* (messis), OHG. *aran*, arn.
[2] Can this magic be alluded to so early as in the Kaiserchronik (2180-87) ?

diu muoter heizit Rachel,	sin sichil smeit schiere
diu hât in gelêret :	mêr dan andere viere ;
swenne sie in hiez sniden gân,	wil er durch einin berc varn,
sin hant incom nie dâr an,	der stêt immer mêr ingegen im ûf getân.

(His mother R. taught him : when she bade him go cut, he never put his *hand* to it, his sickle soon cut more than any other four ; if he will drive through a hill, it opens before him.)

Julius Schmidt too (Reichenfels, p. 119) reports from the Vogtland: The belief in *bilsen-* or *bilver-schnitter* (-reapers) [1] is toler-
ably extensive, nay, there seem to be certain persons who *believe
themselves to be such :* in that case they go into the field before
sunrise on St. John's day, sometimes on Walpurgis-day (May 1),
and cut the stalks with small *sickles tied to their great toes,* stepping slantwise across the field. Such persons must have *small
three-cornered hats* on (bilsenschnitter-hütchen); if during their
walk they are saluted by any one, they must die that year.
These *bilsenschnitter* believe they get half the produce of the
field where they have reaped, and small sickle-shaped instruments have been found in some people's houses, after their death.
If the owner of the field can pick up any stubble of the stalks
so cut, and hangs it in the smoke, the *bilsenschnitter* will gradually waste away (see Suppl.).

According to a communication from Thuringia, there are two
ways of baffling the *bilms-* or *binsen-schneider* (-cutter),[1] whichever he is called. One is, on Trinity Sunday or St. John's day,
when the sun is highest in the sky, to go and sit on an elderbush
with a looking-glass on your breast, and look round in every
quarter, then no doubt you can detect the *binsenschneider,* but
not without great risk, for if he spies you before you see him,
you must die and the binsenschneider remain alive, unless he
happen to catch sight of himself in the mirror on your breast,
in which case he also loses his life that year. Another way is,
to carry some ears that the *binsenschneider* has cut to a newly
opened grave in silence, and not grasping the ears in your bare
hand; if the least word be spoken, or a drop of sweat from your
hand get into the grave with the ears, then, as soon as the ears
rot, he that threw them in is sure to die.

What is here imputed to human sorcerers, is elsewhere laid
to the *devil* (Superst. no. 523), or to elvish goblins, who may at
once be known by their small hats. Sometimes they are known
as *bilgenschneider,* as *pilver-* or *hilperts-schnitter,* sometimes by
altogether different names. Alberus puts *sickles in the hands* of
women travelling in Hulda's host (supra, p. 269 note). In some
places, acc. to Schm. 1, 151, they say *bockschnitt,* because the

---

[1] *Bilse* is henbane, and *binse* a rush, which plants have no business here. 'They
are merely an adaptation of bilwiz, when this had become unintelligible.—TRANS.

goblin is supposed to ride through the cornfield on a he-goat, which may well remind us of Dietrich with the boar (p. 214). The people about Osnabrück believe the *tremsemutter* walks about in the corn: she is dreaded by the children. In Brunswick she is called *kornwif*: when children are looking for cornflowers, they will not venture too far into the green field, they tell each other of the cornwife that kidnaps little ones. In the Altmark and Mark Brandenburg they call her *roggenmöhme* (aunt in the rye), and hush crying children with the words: 'hold your tongue, or *roggenmöhme* with the long black teats will come and drag you away!'[1] Others say 'with her long *iron* teats,' which recals *iron* Berhta: others again name her *rockenmör*, because like Holla and Berhta, she plays all manner of tricks on idle maids who have not spun their distaffs clear during the Twelves. Babes whom she puts to her black breast are likely to die. Is not the Bavarian *preinscheuhe* the same kind of corn-spectre? In the Schräckengast, Ingolst. 1598, there are coupled together on p. 73, '*preinscheuhen* und meerwunder,' and p. 89 'wilde larvenschopper und *preinscheuhen*.' This prein, brein, properly pap (puls), means also grain-bearing plants like oats, millet, panicum, plantago (Schm. 1, 256-7); and *breinscheuhe* (-scare) may be the spirit that is the bugbear of oat and millet fields?

In all this array of facts, there is no mistaking the affinity of these *bilwisses* with divine and elvish beings of our heathenism. They mat the hair like dame Holla, dame Berhta, and the alb, they wear the small hat and wield the shot of the elves, they have at last, like Holla and Berhta, sunk into a children's bugbear. Originally 'gute holden,' sociable and kindly beings, they have twisted round by degrees into uncanny fiendish goblins, wizards and witches. And more, at the back of these elvish beings there may lurk still higher divine beings. The Romans worshipped a *Robigo*, who could hinder blight in corn, and perhaps, if displeased, bring it on. The walking of the *bilwiss*, of the *Roggenmuhme* in the grain had at first a benevolent motive: as the names *mutter, muhme, mör* teach us, she is a motherly

---

[1] Conf. Deut. sagen, no. 89. Kuhn, p. 373. Temme's Sagen, p. 80. 82, of the Altmark. The Baden legend makes of it a *rockert-weibele* and an enchanted countess of Eberstein, who walks about in a wood named Rockert (Mone's Anzeiger, 3, 145).

guardian goddess of spindle and seedfield. *Fro upon his boar*
must have ridden through the plains, and made them productive,
nay, even the picture of Siegfried riding through the corn I
incline to refer to the circuit made by a god; and now for the
first time I think I understand why the Wetterau peasant to this
day, when the corn-ears wave in the wind, says *the boar walks in
the corn.* It is said of the god who causes the crops to thrive.
Thus, by our study of elves, with whom the people have kept up
acquaintance longer, we are led up to gods that once were. The
connexion of elves with Holla and Berhta is further remarkable,
because all these beings, unknown to the religion of the Edda,
reveal an independent development or application of the heathen
faith in continental Germany (see Suppl.).[1]

What comes nearest the hairy shaggy elves, or bilwisses, is a
spirit named *scrat* or *scrato* in OHG. documents, and *pilosus* in
contemporary Latin ones. The Gl. mons. 333 have *scratun*
(pilosi) ; the Gl. herrad. 200^b *waltschrate* (satyrus) ; the Sumerlat.
10, 66 *srate* (lares mali); so in MHG. *scráz*; Reinh. 597 (of the
old fragment), 'ein wilder *waltschrat;*' Barl. 251, 11. Aw. 3,
226. Ulr. Lanz. 437 has 'von dem *schraze*'=dwarf; 'sie ist
villîhte ein *schrat*, ein geist von helle;' Albr. Titur. 1, 190
(Hahn 180). That a small elvish spirit was meant, is plain
from the dimin. *schretel*, used synonymously with wihtel in that
pretty fable, from which our Irish elf-tales gave an extract, but
which has since been printed entire in Mone's treatise on heroic
legend, and is now capped by the original Norwegian story in
Asbiörnsen and Moe, No. 26 (one of the most striking examples

---

[1] The Slavs too have a *field-spirit* who paces through the corn. Boxhorn's Resp.
Moscov., pars 1, p. ....: " Daemonem quoque meridianum Moscovitae metuunt et
colunt. Ille enim, dum jam maturae resecantur fruges, habitu *viduae lugentis* ruri
obambulat, operariisque uni vel pluribus, nisi protinus viso spectro in terram proni
concidant, brachia frangit et crura. Neque tamen contra hanc plagam remedio
destituuntur. Habent enim in vicina silva arbores religione patrum cultas : harum
cortice vulneri superimposito, illum non tantum sanant, sed et dolorem loripedi
eximunt." Among the Wends this corn-wife is named *pshipolnitsa* [prop. *prepoln.*,
from polno, full, *i.e.* full noon], at the hour of noon she creeps about as a *veiled
woman.* If a Wend, conversing with her by the hour on flax and flax-dressing, can
manage to contradict everything she says, or keep saying the Lord's prayer backwards without stumbling, he is safe (Lausitz. monatsschr. 1797, p. 744). The Bohemians call her *baba* (old woman), or *polednice, poludnice* (meridiana), the Poles
dsiewanna, dsiewice (maiden), of whom we shall have to speak more than once, conf.
chap. XXXVI. Here also there are plainly gods mixed up with the spirits and
goblins.

of the tough persistence of such materials in popular tradition);
both the *schretel* and the word wazzerbern answer perfectly to
the *trold* and the hvidbiörn. Vintler thinks of the *schrättlin* as a
spirit light as wind, and of the size of a child. The Vocab. of
1482 has *schretlin* (penates); Dasypodius *nachtschrettele* (ephialtes); later ones spell it *schrättele, schrättel, schrettele, schrötls,*
conf. Stald. 2, 350. Schmid's Schwäb. wörtb. 478. In the Sette
comm. *schrata* or *schretele* is a butterfly, Schm. 3, 519. A
Thidericus *Scratman* is named in a voucher of 1244; Spilcker 2,
84. A district in Lower Hesse is called the *Schratweg,* Wochenbl.
1833, 952. 984. 1023. And other Teutonic dialects seem to
know the word: AS. *scritta,* Eng. *scrat* (hermaphroditus),[1] ON.
skratti (malus genius, gigas); a rock on the sea is called
skrattasker (geniorum scopulus), Fornm. sög. 2, 142. Comparing these forms with the OHG. ones above, we miss the usual
consonant-change: the truth is, other OHG. forms do shew a
s in place of the *t*: *scras,* Gl. fuld. 14; *screza* (larvae, lares mali),
Gl. lindenbr. 996[b]; '*srezze* vel strate' (not: screzzol scraito),
Sumerlat. 10, 66; 'unreiner *schráz,*' Altd. w. 3, 170 (rhymes
vráz).[2] And Upper Germ. dictionaries of the 16th cent. couple
schretzel with alp; Höfer 3, 114, has 'der *schretz,*' and Schm.
3, 552, 'der *schretzel, das schretzlein.*' According to Mich.
Beham 8. 9 (Mone's Anz. 4, 450-1), every house has its *schrez-
lein;* if fostered, he brings you goods and honour, he rides or
drives the cattle, prepares his table on Brecht-night, etc.[3]

The agreement of Slavic words is of weight. O. Boh. *scret*
(daemon), Hanka's Zbirka 6[b]; *screti, scretti* (penates intimi et
secretales), ibid. 16[b]; Boh. *skřet, skřjtek* (penas, idolum); Pol.
skrzot, skrzitek; Sloven. *zhkrát, zhkrátiz, zhkrátelj* (hill-mannikin).
To the Serv. and Russ. dialects the word seems unknown.

I can find no satisfactory root for the German form.[4] In Slavic

[1] Already in Sachsensp. 1, 4 *altvile* and *dverge* side by side; conf. RA. 410.
[2] A contraction of *schrawas?* Gudr. 448, *schrawas* und merwunder; Albr. Titur.
27, 299 has *schrabas* together with pilwiht; *schrawatzen* und merwunder, Casp. von
der Rön's Wolfdieterich 195. Wolfd. und Saben 496. ['Probably of different
origin,' says Suppl.]
[3] Muchar, Römisches Noricum 2, 37, and Gastein 147, mentions a capricious
mountain-spirit, *schranel.*
[4] The ON. skratti is said to mean terror also. The Swed. skratta, Dan. skratte,
is to laugh loud. Does the AS. form *scritta* allow us to compare the Gr. σκιρρος,
a hopping, leaping goblin or satyr (from σκιρτάω, I bound)? Lobeck's Aglaoph.,
1311.

skrẏti (celare, occulere) is worth considering. [A compound of krẏti, to cover, root krẏ, krov, κρύπτω. If Slav. skrẏ, why not AS. scrûd, shroud ?].

Going by the sense, *schrat* appears to be a wild, rough, shaggy wood-sprite, very like the Lat. faun and the Gr. satyr, also the Roman *silvanus* (Livy 2, 7); its dimin. *schrätlein*, synonymous with wichtel and alp, a home-sprite, a hill-mannikin. But the male sex alone is mentioned, never the female; like the fauns, therefore, they lack the beauty of contrast which is presented by the elfins and bilwissins. We may indeed, on the strength of some similarity, take as a set-off to these schrats those wild women and wood-minnes treated of at the end of chapter XVI. The Greek fiction included *mountain-nymphs* (νύμφαι ὀρεσκῷοι) and *dryads* (δρυάδες, Englished *wuduœlfenne* in AS. glosses), whose life was closely bound up with that of a tree (loc. princ., Hymn to Aphrodite 257-272; and see Suppl.).

Another thing in which the schrats differ from elves is, that they appear one at a time, and do not form a people.

The Fichtelberg is haunted by a wood-sprite named the *Katzenveit*, with whom they frighten children : ' Hush, the *Katzenveit* will come !' Similar beings, full of dwarf and goblin-like humours, we may recognise in the *Gübich* of the Harz, in the *Rübezal* of Riesengebirge. This last, however, seems to be of Slav origin, Boh. *Rybecal, Rybrcol.*[1] In Moravia runs the story of the *seehirt*, sea-herd, a mischief-loving sprite, who, in the shape of a herdsman, whip in hand, entices travellers into a bog (see Suppl.).[2]

The gloss in Hanka 7[b]. 11[a] has '*vilcodlac* faunus, *vilcodlaci* faunificarii, incubi, dusii '; in New Boh. it would be *wlkodlak*, wolf-haired; the Serv. *vukodlac* is vampire (Vuk sub v.). It is not surprising, and it offers a new point of contact between elves, bilwisses, and schrats, that in Poland the same matting of hair is ascribed to the *skrzot*, and is called by his name, as the *skřjtek* is in Bohemia ;[3] in some parts of Germany schrötleinzopf.

---

[1] In Slav. ryba is fish, but cal, or col (I think) has no meaning. The oldest Germ. docs. have Rube-zagil, -zagel, -zagl (-tail); Rube may be short for the ghostly 'knecht Ruprecht,' or Robert. Is Rubezagel our bobtail, of which I have seen no decent etymology ?—TRANS.

[2] Sagen aus der vorzeit Mährens (Brünn, 1817), pp. 186-171.

[3] The plica is also called *koltun*, and again *koltki* are Polish and Russian home-sprites.

People in Europe began very early to think of dæmonic beings as *pilosi*. The Vulgate has 'et *pilosi* saltabunt ibi,' Isaiah 13, 21, where the LXX. had δαιμόνια ἐκεῖ ὀρχήσονται, conf. 34, 14.[1] Isidore's Etym. 8, cap. ult. (and from it Gl. Jun. 399): '*pilosi* qui graece panitae, latine *incubi* nominantur,— hos daemones Galli *dusios* nuncupant.[2] Quem autem vulgo *incubonem* vocant, hunc Romani faunum dicunt.' Burcard of Worms (App. Superst. C) is speaking of the superstitious custom of putting playthings, shoes, bows and arrows, in cellar or barn for the home-sprites,[3] and these genii again are called '*satyri* vel *pilosi*.' The monk of St. Gall, in the Life of Charles the Great (Pertz 2,741), tells of a *pilosus* who visited the house of a smith, amused himself at night with hammer and anvil, and filled the empty bottle out of a rich man's cellar (conf. Ir. elfenm. cxi. cxii.). Evidently a frolicking, dancing, whimsical homesprite, rough and hairy to look at, 'eislich getân,' as the Heidelberg fable says, and rigged out in the red little cap of a dwarf, loving to follow his bent in kitchens and cellars. A figure quite in the foreground in Cod. palat. 324 seems to be his very portrait.

Only I conceive that in earlier times a statelier, larger figure was allowed to the *schrat*, or wood-schrat, then afterwards the merrier, smaller one to the *schrettel*. This seems to follow from the ON. meaning of *skratti* gigas, giant. These *woodsprites* must have been, as late as the 6-7th cent., objects of a special worship: there were trees and temples dedicated to them. Quotations in proof have already been given, pp. 58. 68: 'arbores *daemoni* dedicatae,' and among the Warasken, a race akin to the Bavarian, '*agrestium* fana, quos vulgus *faunos* vocat.'

Some remarkable statements are found in Eckehart's Waltharius. Eckevrid of Saxony accosts him with the bitter taunt (761):

---

[1] Luther translates *feldteufel*; the Heb. *sagnir* denotes a shaggy, goat-like being. Radevicus frising. 2, 18, imitates the whole passage in the prophet: 'ululae, upupae, bubones toto anno in ectis funebria personantes lugubri voce aures omnium repleverunt. *Pilosi* quos *satyros* vocant in domibus plerunque auditi.' Again 2, 24: 'in aedibus tuis lugubri voce respondeant ululae, *saltent pilosi*.'

[2] 'Daemones quos *dusios* Galli nuncupant.' Augustine, Civ. Dei, c. 23. The name *dus* still lives in Bretagne, dimin. *dusik* (Villemarqué 1, 42).

[3] In the same way the *jüdel* (I suppose *güetel*, the same as guote holde) has toys placed for him, Superst. I, no. 62; conf. infra, the homesprites.

Dic, ait, an corpus vegetet tractabile temet,
sive per aërias fallas, *maledicte*, figuras ?
saltibus assuetus faunus mihi quippe videris.

Walthari replies in mockery (765) :

Celtica lingua probat te ex illa gente creatum,
cui natura dedit reliquas ludendo praeire;
at si te propius venientem dextera nostra
attingat, post Saxonibus memorare valebis,
te nunc in Vosago *fauni fantasma* videre.

If you come within reach of my arm, I give you leave then
to tell your Saxon countrymen of the 'schrat' you now see in
the Wasgau (Vosges). When Eckevrid has hurled his spear at
him in vain, Walthari cries :

Haec tibi *silvanus* transponit munera *faunus*.

Herewith the 'wood-schrat' returns you the favour.[1]

Here the faun is called *fantasma*, phantom ; OHG. *giscin*, T.
81 (Matt. xiv. 26), otherwise *scinleih* (monstrum), Gl. hrab. 969[b].
Jun. 214; AS. *scinlác* (portentum) ; or *gitroc*, p. 464. *Phantasma vagabundum* (Vita Lebuini, Pertz 2, 361) ; '*fantasma* vult
nos pessundare' (Hroswitha in Dulcicius) ; '*fantasia* quod in
libris gentilium *faunus* solet appellari,' Mabillon, Analect. 3, 352.
A 'municipium,' or 'oppidum *mons fauni*,' in Ivonis Carnot.
epist. 172, and conf. the doc. quoted in the note thereon, in
which it is *monsfaunum*.   Similarly in OFr. poems : '*fantosme*
nous va *faunoiant*' Méon 4, 138; *fantosme* qui me desvoie,
demaine,' ibid. 4, 140. 4. 402. A passage from Girart de
Rossillon given in Mone's Archiv 1835. 210 says of a mountain : 'en ce mont ha moult de grans secrez, trop y a de *fantomes*.'
Such are the *fauni ficarii* and *silvestres homines*, with whom
Jornandes makes his Gothic *aliorunes* keep company (p. 404).
Yet they also dip into the province of demigod heroes.   Miming
silvarum satyrus, and *Witugouwo* (silvicola) seem to be at once
cunning smith-schrats and heroes (pp. 376-379). A valkyr unites
herself with satyr-like Völundr, as the aliorunes did with fauns.
The *wild women*, *wood-minne* (pp. 432-4), and the *wilde man*

---

[1] The dialogue is obscure, and in the printed edition, p. 86, I have endeavoured
to justify the above interpretation.

(Wigamur 203) come together. Wigal. 6286 has *wildez wîp*, and 6602 it is said of the dwarf Karriôz:

Sîn muoter was ein wildez wîp	His mother was a wild woman,
dâ von was sîn kurzer lîp	therefrom was his short body
aller *rûch* unde *stark*,	all over hairy and strong,
sîn gebein was âne mark	his bones without marrow (solid)
nach dem geslehte der muoter sîn,	after his mother's stock,
deste sterker muoser sîn.	the stronger must he be.

In the Wolfdietrich a wild man like this is called *waltluoder*, and in Laurîn 173. 183 *waltmann*. The ON. mythology knows of wild wood-wives by the names *íviðjur*, Sæm. 88ª. 119ᵇ, and *iarn-viðjur*, Sn. 13. About the *íviðja* we find at the beginning of the Hrafnagaldr the obscure statement ' elr íviðja,' alit, anget, parit, gignit dryas; *íviðja* is derived from a wood or grove *íviðr*, of which the Völuspâ 1ª makes mention: 'nio man ek heima, nio íviði' ; so *iarnviðja* from *iarnviðr*, iron wood (see Suppl.).[1]

I cannot properly explain these ON. *íviðjur* and *iarnviðjur*. The popular belief of to-day in South-eastern Germany presents in a more intelligible shape the legend of the *wild-folk, forest-folk, wood-folk, moss-folk*, who are regarded as a people of the dwarf kind residing together, though they come up singly too, and in that case the females especially approximate those higher beings spoken of on p. 432. They are small of stature, but somewhat larger than elves, grey and oldish-looking, hairy and clothed in moss: ' ouch wâren ime die ôren als eime *walttôren vermisset,*' his ears like a forest-fool's bemossed (?), Iw. 440. Often *holz-weibel* alone are mentioned, seldomer the males, who are supposed to be not so good-natured and to live deeper in the woods, wearing green garments faced with red, and black three-cornered hats. H. Sachs 1, 407ª brings up *holzmänner* and *holzfrauen*, and gives 1, 348ᵉ the lament of the *wild woodfolk* over the faithless world. Schmidt's Reichenfels, pp. 140-8 tells us the Voigtland tradition, and Börner, pp. 188-242 that of the Orlagau; from them I borrow what is characteristic. The little wood-wives come up to wood-cutters, and beg for something to eat, or take it themselves out

---

[1] Afzelius 2, 145-7, mentions Swed. *löfjerskor*, leaf-maids, forest-maids, and compares them with *Laufey* (p. 246), but the people have little to say about them.

of their pots; but whatever they have taken or borrowed they
make good in some other way, not seldom by good advice. At
times they help people in their kitchen work and at washing,
but always express a great fear of the wild huntsman that pursues
them.   On the Saale they tell you of a *bush-grandmother* and her
moss-maidens; this sounds like a queen of elves, if not like the
'weird lady of the woods' (p. 407). The little wood-wives are
glad to come when people are baking, and ask them, while they
are about it, to bake them a loaf too, as big as half a millstone,
and it must be left for them at a specified place; they pay it back
afterwards, or perhaps bring some of their own baking, and lay
it in the furrow for the ploughmen, or on the plough, being
mightily offended if you refuse it. At other times the wood-wife
makes her appearance with a broken little wheelbarrow, and begs
you to mend the wheel; then, like Berhta she pays you with the
fallen chips, which turn into gold; or if you are knitting, she
gives you a ball of thread which you will never have done un-
winding. Every time a man twists (driebt, throws) the stem of
a young tree till the bark flies off, a wood-wife has to die. When
a peasant woman, out of pity, gave the breast to a crying wood-
child, the mother came up and made her a present of the bark in
which the child was cradled; the woman broke a splinter off and
threw it in to her load of wood, but when she got home she found
it was of gold (see Suppl.).

Wood-wives, like dwarfs, are by no means satisfied with the
ways of the modern world; but to the reasons given on p. 459
they add special ones of their own. There's never been a good
time since people took to counting the dumplings they put in the
pot, the loaves they put in the oven, to 'pipping' their bread
and putting caraway-seeds in it. Hence their maxim:

Schäl keinen baum,	No tree ever shell,
erzähl keinen traum,	no dream ever tell,
back keinen kümmel ins brot,	bake in thy bread no cummin-seed,
so hilft dir Gott aus aller noth.	and God will help in all thy need.

The third line may be 'pip kein brod,' don't pip a loaf. A

wood-wife, after tasting some newly-baked bread, ran off to the forest, screaming loud:

Sie haben mir gebacken kümmelbrot, •
das bringt diesem hause grosse noth!

(They've baked me caraway-bread, it will bring that house great trouble). And the farmer's prosperity soon declined, till he was utterly impoverished. To 'pip' a loaf is to push the tip of your finger into it, a common practice in most places. Probably the wood-wives could not carry off a pricked loaf, and therefore disliked the mark; for a like reason they objected to counting. Whether the seasoning with cummin disgusted them as an innovation merely, or in some other connection, I do not know. The rhyme runs thus: 'kümmelbrot, unser tod!' the death of us; or—'kümmelbrot macht angst und noth.'——Some wood-mannikins, who had long done good service at a mill, were scared away by the miller's men leaving out clothes and shoes for them, Jul. Schmidt, p. 146 (see Suppl.).[1] It is as though, by accepting

---

[1] This agrees wonderfully with what Reusch, pp. 53-5, reports from Prussian Samland:——A householder at Lapöhnen, to whom the subterraneans had done many services, was grieved at their having such poor clothes, and asked his wife to put some new little coats where they would find them. Well, they took their new outfit, but their leave at the same time, crying, 'paid up, paid up!' Another time they had been helping a poor smith, had come every night and turned out a set of little pots, pans, plates and kettles as bright as could be; the mistress would set a dish of milk for them, which they fell upon like wolves, and cleared to the last drop, washed up the plates and then set to work. The smith having soon become a rich man, his wife sewed them each a pretty little red coat and cap, and left them lying. 'Paid up, paid up!' cried the undergrounders, then quickly slipt into their new finery, and were off, without touching the iron left for them to work at, or ever coming back.——Another story of the Seewen-weiher (-pond), near Rippoldsau, in the Black Forest (Mone's Anz. 6, 175):—A lake-mannikin liked coming to the folks at Seewen farm, would do jobs there all day, and not return into his lake till evening; they used to serve him up breakfast and dinner by himself. If in giving out tasks they omitted the phrase 'none too much and none too little,' he turned cross, and threw all into confusion. Though his clothes were old and shabby, he never would let the Seewen farmer get him new ones; but when this after all was done, and the new coat handed to the lake-mannikin, one evening, he said, 'When one is paid off one must go; beginning from to-morrow, I come to you no more;' and in spite of all the farmer's apologies he was never seen again.——Jos. Rank's Böhmerwald, p. 217, tells a pretty story of a waschweiberl (wee washerwife), for whom the people of the house wanted to have shoes made, but she would not hold out her little foot to be measured. They sprinkled the floor with flour, and took the measure by her footprints. When the shoes were made and placed on the bench for her, she fell a-sobbing, turned her little smock-sleeves down again, unlooped the skirt of her frock, then burst away, lamenting loudly, and was seen no more.' That is to say, the wee wife, on coming into the house, had turned up the sleeves of her smock, and looped up her frock, that she might the more easily do any kind of work. Similar tales are told of the *brownie*, R. Chambers, p. 33. And the same idea lies at the bottom of the first story about wichtelmännerchen in Kinderm. 39.

clothes, the spirits were afraid of suddenly breaking off the relation that subsisted between themselves and mankind. We shall see presently that the home-sprites proper acted on different principles, and even bargained for clothes.

The more these wood-folk live a good many together, the more do they resemble elves, wichtels, and dwarfs; the more they appear singly, the nearer do the females stand to wise women and even goddesses, the males to gigantic fauns and wood-monsters, as we saw in Katzenveit, Gübich and Rübezahl (p. 480). The *salvage man* with uprooted fir-tree in his hand, such as supports the arms of several princes in Lower Germany, represents this kind of faun; it would be worth finding out at what date he is first mentioned. Grinkenschmied in the mountain (Deut. sag. 1, 232) is also called ' der *wilde man.*'

In the Romance fairy-tales an old Roman god has assumed altogether the nature of a wood-sprite; out of *Orcus*[1] has been made an Ital. *orco*, Neapol. *huorco*, Fr. *ogre* (supra, p. 314) : he is pictured *black, hairy, bristly*, but of great stature rather than small, almost *gigantic*; children losing their way in the wood come upon his dwelling, and he sometimes shews himself good-natured and bestows gifts, oftener his wife (orca, ogresse) protects and saves.[2] German fairy-tales hand over his part to the *devil*, who springs even more directly from the ancient god of the lower world. Of the invisible-making helmet the orco has nothing left him, on the other hand a dæmonic *acuteness of scent* is made a characteristic feature, he can tell like a sea-monster the approach of human flesh : ' je sens la chair fraiche,' ' ich rieche, rieche menschenfleisch,' ' ich wittere, wittere menschenfleisch,' ' i schmöke ne Crist,' ' I smell the blood,' ' jeg lugter det paa min höire haand (right hand),' ' her lugter saa kristen mands been,'[3] exactly as the meerminne already in

---

It is a common characteristic, that holds good of wichtels, of subterraneans, of lake-sprites and of wood-folk, but chiefly of male ones who do service to mankind. [Might the objection to shewing their feet arise from their being web-footed, like the Swiss härdmändle, especially in the case of water-sprites?]

[1] See App., Superst. A, ' *Orcum* invocare' together with Neptune and Diana; Superst. G, extr. from Vintler, l. 88 : ' er hab den *orken* gesechen.' Beow. 224 has *orcneas*, pl. of *orcne*.

[2] Pentamerone, for the orco 1, 1. 1, 5. 2, 3. 3, 10. 4, 8. For the orca 2, 1. 2, 7. 4, 6. 5, 4.

[3] Perrault's Petit poucet; Kinderm. 1, 152. 179. 2, 350. 3, 410; Musæus 1, 21 ; Danske viser 1, 220 ; Norske folkeeventyr, p. 35.

Morolt 3924 says: 'ich smacke diutsche îserngewant,' coats of mail (see Suppl.). The Ital. however has also an *uom foresto*, Pulci's Morgante 5, 38.

The Gothic neut. *skôhsl*, by which Ulphilas renders δαιμόνιον, Matth. 8, 31. Lu. 8, 27 (only in margin; text reads unhulþô). 1 Cor. 10, 20. 21, I am disposed to explain by supposing a *skôhs*, gen. skôhis, or rather *skôgs* (the *h* being merely the *g* softened before *sl*). It would answer to the ON. *skôgr* (silva); in all our Gothic fragments the word for forest never occurs, so that in addition to a vidus (p. 376) we may very well conjecture a skôgs. In Sweden the provincialisms *skogsnerte*, *skogsnufva*[1] are still used; snerte appears to contain snert gracilis, and snufva to mean anhelans.[2] Now if *skôhsl* is wood-sprite,[3] there may have been associated with it, as with δαιμόνιον, the idea of a higher being, semi-divine or even divine. When we call to mind the sacred, inviolable trees inhabited by spirits (chap. XXI, and Superst. Swed. no. 110, Dan. no. 162), and the forest-worship of the Germani in general (pp. 54-58. 97-8); we can understand why *wood-sprites* in particular should be invested with a human or divine rather than elvish nature.

Water-sprites exhibit the same double aspect. Wise-women, valkyrs, appear on the wave as swans, they merge into prophetic *merwomen* and *merminnes* (p. 434). Even Nerthus and dame Holla bathe in lake or pool, and the way to Holla's abode is through the well, Kinderm. 24. 79.

Hence to the general term *holde* or *guoter holde* (genius, bonus genius) is added a *wazzerholde* (p. 266), a *brunnenholde* (p. 268); to the more general *minni* a *meriminni* and *marmennill* (p. 433). Other names, which explain themselves, are: MHG. wildiu

---

[1] Linnæus's Gothlandske resa, p. 312. Faye, p. 42.

[2] In 1298 Torkel Knutson founded on the Neva a stronghold against the Russians, called Landskrona. An old folk-tale says, there was heard in the forest near the river a continual knocking, as of a stone-cutter. At last a peasant took courage and penetrated into the forest; there he found a wood-sprite hewing at a stone, who, on being asked what that should mean, answered: 'this stone shall be the boundary between the lands of the Swedes and Moskovites.' Forsell's Statistik von Schweden, p. 1.

[3] To make up an OHG. skuoh and skuohisal is doubtless yet more of a venture. Our *scheusal* (monstrum), if it comes from scheuen (sciuhan), to shy at, has quite another fundamental vowel; it may however be a corruption. The only very old form I know is the *schusel* given in the foot-note on p. 269. But the Vocab. of 1482 has scheuhe (larva).

merkint, wildiu *merwunder*, Gudrun 109, 4. 112, 3. wildez *merwíp*, Osw. 653. 673; Mod. HG. *meerwunder*, *vassermann* (Slav. *vodnik*), *seejungfer*, *meerweib*; ON. *haf-frú*, *œs-kona*, *hafgýgr*, *margýgr*; Dan. *havmand*, *bröndmand* (man of the burn or spring), Molb. Dial. p. 58; Swed. *hafsman*, *hafsfru*, and more particularly *strömkarl* (river sprite or man). Wendish *vodny mus*, water man. The notion of a *water-king* shews itself in *waterconink*, Melis Stoke 2, 96. Certain elves or dwarfs are represented as watersprites: *Andvari*, son of *Oin*, in the shape of a pike inhabited a fors, Sæm. 180-1; and *Alfrikr*, acc. to Vilk. saga, cap. 34, haunted a river (see Suppl.).

The peculiar name of such a watersprite in OHG. was *nihhus*, *nichus*, gen. nichuses, and by this term the glossists render crocodilus, Gl. mons. 332, 412. Jun. 270. Wirceb. 978[b]; the Physiologus makes it neuter: das *nikhus*, Diut. 3, 25. Hoffm. Fundgr. 23. Later it becomes *niches*, Gl. Jun. 270. In AS. I find, with change of *s* into *r*, a masc. *nicor*, pl. *niceras*, Beow. 838. 1144. 2854, by which are meant monstrous spirits living in the sea, conf. *nicorhús*, Beow. 2822. This AS. form agrees with the M. Nethl. *nicker*, pl. nickers, (Horae Belg. p. 119); Reinaert prose MIIII[b] has '*nickers* ende wichteren'; *necker* (Neptunus), Diut. 2, 224[b]. 'hêft mi die *necker* bracht hier?' (has the devil brought me here?), Mone's Ndrl. volkslit. p. 140. The Mod. Nethl. *nikker* means evil spirit, devil, 'alle *nikkers* uit de hel;' so the Engl. 'old *Nick*.' We have retained the form with *s*, and the original sense of a watersprite, a male *nix* and a female *nixe*, i.e., niks and nikse, though we also hear of a *nickel* and *nickelmann*. In MHG. Conrad uses *wassernixe* in the sense of siren: 'heiz uns leiten ûz dem bade der vertânen (accursed) *wassernixen*, daz uns ir gedœne (din) iht schade' (MS. 2, 200[b]).[1]

The ON. *nikr* (gen. niks?) is now thought to mean hippopotamus only; the Swed. *näk*, *nek*, and the Dan. *nök*, *nok*, *nocke*, *aanycke* (Molb. Dial. p. 4) express exactly our watersprite, but always a male one. The Danish form comes nearest to a Mid. Lat. *nocca*, spectrum marinum in stagnis et fluviis; the Finn.

---

[1] Gryphius (mihi 748) has a rhyme: 'die *wasserlüss* auf erden mag nicht so schöne werden,' apparently meaning a water-wife or nixe. In Ziska's Östr. volksm. 54 a kind *wassernix*, like dame Holla, bestows wishing-gifts on the children.

näkki, Esth. *nek* (watersprite) seem borrowed from the Swedish. Some have brought into this connexion the much older *neha nehalennia* (pp. 257, 419), I think without good reason: the Latin organ had no occasion to put *h* for *c*, and where it does have an *h* in German words (as Vahalis, Naharvali), we have no business to suppose a tenuis; besides, the images of Nehalennia hardly indicate a river-goddess.

I think we have better reason for recognising the water-sprite in a name of Oðinn, who was occasionally conceived of as *Neptune* (p. 148), and often appears as a sailor and ferryman in his bark. The AS. Andreas describes in detail, how *God Himself*, in the shape of a divine shipman escorts one over the sea; in the Legenda Aurea it is only an angel. Oðinn, according to Sn. 3, is called *Nikarr* or *Hnikarr*, and *Nikuz* or *Hnikuðr*. In Sæm. 46[a, b] we read *Hnikarr, Hnikuðr*, and in 91[a] 184[a, b] *Hnikarr* again. *Nikarr* would correspond to AS. *Nicor*, and *Nikuz* to OHG. *Nichus*. Snorri's optional forms are remarkable, he must have drawn them from sources which knew of both; the prefixing of an aspirate may have been merely to humour the metre. Finn Magnusen, p. 438, acutely remarks, that wherever Oðinn is called *Hnikarr*, he does appear as a sea-sprite and calms the waves. For the rest, no nickar (like álfar and dvergar) are spoken of in either Edda. Of the metamorphoses of the nickur (hippop.) the ON. uses the expression "*nykrat eða finngálkat*," Sn. 317 (see Suppl.).

Plants and stones are named after the nix, as well as after gods. The nymphæa (νυμφαία from νύμφη) we still call *nixblume* as well as seeblume, seelilie, Swed. *näckblad*, Dan. *nökkeblomster, nökkerose*; the conferva rupestris, Dan. *nökkeskäg* (nix-beard); the haliotis, a shellfish, Swed. *näcköra* (nix-ear); the crumby tufa-stone, tophus, Swed. *näckebröd*, the water-sprite's bread. Finn. *näkinkenka* (mya margaritifera) *näkin waltikka* (typha angustifolia); the Lausitz Wends call the blossoms or seedpods of certain reeds '*vodneho muzha porsty, potaczky* [*piorsty, perczatky*?], *lohszy*,' water-man's fingers or gloves. We ourselves call the water-lily *wassermännlein*, but also *mummel, mümmelchen* = müemel, aunty, water-aunt, as the merminne in the old lay is expressly addressed as Morolt's '*liebe muome*,' and in Westphalia to this day *watermöme* is a ghostly being; in Nib. 1479, 3 Siglint the one merwoman says of Hadburc the other :

> Durch der wæte liebe hât *min muome* dir gelogen,

'tis through love of raiment (weeds) mine aunt hath lied to thee; these merwomen belong, as swan-maidens, to one sisterhood and kindred (p. 428), and in Oswald 673-9 'ein ander merwîp' is coupled with the first. Several lakes inhabited by nixes are called *mummelsee* (Deut. sag. nos. 59. 331. Mone's Anz. 3, 92), otherwise *meumke-loch*, *e.g.*, in the Paschenburg of Schaumburg. This explains the name of a little river *Mümling* in the Oden-wald, though old docs. spell it Mimling. Mersprites are made to favour particular pools and streams, *e.g.*, the Saale, the Danube, the Elbe,[1] as the Romans believed in the bearded river-gods of individual rivers; it may be that the name of the *Neckar* (Nicarus) is immediately connected with our *nicor*, *nechar* (see Suppl.).

Biörn gives *nennir* as another ON. name for hippopotamus, it seems related to the name of the goddess *Nanna* (p. 310).[2] This *nennir* or *nikur* presents himself on the sea-shore as a hand-some *dapple-grey horse*, and is to be recognised by his hoofs looking the wrong way; if any one mounts him, he plunges with his prey into the deep. There is a way however to catch and bridle him, and break him in for a time to work.[3] A clever man at Morland in Bahus fastened an artfully contrived bridle on him, so that he could not get away, and ploughed all his land with him; but the bridle somehow coming loose, the 'neck' darted like fire into the lake, and drew the harrow in after him.[4] In the same way German legends tell of a great hulking *black horse*, that had risen out of the sea, being put to the plough, and going ahead at a mighty pace, till he dragged both plough and plough-man over the cliff.[5] Out of a marsh called the 'taufe,' near

---

[1] The Elbjungfer and Saalweiblein, Deut. sag. no. 60; the river-sprite in the Oder, ibid. no. 62.

[2] Muchar, in Norikum 2, 37, and in Gastein p. 145, mentions an Alpine sprite *Donanadel*; does nadel here stand for nandel? A misprint for madel (girl) is scarcely conceivable.

[3] Landnámabók, 2, 10 (Islend. sög. 1, 74). Olafsen's Reise igiennem Island, 1, 55. Sv. vis. 3, 128.

[4] P. Kalm's Westgöta och Bahusländska resa, 1742, p. 200.

[5] Letzner's Dasselsche chronik 5, 13.

Scheuen in Lower Saxony, a *wild bull* comes up at certain times, and goes with the cows of the herd (Harry's Sagen, p. 79). When a thunderstorm is brewing, a great *horse* with enormous hoofs will appear on the water (Faye, p. 55). It is the vulgar belief in Norway, that whenever people at sea go down, a *söedrouen* (sea sprite) shews himself in the shape of a headless old man (Sommerfelt, Saltdalens prästegjeld, Trondhjem 1827, p. 119). In the Highlands of Scotland a water-sprite in the shape of a horse is known by the name of *water-kelpie* (see Suppl.).

Water-sprites have many things in common with mountain-sprites, but also some peculiar to themselves. The males, like those of the schrat kind, come up singly rather than in companies. The water man is commonly represented as *oldish* and with a *long beard*, like the Roman demigod out of whose urn the river spouts; often he is *many-headed* (conf. p. 387), Faye p. 51. In a Danish folk-song the nökke lifts his beard aloft (conf. Svenska visor 3, 127. 133), he wears a *green hat*, and when he grins you see his *green teeth* (Deut. sag. no. 52). He has at times the figure of a *wild boy* with *shaggy hair*, or else with *yellow curls* and a *red cap* on his head.[1] The näkki of the Finns is said to have *iron teeth*.[2] The *nixe* (fem.), like the Romance fay and our own wise-women, is to be seen sitting in the sun, *combing* her long hair (Svenska vis. 3, 148), or emerging from the waves with the upper half of her body, which is exceedingly beautiful. The lower part, as with sirens, is said to consist of a fish-like tail; but this feature is not essential, and most likely not truly Teutonic, for we never hear of a tailed nix,[3] and even the nixe, when she comes on shore among men, is shaped and attired like the daughters of men, being recognised only by the *wet skirt* of

---

[1] The small size is implied in the popular rhyme: ' *Nix in der grube* (pit), du bist ein *böser bube* (bad boy); wasch dir deine beinchen (little legs) mit rothen ziegelsteinchen (red brick).'

[2] On the grass by the shore a girl is seized by a pretty boy wearing a handsome peasant's belt, and is forced to scratch his head for him. While she is doing so, he slips a girdle round her unperceived, and chains her to himself; the continued friction, however, sends him to sleep. In the meantime a woman comes up, and asks the girl what she is about. She tells her, and, while talking, releases herself from the girdle. The boy was more sound asleep than ever, and his lips stood pretty wide apart; then the woman, coming up closer, cried out: ' why, that's a *neck*, look at his *fish's teeth* !' In a moment the neck was gone (Etwas über die Ehsten, p. 51).

[3] But we do of nixes shaped like men above and like *horses* below; one water-sprite takes his name from his *slit ears*, Deut. sag. no. 63.

her dress, the *wet tips* of her apron.[1] Here is another point of
contact with swan-maidens, whose swan-foot betrays them : and
as they have their veils and clothes taken from them, the nixe
too is embarrassed by the removal and detention of her gloves
in dancing (Deut. sag. nos. 58. 60). Among the Wends the
water-man appears in a linen smockfrock with *the bottom of its
skirt wet*; if in buying up grain he pays more than the market
price, a dearth follows, and if he buys cheaper than others, prices
fall (Lausitz. monatschr. 1797, p. 750). The Russians name
their water-nymphs *rusálki*: fair maidens with green or garlanded hair, combing themselves on the meadow by the waterside,
and bathing in lake or river. They are seen chiefly on Whit-
sunday and in Whitsun-week, when the people with dance and
song plait garlands in their honour and throw them into the
water. The custom is connected with the German river-worship
on St. John's day. Whitsun-week itself was called by the
Russians *rusaldnaya*, in Boh. *rusadla*, and even in Wallachian
rusalie.[2]

Dancing, song and *music* are the delight of all water-sprites, as
they are of elves (p. 470). Like the sirens, the nixe by her
song draws listening youth to herself, and then into the deep.
So Hylas was drawn into the water by the nymphs (Apollod.
i. 9, 19. Apollon. rhod. 1, 131). At evening up come the *dam-
sels from the lake*, to take part in the human dance, and to visit
their lovers.[3] In Sweden they tell of the *strömkarl's* alluring
enchanting strain : the strömkarls-lag (-lay) is said to have
eleven variations, but to only ten of them may you dance,
the eleventh belongs to the night-spirit and his band; begin

---

[1] In Olaf the Saint's saga (Fornm. sög. 4, 56. 5, 162) a *margýgr* is pictured as a
beautiful woman, from the girdle downward ending in a fish, lulling men to sleep
with her sweet song; evidently modelled on the Roman siren. Pretty stories of
nixes are told in Jul. Schmidt's Reichenfels, p. 150 (where the word *docken*=dolls,
puppets) and 151. Water-wives when in labour send for human assistance, like
she-dwarfs (p. 457). ' They spake at Dr. M. L.'s table of spectra and of changelings,
then did Mistress Luther, his goodwife, tell an history, how a midwife at a place
was fetched away by the *devil* to one in childbed, with whom the devil had to do,
and that lived *in a hole in the water in the Mulda*, and the water hurt her not at
all, but in the hole she sat as in a fair chamber.' Table-talk 1571. 440b.

[2] Schafarik in the Časopis česk. mus. 7, 259 has furnished a full dissertation on
the rusalky [from rusy, blond ; but there is also ruslo, river's bed, deepest part].

[3] Hebel doubtless founds on popular tradition when (p. 281) he makes the
' *jungfere usem see* ' *roam through the fields* at midnight, probably like the roggenmuhme to make them fruitful. Other stories of the *meerweiblein* in Mone's Anz. 8,
178, and Bechstein's Thür. sagen 3, 236.

to play that, and tables and benches, cup and can, gray-beards and grandmothers, blind and lame, even babes in the cradle would begin to dance.[1] This melodious *strömkarl* loves to linger by mills and waterfalls (conf. Andvari, p. 488).   Hence his Norwegian name *fossegrim* (fos, Swed. and ON. fors, waterfall). On p. 52 it was cited as a remnant of heathen sacrifices, that to this dæmonic being people offered a *black lamb,* and were taught music by him in return.   The fossegrim too on calm dark evenings entices men by his music, and instructs in the fiddle or other stringed instrument any one who will on a Thursday evening, with his *head turned away,* offer him a little *white he-goat* and throw it into a ' forse' that falls *northwards* (supra, p. 34). If the victim is lean, the pupil gets no farther than the tuning of the fiddle ; if fat, the fossegrim clutches hold of the player's right hand, and guides it up and down till the blood starts out of all his finger-tips, then the pupil is perfect in his art, and can play so that the trees shall dance and torrents in their fall stand still (see Suppl.).[2]

Although Christianity forbids such offerings, and pronounces the old water-sprites diabolic beings, yet the common people retain a certain awe and reverence, and have not quite given up all faith in their power and influence : accursed beings they are, but they may some day become partakers of salvation.   This is the drift of the touching account, how the strömkarl or neck wants you not only to sacrifice to him in return for musical instruction, but to *promise him resurrection and redemption.*[3] Two boys were playing by the riverside, the neck sat there touching his harp, and the children cried to him : ' What do you sit and play here for, neck ? you know you will never be saved.' The neck began to weep bitterly, threw his harp away, and sank to the bottom.   When the boys got home, they told their father

---

[1] Arndt's Reise nach Schweden 4, 241 ; similar dances spoken of in Herrauds-saga, cap. 11. pp. 49—52.

[2] Faye p. 57. Conf. Thiele 1, 185 on the *kirkegrim.*

[3] Ödman's Bahuslän, p. 80 : Om spelemän i högar ok forsar har man ok ätskilliga sagor ; för 15 år tilbacka har man här uti högen under Gären i Tanums gäll belägit hört spela som the bäste musicanter.   Then som har viol ok vill lära spela, blir i ögnableket lärd, allenast han *lofvar upståndelse* ; en som ej lofte thet, fick höra huru the i högen *slogo sonder sina violer ok greto bitterliga.*   (He that has a fiddle and will learn to play, becomes in a moment learned, only he promises resurrection ; one who promised not that, did hear how they in the hill beat asunder their fiddles and wept bitterly.)

what had happened. The father, who was a priest, said 'you have sinned against the neck, go back, *comfort* him and *tell him he may be saved.*' When they returned to the river, the neck sat on the bank weeping and wailing. The children said: 'Do not cry so, poor neck, father says that your Redeemer liveth too.' Then the neck joyfully took his harp, and played charmingly till long after sunset.[1] I do not know that anywhere in our legends it is so pointedly expressed, how badly the heathen stand in need of the Christian religion, and how mildly it ought to meet them. But the harsh and the compassionate epithets bestowed on the nixes seem to turn chiefly upon their *unblessedness,* their damnation.[2]

But beside the *freewill offering* for instruction in his art, the nix also exacted cruel and *compulsory* sacrifices, of which the memory is preserved in nearly all popular tradition. To this day, when people are drowned in a river, it is common to say: 'the river-sprite *demands his yearly victim,*' which is usually 'an *innocent child.*'[3] This points to actual human sacrifices offered to the nichus in far-off heathen times. To the nix of the Diemel they throw *bread and fruit* once a year (see Suppl.).

On the whole there runs through the stories of water-sprites a vein of *cruelty* and *bloodthirstiness,* which is not easily found among dæmons of mountains, woods and homes. The nix not only kills human beings who fall into his clutches, but wreaks a bloody vengeance on his own folk who have come on shore, mingled with men, and then gone back. A girl had passed fifteen years in the sea-wife's house (i haf-fruns gård), and never seen the sun all that time. At last her brother ventures down, and brings his beloved sister safely back to the upper world. The hafsfru waited her return seven years, then seized her staff, and lashing the water till it splashed up high, she cried:

---

[1] Sv. visor 3, 126. Ir. Elfenm. p. 24; similar Irish, Scotch, and Danish traditions, pp. 200-2. Conf. Thiele 4, 14. Holberg's Julestue sc. 12: 'Nisser og underjorske folk, drive store fester bort med klagen og hylen, eftersom de ingen del har derudi' (because they have no part therein).

[2] 'Vertöns wassernixe,' fordone, done for (p. 488); 'den *fula stygga* necken,' Sv. vis. 3, 147; 'den *usle* havfrue, *usle* maremind,' 'den *arme* mareviv,' 'du *fule* og *lede* spaaqvinde!' Danske visor 1, 110. 119. 125. Holberg's Melampus 3, 7 cites a Danish superstition: 'naar en fisker ligger hos sin fiskerinde paa söen, saa föder hun en havfrue.'

[3] Deut. sag., nos. 61. 62. Faye, p. 51. The River Saale yearly demands her victim on Walburgis or St. John's day, and on those days people avoid the river.

Hade jag trott att du varit så falsk,
Så skulle jag knackt dig din tiufvehals!

(had I trowed thou wert so false, I'd have nicked thy thievish
neck), Arvidsson 2, 320-3. If the sea-maidens have stayed too
long at the dance, if the captive Christian have born a child to
the nix, if the water-man's child is slow in obeying his call, one
sees a *jet of blood* shoot up from the water's bed in sign of the
vengeful deed.[1] As a rule, there was likewise a favourable sign

---

[1] Deut. sag., nos. 49. 58-9. 60. 304-6. 318, 1. Here I give another Westphalian
legend, written down for me by Hr Seitz, of Osnabrück:——Dönken von den *smett
uppn Darmssen.* Dichte bei Braumske liggt en lütken see, de Darmssen; do stönd
vörr aulen tiën (olden tide) en klauster ane. de miönke åber in den klauster liabeden
nig nå Goddes willen; drumme gönk et unner. Nig lange nå hiar hörden de buren
in der nauberskup, in Epe, olle nachte en kloppen un liarmen bi den Darmssen, osse
wenn me upn ambold slêt, und wecke lüe seigen wott (some folk saw somewhat)
midden up den Darmssen. Se sgeppeden drup to; då was et *n smett, de bet ant lîf*
(bis an's leib) *inn water seit,* mitn hâmer in de fûst, dâmit weis he jümmer up den
ambold, un bedudde (bedeutete) de buren, dat se em wot to smïen bringen sollen.
Sit der tit brochten em de lüe ut der burskup jümmer isen to smïen (iron to forge),
un ninminske hadde so goe plogisen (good ploughshares) osse de Eper. Ens wol
Koatman to Epe rêt (reed) ut den Darmssen hâlen, do feind he n *tülk kind* annen
öwer, dat was *ruw upn gansen liwe.*[*] Do sgreggede de *smett:* '*nimm mi meinen
süennen nig weg!*' åber Koatman neim dat kind inn back full, un löp dermit nå
huse. Sit der tit was de *smett* nig mehr to sehn or to hören. Koatman fårde
(futterte) den *ruwwen* up, un de wörd sin beste un flïtigste knecht. Osse he åber
twintig jår ault wör, sia he to sinen buren: '*bûr, ik mot von ju gaun, min vår het
mi ropen.*' 'Dat spit mi je,' sia de bûr, 'gift et denn gar nin middel, dat du bi mi
bliwen kannst?' 'Ik will es (mal) sehn,' sia dat *waterkind,* 'gåt erst es (mal) no
Braumske un hâlt mi en niggen djangen (degn); mer ji mjöt do förr giebn wot de
kaupmann hebben will, un jau *niks afhanneln.*' De bûr gönk no Braumske un
kofde en djangn, hannelde åber doch wot af. Nu göngen se to haupe no'n Darmssen,
do sia de *ruwwe:* 'Nu passt upp, wenn ik int water slåe un et *kümmt blôt,* dann
mot ik weg, *kümmt mjalke,* dann darf ik bi ju bliwwen.' He slög int water, då
kwamm kene mjalke un auk kên blôd. gans iargerlik sprak de *ruwwe:* 'ji hebt mi
wot wis maket, un wot afhannelt, dorümme kömmt kên blôd un kene mjalke. spöt
ju, un kaupet in Braumske en ännern djangn.' De bûr göng weg un kweim wïr;
åber erst dat drüdde mal brâchte he en djangen, wå he niks an awwehannelt hadde.
Osse de *ruwwe* då mit int water slög, *do was et so raut osse blôd,* de *ruwwe* störtede
sik in den Darmssen, un ninminske hef en wïer sehn.——[Epitome:—*The smith in
Darmssen lake.* Once a monastery there; bad monks, put down. Peasants at Epe
heard a hammering every night, rowed to middle of lake, found a *smith sitting
up to his waist in water;* he made them signs to bring him work, they did so
constantly, and the Epe ploughshares were the best in the country. Once farmer
Koatman found a *child* on the bank, *all over hairy.* Smith cried, 'don't take *my
son*'; but K. did, and reared him. Smith never seen again. The Shaggy one, when
aged 20, said, 'I must go, *father has called me.*'—'Can't you stay anyhow?'—
'Well, I'll see; go buy me a new sword, give the price asked, *don't beat down.*' K.
bought one, but cheapened. They go to the Darmssen; says Shag, 'Watch, when
I strike the water; *if blood comes,* I must go, *if milk,* I may stay.' But neither came:
'You've cheapened! go buy another sword.' K. cheapened again, but the third time
he did not. Shag struck the water, it was *red as blood,* and he plunged into the
Darmssen.]——The same sign, of *milk or blood* coming up, occurs in another folk-
tale, which makes the water-nymphs into white-veiled nuns, Mone's Anz. 3, 93.

[*] So in Casp. von der Rön, pp. 224-5 the meerwunder is called 'der *rauhe,* der
rausche.' Conf. supra, pp. 481. 491.

agreed upon (a jet of milk, a plate with an apple), but withheld
in such a case as this.

And here is the place to take up *Grendel* again, whom we
likened (p. 243) to the malicious god Loki, though Loki, even
apart from that, seemed related to Oegir. Grendel is cruel and
bloodthirsty: when he climbs out of his marsh at night, and
reaches the hall of the sleeping heroes, he clutches one and drinks
the blood out of another (Beow. 1478). His mother is called a
merewíf (3037), *brimwylf* (she-wolf of the breakers, 3197), and
grundwyrgen (3036) which means the same thing (from wearg,
lupus, comes wyrgen, lupa). This pair, Grendel and mother, have
a *water-house*, which is described (3027 seq.) almost exactly as
we should imagine the Norse Oegir's dwelling, where the gods
were feasted: indoors the water is excluded by walls, and there
burns a pale light (3033).[1] Thus more than one feature leads on
to higher beings, transcending mere watersprites (see Suppl.).

The notion of the nix drawing to him those who are *drowning*
has its milder aspect too, and that still a heathen one. We saw
on p. 311 that drowned men *go to the goddess Rân;* the popular
belief of later times is that they are received into the abode of the
nix or nixe. It is not the river-sprite kills those who sink in the
element of water; kindly and compassionately he bears them to
his dwelling, and harbours their souls.[2] The word *rân* seems to
have had a more comprehensive meaning at first: ' mæla *rân* ok
regin' was to invoke all that is bad, all evil spirits, upon one. It
has occurred to me, whether the unexplained Swed. *râ* in the
compounds *sjörâ* (nix), *skogsrâ* (schrat), *tomtrâ* (homesprite), which
some believe to be râ angulus, or a contraction of râdande, may
not have sprung from this *rân*, as the Scandinavian tongue is so
fond of dropping a final *n*. Dame *Wâchilt* too (p. 434) is a
succouring harbouring water-wife. The water man, like Hel and
Rân, *keeps with him the souls* of them that have perished in the
water, ' in pots turned upside down,' to use the naïve language of
one story (no. 52); but a peasant visiting him tilts them up, and
in a moment the souls all mount up through the water. Of the

---

[1] Conf. the dolphin's house in Musäus's märchen of the Three Sisters.
[2] Probably there were stories also of *helpful succouring* river-gods, such as the
Greeks and Romans told of Thetis, of Ino-Leucothea (Od. 5, 333-353), Albunea,
Matuta.

drowned they say 'the nix has drawn them to him,' or 'has sucked them,' because bodies found in the water have the nose red.[1] 'Juxta pontem Mosellae quidam puerulus naviculam excidens submersus est. quod videns quidam juvenis vestibus abjectis aquae insilivit, et inventum extrahere volens, *maligno spiritu retrahente,* quem *Neptunum* vocant, semel et secundo perdidit; tertio cum nomen apostoli invocasset, mortuum recepit.' Miracula S. Matthiae, cap. 43. Pez, Thes. aneod. 2, 3, pag. 26. Rollenhagen in the Froschmeuseler (Nn II[b]) :

<blockquote>
'das er
elend im wasser wer gestorben,
da die seel mit dem leib verdorben,
oder beim geist blieb, der immer frech
den *ersofnen die hels abbrech.'*
</blockquote>

(that he had died miserably in the water, and his soul had perished with the body, or abode with the spirit that ever without ado breaketh the necks of the drowned). The Swedish superstition supposes that *drowned* men whose bodies are not found have been drawn into the dwelling of the *hafsfru* (Sv. vis. 3, 148). In some German fairy-tales (no. 79) children who fall into the well come under the power of the *water-nixe;* like dame Holla, she gives them tangled flax to spin.

Faye, p. 51, quotes a Norwegian charm, to be repeated on the water against the nix :

<blockquote>
nyk, nyk, naal i vatn !
jomfru Maria kastet staal i vatn :
du säk, äk flyt.[2]
</blockquote>

(nick, nick, needle in water ! Virgin casteth steel in water. Thou sink, and I flee). A similar one for bathers is given in Superst. Swed. no. 71 [with the addition: 'thy father was a steel-thief, thy mother was a needle-thief,' etc.]. Steel stops a spirit's power to act upon you (supra, p. 466-7 n.).

A sepulchral cry of the nix, similar to death groans, is said to portend drowning (Faye, p. 51). Some very old writings ascribe

---

[1] Dan. 'nökken har taget ham,' 'nökken har suet dem,' Tullin's Skrifter 2, 13.
[2] So Brynhildr calls out at last to the giantess: '*seykstu,* gŷgjar kyn !' Sæm. 229[b].

to watersprites in general *wailing voices* and *doleful speeches*, that
resound from lakes and pools: they tell each other of their
baffled schemes, or how they have to vacate the land before the
christians.   Gregory of Tours, in De glor. confess. cap. 31, remembers an incident of his young days 'apud Arvernos gestum.'
A man setting out early to the forest has his morning meal
blessed before he takes it: Cumque ad amnem adhuc ante-
lucanum venisset, imposito plaustro cum bobus in ponte qui
super navem locatus erat, alterum transmeare coepit in littus.
Verum ubi *in medium amnis* devenit, audivit vocem dicentis
'*merge, merge, ne morēris!*'   Cui respondens vox alia ait: 'sine
tua etiam admonitione quae proclamas fecissem, si res sacra meis
conatibus non obstaret; nam scias eum eulogiis sacerdotis esse
munitum, ideo ei nocere non possum' (see Suppl.)—In the
Vita Godehardi Hildesiensis (first quarter of 11th cent.), cap. 4
(Leibn. 1, 492), we read: Erat etiam in orientali parte civitatis
nostrae (Hildenes-hem) *palus horrifica* et circummanentibus
omnino plurali formidine invisa, eo quod ibi, ut opinabantur, tam
meridiano quam et nocturno tempore *illusiones* quasdam *horri-
biles* vel audirent vel viderent, quae (sc. palus) a fonte salsuginis
quae ibidem in medio bulliebat *Sulza* dicitur.   Qua ille (Gode-
hardus) spectata, et *illusione* etiam *phantastica,* qua bruta plebs
terrebatur, audita, eandem paludem secundo sui adventus anno
cum cruce et reliquiis sanctorum invasit, et habitationem suam
ibidem aptavit, et in medio periculo oratorium in honorem S.
Bartholomaei apostoli fundavit, quo sequenti anno consummato et
dedicato, omne *daemonum phantasma* (conf. p. 482) exinde fundi-
tus extirpavit, et eundem locum omnibus commorantibus vel
advenientibus gratum et sine qualibet tentatione habitabilem
reddidit.—My third quotation is a continuation of that given
on p. 108 from the Vita S. Galli (Pertz 2, 7): Volvente deinceps
cursu temporis electus Dei Gallus retia lymphae laxabat in silentio
noctis, sed inter ea audivit *demonem de culmine montis* pari suo
clamantem, qui erat *in abditis maris.*   Quo respondente 'adsum,'
montanus econtra: 'Surge' inquit 'in adjutorium mihi.   Ecce
peregrini venerunt, qui me de templo ejecerunt (nam deos con-
terebant quos incolae isti colebant, insuper et eos ad se conver-
tebant); veni, veni, adjuva nos expellere eos de terris.'   *Marinus
demon* respondit:

' En unus eorum est in pelago,
cui nunquam nocere potero,
volui enim retia sua ledere,
sed me victum proba lugere :
signo orationis est semper clausus,
nec umquam somno oppressus.'

Electus vero Gallus haec audiens munivit se undique signaculo
Christi, dixitque ad eos :

' In nomine Jesu Christi praecipio vobis,
ut de locis istis recedatis,
nec aliquem hic ledere presumatis ! '

et cum festinatione ad littus rediit, atque abbati suo quae audierat
recitavit.[1] Quod vir Dei Columbanus audiens, convocavit fratres
in ecclesiam, *solitum signum tangens*. O mira dementia diaboli !
voces servorum Dei praeripuit *vox fantasmatica,* cum *hejulatus*
atque *ululatus diræ vocis* audiebatur *per culmina*.—Read further
on (2, 9) the story of two *lake-women* who stand naked on the
shore and *throw stones*. Everywhere we see the preachers con-
front the pagan dæmons with cross and holy spell, as something
real; the mournful howl of the spirits yields to the ringing of
bells. Gods and spirits are not distinguished : the god cast out
of the temple, whose image has been broken, is the elf or nix
meditating revenge. It is remarkable, too, that *mountain* and
water sprites are set before us as fellows (pares) ; in folk-tales of
a later time their affinity to each other seems abundantly established.

We have now considered genii of mountains, of woods and of
rivers; it remains to review the large and variously named group
of the friendly familiar *Home-sprites*.

They of all sprites stand nearest to man, because they come
and seek his fellowship, they take up their abode under his very
roof or on his premises.

Again, it is a feature to be marked in home-sprites, that they
are *purely male*, never female ; there appears a certain absence
of sex in their very idea, and if any female beings approach this

[1] Conf. the conversations of trolls overheard by two of St. Olaf's men, Fornm.
sög. 1, 185–188.

goblin kind, it is former goddesses who have come down in the world.[1]

What the Romans called *lar*,[2] *lar familiaris* (see the prologue to Plautus's Aulularia) and *penas*, is named in our older speech *húsing* or *stetigot* (genius loci) ; conf. ' húsinga (penates) ' in Notker's Capella 51. In Cap. 142 N. renders lares by ' *ingoumen* (hiusero alde burgo)' ; the literal meaning of *ingoumo* would be guard of the interior. In Cap. 50 he uses *ingeside* for penates, *i.e.* our ingesinde, inmates, domestics ; the form continued to be used in MHG. : daz liebe heilige *ingeside*, Rol. 115, 1. 226, 18. Similarly the Span. *duende*, *duendecillo* (goblin) seems derivable from domus, dueño is house-owner (dominus, distinct from don, p. 299 note), and duendo domestic, retired. The ON. tôft, Swed. tomt, means area, domus vacua, and the home-sprite's name is in Swed. *tomtekarl*, *tomtegubbe* (old fellow on the premises), *tomtrå*, *tomtebiss*, som styr i källrars rike (Hallman, p. 73) : Norw. *tomtevätte*, *toftvätte*. Another ON. name is *skúrgoð*, p. 112. We can trace in them a peculiar connexion with the *hearth* of the house ; they often come out from under it (p. 456 n.), it seems to be the door, as it were, to their subterranean dwelling : they are strictly *hearth-gods*. Here and there in Germany we also meet with the name *gesell*, fellow (supra, p. 464, selle, selke), *gutgesell*, *nachbar*, *lieber nachbar*, in the Netherlands *goede kind* (Horae Belg. 119), in England *goodfellow*, in Denmark *god dreng*, good boy, *kiäre granne*, dear neighbour, (conf. *bona socia*, p. 283-8, and *guote holde*, p. 266). The Eng. *puck* we may indeed connect with the Ir. *phuka*, Wel. *pwcca*,[3] but with more justice perhaps with the Dan. *pog* (lad), which is simply the Swed. *pojke*, ON. *púki* (puer), and comes from Finn. *poica* (filius) ; in Lower Germany too they say *pook* for a puny stunted man (Brem. wb. 3, 349). Heimreich's Nordfries. chron. 2, 348 has hus*puke* (see Suppl.).

From the 13th century (and possibly earlier, if only we had authorities)[4] down to the present time the name *kobold* has been

---

[1] *Holla, Berhta, Werra, Stempe.* Female are the Gr. Μορμώ and Λαμία, the Rom. Lamia, Mania, Maniola. The Poles too have a fem. *Omacnica* : ' Aniculae vetant pueros edere in tenebris, ne spectrum hoc devorent, quod eos insatiabiles reddat,' Linde sub v. ' omacać,' to burden. OHG. *âgenggun* lamiae, Graff 1, 132.

[2] *Larva* (spectre, dæmon) is conn. with *lar*, as arvum, arvus with arare. The Monachus Sangall. calls the pilosus (p. 481) *larva*.

[3] Croker's Fairy legends 3, 230-2. 262.

[4] ' Acc. to Falke, a *Koboltesdorp* (ann. 946), Trad. corv. ; Adalpertus *chobolt*, *kobolt* (ann. 1185), MB. 27, 36. 42.'——Extr. from SUPPL.

in use. A doc. of 1250 in Böhmer's Cod. francof. 1, 83 has a
'Heinricus dictus *Coboldus*.' Even before that date *coboldus*
occurs (Zeitschr. des Hess. vereins 3, 64). Conrad of Würzburg,
MS. 2, 206ᵃ, has: 'mir ist ein lôser hoveschalk als ein *kobolt*
von buhse,' no better than a k. of boxwood; and the Mîsnære
(Amgb. 48ᵃ): 'wê den *kobolden*, die alsus erstummen (are so
struck dumb)! mir ist ein holzîn (wooden) bischof vil lieber
dan ein stummer herre.' The notions of *kobold, dwarf, thumbkin, puppet, idol* largely run into one another (conf. supra, malik,
p. 104 note). It seems, they used to carve little home-sprites
of boxwood and set them up in the room for fun, as even now
wooden nutcrackers and other mere playthings are cut in the
shape of a dwarf or idol; yet the practice may have had to do
with an old heathen worship of small lares, to whom a place was
assigned in the innermost part of the dwelling; in time the
earnest would turn into sport, and even christian sentiment tolerate the retention of an old custom.[1] They must also have tied
rags and shreds into dolls, and set them up. The dumb wooden
kobold is kept in countenance by the 'wooden bishop' mentioned
immediately after by the Mîsnære.[2] In the oft-quoted poem of
Rüediger we find (17ᵈ of the Königsb. MS.) 'in *koboldes* sprâche,'
[*i.e.*, speaking low]. In Altd. w. 2, 55 'einen *kobold* von wahse
machen,' one of wax. Hoffmann's Fundgruben give us in the
Glossary 386, from a Vocab. of the 14th century, *opold* for
kopold. Hugo von Trimberg has several allusions to kobolds:
line 5064, 'und lêrn einander goukelspil, unter des mantel er
kobolte mache, der (whereat) manic man tougen (secretly) mit im
lache'; 5576, 'der mâle ein andern *kobolt* dar, der ungessen bî
im sitze'; 10277, 'einer siht den andern an, als *kobolt* hern *taterman*'; 10843, 'ir abgot (the heathens' gods), als ich gelesen
hân, daz waren *kobolt* und *taterman*'; 11527, 'Got möhte wol
lachen, solte ez sîn, wan sîne *tatermennelin* (same in Roth's
Fragment, p. 65) sô wunderlîch ûf erden leben,' God might
laugh to see his little mannikins behave so strangely. Jugglers

---

[1] One ought to search out the age and design of the various gear that is set out
(as mere ornament this long while) on shelves and tables; from this and from
long-established moulds for pastry, we may arrive at some conclusions about the
heathen custom of carving or 'doughing' idols (conf. pp. 15. 105. 112. 114): teig
(dough) including any soft substance, clay, wax or flour-paste.

[2] On 'papa salignus' conf. Reinh. p. xciv.

bring kobolds out from under their cloak, kobolds are painted
on the wall, the heathen gods were nothing but kobolds and
tatermen, to stare at each other like kobold and taterman,——
all through, the kobold appears as the tiny tricky home-sprite.
In writers of the 17th century I find the remarkable phrase 'to
laugh *like a kobold*,' Ettner's Unwürd. doct. p. 340, and App. p.
53; 'you laugh as though you'd empty yourself, *like a kobolt*,'
Reimdich p. 149. This must either mean, to laugh with mouth
agape, like a carved kobold, who may have been so represented,
or simply to laugh loud and heartily.[1] Again, 'to laugh like a
hampelmann,' Deutschfranzos p. 274; 'ho, ho, ho! the loud
laugh of Robin Goodfellow,' Anecd. and Trad., ed. by W. J.
Thoms, Lond. 1839, p. 115. In the poem of Zeno 867. 1027
this dæmonic laughter is expressed by *skraken* (Brem. wb. 4,
686 schrachtern). Schweinichen 1, 260 tells of an unquiet spirit
laughing loud and shrill; it may be a laugh of mirth or mockery.

In the Netherlands too we find at an early time the form
koubout (pl. coubouten, Horae Belg. 1, 119); now *kabout*, and in
Belgium *kabot, kabotermanneken*.[2] The Scandinavian languages
have not the word.

It is a foreign word, sprung no doubt from the Gr. κόβαλος
(rogue), Lat. *cobalus*,[3] with a *t* added, as our language is partial
to forms in *-olt* for monstrous and ghostly beings. From cobalus,
in Mid. Lat. already *gobelinus*, the Fr. has formed its *gobelin*,
whence the Engl. *goblin*, strengthened into *hobgoblin*. Hanka's
O. Boh. glosses render 79[b] gitulius (getulius, gaetulius) by *kobolt*,
and directly after, aplinus (l. alpinus, *i.e.* alphinus, the 'fool'
or queen in chess) by *tatrman*: here are kobolt and tatrman
together, just as we saw them staring at each other in the
Renner; hence also the Cod. pal. 341, 126ᶜ speaks of 'einen
taterman mâlen,' painting a t., and the Wahtelmære 140 of
guiding him with strings, 'rihtet zuo mit den snüeren die *tater-*

---

[1] 'Hlahtar *kiscutitas*,' laughed till he shook, K. 24ᵃ. Notk. Cap. 33 has: 'taz
lahter *scutta* sia; Petronius, cap. 24, 'risu dissolvebat ilia sua'; Reinardus 3,
1929, 'cachinnus viscera fissurus'; or, as we say, to split with laughing, laugh
yourself double, short and small, to pieces, to a hölzlin (Gryphius p. m. 877), brown,
out of your senses; 'einen schübel voll lachen'; perish, die with laughing, MHG.
'man swindet under lachen,' Ben. 330. A Breton song in Villemarqué 1, 39 speaks
of the loud laugh of the korred (see Suppl.).
[2] Schayes sur les usages et traditions des Belges. Louvain 1834, p. 230.
[3] Lobeck's Aglaoph. 1308-1328.

manne' (supra, p. 410 *g*.). To explain this taterman by the Engl. tatter has some plausibility, but then our HG. ought to have had zaterman (conf. OHG. zata, zatar, Graff 5, 632-3, with AS. tættera, panniculus). The glossist above may have meant by gaetulius an African savage, by alpinus a Tartar (MHG. tater, tateler), or still better, a fool;[1] the word *taterman* occurs in other O. Boh. documents besides, and signifies doll and idol (Jungmann 3, 554b); foreign to all other Slavic dialects, it seems borrowed from German.[2] Its proper meaning can only be revealed by a fuller insight into the history of puppet-shows. Perhaps the Hung. tatos (juggler) has a claim to consideration.[3]

Several MSS. however and the first printed edition of the Renner have not taterman at all, but *katerman* (Cod. francof. 164b reads verse 10843 kobülde unde *katirman*), which is not altogether to be rejected, and at lowest offers a correct secondary sense. *Katerman*, derived from kater (tom-cat), may be compared with *heinzelman, hinzelman, hinzemännchen*, the name of a home-sprite,[4] with *Hinze* the cat in Reineke, and the wood-sprite *Katzenveit* (p. 480). The *puss-in-boots* of the fairy-tale plays exactly the part of a good-natured helpful kobold; another one is called stiefel (boot, Deut. sag. no. 77), because he wears a large boot: by the boot, I suppose, are indicated the *gefeite schuhe* (fairy shoes) of older legend, with which one could travel faster on the ground, and perhaps through the air; such are the *league-boots* of fairy-tales and the *winged shoes* of Hermes. The name of *Heinze* is borne by a mountain-sprite in the Frosch-meuseler. Heinze is a dimin. of Heinrich, just as in Lower Germany another noisy ghost is called *Chimke*, dimin. of Joachim (conf. 'dat *gimken*,' Brem. wb. 5, 379): the story of *Chimmeken*

---

[1] There is in the kobold's character an unmistakable similarity to the witty court-fool; hence I feel it significant, that one described in Schweinichen 1, 260-2 expressly carries a *bawble*. The Engl. *hobgoblin* means the same as *clowngoblin* (Nares sub v. hob).

[2] Hanusch (Slav. myth. 299) takes the *taterman* (he says, hasterman also occurs) for a water-sprite.

[3] 'In Tyrol *tatterman* = scarecrow, coward, kobold, from tattern, zittern, to quake, skedaddle; Frommann 2, 327. Leoprechting p. 177 says, tattern to frighten; at Gratz in Styria, the night before solstice, *tattermann*, a bugbear, is carried round and set on fire in memory of extirpated heathenism.'—Extr. from SUPPL.

[4] Deut. sag. no. 75; the story is 100 years later than the composition of the Reineke. Hinzelmann leaves a dint in the bed, as if a cat had lain in it. Luther's Table-talk (ed. 1571, p. 441a) had previously related the like concerning a spirit *Heinslin*.

(of about 1327) is to be found in Kantzow's Pomerania 1, 333. The similar and equally Low-German name *Wolterken* seems to have a wider circulation. Samuel Meiger in his Panurgia lamiarum (Hamb. 1587. 4), bok 3 cap. 2, treats 'van den laribus domesticis edder husknechtkens, de men ok *Wolterken* unde *Chimken* an etliken örden nömet.' These Wolterkens are also mentioned by Arnkiel (Cimbr. heidenth. 1, 49); in the Netherlands they are called *Wouters, Wouterken,* and Tuinman 2, 201 has a proverb ''t is een wilde *Wouter,'* though incorrectly he refers it to wout (silva). Wouter, Wolter is nothing but the human proper name Walter bestowed on a home-sprite. It is quite of a piece with the familiar intercourse between these spirits and mankind, that, beside the usual appellatives, certain proper names should be given them, the diminutives of Henry, Joachim, Walter. Not otherwise do I understand the *Robin* and *Nissen* in the wonted names for the English and Danish goblins *Robin goodfellow* and *Nissen god dreng.* Robin is a French-English form of the name Robert, OHG. Hruodperaht, MHG. Ruotperht, our Ruprecht, Rupert, Ruppert; and *Robin fellow* is the same home-sprite whom we in Germany call *knecht Ruprecht,* and exhibit to children at Christmas, but who in the comedies of the 16-17th centuries becomes a mere *Rüpel* or *Rüppel, i.e.* a merry fool in general.[1] In England, Robin Goodfellow seems to get mixed up with Robin Hood the archer, as Hood himself reminds us of Hôdeken (p. 463); and I think this derivation from a being of the goblin kind, and universally known to the people, is preferable to the attempted historical ones from Rubertus a Saxon mass-priest, or the English Robertus knight, one of the slayers of Thomas Becket. *Nisse, Nissen,* current in Denmark and Norway, must be explained from *Niels, Nielsen,*

---

[1] Ayrer's Fastnachtspiele 79d confirms the fact of *Rupel* being a dimin. of Ruprecht. Some dialects use *Rüpel, Riepel* as a name for the tom-cat again; in witch-trials a little young devil is named *Rubel.* Acc. to the Leipzig Avanturier 1, 22-3, *knecht Ruprecht* appears in shaggy clothes, sack on back and rod in hand.——[If *Hob* in hobgoblin stands for Robert, it is another instance of the friendly or at least conciliatory feeling that prompted the giving of such names. In Mids. N. Dream ii. 1, the same spirit that has just been called *Robin* Goodfellow, is thus addressed:

> Those that *Hob*-goblin call you, and sweet Puck,
> You do their work, and they shall have good luck.

Of course Hob as a man's name is Robert, as Hodge is Roger.—Trans.]

i.e. Nicolaus, Niclas,[1] not from our HG. common noun 'nix' the watersprite, which is in Danish nök, nok (p. 488), and has no connexion with Nisse; and the Swed. form is also *Nilson*. I find a confirmation of this in our habit of assigning to *Niclaus, Claus* or *Clobes* the selfsame part that in some districts is played by Ruprecht. To this latter I am inclined to refer even the words of so early a writer as Ofterdingen, MS. 2, 2ᵇ : '*Rupreht min knecht* muoz iuwer hâr gelîch den tôren schern,' R. my man must shear your hair like that of fools. A home-sprite *Rüdy* (for Rudolf) in Mone's Anz. 3, 365.

Another set of names is taken from the noises which these spirits keep up in houses : you hear them jumping softly, knocking at walls, racketing and tumbling on stairs and in lofts. Span. *trasgo* (goblin), and trasguear (to racket); Fr. *soterai, sotret* (jumper), Mém. de l'acad. celt. 4, 91; *ekerken* (eichhörnchen, squirrel), Deut. sag. no. 78; *poltergeist, rumpelgeist, rumpelstilz* in the Kindermärchen no. 55, *rumpelstilt* in Fischart;[2] one particular goblin is called *klopfer*, knocker (Deut. sag. no. 76), and it may be in this connexion that *hämmerlein, hemerlein* (supra, p. 182) has come to be applied to home-sprites of diabolic nature. Nethl. *bullman, bullerman, bullerkater*, from bullen, bullern, to be boisterous. Flem. *boldergeest*, and hence 'bi holder te bolder,' our 'holter die polter,' helter-skelter. A *pophart*, identical with rumpelstilt in Fischart, is to be derived from popeln, popern, to keep bobbing or thumping softly and rapidly;[3] a house-goblin in Swabia was called the *poppele;* in other parts *popel, pöpel, pöpelmann, popanz*, usually with the side-meaning of a muffled ghost that frightens children, and seldom used of playful good-humoured goblins. At the same time *pöpel* is that which muffles (puppt) itself: about Henneberg, says Reinwald 2, 78, a dark cloud is so called ; it contains the notion

[1] Not only Nielsen, but *Nissen* is a family name in Denmark, and can only mean the same, by no means nix or goblin. [I suppose Niels is rather Nigellus, Nigel, which breaks down the connexion with Nicolas or Claus; still the two can stand independently.—TRANS.]

[2] Is *stilt, stils* the old *stalt* in compounds? Gramm. 2, 527. What the fairy-tale says of *Rumpelstilt*, and how his name has to be guessed, other stories tell of *Eisenhütel* or *Hopfenhütel* (who wear an iron hat or one wreathed with hop-leaves), Kletke's Alman. v. volksm. 67 ; or of the dwarf *Holzrührlein, Bonneführlein*, Harrys 1, 18 [of *Knirftker, Gebhart, Tepentiren*, Müllenh. 306-8, of *Titteli Ture*, Sv. folkv. 1, 171.—SUPPL.]; and we shall meet with the like in giant-stories.

[3] Stald. 1, 204. Schm. 1, 293. 323.

of mask and tarnkappe (p. 333). In connexion with Holda, a *Hollepöpel, Hollepeter* is spoken of.

The same shifting of form appears in the words *mumhart* (already in Cæsarius heisterb. 7, 46 : 'mummart momordit me '), *mummel, mummelmann, mummanz*,[1] which express the very same notion, 'mummen, mummeln' signifying to mumble, to utter a muffled sound. Or can we connect it with *mumel, muomel*, the name of the watersprite (p. 490)? In that case, vermummen (to disguise), mummerei (mumming, larva) would seem to mean acting like the spectre, instead of the spectre having taken his name from mumming (see Suppl.).

The word *butze* as far back as the 12th-13th century had the same meaning as mummart and poppart : a place called *Puzi-prunnun, Pucivrunnen*, MB. 6, 60. 62. 9, 420 (12th century), unless puzi=puteus be meant, might take its name from a well, haunted by such a home-sprite. 'Ein ungehiurer (uncanny) *butze*,' Martina 116° 224ª ; 'si sehent mich nicht mêr an in *butzen* wîs,' they look at me no more in butze wise, Walth. 28, 37 ; 'in butzenwise gehn,' Oberlin sub v. ; 'den *butzen* vorht er kleine, als man dô seit von kinden,' he little fears the b., as we say of children, Albr. Tit. x. 144 (Hahn 1275) ; butzengriul, -horror, Walth. 140, 2. MsH. 3, 451ª ; 'geloub ich daz, sô bîz mich *butze*,' b. bite me if I believe it, Hätzlerin 287ª, which agrees with 'mummart momordit me' above ; 'ein *kinderbutze*,' Ls. 1, 617 ; 'forht ich solchen *bützel*,' Ls. 1, 380, where a wihtel is spoken of. So, to frighten with the *butze*, to tear off the *butze* (mask) ; *butzen* antlüt (face) and *butzen* kleider (clothes)=larva in Kaisersperg (Oberlin 209) ; *winterbutz* in Brant's Narrenschiff 129 (winterbutte in the Plattdeutsch translation 140ᵇ). I do not understand the *butzenhänsel* in Weisth. 1, 691. All over Germany almost, we hear to this day : 'der *butz* kommt,'[2] or 'der *butzemann, butzelmann*,' and in Elsass *butzmummel*, the same as butz or mummel alone. *buz*, Jäger's Ulm, p. 522. *butzenmann*, Fischart's Bienkorb 194ª. *butz*, Garg. 231ª. *butzemann*, Simpl. 2, 248. In Bavaria, *fasnachtbutz*, Shrovetide b., *buzmann, buzi-bercht*, b. coupled with the Bercht or Berchta of our pp. 272-9 ;

---

[1] For mum·hans (muffle-jack), as popanz is for pop-hans (bob-jack), and as there were likewise blindhans, grobhans, karsthans, scharrhans, etc.

[2] In Normandy : 'hush, the gobelin will eat you up.'

butzwinkel, lurking-place, *butzlfinster*, pitch-dark, when the apparition is most to be dreaded; 'the *putz* would take us over hill and dale,' Schm. 1, 229. 230; the *butz* who leads travellers astray (Muchar's Gastein, p. 145). In Swabia *butzenmaukler* (from maucheln, to be sly), *butzenbrecht, butzenraule, butzenrolle, rollputz, butzenbell* (because his rattle rolls and his bell tinkles), Schmid 111. About Hanau I have heard the interjection, *katza-butza-rola!* the 'katze-butze' bringing up the connexion between cat and goblin (p. 503) in a new form. In Switzerland *bootzi, bozi,* St. 1, 204. Here several meanings branch out of one another: first we have a monstrous *butz* that drags children away, then a tiny *bützel*, and thence both *bützel* and *butz-igel* (-urchin) used contemptuously of little deformed creatures. In like manner *but* in Low Germ. stands for a squat podgy child; butten, verbutten is to get stunted or deformed, while the bugbear is called *butte, butke, budde, buddeks*: 'dat di de *butke* nig bit,' (that thee the bogie bite not!) is said satirically to children who are afraid of the dark, Brem. wb. 1, 173-5; and here certainly is the place for the watersprite *butt* or *buttje* in the Kindermärchen no. 19, the name having merely been transferred to a blunt-headed fish, the rhombus or passer marinus.[1] There is also probably a *butte-mann, buttmann*, but more commonly in the contracted form *bu-man* (Br. wb. 1, 153). Nethl. *bytebauw*, for buttebauw, which I identify with Low Germ. *bu-ba* (Br. wb. 1, 152). The Dan. *bussemand, bussegroll, bussetrold* (Molbech, p. 60) seems to be formed on the German (see Suppl.).—The origin of this *butze, butte* is hard to ascertain: I would assume a lost Goth. biuta (tundo, pulso), báut, butum, OHG. piuzu, pôz, puzum, whence OHG. anapôz, our amboss, anvil, MHG. bôzen (pulsare), and gebiuze, thumping, clatter [Engl. to butt?], conf. Lachmann on Nib. 1823, 2. Fragm. 40, 186; *butze* would be a thumping rapping sprite, perfectly agreeing with mamhart and pophart,[2] and we may yet hear of a bôzhart or buzhart. But, like

[1] Homesprite and water-sprite meet in this soothsaying wish-granting fish. The story of the butt has a parallel in the OFr. tale of an elvish spirit and enchanter Merlin, who keeps fulfilling the growing desires of the charcoal burner, till they pass all bounds, then plunges him back into his original poverty (Méon, nouv. rec. 2, 242-252. Jubinal 1, 128-135.

[2] As the monstrous includes the repulsive and unclean, it is not surprising that both *butze* and *popel* signify mucus, filth (Oberlin 210. Schm. 1, 291). The same with Swiss *böög*, St. 1, 203.

butzenhänsel, there is also a *hanselmann* used for spiritus familiaris (Phil. v. Sittew. 5, 328, ed. Lugd.), and the similar *hampelmann* for goblin, puppet and mannequin (= männeke, mannikin). Bavar. *hämpel, haimpel,* both devil and simpleton (Schm. 2, 197), Austr. *henparl* (Höfer 2, 46).

The Fr. *follet,* It. *foletto,* is a diminuitive of *fol,* fou; which, like *follis* (bellows), seems to be derived from an obsolete follere (to move hither and thither), and brings us to a fresh contact of the home-sprite with the fool.[1] Then *lutin,* also *luton,* perhaps from the Lat. luctus: a sprite who wails and forebodes sorrow? Lithuan. *bildukkas, bildunas, bildziuks* (noisy sprite), from bildenti (to racket, rattle); *grozdunas* from gródzia (there is a racket made). Sloven. *ztrazhnik,* Serv. *strashilo,* Boh. *strašidlo,* Pol. *straszydlo,* from strašiti (terrere); Boh. *bubák* (noisy sprite). Somewhat stronger is the Pol. *dzieciojad,* child-eater, like the Lat. manducus. Irish home-sprites are called *Cluricauns* (Elfenm. p. 85–114), *Leprechaun, Logheriman* (Keightley 2, 179; and see Suppl.).

But enough of these names: no doubt many more could be added. It is time to consider the nature and functions of these Home-sprites.

In stature, appearance and apparel they come very near to elves and dwarfs; legend loves to give them *red hair* or a *red beard,* and the *pointed red hat* is rarely missing. *Hütchen* (Hodeke, Hoidike), the Hildesheim goblin, and *Hopfenhütel, Eisenhütel* take their names from it. A broad-topped mushroom is in Dan. called *nissehat.* The Norwegian Nissen is imagined small like a child, but strong, clothed in grey, with a *red peaky cap,* and carrying a *blue light* at night.[2] So they can make themselves visible or invisible to men, as they please. Their *fairy shoes* or *boots* have been noticed, p. 503; with these they can get over the most difficult roads with the greatest speed: it was just over mountains and forests that Hütchen's *rennpfad* extended (Deut. sag. 1, 100), and the *schratweg* (p. 479) means much the

---

[1] Ratherius, ed. Ballerini, p. 814: 'merito ergo *follis* latiali rusticitate vocaris, quoniam veritate vacuus.' Wilhelm. metens. ep. 8: '*follem* me rustico verbo appellasti.'

[2] J. N. Wilse's Beskrivelse over Spydeberg, Christiana 1779, p. 418. Conf. the blue light of the black mannikin, Kinderm. no. 116.

same.[1] With this walking apparatus and this swiftness there is associated now and then some *animal's form* and name : Heinze, Heinzelmann, polterkater, katermann, boot-cat, squirrel; their shuffling and bustling about the house is paralleled by the nightly turbulence of obstreperous cats.[2] They like to live in the *stable*, *barn* or *cellar* of the person whose society they have chosen, sometimes even in a *tree* that stands near the house (Swed. *bo-trä*, dwelling-tree). You must not break a bough off such a tree, or the offended goblin will make his escape, and all the luck of the house go with him; moreover, he cannot abide any chopping in the yard or spinning on a Thursday evening (Superst. Swed. no. 110).[3] In household occupations they shew themselves friendly and furthersome, particularly in the *kitchen* and *stable*. The dwarf-king *Goldemar* (pp. 453. 466) is said to have lived on intimate terms with Neveling of Hardenberg at the Hardenstein, and often shared his bed. He played charmingly on the harp, and got rid of much money at dice ; he called Neveling brother-in-law, and often admonished him, he spoke to everybody, and made the clergy blush by discovering their secret sins. His hands were lean like those of a frog, cold and soft to the grasp; he would allow himself to be felt, but *never to be seen*. After a stay of three years he made off without injuring any one. Other accounts call him *king Vollmar*, and they say the room he lived in is called *Vollmar's kammer* to this day : a place at table had to be kept for him, and one in the stable for his horse; meats, oats and hay were consumed, but of horse or man you *saw nothing but the shadow*. Once an inquisitive man having sprinkled ashes and peas to make him fall and to get sight of his footprints, he sprang upon him as he was lighting the fire, and chopped him up into pieces, which he stuck on a spit and roasted, but the head and legs he thought proper to boil. The dishes, when ready, were carried to Vollmar's chamber, and one could hear them being consumed with cries of joy. After this, no more was heard

---

[1] So a *chemin de fées* is spoken of in Mém. celt. 4, 240, and a *tröllaskeid* (curriculum gigantum) in Laxd. saga 66.
[2] Witches and fays often assume the *shape of a cat*, and the cat is a creature peculiarly open to suspicions of witchcraft.
[3] Wilse, ubi supra, entirely agrees : ' tomtegubben skal have sin til hold unde *gamle träer* ved stuehuset (*boeträer*), og derfor har man ej tordet fälde disse gand-ske.' To this connexion of home-sprites with tree-worship we shall have to return further on.

of king Vollmar ; but over his chamber-door it was found written, that from that time the house would be as unlucky as it had been prosperous till then, and the scattered estates would never come together again till there were three Hardenbergs of Hardenstein living at once.   Both spit and gridiron were long preserved, till in 1651 they disappeared during the Lorrain war, but the pot is still there, let into the kitchen wall.[1]   The home-sprite's parting prophecy sounds particularly ancient, and the grim savagery of his wrath is heathen all over.   Sam. Meiger says of the *wolter-kens* : ' Se vinden sik gemeinichlich in den hüseren, dar ein god vörrad (store) van allen dingen is.   Dar schölen se sik bedenst-haftigen (obsequious) anstellen, waschen in der köken up, böten vür (beet the fire), schüren de vate, schrapen de perde im stalle, voderen dat quik, dat it vet und glat herin geit, theen (draw) water und dragent dem vehe (cattle) vör.   Men kan se des nachtes hören de ledderen edder treppen (or stairs) up und dal stigen, lachen, wen se den megeden efte knechte de decken aftheen (pull off), se richten to, houwen in, jegen (against) dat geste kamen schölen,[2] smiten de ware in dem huse umme, de den morgen gemeinliken darna verkoft wert.'   The goblin then is an obliging hardworking sprite, who takes a pleasure in waiting on the men and maids at their housework, and secretly dispatching some of it himself.   He curries the horses, combs out their manes,[3] lays fodder before the cattle,[4] draws water from the well and brings it them, and cleans out the stable.   For the maids he makes up fire, rinses out the dishes, cleaves and carries wood, sweeps and scrubs.   His presence brings prosperity to the house, his departure removes it.   He is like the helpful earth-mannikins who lend a hand in field labour (p. 451 n.).   At the same time he oversees the management of the house, that everything be done orderly ; lazy and careless workers get into trouble with him (as with Holla and Berhta, pp. 269. 273), he pulls the coverlets off

---

[1] Von Steinen's Westph. gesch. pp. 777–9.

[2] When the *cat* trims her whiskers, they say it is a sign of guests.

[3] Like the white lady (Berhta), whose nightly visits are indicated the next morning by the wax that has dropt from her taper on the manes (Deut. sag. no. 122). In Wales the people believe that goats have their beards combed out every Friday night by the elves (Croker 8, 204).

[4] Hence the name *futtermännchen*, (confounded at times with *Petermännchen*) ; but often he has one favourite horse that he pays special attention to, taking hay out of the others' cribs to bring to him. Faye p. 44.

the beds of sluggards, blows their light out, turns the best cow's neck awry, kicks the dawdling milkmaid's pail over, and mocks her with insulting laughter; his good-nature turns into worrying and love of mischief, he becomes a 'tormenting spirit.' *Agemund* in the Reinardus 4, 859–920 seems to me no other than a house-dæmon, distorted and exaggerated by the poet, disturbing the maid in her sleep, her milking and churning (see Suppl.).[1]

Servants, to keep on good terms with him, save a little potful of their food on purpose for him, which is surely a vestige of little sacrifices that were offered him of old (p. 448). That is probably why one Swiss goblin bears the name *Napfhans*, Potjack. But in many cases it is only done on holidays, or once a week. The sprite is easily satisfied, he puts up with a saucerful of porridge, a piece of cake and a glass of beer, which are left out for him accordingly; on those evenings he does not like any noisy work to be going on, either in or out of doors. This they call in Norway 'at holde qvelvart (qvellsvart),' to hold evening rest. Those who desire his goodwill, give him good words: '*kiäre granne*, giör det!' dear neighbour, do this; and he replies conformably. He is said at times to carry his preference for the goodman so far as to pilfer hay and straw from other farmers' barns or stables, and bring it to him (see Suppl.).

The Nissen loves the moonlight, and in wintertime you see him merrily skipping across the farmyard, or skating. He is a good hand at dancing and music, and much the same is told of him as of the Swedish strömkarl (p. 493), that *for a grey sheep* he teaches people to play the fiddle.[2]

The home-sprite is contented with a trifling wage: a new hat, a red cap, a parti-coloured coat with tinkling bells he will make shift with. The *hat* and *cap* he has in common with dwarfs (p. 463), and therefore also the power to make himself invisible. Petronius (Satir. cap. 38) shows it was already a Roman superstition: 'sed quomodo dicunt, ego nihil scivi, sed audivi, quomodo *incuboni pileam* rapuisset, et thesaurum invenit.' Home-

---

[1] The description of his figure (a horse's mane, hawk's bill, cat's tail, goat's beard, ox's horns and cock's feet) can hardly have been all invented there and then.
[2] Unless Wilse (Beskriv. over Spyd. 419) has confounded Nissen with nöcken; yet the German goblin *Goldemar* was likewise musical (Ir. Elfenm. lxxxiii.). Wilse, and Faye, pp. 43-45, give the best account of the Norwegian Nissen, and Thiele i. 134-5 of the Danish.

sprites guard treasures, and in Nib. 399 Siegfried becomes
master of the hoard as soon as he has taken Alberich's tarnkappe
from him.   In Calderon's Dama duende the little goblin wears a
large hat: 'era un *frayle tamañito*, y tenia un *cucurucho tamaño*.'
The Swedish 'tomte i gården' looks like a year-old child, but
has an old knowing face under his red cap.   He shews himself at
midday (see chap. XXXVI., daemon meridianus) in summer and
autumn, slow and panting he drags a single straw or an ear
(p. 459); when the farmer laughed and asked, 'What's the
odds whether you bring me that or nothing?' he quitted the
farm in dudgeon, and went to the next.   From that time prosperity forsook the man who had despised him, and went over to
his neighbour.   The farmer who respected the busy tomte and
cared for the tiniest straw, became rich, and cleanliness and
order reigned in his household.   Many Christians still believe in
such home-sprites, and present them an offering every year, ' pay
them their wage' as they call it.   This is done on the morn of
Yule, and consists of grey cloth, tobacco and a *shovelful of earth*,
Afzelius 2, 169.   A *pück* served the monks of a Mecklenburg
monastery for thirty years, in kitchen, stall and elsewhere; he
was thoroughly good-natured, and only bargained for '*tunicam
de diversis coloribus, et tintinnabulis plenam.*'[1]   In Scotland there
lived a goblin *Shellycoat*, and we saw (p. 465) that the dwarfs
of the Mid. Ages also loved *bells* [schellen; and schellenkappe is
Germ. for cap and bells].   The bells on the dress of a fool still
attest his affinity to the shrewd and merry goblin (fol, follet);
see Suppl.

He loves to play merry pranks, and when he has accomplished
one, he is fain to laugh himself double for delight: hence that
goblin laughter (p. 502) and *chuckling*.   But also when he sulks,
and means mischief to those who have brought him into trouble
and difficulty, he utters a scornful laugh at the top of his voice.[2]

As *henchman true*, he abides by the master he once takes up
with, come weal come woe.   But his attachment is often found
irksome, and one cannot be rid of him again.   A farmer set fire

[1] The story (as written down in 1559) is given in Ern. Joach. Westphal's Speci-
men documentorum ineditorum, Rostock 1726, pp. 156-166.
[2] Scott's Minstrelsy I. civ. mentions a North English *Brag* or *Barguest*: 'he
usually ended his mischievous frolics with a *horselaugh*.'   Conf. Hone's Tablebook
2, 656.

to his barn, to burn the goblin that haunted it; when it is all ablaze, there sits the sprite at the back of the cart in which they were removing the contents (Deut. sag. no. 72).[1] In Mone's Anzeiger 1835, 312 we read of a little *black man* that was bought with a chest, and when this was opened, he hopped out and slipped behind the oven, whence all efforts to rout him out were fruitless; but he lived on excellent terms with the household, and occasionally shewed himself to them, though never to strangers. This black figure reminds one both of the Scandinavian dwarfs, and of the devil. Some thoroughly good goblin-stories are in Adalb. Kuhn's collection, pp. 42. 55. 84. 107. 159. 191-3. 372.[2]

There are also goblins who, like nix and watersprite, are engaged in no man's service, but live independently; when such a one is caught, he will offer you gifts or tell your fortune, to be set at liberty again. Of this sort is the *butt* in the nursery-tale

---

[1] Very similar stories in Kuhn, no. 108, Thiele 1, 136, and the Irish tale of the cluricaun (pp. 92. 213 of the transl.). Also a capital Polish story about Iskrzycki, in Wóycicki's Klechdy 1, 198: An unknown person, who called himself Iskrzycki [flinty, from iskra = spark, says Grimm; there is also a Slav. iskri = near, iskrenny = neighbour, friendly] came and offered his services to a man of noble family. The agreement was drawn up, and even signed, when the master observed that Iskrzycki had horse's feet, and gave him notice of withdrawal. But the servant stood on his rights, and declared his intention of serving his master whether he would or no. He lived invisible by the fireplace, did all the tasks assigned him, and by degrees they got used to him; but at last the lady pressed her husband to move, and he arranged to take another estate. The family all set out from the mansion, and had got through the better part of the way, when, the log-road being out of repair, the carriage threatens to upset, and the lady cries out in alarm. Suddenly a voice from the back of the carriage calls out: Never fear, my masters! Iskrzycki is with you (nie bój się, pani; Iskrzycki z wami). The 'masters' then perceiving that they could not shake him off, turned back to their old house, and lived at peace with the servant until his term expired. [English readers will remember Tennyson's 'Yes, we're flitting, says the ghost.']——The *alraun* or *gallows-mannikin* in Deutsche sagen nos. 83. 84 is not properly a kobold, but a semi-diabolic being carved out of a root, and so diminutive that he can be kept in a glass; like an idol, he has to be bathed and nursed. In one thing however he resembles the home-sprite, that he will not leave his owner, and even when thrown away he always comes back again, unless indeed he be sold [orig. 'bought'] for less than he cost. The last purchaser has to keep him. Simpliciss. 2, 184. 208. Conf. Schm. 8, 96-7. [Home-sprites can be bought and sold, but the third buyer must keep him, Müllenhoff p. 822. With ref. to the 'idol (götze)': As the figure of the child Jesus has its shirt washed (Sommer, pp. 38. 173), so the *heckmännchen* must be dressed up anew at a certain time every year, 10 Ehen, p. 285.—Extr. from SUPPL.]

[2] To *escape* the futtermännchen, a farmer built a new house, but the day before he moved, he spied the f. dipping his grey coat in the brook: 'My little coat here I swill and souse, To-morrow we move to a fine new house.' Börner's Orlagau, p. 246. Whoever has the kobold must *not wash* or *comb* himself (Sommer p. 171. Müllenh. 209); so in the case of the devil, ch. XXXIII.—Extr. from SUPPL.

(p. 507), likewise the *folet* in Marie de Fr. 2, 140, who grants three wishes (oremens). And the captive marmennill (p. 434), or the sea-wife, does the same.

The unfriendly, *racketing* and *tormenting* spirits who take possession of a house, are distinguished from the friendly and good-natured by their commonly forming a whole gang, who disturb the householder's rest with their *riot and clatter*, and *throw stones* from the roof at passers by. A French comedy of the 16th century, 'Les Esprits,'[1] represents goblins racketing in a house, singing and playing at night, and *aiming tiles* at passers by in the daytime; they are fond of fire, but make a violent uproar every time the master spits.[2] In Gervase of Tilbury, cap. 18, the folleti also *pelt with stones*, and this of stone-throwing is what we shall meet with in quite early stories of devils; altogether the racketing sprites have in this respect more of the devil or spectre in them than of the elf: it is a darkening and distortion of their original nature in accordance with Christian sentiment.

So it becomes clear, at last, how the once familiar and faithful friend of the family under heathenism has gradually sunk into a bugbear or a taunt to children : a lot which he shares with goddesses and gods of old. As with Holle and Berhte, so people are threatened with the Lamia, the Omacmica, the manducus and goblin (pp. 500. 507) : ' le gobelin vous mangera, le gobelin vous attrapera ! ' Little bützel no more, but a frightful butze-mann or katzenveit, in mask (strawbeard) or with sooty visage he scares (like the roggenmuhme, p. 477). And it is worth remarking how, in some districts at least, *knecht Ruprecht, knecht Nicolas*, appear at Christmas-time not by themselves, but in

---

[1] Comedies facecieuses de Pierre de l'Arivey, champenois, Lyon 1597. Rouen, 1611, p. 242 seq.

[2] Legenda aurea, cap. 177: Hujus Ludovici tempore, anno Domini 856, ut in quadam chronica habetur, in parochia Maguntina *malignus spiritus parietes domorum quasi malleis pulsando* et manifeste loquendo et discordias seminando adeo hominis infestabat, ut quocumque intrasset, *statim illa domus exurereter*. Presbyteris autem letanias agentibus et aquam benedictam spargentibus inimicus *lapides jactabat* et multos cruentabat. Tandem aliquando conquiescens confessus est se, quando aqua spargebatur, *sub capa talis sacerdotis quasi familiaris sui* latuisse, accusans eum quod eum filia procuratoris in peccatum lapsus fuerit. [This incident, said to have occurred at Capmunti (Kembden) near Bingen, is derived from Rudolfi Fuldensis Annal. ann. 858, in Pertz 1, 872, where further details are given.—Extr. from SUPPL.

attendance on the real gift-giver, the infant Christ or dame
Berhta: while these dole out their favours, those come on with
rod and sack, threatening to thrash disobedient children, to
throw them into the water, to puff their eyes out (Rockenphilos.
6, 353). Their pranks, their roughness, act as foil to the gracious
higher being from whom the gifts proceed; they are almost as
essential to the festival as Jackpudding to our old comedy. I
can well imagine that even in heathen times the divinity, whose
appearing heralded a happy time, had at his side some merry elf
or dwarf as his *attendant* embodying to the vulgar eye the blessings that he brought.[1] Strongly in favour of this view are the
North Franconian names *Hullepöpel* (Popowitsch 522), *Hollepeter*
(Schm. 2, 174), the Bavarian *Semper*, of whom they say he cuts
naughty children's bodies open and stuffs them with pebbles
(Schm. 3, 12. 250), exactly after the manner of Holla and Berhta
(p. 273)[2]; and consider faithful Eckart, who escorts Holla.
In Christian times they would at first choose some saint to
accompany the infant Christ or the mother of God in their dis-
tribution of boons, but the saint would imperceptibly degenerate
into the old goblin again, but now a coarser one. The Christmas
plays sometimes present the Saviour with His usual attendant
Peter, or else with Niclas, at other times however Mary with
Gabriel, or with her aged Joseph, who, disguised as a peasant,
acts the part of knecht Ruprecht. Nicolaus again has converted
himself into a ' man Clobes ' or Rupert; as a rule, it is true,
there is still a *Niclas*, a saintly bishop and benevolent being,
distinct from the ' man ' who scares children; but the characters
get mixed, and *Clobes* by himself acts the 'man' (Tobler 105^b,
106^a); the Austrian *Grampus* (Höfer 1, 313. Schm. 2, 110),
Krämpus, Krambas, is possibly for Hieronymus, but how to explain the Swiss *Schmutzli* (Stald. 2, 337) I do not rightly know,
perhaps simply from his smutty sooty aspect? Instead of Grampus
there is also in Styria a *Bärthel* (pointing to Berhta, or Bartho-
lomew?) *Schmutzbartel*[3] and *Klaubauf*, who rattles, rackets, and

---

[1] *Heinrich* and *Ruprecht* were once common names for serving-men, as Hans
and Claus are now.
[2] *Zember* about Eger in German Bohemia (Popowitsch 523); at the same time
the Lausitz idol *Sompar* (supra, p. 71 note) is worth considering.
[3] The phrase ' he knows where Barthel gets his must,' notwithstanding other
explanations, may refer to a home-sprite well-known in the cellar.

throws nuts (Denis, Lesefr. 1, 181 ; see Suppl.). Further, on this
point I attach weight to the Swedish *jullekar*, Dan. *juleleger*,
yule-lays, undoubtedly of heathen origin, which at Christmas-
time present Christ and certain saints, but replace our man
Ruprecht by a *julbock, julebuk, i.e.* a manservant disguised as
a goat.[1] This interweaving of jackpudding, fool, Klobes and
Rüpel, of the yule-buck and at last of the devil himself, into the
rude popular drama of our Mid. Ages, shows what an essential
part of it the wihtels and tatermans formerly were, how ineradi-
cable the elvish figures and characters of heathenism. The
Greeks enlivened the seriousness of their tragedy by satyric
plays, in which *e.g.* Proteus, similar to our sea-sprite (p. 434),
played a leading part.[2]

There is yet another way in which a former connexion between
gods, wise-women and these genii now and then comes to light.
The elf who showers his darts is *servant* or *assistant* to the high
god of thunder, the cunning dwarf has forged his thunderbolts
for him ; like gods, they wear divine helmets of invisibility, and
the home-sprite has his feet miraculously shod as well ; water-
sprites can assume the shape of fishes and sea-horses, and home-
sprites those of cats. The weeping nix, the laughing goblin are
alike initiated in the mystery of magic tones, and will even un-
veil it to men that sacrifice. An ancient worship of genii and
daemons is proved by *sacrifices* offered to spirits of the mountain,
the wood, the lake, the house. Goblins, we may presume, accompanied the manifestation of certain deities among men, as
Wuotan and Holda, and both of these deities are also connected
with watersprites and swan-maids. Foreknowledge of the future,
the gift of prophecy, was proper to most genii ; their inexhaust-
ible cheerfulness stands between the sublime serenity of gods

---

[1] Read Holberg's Julestue, and look up *julvätten* in Finn Magn. lexicon, p. 326
note.
[2] They frightened children with sooty Cyclops, and acc. to Callimachus (Hymn
to Diana 66-71), Hermes, like our Ruprecht blackened with soot, struck terror
into disobedient daughters even of gods :

> ἀλλ' ὅτε κουράων τις ἀπειθέα μητέρι τεύχοι,
> μήτηρ μὴν κύκλωπας ἐῇ ἐπὶ παιδὶ καλιστρεῖ
> Ἄργην ἢ Στερόπην · ὁ δὲ δώματος ἐκ μυχάτοιο
> ἔρχεται Ἑρμείης, σποδιῇ κεχρημένος αἰθῇ,
> αὐτίκα τὴν κούρην μορμύσσεται · ἡ δὲ τεκούσης
> δύνει ἔσω κόλπους θεμένη ἐπὶ φάεσι χεῖρας.

and the solemn fates of mortals. They feel themselves drawn to men, and repelled by them. The downfall of heathenism must have wrought great changes in the old-established relationship: the spirits acquired a new and terrible aspect as ministers and messengers of Satan.[1] Some put on a more savage look that savours of the giant, especially the woodsprites. Grendel's nature borders on those of giants and gods. Not so with the females however: the wild women and female nixes drop into the class of fortune-telling swan-maids who are of human kind, while the elfins that present the drinking-horn melt into the circle of valkyrs; and here again we recognise a general beauty pervading all the female spirits, and raising them above the males, whose characteristics come out more individually. In wichtels, dwarfs and goblins, especially in that children's bugbear the man Ruprecht, there shews itself a comic faculty derived from the oldest times.

Through the whole existence of elves, nixes, and goblins there runs a low under-current of the unsatisfied, disconsolate: they do not rightly know how to turn their glorious gifts to account, they always require to lean upon men. Not only do they seek to renovate their race by intermarriage with mankind, they also need the counsel and assistance of men in their affairs. Though acquainted in a higher degree than men with the hidden virtues of stones and herbs, they yet invoke human aid for their sick and their women in labour (pp. 457. 492), they borrow men's vessels for baking and brewing (p. 454 n.), they even celebrate their weddings and hightides in the halls of men. Hence too their doubting whether they can be partakers of salvation, and their unconcealed grief when a negative answer is given.

---

[1] *Bruder Rausch* (friar Rush) a veritable goblin, is without hesitation [described as being] despatched from hell among the monks; his name is to be derived from russ = fuligo (as kohlrausch was formerly spelt kolruss).

CHAPTER XVIII.

GIANTS.

The relation in which giants stand to dwarfs and men has been touched upon in p. 449. By so much of bodily size and strength as man surpasses the elf or dwarf, he falls short of the giant; on the other hand, the race of elves and dwarfs has a livelier intellect and subtler sense than that of men, and in these points again the giants fall far below mankind. The rude coarse-grained giant nature is defiant in its sense of material power and might, the sly shy dwarf is conscious of his mental superiority. To man has been allotted a happy mean, which raises him above the giant's intractableness and the dwarf's cunning, and betwixt the two he stands victorious. The giant both does and suffers wrong, because in his stupidity he undervalues everybody, and even falls foul of the gods;[1] the outcast dwarf, who does discern good and evil, lacks the right courage for free and independent action. In order of creation, the giant as the sensuous element came first, next followed the spiritual element of elvish nature, and lastly the human race restored the equilibrium. The abruptness of these gradations is a good deal softened down by the giants or dwarfs forming frequent alliances with men, affording clear evidence that ancient fiction does not favour steep contrasts: the very earliest giants have sense and judgment ascribed to them (see Suppl.).

On one side we see giants forming a close tie of brotherhood or servile dependence with human heroes, on the other side shading off into the type of schrats and woodsprites.

There is a number of ancient terms corresponding in sense to our present word riese (giant).[2]

---

[1] Not a trace of the finer features of gods is to be seen in the Titans. O. Müller's Proleg. 378.

[2] Some are mere circumlocutions (a counterpart to those quoted on p. 450): der grôse man, Er. 5380. der michel man, Er. 5475. der michel knabe, Iw. 5056.

The oldest and most comprehensive term in Norse is *iötunn*, pl. iötnar (not jötunn, jötnar) ; it is backed up by an AS. *eoten*, pl. eotenas, Beow. 223 (eotena cyn, 836. eotonisc, 5953), or *eten*, Lye sub v.; OE. *etin, ettin*, Nares sub v.; Scot. *ettyn, eyttyn*, Jamieson sub v.; an OS. *etan, eten* can be inferred with certainty from the name of a place in old docs., Etanasfeld, Etenesfeld (campus gigantis), Wigand's Archiv i. 4, 85. Möser nos. 2. 13. 18. 19. And what is more, the word must have lived on in later times, down to the latest, for I find the fem. *eteninne* (giantess) preserved at least in nursery-tales. Laurenberg (ed. Lappenberg, p. 26) [1] has ' de olde *eteninne*,' and another Rostock book of the beginning of the 18th century [2] ' die alte *eteninne* ' ; I should like to know whence Adelung sub v. mummel gets the fact, that in Westphalia a certain terrible female with whom they frighten children is called *etheninne?* I have no doubt it is correct. The Saxon etan warrants us in conjecturing an OHG. *ëzan, ëzzan*, a Goth. *itans*, having for root the ON. eta, AS. etan, OHG. ezzan, Goth. ïtan (edere), and for meaning edo (gen. edonis), manducus, πολυφάγος, devourer. An AS. poem in Cod. exon. 425, 26 says: 'ic *mesan* mæg meahtelîcor and efn *etan* ealdum þyrre,' I can chew and eat more mightily than an old giant. Now the question arises, whether another word, which wants the suffix -n, has any business here, namely the ON. *iotr*,[3] AS. *eot*, now only to be found in the compound Forniotr, Forneot (p. 240) and the national name Iotar, the Jutes? One thing that makes for it is the same omission of -n in the Swed. *jätte* (gigas), Dan. *jette*, pl. jetter; then, taking iötnar as = iotar (Goth. ïtanôs = ïtôs), we should be justified in explaining the names Jotar, Jotland by an earlier (gigantic?) race whom the advancing Teutons crowded out of the peninsula.[4] In that case we might expect an OS. et, etes, an OHG. ez, ezes, with the

---

[1] Johann Laurenberg, a Rostock man, b. 1590, d. 1658. The first ed. of his poem appeared 1652.

[2] Ern. Joach. Westphal, De consuetudine ex sacco et libro, Rost. 1726. 8. pp. 224-5 ; the catalogue there given of old stories of women is copied in Joh. Pet. Schmidt's Fastelabendssamlungen, Rostock (1742) 4. resp. 1752, p. 22, but here incorrectly ' von der *Arden Inn* ' instead of Westphal's ' von der alten *Eten Inne*.'

[3] For iötr, as miolk for miölk, see Gramm. 1, 451. 482.

[4] Beda 1, 15 has Juti, which the AS. version mistakenly renders Geátas (the ON. Gautar), though at 4, 16 it more correctly gives Eotaland for Jutorum terra, and the Sax. Chron. (Ingr. p. 14) has Iotum for Iutis, Iutnacynn for Iutorum gens.

meaning of giant.[1] Possibly there was beside *iötunn*, also an
ON. *iötull*, OHG. *ezal* (edax) ;[2] that would explain the present
Norwegian term for giant: *jötul, jutul*, Hallager 52. Faye 7
(see Suppl.).[3]

Our second term is likewise one that suggests the name of
a nation. The ON. *þurs* seems not essentially different from
iötunn ; in Sn. 6 Ymir is called ancestor of all the hrîmþurses, in
Sæm. 118[a] all the iötnar are traced up to him. In particular
songs or connexions the preference is given to one or the other
appellative : thus in the enumeration of dialects in the Alvîsmâl
the giants are always iötnar, never þursar, and there is no
Thursaheimr in use for Iötunheimr, Iötnaheimr; but Thrymr,
though dwelling in Iötnaheimr, is nevertheless called þursa
drôttinn (Sæm. 70. 71) and not iötna drôttinn, but he summons
the iötnar (73[a]), and is a iötunn himself (74[a]). In Sæm. 85[b]
both iötnar and hrîmþursar are summoned one after the other,
so there must be some nice distinction between the two, which
here I would look for in the prefix hrîm: only hrîmþursar, no
hrîmiötnar, are ever met with ; of this hrîmþurs an explanation
will be attempted further on. Instead of þurs there often occurs,
especially at a later stage of the language, the assimilated form
þuss, particularly in the pl. þussar, hrîmþussar ; a dæmonic being
in the later sagas is called *Thusselin* (Müller's Sagab. 1, 367-8),
nay, the Danish tongue has retained the assimilation in its *tosse*,
clumsy giant, dolt (a folk-song has *tossegrefve*),[4] and a Norwegian
dæmon bears the name *tussel*. The ON. þurs, like several names
of gods, is likewise the title of a rune-letter, the same that the
Anglo-Saxons called þorn (conf. 'þurs rîsta,' Sæm. 86[a]) : a
notable deviation, as the AS. tongue by no means lacks the
word ; in Beow. 846 we find *þyrs*, and also in the menology in

---

[1] Can the witch *Jettha* of the Palatinate (p. 96 note) be a corruption of Eta, Eza ?
Anyhow the Jettenbühel (Jetthæ collis) reminds us of the Bavarian *Jettenberg*
(Mon. boica 2, 219, ann. 1817), and Mount *Jetten* in Reinbote's Georg 1717, where
it is misprinted Setten. Near Willingshausen in Hesse is another *Jettenberg*, see
W. Grimm On the runes, p. 271.

[2] The ruined Weissenstein, by Werda near Marburg, was acc. to popular legend
the abode of a giant named *Essel* (ezzal?), and the meadow where at the fall of his
castle he sank its *golden door* in the R. Lahn, is still called *Esselswerd*.

[3] Isidore's glosses render the Gallic name of a people *ambro* by devorator, which
agrees with the OHG. transl. *manezo*, man-eater (Graff 1, 528), the well-known
MHG. *manezze*.

[4] So the Dan. fos, fossen, for the ON. fors.

Hickes (Gramm. AS. p. 207) : '*þyrs* sceal on fenne gewunian,'
and elsewhere *þyrs*, pl. *þyrsas*, renders the Lat. cyclops, orcus.
The passage already given from the Cod. exon. 425, 28 has *þyrre*
with the *s* assimilated, as in irre for irse. And we find an
Engl. *thurst* surviving in *hobthurst* (woodsprite), conf. hobgoblin
p. 502 [hob o' t' hurst ?] The OHG. form ought to be *durs*, pl.
dursâ, or *duris*, gen. durises, which last does occur in a gloss for
the Lat. Dis, Ditis (Schm. 1, 458), and another gloss more Low
Germ. gives *thuris* for orcus (Fr. ogre) ; yet Notker ps. 17, 32
spells it *turs* (daemonium), pl. tursa, and MHG. has *turse*, gen.
tursen (Aw. 3, 179), perhaps *türse*, türsen (as in Massm. denkm.
109 *türsen* rhymes kürsen), and even *türste*, gen. türsten (MS. 2,
205ᵃ) ; on the other hand, Albr. Tit. 24, 47 has 'spil von einem
dürsen' (Hahn 3254 *tursen*) = play of a d., from which passage we
gather that türse-shows as well as wihtel-shows (p. 441n.) were
exhibited for pastime : Ls. 3, 564 says, alluding to a well-known
fable, 'des kunt der *dürsch*, und sprichet schuo !' the d. knows
that, etc., where the notion of satyr and wild man (p. 482)
predominates. The Latin poem of Wilten monastery in Tyrol,
which relates the story of the giant Haimo, names another giant
Thyrsis, making a proper name of the word :

> Forte habitabat in his alius truculentior oris
> Cyclops, qui dictus nomine *Thyrsis* erat,
> *Thyrsis* erat dictus, Seveldia rura colebat.[1]

The name of a place *Tursinriut*, *Tursenriut* (Doc. of 1218-9 in
Lang's Reg. 2, 88. 94) [2] contains our word unmistakably, and so
to my thinking does the earlier Tuzzinwanc near Neugart, standing for *Tussinwanc*, *Tursinwanc* (campus gigantis), the present
Dussnang. Nor does it seem much more hazardous to explain
Strabo's Θουσνέλθα (7, 1. Tzsch. 2, 328) by Thurshilda, Thuss-
hilda, Thursinhilda,[3] though I cannot produce an ON. Thurshildr.
In Switzerland to this day *dürst* is the Wild Hunter (St. 1, 329),
on the Salzburg Alp *dusel* is a night-spirit (Muchar's Gastein,
p. 145), and in Lower Germany *dros* or *drost* is devil, dolt, giant.[4]

---

[1] Mone's Untersuchung, pp. 288-9.
[2] Now Tirschenreit, Tirschengereith, Schmeller's birthplace in the Up. Palatinate, Schm. 1, 458. So Türschenwald, Thyrsentritt, Türstwinkel, et .—SUPPL.
[3] Conf. Pharaïldis, Verelde, p. 284-5 ; Grimild for Grimhild.
[4] Brem. wb. 1, 257. Richey sub v. druus, Schütze sub v. drost, Strodtmann sub

Whether *Thorsholt, Thosholt,* the name of a place in Oldenburg,
is connected with þurs, I cannot tell.—In Gothic the word
would have to be *þaúrs,* pl. þaúrsôs (or þaúrsis, pl. þaúrsjôs?
þaúrsus, þaúrsjus? þaúrsja, þaúrsjans?); and of these forms the
derivation is not far to seek. The Goth. þaúrsus means dry,
þaúrsjan to thirst, þaúrstei thirst; þaúrsus, þaúrsis becomes in
OHG. durri for dursi (as airzis becomes irri for irsi), while the
noun durst (thirst) retains the *s,* and so does our durs (giant)
and the ON. þurs by the side of the adjective þurr (dry). So that
þaúrs, þurs, durs signify either fond of wine, thirsty, or drunken,
a meaning which makes a perfect pair with that we fished out of
ïtans, iötunn. The two words for giant express an inordinate
desire for eating and drinking, precisely what exhibits itself in
the Homeric cyclop. Herakles too is described as edax and
bibax, *e.g.* in Euripides's Alcestis; and the ON. giant Suttûngr
(Sæm. 23. Sn. 84) apparently stands for *Suptúngr* (Finn Magn.
p. 738), where we must presuppose a noun supt = sopi, a sup
or draught.

Now, as the Jutes, a Teutonic race, retained the name of the
former inhabitants whom they had expelled,[1] these latter being
the real Iötnar or Itanôs; so may the þursar, dursâ, in their mythic
aspect [as giants] be connected with a distant race which at a
very early date had migrated into Italy. I have already hinted
(p. 25) at a possible connexion of the þaúrsôs with the Τυρσηνοί,
Τυῤῥηνοί, Tusci, Etrusci: the consonant-changes are the very
thing to be expected, and even the assimilations and the
transposition of the *r* are all found reproduced. Niebuhr makes
Tyrrhenians distinct from Etruscans, but in my opinion wrongly;
as for the θύρσος carried in the Bacchic procession, it has no claim
to be brought in at all (see Suppl.).

There is even a third mode of designating giants in which we
likewise detect a national name. Lower Germany, Westphalia
above all, uses *hüne* in the sense of giant; the word prevails in
all the popular traditions of the Weser region, and extends as far
as the Gröningen country and R. Drenthe; giants' hills, giants'

---

v. droost: 'dat di de *droost* sla!' may the d. smite thee; in the Altmark: 'det di
de *druse* hal (fetch)!' and elsewhere 'de *drôs* in de helle.' At the same time the
HG. druos, truos (plague, blain) is worth considering.
　　[1] A case that often occurs; thus the Bavarians, a Teutonic people, take their
name from the Celtic Boii. [And the present Bulgarians, a Slav race, etc.]

tombs are called *hünebedde, hunebedden,* bed being commonly
used for grave, the resting-place of the dead. ' Grot as en *hüne* '
expresses gigantic stature. Schüren's Teutonista couples 'rese '
with *huyne.* Even H.Germ. writers of the 16th-17th centuries,
though seldomer, use *heune;* Mathesius : 'Goliath der grosse
heune ; ' the Vocab. of 1482 spells *hewne.* Hans Sachs 1, 453ᵃ
uses *heunisch* (like entisch) for fierce, malignant. But the word
goes back to MHG. too; Herbort 1381 : 'grôz alsam ein *hûne,*'
rhym. 'mit starkem gelûne ; ' Trist. 4034 : ' an geliden und an
geliune gewahsen als ein *hiune.*'[1] In OHG. writings I do not find
the word in this sense at all. But MHG. has also a *Hiune* (gen.
Hiunen) signifying, without any reference to bodily size, a Hungarian, in the Nibelunge a subject of Etzel or Attila (1110, 4.
1123, 4. 1271, 3. 1824, 3. 1829, 1. 1831, 1. 1832, 1), which
in Lat. writings of the Mid. Ages is called *Hunnus,* more exactly
Hunus, Chunus. To this Hiune would correspond an OHG.
Hûnio; I have only met with the strong form *Hûn,* pl. Hûnî,
gen. Hûnio, Hûneo,[2] with which many names of places are compounded, *e.g.* Hûniofeld, a little town in Fulda bishopric, now
Hünfeld; also names of men, Hûnolt, Hûnperht (Humprecht), Hûnrât, Althûn, Folchûn, etc. The AS. *Hûna* cyning (Beda 1, 13)
requires a sing. Hûn; but to the ON. nom. pl. *Hûnar* there is said
to belong a weak sing. Hûni (Gl. Edd. havn. 2, 881). It is plain
those Hûnî have a sense that shifts about pretty much with time
and place, now standing for Pannonians, then for Avars, then
again for Vandals and Slavs, always for a nation brought into
frequent contact with Germany by proximity and wars. The
Hiunenlant of the 13th century (Nib. 1106, 3. 1122, 3) cannot
possibly be the *Hûnaland* which the Eddic lays regard as Sigurð's
home (Deutsche heldens. 6. 9). At the time when proper names
like Hûnrât, Hûnperht first arose, there could hardly as yet be
any thought of an actual neighbouring nation like Pannonians
or Wends; but even in the earliest times there might circulate
talk and tale of a primitive mythic race supposed to inhabit some
uncertain region, much the same as Iötnar and Thursar. I incline

---

[1] Wolfdietr. 661 has, for giant, *hœne* rhym. schœne, but only in the place of the
ancient cæsura, so that the older reading was most likely *hiune.*
[2] In Hildeb. lied ' Hûneo truhtin (lord of Huns), and ' altêr Hûn ; ' Diut. 2, 182
Hûnî (Pannonii) ; 2, 353ᵇ Hûni for Hûn (Hunnus) ; 2, 370 Hûnî (Vandali).

therefore to guess, that the sense of 'giant,' which we cannot
detect in Hûn till the 13th century, must nevertheless have lain
in it long before: it is by such double meaning that Hadubrant's
exclamation 'altêr Hûn!' first acquires significance.   When
Gotfried used hiune for giant, he must have known that Hiune
at that time also meant a Hungarian; and as little does the
distinctness of the nationality rendered Hûnî in OHG. glosses
exclude the simultaneous existence of a mythic meaning of the
word.   It may have been vivider or fainter in this place or that:
thus, the ON. hûnar is never convertible with iötnar and þursar.
I will not touch upon the root here (conf. p. 529 note), but only
remark that one Eddic name for the bear is *húnn*, Sn. 179. 222ª,
and acc. to Biörn *hún* and *húnbiörn* = catulus ursinus (see Suppl.).

One AS. term for giant is *ent*, pl. entas : Ælfred in his Orosius
p. 48 renders Hercules gigas by 'Ercol se *ent*.'   The poets like
to use the word, where ancient buildings and works are spoken
of: '*enta* geweorc, *enta* ærgeweorc (early work of giants), eald
enta geweorc,' Beow. 3356. 5431. 5554.   Cod. exon. 291, 24.
476, 2.   So the adj. : '*entisc* helm,' Beow. 5955 ; Lipsius's glosses
also give *eintisc* avitus, what dates from the giants' days of yore.
Our OHG. *entisc* antiquus does not agree with this in consonant-
gradation [*t* should be *z*] ; it may have been suggested by the
Latin word, perhaps also by the notion of enti (end) ; another
form is *antrisc* antiquus (Graff 1, 387), and I would rather associate it with the Eddic '*inn aldni iötunn*' (grandævus gigas), Sæm.
23ª 46ᵇ 84ᵇ 189ᵇ.   The Bavarian patois has an intensive prefix
enz, enzio (Schmeller , 188), but this may have grown out of the
gen. of end, ent (Schm. 1, 77) ; or may we take this *ent-* itself in
the sense of monstrous, gigantic, and as an exception to the law
of consonant-change?   They say both *enterisch* (Schm. 1, 77) and
enzerisch for monstrous, extraordinary.   And was the *Enzenberc*,
MS. 2, 10ᵇ a giant's hill?[1] and is the same root contained in
the proper names *Anzo, Enzo, Enzinchint* (Pez, thes. iii. 3, 689ᵉ),
Enzawip (Meichelb. 1233. 1305), *Enzeman* (Ben. 325)?   If
Hûnî alluded to Wends and Slavs, we may be allowed to identify
entas with the ancient *Antes* ; as for the Indians, whom Mone

---

[1] The present *Inselberg* near Schmalkalden ; old docs., however, spell it Emise-
berc, named apparently from the brook Emise, Emse, which rises on it.   Later
forms are Enzelberg, Einzelberg, Einselberg.

(Anz. 1836, 1. 2) would bring in, they may stay outside, for in OHG. itself antisc, entisc (antiquus) is distinct from indisc (Indicus), Graff 1, 385-6 ; and see Suppl.

The AS. poets use also the Greek, Latin,[1] and Romance appellative *gigant*, pl. gigantas, Beow. 225. *giganta* cyn 3379. *gigantmæcg*, Cædm. 76, 36 ; conf. Ital. Span. *gigante*, Prov. *jayan* (Ferab. 4232), O.Fr. *gaiant* (Ogier 8092. 8101), Fr. *géant*, Eng. *giant;* also OHG. *gigant* (O. iv. 12, 61), MHG. *gigante die mâren* (Diut. 3, 60),[2] M. Nethl. *gigant*. The ON. word which is usually compared with this, but which wants the *nt*, and is only used of giantesses, seems to me unconnected: fem. *gŷgr*, gen. *gŷgjar*, Sæm. 39, Sn. 66. 68 ; a Swed. folk-song still has ʻden leda *gijger*,' Arvidsson, 2, 302. It is wanting in the other Teut. dialects, but if translated into Gothic it would be *giugi* or *giugja;* I trace it to the root giugan, and connect it with the words quoted in my Gramm. 2, 50 no. 536 (see Suppl.).

Our *riese* is the OHG. *risi* (O. iv. 12, 61) or *riso* (N. ps. 32, 16), MHG. *rise*, MLG. *rese* (En. 7096), ON. *risi* (the elder Edda has it only in Grôttas. 12), Swed. *rese*, Dan. *rise*, M. Nethl. *rese, rose* (Huyd. op St. 3, 33. 306), now *reus*. To these would correspond a Gothic *vrisa*, as may be gathered from the OS. form *wriso* which I confidently infer from the adj. *wrisilic* giganteus, Hel. 42, 5. The Anglo-Saxons seem to have had no analogous *wrisa*, as they confine themselves to þyrs, gigant [and ent]. The root of vrisa is unknown to me; it cannot belong to reisan surgere, therefore the OHG. riso does not mean elatus, superbus, excelsus.[3]

Again, *lubbe, lübbe* seems in parts of Lower Saxony to mean

---

[1] Strange that the Latin language has no word of its own for giant, but must borrow the Greek gigas, titan, cyclops ; yet Italy has indigenous folk-tales of Campanian giants.

[2] The Biblical view adopted in the Mid. Ages traced the giants to *Cain*, or at least to mixture with his family : ' *gigantes*, quales propter iracundiam Dei per filios Seth de *filiabus Cain* narrat scriptura procreatos,' Pertz 2, 755. For in Genesis 6, 4 it is said : ' gigantes autem erant super terram in diebus illis ; postquam enim ingressi sunt filii Dei ad filias hominum, illæque genuerunt, isti sunt potentes a seculo viri famosi.' The same view appears in Cædm. 76. 77 ; in Beow. 213 Grendel's descent is derived from *Caines cynne*, on whom God avenged the murder of Abel : thence sprang all the *untydras* (neg. of tudor proles, therefore misbirths, evil brood), *eotenas, ylfe, orcneas* and *gigantas* that war against God. This partly fits in with some heathen notions of cosmogony.

[3] Mone in Anz. 8, 133, takes *wrise* for *frise*, and makes Frisians and Persians out of it. [What of ' writhe, wris-t, wrest, wrestle,' (as wit, wis-t becomes wise) ? Or Slav. vred-íti, to hurt, AS. wreðe ? A Russ. word for giant is verzílo, supposed to be from verg-áti, to throw.]

unwieldy giant, *lübben-stones* are shown on the Corneliusberg near Helmstadt, and *lubbe* acc. to the Brem. wb. 3, 92 means a slow clumsy fellow; it is the Engl. *lubber*, *lobber*, and Michel Beham's *lüpel* (Mone's Anz. 1835, 450ᵇ), conf. ON. *lubbi* (hirsutus). To this add a remarkable document by Bp. Gebhard of Halberstadt, bewailing as late as 1462 the heathenish worship of a being whom men named *den guden lubben*, to whom they offered bones of animals on a hill by Schochwitz in the county of Mansfeld. Not only have such ancient bone-heaps been discovered on the *Lupberg* there (conf. the Augsburg perleich, p. 294), but in the church of the neighbouring Müllersdorf an idol image let into the wall, which tradition says was brought there from the Lupberg (see Suppl.).[1]

The ON. has several words for giantess, beside the *gýgr* mentioned above: *skass*, neut., Sæm. 144ᵇ 154ᵇ, and *skessa*, fem.; *griðr* f., *mella* f.; *gîfr* f., Sæm. 143ᵇ, Norweg. *jyvri* (Hallag. 53) or *gyvri*, *gurri*, *djurre* (Faye 7. 9. 10. 12). This gîfr seems to mean saucy, defiant, greedy.

Tröll neut., gen. trölls (Sæm. 6ᵃ), Swed. *troll*, Dan. *trold*, though often used of giants, is yet a more comprehensive term, including other spirits and beings possessed of magic power, and equivalent to our monster, spectre, unearthly being. By trold the Danish folk-tales habitually understand beings of the elf kind. The form suggests a Gothic *trallu*; does our *getralle* in Renner 1365, 'der gebûre ein getralle,' rhym. 'alle,' mean the same thing? (see Suppl.).

Giant is in Lith. *milžinas*, *milžinis*, Lett. *milsis*, *milsenis*; but it would be overbold to connect with it German names of places, Milize (Trad. fuld. 2, 40), Milsenburg, Melsungen. The Slovak *obor*, Boh. *obr*, O. Pol. *obrzym*,[2] Pol. *olbrzym*, is unknown to the South Slavs, and seems to be simply *Avarus*, Abarus. Nestor calls the Avars Obri (ed. Schlözer 2, 112-7). The 'Græcus Avar' again in the legend of Zisa (p. 292-5) is a giant. Now,

---

[1] Neue mitth. des thür. sächs. vereins 8, 180–6. 5, 2. 110–132. 6, 87-8. The picture, however, contains nothing giant-like, but rather a goddess standing on a wolf. Yet I remark, that a giant's tomb on Mt. Blanc is called 'la tombe du *bon homme*, de la *bonne femme*,' an expression associated with the idea of a sacred venerated man (supra, p. 89). Conf. also *godgubbe* used of Thôrr, p. 167, and *godmor*, p. 480.

[2] Psalter of queen Margareta, Vienna 1834, p.17ᵇ: *obrzim*, the -im as in qyczim, pielgrzym.

as the Avari in the Mid. Ages are = Chuni, the words hûn and obor alike spring out of the national names Hun and Avar.[1] To the Slavs, *Tchud* signifies both Finn and giant, and the Russ. *ispolin* (giant) might originally refer to the 'gens *Spalorum*' of Jornandes; conf. Schafarik 1, 286. 310. So closely do the names for giant agree with those of ancient nations: popular belief magnified hostile warlike neighbours into giants, as it diminished the weak and oppressed into dwarfs. The Sanskrit *râkshasas* can have nothing to do with our riese, nor with the OHG. recchio, MHG. recke, a designation of human heroes (see Suppl.).

We find plenty of proper names both of giants and giantesses preserved in ON., some apparently significant; thus *Hrûngnir* suggests the Gothic hrugga (virga, rod, pole) and our runge (Brem. wb. 3, 558); Herbort 1385: 'grôz alsam ein runge.' Our MHG. poems like giant's names to end in -*olt*, as *Witolt*, *Fasolt*, *Memerolt*, etc.

A great stature, towering far above any human size, is ascribed to all giants: stiff, unwieldy, they stand like hills, like tall trees. According to the Mod. Greeks, they were as tall as poplars, and if once they fell, they could not get up again [like Humpty Dumpty]. The one eye of the Greek cyclops I nowhere find imputed to our giants; but like them[2] and the ancient gods, (p. 322), they are often provided with *many hands* and *heads*. When this attribute is given to heroes, gigantic ones are meant, as Heimo, Starkaðr, Asperian (p. 387). But Sæm. 85[b] expressly calls a þurs *þríhöfðuðr*, exactly as the MHG. Wahtelmære names a *drîhouptigen* tursen (Massm. denkm. 109): a remarkable instance of agreement. In Sæm. 35[a] appears a giant's son with *six heads*, in 56[a] the *many-headed* band of giants is spoken of, and in 53 a giantess with *900 heads*. Brana's father has *three* (invisible) *heads*, Fornald. sög. 3, 574, where also it is said: 'þa

<hr>

[1] Schafarik explains *obor* by the Celtic *ambro* above (p. 520n.); but in that case the Polish would have been ąbr.

[2] Briareus or Ægæon has a *hundred arms* (ἑκατόγχειρος, Il. 1, 402) and *fifty heads*, Geryon *three heads* and *six hands*; in Hesiod's Theog. 150, Kottus, Gyges and Briareus have *one hundred arms* and *fifty heads*. The giant in the Hebrew story has only an *additional finger* or *toe* given to each hand and foot: vir fuit excelsus, qui senos in manibus pedibusque habebat digitos, *i.e.* viginti quatuor (instead of the human twenty), 2 Sam. 21, 20. Bertheau's Israel, p. 143. O. Fr. poems give the Saracen giant *four arms, two noses, two chins*, Ogier 9817.

fell margr (many a) *tvíhöfðaðr* iötunn.' Trolds with 12 heads, then with 5, 10, 15 occur in Norske event. nos. 3 and 24. In Scotland too the story 'of the *reyde eyttyn* with the *thre heydis*' was known (Complaynt, p. 98), and Lindsay's Dreme (ed. 1592, p. 225) mentions the 'history of *reid etin.*' The fairy-tale of *Red etin wi' three heads* may now be read complete in Chambers,[1] pp. 56-58; but it does not explain whether the red colour in his name refers to skin, hair or dress. A black complexion is not attributed to giants, as it is to dwarfs (p. 444) and the devil, though the half-black Hel (p. 312) was of giant kin. Hrûngnir, a giant in the Edda, has a *head of stone* (Sæm. 76[b], Sn. 109), another in the Fornald. sög. 3, 573 is called *Iarnhaus*, iron skull. But giants as a rule appear well-shaped and symmetrical; their daughters are capable of the highest *beauty, e.g.* Gerðr, whose gleaming arms, as she shuts the house-door, make air and water shine again, Sæm. 82[a], Sn. 39 (see Suppl.).

In the giants as a whole, an untamed natural force has full swing, entailing their excessive bodily size, their overbearing insolence, that is to say, abuse of corporal and mental power, and finally sinking under its own weight. Hence the iötunn in the Edda is called *skrautgiarn* (fastosus), Sæm. 117[b]; sa inn *âmâttki* (præpotens) 41[b] 82[h]; *storûðgi* (magnanimus) 76[b]; *þrûngmóðgi* (superbus) 77[a]; *hardrâðr* (sævus) 54[a]; our derivation of the words iötunn and þurs finds itself confirmed in poetic epithet and graphic touch: *kostmóðr* iötunn (cibo gravatus), Sæm. 56[b]; '*ölr* (ebrius) ertu Geirröðr, hefir þû ofdruccit (overdrunk)' 47[a] (see Suppl.).

From this it is an easy step, to impute to the giants a *stupidity* contrasting with man's common sense and the shrewdness of the dwarf. The ON. has '*ginna alla sem þussa*' (decipere omnes sicut thursos), Nialssaga p. 263. *Dumm* in our old speech was mutus as well as hebes, and *dumbr* in ON. actually stands for gigas; to which *dumbi* (dat.) the adj. *þumbi* (hebes, inconcinnus) seems nearly related. A remarkable spell of the 11th cent. runs thus: '*tumbo* saz in berke mit *tumbemo* kinde in arme, *tumb* hiez der berc, *tumb* hiez daz kint, der *heilego tumbo* versegene tisa wunda!' *i.e.* dummy sat on hill with d. child in arm, d. was

---

[1] Popular rhymes, fireside stories, and amusements of Scotland, Edinb. 1842.

called the hill and d. the child, the holy d. bless this wound away [the posture is that of Humpty Dumpty]. This seems pointed at a sluggish mountain-giant, and we shall see how folk-tales of a later period name the giants *dumme dutten;* the term *lubbe,* *lübbe* likewise indicates their clumsy lubberly nature, and when we nowadays call the devil *dumm* (stupid), a quondam giant is really meant (see Suppl.).[1]

Yet the Norse lays contain one feature favourable to the giants. They stand as specimens of a fallen or falling race, which with the strength combines also the innocence and wisdom of the old world, an intelligence more objective and imparted at creation than self-acquired. This half-regretful view of giants prevails particularly in one of the finest poems of the Edda, the Hȳmisqviða. Hȳmir[2] is called *forn* iötunn (the old) 54ᵃ, as Πολύφαμος in Theocr. 11, 9 is ἀρχαῖος, and another giant, from whom gods are descended, has actually the proper name *Forniotr,* *Forneot* (p. 240), agreeing with the '*aldinn* iötunn' quoted on p. 524; then we have the epithet *hundvíss* (multiscius) applied 52ᵇ, as elsewhere to Loðinn (Sæm. 145ᵃ), to Geirröðr (Sn. 113), and to Starkaðr (Fornald. sög. 3, 15. 32).[3] Oegir is called *fiölkunnigr* (much-knowing), Sæm. 79, and *barnteitr* (happy as a child) 52ᵃ; while Thrymr sits fastening golden collars on his hounds, and stroking his horses' manes, Sæm. 70ᵇ. And also the faithfulness of giants is renowned, like that of the men of old : *trölltryggr* (fidus instar gigantis), Egilss. p. 610, and in the Faröe dialect '*trúr sum tröðlir,*' true as giants (Lyngbye, p. 496).[4] Another lay is founded on the conversation that Oðinn himself is anxious to hold with a giant of great sense on matters of antiquity (å fornom stöfum) : Vafþrúðnir again is called 'inn *alsvinni* iötunn,' 30ᵃ 35ᵇ; Örgelmir and Bergelmir 'sa inn *fróði*

---

[1] The familiar fable of the devil being taken in by a peasant in halving the crop between them, is in the Danish myth related of a trold (Thiele 4, 122), see Chap. XXXIII.

[2] ON. hûm is crepusculum, hûma vesperascere, hȳma dormiturire; is Hȳmir the sluggish, sleepy? OHG. *Hiumi?* How if the MHG. *hiune* came from an OHG. hiumi? An *m* is often attenuated into *n*, as OHG. sliumi, sniumi (celer), MHG. sliune, sliunic, our schleunig. That would explain why there is no trace of the word hiune in ON.; it would also be fatal to any real connexion with the national name Hûn.

[3] Hund (centum) intensifies the meaning : hundmargr (permultus), hundgamall (old as the hills).

[4] We find the same faithfulness in the giant of Christian legend, St. *Christopher,* and in that of Carolingian legend, *Ferabras.*

iötunn,' Sæm. 35ᵃˑᵇ; Fenja and Menja are *framvísar* (Grôttas. 1, 13). When the verb þreya, usually meaning exspectare, desiderare, is employed as characteristic of giants (Sæm. 88ᵃ), it seems to imply a dreamy brooding, a half-drunken complacency and immobility (see Suppl.).

Such a being, when at rest, is good-humoured and unhandy,[1] but when provoked, gets wild, spiteful and violent. Norse legend names this rage of giants *iötunmôðr*, which pits itself in defiance against âsmôðr, the rage of the gods: ' vera î iötunmôði,' Sn. 150ᵇ. When their wrath is kindled, the giants hurl rocks, rub stones till they catch fire (Roth. 1048), squeeze water out of stones (Kinderm. no. 20. Asbiörnsen's Möe, no. 6), root up trees (Kinderm. no. 90), twist fir-trees together like willows (no. 166), and stamp on the ground till their leg is buried up to the knee (Roth. 943. Vilk. saga, cap. 60): in this plight they are chained up by the heroes in whose service they are to be, and only let loose against the enemy in war, *e.g.* Witolt or Witolf (Roth. 760. Vilk. saga, cap. 50). One Norse giant, whose story we know but imperfectly, was named *Beli* (the bellower); him Freyr struck dead with his fist for want of his sword, and thence bore the name of ' bani Belja,' Sn. 41. 74.

Their relation to gods and men is by turns friendly and hostile. *Iötunheimr* lies far from *Asaheimr*, yet visits are paid on both sides. It is in this connexion that they sometimes leave on us the impression of older nature-gods, who had to give way to a younger and superior race; it is only natural therefore, that in certain giants, like Ecke and Fasolt, we should recognise a precipitate of deity. At other times a rebellious spirit breaks forth, they make war upon the gods, like the heaven-scaling Titans, and the gods hurl them down like devils into hell. Yet there are some gods married to giantesses : Niörðr to Skaði the daughter of Thiassi, Thôrr to Iarnsaxa, Freyr to the beautiful Gerðr, daughter of Gŷmir. Gunnlöð a giantess is Oðin's beloved. The âsin Gefun bears sons to a giant; Borr weds the giant Bölþorn's daughter Bestla. Loki, who lives among the âses, is son to a giant Farbauti, and a giantess Angrboða is his

---

[1] Unformed, inconcinnus; MHG. *ungevüege*, applied to giants, Nib. 456, 1. Iw. 444. 6051. 6717. der ungevüege knabe, Er. 5552; ' knabe,' as in ' der michel knabe,' p. 518n.

wife. The gods associate with Oegir the iötunn, and by him are bidden to a banquet. Giants again sue for âsins, as Thrymr for Freyja, while Thiassi carries off Iðunn. Hrûngnir asks for Freyja or Sif, Sn. 107. Starkaðr is henchman to Norse kings; in Rother's army fight the giants Asperiân (Asbiörn, Osbern) and Witolt. Among the âses *the great foe of giants* is *Thôrr*, who like *Jupiter* inflicts on them his thunder-wounds;[1] his hammer has crushed the heads of many: were it not for Thôrr, says a Scandinavian proverb, the giants would get the upper hand;[2] he vanquished Hrûngnir, Hŷmir, Thrymr, Geirröðr, and it is not all the legends by any means that are set down in the Edda (see Suppl.). *St. Olaf* too keeps up a hot pursuit of the giant race; in this business heathen and Christian heroes are at one. In our heroic legend Sigenôt, Ecke, Fasolt succumb to *Dietrich's* human strength, yet other giants are companions of Dietrich, notably Wittich and Heime, as Asperiân was Rother's. The kings Nibluuc and Schilbunc had twelve strong giants for friends (Nib. 95), *i.e.* for vassals, as the Norse kings often had twelve berserks. But, like the primal woods and monstrous beasts of the olden time, the giants do get gradually extirpated off the face of the earth, and with all heroes giant-fighting alternates with dragon-fighting.[3]

King Frôði had two captive giant-maidens *Fenja* and *Menja* as mill-maids; the grist they had to grind him out of the quern Grôtti was gold and peace, and he allowed them no longer time for sleep or rest than while the gowk (cuckoo) held his peace or they sang a song. We have a startling proof of the former prevalence of this myth in Germany also, and I find it in the bare proper names. *Managold, Manigold* frequently occurs as a man's name, and is to be explained from mani, ON. men = monile; more rarely we find *Fanigold, Fenegold*, from fani, ON. fen = palus, meaning the gold that lies hidden in the fen. One Trad. patav. of the first half of the twelfth cent. (MB. 28ᵇ, pp. 90-1)

---

[1] The skeleton of a giantess struck by lightning, hung up in a sacristy, see Widegren's Ostergötland 4, 527.
[2] Swed. ' vore ej thordön (Thor-din, thunder) till, lade troll verlden öde.'
[3] In British legend too (seldomer in Carolingian) the heroes are indefatigable giant-quellers. If the nursery-tale of Jack the giantkiller did not appear to be of Welsh origin, that hero's deeds might remind us of Thôr's; he is equipped with a cap of darkness, shoes of swiftness, and a sword that cuts through anything, as the god is with the resistless hammer.

furnishes both names *Manegolt* and *Fenegolt* out of the same
neighbourhood. We may conclude that once the Bavarians well
knew how it stood with the fanigold and manigold ground out by
Fania and *Mania* (see Suppl.).

Ymir, or in giant's language Örgelmir, was the *first-created*,
and out of his body's enormous bulk were afterwards engendered
earth, water, mountain and wood. Ymir himself originated in
melted hoarfrost or rime (brîm), hence all the giants are called
hrîmþursar, rime-giants, Sn. 6. Sæm. 85[a.b]; *hrîmkaldr*, rime-
cold, is an epithet of þurs and iötunn, Sæm. 33[b] 90[a], they still
drip with thawing rime, their beards (kinnskôgr, chin-forest) are
frozen, Sæm. 53[b]; *Hrîmnir, Hrîmgrîmr, Hrîmgerðr* are proper
names of giants, Sæm. 85[a] 86[a] 114. 145. As hrîm also means
grime, fuligo, Ymir may perhaps be connected with the obscure
MHG. om, ome (rubigo), see Gramm. 3, 733. At the same time
the derivation from ymja, umði (stridere) lies invitingly near, so
that Ymir would be the blustering, noisy, and one explanation of
Örgelmir would agree with this; conf. chap. XIX. (see Suppl.).

Herbs and heavenly bodies are named after giants as well
as after gods: *þursaskegg*, i.e. giant's beard (fucus filiformis);
Norw. *tussegras* (paris quadrifolia); *Brönugras* (satyrium, the
same as Friggjargras, p. 302), because a giantess Brana gave it
as a charm to her client Hâlfdân (Fornald. sög. 3, 576); *Forneotes
folme*, p. 240; Oðinn threw *Thiassi's eyes*, and Thôrr *Örvandil's
toe*, into the sky, to be shining constellations, Sn. 82-3. 111.

Giants, like dwarfs, shew themselves *thievish*. Two lays of the
Edda turn upon the recovery of a hammer and a cauldron which
they had stolen.

The giants form a separate people, which no doubt split into
branches again, conf. Rask's Afhand. 1, 88. Thrymr is called
þursa drôttinn, Sæm. 70–74; a *þursa þioð* (nation) is spoken of,
107[a], but *iötunheimr* is described as their usual residence. Even
our poem of Rother 767 speaks of a *riesenlant*. On the borders
of the giant province were situate the *griottûna garðar*, Sn. 108-9.
We have already noticed how most of the words for giant coincide with the names of ancient nations.

Giants were imagined dwelling on *rocks* and *mountains*, and
their nature is all of a piece with the mineral kingdom: they are
either animated masses of stone, or creatures once alive petrified.

Hrûngnir had a three-cornered stone heart, his head and shield were of stone, Sn. 109. Another giant was named *Vagnhöfði* (waggon-head), Sn. 211ª, in Saxo Gram. 9. 10. Dame *Hütt* is a petrified queen of giants, Deut. sag. no. 233.

Out of this connexion with mountains arises another set of names: *bergrisi*, Sn. 18. 26. 30. 45-7. 66. Grôttas. 10. 24. Egilss. 22;[1] *bergbúi*, Fornald. sög. 1, 412; *hraunbúi* (saxicola), Sæm. 57ᵇ 145ª; *hraunhvalr* (-whale) 57ᵇ; *þussin af biargi*, Fornald. sög. 2, 29; *bergdanir* (gigantes), Sæm. 54ᵇ; *bergrisa brûðr* (bride), *mœr bergrisa*, Grôttas. 10. 24, conf. the Gr. ὀρειάς: on this side the notion of giantess can easily pass into that of elfin. Thrymheimr lies up in the mountains, Sn. 27. It is not to be overlooked, that in our own Heldenbuch Dietrich reviles the giants as mountain-cattle and forest-boors, conf. *bercrinder*, Laurin 2625, and *waltgebûren* 534. 2624. Sigenôt 97. walthunde, Sigenôt 13. 114. waldes diebe (thieves), 120. waldes tôre (fool), waldes affe (ape), Wolfd. 467. 991 (see p. 481-2 and Suppl.).

Proper names of giants point to stones and metals, as *Iarnsaxa* (ironstony), *Iarnhaus* (ironskull); possibly our still surviving compound *steinalt*, old as stone (Gramm. 2, 555), is to be explained by the great age of giants, approaching that of rocks and hills; *gîfur rata* (gigantes pedes illidunt saxis) is what they say in the North.

Stones and rocks are *weapons* of the giant race; they use only stone clubs and stone shields, no swords. Hrûngni's weapon is called *hein* (hone); when it was flung in mid air and came in collision with Thôr's hammer, it broke, and a part fell on the ground; hence come all the 'heinberg,' whinstone rocks, Sn. 108-9. Later legends add to their armament *stahelstangen* (steel bars) 24 yards long, Roth. 687. 1662. Hürn. Sifr. 62, 2. 68, 2. Sigenôt (Lassb.) 14, (Hag.) 69. 75. Iwein 5022 (-*ruote*, rod 5058. -*kolbe*, club 6682. 6726). Trist. 15980. 16146; *isenstange*, Nib. 460, 1. Veldek invests his Pandurus and Bitias (taken from Aen. 9, 672) with giant's nature and *iserne kolven*, En. 7089; king Gorhand's giant host carry *kolben stähelin*, Wh. 35, 21. 395, 24. 396, 13; and giant Langben a *staalstang* (Danske viser 1, 29). We are expressly told in Er. 5384, ' wâfens wâren

----

[1] In the case of mixed descent: *hâlf bergrisi, hâlfrisi, hâlftröll*, Egilss. p. 22. Nialss. p. 164; see Gramm. 2, 633.

si blôz,' i.e. bare of knightly weapon, for they carried '*kolben swære, grôze unde lange.*'[1] Yet the '*eald sweord* eotonisc' probably meant one of stone, though the same expression is used in Beow. 5953 of a metal sword mounted with gold; even the '*entisc helm,*' Beow. 5955 may well be a stone helmet. It may be a part of the same thing, that no iron sword will cut into giants; only with the *pommel of the sword* can they be killed (Ecke 178), or with the *fist*, p. 530 (see Suppl.).

Ancient *buildings* of singular structure, which have outlasted many centuries, and such as the men of to-day no longer take in hand, are vulgarly ascribed to *giants* or to the *devil* (conf. p. 85, note on devil's dikes): ' burg an berge, hô holmklibu, *wrisilic* giwerc' is said in Hel. 42, 5 of a castle on a rock (risônburg, N. Bth. 173); a *Wrisberg*, from which a Low Saxon family takes its name, stood near the village of Petze. These are the *enta geweorc* of AS. poetry (p. 524): 'efne swâ wîde swâ *wegas* tô lâgon enta œr̃geweorc innan burgum, *stræte stânfâge,*' Andr. 2466. ' *stapulas* storme bedrifene, *eald enta geweorc,*' 2986. Our Annolied 151 of Semiramis : ' die alten Babilônie stiphti si van cigelin den alten, die die *gigandi* branten,' of bricks that giants burnt. And Karlmeinet 35 : ' we dise *burg* stichte? ein *rise in den alten ziden.*' In O. French poems it is either *gaiant* or *paian* (pagans) that build walls and towers, *e.g.* in Gerars de Viane 1745 :

> Les *fors tors*, ke sont dantiquitey,
> ke *paian* firent par lor grant poestey.

Conf. Mone's Unters. 242-4-7. 250. Whatever was put together of enormous blocks the Hellenes named *cyclopean walls*, while the modern Greeks regard the *Hellenes* themselves as giants of the old world, and give them the credit of those massive structures.[2] Then, as ancient military roads were constructed of great blocks of stone (strâta felison gifuogid, Hel. 164, 27), they also were laid to the account of giants : *iötna vegar* (viæ gigantum), Sæm. 23[b]; ' usque ad giganteam viam: *entisken wec,*' MB. 4, 22 (about 1130). The common people in Bavaria and Salzburg call such a road, which to them is world-old and uncanny, *enterisch* (Schm.

---

[1] Goliath too, 1 Sam. 17, 7, and 2 Sam. 21, 19 is credited with a hastile (spearstaff) quasi liciatorium texentium (like a weaver's beam).
[2] Conf. Niebuhr's Rom. Hist. i. 192-5. An ancient wall is in Mod. Greek τὸ ἑλληνικό, Ulrich's Reise 1, 182.

4, 44) ; the *tröllaskeid* was mentioned p. 508-9, and *tröllahlað* is
septum gigantum. Some passages in Fergût are worthy of
notice ; at 1576 :

> Die roke was swert ende eiselike,
> waut wîlen êr ên *gigant*,
> hie hieu hare ane enen cant
> ên *padelkin* tote in den top,
> daer en mach ghên paert op,
> ên man mochter opgaen te voet..

And at 1628 seq. is described the brazen statue of a *dorper*,[1]
standing outside the porch of a door :

> het dede maken ên *gigant*,
> die daer wilen woende int lant (see Suppl.).

Giant's-mountains, giant's-hills, hünen-beds may be so named
because popular legend places a giant's grave there, or sees in
the rock a resemblance to the giant's shape, or supposes the
giant to have brought the mountain or hill to where it stands.

We have just had an instance of the last kind : the Edda
accounts for all the *hein-rocks* by portions of a *giant's club* having
dropt to the ground, which club was made of smooth whinstone.
There is a pleasing variety about these folk-tales, which to my
thinking is worth closer study, for it brings the living conception
of giant existence clearly before us. One story current in the
I. of Hven makes Grimild and Hvenild two giant sisters living
in Zealand. Hvenild wants to carry some slices of Zealand to
Schonen on the Swedish side ; she gets over safely with a few
that she has taken in her apron, but the next time she carries off
too large a piece, her *apron-string breaks* in the middle of the
sea, she drops the whole of her load, and that is how the Isle of
Hven came to be (Sjöborg's Nomenkl. p. 84). Almost the same
story is told in Jutland of the origin of the little isle of
Worsöekalv (Thiele 3, 66). Pomeranian traditions present differences in detail : a giant in the Isle of Rügen grudges having
to wade through the sea every time to Pomerania ; he will build
a causeway across to the mainland, so, tying an apron round him,
he fills it with earth. When he has got past Rodenkirchen with

---

[1] This *dorper grôt* again we are tempted to take for the old thundergod, for it
says : ' hi hilt van *stale* (of steel) enen *hamer* in sine hant.'

his load, *his apron springs a leak,* and the earth that drops out
becomes the nine hills near Rambin. He darns the hole, and
goes further. Arrived at Gustow, he bursts another hole, and
spills thirteen little hills; he reaches the sea with the earth that
is left, and shoots it in, making Prosnitz Hook and the peninsula
of Drigge. But there still remains a narrow space between
Rügen and Pomerania, which so exasperates the giant that he
is struck with apoplexy and dies, and his dam has never been
completed (E. M. Arndt's Märchen 1, 156). Just the other way,
a giant girl of Pomerania wants to make a bridge to Rügen, 'so
that I can step across the bit of water without wetting my bits
of slippers.' She hurries down to the shore with an apronful of
sand; but the *apron had a hole* in it, a part of her freight ran
out 'tother side of Sagard, forming a little hill named Dubber-
worth. 'Dear me! mother will scold,' said the hüne maiden, but
kept her hand under, and ran all she could. Her mother looked
over the wood: 'Naughty child, what are you after? come, and
you shall have the stick.' The daughter was so frightened she let
the apron slip out of her hands, the sand was all spilt about, and
formed the barren hills by Litzow.[1] Near Vî in Källasocken lies
a huge stone named Zechiel's stone after a giantess or merwoman.
She lived at Edha castle in Högbysocken, and her sister near the
Skäggenäs (shag-ness) in Småland. They both wished to build
a bridge over the Sound; the Småland giantess had brought
Skäggenäs above a mile into the sea, and Zechiel had gathered
stones in her apron, when a man shot at her with his shafts, so
that she had to sit down exhausted on a rock, which still bears
the impress of her form. But she got up again, and went as far
as Pesnässocken, when *Thor began to thunder* (då hafver *gogubben*
begynt at åka); she was in such a fright that she fell dead,
scattering *the load of stones out of her apron* higgledy-piggledy
on the ground; hence come the big masses of rock there of two
or three men's height. Her kindred had her buried by the side
of these rocks (Ahlqvist's Öland, 2, 98-9). These giants' dread
of Thor is so great, that when they hear it thunder, they hide
in clefts of rocks and under trees: a *högbergsgubbe* in Gothland,

---

[1] Lothar's Volkssagen, Leipz. 1825, p. 65. Temme's Pomm. sagen, nos. 190-1;
see Barthold's Pommern 1, 580, who spells Dobberwort, and explains it by the Pol.
wor (sack).

whom a peasant, to keep him friendly, had invited to a christening, refused, much as he would have liked to share in the feast, because he learnt from the messenger that not only Christ, Peter and Mary, but Thor also would be there; he would not face him (Nyerup's Morskabsläsning, p. 243). A giant in Fladsöe was on bad terms with one that lived at Nestved. He took his wallet to the beach and filled it with sand, intending to bury all Nestved. On the way the sand ran out through a *hole in the sack,* giving rise to the string of sandbanks between Fladsöe and Nestved. Not till he came to the spot where Husvald then stood, did the giant notice that the greater part was spilt; in a rage he flung the remainder toward Nestved, where you may still see one sandbank by itself (Thiele 1, 79). At Sonnerup lived another giant, Lars Krands by name, whom a farmer of that place had offended. He went to the shore, filled his glove with sand, took it to the farmer's and emptied it, so that the farmhouse and yard were completely covered; what had *run through the five finger holes* of the glove made five hills (Thiele 1, 33). In the Netherlands the hill of Hillegersberg is produced by the sand which a giantess lets fall through *een schortekleed* (Westendorp's Mythol. p. 187). —And these tales are not only spread through the Teutonic race, but are in vogue with Finns and Celts and Greeks. Near Päjände in Hattulasocken of Tawastoland there stand some rocks which are said to have been carried by giant's daughters *in their aprons* and then tossed up (Ganander's Finn. myth. pp. 29. 30). French traditions put the holy Virgin or fays (p. 413) in the place of giantesses. Notre dame de Cléry, being ill at ease in the church of Mezières, determined to change the seat of her adoration, took *earth in her apron* and carried it to a neighbouring height, pursued by Judas: then, to elude the enemy, she took *a part of the earth up again,* which she deposited at another place not far off: oratories were reared on both sites (Mém. de l'acad. celt. 2, 218). In the Charente country, arrond. Cognac, comm. Saintfront, a huge stone lies by the Ney rivulet; this the holy Virgin is said to have carried on her head, beside four other pillars *in her apron;* but as she was crossing the Ney, she *let one pillar fall* into Saintfront marsh (Mém. des antiquaires 7, 31). According to a Greek legend, Athena was fetching a mountain from Pallene to fortify the Acropolis, but, startled at the ill news

brought by a crow, she *dropt it on the way*, and there it remains
as Mount Lykabettos.[1] As the Lord God passed over the
earth scattering stones, his bags burst over Montenegro, and the
whole stock came down (Vuk. 5).

Like the goddess, like the giants, the devil takes such burdens
upon him. In Upper Hesse I was told as follows: between
Gossfelden and Wetter there was once a village that has now
disappeared, Elbringhausen; the farmers in it lived so luxuriously
that the devil got power over them, and resolved to shift them
from their good soil to a sandy flat which is flooded every year
by the overflowing Lahn. So he took the village up in his
basket, and carried it through the air to where Sarenau stands:
he began picking out the houses one by one, and setting them
up side by side; by some accident *the basket tipped over*, and the
whole lot tumbled pellmell on the ground; so it came about, that
the first six houses at Sarenau stand in a straight row, and all
the others anyhow. Near Saalfeld in Thuringia lies a village,
Langenschade, numbering but 54 houses, and yet a couple of
miles long, because they stand scattered and in single file. The
devil flew through the air, carrying houses *in an apron*, but a
hole in it let the houses drop out one by one. On looking back,
he noticed it and cried ' there's a pity (schade) ! ' (see Suppl.).

The pretty fable of the giant's daughter picking up the *ploughing husbandman* and taking him home to her father *in her apron*
is widely known, but is best told in the Alsace legend of Nideck
castle :

Im waldschloss dort am wasserfall	In forest-castle by waterfall
sinn d'ritter rise gainn (gewesen) ;	the barons there were giants ;
ä mol (einmal) kummt's fräule hrab ins thal,	once the maiden comes down into the dale,
unn geht spaziere drinn.	and goes a-walking therein.
sie thut bis schier noch Haslach gehn,	She doth as far as Haslach go ;
vorm wald im ackerfeld	outside the wood, in the cornfield
do blibt sie voll verwundrung stehn	she stands still, full of wonder,
unn sieht, wie's feld wurd bestellt.	and sees how the field gets tilled.
sie liiegt dem ding ä wil so zu ;	She looks at the thing a while,
der *pftui*, die *ros*, die *lütt*	the *plough*, the *horses*, the *men*
ischer ebs (ist ihr etwas) neus ; sie geht derzu	are new to her ; she goes thereto

¹ Antigoni Carystii hist. mirab. cap. 12, Lips. 1791 p. 22: τῇ δὲ Ἀθηνᾷ, φερούσῃ τὸ ὄρος, ὃ νῦν καλεῖται Λυκαβηττὸς, κορώνην φησὶν ἀπαντῆσαι καὶ εἰπεῖν, ὅτι Ἐριχθόνιος ἐν φανερῷ · τὴν δὲ ἀκούσασαν ῥίψαι τὸ ὄρος, ὅπου νῦν ἐστι· τῇ δὲ κορώνῃ διὰ τὴν κακαγγελίαν εἰπεῖν, ὡς εἰς ἀκρόπολιν οὐ θέμις αὐτῇ ἔσται ἀφικέσθαι.

unn denkt ' die nimm i mit.'
D'rno huurt sie an de bode hin
unn *spreit ihr fürti uss,*
fangt alles mit der hand, thut's 'niin,
unn lauft gar froh noch hus.
sie springt de felswei 'nuf ganz frisch,
dort wo der berg jetzt isch so gäh
unn me (man) so krattle mus in d'höh,
macht sie nur eine schritt.
Der ritter sitzt just noch am tisch :
' min kind, was bringste mit ?
d' freud lüegt der zu de auge 'nuss ;
se krom nur geschwind din fürti uss ;
was hest so zawelichs drin ? '
'o vatter, *spieldings* gar ze nett,
i ha noch nie ebs schöns so g'hett,'
unn stelltem (ihm) alles hin.
Unn uf de tisch stellt sie den *pflui,*
d' *bure* unn ihri *ros,*
lauft drum herum unn lacht derzu,
ihr freud isch gar ze gross.
' Ja, kind, diss isch ken *spieldings* nitt,
do hest ebs schöns gemacht'
saht der herr ritter glich und lacht,
' geh nimm's nur widder mit !
die bure sorje uns für brot,
sunsch sterbe mir de hungertod ;
trah alles widder furt ! '
's fräule krint, der vatter schilt :
' ä bur mir nitt als spieldings gilt,
i liid (ich leide) net dass me murrt.
pack alles sachte widder iin
unn trah's ans nämli plätzel hin,
wo des (du's) genumme hest.
baut nit der bur sin ackerfeld,
se fehlt's bi uns an brot unn geld
in unserm felsennest.'

and thinks ' I'll take them with me.'
Then plumps down on the ground
and *spreads her apron out,*
grasps all in her hand, pops it in,
and runs right joyful home ;
leaps up the rock-path brisk,
where the hill is now so steep
and men must scramble up,
she makes but one stride.
The.baron sits just then at table :
' my child, what bringst with thee ?
joy looks out at thine eyes ;
undo thine apron, quick,
what hast so wonderful therein ? '
' O father, *playthings* quite too neat,
I ne'er had aught so pretty,'
and sets it all before him.
On the table she sets the *plough,*
the *farmers* and their *horses,*
runs round them and laughs,
her joy is all too great.
' Ah child, this is no plaything,
a pretty thing thou hast done ! '
saith the baron quick, and laughs,
' go take it back !
the farmers provide us with bread,
else we die the hunger-death;
carry it all away again.'
The maiden cries, the father scolds :
' a farmer shall be no toy to me.
I will have no grumbling ;
pack it all up softly again
and carry it to the same place
where thou tookst it from.
Tills not the farmer his field,
we are short of bread and money
in our nest on the rock.'

Similar anecdotes from the Harz and the Odenwald are given in Deut. sag. nos. 319. 324. In Hesse the giant's daughter is placed on the Hippersberg (betw. Kölbe, Wehrda and Goss-felden) : her father rates her soundly, and sets the ploughman at liberty again with commendations. The same story is told at Dittersdorf near Blankenburg (betw. Rudolstadt and Saalfeld). Again, a hünin with her daughter dwelt on Hünenkoppe at the entrance of the Black Forest. The daughter found a *peasant* ploughing on the common, and put him *in her apron, oxen, plough* and all, then went and showed her mother 'the *little fellow*

and his *pussy-cats.*' The mother angrily bade her carry man,
beast and plough directly back to where she found them : ' they
belong to a people that may do the hünes much mischief.' And
they both left the neighbourhood soon after.[1] Yet again : when
the Grüngrund and the country round about were still inhabited
by giants, two of them fell in with an ordinary man : ' what sort
of *groundworm* is this ? ' asked one, and the other answered,
' these *groundworms* will make a finish of us yet ! ' (Mone's Anz.
8, 64). Now sentiments like these savour more of antiquity than
the fair reasons of the Alsatian giant, and they harmonize with
a Finnish folk-tale. Giants dwelt in Kemisocken, and twenty
years ago[2] there lived at Rouwwanjemi an old woman named
Caisa, who told this tale : A giant maiden (kalewan tyttären)
took up *horse and ploughman and plough* (bewosen ja kyntäjän
ja auran) *on her lap*, carried them to her mother and asked,
' what kind of *beetle* (sontiainen) can this be, mother, that I found
rooting up the ground there ? ' The mother said, ' put them
away, child ; we have to leave this country, and they are to live
here instead.' The old giant race have to give way to agri-
cultural man, agriculture is an eye-sore to them, as it is to dwarfs
(p. 459). The honest coarse grain of gianthood, which looks
upon man as a tiny little beast, a beetle burrowing in the mud,
but yet is secretly afraid of him, could not be hit off more
happily than in these few touches. I believe this tradition is
domiciled in many other parts as well (see Suppl.).

Not less popular or naïve is the story of the giant on a journey
being troubled with a *little stone in his shoe :* when at last he
shakes it out, there is a rock or hill left on the ground. The
Brunswick Anzeigen for 1759 inform us on p. 1636 : ' A peasant
said to me once, as I travelled in his company past a hill on the
R. Elm : Sir, the folk say that here a hüne *cleared out his shoe*,
and that's how this hill arose.' The book ' Die kluge trödelfrau '
by E. J. C. P. N. 1682, p. 14, mentions a large stone in the
forest, and says : ' Once a great giant came this way with a
pebble in his shoe that hurt him, and when he *untied the shoe*,
this stone fell out.' The story is still told of a smooth rock near
Goslar, how the great Christopher carried it in his shoe, till he

---

[1] L. A. Walther's Einl. in die thür. schwarzb. gesch., Rudolst. 1788, p. 52.
[2] In Ganander's time (Finn. myth. p. 30).

felt something gall his foot; he *pulled off the shoe and turned it down*, when the stone fell where it now lies. Such stones are also called *crumb-stones*. On the Solling near Uslar lie some large boundary-stones, 16 to 20 feet long, and 6 to 8 thick: time out of mind two giants were jaunting across country; says the one to the other, 'this shoe hurts me, some bits of gravel I think it must be,' with that he *pulled off the shoe and shook these stones out*. In the valley above Ilfeld, close to the Bähr, stands a huge mass of rock, which a giant once *shook out of his shoe*, because the grain of sand galled him. I am confident this myth also has a wide circulation, it has even come to be related of a mere set of men: 'The men of Sauerland in Westphalia are fine sturdy fellows; they say one of them walked to Cologne once, and on arriving at the gate, asked his fellow-traveller to wait a moment, while he looked in his shoe to see what had been teazing him so all the while. "Nay" said the other, "hold out now till we get to the inn." The Sauerlander said very well, and they trudged up and down the long streets. But at the market-place he could stand it no longer, he *took the shoe off and threw out a great lump of stone*, and there it has lain this long while to prove my words.' A Norwegian folk-tale is given by Hammerich (om Ragnaröks-mythen, p. 93): a jutel had got something into his eye, that pricked him; he tried to ferret it out with his finger, but that was too bulky, so he took a sheaf of corn, and with that he managed the business. It was a fir-cone, which the giant felt between his fingers, and said: 'who'd have thought a little thing like that would hurt you so?' (see Suppl.).

The Edda tells wonderful things of giant Skrŷmir,[1] in the thumb of whose glove the god Thôrr found a night's lodging. Skrŷmir goes to sleep under an oak, and snores; when Thôrr with his hammer strikes him on the head, he wakes up and asks if *a leaf has fallen on him*. The giant lies down under another oak, and snores so that the forest roars; Thôrr hits him a harder blow than before, and the giant awaking cries, '*did an acorn fall on my face?*' He falls asleep a third time, and Thôrr repeats his blow, making a yet deeper dint, but the giant merely strokes his cheek, and remarks, 'there must be birds roosting in those

---

[1] In the Farôe dialect *Skrujmsli* (Lyngbye, p. 480). ON. *skraumr* blatero, babbler.

boughs; I fancied, when I woke, they *dropt something* on my head.' Sn. 51–53. These are touches of genuine gianthood, and are to be met with in quite different regions as well. A Bohemian story makes the giant Scharmak sleep under a tower, which his enemies undermine, so that it tumbles about his ears; he shakes himself up and cries : 'this is a bad place to rest in, the *birds drop things on your head*.' After that, three men drag a large bell up the oaktree under which Scharmak is asleep, snoring so hard that the leaves shake; the bell is cut down, and comes crashing on the giant, but he does not even wake. A German nursery-tale (1, 307) has something very similar; in another one, millstones are dropt on a giant in the well, and he calls out, ' drive those *hens* away, they scratch the sand up there, and make the *grains come in my eyes* ' (2, 29).[1]

A giantess (gŷgr) named *Hyrrokin* (igne fumata) is mentioned in the Edda, Sn. 66 on occasion of Baldr's funeral: nothing could set the ship Hrînghorn, in which the body lay, in motion; they sent to the giants, and Hyrrokin came riding on a wolf, with a snake for bridle and rein; she no sooner stept up to the vessel and touched it with her foot, than fire darted out of the beams, and the firm land quaked. I also find in a Norwegian folk-tale (Faye, p. 14), that a giantess (djurre) by merely kicking the shore with her foot threw a ship into the most violent agitation.

Rabelais[2] and Fischart have glorified the fable of *Gargantua*. It was, to begin with, an old, perhaps even a Celtic, giant-story, whose genuine simple form may even yet be recoverable from unexpired popular traditions.[3] Gargantua, an enormous eater and drinker, who as a babe had, like St. Christopher, taxed the resources of ten wetnurses, stands with each foot on a high mountain, and *stooping down drinks up the river that runs between*

---

[1] Conf. the story of the giant Audsch in Hammer's Rosenöl 1, 114.

[2] Rabelais took his subject-matter from an older book, printed already in the 15th century, and published more than once in the 16th : Les chroniques admirables du puissant roi Gargantua s. l. et a. (gothique) 8; Lyon 1532. 4; La plaisante et joyeuse histoire du grand Gargantua. Valence 1547. 8; at last as a chap-book: La vie du fameux Gargantua, le plus terrible géant qui ait amais paru sur la terre. Conf. Notice sur les chroniques de Garg., par l'auteur des nouv. rech. bibl. Paris 1834.

[3] A beginning has been made in Traditions de l'ancien duché de Retz, sur Garg. (Mém. de l'acad. celt. 5, 392–5), and in Volkssagen aus dem Greyersland (Alpenrosen 1824, pp. 57–8). From the latter I borrow what stands in the text.

(see Suppl.). A Westphalian legend of the Weser has much the same tale to tell : On the R. Solling, near Mt. Eberstein, stands the Hünenbrink, a detached conical hill [brink = grassy knoll]. When the hüne who dwelt there of old wanted to wash his face of a morning, he would plant one foot on his own hill, and with the other stride over to the Eichholz a mile and a half away, and *draw from the brook that flows through the valley.* If his neck ached with stooping and was like to break, he stretched one arm over the Burgberg and laid hold of Lobach, Negenborn and Holenberg to support himself. •

We are often told of *two giant comrades* or neighbours, living on adjacent heights, or on two sides of a river, and holding converse. In Ostergötland, near Tumbo in Ydre-härad, there was a jätte named *Tumme ;* when he wished to speak to his chum *Oden* at Hersmåla two or three miles off, he went up a neighbouring hill Högatoft, from which you can see all over Ydre (Widegren's Ostergötland 2, 397). The first of the two names is apparently the ON. þumbi (stultus, inconcinnus, conf. p. 528), but the other is that of the highest god, and was, I suppose, introduced in later legend by way of disparagement. German folktales make such giants throw *stone hammers* and *axes* to each other (Deut. sag. no. 20), which reminds one of the thundergod's hammer. Two hünes living, one on the Eberstein, the other on Homburg, had but one axe between them to split their wood with. When the Eberstein hüne was going to work, he shouted across to Homburg four miles off, and his friend immediately *threw the axe over ;* and the contrary, when the axe happened to be on the Eberstein. The same thing is told in a tradition, likewise Westphalian, of the hünes on the Hünenkeller and the Porta *throwing their one hatchet.*[1] The hünes of the Brunsberg and Wiltberg, between Godelheim and Amelunxen, *played at bowls* together across the Weser (Deut. sag. no. 16). Good neighbours too were the giants on Weissenstein and Remberg in Upper Hesse ; they had a *baking-oven* in common, that stood midway in the field, and when one was kneading his dough, he threw a stone over as a sign that wood was to be fetched from his neighbour's fort to heat the oven. Once they both happened to be throwing at the

---

[1] Redeker's Westfälische sagen, no. 36.

same time, the *stones met in the air*,[1] and fell where they now lie in the middle of the field above Michelbach, each with the marks of a big giant hand stamped on it. Another way of signalling was for the giant to *scratch his body*, which was done so loud that the other heard it distinctly. The three very ancient chapels by Sachsenheim, Oberwittighausen and Grünfeldhausen were built by giants, who fetched the great heavy stones *in their aprons*. When the first little church was finished, the giant flung his *hammer* through the air : wherever it alighted, the next building was to begin. It came to the ground five miles off, and there was erected the second church, on completing which the giant flung the hammer once more, and where it fell, at the same distance of five miles, he built the third chapel. In the one at Sachsenheim a huge rib of the builder is preserved (Mone's Anz. 8, 63). The following legends come from Westphalia : Above Nettelstädt-on-the-hill stands the Hünenbrink, where hünes lived of old, and kept on friendly terms with their fellows on the Stell (2½ miles farther). When the one set were baking, and the other wanted a *loaf* done at the same time, they *just pitched it over* (see Suppl.). A hüne living at Hilverdingsen on the south side of the Schwarze lake, and another living at Hille on the north side, used to *bake their bread* together. One morning the one at Hilverdingsen thought he heard his neighbour emptying his kneading-trough, all ready for baking ; he sprang from his lair, snatched up his dough, and leapt over the lake. But it was no such thing, the noise he had heard was only his neighbour *scratching his leg*. At Altehüffen there lived hünen, who had but one knife at their service; this they kept stuck in the trunk of a tree that stood in the middle of the village, and whoever wanted it fetched it thence, and then put it back in its place. The spot is still shown where the tree stood. These hünes, who were also called *duttes*, were a people exceedingly scant of wit, and to them is due the proverb ' Altehüffen *dumme dutten*.' As the surrounding country came more and more under cultivation, the hünen felt no longer at ease among the new settlers, and they retired. It was then that the *duttes* of Altehüffen also made up their minds to emigrate; but what they wanted was to go and find the

---

[1] Like Hrûngni's hein and Thôr's hammer, p. 538.

entrance into heaven. How they fared on the way was never
known, but the joke is made upon them, that after a long march
they came to a great calm, clear sheet of water, in which the
bright sky was reflected; here they thought they could plunge
into heaven, so they jumped in and were drowned.[1] From so
remarkable a consensus[2] we cannot but draw the conclusion, that
the giants held together *as a people*, and were settled in the
mountains of a country, but that they gradually gave way to
the human race, which may be regarded as a nation of invaders.
Legend converts their stone weapons into the woodman's axe or
the knife, their martial profession into the peaceable pursuit of
baking bread. It was an ancient custom to stick swords or
knives into a tree standing in the middle of the yard (Fornald.
sög. 1, 120-1); a man's strength was proved by the depth to
which he drove the hatchet into a stem, RA. 97. The jumping
into the blue lake savours of the fairy-tale, and comes before us
in some other narratives (Kinderm. 1, 343. 3, 112).

But, what deserves some attention, Swedish folktales make the
divine foe of giants, him that hurls thunderbolts and throws
hammers, himself play with stones as with balls. Once, as Thor
was going past Linneryd in Småland with his henchman (the
Thiâlfi of the Edda), he came upon a giant to whom he was not
known, and opened a conversation: 'Whither goes thy way?'
'I go to heaven to fight Thor, who has set my stable on fire.'
'Thou presumest too much; why, thou hast not even the strength
to lift this little stone and set it on the great one.' The giant
clutched the stone with all his might, but could not lift it off the
ground, so much weight had Thor imparted to it. Thor's servant
tried it next, and lifted it lightly as he would a glove. Then
the giant knew it was the god, and fell upon him so lustily that
he sank on his knees, but Thor swung his hammer and laid
the enemy prostrate.

All over Germany there are so many of these stories about
stones and hammers being hurled, and giant's fingers imprinted

---

[1] The last four tales from Redeker, nos. 37 to 40. *Dutten* means stulti, and is
further intensified by the adj. In the Teutonist dod = gawk, conf. Richthofen sub
v. *dud*, and supra, p. 528 on tumbo. Similar tales on the Rhön mts., only with
everything giant-like effaced, about the *tollen dittisser* (Bechstein pp. 81-91).

[2] I do not know that any tract in Germany is richer in giant-stories than Westphalia and Hesse. Conf. also Kuhn's Märkische sagen, nos. 22. 47. 107. 132. 141.
149. 158. 202. Temme's Pommersche sagen, nos. 175-184. 187.

on hard rock, that I can only select one here and there as samples
of the style and spirit of the rest. Ruins of a castle near Homberg in Lower Hesse mark the abode of a giantess; five miles
to one side of it, by the village of Gombet, lies a *stone* which
she *hurled* all the way from Homberg at one throw, and you see
the *fingers of her hand* imprinted on it. The *Scharfenstein* by
Gudensberg was *thrown* there by a giant in his rage. On the
Tyrifjordensstrand near Buru in Norway is a large *stone*, which
one jutul fighting with another is said to have *flung obliquely
across the bay*, and plain *marks of his fingers* remain on the stone
(Faye, p. 15). Two or three miles from Dieren in the Meissen
country there lie a *block of quartz* and one of *granite*; the former
was thrown by the giant of Wantewitz at the giant of Zadel, the
latter by the Zadeler at the Wantewitzer; but they both missed,
the stones having fallen wide of the mark.[1] So two combatants
at Refnäs and Asnäs threw enormous stones at each other, one
called *sortensteen*, the other *blak*, and the latter still shews the
fingers of the thrower (Thiele 1, 47). A kind of slaty stone in
Norway, says Hallager 53ª, is called *jyvrikling*, because the jyvri
(giantess) is said to have smeared it over with butter, and you
may see the *dint of her fingers* on it. Two giants at Nestved
tried their hands at *hurling stones*; the one aimed his at Rüislöv
church, but did not reach it, the other threw with such force that
the stone flew right over the Steinwald, and may still be seen
on the high road from Nestved to Ringsted (Thiele 1, 80; conf.
176). In the wood near Palsgaard lies a huge stone, which a
jette *flung* there because the lady of the manor at Palsgaard,
whom he was courting, declined his proposals; others maintain
that a jette maiden *slung it over* from Fünen *with her garter*
(Thiele 3, 65-6; conf. 42).

When giants fight, and one pursues another, they will in their
haste leap over a village, and *slit their great toe* against the
church-spire, so that the blood spirts out in jets and forms a
pool (Deut. sag. no. 325); which strikingly resembles Wäinä-
möinen, rune 3. In leaping off a steep cliff, their foot or their
horse's hoof leaves *tracks in the stone* (ibid. nos. 318-9). Also,
when a giant *sits down to rest* on a stone, or *leans* against a rock,

---

[1] Preusker in Kruse's Deutsch. alterth. iii. 3, 37.

his figure prints itself on the hard surface,[1] *e.g.* Starcather's in Saxo Gram. 111.

It is not as *smiths*, like the cyclops, that giants are described in German legend, and the forging of arms is reserved for dwarfs. Once in our hero-legend the giant Aspriân *forges shoes* (Roth. 2029); also the giant Vade makes his son Velint learn *smith-work*, first with Mîmir, then with dwarfs.

As for *smiðr* in the ON. language, it does not mean faber, but artificer in general, and particularly *builder*; and to be accomplished builders is a main characteristic of giants, the authors of those colossal structures of antiquity (p. 534). On the nine giant-pillars near Miltenberg the common folk still see the handmarks of the giants who intended therewith to *build a bridge* over the Main (Deut. sag. no. 19).

The most notable instance occurs in the Edda itself. A iötunn had come to the âses, professing to be a smiðr, and had pledged himself to build them a strong castle within a year and a half, if they would let him have *Freyja* with the *sun and moon* into the bargain. The gods took counsel, and decided to accept his offer, if he would undertake to finish the building by himself without the aid of man, *in one winter*; if on the first day of summer anything in the castle was left undone, he should forfeit all his claims. How the 'smith,' with no help but that of his strong *horse Svaðilfari*, had nearly accomplished the task, but was hindered by Loki and slain by Thôrr, is related in Sn. 46-7.

Well, this myth, obeying that wondrous law of fluctuation so often observed in genuine popular traditions, lives on, under new forms, in other times and places. A German fairy tale puts the *devil* in the place of the *giant* (as, in a vast number of tales, it is the devil now that executes buildings, hurls rocks, and so on, precisely as the giant did before him): the devil is to build a house for a peasant, and get *his soul* in exchange; but he must *have done before the cock crows*, else the peasant is free, and the devil has lost his pains. The work is very near completion, one tile alone is wanting to the roof, when the peasant imitates the

---

[1] Herod. 4, 82 : ἴχνος Ἡρακλέος φαίνουσι ἐν πέτρῃ ἐνεόν, τὸ οἶκε μὲν βήματι ἀνδρὸς, ἔστι δὲ τὸ μέγαθος δίπηχυ, παρὰ τὸν Τύρην ποταμόν, in Scythia. (Footprint of Herakles in stone, like a man's, but two cubits long.)

crowing of a cock, and immediately all the cocks in the neighbourhood begin to crow, and the enemy of man loses his wager.
There is more of the antique in a Norrland saga :[1] King Olaf of
Norway walked 'twixt hill and dale, buried in thought; he had
it in his heart to build a church, the like of which was nowhere
to be seen, but the cost of it would grievously impoverish his
kingdom. In this perplexity he met a man of strange appearance,
who asked him why he was so pensive. Olaf declared to him
his purpose, and the *giant* (troll) offered to complete the building
by his single self within a certain time; for wages he demanded
the *sun and moon*, or *St. Olaf himself.* To this the king agreed,
but projected such a plan for the church, as he thought impossible
of execution: it was to be so large, that seven priests could
preach in it at once without disturbing each other; pillar and
ornament, within and without, must be wrought of hard flint,
and so on. Erelong such a structure stood completed, all but
the roof and spire. Perplexed anew at the stipulated terms,
Olaf wandered over hill and dale; suddenly inside a mountain he
heard a child cry, and a giant-woman (jätteqvinna) hush it with
these words: 'tyst, tyst (hush)![2] to-morrow comes thy father
Wind-and-Weather home, bringing both sun and moon, or saintly
Olaf's self.' Overjoyed at this discovery,[3] for to name an evil
spirit brings his power to nought, Olaf turned home: all was
finished, the spire was just fixed on, when Olaf cried: ' *Vind och
Veder!* du har satt spiran sneder (hast set the spire askew).'
Instantly the giant, with a fearful crash, fell off the ridge of
the church's roof, and burst into a thousand pieces, which were
nothing but flintstones. According to different accounts, the
jätte was named *Bläster*, and Olaf cried: 'Bläster, sätt spiran
väster (set the spire west-er)!' or he was called *Slätt*, and the
rhyme ran: ' Slätt, sätt spiran rätt (straight)!' They have the
same story in Norway itself, but the giant's name is *Skalle*, and
he reared the magnificent church at Nidarös. In Schonen the
giant is *Finn*, who built the church at Lund, and was turned into

---

[1] Extracted, from Zetterström's collection, in the third no. of the Iduna, 2 ed.
Stockh. 1816, pp. 60-1. Now included, with others like it, in Afzelius's Sagohäfder 8, 83-86.

[2] Conf. the interj. 'ziss, ziss!' in H. Sachs iv. 3, 3ᵇ.

[3] Almost in the same way, and with similar result, the name of Rumpelstilz is
discovered in Kinderm. 55; conf. 3, 98, and supra p. 505 n.

stone by St. Lawrence (Finn Magnusen's Lex. myth. 351-2; and see Suppl.).

It is on another side that the following tale from Courland touches the story in the Edda. In Kintegesinde of the Dzervens are some old wall-stones extending a considerable length and breadth, and the people say: Before the plague (i.e. time out of mind) there lived in the district of Hasenpot a *strong man* (giant) of the name of Kinte. He could hew out and polish huge masses of stone, and carted even the largest blocks together with his one *white mare*. His dwelling-house he built on rocks, his fields he fenced with stone ramparts. Once he had a quarrel with a merchant of Libau; to punish him, he put his *white mare* to draw a stone equal to twelve cartloads all the way to Libau, intending to drop it at the merchant's door. When he reached the town, they would not let him cross the bridge, fearing it would break under the load, and insisted on his removing the stone outside the liberties. The strong man, deeply mortified, did so, and dropt the stone on the road that goes to Grobin by Battenhof. There it lies to this day, and the Lettons, as they pass, point to it in astonishment.[1] Kinte's white mare may stand for the Scandinavian smith's Svaðilfari; the defeat of the giant's building designs is effected in a different way.

King Olaf brooked many other adventures with giants and giantesses. As he sailed past the high hills on the Horns-herred coast, in which a giantess lived, she called out to him:

> S. Olaf med dit röde skiäg,
> du seilar for när ved min kjeldervåg!

(St. Olaf with thy red beard, thou sailest too near my cellar wall). Olaf was angry, and instead of steering his vessel between the cliffs, he turned her head on to the hill, and answered:

> hör du kjerling med rok og med teen,
> her skal du sidde og blive en steen!

(hear, thou carlin with distaff and spool, here shalt thou sit and become a stone). He had scarce finished speaking, when the hill split open, the giantess was *changed into a stone*, and you still see her sitting *with spindle and distaff* on the eastern cliff; a

---

[1] Communic. by Watson in Jahresverhandl. der kurl. gesellsch. 2, 311-2.

sacred spring issued from the opposite cliff.[1] According to a
Swedish account, Olaf wished to sail through Värmeland and by
L. Väner to Nerike, when the troll shouted to him :

> kong Olaf med dit pipuga skägg (peaky beard),
> du seglar för när min badstuguvägg (bathroom wall) !

Olaf replied :

> du troll med din råk och ten
> skal bli i sten
> och aldrig mer göra skeppare men !

(shalt turn to stone, and never more make skipper moan). The
giantess *turned into stone*, and the king erected a cross at Dalky
church in Elfdals herred.[2] The Danish rhyme is also quoted as
follows :

> hör du Oluf rodeskjäg,
> hvi seiler du igjennem vor stuevägg (through our chamber wall) ?

And :

> stat du der og bliv til steen,
> og (gjör) ingen dannemand (no Dane) mere til meen ![3]

In Norway itself the legend runs thus : The Hornelen Mountains
in Bremanger were once connected with Maröe, but are now
divided from it by a sound. St. Olaf sailed up to them, and
commanded the cliffs to part and let him pass through. They
did so, but instantly a giantess leapt out of the mountain and
cried :

> sig (see), du mand med det hvide skäg (white beard),
> hvi splitter du saa min klippeväg ?

Olaf :

> stat (stand) trold nu evig der i steen,
> saa gjör du ei nogen mand (not any man) meer meen.

His word came to pass, and the stone figure stands yet on the
cliff (Faye 124).   Olaf's *red beard* (like those of our hero-kings
Otto and Friedrich) reminds us of Thôrr the foe of giants (p. 177) ;
'*pipuga* skägg ' is apparently the same as the *pipskägg*, wedge-

---

[1] Danske viser 2, 12-8. Thiele 1, 82 ; conf. Faye, 118-9.
[2] Fernow's Värmeland, p. 223.
[3] Nyerup's Karakteristik af Christian 4, p. 17.

like or peaked beard, quoted by Ihre; but the Norwegian rhyme
has *white beard* (the barbe fleurie of Charlemagne). Such
divergences, and the changes rung on ' cellar wall, bathroom
wall, cliff wall,' vouch for the popular character of the tradition
(see Suppl.). It will surprise no one, if I produce a still older
type of the whole story from the Edda itself. When Brynhildr
in her decorated car was faring the ' hel-veg,' she went past
the dwelling of a *gŷgr*; the giantess accosts her with the words
(Sæm. 228ᵃ) :

> skaltu î gögnom gânga eigi
> griôti studda garða mîna !

(shalt not go through my stone-built house). This brings on a
dialogue, which is closed by Brynhildr with the exclamation:
' seykstu gŷgjarkyn!' (conf. p. 497n.). The giantess's house is
of stones skilfully put together, and the later rhymes speak of
cellar and bathroom : she herself is quite the housewife with
distaff and spindle. The sacred rights of domesticity are in-
fringed, when strangers burst their way through. There are
other instances in which the giantess, like the elfin, is described
with spindle and distaff : ' tolv troldqvinder (12 trold-women) de
stode for hannem med *rok og ten*' (Danske viser 1, 94).[1]

Close to the Romsdalshorn in Norway is a mountain called
Troldtinder, whose jutting crags are due to giants whom Olaf
converted into stones, because they tried to prevent his preaching
christianity in Romsdal.[2]

It would appear, from Sæm. 145ᵇ, that giants, like dwarfs,
have reason to dread the daylight, and if surprised by the break
of day, they *turn into stone* : ' dagr er nû,' cries Atli to Hrîmgerðr,
' hafnar mark þyckir hlœgeligt vera, þars þu î steins lîki stendr.'

Grotesque humanlike shapes assumed by stalactite, flint and
flakestone on the small scale, and by basalt and granite rocks on
the great, have largely engendered and fed these fancies about

---

[1] The Celtic fay carries huge stones on her spindle, and spins on as she walks,
Keightley 2, 286. Conf. supra, p. 413.

[2] Faye 124, who follows Schöning's Reise 2, 128. Sanct Olafs saga på svenske
rim, ed. Hadorph. p. 87: 'ell troll, som draap X män, han *giordit i stena*, och
stander än ; flere troll han och bortdref, sidan folckit i frijd blef.' Certain round
pot-shaped holes found in the mountains, the Norwegian people believe to be the
work of giants. They call them *jättegryter*, *troldgryter*, yet also *S. Oles gryter*
(Hallager 53ᵇ).

petrified giants. Then the myth about stone-circles accounts for
their form by dances of giants ; [1] many rocks have stories attached
to them of wedding-folk and dancing guests being turned into
stone (see Suppl.). The old and truly popular terminology of
mountains everywhere uses the names of different parts of the
body ; to mountains are given a head, brow, neck, back, shoulder,
knee, foot, etc. (RA. 541).

And here we come across numerous approximations and over-
lappings between the giant-legend and those of dwarfs, schrats
and watersprites, as the comprehensive name *troll* in Scandinavian
tradition would of itself indicate. Dwarfs of the mountains are,
like giants, liable to transformation into stone, as indeed they
have sprung out of stone (p. 532-3). Rosmer havmand (merman)
springs or *flies*, as the graphic phrase is, *into stone*.[2]
Then on the other side, the notion of the giant gets a good deal
mixed up with that of the hero, usually his opposite. *Strong
Jack* in our nursery-tales assumes quite the character of a giant ;
and even *Siegfried*, pure hero as he is in the Mid. Age poems,
yet partakes of giant nature when acting as a smith, like *Wielant*,
who is of giant extraction. Moreover, both Siegfried slightly,
and Strong Jack more distinctly, acquire a tinge of that Eulen-
spiegel or Rübezahl humour (p. 486) which is so amusing in the
Finnish stories of *Kalewa, Hisi*, and especially *Soini* (conf.
Kalewala, rune 19). This *Soini* or *Kullervo* bears the nickname
of Kalki (schalk, rogue); when an infant three days old, he tore
up his baby-linen; sold to a Carelian smith, and set to mind the
baby, he dug its eyes out, killed it, and burnt the cradle. Then,
when his master ordered him to fence the fields in, he took whole
fir-trees and pines, and wattled them with snakes; after that, he

---

[1] Stonehenge, AS. Stânhenge (-hanging), near Salisbury, in Welsh Choirgaur,
Lat. *chorea gigantum ;* acc. to Giraldus Cambr. cap. 18, a cairn brought by giants
from Africa to Spain (Palgrave's Hist. of AS., p.. 50) ; conf. Diefenbach's Celtica
ii. 101. In Trist. 5887, Gurmun is said to be ' born of Africa.'

[2] Danske viser 1, 228 : ' han sprang saa vildt i bjerget om, og blev til *flintesten*
sorte.' 1, 228 : ' han blev til en *kampesteen* graa.' 1, 233 : ' saa *flöj* han bort *i
röden flint*, og blev saa borte med alle.' 1, 185 of a cruel stepmother : ' hun *sprang
bort i flintesteen*.' But H. Sachs too has, iii. 3, 31ᵃ. 426, ' vor zorn *zu einem stein
springen ;*' ib. 53ᵇ, ' vor sorg *zu eim stein springen ;*' iv. 8, 97ᵈ, ' vor leid wol *zu eim
stein* möcht *springen*.' Overpowering emotions make the life stand still, and curdle
it into cold stone. Conf. Chap. XXXII. on the heroes entrapped in mountains, and
Suppl.

had to pasture the flock, but the goodwife having baked a stone in his bread, Soini was in such a rage that he called bears and wolves to aid him, who tore the woman's legs and worried the flock. The Esthonians also tell of a giant's son (Kallewepoeg), who furrowed up grassy lands with a wooden plough, and not a blade has grown on them since (see Suppl.). This trickiness of the Finnish giants is a contrast to the rough but honest ways of the German and Scandinavian.

Above all, there is no clear line to be drawn between giants and the wild hairy *woodsprites* dealt with in pp. 478-486. In the woods of the Bingenheim Mark are seen the stone seats of the *wild folk* (conf. p. 432) who once lived there, and the print of their hands on the stones (Deut. sag. no. 166). In the vale of Gastein, says Muchar, p. 137, *wild men* have lived within the memory of man, but the breed has died out since; one of them declared he had seen the forest of Sallesen near Mt. Stubner-kogel get 'mair' (die out and revive again) nine times: he could mind when the Bocksteinkogl was no bigger than a kranawetvogl (crossbill?), or the mighty Schareck than a twopenny roll. Their strength was gigantic: to *hurl a ploughshare the whole breadth of the valley* was an easy throw for them. One of these 'men' leant his staff against the head farmer's house, and the whole house shook. Their dwelling was an inaccessible cavern on the left bank of the Ache, at the entrance to the Klamm; outside the cave stood some appletrees, and with the *apples* they would *pelt* the passers-by in fun; remains of their household stuff are still to be seen. To the inhabitants of the valley they were rather friendly than otherwise, and often put a quantity of butter and milk before their house-doors. This last feature is more of a piece with the habits of dwarfs and elves than of giants.

Just as the elves found the spread of agriculture and the clearing of their forests an abomination, which compelled them to move out; so the giants regard the woods as their own property, in which they are by no means disposed to let men do as they please. A peasant's son had no sooner begun to cut down a bushy pinetree, than a great stout trold made his appearance with the threat: 'dare to cut in my wood, and I'll strike thee dead' (Asbiörnsen's Möe, no. 6); the Danish folk-song of Eline af Villenskov is founded on this, D.V. 1, 175. And no less do giants (like dwarfs, p. 459) hate the ringing of bells, as in the Swedish tale of the old giant in the mountain (Afzelius 3, 88) ; therefore they sling rocks at the belfries. Gargantua also carries off bells from churches.

In many of the tales that have come before us, *giant* and *devil* are convertible terms, especially where the former has laid aside his clumsiness. The same with a number of other resemblances between the two. The devil is described as many-headed like the giant, also, it is true, like the dragon and the hellhound. Wherever the devil's hand clutches or his foot treads, indelible traces imprint themselves even on the hardest stone. The titans chased from Olympus resemble the angels thrust out of heaven and changed into devils. The abode of the giants, like that of heathens and devils in general (p. 34), is supposed to be *in the north :* when Freyr looks from heaven toward Iötunheim (Sæm. 81) and spies the fair giantess, this is expressed in Snorri 39 by 'Freyr leit *i norðrætt.*' In the Danish folk-song of the stolen hammer, Thôrr appears as *Tord* (thunder) af Hafsgaard (sea-burgh), while the giant from whom Loke is to get the hammer back dwells in *Nordenfjeld ;* the Swedish folk-song says more vaguely 'trolltrams gård.' [1]

But what runs into gianthood altogether is the nature of the *man-eating* huorco or ogre (p. 486). Like him the stone-hurling cyclops in the Odyssey hanker after human flesh; and again a Tartar giant *Depêghöz* (eye on top of head) [2] stands midway between *Polyphemus,* who combs with a harrow and shaves with a scythe (Ov. Metam. 13, 764), and *Gargantua.* As an infant he sucks all the nurses dry, that offer him the breast; when grown up, the Oghuzes have to supply him daily with 2 men and 500 sheep. Bissat, the hero, burns out his eye with a red-hot knife ; the blinded giant sits outside the door, and feels with his hands each goat as it passes out. An arrow aimed at his breast would not penetrate, he cried 'what's this fly here teazing me?' The Laplanders tell of a giant *Stalo,* who was one-eyed, and went about in a garment of iron. He was feared as a man-eater, and

---

[1] To wish a man '*nordan till fjälls*' (Arvidsson 2, 163) is to wish him in a disagreeable quarter (Germ. 'in pepperland,' at Jericho).
[2] Diez : The newly discovered Oghuzian cyclop compared with the Homeric. Halle & Berlin 1815.

received the by-name of yityatya (Nilsson 4, 32). The Indian Mahâbhârata also represents *Hidimbas* the râkshasa (giant) [1] as a man-eater, misshapen and red-bearded : man's flesh he *smells from afar*,[2] and orders Hidimba his sister to fetch it him ; but she, like the monster's wife or daughter in the nursery-tales, pities and befriends the slumbering hero (see Suppl.).

Our own giant-stories know nothing of this grim thirst for blood, even the Norse iötunn is nowhere depicted as a cannibal, like the Greek and Oriental giants ; our giants are a great deal more genial, and come nearer to man's constitution in their shape and their way of thinking : their savagery spends itself mainly in hurling huge stones, removing mountains and rearing colossal buildings.

Saxo Gram. pp. 10. 11 invests the giantess Harthgrepa with the power to *make herself small or large* at pleasure. This is a gift which fairy-tales bestow on the ogre or the devil, and folk-tales on the haulemutter (Harrys 2, 10 ; and Suppl.).

It is in living legend (folktale) that the peculiar properties of our native giants have been most faithfully preserved ; the poets make their giants far less interesting, they paint them, especially in subjects borrowed from Romance poetry, with only the features common to all giants. Harpîn, a giant in the Iwein, demands a knight's daughter, hangs his sons, and lays waste the land (4464. 4500) :[3] when slain, he falls to the ground like a tree (5074).[4] Still more vapid are the two giants introduced at 6588 seq. Even in the Tristan, the description of giant Urgân (15923) is not much more vivid : he levies blackmail on oxen and sheep, and when his hand is hewn off, he wants to heal

---

[1] Tevetat's second birth (Reinhart cclxxxi.) is a râkshasî, giantess, not a beast.

[2] 'Mightily works man's smell, and amazingly quickens my nostrils,' Arjuna's Journey, by Bopp, p. 18. The same in our fairy-tales (supra, p. 486). Epithets of these Indian dæmons indicate that they *walk about by night* (Bopp's gloss. 91. 97).

[3] One giant is 'hagel al der lande,' hail-storm to all lands, Bit. 6482.

[4] N.B., his bones are treasured up *outside the castle-gate* (5881), as in Fischart's Garg. 41ª: 'they tell of riesen and haunen, shew their bones in churches, under town halls.' So there hangs in a church the *skeleton* of the giantess struck by lightning (p. 531n.), the heathen maiden's *dripping rib* (Deut. sag. 140), and her *yellow locks* (ibid. 317) ; in the castle is kept the *giant's bone* (ibid. 324). At Alpirsbach in the Black Forest a giant's skeleton hangs outside the gate, and in Our Lady's church at Arnstadt the 'riesenribbe,' Bechst. 3, 129; conf. Jerichow and Werben in Ad. Kuhn, no. 56. The horns of a giant ox nailed up in the porch of a temple (Niebuhr's Rom. Hist. 1, 407).

it on again (16114).[1]   The giants shew more colour as we come
to poems in the cycle of our hero-legend.   Kuperân in the Hürn.
Sîfrit (Cüpriân of the Heldens. 171) rules over 1000 giants, and
holds in durance the captive daughter of a king.   The Rother
brings before us, all alive, the giants Aspriân, Grimme, Widolt,
the last straining like a lion at his leash, till he is let loose for
the fight (744. 2744. 4079) ; in the steel bar that two men could
not lift he buries his teeth till fire starts out of it (650. 4653-74),
and he smites with it like a thunderbolt (2734) ; the noise of his
moving makes the earth to quake (5051), his hauberk rings
when he leaps over bushes (4201) ; he pitches one man over the
heads of four, so that his feet do not touch the ground (1718),
smashes a lion against the wall (1144-53), rubs fire out of millstones (1040), wades in mould (646. 678) up to the knee (935),
a feature preserved in Vilk. saga, cap. 60, and also Oriental
(Hammer's Rosenöl 1, 36).   Aspriân sets his foot on the mouth
of the wounded (4275).   And some good giant traits come out in
Sigenôt : when he breathes in his sleep, the boughs bend (60),[2]
he plucks up trees in the fir-wood (73-4), prepares lint-plugs
(schübel) of a pound weight to stuff into his wounds (113), *takes
the hero under his armpit* and carries him off (110. 158. Hag. 9,
Lassb.).   A giantess in the Wolfdiet. *picks up horse and hero,*
and, bounding like a squirrel, takes them 350 miles over the
mountains to her giant cell ; another in the folk-song (Aw. 1,
161) carries *man and horse* up a mountain five miles high, where
are two ready boiled and one on the spit (a vestige of androphagi
after all) ; she offers her daughter to the hero, and when he
escapes, she beats her with a club, so that all the flowers and
leaves in the wood quiver.   Giant Welle's sister Rütze in the
Heldenbuch takes for her staff a *whole tree*, root and branch,
that two waggons could not have carried ; another woman 'of
wild kin' walks over all the trees, and requires two bullocks'
hides for a pair of shoes, Wolfd. 1513.   Giant Langbein (Danske
viser 1, 26) is asleep in the wood, when the heroes wake him up
(see Suppl.).

A good many giant-stories not yet discovered and collected

---

[1] The Romance giants are often porters and bridge-keepers, conf. the dorper in
Fergût (supra, p. 535) ; yet also in Nib. 457, 4.   458, 1 : 'rise portenære.'
[2] The same token of gianthood is in Vilk. saga, cap. 176, and in a Servian lay.

must still be living in the popular traditions of Norway and Sweden,[1] and even we in Germany may gather something from oral narration, though not much from books. The monk of St. Gall (Pertz 2, 756) has an Eishere (*i.e.* Egisheri, terribilis) of Thurgau, but he is a giant-like hero, not a giant.[2]

Of sacrifices offered to giants (as well as to friendly elves and home-sprites), of a worship of giants, there is hardly a trace. Yet in Kormakssaga 242 I find *blôtrisi*, giant to whom one sacrifices; and the buttered stóne (p. 546) may have been smeared *for* the giantess, not by her, for it was the custom of antiquity to anoint sacred stones and images with oil or fat, conf. p. 63. As to the 'gude lubbe' whose worship is recorded by Bp. Gebhard (p. 526), his gianthood is not yet satisfactorily made out. Fasolt, the giant of storm, was invoked in exorcisms; but here we may regard him as a demigod, like Thorgerðr and Irpa, who were adored in Scandinavia (see Suppl.).

The connexion pointed out between several of the words for giant and the names of ancient nations is similar to the agreement of certain heroic names with historic characters. Mythic traits get mysteriously intergrown with historic, and as Dietrich and Charles do duty for a former god or hero, Hungarians and Avars are made to stand for the old notion of giants. Only we must not carry this too far, but give its due weight to the fact that iötunn and þurs[3] have in themselves an intelligible meaning.

---

[1] Hülphers 3, 47 speaks of 'löjlige berättelse om *fordna jättar*,' without going into them.

[2] It is quite another thing, when in the debased folktale Siegfried the hero degenerates into a giant (Whs. heldensage, pp. 301-16), as divine Oden himself (p. 155) and Thôrr are degraded into düvels and dolts. A still later view (Altd. bl. 1, 122) regards riese and recke (hero) as all one.

[3] Schafarik (Slov. star. 1, 258) sees nothing in them but Geta and Thyrsus; at that rate the national name Thussagetæ must include both.

CHAPTER XIX.

CREATION.

Now that we have treated of gods, heroes, elves, and giants, we are at length prepared to go into the views of ancient times on cosmogony. And here I am the more entitled to take the Norse ideas for a groundwork, as indications are not wanting of their having equally prevailed among the other Teutonic races.

Before the creation of heaven and earth, there was an immense chasm called *gap* (hiatus, gaping), or by way of emphasis *gap ginnûnga* (chasm of chasms), corresponding in sense to the Greek χάος.[1] For, as χάος means both abyss and darkness, so *ginnûnga-gap* seems also to denote the world of mist, out of whose bosom all things rose. How the covering and concealing 'hel' was likewise conceived of as 'nifl-hel' with yawning gaping jaws, has been shewn above, pp. 312–314.

Yet this void of space had two extremities opposed to one another, *muspell* (fire) the southern, and *nifl* (fog) the northern; from Muspellsheim proceed light and warmth, from Niflheim darkness and deadly cold. In the middle was a fountain *Hvergelmir*, out of which flowed twelve rivers named *elivâgar*. When they got so far from their source, that the drop of fire contained

---

[1] Χάος, from χαίνω = OHG. gînan, ON. gîna = Lat. hiare; conf. OHG. ginunga, hiatus. But we need not therefore read 'gap ginûnga,' for the ON. ginna, which has now only the sense of allicere, must formerly have had that of findere, secare, which is still found in OHG. inginnan, MHG. enginnen (see above, p. 403, Ganna): Otfried iii. 7, 27 says of the barleycorn, 'thoh findu ih melo thâr inne, inthiu ih es *biginne* (if I split it open); inkinnan (aperire), Graff 4, 209; ingunnen (sectus), N. Ar. 95. So in MHG., 'sîn herze wart ime engunnen' (fissum), Fundgr. 2, 268; enginnen (secare), En. 2792. 5722; engunnen (secuerunt), En. 1178. Nearly related is ingeinan (fissiculare), N. Cap. 136. From a literal 'splitting open' must have arisen the more abstract sense of 'beginning,' Goth. duginnan, AS. onginnan, OHG. inkinnan, pikinnan. Then gîna hiare, gin hiatus, further suggest gin (amplus), and ginregin (p. 320). Singularly Festus, in discussing *inchoare*, comes upon chaos, just as 'begin' has led us to gînan. *Cohus*, from which some derive incohare = inchoare, is no other than *chaos*. Fest. sub v. cohum. [Nearly all the above meanings appear in derivatives of the Mongol. root *khag, khog* to crack, etc., including *khoghôson* empty, chaos]. 'Beside gînan, the OHG. has a *chînan* hiscere (Graff 4, 450), Goth. *keinan*, AS. *cîne* (rima, chine, chink). The AS. has also a separate word *dwolma* for hiatus, chaos.—Extr. from SUPPL.

in them hardened, like the sparks that fly out of flame, they turned into rigid ice. Touched by the mild air (of the south), the ice began to thaw and trickle : by the power of him who sent the heat, the drops quickened into life, and a man grew out of them, *Ymir*, called *Örgelmir* by the Hrîmþurses, a giant and evil of nature.

Ymir went to sleep, and fell into a sweat, then under his left hand grew man and wife, and one of his feet engendered with the other a six-headed son ; hence are sprung the families of giants.

But the ice dripped on, and a cow arose, *Auðumbla*, from whose udder flowed four streams of milk, conveying nourishment to Ymir. Then the cow licked the salty ice-rocks, and on the evening of the first day a man's hand came forth, the second day the man's head, the third day the whole man ; he was beautiful, large, strong, his name was *Buri*, and his son's name *Börr* (p. 349).[1] Börr took to him *Bestla*, the giant *Bölþorn's* daughter, and begat three sons, *Oðinn, Vili, Ve* (p. 162), and by them was the giant Ymir slain. As he sank to the ground, such a quantity of blood ran out of his wounds, that all the giants were drowned in it, save one, *Bergelmir*,[2] who with his wife escaped in a lûðr (Sæm. 35[b], Sn. 8), and from them is descended the (younger) race of giants (see Suppl.).[3]

The sons of Börr dragged the dead Ymir's body into the middle of ginnûnga-gap, and created out of his *blood* the sea and water, of his *flesh* the earth, of his *bones* the mountains, of his *teeth* and *broken bones* the rocks and crags. Then they took his *skull* and made of it the sky, and the sparks from Muspellsheim that floated about free they fixed in the sky, so as to give light to all. The earth was round, and encircled by deep sea,[4] on

---

[1] In the Zend system, the firs man proceeds from the haunch of the primeval *bull* Kayomer.

[2] Ymir, *i.e.*, *Örgelmir*, begot *Thrúðgelmir*, and he *Bergelmir*.

[3] The meaning of *lûðr* has not been ascertained ; elsewhere it stands for culeus, tuba, here it is supposed to be a mill-chest. The OHG. *lúdara* f. means a cradle (Graff 2, 201) as well as pannus, involucrum (swaddling-band), and this would fit remarkably well, as some accounts of the Deluge do make the rescued child float in its cradle. True, Snorri speaks not of a child, but of a grown-up giant, who sits in the lúðr with his wife ; this may be a later version. [Slav. *lôt* is shallow basket, trough, tray.]

[4] Snorri at all events conceived the earth to be *round*, he says p. 9 : ' hon er kringlótt utan, ok þar utan um liggr hinn diupi siâr.' So in the Lucidarius : ' dise

whose shore the giants were to dwell; but to guard the inland
parts of the earth against them, there was built of Ymir's *brows*
a castle, *Miðgarð*. The giant's *brain* was thrown into the air,
and formed the clouds, Sn. 8, 9.

Sæmund's account 45ᵇ (conf. 33ᵇ) differs in some points:

> or Ymirs *holdi* var iörð um scöput,
> enn or *sveita* sær,
> biörg or *beinom*, baðmr or *hári*,
> enn or *hausi* himinn,
> enn or hans *brám* gerðo blíð regin
> miðgarð manna sonom,
> enn or hans *heila* voro þau in harðmóðgo
> skŷ öll um scöput.

Here the teeth are not made use of, but we have instead the
formation of trees out of the giant's *hair*.

When all this was done, the sons of Börr went to the seashore,
and found *two trees*, out of which they created two human beings,
Askr and *Embla*. To these Oðinn gave soul and life, Vili wit
and feeling (sense of touch), Ve countenance (colour?), speech,
hearing and sight, Sn. 10. More exactly in Sæm. 3ᵇ:

> unz þrîr komo or þvî liði
> öflgir ok âstgir æsir at sûsi (uproar).
> fundo â landi litt megandi
> *Ask* ok *Emblo* örlöglausa :
> önd (spirit) þau ne âtto, óð (mind) þau ne höfðo,
> lâ (blood) ne læti, ne lito (colours) góða.
> önd gaf Oðinn, óð gaf Hœnir,
> lâ gaf Loðr ok litu góða.

In this account the three âses are named Oðinn, Hœnir, Loðr
(p. 241) instead of Oðinn, Vili, Ve (p. 162); they come to the
roaring (of the sea, ad aestum, παρὰ θῖνα πολυφλοίσβοιο θα-
λάσσης), and find Askr and Embla powerless and inert. Then

---

welt ist sinwel (spherical), und umbeflozzen mit dem wendelmer, darin swebt die
erde als daz *tutter in dem wizen des eies* ist,' conf. Berthold p. 287, and Wackern.
Basel MSS. p. 20. The creation of heaven and earth *out of the parts of an egg* is
poetically painted in Kalewala, rune 1 (see Suppl.).—'Indian legend has likewise
a creation out of the egg, heaven and earth being eggshells, Somadeva 1, 10. Conf.
the birth of Helen and the Dioscuri out of an egg.'—Extr. from SUPPL.

Oðinn endowed them with spirit, Hœnir with reason, Loðr with blood and complexion (see Suppl.).

The creation of *dwarfs* is related in two passages which do not altogether agree. Sn. 15 tells us, when the gods sat in their chairs judging, they remembered that in the dust and the earth dwarfs had come alive, as maggots do in meat (see Suppl.). They were created and received life first of all in *Ymir's flesh.* By the decree of the gods these maggots now obtained understanding and human shape, but continued to live in the earth and in stones. Sæm. 2 says on the contrary, that the holy gods in their chairs consulted, who should make the nation of dwarfs out of *Brímir's flesh* and his black *bones ;* then sprang up *Mótsognir,* prince of all dwarfs, and after him *Durinn,* and they two formed a multitude of manlike dwarfs out of the earth.

Taking all these accounts together, it is obvious in the first place, that only the men and dwarfs are regarded as being really *created,* while the giants and gods come, as it were, of themselves out of chaos. To the production of men and dwarfs there went a formative agency on the part of gods; giants and gods, without any such agency, made their appearance under the mere action of natural heat and the licking of a cow. Giants and gods spring out of a combination of fire with water, yet so that the element converted into ice must recover its fluidity before it becomes capable of production. The giant and the cow drip out of the frost, Buri slowly extricates himself in three days from the thawing mass of ice. This *dripping* origin reminds us of some other features in antiquity ; thus, Oðinn had a gold ring Draupnir (the dripper), from which every ninth night there dripped eight other rings of equal weight (Sæm. 84ª. Sn. 66). Sæm. 195ᵇ speaks, not very lucidly, of a hausi Heiðdraupnis (cranio stillantis) ; Styrian legend commemorates a giant's rib from which a drop falls once a year (D.S. no. 140).[1] And Eve may be said to drip out of Adam's rib. With the giant's birth out of ice and rime we may connect the story of the snow-child (in the Modus Liebinc), and the influence, so common in our fairy-tales, of snow and blood on the birth of a long wished for child. All this seems allied to heathen notions of creation, conf.

[1] No doubt the familiar name Ribbentrop is founded on some such tradition.

Chap. XXX. Also I must call attention to the terms *eitrdropi*
Sæm. 35ᵃ, *eitrqvikja* Sn. 5, *qvikudropi* Sn. 6: it is the vivifying
fiery drop, and we do bestow on fire the epithet 'living.' Eitr
is our eiter, OHG. eitar, AS. átor, coming from OHG. eit, AS.
âd ignis; and its derivative sense of venenum (poison, φάρμακον)
seems inapplicable to the above compounds.

It tallies with the views expressed at p. 316 on the gods having
a beginning and an end, that in this system of creation too they
are not described as existing from the first: the god appears in
ginnûngagap after a giant has preceded him. It is true, Snorri
6 makes use of a remarkable phrase: 'svâ at qviknaði með
krapti þess er til sendi hitann,' the quickening is referred to the
might of him that sent the heat, as if that were an older eternal
God who already ruled in the chaos. The statement would have
more weight, were it forthcoming in the Völuspâ or any of the
Eddic songs themselves; as it is, it looks to me a mere shift of
Snorri's own, to account for the presence and action of the heat,
and so on a par with the formulas quoted in pp. 22-3-4.[1] Buri,
who is thawed into existence out of ice, to set limits to the rude
evil nature of the giant that was there before him, shews himself
altogether an ancestor and prototype of the heroes, whose mission
it was to exterminate the brood of giants. From him are descended all the âses, Oðinn himself being only a grandson.

Again, there is no mistaking the distinct methods by which
giants, gods and men propagate their kind. Only one giant had
sprung out of ice, he has to beget children of himself, an office
performed by his hands and feet together, as in other ways also
the hand and foot are regarded as akin and allied to one another.[2]
Ymir's being asleep during the time is like Adam's sleep while
Eve was fashioned out of his rib; Eve therefore takes her rise
in Adam himself, after which they continue their race jointly.
How Buri begat Börr we are not informed, but Börr united himself to a giant's daughter, who bore him three sons, and from
them sprang the rest of the âses. It was otherwise with men,

---

[1] We might indeed imagine that regin and ginregin ruled before the arrival
of the âses, and that this force of heat proceeded from them. But the Edda must
first have distinctly said so.
[2] Conf. Haupt's Zeitschr. 3, 156-7. Brahma too makes a man out of his own
arm, Polier 1, 168.

who were not created singly, like the giant or the god, but two at once, man and wife, and then jointly propagate their species.

While the huge mass of the giant's body supplied the gods with materials, so that they could frame the whole world out of his different parts, and the dwarfs swarmed in the same giant's flesh as worms; mankind are descended from two trees on the seashore, which the gods endowed with breath and perfect life. They have therefore no immediate connexion with giants.

In the *âses* we see a superior and successful second product, in contrast with the first half-bungled giant affair. On the *giants* an undue proportion of inert matter had been expended; in the *âses* body and soul attained a perfect equilibrium, and together with infinite strength and beauty was evolved an informing and creative mind. To *men* belongs a less full, yet a fair, measure of both qualities, while *dwarfs*, as the end of creation, form the antithesis to giants, for mind in them outweighs the puny body. Our Heldenbuch on the contrary makes the dwarfs come into being first, the giants next, and men last of all.

As the *giants* originated in the ice of streams that poured out of the fountain *Hvergelmir*, we may fairly assume some connexion between it and the names *Örgelmir, Thruðgelmir, Bergelmir.* I derive *gelmir* from gialla (stridere), and connect it with the OHG. galm (stridor, sonitus). Hvergelmir will therefore mean a roaring cauldron; and the same notion of uproar and din is likely to be present in the giants' names, which would support the derivation of Ymir from ymja, p. 532. The reading Örgemlir would indeed accord with the notion of great age associated with the giant nature (p. 524), but would sever the link between giants and the cauldron of chaos.

Thus far the Scandinavian theory : now to prove its general diffusion.

Though the word ginnûngagap has no exact parallel in OHG. or AS., it may for all that be the thing described in the following verses of the Wessobrunn Prayer :

> Dat gafregin ih mit firahim firiwizzo meista (wisest men),
> dat ero ni was noh ûfhimil (earth was not, nor sky),
> noh paum (tree) nohheinig noh pereg (mountain) ni was,
> noh sunnâ ni scein [noh sterno ni cleiz (glistened)],

no mâno (moon) ni liuhta noh der mareoseo (sea).

dô dâr niwiht ni was enteo ni wenteo,

enti dô was der eino almahtico Cot (Almighty God alone).

The last line may sound completely christian, and tho preceding
ones may have nothing directly opposed to christian doctrine ;
yet the juxtaposition of earth and heaven, tree and mountain,
sun [and star], moon and sea, also the archaic forms ero (terra),
ûfhimil (cœlum), mareoseo (mare, Goth. marisáivs), which must
be thrown into the scale,—all have a ring of the Edda :

> Vara sandr ne sær, ne svalar unnir,
>
> iörð fanz æva ne upphiminn,
>
> gap var ginnûnga, enn gras hvergi.
>
> sôl þat ne vissi hvar hon sali âtti,
>
> stiörnor þat ne visso hvar þær staði âtto,
>
> mâni þat ne vissi hvat hann megins âtti.

The words 'niwiht ni was enteo ni wenteo' give in roundabout
phrase exactly the notion of ginnûngagap.[1]

These hints of heathenism have gained additional force, now
that OHG. and OS. songs are found to retain the technical term
muspilli = ON. *muspell ;* the close connexion between *nifl, Niflheim,* and the *Nibelungen* so intergrown with our epos (p. 372) does
not in any case admit of doubt. Now if these two poles of the
Scandinavian chaos entered into the belief of all Teutonic nations,
the notion of creation as a whole must have been as widely
spread. It has been shewn that the Old-German opinion about
giants, gods, men and dwarfs closely agreed with the Norse; I
am now able further to produce, though in inverted order, the
same strange connexion described in the Edda between a giant's
body and the world's creation.

Four documents, lying far apart in respect of time and place
(and these may some day be reinforced by others) transmit to us
a notable account of the creation of the first man. But, while
the Edda uses up the giant's gutted and dismembered frame to
make a heaven and earth, here on the contrary the whole world
is made use of to create man's body.

---

[1] Conf. also Otfr. ii. 1, 3: 'êr sê ioh *himil* wurti, ioh *erda* ouh sô herti,' and
the description of chaos in Cædmon 7. 8, particularly the term *heolstersceado* 7,
11 ; though there is little or nothing opposed to Bible doctrine. Conf. Aristoph.
Aves 693-4.

The oldest version is to be found in the Rituale ecclesiae Dunelmensis (Lond. 1839), in which a scribe of the 10th century has interpolated the following passage, an A.S. translation being interlined with the Latin:

Octo pondera, de quibus factus est Adam. pondus limi, inde factus (sic) est *caro*; pondus ignis, inde rubens est *sanguis* et calidus; pondus salis, inde sunt salsae *lacrimae*; pondus roris, unde factus est *sudor*; pondus floris, inde est varietas *oculorum*; pondus nubis, inde est instabilitas *mentium*; pondus venti, inde est anhela *frigida*; pondus [1] gratiae, inde est *sensus* hominis.

Æhte pundo, of þæm âworden is Adam. pund lâmes, of þon âworden is *flæsc*; pund fîres, of þon reád is *blôd* and hât; pund saltes, of þon sindon salto *tehero*; pund þeáwes, of þon âworden is *swât*; pund blôstmes, of þon is fâgung *égena*; pund wolcnes, of þon is onstydfullnisse *þohta*; pund windes, of þon is *oroð cald*; pund [1] gefe, of þon is *þoht* monnes.

A similar addition is made to a MS. of the Code of Emsig (Richthofen, p. 211):—'God scôp thene êresta meneska, thet was Adam, fon *achta wendem*. thet *bênete* fon tha stêne, thet *flâsk* fon there erthe, thet *blôd* fon tha wetere, tha *herta* fon tha winde, thene thochta fon tha wolken, thene *suêt* fon tha dawe, tha *lokkar* fon tha gerse, tha *âgene* fon there sunna, and tha blêrem on (blew into him) thene helga ôm (breath), and tha scôp he Eva fon sîne ribbe, Adames liana.' The handwriting of this document is only of the 15th cent., but it may have been copied from an older MS. of the Emsig Code, the Code itself being of the 14th cent.

[1] This 'pound of grace' comes in so oddly, that I venture to guess an omission between the words, of perhaps a line, which described the 8th material. The two accounts that follow next, after naming eight *material* ingredients, bring in the holy breath or spirit as something additional, to which this gift of 'grace' would fairly correspond. Another AS. version, given in SUPPL, from the Saturn and Solomon (Thorpe's Anal. p. 95, ed. Kemble p. 180), is worth comparing: here 'foldan pund' becomes '*flæsc*, fyres pund *blôd*, windes p. *æðung*, wolcnes p. *môðes* unstaðelfæstnes, gyfe p. *fat and geþang*, blôstmena p. *eágena* missenltenist, deawes p. *swât*, sealtes p. *tearas*.'—Here 'gyfe' is right in the middle of the sentence: can it be, that both 'gefe' and 'gyfe' are a corruption of Geofon the sea god, gifen the sea (supra, p. 239), which in christian times had become inadmissible, perhaps unintelligible? It would be strange if water, except as dew, were made no use of: and the 'sea supplying thought' would agree with the French account, which ascribes wisdom to him that has an extra stock of sea in him.—TRANS.

The third passage is contained in a poem of the 12th cent. on the four Gospels (Diemer 320, 6–20 ; conf. the notes to 95, 18. 27, and 320, 6) :

Got mit sîner gewalt
der wrchet zeichen vil manecvalt,
der worhte den mennischen einen
ûzzen von *aht teilen :*
von dem leime gab er ime daz *fleisch,*
der tow becêchenit den *sweihc* (sweat),
von dem steine gab er im daz *pein* (bone),
des nist zwîvil nehein (is no doubt),
von den wrcen (worts) gab er ime di *âdren* (veins),
von dem grase gab er ime daz *hâr,*
von dem mere gab er ime daz *plût* (blood),
von den wolchen (clouds) daz *mût* (mood, mind),
dû habet er ime begunnen
der *ougen* (eyes) von der sunnen.
Er verlêh ime sînen âtem (his own breath),
daz wir ime den behilten (keep it for him)
unte sînen gesîn (and be his)
daz wir ime imer wuocherente sîn (ever bear fruit).

Lastly, I take a passage from Godfrey of Viterbo's Pantheon, which was finished in 1187 (Pistorii Scriptor. 2, 53) :—'Cum legimus Adam de limo terrae formatum, intelligendum est ex quatuor elementis. mundus enim iste major ex quatuor elementis constat, igne, aere, aqua et terra. humanum quoque corpus dicitur microcosmus, id est minor mundus. habet namque ex terra *carnem,* ex aqua humores, ex aere flatum, ex igne calorem. caput autem ejus est rotundum sicut coelum, in quo duo sunt *oculi,* tanquam *duo luminaria* in coelo micant. venter ejus tanquam mare continet omnes liquores. pectus et pulmo emittit voces, et quasi coelestes resonat harmonias. pedes tanquam terra sustinent corpus universum. ex igni coelesti habet visum, e superiore aere habet auditum, ex inferiori habet olfactum, ex aqua gustum, ex terra habet tactum. in *duritie* participat cum lapidibus, in *ossibus* vigorem habet cum arboribus, in *capillis* et *unguibus* decorem habet cum graminibus et floribus. *sensus* habet cum brutis animalibus. ecce talis est hominis substantia corporea.'—

Godfrey, educated at Bamberg, and chaplain to German kings, must have heard in Germany the doctrine of the eight parts; he brings forward only a portion of it, such as he could reconcile with his other system of the four elements; he rather compares particular parts of the body with natural objects, than affirms that those were created out of these.

Not one of the four compositions has any direct connexion with another, as their peculiarities prove; but that they all rest on a common foundation follows at once from the ' octo pondera, achta wendem, aht teilen,' among which the alleged correspondences are distributed. They shew important discrepancies in the details, and a different order is followed in each. Only three items go right through the first three accounts, namely, that lime (loam, earth) was taken for the flesh, dew for the sweat, clouds for the mind. But then the MHG. and Frisian texts travel much further together; both of them make bone spring out of stone, hair (locks) from grass, eyes from the sun, blood from the sea (water), none of which appear in the AS. Peculiar to the MHG. poem is the derivation of the veins from herbs (würzen), and to the AS. writer that of the blood from fire, of tears from salt, of the various colours in the eye from flowers,[1] of cold breath from wind, and of sense from grace; which last, though placed beyond doubt by the annexed translation, seems an error notwithstanding, for it was purely out of material objects that creation took place; or can the meaning be, that man's will is first conditioned by the grace of God? Fitly enough, tears are likened to salt (salsae lacrimae); somewhat oddly the colours of the eye to flowers, though it is not uncommon to speak of an opening flower as an eye. The creation of hearts out of wind is found in the Frisian account alone, which is also the only one that adds, that into this mixture of eight materials God blew his holy breath, and out of Adam's rib created his companion Eve [the MHG. has: ' imparted his breath '].[2]

---

[1] Variegated eyes are the oculi varii, Prov. vairs huelhs (Rayn. sub v. var), O.Fr. vairs iex (Roquef. sub v.). We find in OHG. bluomféh, and 'gevéhet náh tien bluomon,' Graff 3, 426; the AS. fágung above.

[2] Well, here is already our fifth version, from a Paris MS. of the 15th century (Paulin Paris, MSS. français de la bibl. du roi 4, 207) : ' Adam fu formé ou champ damacien, et fu fait si comme nous trouvons de huit parties de choses : du limm de la terre, de la mer, du soleil, des nues, du vent, des pierres, du saint esprit, et de la clarté du monde. De la terre fu la char, de la mer fu le sang, du soleil furent les

If now we compare all the statements with those taken from the Edda, their similarity or sameness is beyond all question : blood with sea or water, flesh with earth, bone with stone, hair with trees or grass, are coupled together in the same way here. What weighs more than anything with me is the accordance of 'brain and clouds' with 'thoughts and clouds.' The brain is the seat of thought, and as clouds pass over the sky, so we to this day have them flit across the mind ; 'clouded brow' we say of a reflective pensive brooding one, and the Grímnismâl 45[b] applies to the clouds the epithet harðmôðagr, hard of mood. It was quite in the spirit of the Edda to make the skull do for the sky, and the eyebrows for a castle ; but how could sky or castle have furnished materials for the human frame ? That the striking correspondence of the sun to the *eye* should be wanting in the Edda, is the more surprising, as the sun, moon and stars are so commonly spoken of as *eyes* (Superst. 614), and antiquity appears even to have seen *tongues* in them, both of which points fall to be discussed in Chap. XXII. ; meanwhile, if these enu-merations are found incomplete, it may be that there were plenty more of such correspondences passing current. If Thôrr flung a toe into the sky as a constellation, there may also have been tongues that represented stars.

The main difference between the Scandinavian view and all the others is, as I said before, that the one uses the microcosm as material for the macrocosm, and the other inversely makes the universe contribute to the formation of man. There the whole of nature is but the first man gone to pieces, here man is put together out of the elements of nature. The first way of think-ing seems more congenial to the childhood of the world, it is all

yeulx, des nues furent les *pensées*, du vent furent les *allaines*, des pierres furent les *os*, du saint esprit fu la *vie*, la clarté du monde signifie *Crist* et sa créance. Saichez que se il y a en l'omme plus de limon de la terre, il sera paresceux en toutes man-ières ; et se il y a plus de la mer, il sera sage ; et se il y a plus de soleil, il sera beau ; et se il y a plus de nues, il sera pensis ; et se il y a plus du vent, il sera ireux ; et se il y a plus de pierre, il sera dur, avar et larron ; et se il y a plus de saint esprit, il sera gracieux ; et se il y a plus de la clarté du monde, il sera beaux et amez.'——These eight items are again somewhat different from the preceding, though six are the same : earth, sea, cloud, wind, stone and sun ; the Holy Ghost and the light of the world are peculiar, while veins, hair, tears, and motley eyes are wanting. The 'champ damacien' is 'ager plasmationis Adæ, qui dicitur *ager damascenus*,' conf. Fel. Fabri Evagator, 2, 341. [Is 'du monde' the mistranslation of a Germ. 'des mondes,' the moon's ? Like the sun, it bestows 'beauty,' and that has nothing to do with Christ, who is however 'the light of the world.'—Tr.]

in keeping to explain the sun as a giant's eye, the mountains as
his bones, the bushes as his hair; there are plenty of legends
still that account for particular lakes and marshes by the
gushing blood of a giant, for oddly-shaped rocks by his ribs
and marrow-bones; and in a similar strain the waving corn was
likened to the hair of Sif or Ceres. It is at once felt to be more
artificial for sun and mountain and tree to be put into requisition
to produce the human eye and bones and hair. Yet we do speak
of eyes being sunny, and of our flesh as akin to dust, and why
may not even the heathens have felt prompted to turn that cosmogonic view upside down? Still more would this commend
itself to Christians, as the Bible expressly states that man was
made of earth or loam,[1] without enlarging on the formation of
the several constituent parts of the body. None of the Fathers
seem to be acquainted with the theory of the eight constituents
of the first man; I will not venture to decide whether it was
already familiar to heathen times, and maintained itself by the
side of the Eddic doctrine, or first arose out of the collision of
this with christian teaching, and is to be regarded as a fuller
development of the Adamic dogma. If Adam was interpreted
to mean clay, it was but taking a step farther to explain, more
precisely, that the flesh only was borrowed from earth, but
the bones from stones, and the hair from grass. It is almost
unscriptural, the way in which the MHG. poetizer of Genesis
(Fundgr. 2, 15) launches out into such minutiæ:—'Duo Got
zeinitzen stucchen den man zesamene wolte rucchen, duo nam er,
sôsich wâne, einen *leim* zâhe (glutinous lime), dâ er wolte daz
daz lit zesamene solte (wished the limbs to come together),
streich des unterzuisken (smeared it between), daz si zesamene
mohten haften (stick). denselben *letten* (clay) tet er ze âdaren
(made into veins), uber ieglich lit er zôch denselben *leim* zâch,
daz si vasto chlebeten, zesamene sich habeten. ûz *hertem leime*
(hard lime) tet er daz gebeine, uz *prôder erde* (crumbly earth)
hiez er daz fleisk werden, ûz *letten* deme *zâhen* machet er die
âdare. duo er in allen zesamene gevuocte, duo bestreich er in
mit einer *slôte* (bedaubed him with a slime), diu selbe *slôte* wart
ze dere hûte (became the skin). duo er daz pilede (figure) êrlich

---

[1] 'Die *leiminen*,' the loamen folk, Geo. 8409, is said of men, as we say ' e luto,
ex meliori luto ficti.'

gelegete fure sich, duo stuont er ime werde obe der selben erde.
sînen geist er in in blies, michelen sin er ime firliez, die âdare
alle würden pluotes folle, ze fleiske wart diu *erde*, ze peine der
leim herte, die âdare pugen sich swâ zesamene gie daz lit (blew
his spirit in, imparted mickle sense, the veins filled with blood,
the earth became flesh, the hard lime bone, etc.).'——These
distinctions between lime, clay, earth and slime have a tang of
heathenism; the poet durst not entirely depart from the creation
as set forth by the church, but that compounding of man out of
several materials appears to be still known to him. And traces
of it are met with in the folk-poetry.[1]

It is significant how Greek and, above all, Asiatic myths of
the creation coincide with the Norse (and what I believe to have
been once the universal Teutonic) view of the world's origin out
of component parts of the human body: it must therefore be
of remote antiquity. The story lasts in India to this day, that
Brahmâ was slain by the other gods, and the sky made out of his
skull: there is some analogy to this in the Greek notion of Atlas
supporting on his head the vault of heaven. According to one
of the Orphic poets, the body of Zeus is understood to be the
earth, his bones the mountains, and his eyes the sun and moon.[2]
Cochin-Chinese traditions tell, how Buddha made the world out
of the giant Banio's body, of his skull the sky, of his eyes the
sun and moon, of his flesh the earth, of his bones rocks and hills,
and of his hair trees and plants. Similar macrocosms are met
with in Japan and Ceylon; Kalmuk poems describe how the
earth arose from the metamorphosis of a mountain-giantess, the
sea from her blood (Finn Magn. Lex., 877-8, and Suppl.).

But Indian doctrine itself inverts this macrocosm, making the
sun enter into the eye, plants into the hair, stones into the bones,
and water into the blood of created man, so that in him the

---

[1] The giants mould a man out of *clay* (leir), Sn. 109. The Finnish god Il-
marinen hammers himself a wife out of *gold*, Rune 20. Pintosmauto is baked of
sugar, spice and scented water, his hair is made of gold thread, his teeth of pearls,
his eyes of sapphires, and his lips of rubies, Pentam. 5, 3. In a Servian song
(Vuk no. 110), two sisters spin themselves a brother of red and white silk, they
make him a body of boxwood, eyes of precious stones, eyebrows of sea-urchins,
and teeth of pearls, then stuff sugar and honey into his mouth: ' Now eat that,
and talk to us (to nam yèdi, pa nam probesèdi) !' And the myth of Pygmalion is
founded on bringing a stone figure to life (see Suppl.).
[2] Ὄμματα δ᾽ ἠέλιος τε καὶ ἀντιόωσα σελήνη.   Euseb. Προπαρασκ. εὐαγγ. 3, 9.
Lobeck, De microc. et macroc. p. 4.

whole world is mirrored back. According to a Chaldean cosmogony, when Belus had cut the darkness in twain, and divided
heaven from earth, he commanded his own head to be struck off,
and the blood to be let run into the ground; out of this arose
man gifted with reason. Hesiod's representation is, that Pandora
was formed by Hephæstus out of earth mingled with water, and
then Hermes endowed her with speech, Ἔργα 61–79. The
number of ingredients is first reduced to earth and blood (or
water), then in the O. T. to earth alone.

And there are yet other points of agreement claiming our
attention. As Ymir engendered man and wife out of his hand,
and a giant son out of his foot, we are told by the Indian Manus,
that Brahmâ produced four families of men, namely from his
mouth the first brahman (priest), from his arm the first kshatriya
(warrior), from his thigh the first vizh (trader and husbandman),[1]
from his foot the first sûdra (servant and artizan). And so, no
doubt, would the Eddic tradition, were it more fully preserved,
make a difference of rank exist between the offspring of Ymir's
hand and those of his foot; a birth from the foot must mean a
lower one. There is even a Caribbean myth in which Luguo,
the sky, descends to the earth, and the first parents of mankind
come forth from his navel and thigh, in which he had made an
incision.[2] Reading of these miraculous births, who can help
thinking of Athena coming out of Zeus's head (τριτογένεια), and
Dionysus out of his thigh (μηρορραφής)? As the latter was
called διμήτωρ (two-mothered), so the unexplained fable of the
nine mothers of Heimdallr (p. 234) seems to rest on some
similar ground (see Suppl.).

From these earlier creations of gods and giants the Edda and,
as the sequel will shew, the Indian religion distinguish the creation of the *first human pair*. As with Adam and Eve in Scripture, so in the Edda there is presupposed some material to be
quickened by God, but a simple, not a composite one. Trê
means both tree and wood, askr the ash-tree (fraxinus); the
relation of *Askr* to the Isco of heroic legend has already been
discussed, p. 350. If by the side of *Askr*, the man, there stood

---

[1] E femoribus natus = ûravya, ûruja, Bopp's Gloss. 54ᵃ.
[2] Majer's Mythol. taschenbuch 2, 4.

an *Eskja*, the woman, the balance would be held more evenly;
they would be related as Meshia and Meshiane in the Persian
myth, man and woman, who likewise grew out of plants. But
the Edda calls them *Askr* and *Embla* : embla, emla, signifies a
busy woman, OHG. emila, as in fiur-emila (focaria), a cinderella
(Graff 1, 252), from amr, ambr, aml, ambl (labor assiduus),
whence also the hero's name Amala (p. 370). As regards *Askr*
however, it seems worthy of notice, that legend makes the first
king of the Saxons, *Aschanes* (Askanius), grow up out of the
Harz rocks, by a fountain-head in the midst of the forest. Seeing that the Saxons themselves take their name from sahs (saxum,
stone), that a divine hero bears the name of Sahsnôt (p. 203),
that other traditions derive the word Germani from germinare,
because the Germans are said to have grown on trees ;[1] we have
here the possibility of a complex chain of relationships. · The
Geogr. of Ravenna says, the Saxons removed from their ancient
seats to Britain ' cum principe suo, nomine *Anchis*.' This may
be Hengist, or still better his son *Oesc*, whom I have identified
with Askr.[2]

Plainly there existed primitive legends, which made the first
men, or the founders of certain branches of the Teutonic nation,
grow out of trees and rocks, that is to say, which endeavoured
to trace the lineage of living beings to the half-alive kingdom of
plants and stones. Even our leut (populus), OHG. liut, has for
its root liotan (crescere, pullulare), OS. liud, liodan ;[3] and the
sacredness of woods and mountains in our olden time is heightened by this connexion. And similar notions of the Greeks fit
in with this. One who can reckon up his ancestors is appealed
to with the argument (Od. 19, 163) :

οὐ γὰρ ἀπὸ δρυός ἐσσι παλαιφάτου οὐδ' ἀπὸ πέτρης ·

for not of fabled *oak* art thou, nor *rock* ;[4] and there must have

---

[1] D. S. no. 408. Aventin 18[b] ; conf. the popular joke, prob. ancient, on the
origin of Swabians, Franks and Bavarians, Schm. 3, 524.

[2] In the Jewish language, both learned and vulgar, *Ashkenaz* denotes Germany or a German. The name occurs in Gen. 10, 3 and Jer. 51, 27 ; how early
its mistaken use began, is unknown even to J. D. Michaëlis (Spicil. geogr. Hebr.
1, 59) ; it must have been by the 15th century, if not sooner, and the rabbis may
very likely have been led to it by hearing talk of a derivation of the Germans from
an ancestor *Askanius*, or else the Trojan one.

[3] Pŏpulus however is unconn. with pōpulus a poplar.

[4] Such an ' e quercu aut saxo natus,' who cannot name his own father, is vul-

'been fairy tales about it, which children told each other in confidential chat (ὀαριζέμεναι ἀπὸ δρυὸς ἠδ' ἀπὸ πέτρης, Il. 22, 126.[1] ἀλλὰ τίη μοι ταῦτα περὶ δρῦν ἢ περὶ πέτρην; Hes. Theog. 35). In marked unison with the myth of Askr is the statement of Hesiod, that Zeus formed the third or brazen race out of ash-trees (ἐκ μελιᾶν, Op. 147); and if the allusion be to the stout ashen shafts of the heroes, why, Isco or Askr may have brandished them too. One remembers too those wood-wives and fays, who, like the Greek meliads and dryads, had their sole power of living bound up with some particular oak or ash, and, unlike the tree-born man, had never got wholly detached from the material of their origin. Then, a creation out of *stones* is recorded in the story of Deucalion, whom after the deluge Hermes bade throw stones behind his back : those that he threw, all turned into men, and those that his wife Pyrrha threw, into women. As in the Edda, after the great flood comes a new creation ; only in this case the rescued people are themselves the actors.[2] Even the Jews appear to have known of a mythical creation out of stones, for we read in Matth. 3, 9 : ὅτι δύναται ὁ Θεὸς ἐκ τῶν λίθων τούτων ἐγεῖραι τέκνα τῷ Ἀβραάμ (see Suppl.).

The creation of *dwarfs* is described ambiguously in the Edda : according to one story they bred as worms in the proto-giant's flesh, and were then endowed by the gods with understanding and human shape ; but by the older account they were created out of the flesh and bones of another giant Brímir. All this has to do with the black elves alone, and must not be extended to the light ones, about whose origin we are left in the dark. And other mythologies are equally silent.

It is important and interesting to get a clear view of the gradation and sequence of the several creations. That in the Edda giants come first, gods next, and then, after an intervening deluge,

---

garly spoken of as one ' whose father got drowned on the apple (or nut) tree.' Also, ' *not* to have sprung from an oak-stem,' Etner's Unw. doct. 585. ' Min gof ist au nüd abbem nossbom aba ohoh,' ' and my dad didn't come off the nut-tree,' Tobler 337ᵇ, who wrongly refers it to the Christmas-tree.

[1] Homer's phrase is: 'chat *from* oak or rock, as youth and maiden do.'— TRANS.

[2] As Deucalion and Pyrrha create the race of men, so (acc. to a myth in the Reinhartssage, whose source I never could discover) do Adam and Eve create that of beasts by smiting the sea with rods. Only, Adam makes the good beasts, Eve the bad ; so in Parsee legend Ormuzd and Ahriman hold a creating match.

men and dwarfs are created, appears in surprising harmony with a theological opinion largely adopted throughout the Mid. Ages, according to which, though the O. T. begins with the work of the six days, yet the existence and consequently the creation of angels and the apostasy of devils had gone before, and then were produced heaven and earth, man and all other creatures.[1] Afterwards, it is true, there comes also a destructive flood, but does not need to be followed by a new creation, for a pious remnant of mankind is saved, which peoples the earth anew. The Muhammedan eblis (by aphæresis from dieblis, diabolus) is an apostate spirit indeed, but created after Adam, and expelled from Paradise. Our Teutonic giants resemble at once the rebel angels (devils) and the sinful men swept away by the flood; here deliverance was in store for a patriarch, there for a giant, who after it continues his race by the side of men. A narrative preserved in the appendix to our Heldenbuch offers some fragments of cosmogony: three creations follow one another, that of dwarfs leading the way, after whom come giants, and lastly men; God has called into being the skilful dwarfs to cultivate waste lands and mountain regions, the giants to fight wild beasts, and the heroes to assist the dwarfs against disloyal giants; this connexion and mutual dependence of the races is worthy of note, though on the manner of creating there is not a word. Lastly, the threefold *arrangement of classes* instituted by Heimdallr[2] may, I think, be regarded as a later act in the drama of creation, of which perhaps a trace is yet to be seen even in modern traditions (p. 234).[3]

Another thing I lay stress on is, that in the Edda man and woman (Askr and Embla) come into existence together, but the

---

[1] Conf. the poetical representations in Cædmon and Fundgr. 2, 11. 12; of course they rest on opinions approved or tolerated by the church. Scripture, in its account of the creation, looks only to the human race, leaving angels and giants out of sight altogether, though, as the narrative goes on, they are found existing.

[2] The Mid. Ages trace the origin of freemen to Shem, that of knights and serfs to Japhet and Ham; Wackern. Bas. MSS. 2, 20.

[3] I have since lighted on a Muhammedan legend in Wolfg. Menzel's Mythol. forschungen 1, 40 : Eve had so many children, that she was ashamed, and once, when surprised by God, she hid some of them away. God then called the children to him, and divided all the goods and honours of the earth among them. Those that were hidden got none, and from them are descended beggars and fakirs. Unfortunately no authority is given, but the agreement with the German drama of the 16th cent. is undeniable, and makes me doubt the supposed connexion of the latter with the ON. fable. That the concealed children are not called up, is at variance with all German accounts.

Bible makes two separate actions, Adam's creation coming first, and Eve's being performed afterwards and in a different manner.[1] So, by Hesiod's account, there already existed men descended from the gods themselves, when the first woman Pandora, the all-gifted, fair and false, was formed out of earth and flood (p. 571). It is difficult to arrive at the exact point of view in the Hesiodic poems. In the Theogony, there ascend out of chaos first Gaia (earth) the giantess, then Erebus (corresp. to Niflheim) and Night; but Gaia by herself brought forth Uranus (sky) and seas and mountains, then other children by Uranus, the last of them Kronus the father of Zeus and ancestor of all the gods. As the Edda has a Buri and Börr before Oðinn, so do Uranus and Kronus here come before Zeus; with Zeus and Oðinn begins the race of gods proper, and Poseidon and Hades complete the fraternal trio, like Vili and Ve. The enmity of gods and titans is therefore that of âses and giants; at the same time, there is just as much resemblance in the expulsion of the titans from heaven (Theog. 813) to the fall of the rebel angels into the bottomless pit; so that to the giant element in the titans we may add a dæmonic. When the 'Works and Days' makes the well-known five races fill five successive ages, the act of creation must needs have been repeated several times; on which point neither the poem itself nor Plato (Cratyl. 397-8, Steph.) gives sufficient information. First came the golden race of blissful daimones, next the silver one of weaker divine beings, thirdly, the brazen one of warriors sprung from ash-trees, fourthly, the race of heroes, fifthly, the iron one of men now living. The omission of a metal designation for the fourth race is of itself enough to make the statement look imperfect. Dimmest of all is the second race, which also Plato passes over, discussing only dæmons, heroes and men: will the diminutive stature of these shorter-lived genii warrant a comparison with the wights and elves of our own mythology? In the third race giants seem to be portrayed, or fighters of the giant sort, confronting as they do the rightful

---

[1] The rabbinic myth supposes a first woman, Lilith, made out of the ground like Adam. [The Bible, we know, has two different accounts of man's creation: the first (Elohistic) in Gen. 1, 27, 'male and female created he them;' the second (Jehovistic) in Gen. 2, 7, 'formed man of the dust,' and in vv. 21. 22, 'took one of his ribs, . . . and the rib . . . made he a woman.' The first account seems to imply simultaneous creations.—TRANS.]

heroes of the fourth. The latter we might in Mosaic language call sons of Elohim, and the former sons of men; at the same time, their origin from the ash would admit of their being placed beside the first-created men of the Edda. The agreement of the myths would be more striking if we might bestow the name of *stone* race on the third, and shift that of *brazen*, together with the creation from the ash, to the fourth; stones being the natural arms of giants. Apollodorus however informs us it was the *brazen* race that Zeus intended to destroy in the great flood from which Deucalion and Pyrrha were saved, and this fits in with the Scandinavian overthrow of giants. The creation of Askr and Embla has its parallel in the stone-throwing of the Greek myth, and the race of heroes might also be called stone-created (see Suppl.).

It will be proper, before concluding, to cast a glance at the *Story of the Deluge*: its diffusion among the most diverse nations of the earth gives a valuable insight into the nature of these myths.[1]

From the sons of God having mingled with the daughters of men sprang robbers and wrongdoers; and it repented Jehovah that he had made man, and he said he would destroy everything on earth. But *Noah* found favour in his eyes, and he bade him build a great ark, and enter therein with his household. Then it began to rain, until the waters rose fifteen cubits above the highest mountains, and all that had flesh and breath perished, but the ark floated on the flood. Then Jehovah stayed the rain, the waters returned from off the earth, and the ark rested on the mountains of *Ararat*. But Noah let out first a raven, then a dove, which found no rest for her foot and returned into the ark; and after seven days he again sent forth a dove, which came back with an olive leaf in her mouth; and after yet other seven days he sent forth a dove, which returned not any more.[2] Then Noah came out on the dry earth, and offered a clean burntoffering, and

---

[1] Ulph. renders κατακλυσμὸς by *midjasveipdins*, sveipan meaning no doubt the same as κλόζειν, to flush, rinse, conf. AS. swâpan verrere. Diluvium is in OHG. *unmezfluot* or *sinfluot* (like sinwâki gurges, MHG. sinwæge); not so good is the OHG. and MHG. sintvluot, and our sündfluth (*sin*-flood) is a blunder.

[2] Sailors let birds fly, Pliny 6, 22. Three ravens fly as guides, Landnâmabôk 1, 2.

Jehovah made a covenant with man, and set his bow in the cloud for a token of the covenant.

After this beautiful compact picture in the O. T., the Eddic narrative looks crude and unpolished. Not from heaven does the flood rain down, it swells up from the blood of the slain giant, whose carcase furnishes material for creating all things, and the human race itself. The insolence and violence of the annihilated giants resemble those of the sons of Elohim who had mingled with the children of men ; and Noah's box (κιβωτός) is like *Bergelmi's* lûðr. But the epic touches, such as the landing on the mountain, the outflying dove, the sacrifice and rainbow, would surely not have been left out, had there been any borrowing here.

In the Assyrian tradition,[1] Kronos warns *Sisuthros* of the coming downpour, who thereupon builds a ship, and embarks with men and beasts. Three days after the rain has ceased, birds are sent out, twice they come flying back, the second time with slime on their feet, and the third time they staid away. Sisuthros got out first with his wife and daughter and pilot, they prayed, sacrificed, and suddenly disappeared. When the rest came to land, a voice sounded in the air, saying the devout Sisuthros had been taken up to the gods ; but they were left to propagate the human race. Their vessel down to recent times lay on the mountains of *Armenia*.[2] Coins of Apamêa, a city in Phrygia, show an ark floating on the water, with a man and woman in it ; on it sits a bird, another comes flying with a twig in its claws. Close by stand the same human pair on firm land, holding up their right hands. Beside the ark appear the letters ΝΩ (Noah), and this Apamêa is distinguished by the by-name of κιβωτός.[3]

According to Greek legend, Zeus had determined to destroy mankind ; at the prompting of Prometheus, *Deucalion* built an ark, which received him and *Pyrrha* his wife. Zeus then sent a mighty rain, so that Hellas was flooded, and the people perished. Nine days and nights Deucalion floated on the waters, then landed on *Parnassus*, and offered sacrifice to Zeus ; we have seen how this couple created a new generation by casting stones. Plutarch adds, that when Deucalion let a dove out of the ark, he could tell

---

[1] Buttmann On the myth of the Deluge, p. 21.
[2] Conf. the Annolied 308 seq., which brings the Bavarians from Armenia.
[3] All this in Buttmann, pp. 24–27.

the approach of storm by her flying back, and of fair weather by
her keeping away. Lucian (De dea Syria, cap. 12. 13) calls him
Δευκαλίωνα τὸν Σκύθεα (the Scythian); if that sprang out of
Σισύθεα,[1] it may have long had this altered form in the legend
itself. Some branches of the Greek race had their own stories
of an ancient flood, of which they called the heroes *Ogyges* and
Ogygos;[2] but all these accounts are wanting in epic details.[3]

A rich store of these opens for us in the Indian Mahâbhârata.[4]
King *Manus* stood on a river's bank, doing penance, when he
heard the voice of a little fish imploring him to save it. He
caught it in his hand and laid it in a vessel, but the fish began to
grow, and demanded wider quarters. Manus threw it into a large
lake, but the fish grew on, and wished to be taken to Gangâ the
bride of the sea. Before long he had not room to stir even there,
and Manus was obliged to carry him to the sea; but when
launched in the sea, he foretold the coming of a fearful flood,
Manus was to build a ship and go on board it with the seven
sages, and preserve the seeds of all things, then he would shew
himself to them horned. Manus did as he was commanded, and
sailed in the ship; the monster fish appeared, had the ship
fastened to his horn by a rope, and towed it through the sea for
many years, till they reached the summit of the *Himavân*, there
he bade them moor the ship, and the spot to which it was tied
still bears the name of *Naubandhanam* (ship-binding). Then
spake the fish: I am Brahmâ, lord of created things, a higher
than I there is not, in the shape of a fish have I delivered you;

---

[1] CKTΘEA from CICTΘEA is Buttmann's acute suggestion; but he goes
farther, taking this Sisythes or Sisuthros to be Sesothris, Sothis, Seth; and Noah
to be Dionysos, and a symbol of water.

[2] Buttm. p. 45 seq., who connects it with Okeanos and Ogenos.

[3] It is remarkable, that in a beautiful simile, therefore without names or places,
Homer depicts a kind of Deluge, Il. 16, 884:

> ὡς δ' ὑπὸ λαίλαπι πᾶσα κελαινὴ βέβριθε χθών
> ἤματ' ὀπωρινῷ, ὅτε λαβρότατον χέει ὕδωρ
> Ζεύς, ὅτε δή ῥ' ἄνδρεσσι κοτεσσάμενος χαλεπήνῃ,
> οἳ βίῃ εἰν ἀγορῇ σκολιὰς κρίνωσι θέμιστας,
> ἐκ δὲ δίκην ἐλάσωσι, θεῶν ὄπιν οὐκ ἀλέγοντες.
> . . . . . . μινύθει δέ τε ἔργ' ἀνθρώπων.

Even as crouches the darkening land, overcrowed by the tempest, All on a summer's
day, when Jove doth the down-rushing water Suddenly pour, and wreak his wrath
on the proud men, Men of might, who sit dealing a crooked doom in the folkmote,
Forcing justice aside, unheeding of gods and their vengeance; (rivers swell, etc.)
and the works of man are all wasted.

[4] Bopp's Die sündflut, Berl. 1829.

now shall Manus make all creatures, gods, asuris and men, and all the worlds, things movable and immovable. And as he had spoken, so it was done.

In the Bhâgavatam, *Satyâvratas* (supra, p. 249) takes the place of Manus, Vishnus that of Brahmâ, and the facts are embellished with philosophy.

The Indian myth then, like the Teutonic, makes the Deluge precede the real creation, whereas in the Mosaic account Adam lives long before Noah, and the flood is not followed by a new creation. The seven rishis in the ship, as Bopp remarks, are of divine rather than human nature, sons of Brahmâ, and of an older birth than the inferior gods created by Manus or their enemies the asuris (elsewhere daityas and dânavas = titans, giants). But it is a great point gained for us, that *Manus* (after whom manushyas, homo, is named) comes in as a creator; so that in our German *Mannus* (whence manna and manniskja, homo) we recognise precisely Börr and his creator sons (p. 349). Askr and Embla are simply a reproduction of the same idea of creation, and on a par with Deucalion and Pyrrha, or Adam and Eve.

I must not pass over the fact, that the first part of the Indian poem, where Brahmâ as a fish is caught by Manus, and then reveals to him the future, lingers to this day in our nursery tale of the small all-powerful turbot or pike, who gradually elevates a fisherman from the meanest condition to the highest rank'; and only plunges him back into his pristine poverty, when, urged by the counsels of a too ambitious wife, he desires at last to be equal with God. The bestowal of the successive dignities is in a measure a creation of the different orders.[1]

One more story of the Deluge, which relates the origin of the Lithuanians, deserves to be introduced.[2] When Pramžimas the most high god looked out of a window of his heavenly house (like Wuotan, p. 135) over the world, and perceived nothing but war and wrong among men, he sent two giants Wandû and Weyas (water and wind) upon the sinful earth, who laid all things waste for twenty nights and days. Looking down once

---

[1] Conf. the capture of the soothsaying marmennil, p. 434.
[2] Dzieje starożytne narodu Litewskiego, przez Th. Narbutta. Wilno 1835.
1, 2.

more, when he happened to be eating celestial nuts, Pramžimas dropt a nutshell, and it lighted on the top of the *highest mountain*, to which beasts and several human pairs had fled for refuge. They all climbed into the shell, and it drifted on the flood which now covered all things. But God bent his countenance yet a third time upon the earth, and he laid the storm, and made the waters to abate. The men that were saved dispersed themselves, only one pair remained in that country, and from them the Lithuanians are descended. But they were now old, and they grieved, whereupon God sent them for a comforter (linxmine) the rainbow, who counselled them to leap over the earth's bones : nine times they leapt, and nine couples sprang up, founders of the nine tribes of Lithuania. This incident reminds us of the origin of men from the stones cast by Deucalion and Pyrrha ; and the rainbow, of the Bible account, except that here it is introduced as a person, instructing the couple what to do, as Hermes (the divine messenger) did Deucalion. It were overbold perhaps to connect the nutshell with that nut-tree (p. 572-3), by which one vaguely expresses an unknown extraction.

Not all, even of the stories quoted, describe a universal deluge desolating the whole earth : that in which Deucalion was rescued affected Greece alone, and of such accounts of partial floods there are plenty. *Philemon* and *Baucis* in Phrygia (where Noah's ark rested, p. 577), had given shelter to the wayfaring gods, and being warned by them, fled up the mountain, and saw themselves saved when the flood rose over the land (Ovid. Met. 8, 620) ; they were changed into trees, as Askr and Embla were trees. A Welsh folktale says, that in Brecknockshire, where a large lake now lies, there once stood a great city. The king sent his messenger to the sinful inhabitants, to prove them; they heeded not his words, and refused him a lodging. He stept into a miserable hut, in which there only lay a child crying in its *cradle* (conf. lûdara, p. 559 n.) ; there he passed the night, and in going away, dropt one of his gloves in the cradle. He had not left the city long, when he heard a noise and lamentation ; he thought of turning back to look for his glove, but the town was no longer to be seen, the waters covered the whole plain, but lo, in the midst of the waves a *cradle* came floating, in which there lay both child and glove. This child he took to the king, who had it reared as

the sole survivor of the sunken city.[1] Conf. the story of *Dold* at
the end of Ch. XXXII. Another and older narrative, found even
in the British Triads, comes much nearer to those given above :
When the lake of Llion overflowed and submerged all Britain,
the people were all drowned save *Dwyvan* and *Dwyvach,* who
escaped in a naked (sailless) ship, and afterwards repeopled the
land. This ship is also named that of Nevydd nâv neivion, and
had on board a male and female of every creature ; again it is
told, that the oxen of Hu Gadarn dragged the avanc (beaver)
ashore out of the Llion lake, and it has never broken out since.[2]

Of still narrower limits are our German tales, as that of the
dwarf seeking a lodging at Ralligen on L. Thun (no. 45), which
is very like the Philemon-myth ; of Arendsee (no. 111), where
again only a husband and wife are saved; of Seeburg (no. 131) ;
and Frauensee (no. 239). A Danish folktale is given by Thiele
1, 227. Fresh and graceful touches abound in the Servian lay of
the three angels sent by God to the sinful world, and the origin
of the Plattensee or Balatino yezero, Vuk 4, 8–13 (2nd ed. 1,
no. 207).[3]

There is above all a dash of German heathenism about the
lakes and pools said to have been formed by the streaming blood
of giants (Deut. sag. no. 325), as the destructive Deluge arose
from Ymir's blood.

It appears to me impossible to refer the whole mass of these
tales about the great Flood and the Creation of the human species
to the Mosaic record, as if they were mere perversions and distortions of it ; the additions, omissions and discrepancies peculiar
to almost every one of them are sufficient to forbid that. And
I have not by a long way exhausted this cycle of legends (see
Suppl.) : in islands of the Eastern Archipelago, in Tonga and
New Zealand, among Mexicans and Caribs there start up accounts, astonishingly similar and yet different, of creation and
the first human pair, of a flood and deliverance, and the murder
of a brother.[4]

[1] Edw. Davies's Brit. Mythol. 146-7.
[2] Ibid. 95. 129. Villemarqué, Contes bretons 2, 294. Mabinogion 2, 341. 381.
[3] Sole example of a Deluge-story among Slavs, by whom cosmogonic ideas in
general seem not to have been handed down at all.
[4] W. von Humboldt's Kawisprache 1, 240. 3, 449. Majer's Mythol. taschenb.
2, 5. 131.

CHAPTER XX.

ELEMENTS.

From gods, half-gods and heroes, from the whole array of friendly or hostile beings that, superior to man in mind or body, fill up a middle space betwixt him and deity, we turn our glance to simple phenomena of nature, which at all times in their silent greatness wield an immediate power over the human mind. These all-penetrating, all-absorbing primitive substances, which precede the creation of all other things and meet us again everywhere, must be sacred in themselves, even without being brought into closer relation to divine beings. Such relation is not absent in any mythology, but it need not stand in the way of the elements receiving a homage to some extent independent of it and peculiar to themselves.

On the other hand, it is not the religion, properly speaking, of a nation, that ever springs from the soil of this elemental worship; the faith itself originates in a mysterious store of supersensual ideas, that has nothing in common with those substances, but subjugates them to itself. Yet faith will tolerate in its train a veneration of elements, and mix it up with itself; and it may even chance, that when faith has perished or is corrupted, this veneration shall keep its hold of the people longer. The multitude will give up its great divinities, yet persist for a time in the more private worship of household gods; even these it will renounce, and retain its reverence for elements. The history of the heathen and christian religions shews, that long after the one was fallen and the other established, there lived on, nay there live still, a number of superstitious customs connected with the worship of elements. It is the last, the all but indestructible remnant of heathenism; when gods collapse, these naked substances come to the front again, with which the being of those had mysteriously linked itself (see Suppl.).

To this effect I have already expressed myself (pp. 82–84) in

speaking of a worship of nature by our ancestors, which is indeed
supported by early testimonies, but these are often perverted
into an argument against the heathen having had any gods.
The gods stood and fell from other causes.

Water the limpid, flowing, welling up or running dry; Fire
the illuminating, kindled or quenched; Air unseen by the eye,
but sensible to ear and touch; Earth the nourishing, out of
which everything grows, and into which all that has grown dis-
solves;—these, to mankind from the earliest time, have appeared
sacred and venerable; ceremonies, transactions and events in
life first receive their solemn consecration from them. Working
as they do with never-resting activity and force on the whole of
nature, the childlike man bestows on them his veneration, without
any particular god necessarily intervening, though he too will
commonly appear in combination with it. Even to-day the
majesty and might of these eldest born of things awakes our
admiration; how could antiquity have forborne its astonishment
and adoration? Such a worship is simpler, freer and more dignified than a senseless crouching before pictures and idols.

All the elements are cleansing, healing, atoning, and the proof
by ordeal rests mainly upon them; but man had to secure them
in their purest form and at the most seasonable times.

We will consider them one by one.

1. WATER.[1]

Passages proving that the Alamanns and Franks worshipped
rivers and *fountains* are cited at pp. 100-1 and in the Appendix.[2]

---

[1] Goth. *vatô*, ON. *vatn*, OHG. *wazar*, OS. *watar*, AS. *wæter*, Dan. *vand*, Slav.
vodá, Lith. *wandû*, Lett. *uhdens*, Gr. ὕδωρ; then, corresp. in form to Lat. *aqua*, but
meaning fluvius, Goth. *ahva*, OHG. *aha*, AS. *eá*, ON. *á*; the Goth. *vêgs*, OHG.
wâc wâges = fluctus, flow.

[2] When here and elsewhere I use Bp. Burchard's Coll. of Decrees as authority
for *German* superstitions, I do not forget that in most cases (not all) it is drawn
from councils not held in Germany, but in Gaul, Italy or Spain. Yet, if we consider that German nations had been spreading themselves all over those countries
down to the 8-9th cent., that the AS. and Lombard Laws, to say nothing of
Capitularies, declaim equally with those Decrees of Council against water, tree and
stone worship, that Agathias and Gregory of Tours expressly charge the Alamanns
and Franks with such worship; these superstitions are seen to be something common to the Italian, Gallic and German nationalities, of which none of them can be
acquitted. Some have tried to make out from Agathias, that our forefathers had
a mere nature-worship, and no gods. It would be about as uncritical to do what
is to some extent the reverse, and suspect Agathias and Gregory of having adopted
their assertions out of church-prohibitions that were never meant for Germany at

The people *prayed* on the river's bank; at the fountain's brink
they *lighted candles* and laid down *sacrificial gifts*. It is called
'fontibus venerationem exhibere, ad fontanas adorare (conf. Legg.
Liutpr. 6, 30), ad fontes votum facere, reddere, exsolvere, orare
ad fontes, offerre ad fontes, munus deferre, ad fontes luminaria
facere, candelam deferre.' This last no doubt was done only or
chiefly at night, when the flame reflected from the wave would
excite a religious awe.[1] The Saxons also were fonticolae: *wyllas*
and *flótwœter* are named in the AS. laws as objects of reverence. Beside the passage from Cnut (p. 102), the Poenitentiale
Ecgberti says 2, 22: 'gif hwilc man his ælmessan gehâte oððe
bringe tô hwilcon *wylle*'; 4, 19: 'gif hwâ his wæccan æt ænigum
wylle hæbbe (vigilias suas ad aliquem fontem habeat)'; the
Canones Edgari § 16 forbid *wilweorðunga* (well-worship). I am
not sure that a formal worship of water in Scandinavia is implied
in the saga quoted above (p. 102), where *vötn* is mentioned;
but that water was held sacred is a thing not to be doubted.
A lay in the Edda has near the beginning the remarkable words:
'hnigo *heilög vötn* af himinfiöllom,' fell holy waters from heaven's
hills. The Sclaveni as early as Procopius (B. Goth. 3, 14)
σέβουσι ποταμούς (worship rivers); and as late as Helmold
(1, 47) it is said of the Slavs at Faldera: lucorum et *fontium*
ceterarumque superstitionum multiplex error apud eos habetur
(see Suppl.).

Above all was the place honoured, where the wondrous element
leaps up from the lap of earth; a spring is in our older speech
ursprinc (-ges), and also *prunno*.[2]

Often enough the first appearing of a spring is ascribed to
divine agency or a miracle: Wuotan, Balder, Charles the Great,
each made the reviving fountain flow out of earth for his fainting
host (p. 226). Other springs are charmed out of the rock when
struck by a *staff* or a *horse's hoof*;[3] a saint plants a bough in

---

all. Into secular codes such prohibitions seem to have found their way first
through the Capitularies; the older codes had no penalties for idolatry, only the
AS. dômas of Wihtræd cap. 13 impose them on deofolgild in general.

[1] At Christmas people look *into their wells with candles*.

[2] From prinnan (ardere), as *sôt*, another word for well, comes from siodan
(fervere), *welle* (fluctus) from wallan (fervere), *sual* (subfrigidus) from suëlan (ardere),
conf. Gramm. 2, 29. 84; sprudeln to bubble up is from sprühen to fly off as sparks
do. In such words fire and water get wedded together.

[3] The Heliconian horse-fount (ἱπποκρήνη) was struck open by Pegasus: 'novi

the ground, and water bubbles up. But there are two theories even more generally received : that the water of sacred brooks and rivers is in the first instance poured by gods and superior beings out of *bowls* or *urns;* and that springs and wells are guarded by *snakes* or *dragons* lying near them (see Suppl.).

Water drawn at a holy season, at midnight, before sunrise, and in solemn silence, bore till a recent time the name of *heilawâc, heilwâc, heilwœge.* The first form, retaining the connecting vowel after a long syllable, proves the antiquity of the word, whose sacred meaning secured it against change. MS. 2, 149[b] : 'man seit (saith) von *heilawâge* uns vil, wie heil, wie guot ez sî, wie gar vollekomen der êren spil, wie gar sîn kraft verheilet swaz wundes an dem man versêret ist,' how good for healing wounds, etc. Martina 116 : 'Got, du frönde flüzzic *heilawâc*,' and in a like sense 248. 283. Applied to Christ and his cross, Mar. 224 : 'der boum ist gemeizzen, dâ daz *heilwœge* von bechumet, daz aller werlte gefrumet,' the tree whence cometh h. And more generally, 'ein *heilwâge*,' Diut. 1, 352; much later, in Anshelm's Chron. of Bern 1, 308, '*heilwag*' among other charms and magic appliances. Lastly, in Phil. von Sittewald (Strasb. 1677) 1, 483 : 'running spring-water, gathered on holy Christmas night, while the clock strikes twelve, and named *heilwag*, is good for pain of the navel,' Superst. 804. In this heilawâc we discover a very early mingling of heathen customs with christian. The common people believe to this very day, that at 12, or between 11 and 12, on Christmas or Easter night, *spring-water changes into wine* (Superst. 54. 792),[1] Wieselgren p. 412; and this belief rests on the supposition that the first manifestation of the Saviour's divinity took place at the marriage in Cana, where he *turned water into wine.* Now at Christmas they celebrated both his birth (epiphany, theophany, p. 281) and his baptism, and combined with these the memory of that miracle, to which was

---

fontis Dura medusæi quem præpetis ungula rupit,' Ov. Met. 5, 257 seq. So the vein of gold in a hill is laid open by a blow from a hoof. Rhea opens a spring in Arcadia with her staff :

ἀντανύσασα θεὰ μέγαν ὑψόθι πῆχυν
πλῆξεν ὄρος σκήπτρῳ· τὸ δέ οἱ δίχα πουλὺ διέστη,
ἐκ δ' ἔχεεν μέγα χεῦμα. Callimach. hy. Jov. 28.

[1] Zehn ehen eines weibes (her ten marriages), Leipz. 1735, p. 235.

given a special name, bethphania.[1] As far back as 387, Chry-
sostom preaching an Epiphany sermon at Antioch says that
people at that festival *drew running water at midnight, and kept
it a whole year,* and often two or three (no doubt for thaumaturgic
uses), and it remained fresh and uncorrupted.[2]   Superstitious
Christians then believed two things, a hallowing of the water at
midnight of the day of baptism, and a turning of it into wine
at the time of the bethphania: such water the Germans called
heilawâc,[3] and ascribed to it a wonderful power of healing diseases
and wounds, and of never spoiling (see Suppl.).

Possibly even in Syria an old pagan drawing of water became
veiled under new christian meanings.   In Germany other circumstances point undisguisedly to a heathen consecration of
water: it was not to be drawn at midnight, but in the morning *before sunrise, down stream* and *silently* (Superst. 89. 775),
usually on *Easter Sunday* (775-6) to which the above explanations do not so well apply; this water does not spoil, it restores
youth, heals eruptions, and makes the young cattle strong.[4]
Magic water, serving for unchristian divination, is to be *collected
before sunrise on a Sunday* in one glass *from three flowing springs;*
and *a taper is lighted* before the glass, as before a divine being
(Superst. H. c. 55–57).[5]   Here I bring in once again the Hessian

[1] The first manifestation of Christ was his birth, the second his baptism
(Candlemas), the third the marriage in Cana: 'Tertia apparitio fuit postea similiter
eodem die anno revoluto, cum esset 30 annorum et 13 dierum, sive quando
manifestavit se esse Deum *per mutationem aquae in vinum,* quod fuit primum
miraculum apertum, quod Dominus fecit in Cana Galilaeae, vel simpliciter primum
quod fecit. Et haec apparitio dicitur *bethphania* a βῆτω, quod est domus, et φάνειν,
quod est apparitio, quia ista apparitio facta fuit in domo in nuptiis. De his tribus
apparitionibus fit solemnitas in hac die.' Durantis Ration. div. offic. 6, 16. The
church consolidated the three manifestations into one festival.

[2] Tom. 2 (ed. Montfauc., Paris 1718), p. 369 : διὰ τοι τοῦτο καὶ μεσονυκτίῳ κατὰ
τὴν ἑορτὴν ταύτην ἅπαντες ὑδρευσάμενοι οἴκαδε τὰ νάματα ἀποτίθενται, καὶ εἰς ἐνιαυτὸν
ὁλόκληρον φυλάττουσι, ἅτε δὴ σήμερον ἁγιασθέντων τῶν ὑδάτων· καὶ τὸ σημεῖον γίνεται
ἐναργές, οὐ διαφθειρομένης τῆς τῶν ὑδάτων ἐκείνων φύσεως τῷ μήκει τοῦ χρόνου, ἀλλ'
εἰς ἐνιαυτὸν ὁλόκληρον καὶ δύο καὶ τρία ἔτη τοῦ σήμερον ἀντληθέντος ἀκεραίου καὶ
νεαροῦ μένοντος, καὶ μετὰ τοσοῦτον χρόνον τοῖς ἄρτι τῶν πηγῶν ἐξαρπασθεῖσιν ὕδασιν
ἁμιλλωμένου.

[3] And also *heilawîn?*   Frauenlob MS. 2, 213[b] on the 'garden that bears
heilwîn.' Altd. bl. 2, 294.

[4] Jul. Schmidt's Reichenf. p. 121. At Cassel I have heard bathing in the
'drusel' water commended as wholesome, but you must draw with the current, not
against. Probably the right time for it is Walburgis or Midsummer.

[5] The rite, like others cited by Hartlieb (who wrote in 1455), may be of classic
origin. In γαστρομαντεία, *i.e.* divining by a bellied jar (γάστρη) filled with water,
there also occurs the *torch* and the *innocent boy* (Hartl.'s 'ain rain kind'). Potter's
Antiq., 1, 764. Fabricii Bibliogr. antiq., ed. 3, p. 600.

custom mentioned at p. 58: on Easter Monday youths and maidens walk to the Hollow Rock in the mountains, draw *water from the cool spring in jugs to carry home*, and throw flowers in as an offering. Apparently this water-worship was Celtic likewise; the water of the rock-spring Karnant makes a broken sword *whole again*, but

> du muost des urspringes hân
> underm velse, ê in beschin der tac (ere day beshine it).

Parz. 254, 6. Tit. 5456. 5732.[1] Curious customs shew us in what manner young girls in the Pyrenees country *tell their own fortunes in spring water* on May-day morning.

We need not suppose that the peculiar properties of medicinal springs are the point here; no, it is the normal efficacy of the refreshing, strengthening, re-animating element.[2] Many places in Germany are called Heilbrunn, Heilborn, Heiligenbrunn, from the renewing effect of their springs, or the wonderful cures that have taken place at them. Heilbronn on the Neckar is called *Heilacprunno* in the oldest documents.[3] But certain springs and wells may have stood in especial repute. Of high renown are the ON. *Mimisbrunnr* and *Urðarbrunnr* (p. 407), which Sn. 17 calls 'brunnr miöc heilagr.' A Danish folksong (1, 318) tells of a *Maribokilde*, by whose clear waters a body hewn in pieces is *put together* again. Swedish lays celebrate *Ingemos källa* (Vis. 1, 244-5). We remember that old Frisian fount of Forseti, 'whence none drew water save *in silence*,' pp. 229, 230 (see Suppl.). Sacrifices were offered at such springs. Of the salutary effect of *hot* and *chalybeate* springs people must have been aware from immemorial time, witness the Aquae Mattiacae in the Roman time and those

---

[1] The *hardening* and *repairing of swords in water* (sverð herða, Sæm. 136ᵇ) was certainly believed in by the Germans too. The Vilkinasaga, cap. 40 p. 100, says: when dwarf Alberich had fashioned Nailring, he searched nine kingdoms before he found the water in which the sword could be tempered; at last he arrived at the water *Treya*, and there it was tempered. Our Eckenlied, str. 81, agrees with this, but is still more precise: 'dannoch was ez niht vollebrâht, dô fuorten'z zwei wildiu getwerc wol durch niun küneriche, biz daz si kâmen zuo der Drâl, diu dâ ze *Troige* rinnet, daz swert daz was sô liehtgemâl: *si harten'z in der Drôle*, des wart ez alsô fîn' (dwarfs bring it to the Drâl, that runs by Troige, etc.). Who can doubt any longer of real German lays forming the groundwork of the Vilk. saga?

[2] A man bitten by an adder will not die, if he can *leap over the nearest water* before the adder does so. Lenz's Schlangenkunde, p. 208.

[3] Böhmer's Reg. Karolor. nr. 740 (an. 841); Ecc. Fr. orient. 2, 893; 'der Necker vliuzet für Heilicbrunnen (flows past Holy-well),' MS. 2, 68ᵇ.

'aquae calidae' near Luxeuil (p. 83). When the Wetterau
people begin a new jug of chalybeate, they always spill the first
drop or two on the ground, they say 'to clear the dust away,'
for the jugs stand open, but it may have been once a libation to
the fountain-sprite.[1] Not only medicinal, but *salt* springs were
esteemed holy: ancient accounts of these will be presented in a
later chapter. The Mid. Ages cherished the notion of a *jung-brunnen*:[2] whoever bathes in it is both cured of diseases and
guarded from them; in it Ranchels shed her shaggy skin, and
became the beauteous Sigeminne (p. 433-4); such a spring has
sometimes the power even to change the bather's sex (see
Suppl.).[3]

In a spring near Nogent men and women bathed on St.
John's eve (Superst. L. 33); Holberg's comedy of Kilde-reisen
is founded on the Copenhagen people's practice of pilgriming to
a neighbouring spring on *S. Hans aften*, to heal and invigorate
themselves in its waters. On Midsummer eve the people of
Östergötland journeyed according to ancient custom to Lagman's
bergekälla near Skeninge, and drank of the well (Broocman 1,
187. 2, 676). In many parts of Germany some clear fountain is

---

[1] Where the Heathens ascribed the miraculous power of a spring to their wood
or water sprites, the Christians afterwards transferred it to their saints. I take an
instance from the Miracula S. Agili, written in the 12th century: Marvellous cures
were wrought at the *brook of St. Agilus*. Sed interim quorundam vesaniae occur-
rere libet, qui in digito Dei nequaquam haec fieri aestimantes, *daemoniacae*, pro
nefas, attribuunt *potestati*. Cumque miracula diffiteri nequeunt, id solum in
causam calumniae adsumunt, quod in *agresti* fiunt *loco*, ubi nullus Dei cultus, ubi
nullae sanctorum memoriae. O prudentiam! verentur homines sublimi ingenio,
ne ad ludibrium mortalium a *faunis, nymphis* vel *satyris*, ceterisve *ruris numinibus*,
res geratur ejusmodi. Nam ut de fabulis taceam, apud quos historiographorum
veterum sen modernorum legitur daemones visum coecis, mentem amentibus,
manus debilibus, gressum claudicantibus restaurasse? (Acta Bened. sec. 2, p. 333.)
The Swedish people ascribe the healing power of some springs to *white snakes*. In
1809 there flocked thousands from Halland and Vestergötland to the wonder-work-
ing Helsjö, a small lake near Rampegärde; they said, some children tending cattle
on the shore had often during the year seen a beautiful maiden sit on the bank,
holding a snake in her hand and shewing it to them. It is only every hundredth
year that this *water-maiden* with the snake appears (Bexell's Halland 2, 320; 3,
303). Multitudes from Norway and Halland visited a spring named *S. Olafskiälla*,
dropt money-offerings in, and carried on other superstition (Ödman's Bahuslän p.
169). In christian times healing fountains are believed to spring up near the
tombs of holy men, Bex. Hall. 3, 69; or from under a saint's body, Flodoard. re-
mens. 2, 3. I think it is with the hot baths at Aix that we must connect the *water-
maiden* with whose myth Charles the Great is mixed up, p. 435.
[2] Synonymously the OHG. *quecprunno*, MHG. *quecprunne*, Parz. 613, 9.
Fragm. 18, 267.
[3] Conf. the passages quoted in Mus. für altd. lit. 1, 260-3 from Montevilla,
from the Titurel and from H. Sachs.

visited at Whitsuntide, and the water drunk in jugs of a peculiar shape. Still more important is Petrarch's description of the annual bathing of the women of Cologne in the Rhine: it deserves to be quoted in full;[1] because it plainly proves that the cult prevailed not merely at here and there a spring, but in Germany's greatest river. From the Italian's unacquaintance with the rite, one might infer that it was foreign to the country whence all church ceremonies proceeded, and therefore altogether unchristian and heathenish. But Petrarch may not have had a minute knowledge of all the customs of his country; after his time at all events we find even there a lustration on St. John's day [described as an ancient custom then dying out]. Benedict de Falco's Descrizione de luoghi antiqui di Napoli (Nap. 1580) has the statement: 'in una parte populosa della citta giace la chiesa consegrata a S. Giovan battista, chiamata S. Giovan a mare. Era una *antica usanza*, hoggi non al tutto lasciata, che *la vigilia di S. Giovane*, verso la sera e 'l securo del di, *tutti huomini e donne andare al mare, e nudi lavarsi;* persuasi purgarsi de loro peccati, alla focchia degli antichi, che peccando andavano al Tevere lavarsi.' And long before Petrarch, in Augustine's time, the rite was practised in Libya, and is de-

[1] Franc. Petrarchae De rebus familiar. epistolae, lib. i. ep. 4: Aquis digressum, sed prius, unde ortum oppidi nomen putant, aquis bajano more tepentibus ablutum, excepit Agrippina Colonia, quae ad sinistram Rheni latus sita est, locus et situ et flumine clarus et populo. Mirum in terra barbarica quanta civilitas, quae urbis species, quae virorum gravitas, quae munditiae matronarum. Forte *Johannis baptistae vigilia* erat dum illuc applicui, et jam ad occidentem sol vergebat: confestim amicorum monitu (nam et ibi amicos prius mihi fama pepererat quam meritum) ab hospitio traducor ad fluvium insigne spectaculum visurus. Nec fallebar; *omnis enim ripa praeclaro et ingenti mulierum agmine tegebatur.* Obstupui, dii boni, quae forma, quae facies, quis habitus! amare potuisset quisquis eo non praeoccupatum animum attulisset. In loco paullum altiore constiteram, unde in ea quae gerebantur intenderem. Incredibilis sine offensione concursus erat, vicissimque alacres, pars *herbis odoriferis incinctae, reductisque post cubitum manicis, candidas in gurgite manus ac brachia lavabant*, nescio quid blandum peregrino murmure colloquentes. [A few lines omitted.] Unum igitur ex eo [amicorum] numero admirans et ignarus rerum percunctatus vergiliano illo versiculo: 'Quid vult concursus ad amnem, quidve petunt animae?' responsum accepi: *pervetustum gentis ritum esse,* vulgo persuasum, praesertim femineo, *omnem totius anni calamitatem imminentem fluviali illius diei ablutione purgari,* et deinceps laetiora succedere; itaque *lustrationem* esse *annuam,* inexhaustoque semper studio cultam colendamque. Ad haec ego subridens: 'O nimium felices' inquam '*Rheni* accolae, quoniam *ille* miserias purgat, nostras quidem nec *Padus* unquam purgare valuit nec *Tiberis.* Vos vestra mala Britannis Rheno vectore transmittitis; nos nostra libenter Afris atque Illyriis mitteremus, sed nobis (ut intelligi datur) pigriora sunt flumina.' Commoto risu, sero tandem inde discessimus. [A few lines omitted.] The letter is of 1330, and addressed to Card. Colonna. We find it quoted so early as by Kaisersberg (Omeiss 35°).

nounced by that Father as a relic of paganism : ' natali Johannis,
de solemnitate superstitiosa pagana, Christiani *ad mare veniebant*,
et se baptizabant' (Opp., Paris 1683, tom. 5, p. 903); and again:
' ne ullus in festivitate S. Johannis in *fontibus* aut *paludibus* aut
in *fluminibus*, nocturnis aut matutinis horis *se lavare* praesumat,
quia haec infelix consuetudo adhuc de Paganorum observatione
remansit' (Append. to tom. 5 p. 462). Generally sanctioned by
the church it certainly was not, yet it might be allowed here and
there, as a not unapt reminder of the Baptizer in the Jordan,
and now interpreted of him, though once it had been heathen.
It might easily come into extensive favour, and that not as a
christian feast alone : to our heathen forefathers St. John's day
would mean the festive middle of the year, when the sun turns,
and there might be many customs connected with it. I confess,
if Petrarch had witnessed the bathing in the river at some small
town, I would the sooner take it for a native rite of the ancient
Germani; at Cologne, the holy city so renowned for its relics, I
rather suspect it to be a custom first introduced by christian
tradition (see Suppl.).[1]

There are lakes and springs whose waters periodically *rise* and
fall : from either phenomenon mischief is prognosticated, a death,
war, approaching dearth. When the reigning prince is about to
die, the river is supposed to stop in its course, as if to indicate its
grief (Deut. sag. no. 110); if the well runs dry, the head of the
family will die soon after (no. 108). A spring that either *runs
over* or *dries up*, foreboding dearth, is called *hungerquelle, hunger-
brunnen* (Stald. 2, 63). Wössingen near Durlach has a *hunger-
brunnen*, which is said to flow abundantly when the year is going
to be unfruitful, and then also the fish it produces are small.[2]

---

[1] In Poland and Silesia, and perhaps in a part of Russia, girls who have over-
slept matin-time on *Easter* Monday are *soused with water* by the lads, and flogged
with birch twigs ; they are often pulled out of bed at night, and dragged to a *river*
or *cistern*, or a *trough filled with water*, and are ducked. The Silesians call this
schmagostern (even Estor's Oberhess. idiot. has *schmakustern*=giving the rod at
Easter); perh. from Pol. śmić, Boh. smyti, so that śmigust would be rinsing
[Suppl. says, ' better from smagać to flog ']. The Poles say both śmić and dyngo-
wać, dyngus, of the splashing each other with water (conf. Hanusch, p. 197), and
the time of year seems to be St. John's day as well as Easter. In the Russian gov.
of Archangel, the people *bathe in the river* on June 23, and sprinkle kupálnitsa
(ranunculus acris), Karamzin 1, 73-4 [the same is also a surname of St. Agrippina,
on whose day, June 24, river-bathing (kupálnia) commences]. Everywhere a
belief in the sacredness of the Easter-bath and St. John's-bath.
[2] Mone's Anz. 8, 221. 340, who gives a forced and misleading explanation of the

Such a hunger-spring there was by Halle on the Saale; when the peasants came up to town, they looked at it, and if it ran over, they said: 'this year, things 'll be dear.' The like is told of fountains near Rosia in the Siennese, and near Chateaudun in the Orleanese. As Hunger was personified, it was easy to make him meddle with springs. A similar Nornborn was noticed, p. 405. I insert Dietmar of Merseburg's report (1, 3) of lake Glomazi in the Slav parts of the Elbe valley : 'Glomazi[1] est fons non plus ab Albi quam duo milliaria positus, qui unam de se paludem generans, mira, ut incolae pro vero asserunt oculisque approbatum est a multis, saepe operatur. Cum bona pax indigenis profutura suumque haec terra non mentitur fructum, *tritico et avena ac glandine* refertus, laetos vicinorum ad se crebro *confluentium* efficit animos. Quando autem saeva belli tempestas ingruerit, *sanguine et cinere* certum futuri exitus indicium praemonstrat. Hunc omnis incola plus quam ecclesias, spe quamvis dubia, *veneratur et timet.*'[2] But apart from particular fountains, by a mere *gauging of water* a season of dearth or plenty, an increase or decrease of wealth may be divined, according as the water poured into a vessel *rises* or *falls* (Superst. F, 43 ; and no. 958 in Praetor's Saturnalien p. 407). This looks to me like a custom of high antiquity. Saxo Gram. p. 320 says, the image of the god Svantovit in Rügen held in its right hand a horn : 'quod sacerdos sacrorum ejus peritus annuatim mero perfundere consueverat, ex *ipso liquoris habitu sequentis anni copias prospecturus.*
. . . Postero die, populo prae foribus excubante, detractum simulacro poculum curiosius speculatus, si quid *ex inditi liquoris mensura substractum* fuisset, ad *sequentis anni inopiam* pertinere putabat. Si *nihil* ex consuetae foecunditatis habitu *diminutum* vidisset, ventura agrorum ubertatis tempora praedicabat.' The wine was emptied out, and water poured into the horn (see Suppl.).

---

word. Another name is *schändlebach* (beck that brings shame, confusion): such a one was pointed out to me on the plain near Cassel, and Simpliciss. 5, 14 mentions the *schändlibach* by Oberneheim, which only runs when misfortune befalls the land. [SUPPL. adds the MHG. *schantbach*, Weisth. 1, 760, and 'der *schanden bechelin*,' Frauenlob p. 186]. So, when the *Lutterborn* by Herbershausen (Helperhusen) near Göttingen runs, it is a dear season ; but when the spider builds in Helperhouse mill, and the swallow in the millwheel, the times are good.

[1] Al. 'Glomuzi, Zlumici'; now the Lommatsch district.

[2] Capitul. an. 794 (Pertz 3, 74) : 'experimento didicimus, in anno quo illa valida famis irrepsit, *ebullire* vacuas annonas (empty ears), a daemonibus devoratas.'

Whirlpools and *waterfalls* were doubtless held in special veneration; they were thought to be put in motion by a superior
being, a river-sprite. The Danube whirlpool and others still
have separate legends of their own. Plutarch (in his Cæsar,
cap. 19) and Clement of Alex. (Stromat. 1, 305) assure us that
the German prophetesses watched the eddies of rivers, and by
their whirl and noise explored the future. The Norse name for
such a vortex is *fors*, Dan. *fos*, and the Isl. sög. 1, 226 expressly
say, 'blôtaði *forsin* (worshipped the f.).' The legend of the
river-sprite *fossegrim* was touched upon, p. 493; and in such a
fors dwelt the dwarf Andvari (Sæm. 180. Fornald. sög. 1, 152).
But *animal* sacrifices seem to have been specially due to the
whirlpool (δῖνος), as the black lamb (or goat) to the fossegrim;
and the passages quoted from Agathias on pp. 47, 100, about the
Alamanns offering horses to the rivers and ravines, are to the
same purpose. The Iliad 21, 131 says of the Skamander:

$$\text{ᾧ δὴ δηθὰ πολεῖς ἱερεύετε ταύρους,}$$
$$\text{ζωοὺς δ' ἐν δίνῃσι καθίετε μώνυχας ἵππους·}$$

(Lo, to the river this long time many a bull have ye hallowed,
Many a whole-hoofed horse have ye dropped alive in his eddies);
and Pausan. viii. 7, 2 : τὸ δὲ ἀρχαῖον καθίεσαν ἐς τὴν Δεινὴν
(a water in Argolis, conn. with δῖνος) τῷ Ποσειδῶνι ἵππους οἱ
Ἀργεῖοι κεκοσμένους χαλινοῖς. Horace, Od. 3, 13: O fons
Bandusiae, non sine floribus cras donaberis haedo (see Suppl.).

It is pretty well known, that even before the introduction of
Christianity or christian baptism, the heathen Norsemen had a
hallowing of new-born infants by means of water; they called
this *vatni ausa*, sprinkling with water. Very likely the same
ceremony was practised by all other Teutons, and they may have
ascribed a peculiar virtue to the water used in it, as Christians do
to *baptismal water* (Superst. Swed. 116). After a christening,
the Esthonians will bribe the clerk to let them have the water,
and then *splash it up* against the walls, to secure honours and
dignities for the child (Superst. M, 47).

It was a practice widely prevalent to turn to strange superstitious uses the *water of the millwheel* caught as it glanced off the
paddles. Old Hartlieb mentions it (Superst. H, c. 60), and vulgar
opinion approves it still (Sup. I, 471. 766). The Servians call

such water *omaya*, rebound, from omanuti, omakhnuti, to rebound.
Vuk, under the word, observes that women go early on St.
George's day (Apr. 23), to catch it, especially off a small brook-
mill (kashitchara), and bathe in it. Some carry it home the
evening before, and sprinkle it with all manner of broken greens :
they think all evil and harm will then *glance off* their bodies *like
the water off the millwheel* (Vuk sub v. Jurjev dan). Similar,
though exactly the reverse, is the warning not to *flirt the water*
off your hands after washing in the morning, else you *flirt away*
your luck for the day (Sup. I, 21).

Not only brooks and rivers (p. 585), but *rain* also was in the
childlike faith of antiquity supposed to be let fall out of bowls by
gods of the sky; and riding witches are still believed to carry
pitchers, out of which they pour storm and hail upon the plains,
instead of the rain or dew that trickled down before. [1]

When the heavens were shut, and the fields languished in
drought, the granting of *rain* depended in the first instance on a
deity, on Donar, or Mary and Elias, who were supplicated accordingly (pp. 173-6). [2] But in addition to that, a special charm
was resorted to, which infallibly procured 'rainwater,' and in a
measure compelled the gods to grant it. A little girl, *completely
undressed* and led outside the town, had to dig up *henbane* (bilsen-
kraut, OHG. pilisa, hyoscyamus) with the little finger of her
right hand, and tie it to the little toe of her right foot; she was
then solemnly conducted by the other maidens to the nearest
river, and *splashed with water*. This ceremony, reported by
Burchard of Worms (Sup. C, 201ᵇ) and therefore perhaps still in
use on the Rhine or in Hesse in the 11th cent., comes to us with
the more weight, as, with characteristic differences which put all
direct borrowing out of the question, it is still in force among
Servians and Mod. Greeks. Vuk, under the word 'dodole,'
describes the Servian custom. A girl, called the *dodola*, is *stript
naked*, but so *wrapt up in grass, herbs and flowers*, that nothing of

---

[1] The Peruvians believe in a *rain-goddess*, who sits in the clouds with a *pitcher
of water*, ready to pour it out at the right time; if she delays, her *brother* with
thunder and lightning smites the pitcher in pieces. Garcilaso de la Vega's Histt.
Incarum peruanorum 11, 27 ; conf. Talvj's Characteristik der volkslieder, p. 126.

[2] I will here add, from Anton's Coll. on the Slavs, the substance of a Wallachian song, which the children sing when the corn is endangered by drought :
'*Papaluga* (father Luga), climb into heaven, open its doors, and send down rain
from above, that well the rye may grow ! '

her person is to be seen, not even the face.[1] Escorted by other maidens, dodola passes from house to house, before each house they form a ring, she standing in the middle and dancing alone. The goodwife comes out and *empties a bucket of water* over the girl, who keeps dancing and whirling all the while; her companions sing songs, repeating after every line the burden 'oy dodo, oy dodo le!' The second of these rain-hymns (piesme dodolske) in Vuk's Coll. nos. 86–88 (184–8 of ed. 2) runs thus:

To God doth our doda call,   oy dodo oy dodo le!

That dewy rain may fall,   oy dodo oy dodo le!

And drench the diggers all,   oy dodo oy dodo le!

The workers great and small,   oy dodo oy dodo le!

Even those in house and stall, oy dodo oy dodo le!

And they are sure that rain will come at once. In Greece, when it has not rained for a fortnight or three weeks, the inhabitants of villages and small towns do as follows. The children choose one of themselves who is from eight to ten years old, usually a poor orphan, whom they *strip naked* and *deck from head to foot with field herbs and flowers*: this child is called πυρπηροῦνα. The others lead her round the village, singing a hymn, and every housewife has to *throw a pailful of water over the pyrperuna's head*, and hand the children a para (¼ of a farthing). The Mod. Greek hymn is in Theod. Kind's τραγῴδια τῆς νέας Ἑλλάδος, Leipz. 1833, p. 13. Passow, nos. 311–3, p. 627. Neither Greek nor Slavic will explain why the rain-girl should be called *dodola* (caressingly *doda*) and πυρπηροῦνα·[2] Burchard very likely could have given us a German designation equally inscrutable. But the meaning of the performance is clear: as the water from the bucket on the dodola, so is rain out of heaven to stream down on the earth; it is the mystic and genuinely symbolic association of means with end. Just so the rebound off the millwheel was to send evil flying, and the lustration in the stream to wash away all

---

[1] Is this covering merely to protect the maiden's modesty, or has it some further reason? We shall see that personations of spring and summer were in like manner enveloped in foliage.

[2] Kind, pp. 86-7, gives some variant forms, but all the explanations appear to me farfetched. Both the Greek and the Servian names have the reduplication so characteristic of folk-words. [Slav. dozhd is rain, and zhd represents either gd or dd; if this be the root, dodo-la may be a dimin.]

future illnesses. Celtic tradition, without bringing in girl or
child, makes the *pouring out of water* in seasons of great drought
evoke the wished-for rain. The huntsmen go to the fountain of
Barenton in the forest of Breziliande, scoop up the water in their
horns, and *spill it on the stones;* immediately the rain-clouds rise
and refresh the land.[1] The custom, with an addition of church
ceremonial, is kept up to this day. Led by the clergy, amid
chanting and pealing of bells, with five great banners borne in
front, the parish walks in procession to the spring, and the head
of the commune *dips his foot* crosswise in the fountain of Barenton; they are then sure of its raining before the procession
arrives home again.[2] The mayor's foot alone is wetted instead of
the child, or a little water only is poured out as a beginning of
that which is to fall in masses from the sky. The scanty offering
brings the great bounty to our door. In Spain, when hot weather
lasts long, an image of the Virgin arrayed in mourning (imagen
cubierta de luto) is solemnly escorted through the villages, to
obtain the blessing of rain,[3] as in the Liège procession (pp.174-5),
with which again that described by Petronius agrees (p. 175);
only here the symbolic libation is left out. But of those herbs
that were tied round the child, some most likely were of magic
power; such a use of henbane is otherwise unknown to me.
Lastly, the Bavarian *waterbird* seems identical with dodola and
pyrperuna. The man who is the last to drive out on Whitmonday[4]
is led by the other workmen into the nearest wood, and *tied
round and round with leaves and twigs or rushes;* then they ride in
triumph through the village, and everybody that has young legs
follows the procession to the pond or brook, where the *waterbird
is solemnly tumbled* off his horse *into the water* (Schm. 1, 320).
In Austria too the village lads elect a Whitsun king, *dress him
up in green boughs, blacken his face and pitch him into the brook*
(Denis, Lesefr. 1, 130). In these two cases the 'votis vocare

---

[1] Roman de Rou, v. 11514 (the passage extracted in the notes to Iwein, pp.
262-3).
[2] Revue de Paris, tome 41, pp. 47-58. Villemar adds, that children throw
pins into the fountain, while they call out: 'ris donc, fontaine de Berendon, et je
te donnerai une épingle!' and the fay of the fountain is supposed to be made
friendly by the gift. Conf. 'libamina lacui exhibere', p. 596.
[3] Don Quixote 1, 52 (Ideler 2, 435). And in other places it was the custom in
time of drought, to carry the bodies of saints about, Flodoard. rem. 4, 41.
[4] As the girl who oversleeps herself on Easter morning is ducked (p. 590).

imbrem' has dropt out altogether, and been replaced by a mere
Whitsun drollery at the cost of the laziest man;[1] but I have
little doubt that the same purpose lies at the bottom of the
custom (see Suppl.).

Of goddesses, no doubt the bath-loving *Nerthus* and *Holda*
are the most nearly connected with water-worship (Holda lives in
wells, pp. 268, 487) ; and to them must be added swan-maidens,
merminnes (p. 433), water-holdes, spring-holdes (p. 268), water-
muhmes and nixies. To all of them particular rivers, brooks,
pools and springs can be consecrated and assigned as their
abode; *Oegir* (p. 237) and *Rân* (pp. 311, 497) ruled in the sea,
and the waves are called their daughters : all this gives a new
stamp to the veneration of the element. Of this very natural,
but not essential, combination of simple rude water-worship with
a faith in higher beings, I will give a few more specimens.

As those who cross a river by ferry or by bridge have to dread
the power of the dæmon that dwells in it (p. 497), so vulgar
opinion in Sweden (Sup. K, 40) holds it advisable, in crossing
any water in the dark, to *spit three times*, as a safeguard against
evil influences.[2] Precautions are also taken in drawing water from
a well : before drawing any, the Greeks at Mykono *salute three
times* in honour of Teloni (fountain-sprite).[3] For a thief to throw
in the water a little of what he has stolen (Sup. I, 836), means
sacrificing to the water-sprite. The Vita S. Sulpicii Biturig.
(died 644) relates (Acta Bened. sec. 2, p. 172): 'gurges quidam
erat in Virisionensium situs agello (Vierzon, in Biturigibus)
aquarum mole copiosus, utpote *daemonibus consecratus ;* et si
aliquis causa qualibet ingrederetur eundem, repente *funibus
daemoniacis* circumplexus amittebat crudeliter vitam.' A more
decisive testimony to the worship of water itself is what Gregory
of Tours tells of a lake on Mt. Helanus (De gloria confess.,
cap. 2) : 'Mons erat in Gabalitano territorio (Gevaudan) cogno-
mento Helanus, lacum habens magnum. Ad quem certo tempore multitudo rusticorum, *quasi libamina lacui illi exhibens,*

---

[1] Sup. I, 842: the lazy maid, on carrying home her first grass, is ducked or
splashed, to prevent her going to sleep over grass-cutting.
[2] The spirits cannot abide *spitting* (p. 514).
[3] Villoison in Maltebrun, Annales de voy. 2, 180. Artemidorus's Oneirocrit.
2 27 (Reiff 1, 189) admits well-nymphs : νύμφαι τε γάρ εἰσιν ἐν τῷ φρέατι. Fauriel:
τὸ στοιχειὸν τοῦ ποταμοῦ.

linteamina projiciebat ac pannos qui ad usum vestimenti virilis praebentur: nonnulli lanae vellera, plurimi etiam formas casei [1] ac cerae vel panis, diversasque species unusquisque juxta vires suas, quae dinumerare perlongum puto. Veniebant autem cum plaustris potum cibumque deferentes, *mactantes animalia et per triduum epulantes*. Quarta autem die cum discedere deberent, anticipabat eos *tempestas* cum tonitruo et coruscatione valida; et in tantum imber ingens cum lapidum violentia descendebat, ut vix se quisquam eorum putaret evadere. Sic fiebat *per singulos annos*, et involvebatur insipiens populus in errore.'—No god or spirit shews his face here, the yearly sacrifice is offered to the lake itself, and the feast winds up with the coming *tempest*. Gervase of Tilbury (in Leibnitz 1, 982) tells of a lake on Mt. Cavagum in Catalonia: 'in cujus summitate *lacus* est aquam continens subnigram et in fundo imperscrutabilem. Illic *mansio* fertur esse *daemonum* ad modum palatii dilatata et janua clausa; facies tamen ipsius mansionis sicut ipsorum daemonum vulgaribus est incognita ac invisibilis. In lacum si quis aliquam lapideam aut aliam solidam projecerit materiam, statim *tanquam offensis daemonibus tempestas erumpit*.'[2] Then comes the story of a girl who is carried off by the watersprites, and kept in the lake seven years.

Lakes cannot endure to have their depth gauged. On the *Mummelsee*, when the sounders had let down all the cord out of nine nets with a plummet without finding a bottom, suddenly the raft they were on began to sink, and they had to seek safety in a rapid flight to land (Simplic. 5, 10). A man went in a boat to the middle of the *Titisee*, and payed out no end of line after the plummet, when there came out of the waves a terrible cry: 'Measure me, and I'll eat you up!' In a great fright the man desisted from his enterprise, and since then no one has dared

---

[1] Formages, whence fromages.

[2] This raising of a storm by *throwing stones into a lake or wellhead* is a Teutonic, a Celtic and a Finnish superstition, as the examples quoted shew. The watersprite avenges the desecration of his holy stream. Under this head come the stories of the Mummelsee (Deut. sag. no. 59. Simplic. 5, 9), of the Pilatussee (Lothar's Volkssag. 232. Dobenek 2, 118. Gutslaff p. 288. Mone's Anz. 4, 423), of L. Camarina in Sicily (Camarinam movere), and above all, of Berenton well in Breziliande forest, Iwein 553–672, where however it is the well-water poured on the well-rock that stirs up the storm: conf. supra, p. 594, and the place in Pontus mentioned by Beneke, p. 269. The lapis manalis also conjured up rain, O. Müller's Etr. 2, 97.

to sound the depth of the lake (Mone's Anz. 8, 536). There is
a similar story in Thiele 3, 73, about Huntsöe, that some people
tried to fathom its depth with a ploughshare tied to the line,
and from below came the sound of a spirit-voice: 'i maale vore
vägge, vi skal maale jeres lägge!' Full of terror they hauled
up the line, but instead of the share found an old horse's skull
fastened to it.[1]

It is the custom in Esthonia for a newly married wife to drop a
present *into the well* of the house; it is a nationality that seems
particularly given to worshipping water. There is a detailed
account of the *holy Wöhhanda*, a rivulet of Livonia. It rises
near Ilmegerve, a village of Odenpä district in Esthonia, and
after its junction with the Medda, falls into L. Peipus. The
source is in a *sacred grove*, within whose bounds no one dares to
cut a tree or break a twig: whoever does it is sure to die that
year. Both brook and fountain are kept clean, and are put to
rights once a year; if anything is thrown into the spring or
the little lake through which it flows, the weather turns to *storm*
(see Suppl.).

Now in 1641 Hans Ohm of Sommerpahl, a large landowner
who had come into the country in the wake of the Swedes, built
a mill on the brook, and when bad harvests followed for several
years, the Ehsts laid it all to the desecration of the *holy stream*,
who allowed no obstructions in his path; they fell upon the mill,
burnt it down, and destroyed the piles in the water. Ohm went
to law, and obtained a verdict against the peasants; but to
rid himself of new and grievous persecutions, he induced pastor
Gutslaff, another German, to write a treatise[2] specially com-
bating this superstition. Doubtless we learn from it only the
odious features of the heathenish cult. To the question, how
good or bad weather could depend on springs, brooks and lakes,
the Ehsts replied: 'it is our ancient faith, the men of old have
so taught us (p. 25, 258); mills have been burnt down on this

---

[1] The people about L. Baikal believe it has no bottom. A priest, who could
dive to any depth, tried it, but was so frightened by the lôs (dragons, sea-monsters),
that, if I remember rightly, he died raving mad.—TRANS.

[2] A short account of the holy brook (falsely so called) Wöhhanda in Liefland,
whereby the ungodly burning of Sommerpahl mill came to pass. Given from
Christian zeal against unchristian and heathenish superstition, by Joh. *Gutslaff*,
Pomer. pastor at Urbs in Liefland. Dorpt 1644 (8vo, 407 pp. without the Dedic.
and Pref.). An extract in Kellgren (Suomi 9, 72–92).

brook before now (p. 278), he will stand no crowding.' The Esth. name is ' pöha yögge,' the Lettic ' shvèti ubbe,' *i.e.* holy brook. By means of it they could regulate the weather, and when they wanted *rain*, they had only to *throw* something *in* (p. 25). Once, when three oxen were drowned in the lake, there followed snow and frost (p. 26). At times there came up out of the brook *a carl with blue and yellow stockings :* evidently the spirit of the brook.

Another Esthonian story is about *L. Eim* changing his bed. On his banks lived wild and wicked men, who never mowed the meadows that he watered, nor sowed the fields he fertilized, but robbed and murdered, so that his bright wave was befouled with the blood of the slain. And the lake mourned ; and one evening he called his fish together, and mounted with them into the air. The brigands hearing a din cried : ' the Eim has left his bed, let us collect his fish and hidden treasure.' But the fish were gone, and nothing was found at the bottom but snakes, toads and salamanders, which came creeping out and lodged with the ruffian brood. But the Eim rose higher and higher, and swept like a white cloud through the air ; said the hunters in the woods : ' what is this murky weather passing over us ? ' and the herdsmen : ' what white swan is flying in the sky ? ' All night he hung among the stars, at morn the reapers spied him, how that he was sinking, and the white swan became as a white ship, and the ship as a dark drifting cloud. And out of the waters came a voice: 'get thee hence with thy harvest, I come to dwell with thee.' Then they bade him welcome, if he would bedew their fields and meadows, and he sank down and stretched himself in his new couch. They set his bed in order, built dikes, and planted young trees around to cool his face. Their fields he made fertile, their meadows green ; and they danced around him, so that old men grew young for joy.[1]

[1] Fr. Thiersch in Taschenbuch für liebe und freundschaft 1809, p. 179. Must not *Eim* be the same as *Embach* (mother-beck, fr. emma mother, conf. öim mother-in-law) near Dorpat, whose origin is reported as follows ? When God had created heaven and earth, he wished to bestow on the beasts a king, to keep them in order, and commanded them to dig for his reception a deep broad beck, on whose banks he might walk; the earth dug out of it was to make a hill for the king to live on. All the beasts set to work, the hare measured the land, the fox's brush trailing after him marked the course of the stream ; when they had finished hollowing out the bed, God poured water into it out of his golden bowl (Verhandl. der esthn. gesellschaft, Dorpat 1840. 1, 40–42). The two stories differ as to the manner of preparing the new bed.

The Greeks and Romans personified their *rivers* into male beings; a bearded old man pours the flowing spring out of his urn (pp. 585. 593). Homer finely pictures the elemental strife between water and fire in the battle of the *Skamander* with Hephæstus: the river is a god, and is called ἄναξ, Od. 5, 445. 451. The Indian *Ganges* too is an august deity. Smaller streams and fountains had nymphs set over them.[1] In our language, most of the *rivers' names* are feminine (Gramm. 3, 384–6), there must therefore have been female watersprites. Twelve or eighteen streams are specified by name in Sæm. 43ᵇ. Sn. 4. I single out *Leiptr*, by whose clear water, as by Styx or Acheron, oaths were sworn. Sæm. 165ᵃ: 'at eno liosa *Leiptrar* vatni.' A dæmon of the Rhine is nowhere named in our native traditions, but the Edda calls the *Rín* (fem.) svinn, åskunna (prudens, a diis oriunda, Sæm. 248ᵃ). And in the bosom of the Rhine lie treasure and gold. The Goths buried their beloved king Alaric in the bed of a river near Consentia (Cosenza), which they first dug out of its course, and then led back over the corpse (Jornandes, cap. 30); the Franks, when crossing a river, offered sacrifice to it (p. 45).

But where the sacred water of a river sweeps round a piece of meadow land, and forms an *ea* (aue), such a spot is specially marked out for the residence of gods; witness Wunsches ouwe (p. 140), Pholes ouwa (p. 225).[2] Equally venerable were *islands* washed by the pure sea wave, Fosetesland (p. 230), and the island of Nerthus (p. 251).

In the *sea* itself dwelt Oegir (p. 237) and Rån (p. 311), and the waves are their daughters: the Edda speaks *of nine waves*, and gives their names (Sn. 124, conf. the riddles in the Hervararsaga, pp. 478-9); this reminds me of the *nona unda* in the Waltharius 1343, and the 'fluctus decumanus' [every tenth wave being the biggest, Festus, and Ov. Trist. i. 2, 50]. There must also have been another god of the sea, Geban (p. 239, conf. p. 311). Then,

---

[1] The Romans appear to have much elaborated their cultus of rivers and brooks, as may be seen by the great number of monuments erected to river-gods. I will here add the testimony of Tacitus, Ann. 1, 79: 'sacra et lucos et aras *patriis amnibus* dicare.'

[2] Gallus Ohem's Chronik von *Reichenau* (end of 15th cent.) quoted in Schönhuth's Reichenau, Freib. 1836, p. v.: 'the isle is to this day esteemed *honourable* and *holy*; unchristened babes are not buried in it, but carried out and laid beside a small house with a saint's image in it, called the chindli-bild.

according to the Edda, there lies in the deep sea an enormous 'worm,' miðgarðs-ormr, biting his own tail and begirding the whole earth. The immensity of ocean (Goth. *marisáivs*) is expressed in the OHG. names *endilmeri* and *wendilmeri* (Graff 2, 829); conf. enteo and wenteo (p. 564), entil and wentil (p. 375). An AS. term *gârsecg* I have tried to explain in Zeitschr. für d. a. 1, 578. As the running stream will suffer no evil-doer in it, so is 'daz *mer* so reine, daz ez keine bôsheit mac gelîden,' so clean that it no wickedness can bear, Wiener merfart 392 (see Suppl.).

2. FIRE.

Fire,[1] like water, is regarded as a *living* being : corresponding to quecprunno (p. 588n.) we have a *quecfiur*, daz quecke fiwer, Parz. 71, 13; Serv. vatra *zhiva*, ogan *zhivi* (vivus, Vuk 1, xlvi. and 3, 8. 20); τὸ πῦρ θηρίον ἔμψυχον of the Egyptians, Herod. 3, 16; ignis *animal*, Cic. de N. D. 3, 14, *i.e.* a devouring hungry insatiable beast, vorax flamma; frekr (avidus), Sæm. 50[b]; bitar fiur, Hel. 78, 22; bitar logna 79, 20; grâdag logna (greedy lowe), 130, 23; grim endi grâdag 133, 11; eld unfuodi (insatiabilis) 78, 23; it licks with its tongue, eats all round it, *pastures*, νέμεται, Il. 23, 177; the land gets eaten clean by it, πυρὶ χθὼν νέμεται, 2, 780; 'lêztu eld *eta* iöfra bygdir, Sæm. 142ᵃ; it is restless, ἀκάματον πῦρ, Il. 23, 52. To be spoken to is a mark of living things: 'heitr ertu hripuðr!' (hot art thou, Fire), Sæm. 40ᵃ. The ancient Persians made a god of it, and the Indian Agni (ignis) is looked upon as a god. The Edda makes fire a brother of the wind and sea, therefore himself alive and a god, Sn. 126. Our people compare the element to a cock flying from house to house : 'I'll set the *red cock* on your roof' is a threat of the incendiary; 'ein roten han aufs stadel setzen,' H. Sachs iv. 3, 86ᵈ; *rôter schîn*, Gudr. 786, 2.

An antique heathen designation of the great World-fire, ON. *muspell*, OHG. OS. *muspilli, mudspelli, mutspelli*, has already been noticed, p. 558. The mythic allusions here involved can only be unfolded in the sequel; the meaning of the word seems to be ligni perditor, as fire in general is also called *bani viðar*,

[1] Names for it, Gramm. 3, 352; Eddic names, Sæm. 50ᵇ, Sn. 187-8.

grand viðar (bane, crusher, of wood), Sn. 126, *her alls viðar*,
Sæm. 228[b]. Another difficult expression is *eikin fur*, Sæm. 83[b].
Of *vafrlogi* (quivering flame), suggesting the MHG. ' daz *bibende*
fiwer' (Tund. 54, 58), I likewise forbear to speak; conf. Chap.
XXXI., Will o' the wisp (see Suppl.).

A regular worship of fire seems to have had a more limited
range than the veneration of water; it is only in that passage of
the AS. prohibitions quoted p. 102, and in no other, that I find
mention of fire. A part of the reverence accorded to it is no
doubt included in that of the light-giving and warming *sun*, as
Julius Caesar (p. 103 above) names *Sol* and *Vulcanus* together,
and the Edda *fire* and *sun*, praising them both as supreme :
' *eldr* er beztr med ŷta sonum, ok *sólar* sŷn,' fire is best for men,
Sæm. 18[b] (as Pindar says water is). In Superst. B, 17, I understand ' observatio pagana in *foco* ' of the flame on the hearth or in
the oven : where a *hearth-fire* burns, no lightning strikes (Sup. I,
126) ; when it crackles, there will be strife (322. 534). Compare
with this the Norwegian exposition (p. 242) ; so long as a child
is unbaptized, you must *not let the fire out* (Sup. Swed. 22), conf.
kasta eld, tagi i elden (24-5. 54. 68. 107).—The Esthonians
throw *gifts* into fire, as well as into water (Sup. M, 11) ; to
pacify the flame, they *sacrifice a fowl* to it (82).

A distinction seems to have been made between friendly and
malignant fires; among the former the Greeks reckoned brimstone
fire, as they call sulphur θεἳον, divine smoke (Il. 8, 135. Od. 22,
481. 493). In O. Fr. poems I often find such forms of cursing
as : *mal feu* arde ! Tristr. 3791; *maus feus* et *male flambe*
m'arde ! Méon 3, 227. 297. Ren. 19998. This evil fire is what
the Norse Loki represents; and as Loki or the devil breaks loose,
we say, when a fire begins, that it *breaks loose, breaks out, gets out,*
as if from chains and prison : ' worde vür los,' Doc. in Sartorius's
Hanse p. 27 ; in Lower Germany an alarm of fire was given in the
words ' für los ! ' ON. ' einn neisti (spark) warð laus.'

Forms of exorcism treat fire as a hostile higher being, whom
one must encounter with might and main. Tacitus (Ann. 13, 57)
tells us how the Ubii suppressed a fire that broke out of the ground :
Residentibus flammis propius suggressi, ictu fustium aliisque
verberibus *ut feras* (see p. 601) absterrebant, postremo tegmina
corpore direpta injiciunt, quanto magis *profana* et *usu polluta*,

tanto magis oppressura ignes. So, on valuables that have caught
fire, people throw some article of clothing that has been worn
next the skin, or else earth which has first been *stamped on with
the foot*. Rupertus Tuitiensis, De incendio oppidi Tuitii (*i.e.* Deutz,
in 1128), relates that a white altar-cloth (corporale) was thrust
into the middle of the fire, to stifle it, but the flame *hurled back*
the cloth. The cloth remained uninjured, but had a red streak
running through it. Similar to this was the casting of clothes
into the lake (p. 596-7). Fire breaking out of the earth (iarðeldr) is mentioned several times in Icelandic sagas: in the evening you see a great horrible man rowing to land in an iron boat,
and digging under the stable door; in the night earth-fire breaks
out there, and consumes every dwelling, Landn. 2, 5; 'iarðeldr
rann ofan,' 4, 12 (see Suppl.).

NEEDFIRE.—Flame which had been kept some time among
men and been propagated from one fire to another, was thought
unserviceable for sacred uses; as holy water had to be drawn
fresh from the spring, so it made all the difference, if instead of
the profaned and as it were worn out flame, a new one were used.
This was called *wild fire*, as opposed to the tame and domesti-
cated. So heroes when they fought, 'des fiurs ûz den ringen
(harness) hiuwen si genuoc,' Nib. 2215, 1; ûz ir helmen daz
wilde fiwer von den slegen vuor entwer,' Alt. bl. 1, 339; 'daz
fiur wilde wadlende drûze vluoc,' Lanz. 5306; 'si sluogen ûf einander, daz *wilde fiur* erschien,' Etzels hofh. 168 (see Suppl.).
Fire struck or scraped out of stone might indeed have every
claim to be called a fresh one, but either that method seemed
too common (flammam concussis ex more lapidibus elicere, Vita
Severini cap. 14), or its generation out of wood was regarded as
more primitive and hallowed. If by accident such wild fire have
arisen under the carpenter's hand in driving a nail into the mor-
tised timbers of a new house, it is ominous of danger (Superst. I,
411. 500, 707). But for the most part there was a formal kindling
of flame by the rubbing of wood, for which the name known from
the oldest times was *notfeuer* (need fire), and its ritual can with
scarce a doubt be traced back to heathen sacrifices.

So far back as in the Indiculus superstit. 15, we have mention
'de *igne fricato* de ligno, id est *nodfyr*'; the Capitulare Carlomani

of 742 § 5 (Pertz 3, 17) forbids ' illos sacrilegos ignes quos *nied-fyr* vocant.[1]

The preparation of needfire is variously described : I think it worth the while to bring all such accounts together in this place.　Lindenbrog in the Glossary to the Capitularies says : ' Rusticani homines in multis Germaniae locis, et festo quidem S. Johannis Baptistae die, *palum sepi extrahunt, extracto funem circumligant, illumque huc illuc ducunt, donec ignem concipiat :* quem stipula lignisque aridioribus aggestis curate fovent, ac cineres collectos supra olera spargunt, hoc medio erucas abigi posse inani superstitione credentes.　Eum ergo ignem *nodfeur* et *nodfyr*, quasi necessarium ignem, vocant.'—Joh. Reiskius,[2] in Untersuchung des notfeuers, Frankf. and Leipz. 1696, 8. p. 51 : ' If at any time a grievous murrain have broke out among cattle great or small, and they have suffered much harm thereby ; the husbandmen with one consent make a *nothfür* or *nothfeuer*.　On a day appointed there must *in no house be any flame* left on the hearth.　From every house shall be some straw and water and bushwood brought ; then is a stout *oaken stake driven fast into the ground,* and a hole bored through the same, to the which a *wooden roller* well smeared with pitch and tar is let in, and so winded about, until by reason of the great heat and stress (nothzwang) it give out fire.　This is straightway catched on shavings, and by straw, heath and bushwood enlarged, till it grow to a full *nothfeuer,* yet must it stretch a little way along betwixt two walls or hedges, and the cattle and thereto the horses be with sticks and whips driven through it three times or two.　Others in other parts set up *two such stakes,* and stuff *into the holes a windle or roller* and therewith old *rags* smeared with grease.　Others use a hairen or common light-spun rope, collect *wood of nine kinds,* and keep up a violent motion till such time as fire do drop therefrom.　There may be in use yet other ways for the generating or kindling of this fire, nevertheless they all have respect unto the healing of cattle alone.　After thrice or twice passing through, the cattle are driven to stall or field, and the

---

[1] Ignorant scribes made it metfratres, the Capitularia spuria Benedicti 1, 2 (Pertz iv. 2, 46) have nedfratres.
[2] Rector of Wolfenbüttel school, v. Gericke's Schottelius illustratus, Leipz. 1718, p. 66. Eccard's Fr. or. 1, 425.

collected pile of wood is again pulled asunder, yet in such wise in
sundry places, that every householder shall take a brand with him,
quench it in the wash or swill tub, and put the same by for a
time in the crib wherein the cattle are fed. The stakes driven in
for the extorting of this fire, and the wood used for a roller, are
sometimes carried away for fuel, sometimes laid by in safety, when
the threefold chasing of the cattle through the flame hath been
accomplished.'—In the Marburg Records of Inquiry, for 1605, it
is ordered, that a *new cartwheel* with an unused axle be taken
and worked round until it give fire, and with this a fire be
lighted between the gates, and all the oxen driven through it ; but
before the fire be kindled, *every citizen shall put his own fire clean
out*, and afterward fetch him fire again from the other.[1] Kuhn's
Märkische sagen p. 369 informs us, that in many parts of the
Mark the custom prevails of making a *nothfeuĕr* on certain occasions, and particularly when there is disease among swine. Before
sunrise *two stakes* of dry wood are dug into the ground amid solemn
silence, and hempen ropes that go round them are pulled back
and forwards till the wood catches fire ; the fire is fed with leaves
and twigs, and the sick animals are driven through. In some
places the fire is produced by the friction of an *old cartwheel*.—
The following description, the latest of all, is communicated from
Hohenhameln, bailiw. Baldenberg, Hildesheim : In many villages
of Lower Saxony, especially in the mountains, it is common, as a
precaution against cattle plague, to get up the so-called *wild fire*,
through which first the *pigs*, then the *cows*, lastly the *geese* are
driven.[2] The established procedure in the matter is this. The
farmers and all the parish assemble, each inhabitant receives
notice *to extinguish every bit of fire* in his house, so that not a
spark is left alight in the whole village. Then old and young
walk to a hollow way, usually towards evening, the women carrying linen, the men wood and tow. *Two oaken stakes* are driven
into the ground a foot and a half apart, each having a hole on the
inner side, into which fits a cross-bar as thick as an arm. The
holes are *stuffed with linen*, then the cross-bar is forced in as
tight as possible, the heads of the stakes being held together with

[1] Zeitschr. des hess. vereins 2, 281.
[2] Not a word about *sheep* : supposing *cocks and hens* were likewise hunted over
the coals, it would explain a hitherto unexplained proverb (Reinhart xciv.).

cords.   About the smooth round cross-bar *is coiled a rope,* whose long ends, left hanging on both sides, are seized by a number of men ; these make the cross-bar revolve rapidly this way and that, till the friction sets the linen in the holes on fire. The sparks are caught on tow or oakum, and *whirled round* in the air till they burst into a clear blaze, which is then communicated to straw, and from the straw to a bed of brushwood arranged in cross layers in the hollow way.   When this wood has well burnt and nearly done blazing, the people hurry off to the herds waiting behind, and drive them perforce, one after the other, through the glowing embers.   As soon as all the cattle are through, the young folks throw themselves pellmell upon the ashes and coals, sprinkling and blackening one another; those who are most blackened and besmudged march into the village behind the cattle as conquerors, and will not wash for a long time after.[1]   If after long rubbing the linen will not catch, they feel sure there is still fire somewhere in the village, and that the element refuses to reveal itself through friction : then follows a strict searching of houses, any fire they may light upon is extinguished, and the master of the house rebuked or chastised.   But that the *wild fire* should be evoked by friction is indispensable, it cannot be struck out of flint and steel. Some localities perform the ceremony, not yearly as a preventive of murrain, but only upon its actually breaking out.

Accurate as these accounts are, a few minor details have escaped them, whose observance is seen to in some districts at least.   Thus, in the Halberstadt country the ropes of the wooden roller are pulled *by two chaste boys.*[2]   Need fires have remained in use longer and more commonly in North Germany,[3] yet are not quite unknown in the South.   Schmeller and Stalder are silent, but in Appenzell the country children still have a game of *rubbing* a rope against a stick *till it catches fire :* this they call ' *de tüfel häle,*' unmanning the devil, despoiling him of his strength.[4]

---

[1] Is there not also a brand or some light carried home for a redistribution of fire in the village?

[2] Büsching's Wöchentliche nachr. 4, 64 ; so a chaste youth has to strike the light for curing St. Anthony's fire, Superst. I, 710.

[3] Conf. Conring's Epist. ad Baluz. xiii. Gericke's Schottel. p. 70. Dähnert sub v. noodfür.

[4] Zellweger's Gesch. von Appenzell, Trogen 1830. 1, 68 ; who observes, that with the ashes of the fire so engendered they strew the fields, as a protection against vermin.

But Tobler 252[b] says, what boys call *de tüfel häla* is spinning a pointed stick, with a string coiled round it, rapidly in a wooden socket, till it takes fire. The name may be one of those innumerable allusions to Loki, the devil and fire-god (p. 242). Nic. Gryse, in a passage to be quoted later, speaks of *sawing fire* out of wood, as we read elsewhere of symbolically sawing the old woman in two. The Practica of Berthol. Carrichter, phys. in ord. to Maximilian II., gives a description (which I borrow from Wolfg. Hildebrand on Sorcery, Leipz. 1631. p. 226) of a magic bath, which is not to be heated with common flint-and-steel fire: 'Go to an appletree *which the lightning hath stricken*, let a saw be made thee of his wood, therewith shalt thou *saw upon a wooden threshold* that much people passeth over, till it be kindled. Then make firewood of birch-fungus, and kindle it at this fire, with which thou shalt heat the bath, and on thy life see it go not out' (see Suppl.).

Nôtfiur can be derived from nôt (need, necessitas), whether because the fire is forced to shew itself or the cattle to tread the hot coal, or because the operation takes place in a time of need, of pestilence. Nevertheless I will attempt another explanation: notfiur, nodfiur may stand for an older *hnotfiur, hnodfiur*, from the root hniudan, OHG. hniotan, ON. hnioða (quassare, terere, tundere);[1] and would mean a fire elicited by thumping, rubbing, shaking.

And in Sweden it is actually called both *vrideld* and *gnideld*: the one from vrida (torquere, circumagere), AS. wriðan, OHG. rîdan, MHG. rîden; the other from gnida (fricare), OHG. knîtan, AS. cnîdan (conterere, fricare, depsere).

It was produced in Sweden as with us, by violently rubbing two pieces of wood together, in some districts even near the end of last century; sometimes they used boughs of *nine sorts of wood*.[2] The smoke rising from gnideld was deemed salutary,

---

[1] OHG. pihniutit (excutit), Gl. ker. 251. hnotôt (quassat) 229. hnutten (vibrare) 282; N. has fnotôn (quassare), Ps. 109, 6. Bth. 230; conf. nieten, to bump. ON. still has hnioða in hnoð (tudes, malleus), hnoða (depsere), hnuðla (subigere). It might be spelt hnôtfiur or hnotfiur (hnutfiur), acc. as the sing. or pl. vowel-form was used. Perhaps we need not even insist on a lost *h*, but turn to the OHG. niuwan, ON. nûa (terere, fricare), from which a subst. nôt might be derived by suffix. Nay, we might go the length of supposing that nôt, nâuþs, nauðr, need, contained from the first the notion of stress and pressure (conf. Graff 2, 1032. 4, 1125).

[2] Ihre's De superstit. p. 98, and Glossary sub. v. wredeld. Finn. Magn.,

fruit-trees or nets *fumigated* with it became the more productive
of fruit or fish.   On this *fumigation* with *vriden eld*, and on
driving the cattle out over such *smoke*, conf. Superst. Swed. 89.
108.   We can see that the purposes to which needfire was
applied must have been far more numerous in heathen times : in
Germany we find but a fragment of it in use for diseased cattle,
but the superstitious practice of *girls kindling nine sorts of wood*
on Christmas eve (Sup. I, 955) may assure us of a wider meaning
having once belonged to needfire (see Suppl.).

In the North of England it is believed that an angel strikes a
tree, and then needfire can be got from it ; did they rub it only
out of windfall wood ? or does striking here not mean felling ?

Of more significance are the Scotch and Irish procedures,
which I am glad to give in the words of the original communica-
tions.   The following I owe to the kindness of Miss Austin ; it
refers to the I. of Mull (off the W. coast of Scotland), and to
the year 1767.   'In consequence of a disease among the black
cattle the people agreed to perform an incantation, though they
esteemed it a wicked thing.   They carried to the top of Carn-
moor a *wheel* and *nine spindles of oak wood*.   They extinguished
every fire in every house within sight of the hill ; the *wheel* was
then turned from east to west *over the nine spindles* long enough
to produce fire by friction.   If the fire were not produced before
noon, the incantation lost its effect.   They failed for several days
running.   They attributed this failure to the obstinacy of one
householder, who would not let *his fires be put out* for what he
considered so wrong a purpose.   However by bribing his servants they contrived to have them extinguished, and on that
morning raised their fire.   They then *sacrificed a heifer*, cutting
in pieces and burning, while yet alive, the diseased part.   Then
they lighted their own hearths from the pile, and ended by feast-
ing on the remains.   Words of incantation were repeated by an
old man from Morven, who came over as master of the ceremonies, and who continued speaking all the time the fire was
being raised.   This man was living a beggar at Bellochroy.
Asked to repeat the spell, he said the sin of repeating it once had

---

Tidskr. for nord. oldk. 2, 294, following Westerdahl.   Conf. bjäraan, a magic
utensil, Chap. XXXIV.

brought him to beggary, and that he dared not say those words again. The whole country believed him accursed' (see Suppl.).

In the Highlands, and especially in Caithness, they now use needfire chiefly as a remedy for preternatural diseases of cattle brought on by witchcraft.[1] 'To defeat the sorceries, certain persons who have the power to do so are sent for to raise the *needfire*. Upon any small river, lake, or island, a circular booth of stone or turf is erected, on which a *couple* or *rafter of a birch-tree* is placed, and the roof covered over. In the centre is set a *perpendicular post*, fixed by a wooden pin to the couple, the lower end being placed in an oblong groove on the floor; and *another pole is placed horizontally* between the upright post and the legs of the couple, into both of which the ends, being tapered, are inserted. This horizontal timber is called the *auger*, being provided with four short arms or spokes by which it can be turned round. As many men as can be collected are then set to work, having first *divested themselves of all kinds of metal*, and two at a time continue to turn the pole by means of the levers, while others keep driving wedges under the upright post so as to press it against the auger, which by the friction soon becomes ignited. From this the needfire is instantly procured, and *all other fires being immediately quenched*, those that are *rekindled* both in dwelling house and offices are accounted *sacred*, and the cattle are successively made to smell them.' Let me also make room for Martin's description,[2] which has features of its own: 'The inhabitants here did also make use of a fire called *tinegin, i.e.* a forced fire, or fire of necessity,[3] which they used as an antidote against the plague or murrain in cattle; and it was performed thus: *all the fires* in the parish *were extinguished*, and then *eighty-one* (9 × 9) *married men*, being thought the necessary number for effecting this design, took *two great planks* of wood, and *nine* of 'em were employed by turns, who by their repeated efforts *rubbed one of the planks against the other* until the heat

---

[1] I borrow the description of the process from James Logan's 'The Scottish Gaël, or Celtic manners as preserved among the Highlanders,' Lond. 1831. 2, 64; though here he copies almost verbally from Jamieson's Supplem. to the Scot. Dict. sub v. neidfyre.

[2] Descr. of the Western Islands, p. 113.

[3] From tin, Ir. teine (fire), and egin, Ir. eigin, eigean (vis, violentia); which seems to favour the old etymology of nothfeuer, unless it be simply a translation of the Engl. *need*fire [which itself may stand for *knead*fire].

thereof produced fire; and from this forced fire *each family is supplied with new fire*, which is no sooner kindled than a *pot full of water* is quickly *set on it*, and afterwards sprinkled upon the people infected with the plague, or upon the cattle that have the murrain. And this they all say they find successful by experience: it was practised on the mainland opposite to the south of Skye, within these thirty years.' As in this case there is *water boiled* on the frictile fire, and sprinkled with the same effect, so Eccard (Fr. or. 1, 425) tells us, that one Whitsun morning he saw some stablemen *rub fire out of wood*, and *boil their cabbage* over it, under the belief that by eating it they would be proof against fever all that year. A remarkable story from Northamptonshire, and of the present century, confirms that sacrifice of the young cow in Mull, and shows that even in England superstitious people would kill a calf to protect the herd from pestilence: Miss C—— and her cousin walking saw a *fire in a field*, and a crowd round it. They said, 'what is the matter?' '*Killing a calf.*' 'What for?' 'To stop the murrain.' They went away as quickly as possible. On speaking to the clergyman, he made inquiries. The people did not like to talk of the affair, but it appeared that when there is a disease among the cows, or the calves are born sickly, they *sacrifice* (*i.e.* kill and burn) *one* for good luck.' [A similar story from Cornwall in Hone's Daybook 1, 153.]

Unquestionably needfire was a sacred thing to other nations beside the Teutonic and Celtic. The Creeks in N. America hold an annual harvest festival, commencing with a strict fast of three days, during which the *fires are put out* in all houses. On the fourth morning the chief priest by *rubbing* two dry sticks together lights a *new clean fire*, which is distributed among all the dwellings; not till then do the women carry home the new corn and fruits from the harvest field.[1] The Arabs have for fire-friction two pieces of wood called *March* and *Aphar*, the one male, the other female. The Chinese say the emperor Sui was the first who rubbed wood against wood; the inconvenient method is retained as a holy one. Indians and Persians turn a piece of cane round in dry wood, Kanne's Urk. 454-5 (see Suppl.).

[1] Fr. Majer's Mythol. taschenb. 1811, p. 110.

It is still more interesting to observe how nearly the old Roman and Greek customs correspond. Excerpts from Festus (O. Müller 106, 2) say: '*ignis Vestae* si quando interstinctus esset, virgines verberibus afficiebantur a pontifice, quibus mos erat, *tabulam* felicis materiae *tam diu terebrare*, quousque exceptum ignem cribro aeneo virgo in aedem ferret.' The sacred fire of the goddess, once *extinguished*, was not to be rekindled, save by generating the pure element anew. A plank of the choice timber of sacred trees was bored, *i.e.* a pin turned round in it, till it gave out sparks. The act of catching the fire in a sieve, and so conveying it into the temple, is suggestive of a similar carrying of water in a sieve, of which there is some account to be given further on. Plutarch (in Numa 9) makes out that *new fire* was obtained not by friction, but by intercepting the sun's rays in clay vessels destined for the purpose. The Greeks worshipped *Hestia* as the pure hearth-flame itself.[1] But Lemnos, the island on which Zeus had flung down the celestial fire-god Hephæstus,[2] harboured a fire-worship of its own. Once a year *every fire was extinguished* for nine days, till a ship brought some fresh from Delos off the sacred hearth of Apollo: for some days it drifts on the sea without being able to land, but as soon as it runs in, there is fire served out to every one for domestic use, and a *new life* begins. The old fire was no longer holy enough; by doing without it altogether for a time, men would learn to set the true value on the element (see Suppl.).[3] Like Vesta, St. Bridget of Ireland (d. 518 or 521) had a *perpetual fire* maintained in honour of her near Kildare; a wattled fence went round it, which none but women durst approach; it was only permissible to blow it with bellows, not with the mouth.[4] The mode of generating it is not recorded.

The wonderful amount of harmony in these accounts, and the usages of needfire themselves, point back to a high antiquity. The *wheel* seems to be an emblem of the sun, whence light and fire proceed; I think it likely that it was provided with nine

[1] Nec tu aliud Vestam quam *vivam* intellige *flammam*, Ov. Fast. 6, 295.
[2] Acc. to the Finnish myth, the fire created by the gods falls on the sea in balls, it is swallowed by a salmon, and men afterwards find it inside the fish when caught. Runes pp. 6–22.
[3] Philostr. Heroic. pp. 740. Welcker's Trilogie, pp. 247-8.
[4] Acta sanctor., calend. Febr. p. 112ᵇ.

spokes: 'thet niugenspetze fial' survives in the Frisian laws, those nine oaken spindles whose friction against the nave produced fire signify the nine spokes standing out of the nave, and the same sacred number turns up again in the nine kinds of wood, in the nine and eighty-one men that rub. We can hardly doubt that the wheel when set on fire formed the nucleus and centre of a holy and purifying sacrificial flame. Our weisthümer (2, 615-6. 693-7) have another remarkable custom to tell of. At the great yearly assize a *cartwheel*, that had lain six weeks and three days soaking in water (or a cesspool), was placed in a fire kindled before the judges, and the banquet lasts till the *nave*, which must on no account be turned or poked, be consumed to ashes. This I take to be a last relic of the pagan sacrificial feast, and the wheel to have been the means of generating the fire, of which it is true there is nothing said. In any case we have here the use of a cartwheel to feed a festal flame.

If the majority of the accounts quoted limit the use of need-fire to an outbreak of murrain, yet some of them expressly inform us that it was resorted to at *stated times of the year*, especially Midsummer, and that the cattle were driven through the flames to guard them beforehand against future sicknesses. Nicolaus Gryse (Rostock 1593, liii*) mentions as a regular practice on St. John's day: 'Toward nightfall they warmed them by St. John's blaze and *needfire* (nodfür) that they sawed out of wood, kindling the same not in God's name but St. John's; leapt and ran and *drave the cattle therethro'*, and were fulfilled of thousand joys whenas they had passed the night in great sins, shames and harms.'

Of this yearly recurrence we are assured both by the Lemnian worship, and more especially by the Celtic.[1] It was in the great gatherings at annual feasts that needfire was lighted. These the Celtic nations kept at the beginning of May and of November. The grand hightide was the Mayday; I find it falling mostly on the 1st of May, yet sometimes on the 2nd or 3rd. This day is called in Irish and Gaelic *la bealtine* or *beiltine*, otherwise spelt *beltein*, and corrupted into *belton, beltim, beltam.* Lá means day,

---

[1] Hyde remarks of the Guebers also, that they lighted a fire every year.

teine or tine fire, and beal, beil, is understood to be the name of
a god, not directly connected with the Asiatic Belus,[1] but a deity
of light peculiar to the Celts. This Irish *Beal, Beil,* Gaelic
Beal, appears in the Welsh dialect as *Beli,* and his O. Celtic
name of *Belenus, Belinus* is preserved in Ausonius, Tertullian and
numerous inscriptions (Forcellini sub v.). The present custom
is thus described by Armstrong sub v. bealtainn : 'In some parts
of the Highlands the young folks of a hamlet meet in the moors
on the first of May. They cut a table in the green sod, of a
round figure, by cutting a trench in the ground of such circumference as to hold the whole company. They then kindle a fire,
and dress a repast of eggs and milk in the consistence of a
custard. They knead a cake of oatmeal, which is toasted at the
embers against a stone. After the custard is eaten up, they
divide the cake in so many portions, as similar as possible to one
another in size and shape, as there are persons in the company.
They daub one of these portions with charcoal until it is perfectly
black. They then put all the bits of the cake into a bonnet, and
every one, blindfold, draws out a portion. The bonnet-holder is
entitled to the last bit. Whoever draws the black bit is the
devoted person who is *to be sacrificed to Baal, whose favour they
mean to implore in rendering the year productive.* The devoted
person is compelled to *leap three times over the flames.*' Here the
reference to the worship of a deity is too plain to be mistaken :
we see by the leaping over the flame, that the main point was, to
select a human being to propitiate the god and make him merciful, that afterwards an animal sacrifice was substituted for him,
and finally, nothing remained of the bodily immolation but a leap
through the fire for man and beast. The holy rite of friction is
not mentioned here, but as it was necessary for the needfire that
purged pestilence, it must originally have been much more in
requisition at the great yearly festival.

The earliest mention of the *beiltine* is found in Cormac, arch-
bishop of Cashel (d. 908). Two fires were lighted side by side,
and to pass unhurt between them was wholesome for men and
cattle. Hence the phrase, to express a great danger : 'itir dha
theinne beil,' *i.e.* between two fires.[2] That the sacrifice was

---

[1] *Bel, Bal,* Isidor. Etym. 8, 23.
[2] O'Flaherty in Transact. of Irish Acad., vol. 14, pp. 100. 122-3.

strictly superintended by priests, we are expressely assured by Usher (Trias thaumat. p. 125), who founds on Evinus: Lege etiam severissima cavebatur, ut omnes ignes per universas regiones ista nocte exstinguerentur, et nulli liceat ignem reaccendere nisi prius Temoriae (Tighmora, whom we know from Ossian) *a magis rogus sacrificiorum exstrueretur*, et quicunque hanc legem in aliquo transgrederetur non alia mulcta quam capitis supplicio commissi delicti poenam luebat.[1]

Leo (Malb. gl. i, 35) has ingeniously put forward an antithesis between a god of war *Beal* or *Bael*, and a god of peace *Sighe* or *Sithich*; nay, by this distinction he explains the brothers Bellovesus and Sigovesus in Livy 5, 34 as servants (vesus = Gaelic uis, uais, minister) of Beal and Sighe, connecting Sighe with that silent peaceful folk the elves, who are called sighe (supra, p. 444n.) : to Beal were offered the May fires, *bealtine*, to Sighe the November fires, *samhtheine* (peace-fire). In Wales too they lighted fires on May 1 and Nov. 1, both being called *coelcerth* (see Suppl.).

I still hesitate to accept all the inferences, but undoubtedly *Beal* must be taken for a divine being, whose worship is likely to have extended beyond the Celtic nations. At p. 228 I identified him with the German *Phol*; and it is of extraordinary value to our research, that in the Rhine districts we come upon a *Pfultag*, *Pulletag* (P.'s day), which fell precisely on the 2nd of May (Weisth. 2, 8. 3, 748). We know that our forefathers very generally kept the beginning of May as a great festival, and it is still regarded as the trysting-time of witches, *i.e.* once of wisewomen and fays; who can doubt that heathen sacrifices blazed that day? *Pholtag* then answers to *Bealteine*,[2] and moreover *Baldag* is the Saxon form for Paltar (p. 229).

Were the German May-fires, after the conversion, shifted to *Easter* and *Midsummer*, to adapt them to Christian worship ? Or, as the summer solstice was itself deeply rooted in heathenism, is it Eastertide alone that represents the ancient May-fires ? For, as to the Celtic November, the German Yule or Midwinter might easily stand for that, even in heathen times.

---

[1] Conf. the accounts in Mone's Geschichte des heidenth. 2, 485.
[2] All over England on the 1st of May they set up a *May pole*, which may be from pole, palus, AS. pol ; yet Pol, Phol may deserve to be taken into account too.

Whichever way we settle that, our very next investigations will shew, that beside both needfire and bealtine, other fires are to be found almost all over Europe.

It is not unimportant to observe, that in the north of Germany they take place at *Easter*, in the south at *Midsummer*. There they betoken the entrance of spring, here the longest day; as before, it all turns upon whether the people are Saxon or Frank. All Lower Saxony, Westphalia, and Lower Hesse, Gelders, Holland, Friesland, Jutland, and Zealand have Easter fires; up the Rhine, in Franconia, Thuringia, Swabia, Bavaria, Austria, and Silesia, Midsummer fires carry the day. Some countries, however, seem to do homage to both, as Denmark and Carinthia.

EASTER FIRES.—At all the cities, towns and villages of a country, towards evening on the first (or third) day of Easter, there is lighted every year on *mountain* and *hill* a great fire of straw, turf, and wood, amidst a concourse and jubilation, not only of the young, but of many grown-up people. On the Weser, especially in Schaumburg, they tie up a tar-barrel on a fir-tree wrapt round with straw, and set it on fire at night. Men and maids, and all who come, dance exulting and singing, hats are waved, handkerchiefs thrown into the fire. The *mountains* all round are lighted up, and it is an elevating spectacle, scarcely paralleled by anything else, to survey the country for many miles round from one of the higher points, and in every direction at once to see a vast number of these bonfires, brighter or fainter, blazing up to heaven. In some places they marched up the hill in stately procession, carrying white rods; by turns they sang Easter hymns, grasping each other's hands, and at the Hallelujah clashed their rods together. They liked to carry some of the fire home with them.[1]

No doubt we still lack many details as to the manner of keeping Easter fires in various localities. It is worth noting, that at Bräunrode in the Harz the fires are lighted at evening twilight

[1] Joh. Timeus On the Easter fire, Hamb. 1590; a reprint of it follows Reiske's Notfeuer. Letzner's Historia S. Bonif., Hildesh. 1602. 4, cap. 12. Leukfeld's Antiq. ganderah. pp. 4-5. Eberh. Baring's Beschr. der (Lauensteiner) Saala, 1744. 2, 96. Hamb. mag. 26, 302 (1762). Hannöv. mag. 1766, p. 216. Rathlef's Diepholz, Brem. 1767. 3, 36-42. (Pratje's) Bremen und Verden 1, 165. Bragur vi. 1, 35. Geldersche volksalmanak voor 1835, p. 19. Easter fire is in Danish *paaske-blus* or *-blust;* whether Sweden has the custom I do not know, but Olaus Magnus 15, 5 affirms that Scandinavia has Midsummer fires. Still more surprising that England has no trace of an Easter fire; we have a report of such from Carinthia in Sartori's Reise 2, 350.

of the first Easter day, but before that, old and young sally out
of that village and Griefenhagen into the nearest woodlands to
hunt up the *squirrels*. These they chase by throwing stones and
cudgels, till at last the animals drop exhausted into their hands,
dead or alive. This is said to be an old-established custom.[1]

For these ignes paschales there is no authority reaching beyond
the 16th century; but they must be a great deal older, if only for
the contrast with Midsummer fires, which never could penetrate
into North Germany, because the people there held fast by their
Easter fires. Now, seeing that the fires of St. John, as we shall
presently shew, are more immediately connected with the Christian
church than those of Easter, it is not unreasonable to trace these
all the way back to the worship of the goddess *Ostarâ* or *Eástre*
(p. 291), who seems to have been more a Saxon and Anglian
divinity than one revered all over Germany. Her name and her
fires, which are likely to have come at the beginning of May,
would after the conversion of the Saxons be shifted back to the
Christian feast.[2] Those mountain fires of the people are scarcely
derivable from the taper lighted in the church the same day : it
is true that Boniface, ep. 87 (Würdtw.), calls it *ignis paschalis*,[3]
and such Easter lights are still mentioned in the 16th century.[4]
Even now in the Hildesheim country they light the lamp on
Maundy Thursday, and that on Easterday, at an Easter fire which
has been *struck with a steel*. The people flock to this fire, carrying oaken crosses or simply crossed sticks, which they set on fire
and then preserve for a whole year. But the common folk distinguish between this fire and the wild fire elicited by rubbing
wood. Jäger (Ulm, p. 521) speaks of a *consecration of fire* and
of logs.

---

[1] Rosenkranz, Neue zeitschr. f. gesch. der germ. völk. i. 2, 7.
[2] Letzner says (ubi supra), that betwixt Brunstein and Wibbrechtshausen,
where Boniface had overthrown the heathen idol Reto (who may remind us of Beda's
Rheda), on the same Retberg the people ‘did after sunset on Easter day, even
within the memory of man, hold the *Easter fire*, which the men of old named
bocks-thorn.’ On the margin stands his old authority again, the lost Conradus
Fontanus (supra p. 190). How the fire itself should come by the name of buck's or
goat's thorn, is hard to see ; it is the name of a shrub, the tragacanth. Was bocks-
thorn thrown into the Easter flames, as certain herbs were into the Midsummer
fire ?
[3] N.B., some maintain that the Easter candle was ignited by burning-glasses
or crystals (Serrarius ad Epist. Bonif. p. 348).
[4] Franz Wessel's Beschreibung des päbstlichen gottesdienstes, Stralsund ed. by
Zober, 1837, p. 10.

Almost everywhere during the last hundred years the feeble-
ness of governments has deprived the people of their Easter fires
(see Suppl.).[1]

MIDSUMMER FIRES.[2]—In our older speech, the most festive
season of the year, when the sun has reached his greatest height
and must thence decline again, is named *sunewende = sunnewende*
(sun's wending, solstice), commonly in the plural, because this
high position of the sun lasts several days: 'ze einen sunewenden,'
Nib. 32, 4; 'zen næhsten sunewenden,' Nib. 1424, 4. Wigal. 1717;
'vor disen sunewenden,' Nib. 678, 3. 694, 3; 'ze sunewenden,'
Trist. 5987 (the true reading comes out in Groot's variants); 'an
sunewenden âbent,' Nib. 1754, 1; 'nâch sunewenden,' Iw. 2941.[3]
Now, as Midsummer or St. John's day (June 24), 'sant Johans
sunewenden tac,' Ls. 2, 708, coincides with this, the fires in
question are called in Up. German documents of the 14-15th
century *sunwentfeuer, sunbentfeur,*[4] and even now among the
Austrian and Bavarian peasantry *sunäwetsfoir, sunwentsfeuer.*
H. Sachs 1, 423[d]: 'auch schürn die bubn (lads poke) *sunwentfeuer.*' At this season were held great gatherings of the people :
'die nativitatis S. Johannis baptistae *in conventu populi maximo*'
(Pertz 2, 386); this was in 860. In 801 Charles the Great kept
this festival at Eporedia, now Ivrea (Pertz 1, 190. 223); and
Lewis the Pious held assemblies of the Empire on the same day
in 824 and 831. Descriptions of Midsummer fires agree with
those of Easter fires, with of course some divergences. At
Gernsheim in the Mentz country, the fire when lighted is blessed
by the priest, and there is singing and prayer so long as it burns ;
when the flame goes out, the children *jump over the glimmering
coals;* formerly grown-up people did the same. In Superst. I,

---

[1] 'Judic. inquiry resp. the Easter fire burned, contr. to prohib., on the Kogeln-
berg near Volkmarsen, Apr. 9, 1833,' see Niederhess. wochenbl. 1834, p. 2229ª.
The older prohibitions allege the unchristian character, later ones the waste of
timber. Even bonfires for a victory were very near being suppressed.

[2] The best treatise is: Franc. Const. de Khautz de ritu ignis in. natali S.
Johannis bapt. accensi, Vindob. 1759, 8vo.

[3] All the good MSS. have, not sunnewande, but sunewende, which can only
stand for sunwende, formed like suntac. We also find 'zu sungihten,' Scheffer's
Haltaus, pp. 109, 110; *giht* here corresp. to Goth. gahts (gressus), and allows us to
guess an OHG. sunnagaht.

[4] Hahn's Monum. 2, 693. Sutner's Berichtigungen, Münch. 1797, p. 107 (an.
1401).

848 we are told how a garland is plaited of *nine sorts* of flowers.
Reiske (ut supra, p. 77) says: 'the fire is made under the open
sky, the youth and the meaner folk *leap over it*, and all manner
of *herbs are cast into it* : like these, may all their troubles go off
in fire and smoke ! In some places they light lanterns outside
their chambers at night, and dress them with red poppies or
anemones, so as to make a bright glitter.' At Nürnberg the
lads go about begging billets of wood, cart them to the Bleacher's
pond by the Spital-gate, make a fire of them, and *jump over it* ;
this keeps them in health the whole year (conf. Sup. I, 918).
They invite passers by to have a leap, who pay a few kreuzers
for the privilege. In the Fulda country also the boys beg for
wood to burn at night, and other presents, while they sing a
rhyme : ' Da kommen wir her gegangen Mit spiessen und mit
stangen, Und wollen die eier (eggs) langen. Feuerrothe blüme-
lein, An der erde springt der wein, Gebt ihr uns der eier ein
Zum *Johannisfeuer*, Der haber is gar theuer (oats are so dear).
Haberje, haberju! *fri fre frid !* Gebt uns doch ein schiet (scheit,
billet)!' (J. v. u. f. Deutschl. 1790. 1, 313.) Similar rhymes
from Franconia and Bavaria, in Schm. 3, 262. In the Austrian
Donauländchen on St. John's eve they light fires on the hill, lads
and lasses *jump over the flames* amid the joyful cries and songs
of the spectators (Reil, p. 41). 'Everywhere on St. John's eve
there was merry *leaping over the sonnenwendefeuer*, and mead was
drunk over it,' is Denis's recollection of his youthful days (Lesefr.
1, 130). At Ebingen in Swabia they *boiled pease* over the fire,
which were laid by and esteemed wholesome for bruises and
wounds (Schmid's Schwäb. id. 167); conf. the boiling over need-
fires (p. 610). Greg. Strigenitius (b. 1548, d. 1603), in a sermon
preached on St. John's day and quoted in Ecc. Fr. or. i. 425,
observes, that the people (in Meissen or Thuringia) *dance* and
sing round the *Midsummer fires* ; that one man threw a *horse's
head into the flame*, meaning thereby to force the witches to fetch
some of the fire for themselves. Seb. Frank in his Weltbuch
51[b]: ' On St. John's day they make a *simet fire* [corrupt. of sun-
went], and moreover wear upon them, I know not from what
superstition, quaint *wreaths* of *mugwort* and *monks-hood* ; nigh
every one hath *a blue plant named larkspur in hand*, and *whoso
looketh into the fire thro' the same*, hath never a sore eye all that

year; he that would depart home unto his house, *casteth this his
plant into the fire*, saying, So depart all mine ill-fortune and be
burnt up with this herb!'[1]   So, on the same day, were the waves
of water to wash away with them all misfortune (p. 589). But
in earlier times the polite world, even princes and kings, took
part in these bonfires. Peter Herp's Ann. francof. tell us, ad an.
1489 (Senkenb. Sel. 2, 22): 'In vigilia S. Joh. bapt. rogus ingens
fuit factus *ante domum consulum in foro* (francofurtensi), fuerunt-
que multa vexilla depicta posita in struem lignorum, et vexillum
regis in supremo positum, et circa ligna *rami virentes* positi,
fuitque magna *chorea dominorum*, rege inspiciente.' At Augsburg
in 1497, in the Emp. Maximilian's presence, the fair Susanna
Neithard kindled the Midsummer fire *with a torch*, and with
Philip the Handsome led the first *ring-dance round the fire.*[2]
A Munich voucher of 1401 renders account: 'umb gras und
knechten, die dy pänk ab dem haws *auf den margt* trugen
(carried benches to the market-place) an der sunbentnacht, da
herzog Stephan und sein gemachel (consort) und das frawel *auf
dem margt tanzten* mit den purgerinen *bei dem sunbentfur*,' (Sutner's Berichtig. p. 107). On St. John's eve 1578, the Duke of
Liegnitz had a bonfire made *on the Gredisberg*, as herr Gotsch
did on the *Kynast*, at which the Duke himself was present with
his court (Schweinichen 2, 347).

We have a fuller description of a Midsummer fire made in
1823 at Konz, a Lorrainian but still German village on the
Moselle, near Sierk and Thionville. Every house delivers a truss
of straw on the top of the Stromberg, where men and youths
assemble towards evening; women and girls are stationed by the
Burbach spring. Then a *huge wheel* is *wrapt round with straw,*

---

[1] On June 20, 1653, the Nürnberg town-council issued the following order:
Whereas experience heretofore hath shewn, that after the old heathenish use, on
John's day in every year, in the country, as well in towns as villages, money and
wood hath been *gathered by young folk*, and thereupon the so-called *sonnenwendt* or
zimmet fire kindled, and thereat winebibbing, *dancing about the said fire, leaping
over the same, with burning of sundry herbs and flowers*, and *setting of brands from
the said fire in the fields*, and in many other ways all manner of superstitious work
carried on—Therefore the Hon. Council of Nürnberg town neither can nor ought
to forbear to do away with all such unbecoming superstition, paganism, and peril
of fire on this coming day of St. John (Neuer lit. anz. 1807, p. 818). [Sunwend
fires forbidden in Austria in 1850, in spite of Goethe's ' Fires of John we'll cherish,
Why should gladness perish?'—SUPPL.]

[2] Gasseri Ann. august., ad an. 1497, Schm. 3, 261; conf. Ranke's Roman. u.
German. völk. 1, 102.

so that none of the wood. is left in sight, a strong pole is passed
through the middle, which sticks out a yard on each side, and is
grasped by the guiders of the wheel; the remainder of the straw
is tied up into a number of small torches. At a signal given
by the Maire of Sierk (who, according to ancient custom, earns
a basket of cherries by the service), the wheel is lighted with a
torch, and set rapidly in motion, a shout of joy is raised, all *wave
their torches* on high, part of the men stay on the hill, part follow
the rolling *globe of fire as it is guided downhill to the Moselle.* It
often goes out first; but if alight when it touches the river,
it prognosticates an *abundant vintage,* and the Konz people have
a right to levy a tun of white wine from the adjacent vineyards.
Whilst the wheel is rushing past the women and girls, they
break out into cries of joy, answered by the men on the hill; and
inhabitants of neighbouring villages, who have flocked to the
river side, mingle their voices in the universal rejoicing.[1]

In the same way the butchers of Treves are said to have yearly
sent down a wheel of fire into the Moselle from the top of the
Paulsberg (see Suppl.).[2]

The custom of Midsummer fires and wheels in France is
attested even by writers of the 12th and 13th centuries, John
Beleth, a Parisian divine, who wrote about 1162 a Summa de
divinis officiis, and William Durantis, b. near Beziers in Langue-
doc, about 1237, d. 1296, the well-known author of the Rationale
divinor. offic. (written 1286; conf. viii. 2, 3 de epacta). In the
Summa (printed at Dillingen, 1572) cap. 137, fol. 256, and thence
extracted in the Rationale vii. 14, we find: 'Feruntur quoque
(in festo Joh. bapt.) *brandae* seu *faces ardentes* et fiunt *ignes,*
qui significant S. Johannem, qui fuit lumen et lucerna ardens,
praecedens et praecursor verae lucis . . . ; *rota* in quibusdam
locis *volvitur,* ad significandum, quod sicut sol ad altiora sui
circuli pervenit, nec altius potest progredi, sed tunc sol descendit
in circulo, sic et fama Johannis, qui putabatur Christus, descendit

---

[1] Mém. des antiquaires de Fr. 5, 383–6.

[2] 'In memory of the hermit Paulus, who in the mid. of the 7th cent. hurled
the idol Apollo from Mt. Gebenna, near Treves, into the Moselle,' thinks the writer
of the article on Konz, pp. 387-8. If Trithem's De viris illustr. ord. S. Bened. 4,
201, is to vouch for this, I at least can only find at p. 142 of Opp. pia et spirit.
Mogunt. 1605, that Paulus lived opposite Treves, on Cevenna, named Mons Pauli
after him; but of Apollo and the firewheel not a word [and other authorities are
equally silent].

secundum quod ipse testimonium perhibet, dicens : me oportet minui, illum autem crescere.' Much older, but somewhat vague, is the testimony of Eligius : 'Nullus in festivitate S. Johannis vel quibuslibet sanctorum solemnitatibus *solstitia* (?) aut valla-tiones vel saltationes aut casaulas aut cantica diabolica exerceat.'[1]

In great cities, Paris, Metz, and many more, as late as the 15-16-17th centuries, the pile of wood was reared in the public square before the town hall, decorated with flowers and foliage, and set on fire by the Maire himself.[2] Many districts in the south have retained the custom to this day. At Aix, at Marseille, all the streets and squares are cleaned up on St. John's Day, early in the morning the country folk bring flowers into the town, and everybody buys some, every house is decked with greenery, to which a healing virtue is ascribed if plucked before sunrise : 'aco soun dherbas de san Jean.' Some of the *plants* are *thrown into the flame*, the young people *jump over it*, jokes are played on passers-by with powder trains and hidden fireworks, or they are squirted at and soused with water from the windows. In the villages they ride on mules and donkeys, carrying *lighted branches of fir* in their hands.[3]

In many places they drag some of the *charred brands* and *charcoal* to their homes : salutary and even magical effects are supposed to flow from these (Superst. French 27. 30. 34).

In Poitou, they *jump three times round the fire* with a *branch of walnut in their hands* (Mém. des antiq. 8, 451). Fathers of families whisk a *bunch of white mullein* (bouillon blanc) and a *leafy spray of walnut* through the flame, and both are afterwards *nailed up over the cowhouse door;* while the youth dance and sing, old men put some of the coal in their wooden shoes as a safeguard against innumerable woes (ibid. 4, 110).

In the department of Hautes Pyrénées, on the 1st of May,

---

[1] The Kaiserchronik (Cod. pal. 361, 1ᵇ) on the celebration of the Sunday :

Swenne in kom der sunnintac,
sô vlîzete sich Rôme al diu stat (all R. bestirred itself),
wie si den got mohten geêren (to honour the god),
die allirwîsisten hêrren (wisest lords)
vuorten einiz al umbe die stat (carried a thing round the city)
daz was geschaffen same ein rat (shapen like a wheel)
mit brinnenden liehten (with burning lights) ;
ô wie grôze sie den got zierten (greatly glorified the god) !

[2] Mém. de l'acad. celt. 2, 77-8. 3, 447.
[3] Millin's Voyage dans le midi 3, 28. 341-5.

every commune looks out the *tallest* and *slenderest tree*, a pine or fir on the hills, a poplar in the plains; when they have lopped all the boughs off, they drive into it a number of wedges a foot long, and keep it till the 23rd of June. Meanwhile it splits diamond-shape where the wedges were inserted, and is now rolled and dragged up a mountain or hill. There the priest gives it his blessing, they plant it upright in the ground, and set it on fire (ibid. 5, 387).

Strutt[1] speaks of Midsummer fires in England: they were lighted on Midsummer Eve, and kept up till midnight, often till cock-crow; the youth danced round the flame, in garlands of *motherwort* and *vervain*, with *violets* in their hands. In Denmark they are called Sanct *Hans aftens blus*, but also *gadeild* (street-fire), because they are lighted in public streets or squares, and on hills. [Is not gade conn. with sunna-gaht, p. 617?] Imagining that all poisonous plants came up out of the ground that night, people avoided lingering on the grass; but wholesome plants (chamaemelum and bardanum) they hung up in their houses. Some however shift these street-fires to May-day eve.[2] Norway also knows the custom: 'S. Hans aften brändes der baal ved alle griner (hedged country-lanes), hvilket skal fordrive ondt (harm) fra creaturerne,' Sommerfeldt's Saltdalen, p. 121. But some words quoted by Hallager p. 13 are worth noting, viz. *brandskat* for the wood burnt in the fields, and *brising* for the kindled fire; the latter reminds us of the gleaming necklace of Freyja (p. 306-7), and may have been transferred from the flame to the jewel, as well as from the jewel to the flame.

There is no doubt that some parts of Italy had Midsummer fires: at Orvieto they were exempted from the restrictions laid on other fires.[3] Italian sailors lighted them on board ship out at sea, Fel. Fabri Evagat. 1, 170. And Spain is perhaps to be included on the strength of · a passage in the Romance de Guarinos (Silva, p. 113):

---

[1] Sports and Pastimes of the People of England, by Jos. Strutt. New ed. by WHone, Lond. 1830, p. 359.

[2] Molbech's Dialect. Lex. 150. Lyngbye's Nord. tidskr. for oldk. 2, 352-9. Finn Magn. Lex. myth. 1091-4. Arndt's Reise durch Schweden 3, 72-3.

[3] Statuta urbevetana, an. 1491. 3, 51: Quicunque sine licentia officialis fecerit ignem in aliqua festivitate de nocte in civitate, in xl sol. denarior. puniatur, excepta festivitate S. Johannis bapt. de mense Junii, et qui in illa nocte furatus fuerit vel abstulerit ligna vel tabulas alterius in lib. x den. puniatur.

Vanse dias, vienen dias, venido era el *de Sant Juan*,
donde Christianos y Moros hazen gran solenidad :
los Christianos *echan juncia*, y los Moros *arrayhan*,
los Judios echan *eneas*, por la fiesta mas honrar.

Here nothing is said of fire,[1] but we are told that the Christians
strew *rushes*, the Moors myrtle, the Jews reeds ; and the throwing
of flowers and herbs into the flame seems an essential part
of the celebration, e.g. mugwort, monks-hood, larkspur (p. 618),
mullein and walnut leaves (p. 621). Hence the collecting of
all such *John's-herbs* in Germany (Superst. I, 157. 189. 190), and
of *S. Hans urter* (worts) in Denmark (K, 126), and the like in
France (L, 4). According to Casp. Zeumer's De igne in festo
S. Joh. accendi solito, Jenae 1699, the herb ἄλιδμα (?) was
diligently sought on that day and *hung up over doors*.

In Greece the women make a fire on Midsummer Eve, and
jump over it, crying, ' I leave my sins.' In Servia they think the
feast is so venerable, that the sun halts three times in reverence.[2]
On the day before it, the herdsmen tie birchbark into torches,
and having lighted them, they first march round the sheepfolds
and cattle-pens, then *go up the hills* and let them *burn out* (Vuk
sub v. Ivan dan). Other Slav countries have similar observances.
In Sartori's Journey through Carinthia 3, 349-50, we find the
rolling of St. John's *fiery wheel* fully described. Midsummer-
day or the solstice itself is called by the Slovèns *kres*, by the
Croats *kresz*, i.e. striking of light, from kresáti (ignem elicere),
Pol. krzesać ; and as May is in Irish mi-na-bealtine (fire-month),
so June in Slovenic is kresnik. At the kres there were *leaps of
joy* performed at night ; of lighting by friction I find no mention.
Poles and Bohemians called the Midsummer fire *sobótka*, i.e. little
Saturday, as compared with the great sobóta (Easter Eve) ; the

---

[1] It is spoken of more definitely by Martinus de Arles, canonicus of Pampeluna
(cir. 1510), in his treatise De superstitionibus (Tract. tractatuum, ed. Lugd. 1544.
9, 133): Cum in die S. Johannis propter jucunditatem multa pie aguntur a
fidelibus, puta pulsatio campanarum et *ignes jucunditatis*, similiter summo mane
exeunt ad colligendas herbas odoriferas et optimas et medicinales ex sua natura et
ex plenitudine virtutum propter tempus. . . quidam *ignes accendunt* in compitis
viarum, in agris, ne inde sortilegae et maleficae illa nocte transitum faciant, ut
ego propriis oculis vidi. Alii *herbas* collectas in die S. Johannis *incendentes* contra
fulgura, tonitrua et tempestates credunt suis fumigationibus arcere daemones et
tempestates.

[2] As he is supposed to leap three times at Easter (p. 291).

Bohemians used to *lead their cows over it* to protect them from witchcraft. The Russian name was *kupálo,* which some explain by a god of harvest, *Kupalo* : youths and maidens, garlanded with flowers and girt with holy herbs, assembled on the 24th June, *lighted a fire, leapt* and *led their flocks over it,* singing hymns the while in praise of the god. They thought thereby to shield their cattle from the lèshis or woodsprites. At times a *white cock* is said to have been burnt in the fire amid dance and song. Even now the female saint, whose feast the Greek ritual keeps on this day [Agrippina], has the by-name *kupálnitsa;* a burning pile of wood is called the same, and so, according to Karamzín, is the flower that is strewn on St. John's Day [ranunculus, crowfoot].[1] This fire seems to have extended to the Lithuanians too : I find that with them *kupóles* is the name of a St. John's herb. Tettau and Temme p. 277 report, that in Prussia and Lithuania, on Midsummer Eve fires blaze on all the heights, as far as the eye can reach. The next morning they drive their cattle to pasture over the remains of these fires, as a specific against murrain, magic and milk-drought, yet also against hailstroke and lightning. The lads who lighted the fires go from house to house collecting milk. On the same Midsummer Eve they fasten large burs and mugwort (that is to say, kupóles) over the gate or gap through which the cattle always pass.

Now at a bird's-eye view we perceive that these fires cover nearly all Europe, and have done from time immemorial. About them it might seem a great deal more doubtful than about water-lustration (pp. 585. 590), whether they are of heathen or of Christian origin. The church had appropriated them so very early to herself, and as Beleth and Durantis shew, had made them point to John ; the clergy took some part in their celebration, though it never passed entirely into their hands, but was mainly conducted by the secular authorities and the people itself (see Suppl.).

Paciaudi[2] labours to prove that the fires of St. John have nothing to do with the far older heathenish fires, but have sprung out of the spirit of Christian worship.

---

[1] Karamzín 1. 78. 81. 284. Götze's Russ. volksl. p. 280–2. Dobrovsky denies a god Kupalo, and derives the feast from kúpa (haycock) ; Hanusch p. 201 from kupel, kaupel, kupadlo (bath, pond), because acc. to Slav notions the sun rises out of his bath, or because pouring of water may have been practised at the festival.

[2] De cultu S. Johannis baptistae, Romae 1755, dissert. 8, cap. 1. 2.

In Deut. 18, 10 and 2 Chron. 28, 3 is mentioned the heathen custom of making *sons* and *daughters pass through a fire*. In reference to this, Theodoret bp. of Cyrus (d. 458), makes a note on 2 Kings 16, 3: εἶδον γὰρ ἔν τισι πόλεσιν ἅπαξ τοῦ ἔτους ἐν ταῖς πλατείαις ἁπτομένας πυρὰς καὶ ταύτας τινὰς ὑπεραλλομένους καὶ πηδῶντας οὐ μόνον παῖδας ἀλλὰ καὶ ἄνδρας, τὰ δέ γε βρέφη παρὰ τῶν μητέρων παραφερόμενα διὰ τῆς φλογός. ἐδόκει δὲ τοῦτο ἀποτροπιασμὸς εἶναι καὶ κάθαρσις. (In some towns I saw *pyres* lighted *once a year* in the streets, and not only *children* but *men leaping over them*, and the *infants passed through the flame* by their mothers. This was deemed a protective expiation).[1] He says 'once a year,' but does not specify the day, which would have shewn us whether the custom was imported into Syria from Rome. On April 21, the day of her founding, Rome kept the *palilia*, an ancient feast of herdsmen, in honour of Pales, a motherly divinity reminding us of Ceres and Vesta.[2] This date does not coincide with the solstice, but it does with the time of the Easter fire; the ritual itself, the leaping over the flame, the driving of cattle through the glowing embers, is quite the same as at the Midsummer fire and needfire. A few lines from Ovid's description in the 4th book of the Fasti shall suffice:

727. certe ego *transilui* positas *ter* in ordine flammas.
781. moxque *per ardentes stipulae* crepitantis *acervos*
        trajicias celeri strenua membra pede.
795. pars quoque, quum saxis pastores saxa feribant,
        scintillam subito prosiluisse ferunt;
        prima quidem periit; stipulis excepta secunda est,
        hoc argumentum *flamma palilis* habet.
805. per *flammas saluisse pecus, saluisse colonos;*
        quod fit natali nunc quoque, Roma, tuo (see Suppl.).

The shepherds had struck the fire out of stone, and caught it on straw; the leaping through it was to atone and cleanse, and to secure their flock against all harm. That *children* were *placed in the fire* by their mothers, we are not told here; we know how the infant Demophoon or Triptolemus was put in the fire by

---

[1] Opp., ed. Sirmond, Paris, 1642. 1, 352.
[2] The masc. *Pales*, which also occurs, may remind us of the Slav god of shepherds, Russ. *Volos*, Boh. *Weles*.

Ceres, as Achilles was by Thetis, to insure his immortality.[1] This fire-worship seems equally at home in Canaan, Syria, Greece and Rome, so that we are not justified in pronouncing it a borrowed and imported thing in any one of them. It is therefore hard to determine from what source the Christians afterwards drew, when they came to use it in their Easter and Midsummer festivals, or on other occasions. Canon 65 of the Council of A.D. 680 already contains a prohibition of these superstitious fires at *new moon*: τὰς ἐν ταῖς νουμηνίαις ὑπό τινῶν πρὸ τῶν οἰκείων ἐργαστηρίων ἢ οἴκων ἀναπτομένας πυρκαιὰς, ἃς καὶ ὑπεράλλεσθαί τινες, κατὰ τὸ ἔθος ἀρχαῖον, ἐπιχειροῦσιν, ἀπὸ παρόντος καταργηθῆναι προστάττομεν (The *fires* kindled before workshops and houses at new moon, which some *also leap over* after the *ancient* custom, we command henceforth to be abolished). The same thing was then forbidden, which afterwards, on St. John's day at least, was tolerated, and to some extent connected with church ordinances.

Now, even supposing that the *Midsummer fire* almost universal throughout Europe had, like the Midsummer bath, proceeded more immediately from the church, and that she had picked it up in Italy directly from the Roman palilia; it does not follow yet, that our *Easter fires* in northern Germany are a mere modification of those at Midsummer. We are at liberty to derive them straight from fires of our native heathenism: in favour of this view is the difference of day, perhaps also their ruder form; to the last there was more earnestness about them, and more general participation; Midsummer fires were more elegant and tasteful, but latterly confined to children and common people alone, though princes and nobles had attended them before. Mountain and hill are essential to Easter fires, the Solstitial fire was frequently made in streets and marketplaces. Of jumping through the fire, of flowers and wreaths, I find scarcely a word in connexion with the former; friction of fire is only mentioned a few times at the Midsummer fire, never at the Easter, and yet this friction is the surest mark of heathenism, and—as with needfire in North Germany, so with Easter fires there—may safely be assumed. Only of these last we have no accounts whatever. The Celtic bel-fires, and if my conjecture be right, our Phol-days, stand nearly midway betwixt

---

[1] Conf. the superstitious 'filium *in fornacem ponere* pro sanitate febrium,' and 'ponere infantem *juxta ignem*,' Superst. B, 10. 14, and p. 200ᵃ.

Easter and Midsummer, but nearer to Easter when that falls late.
A feature common to all three, and perhaps to all public fires
of antiquity, is the *wheel*, as friction is to all the ancient Easter
fires.

I must not omit to mention, that fires were also lighted at
the season opposite to summer, at *Christmas*, and in Lent. To
the Yule-fire answers the Gaelic samhtheine (p. 614) of the 1st
November. In France they have still in vogue the *souche de
Noël* (from dies natalis, Prov. natal) or the *tréfué* (log that burns
three days, Superst. K, 1. 28), conf. the *trefoir* in Brand's Pop. antiq.
1, 468. At Marseille they burnt the *calendeau* or *caligneau*, a
large oaken log, sprinkling it with wine and oil; it devolved on
the master of the house to set light to it (Millin 3, 336). In
Dauphiné they called it *chalendul*, it was lighted on Christmas
eve and sprinkled with wine, they considered it holy, and had
to let it burn out in peace (Champol.-Figeac, p. 124). Christmas-
tide was called *chalendes*, Prov. *calendas* (Raynouard 1, 292),
because New-year commenced on Dec. 25. In Germany I find
the same custom as far back as the 12th cent. A document of
1184 (Kindl.'s Münst. beitr. ii. urk. 34) says of the parish priest
of Ahlen in Münsterland : ' et arborem in nativitate Domini *ad
festivum ignem suum* adducendam esse dicebat.' The hewing of
the *Christmas block* is mentioned in the Weisthümer 2, 264. 302.
On the Engl. *yule-clog* see Sup. I, 1109, and the Scandinav.
julblok is well known; the Lettons call Christmas eve *blukku
wakkars*, block evening, from the carrying about and burning of
the log (blukkis).[1] Seb. Frank (Weltbuch 51ª) reports the following *Shrovetide* customs from Franconia: ' In other places they
draw a *fiery plough* kindled by a fire cunningly made thereon, till
it fall in pieces (supra, p. 264). Item, they wrap a *waggon-wheel*
all round in straw, drag it up an high steep mountain, and hold
thereon a merrymaking all the day, so they may for the cold,
with many sorts of pastime, as singing, leaping, dancing, odd or
even, and other pranks. About the time of vespers they *set the
wheel afire*, and let it *run into the vale* at full speed, which to look
upon is like as the sun were running from the sky.' Such a

[1] ' So the Lith. *kalledos* = Christmas, from kalada, a log.'—SUPPL.

'*hoop-trundling*' on Shrove Tuesday is mentioned by Schm. 1,
544; the day is called *funkentag* (spunk.), in the Rheingau *hall-
feuer*, in France '*la fête des brandons.*' [1] It is likely that similar
fires take place here and there in connexion with the vintage.
In the Voigtland on Mayday eve, which would exactly agree with
the bealteine, you may see *fires* on most of the hills, and children
with *blazing brooms* (Jul. Schmidt's Reichenf. 118). Lastly, the
Servians at Christmas time light a log of oak newly cut, *badniak*,
and pour wine upon it. The cake they bake at such a fire and
hand round (Vuk's Montenegro, 105) recalls the Gaelic practice
(p. 613). The Slavs called the winter solstice *koleda*, Pol.
koleda, Russ. koliadá, answering to the Lat. calendae and the
chalendes above; [2] they had games and dances, but the burning
of fires is not mentioned. In Lower Germany too *kaland* had
become an expression for feast and revelry (we hear of kaland-
gilden, kalandbrüder), without limitation to Christmas time, or
any question of fires accompanying it (see Suppl.).

If in the Mid. Ages a confusion was made of the two Johns,
the Baptist and the Evangelist, I should incline to connect with
St. John's fire the custom of *St. John's minne* (p. 61), which by
rights only concerns the beloved disciple. It is true, no fire
is spoken of in connexion with it, but fires were an essential
part of the old Norse minne-drinking, and I should think the
Sueves with their barrel of ale (p. 56) burnt fires too. In the
Saga Hâkonar góða, cap. 16, we are told: '*eldar* scyldo vera â
midjo gôlfi î hofino, oc þar katlar yfir, oc *scyldi full of eld bera,*'
should bear the cups round the fire. Very striking to my mind
is the '*dricka eldborgs skâl*' still practised in a part of Sweden
and Norway (Sup. K, 122-3). At Candlemas two tall candles
are set, each member of the household in turn sits down between
them, takes a drink out of a wooden beaker, then throws the
vessel backwards over his head. If it fall bottom upwards, the
thrower will die; if upright, he remains alive. [3] Early in the
morning the goodwife has been up making her fire and baking;
she now assembles her servants in a half-circle before the oven

---

[1] Sup. K, 16. Mém. des antiquaires 1, 236. 4, 371.
[2] Other derivations have been attempted, Hanusch 192-3. [See note, p. 627,
on Lith. *kalledos.*]
[3] A similar throwing backwards of an emptied glass on other occasions, Sup. I,
514. 707.

door, they all *bend the knee*, take one bite of cake, and *drink
eldborgsskål* (the fire's health) ; what is left of cake or drink is
cast into the flame. An unmistakeable vestige of heathen fire-
worship, shifted to the christian feast of candle-consecration as
the one that furnished the nearest parallel to it.

Our *ofen*, MHG. *oven*, OHG. *ovan*, ON. *ón* represents the Goth.
aúhns, O. Swed. *omn*, *ofn*, *ogn*, Swed. *ugn*, Dan. *on*; they all
mean fornax, i.e. the receptacle in which fire is inclosed (conf.
focus, fuoco, feu), but originally it was the name of the fire itself,
Slav. *ogan*, *ogen*, *ogn*, Boh. *ohen*, Lith. *ugnis*, Lett. *ugguns*, Lat.
ignis, Sanskr. *Agni* the god of fire. Just as the Swedish servants
kneel down before the *ugns-hol*, our German märchen and sagen
have retained the feature of *kneeling before the oven* and *praying
to it*; the unfortunate, the persecuted, resort to the oven, and
bewail their woe, they reveal to it some secret which they dare not
confide to the world.[1] What would otherwise appear childish is
explained : they are forms and formulas left from the primitive
fire-worship, and no longer understood. In the same way people
complain and confess to mother earth, to a stone, a plant, an oak,
or to the reed (Morolt 1438). This personification of the oven
hangs together with Mid. Age notions about orcus and hell as
places of fire. Conf. Erebi fornax (Walthar. 867), and what was
said above, p. 256, on *Fornax*.

The luminous element permitted a feast to be prolonged into
the night, and fires have always been a vehicle for testifying
joy. When the worship had passed over into mere *joy-fires*, *ignis
jocunditatis*, *feux de joie*, Engl. *bon-fires*, these could, without
any reference to the service of a deity, be employed on other
occasions, especially the entry of a king or conqueror. Thus
they made a *torch-waggon* follow the king, which was afterwards
set on fire, like the plough and wheels at the feast of St. John

---

[1] Haus und kinderm. 2, 20. 3, 221. Deutsche sagen no. 513. A children's
game has the rhyme : 'Dear good oven, I pray to thee, As thou hast a wife, send a
husband to me !' In the comedy 'Life and death of honest Madam Slut (Schlam-
pampe),' Leipz. 1696 and 1750, act 3, sc. 8: 'Come, let us go and *kneel to the oven*,
maybe the gods will hear our prayer.' In 1558 one who had been robbed, but had
sworn secrecy, told his story to the Dutch-tile oven at the inn. Rommell's Hess.
gesch. 4, note p. 420. Joh. Müller's Hist. Switz. 2, 92 (A.D. 1838). 'Nota est in
eligiis Tibulli *Januae* personificatio, cui amantes dolores suos narrant, quam orant,
quam increpant ; erat enim daemoniaca quaedam vis januarum ex opinione veterum,'
Dissen's Tib. 1, clxxix. Conf. Hartung's Rel. der Röm. 2, 218 seq.

(RA. 265). ' *Faculis* et faustis acclamationibus, ut prioribus regibus assueverant, obviam ei (non) procedebant,' Lamb. schafn. ad an. 1077. Of what we now call *illumination*, the lighting up of streets and avenues, there are probably older instances than those I am able to quote: ' von kleinen kerzen manec schoup geleit ûf ölboume loup,' of little tapers many a cluster ranged in olive bower, Parz. 82, 25. Detmar (ed. Grautoff 1, 301) on the Emp. Charles IV.'s entry into Lubeck : ' des nachtes weren die luchten bernde ut allen husen, unde was so licht in der nacht als in dem dage.' The church also escorted with torchlight processions : ' cui (abbati) intranti per noctis tenebras adhibent faces et lampadas,' Chapeaville 2, 532 (12th cent.). ' Hirimannus dux susceptus est ab archiepiscopo manuque deducitur ad ecclesiam accensis luminaribus, cunctisque sonantibus campanis,' Dietm. merseb. 2, 18. ' Taceo coronas tam luminoso fulgore a luminaribus pendentes,' Vita Joh. gorziens. (bef. 984) in Mabillon's Acta Ben., sec. 5, p. 395 (see Suppl.).

3. AIR.

The notions ' *air, wind, weather,*' touch one another, and their names often do the same.[1] Like water, like fire, they are all regarded as a being that moves and lives : we saw how the words *animus, spiritus, geist* (pp. 439. 461) come to be used of genii, and the Slav. *dukh* is alike breath, breathing, and spirit. Wuotan himself we found to be the all-pervading (p. 133) ; like Vishnu, he is the fine æther that fills the universe. But lesser spirits belong to this element too : *Gustr, Zephyr, Blaser* (p. 461), *Bläster, Wind-and-weather* (p. 548), proper names of dwarfs, elves, giants. In the Lithuanian legend the two giants Wandû (water) and *Weyas* (wind) act together (p. 579). To the OHG. *wetar*, OS. *wedar*, AS. *weder* (tempestas) corresponds the Slav. *veter, vietar* (ventus, aër) : and to Goth. *vinds*, OHG. *wint*, the Lat. *ventus*. The various names given to wind in the Alvismâl (Sæm. 50ᵃ) are easily explained by its properties of blowing, blustering and so forth : *œpir* (weeper) ejulans, the wailing, conf. OS. wôp (whoop), OHG. wuof ejulatus ; *gneggioðr* (neigher) strepens, quasi hinniens ; *dynfari* cum sonitu iens.

---

[1] Our *luft* I include under the root liuban, no. 530, whose primary meaning is still obscure ; conf. kliuban kluft, skiuban skuft.

Thus personification already peeps out in mere appellatives; in the mythic embodiments themselves it is displayed in the most various ways.

Woodcuts and plates (in the Sachsenspiegel) usually represent the winds, half symbolically, as *blowing faces*, or *heads*, probably a fancy of very early date, and reminding us of the *blowing John's-head* that whirls Herodias about in the void expanse of heaven (p. 285). The winds of the four cardinal points are imagined as *four dwarfs*: ' undir hvert horn (each corner) settu þeir dverg', Sn. 9 (p. 461) [1]; but by the Greeks as *giants* and *brethren*: Zephyrus, Hesperus, Boreas, Notus (Hes. Theog. 371), and Boreas's sons *Zetes* and *Kalaïs* are also *winged winds* (Apollon. Argon. 1, 219). *Aeolus* (αἰόλος nimble, changeful, many-hued), at first a hero and king, was promoted to be governor and guider of winds (ταμίης ἀνέμων, p. 93). In Russia popular tradition makes the four winds *sons of one mother*,[2] the O. Russ. lay of Igór addresses the wind as ' lord,' and the winds are called *Stribogh's grandsons*,[3] his divine nature being indicated by the ' bogh' in his name. So in fairy-tales, and by Eastern poets, the *wind* is introduced talking and acting : ' the wind, the *heavenly child !* '[4]

In the ON. genealogy, Forniotr, the divine progenitor of giants (p. 240), is made father of *Kári* (stridens) '*who rules over the winds ;*' Kári begets *Iökul* (glacies), and Iökul *Snær* (nix), the king whose children are a son *Thorri* and three daughters *Fönn, Drífa, Miöll*, all personified names for particular phenomena of snow and ice (Sn. 358. Fornald. sög. 2, 3. 17). Kári however is brother to Hlêr (p. 241) and Logi (p. 240), to water and fire, by which is expressed the close affinity between air and the other two elements. The old Scandinavian cry ' blås *kári !* ' is echoed in that of the Swedish sailors ' blås *kajsa !* ' a goddess instead of the god (Afzelius 1, 30). Both wind and fire ' blow' and ' emit spray,' nay, fire is called the *red wind :* ' von ir zweier swerte gie der *fiur-rôte wint*,' Nib. 2212, 4. In the same line of thought a higher divinity, Niörðr, has the sovereignty given him alike over

---

[1] And therefore *ôstrôni, westrôni, sundrôni, nordrôni* are masc. nouns ; the Go:hi; forms would be *âustrôneis*, etc.
[2] Russ. volksmärchen, Leipz. 1881. p. 119.
[3] ' Vêtre vêtrilo gospodine,' Hanka's ed. pp. 12. 36.
[4] E.g. in Nalus, p. 180 (Bopp's 2 ed.). Kinderm. nos. 15. 88.

O

water, wind and fire (p. 217) ; and *Loptr* (aëreus) is another name
for Loki (p. 246). A phrase in Cædm. 181, 13 seems worthy of
notice : ' *lyft-helme* beþeaht,' galea aërea tectus (see Suppl.).

When in our language we still call one kind of tempest (OHG.
wiwint, Graff 1, 624), the *windsbraut* (wind's bride), and it was
called the same in our older speech, OHG. *wintes brût*, O. v. 19,
27. *windis prût*, Gl. Hrab. 975ᵇ. Jun. 230. Diut. 2, 182. Gl.
florent. 982ª-3ᵇ-4ᵇ; MHG. *windes brût* (Gramm. 2, 606), Tit. 3733.
swinder (swifter) danne *windes brût*, Ms. 2, 131ª. lief spilnde
als ein w.b. durch daz gras, Fragm. 19ª. alsam in rôre diu w. b.,
Reinfried 159ᵇ. varn mit hurt als ein w. prût, Frauend. 92, 13 ;—
it is only the proper names that seem to be lost.[1] The corrupt
forms wintsprout, -praut (Suchenw. 41, 804), windbrauss (in later
writers, as Matthesius), windsprauch (Schm. 4, 110), have arisen
out of the endeavour to substitute some new meaning for the
no longer intelligible mythic notion. They say it is a woman
snatching up a napkin from the bleaching ground and falling
down with it, Mone's Anz. 8, 278. So in the Netherlands the
whirlwind is called *barende frauw*, Wolf nos. 518–520 (see Suppl.).

This wind's-bride is a whirlwind, at which our mythology
brings the highest gods into play. Even *Wuotan's* ' furious host,'
what is it but an explanation of the stormwind howling through
the air ? The OHG. *ziu*, turbines, we have traced to *Zio*, pp. 203.
285 ; and the storm-cloud was called *maganwetar* (p. 332 last l.).
But the whirlwind appears to be associated with *Phol* also (pp.
229. 285), and with an opprobrious name for the *devil* (schweine-
zagel, säuzagel, sûstert, sow's tail), to whom the raising of the
whirl was ascribed (Superst. I, 522)[2] as well as to *witches* (ibid.
554). It was quite natural therefore to look upon some female
personages also as prime movers of the whirlwind, the gyrating
dancing *Herodias*, and *frau Hilde, frau Holde* (p. 285). In Kilian
693 it is a *fahrendes weib;* in Celtic legend it is stirred up by *fays,*

---

[1] Orithyia carried off by Boreas (Ov. Met. 6, 710) could with perfect justice
be named *windesbrût* by Albrecht.
[2] Two Pol. tales in Woycicki 1, 81 and 89 : When the whirlwind (vikher) sweeps
up the loose sand, it is the evil spirit dancing ; throw a *sharp new knife* into the
middle of it, and you wound him. A magician plunged such a knife into his
threshold, and condemned his man, with whom he was angry, for seven years to ride
round the world on the swift stormwind. Then the whirlwind lifted the man, who
was making haycocks in a meadow, and bore him away into the air. This *knife-
throwing* is also known to Germ. superstition everywhere (I, 554).

and the Irish name for it is *sigh gaoite* ('O'Brien), *sighgaoithe* (Croker III, xxi); in a whirlwind elvish sprites can steal (Stewart p. 122). It is a popular belief in Sweden, that the skogsrå (wood-wife) makes her presence known by a violent *whirlwind* which shakes the trees even to breaking. The Slav. *polednice* (supra, p. 478n.) is a female daemon, who flies up in the dust of the whirlwind (Jungmann sub v.). According to a legend of the Mark (Kuhn no. 167) the whirlwind was a noble damsel who loved the chase above everything, and made havock of the hus- bandman's crops, for which she is doomed to ride along with the storm to all eternity; this again reminds us of Diana and the huntress Holda (see Suppl.).

In addition to these widely spread fancies, there is a peculiar one about the origin of wind, which appears to extend through nearly all Europe. According to the Edda, *Hræsvelgr* is the name of a *giant*, who in the *shape of an eagle* [1] sits at the end of heaven: *from his wings cometh all wind* upon men, Sæm. 35ᵇ. Snorri defines it more minutely: He sits at the north side of heaven, and *when he flaps his wings*, the winds rise from under them (Sn. 22.) And in the formula of the trygdamål (Grågås 2, 170), it is said: 'svå vîða sem *valr* flŷgr vårlångan dag, oc *standi byrr undir bâda vængi*,' far as falcon flies a summerlong day, when stands fair wind under both his wings. Light clouds threatening storm are called in Iceland *klô-sigi* (Biörn spells klôsegi), claw- sinking; acc. to Gunnar Pauli, because the eagle causes storm by letting down one of his claws (Finn Magn. p. 452).[2] It is also an Indian belief that tempest comes from *Garuda's wings*, Somadeva 2, 102: the motion of his flight stirs up the wind.

Then again people in the Shetland isles are said to conjure the storm-wind in the shape of a great *eagle*.[3] Further we are told that Charles the Great had a brazen eagle fixed on the top of his palace at Achen (Aix), and there was some connexion between it and the wind; Richerus 3, 71 (Pertz 5, 622) relates the inroad of the Welsh (Gauls) in 978: 'Aëneam *aquilam*, quae *in vertice palatii* a Karolo magno acsi *volans* fixa erat,[4] in *vul-*

---

[1] The giants often put on the *arnar ham* (erne's coat): Thiazi in Sn. 80. 82, Suttûngr in Sn. 86.

[2] Day also was imaged as a bird, who dug his claws into the clouds.

[3] Scott's Pirate, Edinb., 1822.

[4] It ought not to be overlooked here, that at the west door of Oðin's hall there

turnum converterunt. Nam Germani eam in *favonium* (Up. Germ. föhn) converterant, subtiliter significantes Gallos suo equitatu quandoque posse devinci.' The meaning seems to be, that the French turned the eagle's head to the south-east, the Germans to the west, to signify that like the storm they could make a raid (ride, that is what equitatus comes to) upon the country toward which the bird's head was directed. Dietmar of Merseburg's account 3, 6 (Pertz 5, 761) is as follows : ' Post haec autem imperator ordinavit expeditionem suam adversus Lotharium regem Karelingorum, qui in Aquisgrani palatium et sedem regiam nostrum semper respicientem dominium valido exercitu praesumpsit invadere, sibique *versa aquila* designare. Haec stat in orientali parte domus, morisque fuit omnium hunc locum possidentium *ad sua eam vertere regna.*' This statement appears less accurate than that of Richerus, for each would turn the eagle's head not toward his own kingdom, but the foreign or dependent one ; conf. Jahrb. d. Rheinlande v. vi. 73. But even in the 12th cent. the wind's connexion with the eagle was still known in Germany, for Veldek sings, MS. 1, 21ª: ' jârlanc ist reht daz der *ar* winke dem vil *süezen winde,*' all this year the eagle must beckon to (i.e. bring) a mild wind. How many fancies familiar to the Mid. Ages must be lost to us now, when of all the poets that mention air and wind and storm no end of times, only one happens to allude to this myth ! But not only do *aquila* and *aquilo,*[1] *vultur* and *vulturnus* point to each other ; ἄνεμος (wind) and ἀετός (eagle) are likewise from one root ἄω, ἄημι.[2] According to Horapollo 2, 15 a *sparrowhawk* with outspread wings represents the *wind.* Eagle, falcon, vulture, sparrowhawk, are here convertible birds of prey. The Indian *garuda,* king of birds, is at the same time the wind. The O.T. also thinks of the winds as winged creatures, without specifying the bird, 2 Sam. 22, 11 : ' rode on the *wings of the winds* '; Ps. 18, 11. 104, 3 : ' volavit super *pennas ventorum,*' which

also hung a wolf, and over it an *eagle* (drûpir örn yfir, Sæm. 41ᵇ), and that the victorious Saxons fixed an *eagle* over the city's gate, supra, p. 111.

[1] Festus: ' *aquilo* ventus a vehementissimo volatu ad instar aquilae appellatur '; conf. Hesychius, ἀκιρὸς ὁ βορῥᾶς.

[2] Wackernagel on Ablaut (vowel-change) p. 30. Eustathius on the Il. 87. 15 Rom.

Notker translates 'überfloug die vettacha dero windo'; and
Martina 7ᶜ has, in allusion to the biblical phrase, 'der ûf *der
winde vedern* saz.' The expression used by Herbort 17091, 'der
wint liez ouch dare gân,' shews that the poet imagined it either
flying or riding (see Suppl.).

The Finns call the eagle *kokko* (kotka); but a poem descriptive
of the *northstorm* begins: 'Came the eagle on from Turja, down
from Lappmark sinks a bird,' and ends: 'Neath his wing a
hundred men, thousands on his tail's tip, ten in every quill there
be.'[1] And in a Mod. Greek folk-song the *sparrowhawk* (as in
Horapollo) calls upon the *winds* to hush: ἀπὸ τὰ τρίκορφα βουνὰ
ἱεράκι ἔσυρε λαλιά· πάψετ,' ἀέρες, πάψετε ἀπόψε κ' ἄλλην μιὰν
βραδιά.[2] The winds are under the bird's command, and obey
him. In another song the mother sets three to watch her son
while he sleeps, in the mountains the sun, in the plain the eagle
(ἀετός), on the sea the brisk lord Boreas: the sun sets, the eagle
goes to sleep, and Boreas goes home to his mother;[3] from the
whole context here we must understand by the *eagle* the sweet
soft wind, and by Boreas the cool northwind.

Hræsvelgr (OHG. Hrêosuolah?) means swallower of corpses,
flesh-eater, Sansk. kraviyâda, and is used of birds of prey that
feed on carrion, but may also be applied to winds and storms
which purify the air: they destroy the effluvia from bodies that
lie unburied.

Is that the foundation of the fancy, that *when a man hangs
himself*, a tempest springs up, and the roar of the wind pro-
claims the suicide?[4] Is it the greedy carrion-fowl that comes
on in haste to seize the dead, his lawful prey, who swings unburied on the tree? Or does the air resent the self-murderer's
polluting presence in it? A New-year's storm is thought to
announce pestilence (Sup. I, 330. 910), spreading an odour of
death in anticipation.

Tempest (like fire) the common people picture to themselves as
a *voracious hungry being* (of course a giant, according to the root

[1] Finnish runes, Ups. 1819, pp. 58–60.
[2] Fauriel 2, 236. Wh. Müller 2, 100.
[3] Fauriel 2, 432. Wh. Müller 2, 120.
[4] Sup. I, 343. 1013. Kirchhofer's Schweiz. spr. 327. Cl. Brentano's Libussa
p. 432. Sartori's Reise in Kärnten 2, 164. Leoprechting 102.

idea of iötunn, p. 519), and they try to pacify him by pouring out flour in the air.[1] I take this to be an ancient superstition, and light is thrown upon it now by a Norwegian tale in Asbjörnsen no. 7, of the *northwind* carrying off a poor fellow's meal three times, but compensating him afterwards by costly presents. This *northwind* behaves exactly as a rough good-natured giant. (See Suppl.).

The raising of the *whirlwind* was, as we have seen (p. 632), ascribed to divine, semi-divine and diabolic beings. In Norway they say of whirlwinds and foul weather, 'the *giant* stirs his pots,' Faye p. 7.

In two weather-spells (Append., Exorcism v.) *Mermeut* and *Fasolt* are called upon as evil spirits and authors of storms. *Fasolt* is the well-known giant of our hero-legend, brother of Ecke, who was himself god of tides and waves (p. 239). The two brothers have kindred occupations, being rulers of the dread sea and of the weather. What we gather from the second spell about Fasolt seems to me of importance, and another conclusive proof of the identity of Ecke with Oegir: as Hlêr and Kâri are brothers and giants, so are also Ecke and Fasolt; as Hlêr commands the sea and Kâri the winds, so does Ecke rule the waters and Fasolt the storm. To the Norse poets the *wind* is 'Forniots sonr' and 'Oegis brôðir.'[2] Now, as Hlêr was called by another nation Oegir, i.e. Uogi, Ecke, so Kâri may have been called Fasolt. Fasolt must be an old word, if only because it is hard to explain; does it come under the OHG. fasa, fasôn (Graff 3, 705)? In ON., 'fas' is superbia, arrogantia; the name seems to express the overbearing nature of a giant. *Mermeut*, which occurs nowhere else, perhaps means the sea-mutterer? Schm. 2, 552. 653 has maudern, mutern, murmurare.—These demi-gods and giants stand related to Donar the supreme director of clouds and weather, as Æolus or Boreas to Zeus.

And from *Zeus* it was that the favourable wished-for wind proceeded: $\Delta\iota\grave{o}\varsigma$ $o\check{v}\rho o\varsigma$, Od. 5, 176. *Wuotan* (the all-pervading,

---

[1] Sup. I, 282. Praetorius's Weltbeschr. 1, 429: At Bamberg, when a *violent wind was raging*, an old woman snatched up her mealsack, and emptied it out of window into the air, with the words: 'Dear wind, don't be so wild; take that home to your child!' She meant to appease the hunger of the wind, as of a greedy lion or fierce wolf.

[2] 'Forniots sefar' = sea and wind, Sæm. 90ᵇ.

p. 630) makes the wish-wind, ôska-byrr, p. 144. What notion lies at the bottom of Wolfram's making *Juno* give the ' segels luft,' sail-wind (Parz. 753, 7)? Again in Parz. 750, 7 and 766, 4 : ' Juno fuocte (fitted) daz *weter*,' and ' *segelweter*.' The fruitful breeze that whispers in the corn was due to *Frô* and his boar, pp. 213-4. An ON. name of Oðinn was *Viðrir*, the weatherer : ' at þeir sögðu han veðrum ráða,' he governs weathers (Fornm. sög. 10, 171). Such a god was *Pogóda* to the Slavs, and the Pol. pogoda, Boh. pohoda, still signifies good growing or ripening weather [Russ. gód = time, year; pogóda = weather, good or bad]. *Typhon* in Egyptian legend meant the south wind, Hes. Theog. 301. 862.

The Lettons believed in a god of winds and storms *Okkupeernis*, and thought that from his forehead they came down the sky to the earth.[1]

In an ON. saga (Fornald. sög. 3, 122) appears giant Grîmnir, whose father and brother are named Grîmôlfr and Grîmarr, a sort of Polyphemus, who can excite *storm* or *good wind :* here again it is Oðinn we must think of (p. 144). Two semi-divine beings, honoured with temples of their own and bloody sacrifices, were the giant's daughters *Thorgerðr* and *Irpa* (p. 98). In the Skâldskaparmâl 154 Thorgerðr is called *Hölgabrûðr* or king Hölgi's daughter, elsewhere *hörgabrûðr* and *hörgatröll* (Fornald. sög. 2, 131), sponsa divum, immanissima gigas, which reminds us of our *wind's-bride*. Both the sisters sent *foul weather, storm* and *hail*, when implored to do so, Fornm. sög. 11, 134–7. And ON. legend mentions other dames besides, who make *foul weather* and *fog*, as Heiði and Hamglöm, Fornald. sög. 2, 72, Ingibiörg, ibid. 3, 442 (see Suppl.).[2]

What was at first imputed to gods, demigods and giants, the sending of wind, storm and hail (vis daemonum concitans procellas, Beda's Hist. eccl. 1, 17), was in later times attributed to human sorcerers.

First we find the Lex Visigoth. vi. 2, 3 provides against the ' malefici et *immissores tempestatum*, qui quibusdam incantationibus grandinem in vineas messesque mittere perhibentur.' Then Charles the Great in his Capit. of 789 cap. 64 (Pertz 3, 64) :

[1] Okka, or anka, storm ; peere forehead. Stender's Gramm. 266.
[2] Conf. p. 333, 463 hulizhialmr.

' ut nec cauculatores et incantatores, nec tempestarii vel obligatores non fiant, et ubicunque sunt, emendentur vel damnentur.' Soon after that king's death, about the beginning of Lewis the Pious's reign, bp. Agobard (d. 840) wrote ' Contra insulsam vulgi opinionem de grandine et tonitruis.' From this treatise, following Baluz's edit. of the works of Agobard, I take a few passages.

1, 145 : In his regionibus pene omnes homines, nobiles et ignobiles, urbani et rustici, senes et juvenes, putant *grandines* et *tonitrua* hominum libitu posse fieri. Dicunt enim, mox ut audierint tonitrua et viderint fulgura : ' *aura levatitia* est.' Interrogati vero, quid sit aura levatitia ? alii cum verecundia, parum remordente conscientia, alii autem confidenter, ut imperitorum moris esse solet, confirmant *incantationibus* hominum qui dicuntur *tempestarii, esse levatam,* et ideo dici *levatitiam auram.*

1, 146 : Plerosque autem vidimus et audivimus tanta dementia obrutos, tanta stultitia alienatos, ut credant et dicant, quandam esse regionem quae dicatur *Magonia,* ex qua *naves* veniant *in nubibus, in quibus fruges quae grandinibus decidunt et tempestatibus pereunt, vehantur in eandem regionem,* ipsis videlicet *nautis aëreis* dantibus pretia *tempestariis,* et accipientibus frumenta vel ceteras fruges. Ex his item tam profunda stultitia excoecatis, ut hoc posse fieri credant, vidimus plures in quodam conventu hominum exhibere vinctos quatuor homines, tres viros et unam feminam, quasi qui *de ipsis navibus ceciderint* : quos scilicet, per aliquot dies in vinculis detentos, tandem collecto conventu hominum exhibuerunt, ut dixi, in nostra praesentia, tanquam lapidandos. Sed tamen vincente veritate post multam ratiocinationem, ipsi qui eos exhibuerant secundum propheticum illud confusi sunt, sicut confunditur fur quando deprehenditur.

1, 153 : Nam et hoc quidam dicunt, nosse se tales *tempestarios,* qui *dispersam grandinem et late per regionem decidentem* faciant unum in locum fluminis aut silvae infructuosae, aut *super unam,* ut ajunt, *cupam,* sub qua ipse lateat, defluere. Frequenter certe audivimus a multis dici quod talia nossent in certis locis facta, sed necdum audivimus, ut aliquis se haec vidisse testaretur.

1, 158 : Qui, mox ut audiunt tonitrua vel *cum levi flatu venti,* dicunt ' *levatitia aura* est,' et maledicunt dicentes : ' maledicta lingua illa et arefiat et jam praecisa esse debebat, quae hos facit ! '

1, 159 : Nostris quoque temporibus videmus aliquando, collectis messibus et vindemiis, propter siccitatem agricolas seminare non posse. Quare non obtinetis apud *tempestarios* vestros, ut mittant *auras levatitias,* quibus terra inrigetur, et postea seminare possitis?

1, 161 : Isti autem, contra quos sermo est, ostendunt nobis homunculos, a sanctitate, justitia et sapientia alienos, a fide et veritate nudos, odibiles etiam proximis, a quibus dicunt *vehementissimos imbres, sonantia aquae tonitrua* et *levatitias auras* posse fieri.

1, 162 : In tantum malum istud jam adolevit, ut in plerisque locis sint homines miserrimi, qui dicant, se non equidem nosse immittere tempestates, sed nosse tamen *defendere a tempestate habitatores* loci. His habent statutum, *quantum de frugibus suis donent,* et appellant hoc *canonicum.* Many are backward in tithes and alms, *canonicum* autem, quem dicunt, suis defensoribus (a quibus se defendi credunt a tempestate) nullo praedicante, nullo admonente vel exhortante, *sponte persolvunt,* diabolo inliciente. Denique in talibus ex parte magnam spem habent vitae suae, quasi per illos vivant (see Suppl.).

It was natural for driving hail-clouds to be likened to a *ship* sailing across the sky; we know our gods were provided with cars and ships, and we saw at p. 332 that the very Edda bestows on a cloud the name of *vindflot.* But when the tempest-men by their spells call the air-ship to them or draw it on, they are servants and assistants rather than originators of the storm. The real lord of the weather takes the corn lodged by the hail into the ship with him, and remunerates the conjurors, who might be called his priests. The Christian people said : ' these conjurors sell the grain to the aëronaut, and he carries it away.' But what mythic country can *Magonia* mean ? It is not known whether Agobard was born in Germany or Gaul, though his name is enough to shew his Frankish or Burgundian extraction; just as little can we tell whether he composed the treatise at Lyons, or previously at some other place. The name Magonia itself seems to take us to some region where Latin was spoken, if we may rely on its referring to magus and a magic land.

In later times I find no mention of this *cloud-ship,* except in H. Sachs, who in his schwank of the Lappenhäuser ii. 4, 89ᶜ relates how they made a ship of feathers and straw, and carried it up the hill), with the view of launching out in it *when the mist should fall.* Fischer in Garg. 96ª introduces quite unconnectedly the *nebelschiffs segel* of Philoxenus (the guestfriend or Zeus ?) in a passage that has nothing in Rabelais answering to it.

In the latter part of the Mid. Ages there went a story of the wind-selling inhabitants of Vinland, which I give from a work composed towards 1360 by Glanvil or Bartholomaeus Anglicus, 'De proprietatibus rerum' 15, 172 : 'Gens (Vinlandiae) est barbara, agrestis et saeva, magicis artibus occupata. Unde et navigantibus per eorum litora, vel apud eos propter venti defectum moram contrahentibus, *ventum venalem* offerunt atque vendunt. Globum enim de filo faciunt, et *diversos nodos in eo connectentes, usque ad tres nodos* vel plures de globo *extrahi* praecipiunt, secundum quod voluerint ventum habere fortiorem.[1] Quibus propter eorum incredulitatem illudentes, *daemones aërem concitant* et ventum majorem vel minorem excitant, secundum quod plures *nodos de filo extrahunt* vel pauciores, et quandoque in tantum commovent ventum, quod miseri talibus fidem adhibentes justo judicio submerguntur.'—This selling of wind in Wilandia (as he calls it) is likewise mentioned in Seb. Frank's Weltbuch 60ª, without any description of the method. By Vinland is to be understood a part of the Greenland coast which had been early visited by Norwegians and Icelanders, and in ON. tales is by turns called Vinland and Vindland;[2] the latter form might have suggested the whole story of raising the wind, on which the ON. writings as well as Adam of Bremen are silent. Others however tell the same story of the Finns (Ol. Magnus 3, 15): it seems to me a tradition spread all over the North[3] (see Suppl.).

The Norse legends name wind produced by magic *görninga-veðr.* Ogautan (like Aeolus) had a *veðr-belgr* (-bellows, or leathern bag); when he shook it, storm and wind broke out (Fornald. sög. 2, 412); the same with Möndull (3, 338). The Swedish

---

[1] This globus resembles the Lat. *turbo*, a top or teetotum used in magic : 'citum retro solve, solve turbinem,' Hor. Epod. 17, 7.

[2] Fornm. sög. 2, 246. Isl. sög. 1, 9. 100. 151. Conf. Torfaeus's Hist. Vinlandiae antiquae, Hafn. 1705.

[3] The Esthonians believed that wind could be generated and altered. In the direction whence you wish it to blow, hang up a snake or set an axe upright, and whistle to make it come. A clergyman happened to see some peasants making a great fuss round *three stones*, eating, drinking and dancing to the sound of rustic instruments. Questioned as to the object of the feast, they replied that by means of those stones they could produce *wet weather* or *dry ;* dry, if they set them upright, wet if they laid them along (Ueber die Ehsten, p. 48) ; supra pp. 593–7.

king Eiríkr, son of Ragnar Lodbrok, bore the surname of *veðrhattr* (ventosi pilei) : whichever way he *turned his hat*, from there the *wished for wind* would blow (Saxo Gram. 175. Ol. Magnus 3, 13. Gejer's Häfder 582). One of our nursery-tales even, no. 71, tells of a man who can direct the weather by *setting his hat straight* or *askew*. There is an expression in the Edda, *vindhiâlmr* (Sæm. 168ᵇ), which reminds me of the OHG. name *Windhelm*, Trad. fuld. 2, 167 (see Suppl.).

That is a beautiful fancy in the Edda, of seven-and-twenty valkyrs riding through the air, and when their horses shake themselves, the *dew* dropping out of their manes on the deep valleys, and *hail* on the lofty trees : a sign of a fruitful year, Sæm. 145. So *morning-dew* falls on the earth each day from the foaming bit of the steed Hrîmfaxi (dew-mane), Sn. 11. The ON. meldropi, AS. meledeáw, OHG. militou (Gl. Jun. 224), MHG. miltou (Ms. 2, 124ª), all take us back to mel (lupatum equi) ; conf. note on Elene p. 164, where mel is derived from midl, mittul, and supra p. 421. Antiquity referred all the phenomena of nature to higher powers. The people in Bavaria call a dark rain-cloud ' *anel* mit der laugen,' granny with her ley (Schm. 1, 63) ; in Bohemia light clouds are *babky*, grannies. When mountain mist is rising, the Esthonians say ' the *Old one* is putting his fire out' ; our people ascribe it to animals at least : ' the hare is boiling [his supper], the fox is bathing, brewing,' Reinh. ccxcvi. When shapes keep rising in the mists on the seashore, the Italians call it *fata morgana*, p. 412 (see Suppl.).

The Scythians explained *drifting snow* as flying feathers (Herod. ·4, 31), and our people see in the flakes the feathers out of the goddess's bed, or goose (p. 268). Those snow-women Fönn, Drîfa, Miöll (p. 631) appear also to touch one side of Holda. The Lettish riddles, ' putns skreen, spahrni pill,' and ' putns skreen, spalwas putt '[1] mean a *rain-cloud* and a *snow-cloud*. In Switzerland vulgar opinion looks upon avalanches as ravening beasts, on whom (as on fire) you can put a check (see Suppl.).

4. EARTH.

Of the goddess, and her various names, we have spoken already : Nerthus p. 251, Erda p. 250, Faírguni p. 172. 256, Erce p. 253,

---

[1] Bird flies, wings drip. Bird flies, feathers drop. Stender's Gramm. 260.

Hludana p. 256, and others; in which the ideas of the ancients about Terra, Gaia, Ops, Rhea, Cybele, Ceres repeat themselves. On p. 303 the Indian Prithivî was compared with Freyja, and the closest kinship exists between Freyr and Niörðr (the male Nerthus). But also the bare element itself, the *molte* (mould, pulvis) p. 251, was accounted holy: it is the χθὼν πολυβότειρα, out of its teeming lap rise fruits and trees, into it the dead are laid, and decay or fire restores them to dust and ashes.[1] To die was 'to sink to the earth,' 'til iarðar (til moldar) hníga,' 'to kiss the earth,' still more prettily in ON. 'í móðurætt falla' (Nialss. cap. 45), in maternum genus cadere, to fall back into the womb of terra *mater*.[2] They also said '*iarðar megin* kiosa' (vim telluris eligere, *i.e.* invocare), Sæm. 27[b]; and as the Greeks made the falling giant acquire new strength the moment he touched the ground, the Edda has 'aukinn *iarðar megni*' (auctus vi telluris), 118[b], 119[a].[3] One who had been long away from home kissed the earth on treading it once more; in O.Fr. poems 'baiser la terre' is a sign of humility, Berte pp. 35. 43. 58. Renart 14835. As the pure stream rejects the malefactor, so neither will the earth endure him: 'uns solt diu erde nicht tragen,' Troj. 491 [conf. 'art cursed from the earth,' Gen. 4. 10–12]. Secrets were entrusted to the earth, as well as to fire and oven, p. 629 (see Suppl.).

It is more especially earth grown over with grass, the *greensward*, that has a sacred power; such grass the Sanskrit calls *khusa*, and in particular *durva*, to which correspond the AS. *turf*, ON. *torf*, OHG. *zurba*: 'holy earth and haulms of durva,' Sakuntala (Hirzel pp. 51. 127). I have also accounted for the famous *chrene crud* of the Salic law by our 'reines kraut,' clean herb; and explained 'chreneschruda (dat.) jactare' by the Roman

---

[1] Irstantent (they rise again) fon themo fûlen legare, ûz fon theru *asgu*, fon theru *falawisgu*, fon themo *irdisgen herde*, O. v. 20, 25–8.

[2] Ancient tombs have been discovered, in which the bodies neither lie nor sit, but crouch with the head, arms and legs pressed together, in receptacles nearly square. M. Fréd. Troyon of French Switz., who has carefully explored and observed many old graves, expressed to me his opinion, that by this singular treatment of dead bodies it was prob. intended to replace man in the same posture that he maintained in the womb before birth. Thus the return into mother earth would be at the same time an intimation of the coming new birth and resurrection of the embryo.

[3] The Servians, by way of protesting, say 'tako mit zemlie!' so (help) me earth. A Gaelic saw (Armstrong sub v. coibhi, priest, supra p. 92 note) declares: 'ged is fagus clach do 'n làr, is faigse na sin cobhair choibhi,' near as a stone is to the ground, the coibhi's help is nearer still, which seems to imply the earth's prompt assistance as well as the priest's.

'*puram herbam* tollere,' as the Hel. 73, 7 has *hrêncurni*, an OHG.
gloss *reincurnes* = frumenti, MHG. 'daz *reine gras*,' Iw. 6446, and
grass and 'der melm,' dust, are coupled together, Wh. 24, 28.
The purport of the law is, that *earth* or *dust* must be taken up
from the four corners of the field, and thrown with the hand *over
the nearest kinsman.* It was a solemn legal ceremony of heathen
times, which the christian Capitulars abolished. Against my
interpretation, however, Leo has now set up a Celtic one (cruin-
neach collectus, criadh terra),[1] and I cannot deny the weight
of his arguments, though the German etymology evidently
has a stronger claim to a term incorporated in the text itself
than in the case of glosses [because the Latin text must be
based on a Frankish original]. The mythic use made of the
earth remains the same, whichever way we take the words.

The ON. language of law offers another and no less significant
name: the piece of turf [under which an oath was taken] is
called *iarðmen, iarðar men ;* now 'men' is literally monile, OHG.
mani, meni, AS. mene, as we saw in the case of Freyja's necklace 'Brîsînga men.' But 'iarðar men' must once have been
Iarðar men, Erda's necklace, the greensward being very poetically
taken for the goddess's jewelry. The solemn 'gânga undir
Iarðar men' (RA. 118-9) acquires its true meaning by this. In
other nations too, as Hungarians (RA. 120), and Slavs (Böhme's
Beitr. 5, 141), the administration of oaths took place by the person who swore placing *earth* or *turf* on his head (see Suppl.).

The custom of conquered nations presenting *earth* and *water*
in token of submission reaches back to remote antiquity : when
the Persians declared war, they sent heralds to demand the two
elements of those whose country they meant to invade,[2] which
again reminds us of the Roman 'pura.' Our landsknechts as
late as the 16th century, on going into battle, threw a *clod of
earth* (like him that threw chrenechruda) in token of utter re-
nunciation of life.[3] Among the Greeks too, grasping the *sod*

---

[1] Zeitschr. f. d. alterth. 2, 163 seq. Malb. gl. 2, 149. 150.
[2] Brissonius De regno Pers. 3, 66—71. Herod. 4, 127. 5, 18. Curtius iii. 10,
108. Aristotle Rhet. ii. 22, 87. Also Judith 2, 7 : ἑτοιμάζειν γῆν καὶ ὕδωρ (Cod.
alex. ed. Augusti).
[3] Barthold's Frundsberg p. 58-9. In the Mid. Ages, when a nun was consecrated, her kinsmen, as a sign that she renounced all earthly possessions, threw
earth over the maiden's *arm;* conf. Svenska visor 1, 176 :

    det voro så många grefvar båld,

signified taking possession of land, especially in the case of
emigrants. As Euphamos sits on the prow of the Argo, Triton
appears in human form and presents him with a *clod of earth* as a
gift of hospitality. Euphamos takes the symbolic earth ($\beta\omega\lambda\alpha\kappa\alpha$
$\delta\alpha\iota\mu\nu\nu\iota\alpha\nu$), and gives it to his men to keep, but they drop it
in the sea, and it melts away. Had it been preserved and
deposited at Tainaros, the descendants of Euphamos would have
won the promised land (Cyrene) in the fourth generation. As
it was, they only got it in the 17th (see Suppl.).[1]

In an AS. spell which is elsewhere given, four pieces of *turf*
are cut out, oil, honey, yeast and the milk of all cattle are dropt
on them, and thereto is added some of every kind of tree that
grows on the land, except hard trees,[2] and of every herb except
burs; and then at length the charm is repeated over it. With
their seedcorn people mix *earth* from *three sorts of fields* (Superst.
I, 477); on the coffin, when lowered, *three clods* are dropt (699);
by cutting out the *sod* on which footprints [of a thief or enemy]
are left, you can work magic (524. 556; and see Suppl.).

Of holy *mountains* and *hills* there were plenty; yet there seems
to have been no elemental worship of them: they were honoured
for the sake of the deity enthroned upon them, witness the
Wôdan's and Thunar's hills. When Agathias, without any such
connexion, speaks of $\lambda\acute{o}\phi o\iota$ and $\phi\acute{a}\rho\alpha\gamma\gamma\epsilon\varsigma$ (hills and gullies) as
objects of worship (p. 100); possibly his knowledge of the facts
was imperfect, and there was a fire or water worship connected
with the hill. It is among the Goths, to whom *fairguni* meant
mountain (p. 172), that one would first look for a pure mountain-
worship, if the kinship I have supposed between that word and
the god's name be a matter of fact. Dietmar of Merseburg
(Pertz 5, 855) gives an instance of mountain-worship among the
Slavs: ' Posita autem est haec (civitas, viz. Nemtsi, Nimptch)
in pago silensi, vocabulo hoc a *quodam monte*, nimis excelso et
grandi, olim sibi indito : et hic ob qualitatem suam et quantitatem,
cum execranda gentilitas ibi veneraretur, *ab incolis omnibus nimis*

som hade deraf stor harm (great sorrow),
der de nu *kastade den svarta mull* (black mould)
allt *öfver skön* Valborg's arm.

[1] Pindar's Pyth. 4, 21–44. O. Müller's Orchom. 352, and proleg. 142 seq.;
his Dorier 1, 85. 2, 585.
[2] ' Only of soft wood, not hard,' RA. 506.

honorabatur.' The commentators say it is the Zobtenberg in Silesia (see Suppl.).

Here and there single *stones* and *rocks*, or several in a group, sometimes arranged in circles, were held in veneration (Append. ' vota ad *lapides*,' especially ' *lapides* in ruinosis et silvestribus locis venerari ;' AS. *stânweorðung*, ' bringan tô *stâne*,' Thorpe pp. 380. 396). This worship of stones is a distinguishing character- istic of Celtic religion,[1] less of Teutonic, though amongst our- selves also we meet with the superstition of slipping through *hollow stones* as well as hollow trees, Chap. XXXVI. Cavities not made artificially by human hand were held sacred. In Eng- land they hang such holy-stones or holed-stones at the horses' heads in a stable, or on the bed-tester and the house-door against witchcraft. Some are believed to have been hollowed by the sting of an adder (adderstones). In Germany, holy stones were either mahlsteine of tribunals or sacrificial stones : oaths were taken ' at ursvölum *unnar steini*,' ' at enom *hvíta helga steini*,' Sæm. 165ª. 237ᵇ. *heilög fiöll* 189ᵇ. *Helgafell*, Landn. 2, 12 ; conf. espec. Eyrbygg. saga c. 4. Four holy stones are sunk to cleanse a profaned sea (supra p. 87 note). A great number of stones which the giant or devil has dropt, on which he has left the print of his hand or foot, are pointed out by popular legend, without any holy meaning being thereby imparted to them (see Suppl.).

As giants and men get petrified (p. 551), and still retain, so to speak, an after-sense of their former state, so to rocks and stones compassion is attributed, and interest in men's condition. Snorri 68 remarks, that stones begin to sweat when brought out of the frost into warmth, and so he explains how rocks and stones wept for Baldr. It is still common to say of bitter anguish : ' a stone by the wayside would feel pity,' ' it would move a heart of stone.'[2] Notice the MHG. phrase : ' to squeeze a stone with

---

[1] Conf. Armstrong sub v. carn and clachbrath ; O'Brien sub v. carn ; H. Schreiber's Feen, p. 17 on the menhir and pierres fites, p. 21 on the pierres branlantes. Of spindle-stones I have spoken, p. 419.

[2] This mode of expression is doubtless very old ; here are specimens from MHG. : ez erbarmet einem *steine*, Hart. erst. büchl. 1752. wær sîn *herze steinen*, swer (whoso) si weinen sæhe, ze weinen im geschæhe, Herb. 66ᵈ ; ir klage mohte erbarmen einen *stein* 89ᵇ. erbarmen ein *steinhertez herze*, Flore 1498. ir jâmer daz moht einen *vels* erbarmen, Lohengr. p. 16. ez moht ein stein beweinet hân dise barmunge, Dietr. 48ª. Mark, the stones did not weep of themselves, but were moved to sympathy by the weeping and wailing of the hapless men, which as it

straps, till its veins drop blood,' MsH. 2, 235[b], suggested no
doubt by the veins which run through some stones (see Suppl.).

In closing this chapter, I will group together the *higher* gods
who more immediately govern the four elements.   Water, springs,
rain and sea are under Wuotan (Nichus), Donar, Uogi, Holda.
Fire, lightning under Donar, Loki.   Air, wind under Wuotan,
Frô. Earth under Nerthus and many others, mentioned on
p. 641-2.

---

were penetrated their ears. So in Holberg (Ellefte juni 4, 2): hörte jeg en sukken
og hylen, som en *steen* maatte *gräde ved.* And Ovid (Met. 9, 303): moturæque
duras Verba queror *silices.* Luke 19, 40: οἱ λίθοι κεκράξονται [Habak. 2, 11: the
stones shall cry out of the wall].

CHAPTER XXI.

TREES AND ANIMALS.

As all nature was thought of by the heathen mind as living;[1] as language and the understanding of human speech was allowed to beasts, and sensation to plants (see Suppl.) ; and as every kind of transition and exchange of forms was supposed to take place amongst all creatures : it follows at once, that to some a higher worth may have been assigned, and this heightened even up to divine veneration. Gods and men transformed themselves into trees, plants or beasts, spirits and elements assumed animal forms ; why should the worship they had hitherto enjoyed be withheld from the altered type of their manifestation ? Brought under this point of view, there is nothing to startle us in the veneration of trees or animals. It has become a gross thing only when to the consciousness of men the higher being has vanished from behind the form he assumed, and the form alone has then to stand for him.

We must however distinguish from divinely honoured plants and animals those that were esteemed high and holy because they stood in close relationship to gods or spirits. Of this kind are beasts and vegetables used for sacrifice, trees under which

[1] The way it is expressed in the Eddic myth of Baldr is more to the point than anything else : To ward off every danger that might threaten that beloved god, Frigg exacted oaths from water, fire, earth, stones, plants, beasts, birds and worms, nay from plagues personified, that they would not harm him ; one single shrub she let off from the oath, because he was too young, Sn. 64. Afterwards all creatures weep the dead Baldr, men, animals, plants and stones, Sn. 68. The OS. poet of the Heliand calls dumb nature the *unquethandi*, and says 168, 32 : ' that thar Waldandes dôd (the Lord's death) *unquethandes* sô filo antkennian scolda, that is endagon *ertha* bivôda, hrisidun thia hôhun *bergos*, harda *stênos* clubun, *felisos* after them felde.' It is true these phenomena are from the Bible (Matth. 27, 51-2), yet possibly a heathen picture hovered in the author's mind (as we saw on pp. 148. 307), in this case the mourning for Baldr, so like that for the Saviour. Herbort makes all things bewail Hector : if (says he, 68ᵃ) stones, metals, chalk and sand had wit and sense, they would have sorrowed too. As deeply rooted in man's nature is the impulse, when unfortunate, to bewail his woes to the rocks and trees and woods ; this is beautifully expressed in the song Ms. 1, 8ᵇ, and all the objects there appealed to, offer their help.

higher beings dwell, animals that wait upon them. The two classes can hardly be separated, for incorrect or incomplete accounts will not allow us to determine which is meant.

I. TREES.

The high estimation in which *Woods* and *Trees* were held by the heathen Germans has already been shown in Chap. IV. To certain deities, perhaps to all, there were groves dedicated, and probably particular trees in the grove as well. Such a grove was not to be trodden by profane feet, such a tree was not to be stript of its boughs or foliage, and on no account to be hewn down.[1] Trees are also consecrated to individual dæmons, elves, wood and home sprites, p. 509.

Minute descriptions, had any such come down to us, would tell us many things worth knowing about the enclosure and maintenance of holy woods, about the feasts and sacrifices held in them. In the Indiculus paganiarum we read ' de sacris silvarum, quae *nimidas* vocant.' This German word seems to me uncorrupted, but none the easier to understand: it is a plur. masc. from the sing. *nimid*,[2] but to hit the exact sense of the word, we should have to know all the meanings that the simple verb neman was once susceptible of. If the German nimu be, as it has every appearance of being, the same as νέμω, then nimid also may answer to Gr. νέμος, Lat. nemus, a woodland pasture, a grove, a sacrum silvae (p. 69).[3] Documents of 1086 and 1150

---

[1] *Sacrum nemus, nemus castum* in Tacitus. Ovid, Amor. iii. 1, 1:

> Stat vetus et multos *incaedua silva* per annos,
> credibile est illi numen inesse loco :
> fons sacer in medio, speluncaque pumice pendens,
> et latere ex omni dulce queruntur aves.

Lucan, Phars. 3, 399 : Lucus erat longo *nunquam violatus* ab aevo. So the Semnonian wood, the nemus of Nerthus, the Slav lucus Zutibure, the Prussian grove Romowe. Among the Esthonians it is held infamous to pluck even a single leaf in the sacred grove : *far as its shade extends* (ut umbra pertingit, RA. 57. 105), they will not take so much as a strawberry ; some people secretly bury their dead there (Petri Ehstland 2, 120). They call such woods *hio*, and the I. of Dagö is in Esth. *Hiomah*, because there is a consecrated wood near the farmhouse of *Hiohof* (Thom. Hiärn.).

[2] Like helid (heros), gimeinid (communio), frumid, pl. frumidas (AS. frymðas, primitiae), barid (clamor, inferred from Tacitus's baritus).

[3] Can *nimid* have been a heathen term for sacrifice? Abnemen in the 13th cent. meant mactare, to slaughter (used of cattle), Berthold p. 46, as we still say abthun, abschneiden, Ulph. ufsneiþan ; Schmid's Schwäb. wtb. 405 abnehmen to kill poultry. This meaning can hardly lie in the prefix, it must be a part of the word itself:

name a place *Nimodon, Nimeden* (Möser's Osnabr. gesch., urk. 34. 56. 8, 57. 84) ; the resemblance may lead to something further (see Suppl.).

There can be no doubt that for some time after the conversion the people continued to light candles and offer small sacrifices under particular holy trees, as even to this day they hang wreaths upon them, and lead the ring-dance under them (p. 58). In the church-prohibitions it is variously called : ' vota ad *arbores* facere aut ibi *candelam* seu quodlibet munus deferre; *arborem* colere ; votum ad *arborem* persolvere ; *arbores daemonibus consecratas* colere, et in tanta veneratione habere, ut vulgus nec *ramum* nec *surculum audeat amputare.*' It is the AS. *treow-weorðung* (cultus arborum), the ON. blôta *lundinn* (grove), Landn. 3, 17. The Acta Bened. sec. 2 p. 841 informs us : ' Adest quoque ibi (at Lutosas, now Leuze) non ignoti miraculi *fagus* (beech), *subter quam luminaria* saepe cum *accensa* absque hominum accessu videmus, divini aliquid fore suspicamur.' So the church turned the superstition to account for her own miracles : a convent was founded on the site of the tree. About Esthonians of the present day we are told in Rosenplänter's Beitr. 9, 12, that only a few years ago, in the parish of Harjel, on St. George's, St. John's and St. Michael's night, they used to *sacrifice under certain trees,* i.e. to *kill, a black fowl.*[1] Of the Thunder-god's *holy oak* an account has been given, pp. 72-3-4. 171. 184; and in Gramm. 2, 997 the OHG. *scaldeih* (ilex) is compared with the AS. names of plants scaldhyfel, scaldþyfel and the scaldo quoted above, p. 94. All, this is as yet uncertain, and needs further elucidation.

Among the Langobards we find a worship of the so-called *blood-tree* or *holy tree* (p. 109). The Vita S. Barbati in the Acta sanctor. under Febr. 19, p. 139. The saint (b. cir. 602, d. cir. 683) lived at Benevento, under kings Grimoald and Romuald ;

---

niman, neman would therefore be to cut, kill, divide, and *nimidas* the victims slain in the holy grove, under trees ? Conf. what is said in the text of the Langobardic tree of sacrifice. Celtic etymologies seem rather out of place for this plainly Saxon Indiculus. Adelung already in Mithrid. 2, 65. 77 had brought into the field Nemetes and nemet (templum) ; Ir. naomh is sanctus, neamh (gen. nimhe) coelum, niem- headh land consecrated, belonging to the church.

[1] The superstition of the Lausitz Wends holds that there are woods which *yearly demand a human victim* (like the rivers, p. 494); some person must lose his life in them : 'hohla dyrbi kojzde ljeto janeho czloweka mjecs,' Lausitz mon. schr. 1797, p. 748.

the Lombard nation was baptized, but still clung to superstitious practices: 'Quin etiam non longe a Beneventi moenibus devotissime *sacrilegam colebant arborem*, in qua *suspenso corio* cuncti qui aderant terga vertentes arbori celerius equitabant, calcaribus cruentantes equos, ut unus alterum posset praeire, atque in eodem cursu *retroversis manibus in corium jaculabantur*. Sicque particulam modicam ex eo comedendam superstitiose accipiebant. Et quia stulta illic *persolvebant vota*, ab actione illa nomen loco illi, sicut hactenus dicitur, *votum* imposuerunt.' In vain Barbatus preaches against it: 'illi ferina coecati dementia nil aliud nisi sessorum meditantes usus, optimum esse fatebantur *cultum legis majorum suorum*, quos nominatim bellicosissimos asserebant.' When Romuald was gone to Naples, 'repente beatissimus Barbatus securim accipiens et *ad votum* pergens, suis manibus *nefandam arborem*, in qua *per tot temporis spatia* Langobardi exitiale sacrilegium perficiebant, defossa humo a radicibus incidit, ac desuper terrae congeriem fecit, ut nec indicium ex ea quis postea valuerit reperire.' [1] This part about felling the tree has an air of swagger and improbability; but the description of the heathen ceremony may be true to the life. I have pointed out, p. 174, that the Ossetes and Circassians hung up the *hides of animals on poles* in honour of divine beings, that the Goths of Jornandes *truncis suspendebant exuvias* to Mars (p. 77 note), that as a general thing *animals* were hung on *sacrificial trees* (pp. 75–9); most likely this tree also was sacred to some god through sacrifices, i.e. votive offerings of individuals,[2] hence the whole place was named 'ad votum.' What was the meaning of *hurling javelins through the suspended skin*, is by no means clear; in the North it was the custom to *shoot through a hanging raw oxhide* (Fornm. sög. 3, 18. 4, 61), as a proof of strength and skill. Doing it backwards

---

[1] Another Vita Barbati (ibid. p. 112) relates as follows: 'Nam quid despicabilius credendum est, quam ex mortuis animalibus non carnem sed corium accipere ad usum comestionis, ut pravo errori subjecti Langobardi fecerunt? qui suarum festa solennitatum equis praecurrentibus unus altero praecedente, sicut mos erat *gentilium, arbori* ludificae procul non satis Benevento *vota sua solvebant.* Suspensa itaque putredo corii in hanc *arborem divam*, equorum sessores versis post tergum brachiis ignominiam corii certabant lanceolis vibrare. Cumque lanceolis esse vibrata pellis mortua cerneretur, veluti pro remedio animae ex hac illusione corii partis mediae factam recisionem gustabant. Ecce quali ridiculo vanae mentis homines errori subjacebant pestifero!'

[2] Supra p. 360 note; votum is not only vow, but the oblatio rei votivae: 'votare puerum' in Pertz 2, 93 is equiv. to offerre.

increased the difficulty, and savours of antiquity.[1] Why the
particle of skin that was knocked out should be eaten, it is hard
to say; was it to indicate that they were allowed to participate
in the sacrifice? (p. 46; see Suppl.).

And not only were those trees held sacred, under which men
sacrificed, and on which they hung the head or hide of the
slaughtered beast, but saplings that *grew up on the top of sacrificed animals.* A willow slip set over a dead foal or calf is not
to be damaged (Sup. I, 838); are not these exactly Adam of
Bremen's '*arbores ex morte vel tabo immolatorum divinae*'? (p.
76).[2]

Of hallowed trees (which are commonly addressed as *frau,*
dame, in the later Mid. Ages) the *oak* stands at the head (pp.
72-77): an oak or beech is the arbor frugifera in casting lots
(Tac. Germ. 10). Next to the oak, the *ash* was holy, as we may
see by the myth of the creation of man; the ashtree Yggdrasill
falls to be treated in Chap. XXV. The wolf, whose meeting of
you promises victory, stands under ashen boughs. ' The common
people believe that 'tis very dangerous to break a bough from
the *ask*, to this very day,' Rob. Plot's Staffordshire p. 207. One
variety, the mountain-ash or *rountree*, rowan-tree, is held to have
magical power (Brockett p. 177),[3] (conf. Chap. XXVII., Rönn).
With dame *Hazel* too our folk-songs carry on conversations, and
hazels served of old to hedge in a court of justice, as they still do
cornfields, RA. 810. According to the Östgöta-lag (bygdab. 30),
any one may in a common wood hew with impunity, all but *oaks*
and *hazels,* these have peace, *i.e.* immunity. In Superst. I, 972 we
are told that oak and hazel dislike one another, and cannot agree,
any more than haw and sloe (white and black thorn; see Suppl.).
Then the *elder* (sambucus), OHG. *holantar,* enjoyed a marked
degree of veneration; holan of itself denotes a tree or shrub (AS.
cneowholen=ruscus). In Lower Saxony the sambucus nigra is

---

[1] So the best head had to be touched *backwards*, RA. 396; so men sacrificed
with the head turned away (p. 493), and threw backwards over their heads (p. 628).
[2] A scholium on Ad. of Bremen's Hist. eccl. (Pertz, scr. 7, 879) is worth
quoting: ' Prope illud templum (upsaliense) est *arbor maxima,* late ramos extendens,
aestate et hieme semper virens : cujus illa generis sit, nemo scit. Ibi etiam est fons,
ubi sacrificia Paganorum solent exerceri, et homo vivus immergi, qui dum im-
mergitur (al. invenitur), ratum erit votum populi.' To sink in water was a good
sign, as in the ordeal (RA. 924; conf. Chap. XXXIV., Witch's bath).
[3] Esculus Jovi sacra, Pliny 16, 4 (5).

called *ellorn*, *ell*-horn.[1]   Arnkiel's testimony 1, 179 is beyond
suspicion : ' Thus did our forefathers also hold the ellhorn holy, and
if they must needs clip the same, they were wont first to say this
prayer : " Dame Ellhorn, give me somewhat of thy wood, then will
I also give thee of mine, if so be it grow in the forest."   And this
they were wont to do sometimes with bended knees, bare head and
folded hands, as I have ofttimes in my young days both heard
and seen.'   Compare with this the very similar accounts of *elder
rods* (Sup. I, 866), of planting the *elder* before stables (169), of
pouring water under the *elder* (864), and of the *elder's mother*
(Sup. K, Dan. 162).[2]   The *juniper*, wacholder, plays an important part in the märchen of *machandel*boom ; in the poem of the
Mirror's adventure, fol. 38, occurs the mysterious statement :

Fraw Weckolter, ich sich	Dame Juniper, I see
daz du ir swester bist,	that thou her[3] sister art,
du kund ouch falsche list	thou knewest false cunning too
dô du daz kind verstalt.	when thou stolest the child.

A man in Sudermania was on the point of cutting down a fine
shady juniper, when a voice cried out, ' hew not the juniper ! '
He disregarded the warning, and was about to begin again, when
it cried once more ' I tell thee, hew not down the tree ! ' and he
ran away in a fright.[4]   A similar notion lies at the bottom of
kindermärchen no. 128, only it has a ludicrous turn given it; a
voice out of the tree cries to the hewer, ' he that hews *haspelholz*
(windlass-wood), shall die.'   Under such a tree, the Klinta *tall*
(deal-tree, pine) in Westmanland, dwelt a hafs-fru, in fact the
pine tree's râ (p. 496) ; to this tree you might see snow-white
cattle driven up from the lake across the meadows, and no one
dared to touch its boughs.   Trees of this kind are sacred to individual elves, woodsprites, homesprites ; they are called in Swed.

---

[1] AS. *ellen*. The Canones editi sub Eadgaro rege, cap. 16 (Thorpe, p. 396),
speak of the sorcery practised ' on *ellenum* and eác on oðrum mislicum treowum '
(in sambucis et in aliis variis arboribus).
[2] The god Pushkait lives under the *elder*, and the Lettons used to set bread and
beer for him beside the tree, Thom. Hiärn, p. 43. [In Somersetshire they will not
burn elder wood, for fear of ill luck.—TRANS.]
[3] My faithless lover's.
[4] I find this quoted from Locoenius's Antiq. Sueog. 1, 3 ; it is not in the ed. of
1647, it may be in a later. Afzelius 2, 147 has the story with this addition, that at
the second stroke blood flowed from the root, the hewer then went home, and soon
fell sick.

bo-träd, in Dan. *boe-trä* (p. 509). Under the lime-tree in the Hero-book dwarfs love to haunt, and heroes fall into enchanted sleep: the sweet breath of its blossoms causes stupefaction, D. Heldenb. 1871, 3, 14-5. 135 (see Suppl.). But elves in particular have not only single trees but whole *orchards* and *groves* assigned them, which they take pleasure in cultivating, witness Laurin's *Rosegarden* enclosed by a silken thread. In Sweden they call these gardens *elfträd-gårdar*.

The Greek dryads[1] and hamadryads have their life *linked to a tree*, and as this withers and dies, they themselves fall away and cease to be; any injury to bough or twig is felt as a wound, and a wholesale hewing down puts an end to them at once.[2] A cry of anguish escapes them when the cruel axe comes near. Ovid in Met. 8, 742 seq., tells a beautiful story of Erisichthon's impious attack on the grove of Ceres:

> Ille etiam Cereale nemus violasse securi
> dicitur, et lucos ferro temerasse vetustos.
> Stabat in his *ingens annoso robore quercus,*
> saepe sub hac dryades festas duxere choreas . . .
> Contremuit, gemitumque dedit Deoïa quercus,
> et pariter frondes, pariter pallescere glandes
> coepere, ac longi pallorem ducere rami.

When the *alder* (erle) is hewn, it bleeds, weeps, and begins to speak (Meinert's Kuhländch. 122). An Austrian märchen (Ziska 38-42) tells of the stately *fir*, in which there sits a fay waited on by dwarfs, rewarding the innocent and plaguing the guilty; and a Servian song of the maiden in the *pine* (fichte) whose bark the boy splits with a gold and silver horn. Magic spells banish the ague into *frau Fichte* (see Suppl.).

This belief in spirit-haunted trees was no less indigenous among Celts. Sulpicius Severus (beg. of 5th cent.) reports in his life of St. Martin, ed. Amst. 1665, p. 457: 'Dum in vico quodam templum antiquissimum diruisset, et *arborem pinum,* quae fano erat proxima, esset aggressus excidere, tum vero antistes illius luci ceteraque gentilium turba coepit obsistere; et cum iidem illi, dum templum evertitur, imperante domino quievissent, *succidi arborem*

---

[1] AS. gloss, *wudu-elfenne*, wood-elfins, fem. pl.
[2] 'Non sine hamadryadis fato cadit arborea trabs.' Ausonius.

non patiebantur. Ille eos sedulo commonere, nihil esse religionis in stipite; Deum potius, cui serviret ipse, sequerentur; arborem illam exscindi oportere, quia esset *daemoni* dedicata' (see Suppl.).

A great deal might be written on the sacredness of particular *plants* and *flowers.* They are either dedicated to certain gods and named after them (as Donners bart, p. 183. Baldrs brâ, p. 222. Forneotes folme, p. 240. Lokkes havre, p. 242. Freyju hâr, Friggjar gras, p. 302-3); or they come of the transformation of some afflicted or dying man. Nearly all such plants have power to heal or hurt, it is true they have to be plucked and gathered first: the Chap. on magic will furnish examples. Like sacred tutelary beasts, they are blazoned on the coats-of-arms of countries, towns, and heroes. Thus to the Northwest Germans, especially Frisians and Zeelanders, the *seeblatt* (nymphaea, nenuphar) was from the earliest times an object of veneration. The Hollanders call it *plompe,* the Frisians *pompe :* strictly speaking, the broad leaves floating on the sea are *pompebledden,* and the fragrant white flowers, golden yellow inside, *swanneblommen* (flores cygnei); which recals the names given at p. 489, *nixblume, näckblad, muhme* and *mummel* (*i.e.* swan-maiden). The Frisians put seven 'sea-blades' (zeven plompenbladen) in their escutcheon, and under that emblem looked for victory;[1] our Gudrunlied (1373) knows all about it, and furnishes Herwîc of Sêwen or Sêlanden with a sky-blue flag: ' *sêbleter* swebent (float) dar inne.' This sea-flower is the sacred lotus of old Egypt, and is also honoured in India; the Tibetans and Nepâlese bow down to it, it is set up in temples, Brahma and Vishnu float on its leaf; and it is no other than a M. Nethl. poem that still remembers Thumbkin floating on the leaf (p. 451).

---

[1] J. H. Halbertsma's Het Buddhisme en zijn stichter, Deventer 1843, pp. 3. 10; and he adds, that the people are to this day very careful in picking and carrying the plompen: if you fall with the flower in your hand, you get the falling sickness. Plomben, our plumpfen, ON. pompa, means plumping or plunging down. Acc. to W. Barnes, ' butterpumps – ovary of the yellow waterlily;' conf. Lith. pumpa, Slav. pupa, wen, pimple? Mart. Hamconii Frisia, Franekarae 1620, p. 7, says Friso introduced the cognisance of the *seven sea-blades :* ' insigne Frisonis, ut Cappidus refert, *septem* fuerunt rubra *nympheae herbae* folia, in tribus argenteis constitutae trabibus per *scutum caeruleum* oblique ductis.' Cappidus is said to have been a priest at Stavorn at the beg. of the 10th century, but nothing more is known of him. Conf. Van d. Bergh's Volksoverlev. p. 38. 41. 110. Others connect the division of Friesland into 7 sea-lands with the 7 leaves of the scutcheon; it is not known for certain when that division first began; see De vrije Vries 4, 137.

2. ANIMALS.

We shall have still more to say about sacred *animals*, which enter into more intimate relations with man than dumb nature can; but their cultus will admit of being referred to two or three principal causes. Either they stood connected with particular gods, and to some extent in their *service*, as the boar belongs to Frô, the wolf and raven to Wuotan; or there lies at the basis the *metamorphosis of a higher being* into some animal shape, on the strength of which the whole species comes to be invested with a halo of honour. That is how we may in some instances have to take a bear, bull, cow or snake, presupposing an incarnation, though our mythology may have long ceased to reach so far back as to give a full account of it. Then, bordering close upon such a lowering of the god into the animal, comes the penal *degradation of man into a beast*, the old doctrine of transmigration, in which we discover a third reason for the consecration of animals, though it does not warrant an actual worship of them. Those myths, e.g. of the cuckoo, woodpecker, nightingale, and so on, furnish a fund of beautiful tales, which enter largely into the hero-worship (see Suppl.).

QUADRUPEDS.—Foremost of animals I name the *horse*, the noblest, wisest, trustiest of domestic animals, with whom the hero holds friendly talk (p. 392), who sympathizes in his griefs and rejoices in his victories. As some heroes are named after the horse (Hengest, Hors), the horse too has proper names given him; Norse mythology assigns to nearly every god his separate horse, endowed with miraculous powers. Oðin's steed is named *Sleipnir* (p. 154), and is, like some giants and heroes, an octopod.[1] The other horses of the âses are enumerated by Sæm. 44ª and Sn. 18, without specifying to which they belonged. Several names are formed with 'faxi' (jubatus, comatus, OHG. vahso), as *Skînfaxi* (Sæm. 32. Sn. 11), *Gullfaxi* (Sn. 107-10), *Hrímfaxi* (Sæm. 32. 91. Sn. 11), *Freyfaxi* (Vatnsd. 140-1). Of these, Gullfaxi the gold-maned belonged to giant Hrûngnir, Skînfaxi the shiny-

---

[1] Old riddle on Oðinn and Sleipnir in the Hervararsaga: 'Who are the two that go to Thing (council) together, and have three eyes, ten legs and one tail between them?' A mode of expression quite of a piece with our old habits of speech; thus in the Weisthümer it is said the officers of the court shall come to the assize with 6½ mouths, meaning three men on horseback and a dog.

maned was the steed of Day, and Hrímfaxi the rimy-maned
(p. 641) of Night.   But even *Faxi* by itself is a name for horses,
e.g. Fornald. sög. 2, 168. 508.   *Arvakr* (early-waker), *Alsviðr*
(all-wise) are horses of the sun-chariot, Sæm. 45. Sn. 12; on
Arvakr's ear, on Alsvinn's [1] hoof, there were runes written; also
runes 'á *Sleipnis* tönnom (teeth),' Sæm. 196ª, as well as on the
bear's paw and the wolf's claws.[2] *Svaðilfari* was the horse that
helped the giant in building, Sn. 46. And our hero-legend has
handed down the names of many famous horses (p. 392).   *Bajart*
is described as intelligent, like Alsviðr; he is said to be still alive
in Ardennes forest, where you may hear him neigh every year on
Midsummer day (Quatre fils Aimon 180ᵉ).   The track of Schim-
ming's shoe stands printed on the rock, Vilk. saga cap. 37 (see
Suppl.).

The *Freyfaxi* in Vatnsdælasaga was owned by a man named
Brandr, who is said to have worshipped it (at hann hefði átrúnað
á Faxa), and was therefore called Faxabrandr.   The unpublished
saga of Hrafnkell is known to me only from Müller's Bibl. 1, 108,
but he too had a horse *Freyfaxi* (mispr. Freirfara), which he
had half given to Freyr, vowing at the same time to slay the
man who should mount it without his leave.   I can give the
passage from Joh. Erici de philippia apud priscos boreales, Lips.
1755, p. 122: 'Hrafnkell átti þann grip í eigo sinni, er hánom
þótti betri enn annar, þat var hestr bleikalóttr at lit, er hann
kallaði *Freyfaxa*, hann *gaf Frey vin sinom* (supra, pp. 93. 211)
þenna hest hálfann. á þessom hesti hafði hann svá mikla elsko
(love), at hann strengdi þess heit (vow), at hann skyldi þeim
manni at bana verða, er þeim hesti riði án hans vilja.'   Brand's
'átrúnað' refers, no doubt, to the same circumstance of his horse
being hallowed and devoted to the god.   A striking testimony
to this is found in Olafs Tryggvasonar saga:[3] Tidings came to
the king, that the Trœndir (men of Drontheim) had turned back
to the worship of Freyr, whose statue still stood among them.
When the king commanded them to break the image, they replied: 'ei munum ver brióta *likneski Freys*, þvíat ver höfum leingi

---

[1] Sviðr, gen. svinns, like maðr, manns.
[2] Reminding of the Germ. Beast-apologue (Reinh. cclxiii.).   In Fornald. sög.
1, 169 Rafn prefers, wrongly I think, the reading 'höfði,' head.
[3] Ed. Skalh. 1698. 1690. 2, 190 cap. 49; this cap. is left out in Fornm. sög. 2,
189, but inserted at 10, 312.

honum þionat ok hefr oss vel dûgat.' Olafr summoned them
to an assembly, resolving to destroy the idol himself, and sailed
to the coast where the temple (hof) stood. When he landed, he
found the *horses of the god grazing there* (þâ sâu hans menn stôð-
hross nokr við vegin, er þeir sögðu at hann Freyr sætti). The
king mounted the stallion, and his courtiers the mares, and so
they rode to the temple; Olafr dismounted, walked in and threw
down the idols (goðin),[1] but took Frey's image away with him.
When the Trændir found their gods dishonoured, and Frey's
image carried off, they were ware that the king had done it, and
they came to the place of meeting. The king had the image set
up in the Thing, and asked the people : 'know ye this man ? '
' It is Freyr our god' they answered. ' How has he shewn his
power to you ? ' ' He has often spoken to us, foretold the
future, granted plenty and peace (veitti oss âr oc frið).' ' The
devil spake to you ' said the king ; then taking an axe, he cried
to the image : ' Now help thyself, and defend thee if thou canst.'
Freyr continuing silent, Olafr hewed off both his hands, and then
preached to the people how this idolatry had arisen. The whole
narrative bears the impress of a later age, yet it had sprung out
of Norse tradition, and assures us that *horses were consecrated* to
Freyr, and *maintained* in the hallowed *precincts of his temples.*
Had not the temples of other gods such horses too ? The animals
that Wilibrord found grazing in Fosete's sanctuary (p. 230) can
hardly have been horses, or he would not have had them slaughtered for food; but the practice of rearing cattle consecrated to
the gods is established by it none the less. And apart from this,
it seems that single beasts were maintained by private worship-
pers of the god.

Such breed of pure and dedicated horses was destined for holy
uses, especially sacrifice, divination, and the periodical tours of
deities in their cars. Their manes were carefully cultivated,
groomed and decorated, as the name *Faxi* indicates; probably
gold, silver and ribbons were twined or plaited into the locks
(*Gullfaxi, Skinfaxi*) ; mön glôar (juba splendet), Sæm. 92ª, lýsir
mön af mari (lucet juba ex equo) 32ᵇ, as indeed the Lat. jubar
suggests juba, because a mane does radiate, and light sends out

---

[1] So that there were other statues standing beside Frey's.

beams in the manner of hair.[1] *Gulltoppr, Silfrintoppr* are names of horses whose tails were tied round with gold or silver, Sn. 44. The names *Gyllir* and *Gler* (golden, glittering, ibid.) may be given them for the same reason, or because their hoofs were shod with gold, or from the gilding of the bridle and saddle. Of colours, *white* was esteemed the noblest; a king would make his entry, or bestow a fief, seated on a *milk-white steed.* The Weisthümer often mention the *white horse* (e.g. 3, 342. 857); if an inheritance lie vacant, the governor is to mount a *white foal*, and taking one man before him and the other behind, to set one of them down on the property (3, 831; conf. 2, 541). A foal was esteemed even purer and nobler than a horse (see Suppl.).[2]

Tacitus (Germ. 9, 10), after saying 'lucos ac nemora consecrant,' adds: 'Proprium gentis, *equorum* quoque *praesagia* ac monitus experiri. *Publice aluntur, iisdem nemoribus ac lucis, candidi et nullo mortali opere contacti,* quos pressos sacro curru sacerdos ac rex vel princeps civitatis comitantur, *hinnitusque ac fremitus* observant. Nec ulli auspicio major fides, non solum apud plebem, sed apud proceres, apud sacerdotes: se enim ministros deorum, *illos conscios* putant;' these sacred beasts are in the secrets of the gods, and can reveal their counsels. And in christian times the Indiculus pagan. cap. xiii. speaks 'de *auguriis equorum*,' without describing them further. A *horse's neigh* is an omen of good (Sup. I, 239).[3] To warriors victory was foretokened by their chargers' *neighing* (OHG. hueiôn, MHG. weien, M. Neth. neien, ON. hneggja, Swed. gnägga), and defeat by their withholding the cheerful spirit-stirring strain: see an instance in the Flem. rhyming chron., ed. Kausler 7152. We

---

[1] Single hairs out of the mane or tail of a sacred horse were treasured up. Franz Wessel relates, p. 14, that when the Johannites preached in a town or village, they had a fine stallion ridden round, to which the people offered 'afgehowen woppen (bunch of oat ears)'; any one who could get a hair out of the horse's tail, thought himself lucky, and sewed it into the middle of his milk-strainer, and the milk was proof against witchcraft.

[2] A foal's tooth, it seems, was hung about the person, and worn as a safeguard. A MHG. poet says: 'gevater unde *füli-zant* an grôzen nœten sint ze swach,' godfathers and foal's teeth are too weak in great emergencies, MS. 2, 160ᵇ. To let children ride on a black foal makes them cut their teeth easily, Superst. I, 428. From Eracl. 1320. 1485 *ful-zene* appear to be the milk-teeth shed by a foal (see Suppl.).

[3] What the *breath* of a swine has polluted, is set right again by that *of the horse* (Sup. I, 820. K, 92); the horse is a *clean animal*. It helps a woman in labour, for a *horse to feed out of her apron* (Sup. I, 337).

know how the Persians chose a king by the neighing of his horse, Herod. 3, 84. In the Norwegian tale Grimsborken (Asb. and Moe, no. 38) a foal is suckled by twelve mares, and gets to talk sensibly (see Suppl.).

And as Mîmi's head retained its wisdom after it was cut off (379), heathendom seems to have practised all sorts of magic by cutting off *horse's heads* and sticking them up. In a nursery-tale (no. 89) the trusty Falada's head is *nailed up over the gate*, and carries on converse with the king's daughter. This cutting off and setting up of *horse's heads* has been mentioned at p. 47-8 as an ancient German custom. Pliny 19, 10 (58) notices, as a remedy for caterpillars : ' si *palo imponantur* in hortis *ossa capitis ex equino genere.*' In Scandinavia they stuck a horse's head on a pole, and turned the gaping jaws, propped open with a stick, in the direction whence the man they had a spite against, and wished to harm, was sure to come.[1] This was called a *neidstange* (spite-stake). Saxo Gram. p. 75 : *Immolati diis equi abscissum caput conto excipiens, subjectis stipitibus distentos faucium rictus aperuit,* sperans se primos Erici conatus atrocis spectaculi formidine frustraturum. Arbitrabatur enim ineptas barbarorum mentes oblatae cervicis terriculamento cessuras ; et jam Ericus obvium illis iter agebat. Qui prospecto eminus capite, obscoenitatis apparatum intelligens, silere socios cautiusque se gerere jubet, nec quemquam temere praecipitare sermonem, ne incauto effamine ullum maleficiis instruerent locum, adjiciens, si sermone opus incideret, verba se pro omnibus habiturum. Jamque medius illos amnis secreverat, cum magi, ut Ericum pontis aditu deturbarent, *contum quo equi caput refixerant* fluvio citimum locant. Ille nihilominus pontem intrepide aggressus, 'in latorem' inquit ' gestaminis sui fortuna recidat, nos melior consequatur eventus. Male maleficis cedat, infaustae molis gerulum onus obruat, nobis potiora tribuant omina sospitatem ! ' Nec secus quam optabatur evenit : continuo namque excussa cervice ruens ferentem stipes oppressit.—Egilssaga p. 389 : Egill tôk î hönd ser *heslis staung* (hazel rod), ok geck â bergsnaus nockura, þâ er vissi til lands inn. þâ tôk hann *hross-höfuð ok setti up â staungina.* siðan veitti

---

[1] *Wolves' heads* were in like manner held open with *hazel rods* and *hung up* Isengr. 645-7-8. Reinardus 3, 293. 812. Reinhart, introd. p. lxix.

hann formála ok mælti sva: 'her set ek upp *niðstaung*, ok sný ek þessu nîði á hönd Eiríki konúngi ok Gunnhilda dróttníngu.' hann *sneri hross-höfðinu inn á land.*—At other times they carved a man's head out of wood, and fastened it to a stake which was inserted in the breast of a *slaughtered horse.*[1] Vatnsd. saga, p. 142: Iökull skar karls höfut á súlu endann, ok risti á rúnar með öllum þeim formála sem fyrr var sagdr, síðan *drap* Iökull *mer* eina (killed a mare), ok opnuðu hana hia briostinu, *færðu á súluna,* ok létu horfa þeim á Borg (see Suppl.). It is well worth noticing, that to this very day the peasants' houses in a part of Lower Saxony (Lüneburg, Holstein, Mecklenburg) have *horses' heads carved* on the gables: they look upon it merely as an ornament to the woodwork of the roof, but the custom may reach far back, and have to do with the heathen belief in outward-pointing heads keeping mischief away from houses.[2] The Jahrb. of the Meckl. verein 2, 118 says, these *horses' heads* are nailed transversely on each gable-end (kühlende) of the roof, a reminiscence of the sacred horses of the ancients. Heinr. Schreiber (Taschenb. f. 1840, p. 240 seq.) has likewise noticed these horses rushing at each other on gables of the older houses in Romanic Rhætia (not Germ. Switz., but Tyrol; see Zingerle's Sitten p. 55); he is decidedly over hasty in pronouncing them a Celtic symbol, for if we were to say that the custom in L. Saxony was a legacy from the earlier Celtic inhabitants, criticism would lose all firm footing. To me this custom, as well as horse-worship altogether, seems to belong equally to Celts, Teutons and Slavs; what particular branches of these races were most addicted to it, will by degrees unfold itself to future research (see Suppl.). Prætorius (Weltbeschr. 2, 162-3) relates, that the Non-German people (Wends) used to keep off or extirpate cattle-plagues by fixing round their stables the *heads of mad horses and cows* on

---

[1] Conf. Sup. I, 838, planting the willow in the dead foal's mouth.

[2] Pretty much as they turned the eagle's head on the house, and thought thereby to shift the wind (p. 633-4). The heathen practice of fastening up animals' heads explains many very old names of places in Germ. and France, as *Berhaupten, Tierhaupten, Roshaupten,* Schm. 2, 223. Ad locum qui nuncupatur *caput caballinum,* Pertz 2, 278. Ad locum qui vocatur *caput equi* (Vita S. Magni, in Canisius's Lect. ant. 1, 667), with the addition in Goldast (Scr. rer. Alem. i. 2, 198): 'ět idcirco vocatus est ille locus caput equi, quia omnes venatores reliquerant ibi suos caballos, et pedestres ibant ad venandum.' Obviously a false later interpretation; in fact this life of St. Magnus (Magnoald, Mangold) has a good many interpolations, conf. Mabillon's Acta Bened. sec. 2, p. 505.

hedge-stakes; also that if at night their horses were ridden to exhaustion by the night-hag or leeton, they put a *horse's head* among the fodder in the crib, and this would curb the spirit's power over the beast. Very likely the superstitious burying of a *dead head* in the stable (I, 815) means that of a horse,[1] conf. Chap. XXXVIII., Nightmare. In Holland they hang a *horse's head* over pigstyes (Westendorp p. 518), in Mecklenburg it is placed under a sick man's pillow (Jahrb. 2, 128). We saw the *horse's head* thrown into the Midsummer fire with a view to magical effects (p. 618).[2]

Prætorius's account is enough to shew that Slavs agreed with Germans in the matter of horse-worship. But older and weightier witnesses are not wanting. Dietmar of Merseburg (6, 17. p. 812) reports of the Luitizers, *i.e.* Wilzes: 'Terram cum tremore infodiunt, quo sortibus emissis [imm. ?] rerum certitudinem dubiarum perquirant. Quibus finitis, cespite viridi eas operientes, *equum*, qui maximus inter alios habetur et *ut sacer ab his veneratur, super fixas* in terram *duorum cuspides hastilium inter se transmissorum* supplici obsequio *ducunt*, et praemissis sortibus quibus id explicavere prius, per hunc *quasi divinum* denuo *augurantur*; et si in duabus his rebus par omen apparet, factis completur; sin autem, a tristibus populis hoc prorsus omittitur.' —The Vita beati Ottonis episcopi bambergensis, composed by an unknown contemporary (Canisius iii. 2, 70), relates more fully of the Pomeranians, whom Otto converted A.D. 1124: 'Habebant *caballum mirae magnitudinis*, et pinguem, *nigri coloris*, et acrem valde. Iste toto anni tempore vacabat, tantaeque fuit *sanctitatis* ut nullum dignaretur sessorem; habuitque unum de quatuor sacerdotibus templorum custodem diligentissimum. Quando ergo itinere terrestri contra hostes aut praedatum ire cogitabant, eventum rei hoc modo solebant praediscere. *Hastas novem* disponebantur humo, spatio unius cubiti ab invicem separatae. Strato ergo caballo atque frenato, sacerdos, ad quem pertinebat custodia illius, tentum freno *per jacentes hastas transversum ducebat ter*, atque *reducebat*. Quod si pedibus inoffensis hastisque

---

[1] Conf. Fornald. sög. 2, 168. 300, what is said of Faxi's *hross-haus*.
[2] Why should the monks in the abbey have a *caput caballinum*? Reinhardus 3, 2082. 2153. Does the expression spun out of a *dead horse's head*' in Burchard, Waldis 4, 2, mean enchanted?

indisturbatis equus transibat, signum habuere prosperitatis, et
securi pergebant; sin autem, quiescebant.'—Here the holy steed
is led *across nine* spears lying a cubit apart from one another, in
Dietmar's older narrative *over* the points of *two* crossed spears;
of course the Luitizers may have had a different method from the
Pomeranians. Saxo Gram. p. 321 gives yet a third account of
the matter respecting the Slavs of Rügen: ' Praeterea peculiarem
albi coloris equum titulo possidebat (numen), cujus *jubae aut caudae
pilos convellere* nefarium ducebatur. Hunc soli sacerdoti pascendi
insidendique jus erat, ne *divini animalis* usus quo frequentior hoc
vilior haberetur. In hoc equo, opinione Rugiae, *Svantovitus* (id
simulacro vocabulum erat) adversus sacrorum suorum hostes bella
gerere credebatur. Cujus rei praecipuum argumentum exstabat,
quod is nocturno tempore stabulo insistens adeo plerumque mane
sudore ac luto respersus videbatur,[1] tanquam ab exercitatione
veniendo magnorum itinerum spacia percurrisset. *Auspicia*
quoque per eundem equum hujusmodi sumebantur. Cum bellum
adversum aliquam provinciam suscipi placuisset, ante fanum *tri-
plex hastarum ordo* ministrorum opera disponi solebat, in quorum
quolibet *binae e traverso junctae* conversis in terram cuspidibus
figebantur, aequali spaciorum magnitudine ordines disparante.
Ad quos equus ductandae expeditionis tempore, solenni precatione
praemissa, a sacerdote e vestibulo cum loramentis productus, si
propositos ordines *ante dextro quam laevo pede* transcenderet,
faustum gerendi belli omen accipiebatur. Sin *laevum vel semel
dextro praetulisset*, petendae provinciae propositum mutabatur.'—
This description is still more exact: the sacred horse, here attributed to the deity himself who bestrides him by night, is led
three times over two spears planted crosswise, that is, *over six*
spears, and must, for the omen to be favourable, pass each row
with his right foot foremost; if at even one row he has lifted
the left before the right, misfortune is threatened. The colour
ascribed to the steed is *white* as in Tacitus, not *black* as in the
biographer of Otto.

The Chronica Augustensis ad. an. 1068 (in Freher 1, 349)
says, that Bp. Burcard of Halberstadt (the Buko still known in

---

[1] As the horse ridden by the night-spirit is covered with dust and sweat the
next morning (see p. 287 and Suppl.).

our children's game) took away their sacred horse from the
Lutizers, and rode home to Saxony on it himself: ' Burcardus
Halberstatensis episcopus Luiticiorum provinciam ingressus in-
cendit, vastavit, avectoque *equo quem pro deo* in Rheda[1] *colebant,
super eum sedens* in Saxoniam rediit.'

May we then adopt the hypothesis, that Dietmar and the
Augsburg chronicler mean the sacred horse of Radigast at
Rhetra, and Saxo and the author of the Vita Ottonis that of
Sviatovit at Arkona? Each of these gods[2] had horses hallowed
to him, and others may have had the same. And so in Germany
too, horses may have been dedicated to several deities, and
divination performed with them under similar forms; especially
to the gods Frouwo (p. 656) and Wuotan (p. 154-5-6).

Some accounts of the reverence paid to sacred horses in Ditmarsen have a doubtful look. The Rieswold or Riesumwold on
the confines of N. and S. Ditmarsen is said to have been a holy
wood, in which human sacrifices were offered, and *white horses
consecrated to gods* were maintained.[3] This is simply an unauthor-
ized appropriation of the statement in Tacitus to a particular
locality. There is more of local colour in what Bolten 1, 262 repeats after the suspicious Carsten, that at Windbergen there
stood a grove set apart to Hesus (!), which is still called Hese
or Heseholt.[4] In the grove *two white horses*, a young and an
old, were fed for the god, no one was allowed to mount them, and
good or bad auguries were gathered from their neighing and
leaping. Some talk of ten or even twenty horses. A priest of
the god stuck staves in the ground, led the bridled steed along,
and by certain processes made it *leap* slowly *over the staves.*
Joh. Aldolfi, *i.e.* Neocorus, who is cited in support, says nothing
at all about it. The immunity from mounting is another point of
agreement with those Slav horses.

[1] Not 'in rheda' (Wedekind's Notes 1, 173). Rhetra, a chief place of Slav
heathenism, placed by Adam of Bremen in the land of the Retharii, where stands
the temple of Redigost; Dietmar gives the Lutiz town in the ' grau Riedera' itself
the name of Riedegost.
[2] *Sviatovit* or Svantevit has been confounded with St. Vitus, sanctus Vitus
(conf. Acta sanctor. 15 Jun. p. 1018); but we cannot possibly make the god
Svantevit originate in Vitus.
[3] Falk's Collection of treatises, 5, 103. Tondern, 1828.
[4] This *Hese-wood* may however remind us of the ' silva *Heisi, Hese*' on the
Ruhr in Westph. (Lacombl. no. 6. 17. 64. 260) and the ' silva *caesia*' of Tacitus.

But in the case of the heathen Livonians the Slav custom admits of proof. The Chronicon livonicum vetus relates ad an. 1192 (in Gruber p. 7): 'Colligitur populus, voluntas deorum de immolatione (fratris Theoderici cisterciensis) sorte inquiritur. *Ponitur lancea, calcat equus; pedem vitae deputatum* (the right foot) nutu dei praeponit. Orat frater ore, manu benedicit. Ariolus deum Christianorum equi dorso insidere et pedem equi ad praeponendum movere asserit, et ob hoc equi dorsum tergendum, quo deus elabatur. Quo facto, dum equus *vitae pedem* praeponit ut prius, frater Theodoricus vitae reservatur.' Here a heathen and a christian miracle met.

This worship was also an Old Prussian one : ' Prussorum aliqui *equos nigros,* quidam *albi coloris,* propter deos suos non audebant aliqualiter equitare.' Dusburg 3, 5 (see Suppl.).[1].

The *sacrificing of horses,* and the *eating of horseflesh* inseparable from it, have been noticed (pp. 47-49). Strabo reports, that the Veneti offered a *white horse* to Diomed (v. 1, 9. Siebenk. 2, 111. Casaub. 215. Kramer 1, 339). The Indians get up grand horse-sacrifices with imposing ceremonies. What is told of the Kal-muks appears worthy of notice. Among them you see numbers of scaffolds erected, bearing *horses' hides* and *heads,* the remains of former sacrifices. By the *direction of the horse's head* to east or west, you can tell if the sacrifice was offered to a good or evil spirit.[2] On the one hand it suggests that sacrificial fixing of horses' heads in a particular direction in Germany, which under Christianity was treated as wicked sorcery; and on the other hand the ' pira equinis sellis constructa ' in Jornandes, and the σῆμα of the Scythian kings in Herodotus (see RA. 676, and Suppl.).[3]

Of honours paid to *oxen* I have not so much to tell, though they are not at all a matter of doubt, if only because *bullocks* were sacrificed, and *bulls* drew the car of the Frankish kings, RA. 262. War-chariots continued to have oxen till late in the Mid. Ages: ' capto ducis (Lovaniensis) vexillo, dicto gallice standart,

---

[1] Sup. M, 35 shews that Esthonians ascribe *prophetic* powers to the horse.
[2] Ledebour's Reise nach dem Altai, Berl. 1830. 2, 54-5.
[3] A Sansk. name for the horse is *Srîbhrâtri,* brother of Srî (Lakshmi), because, like her (and Aphrodite) it rose out of the sea-waves, Pott 2, 407. Still more natural is the identification of horse and ship.

opere plumario a regina Angliae ei misso, quod fastu superbiae *quadriga boum* ferebat,' Chapeaville 2, 69 (an. 1129). A chariot drawn by *four white oxen* in Lorraine occurs in Scheffer's Haltaus, p. 251. In Plutarch's Marius cap. 23 is the well-known story of the Cimbrians swearing over a *brazen bull,* by which the Mecklenburgers account for the bull's head in their arms (Mascov 1, 13). At Hvítabær the people worshipped an *ox* (Fornald. sög. 1, 253), at Upsal a *cow* (1, 254. 260-6. 270-2; see Suppl.).

Whilst among horses the stallion is more honoured than the mare, among neat the *cow* seems to take the lead. *Kine* were yoked to the car of Nerthus [and two milch-kine to the ark of Jehovah]. The Edda speaks of a *cow* named *Auðumbla,* which plays a great part in the origin of men and gods (p. 559), and was no doubt regarded as a sacred beast. By the side of that faith in horses (p. 656) we find an 'âtrûnaðr â kû.' King Eysteinn of Sweden put faith in a cow called *Sibilja:* 'hun var svâ miök blôtin (so much worshipped), at menn mâttu eigi standast lât hennar'; they used to lead her into battle, Fornald. sög. 1, 254. 260. King Ögvaldr carried a *sacred cow* with him everywhere, by sea and by land, and constantly drank of her milk (Fornm. sög. 2, 138. 10, 302).[1]

The horns of cows, like the manes of horses, were adorned with gold: '*gullhyrndar* kŷr,' Sæm. 73ᵃ. 141ᵃ; and the herdsman of the Alps still decks the horns of his cattle with ribbons and flowers. Oxen for sacrifice are sure not to have lacked this decoration.

The Sanskrit *gauś* (bos and vacca), root gô, acc. gâm, Pers. ghau, gho, corresponds to Lett. *gohw,* OHG. *chuo,* AS. *cû,* ON. *kŷr.* What is more important, 'gô' likewise means terra and plaga (Bopp's Gram. § 123. Gloss. p. 108ᵇ), so that it touches the Gr. γᾶ, γῆ. Taking with this the presence of *Auðumbla* in the Norse history of creation, we can perhaps connect *rinta* (the earth) and *Rindr* (p. 251) with our *rind* armentum; it is true this 'rind' originally began with *hr* (Graff 4, 1171), and is the

---

[1] What can the *black cow* mean in the following phrases? 'the *b. c.* crushes him' (Hüpel's Livländ. idiot. 181); 'the *b. c.* has trodden him' (Etner's Apoth. 514). The Hor. Belg. 6, 97. 101 (conf. 223) speaks 'van onser goeden *blaren coe,* van miere *blaren coe*'; and Ir. elfenm. cxx. of the *blue cow.* It is dangerous to kill the black cow, Sup. I, 887. A Slovènic name for the rainbow is *mavra* = black cow. [Eng. 'the *b. c.* has trodden on his foot,' of sorrow, esp. bereavement.]

AS. hrýðer, hroðer, but who can tell whether ' rinde' cortex was not once aspirated too?' *Εὐρώπη*, the name of one quarter of the earth, must surely also mean earth (*εὐρεῖα* the broad), and on p. 338 I made a guess that *Europa*, whom Zeus courted in the shape of a bull, must herself have been thought of as a *cow*, like Io; it was not the earth took name from her, but she from the earth. On the worship of cows and oxen by the Indians, Egyptians and Romans, I refer to A. W. Schlegel's learned treatise.[1] The Israelites also made a burnt-offering of 'a red heifer (Goth. kalbô) upon which never came yoke,' Numb. 19, 2 (see Suppl.).

The *boar* and the *he-goat* were holy sacrificial beasts (p. 50-1-2), the boar[2] dedicated to Freyr (p. 213), he and she goats to Thôrr (p. 185), as goats are even yet considered devil's creatures.[3] To that divine *boar's* account I think we are also entitled to set down the old song out of which Notker has preserved a passage (he whose foreign learning so seldom suffers him to put down anything he knew of his own country) :

> Imo sint fuoze fuodermâze,
> imo sint burste ebenhô forste,
> unde zene sîne zuelif-elnîge;

his bristles are even-high with the forest, and his tusks twelve ells long. A reason for the veneration of the boar has been found in the fact that he roots up the ground, and men learnt from him to plough. The Slavs also seem to have worshipped boars : 'Testatur idem antiquitas, errore delusa vario, si quando his saeva longae rebellionis asperitas immineat, ut e mari praedicto (near Riedergost) *aper magnus* et *candido dente e spumis lucescente exeat*, seque in volutabro delectatum terribili quassatione multis ostendat,' Ditm. merseb. p. 812 (see Suppl.).

None but domestic animals were fit for sacrifice, and not all of them, in particular not the *dog*, though he stands on much the same footing with his master as the horse; he is faithful and intelligent, yet there is something mean and unclean about him,

---

[1] Ind. bibl. 2, 288—295.
[2] He enjoys a double appellation : OHG. *epur*, AS. eofor ; and OHG. *pér*, AS. bâr (Goth. báis?).
[3] While God (Wuotan) made the wolf (p. 147), the devil (Donar?) produced the goat. In some places they will not eat goats' feet (Tobler p. 214).

which makes his name a handle to the tongue of the scorner. It seems worthy of notice, that dogs can see spirits (Sup. I, 1111), and recognise an approaching god while he is yet hidden from the human eye. When Grímnir entered the house of Geirröðr, there was 'eingi *hundr* svâ ôlmr, at â hann mundi hlaupa,' the king bade seize the dark-cloaked giant, 'er eigi vildo *hundar* ârûða,' Sæm. 39. 40. So when Hel prowls about, the *dogs* perceive her. The Greeks had exactly the same notion : at Athena's approach, no one espies her, not even Telemachos, only Odysseus and the dogs, Od. 16, 160 :

οὐδ' ἄρα Τηλέμαχος ἴδεν ἀντίον, οὐδ' ἐνόησεν,
οὐ γάρ πὼ πάντεσσι θεοὶ φαίνονται ἐναργεῖς,
ἀλλ' Ὀδυσεύς τε κύνες τε ἴδον, καί ῥ' οὐχ ὑλάοντο,[1]
κνυζηθμῷ ἑτέρωσε διὰ σταθμοῖο φόβηθεν,

(they did not bark, but fled whining through the tent).—The howling of dogs is ominous (Sup. I, 493), and gives notice of fire. Oðinn is provided with dogs, 'Viðris *grey*,' Sæm. 151ᵃ ; so are the norns (p. 410), 'norna *grey*,' 273ᵃ. But whence arose the story in the early Mid. Ages, of St. Peter and his dog ? In the AS. Saturn and Solomon (Kemble p. 186), one asks : 'saga me, hwilc man êrost wære *wið hund sprecende?*' and the other answers : 'ic þe secge, sanctus Petrus.' The Nialss. cap. 158 p. 275 contains a spell to save from the power of the watersprite : 'runnit hefr *hundr* þinn, Petr 'postoli, till Rôms tysvar (twice), ok mundi (would) renna it þriðja sinn, ef þû leyfdir' (see Suppl.).

Among wild beasts of the wood were some that men regarded with awe, and treated with respect : above all, the *bear, wolf* and *fox*. I have shewn that it was an ancient and widespread custom in Europe to bestow names of honour on these three (Reinh. p. lv. ccvii. 446),[2] and that with our ancestors the *bear* passed for the *king of beasts* (p. xlviii. seq. ccxcv.). A doc. of 1290 (Lang's Reg. 4, 467) presents the surname 'Chuonrat der *heiligbär*'; with this connect the name *Halecbern* (Trad. corb. Wig. § 268), the ON. *Hallbiörn*, and the still older names, male and female, ON.

---

[1] In a Dan. folksong 1, 207-9 they bark at a spectre. Barking and not barking are the same thing here.
[2] A striking confirmation appears in V. Hugo's Notre Dame de Paris 2, 272 : he states, from a book or from oral tradition, that the Gipsies call the fox *piedbleu, coureur des bois*, the wolf *piedgris, pieddoré*, and the bear *vieux* or *grandpère*.

Asbiörn, AS. *Osbeorn*, OHG. *Anspero*, and ON. *Asbirna*, OHG. *Anspirin* (in Walth. Ospirn), *Ospirinberg*, MB. 28. 2, 123; apparently the legend of the animal's sacredness was still in full swing among the people. *Biörn* was a side-name of Thôrr, and Welsh legend presents king *Arthur* as a bear and a god, which is not to be accounted for by the mere resemblance of his name to ἄρκτος: the bear in the sky plays a most dignified part. In the Edda a by-name of the bear is *Vetrliði*, hiemem sustinens (Sn. 179. 222), because he sleeps through winter, and winter was called biarnar-nôtt; the name was passed on to men, as '*Vetrliði* skáld' in Fornm. sög. 2, 202, and a *Vetrliði* 3, 107 whose name reproduces his father's name *Asbiörn*.[1] The myth of the *white bear* and the wee wight was alluded to, p. 479. It is not to be overlooked, that certain beast-fables get converted into human myths, and vice versâ: *e.g.*, the parts of *bear* and *fox* are handed over to a *giant* or the *devil*. Thus, the Esthonian tale of the man who goes partners with the bear in raising turnips and oats (Reinhart cclxxxviii.) is elsewhere told of a man and the devil. Such overlapping of the beast-fable with other traditions is an additional guarantee of the epic nature of the former.—Two wolves, *Geri* and *Freki*, were sacred to Oðinn: whatever food was set before him, he gave to them to eat, Sn. 4; they were, so to speak, the hounds of the god (Viðris grey). I should like to know where Hans Sachs picked up that striking notion of the Lord God having chosen wolves to be His hunting dogs.[2] A son of Loki, *Fenrisúlfr*, makes his appearance in *wolf's shape* among the gods; no metamorphosis occurs more frequently in our antiquities than that of men into *were-wolves*.—Both wolf and bear are a favourite cognisance in coats of arms, and a great many names of men are compounded with them: neither fact is true of the *fox*. Hence the dearth of mythical conceptions linked with the fox; a few traces have been pointed out in Reinh. ccxcvi.,[3]

[1] The name *Weturlit* is also found in the Necrolog. augiense (Mone 98ᵇ).
[2] Ed. 1558. i, 499ᵈ: 'die wolf er im erwelen gund ('gan choose), und het sie bei ihm für jagdhund.'
[3] Klaproth finds in Japanese books, that the people in Japan worship the *inari* (fox) as a *tutelar god*: little temples are dedicated to him in many houses, espec. of the commoner folk. They *ask his advice* in difficulties, and set rice or beans for him at night. If any of it is gone in the morning, they believe the fox has consumed it, and draw good omens from it; the contrary is an unlucky sign (Nouv. annales des voyages, Dec. 1883, p. 298). They take him to be a kami i.e. the soul of a good man deceased (ibid.)

and the kindermärchen no. 38 has furnished him with *nine tails*, as Sleipnir had eight legs, and some heroes and gods four arms.

Freyja's car was drawn by two *cats* (tveim köttum), p. 305. Now, as *fres* in ON. means both he-cat and bear, it has lately been contended, not without reason, that köttum may have been substituted for *fressum*, and a brace of bears have been really meant for the goddess, as Cybele's car was drawn by lions, p. 254. For Puss-in-boots see pp. 503-9, and the Norweg. tale in Folkeeventyr no. 29. *Cats* and *weasels* pass for knowing beasts with magical powers, whom one has good reason to indulge, Sup. I, 292 (see Suppl.).

BIRDS.—With *birds* the men of old lived on still more intimate terms, and their greater nimbleness seemed to bespeak more of the spiritual than was in quadrupeds. I will here quote some instances of wild fowl being fed by man. Dietmar of Merseb. relates of Mahtildis, Otto I.'s mother (Pertz 5, 740): ' non solum pauperibus, verum etiam *avibus* victum subministrabat ; ' and we find the same in the Vita Mahtild. (Pertz. 6, 294): ' nec etiam oblita est *volucrum* aestivo tempore in arboribus resonantium, praecipiens ministris sub arbores proicere micas panis.' In Norway they used to put out bunches of corn for the *sparrows* on Yule-eve: ' Jule-aften at sette trende kornbaand paa stöer under aaben himmel ved laden og föe-huset till *spurrens* föde, at de näste aar ikke skal giöre skade (do no harm next year) paa ageren,' Hiorthöi Gulbrands dalen, Kb. 1785. 1, 130 ; it was a sacrifice offered to the birds, to keep them from ravaging the crops. It reminds one of the legacy to birds on Walther von der Vogelweide's tombstone, whose very name denotes ' pascua avium.'

Gods and goddesses often change themselves into *birds*, but giants possess the same power too. The Esthonian god Tarapila *flies* from one place to another, p. 77; the Greek imagination pictured *winged* gods, the Hebrew *winged* angels, the Old German a maiden with *swan's wings*. The Norse gods and giants put on an eagle's coat, *arnar-ham*, p. 633n., the goddesses a falcon's coat, *vals-ham*, p. 302. Wind is described as a giant and *eagle*, p. 633, and sacred *eagles* scream on the mountains: ' örn göl arla,

arar gullo,' Sæm. 142ᵃ 149ᵃ. Wolfram thinks of the earth as a
bird, when he says, Wh. 308, 27:

> sô diu erde ir gevidere rêrt
> unde si der meie lêrt
> ir mûze alsus volrecken (see Suppl.).

Domestic fowl available for sacrifice, notably the cock and the
goose, have but few mythic aspects that I know of.   Fire is de-
cribed as a *red cock* (p. 601): H. Sachs has the phrase ' to make
the red cock ride on one's rooftree,' and the Danes ' den röde
hane galer over taget,' the red cock crows on the thack (the
fire crackles).   Red cocks in preference had to be brought *in
payment of ground rent* (formerly perhaps in sacrifice), RA. 376.
The Völuspâ 54 sets before us 'Fialarr, *fagur-rauðr* hani ' singing
in the forest; a golden-crested cock awakes the heroes, a dark
one crows in the nether world.   In the Danish song 1, 212 there
is meaning in the crowing of a *red* and a *black* cock one after the
other; and another song 1, 208 adds a *white* cock as well.   Another cock in the Edda, Víðofnir, perches on Mîmameiðr, Sæm.
109ᵃ; with him Finn Magnusen (Lex. myth. 824. 1090) would
connect the cock they stick on the *Maypole*.   The Wends erected
cross-trees, but, secretly still heathen at heart, they contrived to
fix at the very top of the pole a *weathercock*.[1]   In one fairy-tale,
no. 108, Hansmeinigel's *cock* sits *on a tree* in the wood.   I do not
know when the gilded *cock on the church-steeple* was introduced ;
it can hardly have been a mere weather-vane at first.   Guibertus
in Vita sua, lib. 1 cap. 22, mentions a *gallus super turri*, so that
the custom prevailed in France at the beginning of the 12th
century; in S. Germany we know it existed two centuries earlier.
Eckehard tells of the great irruption of Hungarians : ' duo ex illis
accendunt *campanarium*, cujus cacuminis *gallum aureum* putantes,
deumque loci sic vocatum, non esse nisi carioris metalli materia
fusum, lancea dum unus, ut eum revellat, se validus protendit, in
atrium de alto cecidit et periit ' (Pertz 2, 105).   The Hungarians
took this gilded cock (gallus) for the divinity of the place, and
perhaps were confirmed in their error by the bird's name being
the same as that of St. Gallus ; they even left the minster stand-

---

[1] Annalen der Churbr. Hannöv. lande, 8 jahrg. p. 284. Some think the cock
referred to Peter's denial.

ing for fear of him: 'monasterio, eo quod *Gallus, deus ejus, ignipotens* sit, tandem omisso' (ibid. 106).[1] Tit. 407: '*úz golde ein ar* gerœtet, gefiuret unde gefunkelt *úf jeglich kriuze* gelœtet.' True, the cock is an emblem of vigilance, and the watchman, to command a wide view, must be highly placed;[2] but it is quite possible that the christian teachers, to humour a heathen custom of tying cocks to the tops of holy trees, made room for them on church-towers also, and merely put a more general meaning on the symbol afterwards (see Suppl.).

At the head of wildfowl the *eagle* stands as *king*, and is the messenger of Jove. In our beast-fables the *raven* seems to take upon him the parts both of wolf and of fox, uniting the greed of the one with the other's cunning. Two ravens, *Huginn* and *Muninn*, are, like the two wolves, constant companions of Oðinn (p. 147); their names express power of thought and remembrance: they bring him tidings of all that happens.[8] Compare the sage *sparrow* (spörr) of the Norse king Dag (Yngl. saga 21), who gathers news for him out of all countries, and whose death he avenges by an invasion. Those scouts of Oðinn seem to be alluded to in several stories, e.g., Olaf Tryggv. cap. 28, where screaming ravens testify that Oðinn accepts the offering presented; and in Nialss. 119 two ravens attend a traveller all day. In like manner St. Gregory is escorted by three flying ravens, Paul. Diac. 1, 26. In the beautiful myth of king Oswald, the *raven* who gets his plumage bound with gold (conf. the falcon, Ms. 1, 38b) acts an essential part: he has nothing of the fiendish nature afterwards imputed to this bird. It shews the same tendency, that where the Bible says of the *raven* sent out of the ark by Noah, simply that he ἐξελθὼν οὐκ ἀνέστρεψε (Gen. 8, 7),

---

[1] All very legendary; for the Hungarian attack on the monastery of Herzfeld (Hirutfeld) on the Lippe is related much in the same way in the Vita S. Idae, viz. that having scaled the nolarius, but not succeeded in wrenching off the bells, they suddenly fled, aliquid ibi esse divalis numinis suspicati sunt (Pertz 2, 573). Here the cock does not come into play, the bells do it all.

[2] Münster's Sinnbilder der alten Christen, p. 55. As Gregory the Great explains *gallus* by 'praedicator' (Opp., Paris 1705. i, 959. 961), and again *speculator* by the same 'praedicator,' he may in the following passage have had the cock in view, without naming him: 'speculator semper in altitudine stat, ut quidquid venturum sit longe prospiciat,' ibid. i, 1283.

[8] In a Slovènic fairy-tale somebody had a raven (*vrána*) who was all-knowing (*védezh*), and used to tell him everything when he came home. Murko's Sloven. deutsches wtb. Grätz 1833. p. 696.

our Teutonic poetizers must make him alight on carrion, Cædm. 87, 11. Diut. 3, 60. King Arthur, whom we lately met as a bear, is said to have been converted into a *raven:* ' que anda hasta ahora convertido en *cuervo*, y le esperan en su reyno por momentos,' Don Quixote 1, 49. In folksongs it is commonly a bird that goes on errands, brings intelligence of what has passed, and is sent out with messages : the Bohemians say ' to learn it of the bird' (dowĕdĕti se po ptačku, see Suppl.).

In our legends, birds converse together on the destinies of men, and foretell the future. *Ravens* reveal to the blind the means of recovering their sight, KM. no. 107. *Domestic fowls* discuss the impending ruin of the castle, Deut. sag. 1, 202. In the Helgaqviða, Sæm. 140-1, a *wise bird* (fugl fróðhugaðr) is introduced talking and prophesying to men, but insists on a *temple* and *sacrifices* before he will tell them more. In one German story, men get to understand the *language of birds* by eating of a *white snake*, KM. no. 17. Sigurðr understands it too, the moment the heart's blood of the dragon Fafnir has got from his finger-tips to his tongue : and then *swallows* (igðor) give him sound advice, Sæm. 190-1. To kill *swallows* brings misfortune : acc. to Sup. I, 378 it occasions four weeks' rain ; and their nests on the houses no one dares knock down. From Saxo's account (p. 327) of the oaken statue of Rugivit, we may conclude that the Slavs had let *swallows* build on it in peace (see Suppl.).

The mythical character of the *swan* is certified by the legend of swan-wives (p. 426) and by the bird's own death-song (see Suppl.). The *stork* too was held inviolable, he is like swallows a herald of spring ; his poetic name certainly reaches back to heathen times, but hitherto has baffled all explanation. OHG. glosses give *odebero*, Graff 3, 155, *udebero*, Sumerl. 12, 16, *otivaro, odebore*, Fundgr. 1, 386, *odeboro*, Gl. Tross; MHG. *adebar* only in Diut. 3, 453; MLG. *edebere*, Brun's Beitr. 47, *adebar*, Reinke, 1777. 2207; M. Neth. *odevare*, hodevare, Rein. 2316. Clignett 191 ; New Neth. *ôyevâr*; New LG. *êber*, äbêr, atjebar; AS. and Norse have nothing similar. The ' bero, boro ' is bearer, but the first word, so long as the quantity of its vowel remains doubtful, is hard to determine ; the choice would lie between luck-bringer (fr. ôt opes) and child-bringer, which last fits in with the faith, still very prevalent, that the stork brings babies. If, beside the OS. partic. ôdan, AS. eáden, ON. auðinn (genitus), we could produce a subst. ôd, eád (proles), all would be straight. The prose word, OHG. *storah*, AS. *storc*, ON. *storkr*, may be just as old. In Frisian superstition there occur metamorphoses of storks into men, and of men into storks. A lay of Wolfram 5, 21 declares that storks never hurt the crops (see Suppl.).

The *woodpecker* was held sacred by ancient peoples of Italy, and ranked as the bird of Mars, Ἄρεος ὄρνις : perched on a wooden pillar (ἐπὶ κίονος ξυλίνου) he prophesied to the Sabines in the grove by Matiena (or Matiera, Dion. hal. 1, 14. Reiske p. 40) ; he had once guided them on their way, ὥρμηνται οἱ Πικεντῖνοι δρυοκολάπτου τὴν ὁδὸν ἡγεσαμένου, Strabo v, p. 240. And he purveyed for Romulus and Remus, when the wolf's milk did not suffice them, Ov. Fasti 3, 37. 54 ; conf. Niebuhr 1, 245. Acc. to Virg. Aen. 7, 189 and Ov. Met. 14, 321 *Picus* was the son of Saturn and father of Faunus,[1] and was changed into the bird. The apparent relationship of this Picus to our poem of *Beowulf* (bee-hunter, *i.e.* woodpecker), was pointed out p. 369. In Norway the red-hooded blackpecker is called *Gertrude's fowl*, and a story in Asbiörnsen and Moe (no. 2) explains its origin : When our Lord walked upon earth with Peter, they came to a woman that sat baking, her name was Gertrude, and she wore a red cap on her head. Faint and hungry from his long journey, our Lord asked her for a little cake. She took a little dough and set it on, but it rose so high that it filled the pan. She thought it too large for an alms, took less dough and began to bake it, but this grew just as big, and again she refused to give it. The third time she took still less dough, and when the cake still swelled to the same size, ' Ye must go without ' said Gertrude, ' all that I bake becomes too big for you.' Then was the Lord angry, and said: ' Since thou hast grudged to give me aught, thy doom is that thou be a little bird, seek thy scanty sustenance twixt wood and bark, and only drink as oft as it shall rain.' No sooner were these words spoken, than the woman was changed into *Gertrude's fowl*, and flew up the kitchen

---

[1] When the Swiss call the black-pecker *merzaçilli* (March-foal, Stald. 2, 199. Tobler 316ᵃ), the simplest explan. is from picus martius ; yet fülli may be for vögeli, and so March-fowl or Martin's fowl ; see more in Chap. XXXV., Path-crossing.

chimney. And to this day we see her in her red cap, and the rest of her body black, for the soot of the chimney blackened her; continually she hacks into the bark of trees for food, and pipes before rain, because, being always thirsty, she then hopes to drink.[1] The green-pecker has the alias *giessvogel*, Austr. *gissvogel* (Stelzhamer's Lieder pp. 19. 177), *goissvogel* (Hofer 1, 306), Low G. *gütvogel, gietvogel, gütfugel* (Ehrentr. 1. 345), Engl. *rainbird, rainfowl*, because his cry of 'geuss, giess, giet' (pour!) is said to augur a downpour of rain. About him there goes a notable story: When the Lord God at the creation of the world ordered the beasts to dig a great well (or pond), this bird abstained from all work, for fear of soiling his handsome plumage (or yellow legs). Then God ordained that to all eternity he should drink out of no well (pond); therefore we always see him sip laboriously out of hollow stones or cart-ruts where rainwater has collected. But when no rain has fallen and there is drought, he is sore athirst, and we hear unceasingly his pain-stricken 'giet!' And the good Lord takes pity, and pours down rain (Reusch in Preuss. provinz. bl. 26, 536; from Samland). Fähl-mann in the Dorpater verhandl. 1; 42 gives an Esthonian myth: God was having the Em-bach (-beck, -brook, p. 599n.) dug, and set all the beasts to work; but the Whitsun-fowl idly flew from bough to bough, piping his song. Then the Lord asked him: 'hast thou nought to do but to spruce thyself?' The bird replied, 'the work is dirty, I can't afford to spoil my golden-yellow coat and silvery hose.' 'Thou foolish fop,' the Lord exclaimed, 'from henceforth thou shalt wear black hose, and never slake thy thirst at the brook, but pick the raindrops off the leaves, and only then strike up thy song when other creatures creep away from the coming storm.'——Now that Norwegian *Gertrude's fowl*, whose thirsty piping brings on rain, is evidently identical, and very likely another story explains the rainbird as the metamorphosis of a vain idle person. Sometimes it is not the woodpecker at all that is meant by *giessvogel, giesser, wasser-vogel, pfingstvogel, regenpfeifer*, but a snipe (Höfer 1, 306. 341), whose cry likewise forebodes a storm (p. 184), or the curlew (numenius arquata), Fr. *pluvier* (pluviarius), Boh. *koliha*, Pol.

---

[1] Rytchkov's Journ. thro' the Russ. Emp., trsl. by Hase, Riga 1774. p. 124.

kulig, kullik, LG. *regenwolp, waterwolp* (Brem. wtb. 5, 286). In our own beast-fables the woodpecker is left without any part to play, only in an altogether isolated episode he is introduced conversing with the wolf (Reinh. 419). The Votiaks pay divine honours to the tree-tapping woodpecker, to induce him to spare their woods.[1] The cry of this woodpecker (zhunia) the Servians call klikchi, kliknuti, kliktati, as they do that of the vila [p. 436, but there wrongly ascribed to the tapping noise]. Woodpeckers by their tapping shew the way to the river (Lay of Igór 79); the old legend of the woodpecker and springwurzel will be examined in Chap. XXXII (see Suppl.).——A near neighbour of the pecker (picus) is the *pie, magpie* (pica). In ON. her name is *skaði* (masc., says Biörn), Swed. *skata*, Dan. *skade*, which may be referred to the abstract notion of damnum, OHG. scado; at the beginning of the Völsunga saga there occurs a man's name *Skaði*, which Finn Magn. (Lex. 699) declares to be the goddess *Skaði*. In Flemish beast-legend the magpie was 'ver Ave,' frau Ave. In Poitou there still lingers a trace of pie-worship; viz. a bunch of heath and laurel is tied to the top of a high tree *in honour of the magpie*, because her chatter warns the people of the wolf's approach: 'porter la crêpe (pancake) à la pie,' Mém. des antiq. 8, 451.

In Old Bohemian songs the *sparrowhawk* (krahui, krahug) is a sacred bird, and is harboured in a grove of the gods (Königinh. MS. 72. 80. 160). On the boughs of an oak that springs out of a murdered man's grave, holy sparrowhawks perch, and publish the foul deed (see Suppl.).

There is no bird to which the gift of prophecy is more universally conceded than the *cuckoo*,[2] whose clear and measured voice rings in the young foliage of the grove. The Old German law designates spring by the set phrase 'wann der *gauch guket*' (RA. 36), as in Hesiod's rules of husbandry the cuckoo's song marks the growing rains of spring. Two old poems describe the quarrel of Spring and Winter about the cuckoo, and the shepherds' lamentation for him: Spring praises the bird, 'tarda hiems'

---

[1] Carniol. žuna, Pol. Boh. zluwa, Boh. also wlha, wolga.
[2] Goth. gáuks? OHG. gouh (Hoffm. 5, 6), AS. geác, ON. gaukr; MHG. gouch, MS. 2, 182ᵇ, also reduplicated (like cuculus) gucgouch, MS. 1, 132ᵃ, guggouch, MS. 1, 166ᵃ; our gukuk, kukuk, Up.G. guggauch, gutzgouch.

chides him, shepherds declare that he is drowned or kidnapped. There is a remarkable line :

Tempus adest veris ; *cuculus,* modo rumpe soporem.[1]

His notes usher in the sweetest season of the year, but his telling men their fortunes is not alluded to. The Cod. Exon. 146, 27 also makes him publish or 'bid' the year : '*geácas* gear budon,' cuculi annum nuntiavere. But the superstition is not yet extinct, that the first time you hear the cuckoo in the spring, you can learn of him how many years you have yet to live (Sup. I, 197. K, Swed. 119. Dan. 128. 146). In Switzerland the children call out : '*gugger,* wie lang leb i no ? ' and in Lower Saxony :

kukuk vam häven,
wo lange sall ik leven ?

then you must listen, and count how many times the bird repeats his own name after your question, and that is the number of years left you to live (Schütze's Holst. idiot. 2, 363). In some districts [2] the rhyme runs :

kukuk beckenknecht,
sag mir recht,
wie viel jar ich leben soll ? [3]

The story is, that the bird was a baker's (or miller's) man, and that is why he wears a dingy meal-sprinkled coat. In a dear season he robbed the poor of their flour, and when God was blessing the dough in the oven, he would take it out, and pull lumps out of it, crying every time 'guk-guk,' look-look ; therefore the Lord punished him by changing him into a bird of prey,

---

[1] Both eclogues in Dornavii Amphith. 456-7, where they are attrib. to Beda ; ditto in Leyser p. 207, who says they were first printed in the Frankf. ed. (1610) of Ovid's Amatoria, p. 190. Meanwhile Oudin (De script. eccles. 2, 327-8, ed. Lips. 1722) gives the Conflictus veris et hiemis under the name of '*Milo,* sancti Amandi elnonensis monachus' (first half of 9th century) ; and the second poem De morte cuculi stands in Mabillon's Anal. 1, 369 as '*Alcuini* versus de cuculo.' Anyhow they fall into the 8th or 9th century ; in shortening the penultima of 'cuculus' they agree with Reinardus 3, 528. Hoffm, Horae belg. 6, 236 has also revived the Conflictus.

[2] Aegid. Albertini narrenhatz, Augsb. 1617. p. 95 : ' Even as befel that old wife, which asked a guguck how many year she had yet to live, and the guguck beginning five times to sing, she supposed that she had five year more to live, etc.' From ' Schimpf und ernst ' c. 391.

[3] So in Mod. Greek : κοῦκο μου, κοῦκάκι μου, κι ἀργυροκουκάκι μου, πόσους χρόνους θὲ νὰ ζήσω ;

which incessantly repeats that cry (conf. Praetorius's Weltbeschr.
1, 656. 2, 491). No doubt the story, which seems very ancient,
and resembles that of the woodpecker (p. 673), was once told
very differently; conf. Chap. XXII., Pleiades. That 'dear
season' may have to do with the belief that when the cuckoo's
call continues to be heard after Midsummer, it betokens dearth
(Sup. I, 228).

In Sweden he tells maidens how many years they will remain
unmarried :

> gök, gök, sitt på quist (on bough),
> säg mig vist (tell me true),
> hur många år (how many years)
> jag o-gift går (I shall un-given go) ?

If he calls more than ten times, they declare he has got 'på *galen
quist*' (on the silly bough, *i.e.* bewitched), and give no heed to
his prophecies. And then a good deal depends on the quarter
whence you hear your cuckoo first. You must pay strict attention in spring; if you hear him from the north (the unlucky
quarter), you will see sorrow that year, from east or west his
call betokens luck, and from the south he is the proclaimer of
butter : ' *östergök* är *tröstegök*, *vestergök* är *bästagök*, *norrgök* är
sorggök, *sörgök* är smörgök.[1]

In Goethe's Oracle of Spring the prophetic bird informs a
loving pair of their approaching marriage and the number of
their children.

It is rather surprising that our song-writers of the 13th century never bring in the cuckoo as a soothsayer; no doubt the
fact or fancy was familiar to all, for even in the Renner 11340 we
read :

> daz weiz der *gouch*, der im für wâr
> hât *gegutzet hundert jâr*.

Caesarius heisterbac. 5, 17: 'Narravit nobis anno praeterito
(? 1221) Theobaldus abbas eberbacensis, quod quidam conversus,
cum nescio quo tenderet, et avem, quae *cuculus* dicitur a voce
nomen habens, *crebrius cantantem* audiret, vices interruptionis
numeravit, et viginti duas inveniens, easque quasi pro omine

---

[1] Arndt's Reise durch Schw. 4, 5—7. The snipe is in Swed. *hrəsjök*, ON.
hrossagaukr (horse-cuckoo), and she too has the gift of divination, p. 184.

accipiens, *pro annis totidem* vices easdem *sibi computavit* : ' eia '
inquit, ' certe viginti duobus annis adhuc vivam, ut quid tanto
tempore mortificem me in ordine ? redibo ad seculum, et seculo
deditus viginti annis fruar deliciis ejus ; duobus annis qui super-
sunt pœnitebo.'—In the Couronnemens Renart, the fox hears the
bird's voice, and propounds to him the query :

> A cest mot Renart le *cucu*
> *entent,* si jeta un faus ris,
> ' jou te conjur ' fait il, ' de cris,
> 215 cucus, que me dies le voir (truth),
> . *quans ans jai à vivre ?* savoir
> le veil.'   Cucu, en preu cucu,[1]
> et deus cucu, et trois cucu,
> quatre cucu, et cinc cucu,
> 220 et sis cucu, et set cucu,
> et uit cucu, et nuef cucu,
> et dis cucu, onze cucu,
> duze cucu, treize cucu.
> Atant se taist, que plus ne fu
> 225 li oisiaus illuec, ains s'envolle.

Renart carries the joyful news to his wife, that the bird has
promised him yet ' treize ans d'aé ' (see Suppl.).

Is it the cuckoo that is meant by ' *timebird* ' in Ms. 1, 88ᵃ : ' diu
vröide vlogzet (joy flies) gelîch dem *zîtvogel* in dem neste '?
What makes me think so is a passage in Pliny, which anyhow is
pertinent here, exhorting the husbandman at the aequinoctium
vernum to fetch up all arrears of work : ' dum sciat inde natam
exprobrationem foedam putantium vites per imitationem cantus
alitis temporarii, quem *cuculum* vocant.   Dedecus enim habetur
opprobriumque meritum, falcem ab illa volucre deprehendi, ut ob
id petulantiae sales etiam cum primo vere ludantur.'

Delight at the first song of the cuckoo is thus expressed in a
Swiss couplet (Tobler 245ᵇ) :

> wenn der *gugger* chond gegugga ond 's *merzaföli* lacht,
> denn wött i gad goh lo, 'swit i koh möcht ;

---

[1] A line seems wanting here, to tell us that Cuckoo, like a sensible cuckoo (en
preu cucu, fugl frôðhugaðr), ' began to sing, One cucu.'

they imagine that he never sings before the 3rd of April, and never after Midsummer :

> am dretta Abarella
> moss der *gugger* grüena haber schnella ;

but he cannot sing till he has eaten a bird's egg. If you have money in your pouch when you hear him sing the first time, you will be well off all that year, if not, you will be short the whole year (Sup. I, 374); and if you were fasting, you will be hungry all the year. When the cuckoo has eaten his fill of cherries three times, he leaves off singing. As the cuckoo's song falls silent at Midsummer, vulgar opinion holds that from that time he *turns into a hawk.* Reusch, N. pr. prov. bl. 5, 338-9.

The Poles call the bird żeżula, the Bohemians 'eżhule (both fem.). The O. Pol. chronicle of Prokosz,[1] p. 113 of the Lat. ed., has a remarkable account of the worship of a Slavic god Zyvie: 'divinitati Zywie fanum exstructum erat in monte ab ejusdem nomine Zywiec dicto, ubi primis diebus mensis Maji innumerus populus pie conveniens precabatur ab ea, quae vitae [2] auctor habebatur, longam et prosperam valetudinem. Praecipue tamen ei litabatur ab iis qui *primum cantum cuculi audivissent,* ominantes superstitiose *tot annos se victuros* quoties vocem repetiisset. Opinabantur enim supremum hunc universi moderatorem *transfigurari in cuculum* ut ipsis annuntiaret vitae tempora : unde crimini ducebatur, capitalique poena a magistratibus afficiebatur, qui cuculum occidisset.' Here the oracular bird is a *god in metamorphosis,* just as that Saxon rhyme called him 'kukuk *vam häven.*'

To the Servian haiduks it betokens evil when the *kukavitsa* comes too soon, and cries out of the black (leafless) forest ; and good luck when it sings from the green wood, Vuk sub v.

In the Eddic Grotta-song the quern-maids are only allowed to rest and sleep *while the cuckoo is silent* (enn gaukrinn þagði).

The cuckoo can prophesy both good and ill ; in dealing with him (as with other birds of enchantment, owls, magpies) you

---

[1] Kronika polska przez Prodosza, Warsz. 1825, and in Latin 'Chronicon Slavosarmaticum Procosii,' Varsav. 1827 ; professedly of the 10th cent. It is not so old as that, yet Dobrowsky (Wien. jahrb. 32, 77—80) goes too far in pronouncing it a pure fabrication ; it is at any rate founded on old traditions.

[2] żywy, alive ; żywić, to sustain life, nourish.

have to weigh your words and questions, so as not to get en-
snared (Arndt's Sweden 3, 18). To kill him without cause is
dangerous, his followers might avenge it. He has power to *teaze*
men, to *delude* them, what Swedish superstition calls *dåra*, and
Danish *gante*. A MHG. poem (Fragm. 38ᵇ) has : 'peterlîn und
louch hât *begucket* mit der *gouch.*' Often his appearing is of evil
omen. Paulus Diac. 6, 55 says of Hildeprand king of the Lombards : 'cui dum contum, sicut moris est, traderent, in ejus *conti
summitate cuculus avis* volitando veniens *insedit*. Tunc aliquibus
prudentibus hoc portento visum est significari, ejus principatum
inutilem fore' (see Suppl.).

As that all-nourishing life-divinity of the Slavs took the shape
of the cuckoo, so does the Grecian Zeus *transform himself into
the bird*, when he first approaches Hera. A seated figure of the
goddess shews a *cuckoo on her staff*, and a bas-relief representing
the wedding procession of Zeus and Hera has a *cuckoo perched* on
Zeus's *sceptre* (as on that of the Lombard king) ;[1] so that this
bird has got mixed up with the most sacred of all weddings,
and we understand why he promises marriage and the fruit of
wedlock. Then, the mountain on which Zeus and Hera came
together, previously called Θρόναξ (from θρόνος, seat of the
Thunderer? supra p. 183) or Θόρναξ, received after that the
name of ὄρος κοκκύγιον (Pausanias ii. 36, 2). Well, and we have
gowk's-hills in Germany : a *Gauchsberg* near Kreuznach (Widder's
Pfalz 4, 36), others near Durlach and Weinsberg (Mone's Anz. 6,
350), a *Guggisberg* in Switzerland (Joh. Müller, 1, 347. 2, 82.
Tschachtlan p. 2), *Göckerliberg* (KM. no. 95); the name might
be accounted for very naturally by the song of the bird being
heard from the hill, but that other traditions also are mixed up
with it. In Freidank 82, 8 (and almost the same in Bonerius 65,
55) :

> wîsiu wort unt tumbiu werc   •
> diu habent die von *Gouchesberc*.

Here the men of Gauchsberg are shown up as talking wisely and
acting foolishly ; Gauchsberg is equivalent to Narrenberg (fool's

---

[1] Welcker on Schwenk 269. 270; usually an *eagle* sits there. The figures of
eagle and cuckoo are not always easy to distinguish ; but to this day the Bavarians
by way of jest call the Prussian eagle 'gukezer,' Schm. 2, 27.

mount).[1] As far back as the 10th cent. *gouh* has the side-mean-ing of fool (N. ps. 48, 11. 93, 8. urheiz*kouh*, war-fool, N. Bth. 175); the same everywhere in the 13th (Walth. 22, 31. Trist. 8631. 18215), though commonly with a qualifying adj. or gen. pl.: ich tumber gouch, MS. 1, 65ᵃ. tumber denn ein gouch, Troj. 8126. tumber gouch, Barl. 319, 25. gouch unwîse 228, 32. sin-neloser gouch, 319, 38. der treit gouches houbet (wears a gowk's head), MsH. 3, 468ᵍ. rehter witze ein gouch, MS. 2, 124ᵇ. der mære ein göichelîn (dim.), and gouchgouolt (augm.), Ben. 209. The ON. gaukr is likewise arrogans morio. Hans Sachs occa-sionally uses *Gauchberg*[2] in the same sense, ii. 4, 110ᵈ (Kempten ii. 4, 220ᵃ), extr. from Göz 1, 52. Yet originally in Gauchsberg the bird himself may very well have been meant in a mystic sense which has fallen dark to us now (see Suppl.).[3]

In other ways too the cuckoo stands in ill repute, he passes for an adulterer, who lays his eggs in other people's nests; hence the Romans used cuculus in the sense of moechus (Plauti Asinaria, twice in last scene), and our *gouch*, *göuchelîn* formerly meant bastard (Nib. 810, 1. Aw. 1, 46), as the Swiss *gugsch* still means an unbidden rival suitor. He even comes out as a fiendish being, or the fiend himself, in phrases everywhere known from of old : 'cuckoo knows, cuckoo take him, cuckoo sent him here' and the like, in all of which the devil's name might be substi-tuted without change of meaning. This seems to me to point to old heathen traditions, to which the diabolic tinge was added only by degrees; and among these I reckon the Low Saxon formula 'the *cuckoo* and his *clerk* (or sexton)'! by which clerk is meant the *hoopoo* (Brem. wtb. 2, 858), a bird that is likewise thought to have received his form by metamorphosis. I cannot trace the story of the *cuckoo* and *hoopoo* any further; does the

---

[1] Hence we find, as substitutes for it, *Affenberc* (Docen's Misc. 2, 187); *Affen-berc* and *Narrental*, MsH. 3, 200ᵇ; *Affental*, ibid. 213ᵃ. Winsbeke 45, 7. Renner 16469; *Apenberg* and *Narrenberg* in the Plattd. 'Narragonia' 77ᵇ. 187ᵇ; *Eselsberc*, Diut. 2, 77. Animals whose stupidity was proverbial of old, are the ox, ass, ape, goat, goose, gowk and jay : viỗ ôsvinna apa, Sæm. 25ᵇ. âtrunnr apa 55ᵃ. Notk. ps. 57, 11 has ruoh (stultus), *i.e.* hruoh, AS. hrôc (graculus, Gramm. 3, 361).

[2] Much oftener *Schalksberg* (rogue's hill) in the phrase 'in den schalksperg hawen (hew)' i. 5, 524ᵃ. iii. 3, 28ᵈ. 54ᵇ. iv. 3, 204ᵈ. 31ᶜ. 40ᵃ; the reason of which I do not know. ' *Schalksberg* wine grows in Franconia.' ' Henricus dictus de *Scalkes-bergh*,' Spilker 2, 148 (an. 1268).

[3] Those who crave other explanations, will find plenty in Mone's Anz. 6, 350 seq. 'Gouchsberg is Caucasus, as Elberich is the spirit of Elburj, diabolus the Parsic div,' and so forth.

one sing to the other? [his note 'ooboo' is like an echo of
'cuckoo']. Döbel i. 1, 68 calls the hoopoo the cuckoo's lackey,
because he comes with him in spring and goes with him in
autumn (see Suppl.). The *peewit* has the same things said of
him.

The froth on willows, caused by the cicada spumaria, we call
kukuks-speichel, Swiss *guggerspeu*, Engl. *cuckoo-spit, -spittle*, Dan.
giögespyt, but in some places witch's spittle, Norweg. trold-
kiäringspye :[1] another proof of the bird's connexion with preternatural things, and reminding us of the bird-spittle (fugls hráki)
which in Sn. 34 goes to make up the band Gleipnir. Several
names of plants assure us of his mythic nature. Sorrel : OHG.
gouchesampfera, Swiss *guggersauer*, A.S. *geácessúre*, Dan. *giöge-
mad, giögesyre*, it being supposed that he loved to eat it; our
kukuksbrot, gauchlauch, Fr. *pain de coucou*, panis cuculi. Cuckoo-
flower : *kukuksblume, gauchblume*, flos cuculi. Pimpernel : *gauch-
heil*, etc., *guckgauchdorn*, Fischart's Geschichtskl. 269[a].

The Slavs all make this bird feminine, and see nothing bad,
nothing fiendish in it : *zezhulice* sits on the oak, and bewails the
passing away of spring, Königinh. MS. 174. The Servian *kukavitsa* was once a maiden, who wept her brother's death till she
was changed into the bird; 'sinia (gray) kukavitsa,' Vuk 3, 66 ;
three women turned into kukavitsas, Vuk 1, no. 321. In songs
of Lit. Russia still a moping melancholy bird ; and in Russian
folktales we have again a young girl changed into a cuckoo by an
enchantress (Götze's Serb. lieder, p. 212).

Of small birds, the *swallow* has been mentioned, p. 672.
'Frau *nachtigall*' is often named by our minnesingers ; but the
myth, that her children are born dead and she sings them alive,
seems not of German origin. The *lark* and *galander* (crested
lark) must have been actors in the animal legend oftener than we
are now aware of; there are still beautiful stories of the *zaunkönig*
(hedgeking, wren), A.S. wrenna. But I have yet to speak of two
little birds, which appear to have been peculiarly sacred in olden
times : redbreast and titmouse.

Robin redbreast is on no account to have his nest disturbed, or
the house will be struck with lightning : it is the *redstart's* nest

---

[1] Summer-freckles in Bavar. *gugker-schegken*, cuckoo-spots, Schm. 2, 27 ; conf.
Höfer 1, 387.

that draws down the flash. The latter the Swiss call *husrötheli* (house-redling) ; if you tease him or take him out, your cows will give red milk (Tobler 281). Were these birds sacred to Donar the red-bearded ? And has that to do with the colour of their throat and tail ? They say the redbreast drops leaves and flowers on the face of a murdered man [or 'babe '] whom he finds in the wood ; did he do this in the service of a god, who therefore would not suffer him to be molested ?

The tiny *titmouse*,[1] whom he called gossip, was able to outwit even Reynard himself. The weisthümer tell us in what estimation this little forest bird was held, by setting the severest penalties on his capture : ' item, si quis sibilando vel alio modo volucrem illum ceperit, qui vulgo *meise* nuncupatur, banni reus erit,' Jura archiep. trever., in Lacombl. arch. 826. ' si quis auceps hanc silvam intraverit, pro nullo genere volucrum componet, nisi capiat *meisam* que dicitur *banmeisa*, et pro illa componat 60 sol. tanquam pro cervo,' ibid. 367. ' wer da fehet ein *bermeisen*, der sal geben ein koppechte hennen und zwelf hunkeln, und sechzig schilling pfenning und einen helbeling,' Dreieicher wildbann (Weisth. 1, 499). ' wer eine *kolmeise* fienge mit limen ader mit slagegarn, der sal unserme herrn geben eine falbe henne mit sieben hünkeln,' Rheingauer w. 1, 535. ' wer ein *sterzmeise* fahet, der ist umb leib u. guet, und in unsers herrn ungnad,' Creuznacher w. 2, 153.—The reason of these laws is hidden from us ; plainly the bird was held sacred and inviolable. And it is perfectly in tune with this, that at the present moment the Lettons, who call the bird *sihle*,[2] regard it as prophetic and auspicious, and even call a soothsayer *sihlneeks*.[3] Also the Spanish name for the titmouse, *cid* (lord), or *cid paxaro* (lord sparrow), is worth considering. Titmouse, wren and woodpecker (bee-wolf) are confounded in popular belief ; what is meant is the tiniest prettiest bird (see Suppl.).

---

[1] Meise, OHG. meisâ, AS. mâse, Nethl. mêze, Fr. mesange, O.Fr. mesenge.

[2] Lith. żyle, żyléle ; Pol. sikora, Boh. sykora, Russ. zinika, sinítsa, Slov. senitsa, Serv. sienitsa. The Lettic name may be derivable from sinnaht, the Lith. from żynoti (scire), so that the full form would be sinnele, żynle, the sage knowing bird ? The jay also is in Lettic sihls. To the Swed. Lapps *taitne* signifies not only wood-pecker, but superstitious divination ; tayetet is to understand. In view of that, our *specht* (woodpecker) seems to belong to a lost root spihan, spah, spâhun, whence also spëhôn (explorare), and spâhi (sapiens, prudens).

[3] Mag. der lett. lit. gesellsch., Mitau 1838. 6, 151.

REPTILES.—*Snakes*, by the beauty of their shape and the terror
of their bite, seem above all animals to command awe and reverence. A great many stories tell of an exchange of form between
men and snakes: an almost infallible sign of their having been
worshipped. Beings that had passed out of human into animal
shapes, and were able to return into the former at need, these
heathenism was inclined to regard as sacred; it worshipped kind
beneficent snakes, whilst in christian opinion the notion of snakes
being malignant and diabolic predominates.

The same Vita Barbati, which we had to thank for information
on the tree-cultus of the Lombards (p. 649), tells us likewise of
a worship of snakes: 'His vero diebus, quamvis sacra baptis-
matis unda Langobardi abluerentur, tamen *priscum gentilitatis
ritum* tenentes, sive bestiali mente degebant, *bestiae simulachro,*
quae vulgo *vipera* nominatur, *flectebant colla,* quae debite suo de-
bebant flectere Creatori. . . . Praeterea Romuald ejusque
sodales, prisco coecati errore, palam se solum Deum colere fatebantur, et in abditis *viperae simulachrum* ad suam perniciem
adorabant.' During the king's absence, Barbatus beseeches his
consort Theodorada to procure for him that image of the snake.
'Illaque respondit: Si hoc perpetravero, pater, veraciter scio me
morituram.' He perseveres and at last persuades her; as soon
as the image is in his hands, he melts it down, and delivers the
metal to goldsmiths to make out of it a plate and a chalice.[1]
Out of these golden vessels the christian sacrament is adminis-
tered to the king on his return, and then Barbatus confesses that
the holy utensils were made by melting down the idol. 'Repente
unus ex circumstantibus ait: Si mea uxor talia perpetrasset, nullo
interposito momento abscinderem caput ejus.' A passage in the
other Vita also is pertinent here: 'Quinetiam *viperam auri
metallo formatam summi pro magnitudine dei* supplici devotione
venerari videbantur. Unde usque hodie, sicut pro voto arboris
Votum, ita et locus ille *Census,* devotiones[2] ubi viperae reddebantur dignoscitur appellari.' About 'votum' I expressed my
mind, p. 650n.; 'census' signifies the Goth. *gild, gilstr,* OHG.
këlt, këlstar (p. 38-9 and RA. 358). The two words votum and

---

[1] As the gold of the swan-rings was made into pots, and what remained over
was the goldsmith's profit.
[2] Printed text: locus ille census devotionis, ubi viperae reddebantur.

census are no slight testimony to the genuineness and oldness of the biography.——Here then we have a striking instance of an idol made of gold, and moreover of the christian teacher's endeavour to preserve the sacred material, only converting it into a christian form. What higher being the snake represented to the Lombards, we can scarcely say for certain ; not the all-encircling world-snake, the miðgarðs-ormr, iörmungandr of Norse mythology, for there is not a hint that even in the North, let alone elsewhere, he was visibly represented and worshipped. *Ofnir* and *Sváfnir* are ON. names of snakes, and side-names of Oðinn (conf. p. 144) ; is it Wuotan that we are to understand by the ' summus deus ' of the Lombards ?[1] But the special characteristics of their snake-worship are entirely lost to us. If the term vipera was deliberately chosen, as I have no doubt it was, it can only mean one of the smaller kinds of snake (coluber berus), OHG. *natara*, AS. *nœdre*, ON. *naðra* (also masc. naðr, like Goth. nadrs), though the simulacrum, of whose gold a plate and chalice could be made, bespeaks a considerable size.

Lombard legend has more to tell us of snakes, and those expressly small ones. The Heldenbuch describes the combat of a small fire-spitting beast on the Gartensee (L. di Garda) with Wolfdietrich and a lion, to both of whom it gives enough to do :

> Nun hörent durch ein wunder, wie das tierlein ist genant :
> es heisst zu welsch ein *sunder*, zu teutsch ein *saribant*,
> in Sittenland nach eren ist es ein *vipper* genant ;

and it is added, that there are but two such vipers alive at once, for the young ones soon after birth eat up their parents. This agrees closely with the statements in the Physiologus (Diut. 3, 29, 30. Hoffm. fundgr. 28). I cannot explain *zunder* from any Italian dialect ; *saribant* is the MHG. *serpant*, Trist. 8994. Sittenland I take to be the canton Valais, from its capital Sitten (Sion) ; there the Romance *vipera* might easily remain in use (Grisons vipra, vivra). In the Jura a never-dying winged snake with a diamond eye is called *vouivre*, Mém. des antiq. 6, 217. In Switzerland this snake in called *stollenwurm* (Wyss's Reise ins Berner Oberland, p. 422), and in Salzburg *birgstutze*, Schm. 1, 196 (see Suppl.).

---

[1] ' Summi *pro* magn. Dei ' may possibly mean ' *instead of* (worshipping) the majesty of the Most High.'—TRANS.

Plenty of old tales are still told of *home-snakes* and *unkes*.[1] On meadows and pastures, and even in houses, snakes come to children when alone, sip milk with them out of their bowl, wear *golden crowns*, which in drinking they take off from their heads and set on the ground, and often forget and leave them; they watch infants in the cradle, and to bigger children they shew treasures : *to kill them is unlucky*. Every village has its own snakes to tell of. So goes the story in Swabia. Some Hessian stories are collected under Kinderm. no. 105, and one from Austria in Ziska's Volksmärchen (Vienna 1822, p. 51) ; nearly all bring in the *milk-drinking*[2] and the *golden crown*. If the parents surprise the snake with the child, and kill it, the child begins to fall away, and dies before long (Temme's Pomm. sagen no. 257). Once, when a woman lay asleep, a snake crept into her open mouth, and when she gave birth to a child, the snake lay tightly coiled round its neck, and could only be got away by a milk-bath; but it never left the baby's side, it lay in bed with it, and ate out of its bowl, without doing it any harm (Mone's Anz. 8, 530). Then other accounts speak of a multitude of snakes filling house and yard, whose *king* was distinguished by a glittering *crown* on his head. When he left the yard, all the rest would accompany him; in the stable where he lived, they swarmed so plentifully, that the maids feeding the cattle would take them out of the crib by armfuls. They were friendly to the cattle and the people; but a new farmer shot their king, and they all departed, and with them vanished wealth and prosperity from the estate (ibid. 6, 174).[3] Here also comes in the *queen of snakes* (Deut. sagen no. 220), and a remarkable story in the Gesta Romanorum (Keller p. 152). To a dairymaid at Immeneich there came a great snake into the cowshed every morning and evening at milking-time, and wore a great crown on its head. The girl

---

[1] MHG. *unk*, gen. *unkes*, MS. 2, 209ᵇ. 206ᵃ: 'from copper one divideth gold with an unke's ashes'; hence an alchymist was called *unken-brenner* (Felix Malleolus de nobilitate et rusticitate, cap. 30). By *unke* is properly meant the rana portentosa (bull-frog ?), but often snake or reptile in general. Like the weasel, it is called caressingly '*mümelein, müemal*,' aunty. Schm. 2, 576.

[2] Down to the recurring formula : ' ding, iss auch brocken ! ' (thing, eat crumbs too) ; ' friss auch mocken, nicht lauter schlappes ! ' (not only slops) Mone's Anz. 8, 530 ; ' friss auch brocken, nicht lauter brühe ! ' ibid. 6, 175.

[3] A similar story of the king of snakes from Lübbenau in the Spreewald of Lausitz (Büsching's Wöch. nachr. 3, 342) in Reusch no. 74.

everytime gave it warm *cow's milk to sup.* She suddenly left the place in a tiff, and when the new maid went for the first time to milk, there lay the *golden crown* on the milking-stool, with the inscription : 'a token of gratitude.' She brought the crown to her master, who gave it to the girl it was intended for; but from that time the snake was never seen again (Mone's Anz. 8, 587). The *adder's crown* (atternkrönlein) makes any one that wears it invisible (Schm. 2, 388) and immensely rich as well. In some districts they say every house has two snakes, a male and a female, but they never shew themselves till the master or mistress of the house dies, and then they undergo the same fate. This feature, and some others, such as the offering of milk, bring the *home-snakes* near to the notion of good helpful home-sprites (see Suppl.).

The snake then comes before us as a beneficent inviolable creature, perfectly adapted for heathen worship. A serpent twined round the staff of Asklepios, and serpents lay beside healing fountains (p. 588n.). The ancient Prussians maintained a large snake for their Potrimpos, and the priests guarded it with care; it lay under ears of corn, and was nourished with *milk*.[1] The Lettons call snakes *milk-mothers* (peena mahtes); they were under the protection of one of the higher goddesses named Brehkina (crier), who cried out to all that entered to leave her 'peena mahtes' unmolested in the house (Mag. der lett. gesellsch. 6, 144). There is *milk* set for them in pots. The Lithuanians also revered *snakes*, harboured them in their houses, and offered them sacrifices.[2] Egyptian snake-worship was witnessed by Herodotus 2, 74. 'Nullus locus sine genio, qui per *anguem* plerumque ostenditur,' Serv. ad Aen. 5, 95.

Snakes were devised as a charm in swords and on helmets (Sæm. 142[b]) :

liggr með eggjo *ormr* dreyfáðr,
enn á valbösto verpr *naðr* hala.

The ormr or yrmlíngr was supposed to run from the sword's hilt

---

[1] Voigt's Geschichte Preussens 1, 584.
[2] Seb. Frank's Weltbuch 55[b]. Mone's Heidenth. 1, 98. Adam. brem. de situ Daniae, cap. 24, of the Lithuanians : '*dracones* adorant cum *volucribus*, quibus etiam vivos litant homines, quos a mercatoribus emunt, diligenter omnino probatos ne maculam in corpore habeant.'

(helz, hialt) to the point and back again (Kormakss. p. 82-4. Vilk. s. p. 101). Vitege had the epithet 'mit dem *slangen*' because of his helmet's crest (Heldensage p. 148). They imparted strength to a helmet, and force to the blade of a sword. It seems much the same thing, when waggoners plait adder's-tongues into their whips, Sup. I, 174 (see Suppl.).

The snake crawls or wriggles along the ground; when provided with wings, it is called *drache*, a non-German word coming from the Lat. draco, Gr. δράκων, and introduced very early, OHG. *traccho*, AS. *draca*, ON. *dreki*. The Elder (or Sæmund's) Edda has dreki only once, in the latish Sôlarl. 127ᵇ; elsewhere it is *ormr*, AS. *wyrm*, OHG. *wurm*, Goth. *vaúrms*, which in a wider sense includes the snake also. The one encountered by Beowulf comes before us emphatically as a winged snake (serpens alatus); 'nihtes fleogeð' 4541, by night he flies, and hence is called *uhtsceaða* 4536 (nocturnus hostis, aggressor), and *lyftsceaða* (aëreus hostis), Cod. exon. 329, 24. Also the dragon that keeps Krimhild prisoner on the Drachenstein comes riding through the air, or flying. But the one that young Siegfried had previously killed, when sent out by the smith, lay beside a linde (lime-tree), and did not fly: this is the *Fâfnir* of the Edda, a man who had assumed the form of a snake; of him the Edda uses skríða (repere, to stride), Sæm. 186. Sn. 138; and he is the wyrm or draca slain by Sigemund and Fitela in Beow. 1765. 1779. In the Nib. 101, 2 and 842, 2 he is called *lintrache*, *lintdrache*, in the Siegfriedslied 8, 2 *lintwurm*: an expression found also in Mar. 148, 28. En. 2947. Troj. 25199, and to be explained, not from linde (tilia) as misunderstood by later legend, but from the OHG. *lint*. With this *lint* (Goth. linþs, AS. lið, ON. linn?) many women's names are formed (Gramm. 2, 505), e.g., Sigilint, ON. Sigrlinn (supra p. 428), and it may have contained the notion of brightness or beauty,[1] suitable alike to snake and woman; the derivative weak form *linni* (masc.) in ON. signifies again coluber, serpens. And Limburg = *Lintburg*, the name of several towns, is more correctly derived from snake than from lime-tree.

About dragons it is a favourite fancy of antiquity, that they

---

[1] Does not the Engl. *lithe*, pliable, give the most suitable meaning, Germ. *gelind* soft, *lindern* to mitigate?—TRANS.

lie upon gold, and are illumined by it; gold itself was poetically named *worm-bed,* ON. ormbeðr or ormbeðs-eldr (wormbed's fire). And with this was linked a further notion, that they guard treasures, and carry them through the air by night. That wyrm slain by Sigemund is called 'hordes hyrde,' Beow. 1767; the one that Beowulf fought with receives the epithet 'se hord beweotode' 4420. Fåfnir, formerly a giant, lay 'in (the shape of) a worm,' wearing the Oegis-hialm, over inherited gold (Sæm. 188ᵇ. 189ᵇ); the expression is 'í lýngvi' (from lýng, heath), and the spot is named Gnîta-heiði; hence in other cases also the word *lýngvi, lýngormr* (heath-worm) stands for dragon. The Völs. saga c. 17 distinguishes *lýngormr* a small snake from *dreki* a large one; so that our OHG. *heimo,* OS. *hêma,* AS. *hâma,* spoken of on p. 387, may be identical with *lýngvi;* Vilk. saga c. 17, p. 31 expressly calls *heima* 'allra orma *skemstr*' (omnium vermium minimus), but as he is venomous, he cannot be the harmless cicada (OHG. muhheimo). Popular belief still dreams of glittering treasures lying on lonesome heaths and guarded by dragons; and *hæðen gold* in Beow. may mean either aurum tesquorum or ethnicorum, for dragons, like giants, were thought of as old and full of years, *e.g.,* eald uhtsceaða, Beow. 4536; wintrum fróð (wise with years) 4548; þreo hund (300) wintra heold on hrusan (earth) 4550; at the same time they are covetous, envious, venomous, spitting flame: *niððraca,* Beow. 4540; *âttorsceaða* 5673, fýre befongen 4541, ongan glêdum spîwan 4619, deorcum nihtum rîcsian 4417. It is said of Fåfnir, Sæm. 186: 'screið af gulli, blês eitri, hristi sik ok barði höfði ok sporði,' stept off the gold, blew poison, shook himself, and struck with head and tail; it was noticed on p. 562 that the two notions of eit (fire) and eiter (poison) run into one. Connect with this the descriptions of MHG. poets: the 'trache' has his haunt in a valley, out of his throat he darts flame, smoke and wind, Trist. 8944-74; he has plumage, wings, he spits fire and venom, Troj. 9764. 9817 (see Suppl.).

Now it was the heroes' province to extirpate not only the giants, but (what was in a measure the same thing) the dragons [1] in the world: Thôrr himself tackles the enormous miðgarðs-orm, Sigemund, Siegfried, Beowulf stand forth as the bravest of

---

[1] The analogy is kept up in the circumstance of the conquered dragon (like the giant's skeleton p. 555n.) being fastened over the town-gate, *e.g.* Pulci 4, 76.

dragon-quellers, backed by a crowd of others, who spring out of the exhaustless fount of living legend, wherever time and place requires them. Frotho, a second Siegfried, overpowers a venomous dragon that lay reposing on his treasure, Saxo Gram. p. 20. The beautiful Thora Borgarhiörtr had a small lýngorm given her, whom she placed in a casket, with gold under him : as he grew, the gold grew also, till the box became too narrow, and the worm laid himself in a ring all round it; soon the chamber was too small, and he lay round that, with his tail in his mouth, admitting none into the room unless they brought him food, and he required an ox at every meal. Then it was proclaimed, that whoever slew him should get the maiden for his bride, and as much gold as lay under the dragon, for her dowry. It was Ragnar Lodbrok that subdued this dragon, Fornald. sög. 1, 237-8. The rapid growth of the worm has a startling similarity to that of the fish, p. 578. But, beside the hoarded gold which the heroes carry off as prize, the adventure brings them other advantages : eating the dragon's heart gives one a knowledge of beasts' language, and painting oneself with his blood hardens the skin against all injury. Both features enter deeply into the legend of Siegfried (see Suppl.).[1]

Nearly all of this has its counterpart in the beliefs of other nations. As the Romans borrowed gigas from the Greeks, so they did draco, for neither serpens nor vermis was adequate (like our slango and wurm) to express the idea. Now δράκων comes from δέρκειν to look, illumine, flash out, φάος δέδορκε expresses illuminating light, and this confirms me in my proposed explanation of our lint and linni. A fox after long burrowing struck upon the cave of a dragon watching hidden treasure, 'ad draconis speluncam ultimam, custodiebat qui thesauros abditos,' Phaedr. 4, 19. Then the story of the gold-guarding griffins must be included, as they are winged monsters like the dragons.

In O. Slavic zmiy m., and zmiya f., signify snake, the one more a dragon, the other an adder. The Boh. zmek is the fiery dragon guarding money, zmiye the adder; Serv. zmay dragon, zmiya adder. Mica, which the zmay shakes off him, is named otresine zmayeve (dragon's offshake), Vuk p. 534. Once more, everything

---

[1] Which reminds Albrecht in Titurel 3313—17 of a similar tale of Rodolz, conf. Parz. 518, 18 and Diut. 3, 59.

leads to glitter, gold and fire. The Lith. *smakas* seems borrowed from Slavic; whether connected with AS. *snaca*, is a question. Jungmann says, *zmek* is not only a dragon, but a spirit who appears in the shape of a wet bird,[1] usually a *chicken*, and brings people money; Sup. I, 143 says you must not hurt *earth-chicks* or *house-adders*; Schm. 1, 104 explains *erdhünlein* (earth-chicken) as a bright round lustre, in the middle of which lies something dark; conf. geuhuon, Helbl. 8, 858.

Renvall thus describes the Finn. *mammelainen*: 'femina maligna, matrix serpentis, divitiarum subterranearum custos.' Here at last the hoard is assigned to a female snake; in Teutonic and also Slavic tales on the contrary it is characteristic of the fierce fiendish dragon (m.) to guard treasure, and the adder or unke (f.) plays more the part of a friendly homesprite: as the one is a man transformed, so the other appears as a crowned maiden with a serpent's tail (Deut. sag. no. 13), or as a fay. But she can no more dispense with her golden crown than the dragon with his guardianship of gold; and the Boh. zmek is at once dragon and adder. A story of the *adder-king* is in Bechstein's Franken p. 290 (see Suppl.).

Amidst all these points of connexion, the being worshipped by the Lombards must remain a matter of doubt; we have only a right to assume that they ascribed to it a benign and gracious character.

INSECTS.—Some traces of *beetle-worship* I am able to disclose.

We have two old and pretty general terms: OHG. *chevor*, *cheviro*, MHG. *kever*, kevere, NHG. *käfer*, N. Neth. *kever*, AS. *ceafor*, Engl. *chafer*. We have no business to bring in the Lat. caper (which is AS. hæfer, ON. hafr); the root seems to be the AS. ceaf, caf=alacer, for the chafer is a brisk lively creature, and in Swabia they still say käfermässig for agilis, vivax (Gramm. 2, 571. 1013). The AS. has ceafortûn, cafertûn, for atrium, vestibulum; 'scarabaeorum oppidum' as it were, because chafers chirp in it?[3] The second term, OHG. *wibil*, *webil*, MHG. *wibel*,

---

[1] Zmokly is drenched, zmoknuti to wet; 'mokrý gako zmok,' dripping like an earth-sprite.

[2] Here again the female being has the advantage over the male.

[3] Helbling, speaking of an ill-shaped garment, starts the query (1, 177), where

NHG. *webel*, *wiebel*, AS. *wifel*, *wefel*, Engl. *weevil*, agrees with
Lith. *wabalas*, *wabalis*, Lett. *wabbols*, and I trace it to weben
(weave, wave) in the sense of our 'leben und weben,' vigere,
moveri; we say, 'kriebeln und wiebeln' of the swarming of
beetles.[1]

To the Egyptians the beetle (scarabaeus, κάνθαρος, κάραβος)
was a sacred being, an emblem of inmost life and mysterious self-
generation. They believed that he proceeded out of matter
which he rolled into globules and buried in manure (see Suppl.).

ON. literature deals in no prose terms, but at once comes out
with the poetic name *iötunox*, *iötunoxi* (giant-ox); as that giant
maiden took the ploughman with his oxen and plough for crawl-
ing beetles (p. 540, Finn. *sontiainen*, sondiainen, dung-beetle
from sonda, fimus), so conversely the real beetle might awaken
the notion of a iötunox. To liken the small animal to the large
was natural.

Our biggest beetle, the stately antlered stag-beetle, the Romans
called *lucanus*, Nigid. in Pliny 11, 28 (34), with which I suppose
is connected the well-known *luca bos*, lucanus or lucana bos, a
name which got shifted from the horned beast to a tusked one,
the elephant (Varro 7, 39. 40. O. Müll. p. 135). But we call
the beetle *hirsch* (stag, Fr. cerf volant), and even ox and goat,
all of them horned beasts, Pol. ielonek, O. Slav. elenetz (both
stagling), Boh. rohač (corniger), Austr. *hörnler*, Swed. *horntroll*.
Again, a Lat. name for scarabaeus terrester was *taurus*, Plin. 30,
5 (12), which keeps my lucanus bos or cervus, in countenance.
To the female the Bohemians give the further name of *babka*
(granny).

On p. 183 we came across a more significant name, *donner-
guegi*, *donnerpuppe*, in obvious allusion to Donar, whose holy tree
the beetle loves to dwell in; and with this, apparently, agrees a
general term for beetles which extends through Scandinavia,
viz. Westergötl. *torbagge*, Swed. *tortyfvel*, Norweg. *tordivel*, Jutl.
torr, *torre*. True, there is no Icelandic form, let alone ON., in
which Thôrr can be detected; yet this 'tor' may have the same

---

might be the back and belly of one that was hidden away in such a *cheverpeunt*?
He calls the ample cloak a chafer-pound or yard, in whose recesses you catch beetles.
This *keverpiunt* answers to the AS. *ceafortún*.

[1] Slavic names are, Boh. chraust, Pol. chraszcz; Boh. brauk, bruk, prob. from
bruchus, βροῦκος. [Russ. xhuk; the 'gueg' of S. Germany?]

force it has in torsdag (p. 126) and tordön (p. 166); 'bagge,' says Ihre p. 122, denotes juvenis, puer, hence servant of the god, which was afterwards exchanged for dyfvel=diefvul, devil. Afzelius (Sagohäfder 1, 12. 13) assures us, that the torbagge was sacred to Thor, that in Norrland his larva is called *mulloxe* (earth-ox, our Swiss donnerpuppe? conf. iötunoxi), and that he who finds a *dung-beetle lying on his back* (ofvältes) unable to help himself, and *sets him on his legs* again, is believed by the Norr-landers to have atoned for seven sins thereby.

This sounds antique enough, and I do not hastily reject the proposed interpretation of tordyfvel, false as it looks. For the AS. *tordwifel* is plainly made up of 'tord,' stercus (Engl. turd) and the 'wifel' above, and answers to the Dan. skarnbasse, skarntorre (dungbeetle); consequently tordyfvel, torbasse crave the same solution, even though a simple 'tord' and 'vivel' be now wanting in all the Scandinavian dialects. The Icelandic has turned tordivel about into *torfdifill*, as if turf-devil, from torf, gleba. There is also the N. Neth. *tor, torre* beetle, and *drektorre* dungbeetle [or devil's coach-horse; also Engl. *dumble-dorr* cockchafer], to be taken into account (see Suppl.).

But who ever saw even a beetle lie struggling on his back, without compassionately turning him over? The German people, which places the stagbeetle in close connexion with thunder and fire, may very likely have paid him peculiar honours once.

Like other sacred harbingers of spring (swallows, storks), the *first cockchafer* (Maikäfer)[1] used to be escorted in from the woods with much ceremony; we have it on good authority, that this

---

[1] *Maikäfer* (like maiblume) sounds too general, and not a people's word. And there is no Lat. name preserved either. The Greek μηλολόνθη designates our mai-käfer or our goldkäfer; boys tied a string to it and played with it (Aristoph. Nub. 763), as our boys do. The It. *scarafaggio* is formed from scarafone (scarabaeus); the Fr. *hanneton* a dim. of the obsolete *hanne* horse, which may have been the term for the stagbeetle (still petzgaul, Bruin's horse, in the Wetterau), Fr. cerf volant, Dan. *seghiort*, Swed. *ekhjort*, i.e. oak-hart. The Mecklenb. *eksäwer*, oak-chafer, as well as the simple *säver, sever, sebber* (Schütze's Holst. idiot. 4, 91) is applied to the maikäfer; in other parts of L. Saxony they say *maisävel, maisäbel*. This *säver, säver* (Brem. wtb. 4, 592. 5, 810) is surely no other than käfer with change of *k* into *s, z*; Chytræus's Nomencl. saxon. has '*sever*, and *goldsever*=goldkäfer.' Or does the HG. *siefer* belong here, contrary to the etymol. proposed on p. 40? In the Westerwald *pöwitz, köwitz* is maikäfer, and in Ravensberg *povömmel* dungbeetle (Kuhn's Westfäl. sagen 2, 188), almost agreeing with Esthon. *poua* chafer, beetle. Like the various names for the stagbeetle, maybeetle, dungbeetle, goldbeetle, the traces of ancient beetle-worship seem also to meet, first in one, then in another of them. A *scarafone* who brings succour occurs in Pentamer. 3, 5 (see Suppl.).

continued to be done by the spinning girls in parts of Schleswig as late as the 17th century.[1]

Folk-tales of Up. Germany inform us : Some girls, not grown up, went one Sunday to a deserted tower on a hill, found the stairs strewn with sand, and came to a beautiful room they had never seen before, in which there stood a bed with curtains. When they drew these aside, the bed was *swarming with gold-beetles*, and jumping up and down of itself. Filled with amazement, the girls looked on for a while, till suddenly a terror seized them, and they fled out of the room and down the stairs, with an unearthly howl and racket at their heels (Mone's Anz. 7, 477). On the castle-hill by Wolfartsweiler a little girl saw a copper pot standing on three legs, quite new and *swarming full of horsebeetles* (roskäfer). She told her parents, who saw at once that the beetles were a treasure, and hastened with her to the hill, but found neither pot nor beetles any more (ibid. 8, 305). Here beetles appear as holy animals guarding gold, and themselves golden.

In Sweden they call the small goldbeetle (skalkräk) Virgin Mary's key-maid (jungfru Marie nyckelpiga), Dybeck's Runa 1844, p. 10; in spring the girls let her creep about on their hands, and say, ' hon märker mig brudhandskar,' she marks (fore-shews) me bride's gloves; if she flies away, they notice in which direction, for thence will come the bridegroom. Thus the beetle seems a messenger of the goddess of love; but the number of the black spots on his wings has to be considered too: if more than seven, corn will be scarce that year, if less, you may look for an abundant harvest, Afzel. 3, 112-3.

The little coccinella septempunctata has mythical names in nearly all our dialects: NHG. *gotteskühlein* (God's little cow),[2] gotteskalb, herrgotteskalb, herrgotts-thierchen (-beastie), *herr-gots-vöglein* (-birdie), Marienvöglein, *Marienkäfer*, Marienkälblein; Engl. *ladycow*, ladybird, ladyfly; Dan. *Marihöne* (-hen); Boh. *krawka, krawicka* (little cow). In Up. Germany they call the small goldbeetle (chrysomela vulg.) *fraua-chüeli*, ladycow (Tobler

---

[1] An old description of the maygrave feast by Ulr. Petersen (in Falck's New staatsb. mag., vol. 1, Schlesw. 1832, p. 655) speaks of it thus : ' A quaint procession of the erewhile amazons of the spinning-wheel at Schleswig, for fetching in of a *cantharis* or *maykäfer* with green boughs, whereat the town-hall of this place was decked out with greenery.' The feast was still held in 1630—40.

[2] The Russ. ' Bóžhia koróvka, has exactly the same meaning.—TRANS.

204^b) and 'der liebe *froue henje*,' our lady's hen (Alb. Schott's Deutsche in Piemont 297), in contrast to *herra-chüeli* the coccinella (Tobler 265ª), though the name probably wavers between the two. By the same process which we observed in the names of plants and stars, Mary seems to have stept into the place of Freyja, and Marihöne was formerly *Freyjuhœna*, which we still have word for word in Froue henje, and the like in Fraua-chüeli. And of Romance tongues, it is only that of France (where the community of views with Germany was strongest) that has a *bête à dieu, vache à dieu;* Span. and Ital. have nothing like it. At all events our children's song :

> *Marienkäferchen*, flieg aus ! (fly away)
> dein häuschen brennt, (burns)
> dein mütterchen flennt, (weeps)
> dein väterchen sitzt auf der schwelle ; (sits on the threshold)
> flieg *in 'n himmel* aus der hölle ! (into heaven out of hell)

must be old, for in England also they sing : '*Ladybird*, ladybird, fly away home, your house is on fire, and your children will burn [all but little Bessie that sits *in the sun*].' With us too the children put the Marienkäfer or sonnenkäfer on their finger, and ask it, like the cuckoo: '*sunnenkieken* (sun's chicken), ik frage di, wo lange schal ik leven ? ' 'Een jaar, twee jaar,' etc., till the chafer flies away, its home being in the sun or in heaven. In Switzerland they hold the goldbeetle on their hand, and say : ' cheferli, cheferli, flüg us ! i getter milech ond brocka ond e silberigs löffeli dezue.' Here the chafer, like the snake, is offered ' milk and crumbs and a silver spoon thereto.' In olden times he must have been regarded as the god's messenger and confidant (see Suppl.).

Lastly the *bee*, the one insect that is tamable and will live among men, and whose wise ways are such a lesson to them, may be expected to have old mythic associations. The bee is believed to have survived from the golden age, from the lost paradise (Chap. XXX.) ; nowhere is her worth and purity more prettily. expressed than in the Servian lay of the rich Gavan, where God selects three holy angels to prove mankind, and bids them descend from heaven to earth, ' as the bee upon the flower,' kako. pchela po tsvetu (Vuk 1, 128 ed. 2). The clear sweet honey,.

which bees suck out of every blossom, is a chief ingredient of the
drink divine (p. 319), it is the ἡδεῖα ἐδωδή of the gods, Hymn. in
Merc. 560 ; and holy honey the first food that touches the lips
of a new-born child, RA. 457. Then, as the gift of poesy is
closely connected with Oðhrœris dreckr, it is bees that bring it
to sleeping Pindar : μέλισσαι αὐτῷ καθεύδοντι προσεπέτοντό τε
καὶ ἔπλασσον πρὸς τὰ χείλη τοῦ κηροῦ· ἀρχὴ μὲν Πινδάρῳ
ποιεῖν ᾄσματα ἐγένετο τοιαύτη, Pausan. ix. 23, 2. And therefore they are called Musarum volucres (Varro de re rust. 3, 16).
A kindermärchen (no. 62) speaks of the queen-bee settling on
her favourite's mouth ;[1] if she flies to any one in his sleep, he
is accounted a child of fortune.

It seems natural, in connexion with these bustling winged
creatures, to think of the silent race of elves and dwarfs, which
like them obeys a queen. It was in the decaying flesh of the first
giant that dwarfs bred as maggots ; in exactly the same way bees
are said to have sprung from the putrefaction of a bullock's body :
' apes nascuntur ex bubulo corpore putrefacto,' Varro, 2, 5;
' amissas reparari ventribus bubulis recentibus cum fimo obrutis,'
Plin. 11, 20 (23); conf. Virg. Georg. 4, 284–558. Ov. Met. 15,
364. To this circumstance some have ascribed the resemblance
between apis bee and Apis bull, though the first has a short a,
and the last a long. What seems more important for us is the
celebrated discovery of a golden bullock's-head amongst many
hundred golden bees in the tomb of the Frankish king Childeric
at Doornik (repres. in Eccard's Fr. or. 1, 39. 40).

Natural history informs us that clouds of bees fall upon the
sweet juice of the ash-tree; and from the life-tree Yggdrasil the
Edda makes a dew trickle, which is called a 'fall of honey,'
and nourishes bees (Sn. 20).[2]

The Yngl. saga cap. 14 says of Yngvifrey's son, king Fiölnir
(Siolm in the O. Swed. chron.), that he fell into a barrel of mead
and was drowned; so in Saxo, king Hunding falls into sweet
mead, and the Greek myth lets Glaucus drown in a honey-jar, the
bright in the sweet. According to a legend of the Swiss Alps,

---

[1] Sederunt in ore infantis tum etiam Platonis, suavitatem illam praedulcis
eloquii portendentes. Plin. 11, 17 (18).
[2] Ceram ex floribus, melliginem e lacrimis arborum quae glutinum pariunt,
salicis, ulmi, arundinis succo.

in the golden age when the brooks and lakes were filled with
milk, a shepherd was upset in his boat and drowned; his body,
long sought for, turned up at last in the foaming cream, when
they were churning, and was buried in a cavity which bees had
constructed of honeycombs as large as town-gates (Mém. de
l'acad. celt. 5, 202). Bees weave a temple of wax and feathers
(Schwenk's Gr. myth. p. 129. Herm. Müller's Griechenth. 455),
and in our Kinderm. no. 107, p. 130-1 a palace of wax and honey.
This reminds us of the beautiful picture in Lohengrin p. 191 of
Henry 2.'s tomb in Bamberg cathedral:

> Sus lît er dâ in sîner stift
> di'er het erbouwen, als diu *bin* ir wîft
> ûz maneger blüete würket, daz man honc-seim nennet.

(he lies in the minster he built, as the bee her web from many a
blossom works, that we name honey-juice). In the various
languages the working bee is represented as female, OHG. pîa,
Lat. apis, Gr. $\mu\acute{\epsilon}\lambda\iota\sigma\sigma\alpha$, Lith. bitte, in contrast with the masc.
fucus the drone, OHG. treno, Lith. tranas; but then the head of
the bees is made a king, our weiser (pointer), MHG. wîsel, OHG.
wîso, dux, Pliny's 'rex apium,' Lith. bittinis, M. Lat. chosdrus
(Ducange sub v.), yet AS. beomôdor, Boh. matka. The Gr.
$\grave{\epsilon}\sigma\sigma\acute{\eta}\nu$ is said to have meant originally the king-bee, and to have
acquired afterwards the sense of king or priest, as $\mu\acute{\epsilon}\lambda\iota\sigma\sigma\alpha$ also
signified priestess, especially of Demeter and Artemis. Even
gods and goddesses themselves are represented by the sacred
animal, Zeus (Aristaeus) as a bee, Vishnu as a blue bee. A
Roman Mellona (Arnob. 4, 131), or Mellonia (Aug. de civ. Dei
4, 24), was goddess of bees; the Lith. Austheia was the same,
jointly with a bee-god Bybylus. Masculine too was the Lett.
Uhsinsh, *i.e.*, the hosed one, in reference to bees' legs being
covered with wax ('waxen thighs,' Mids. Dream 3, 1). From all
these fancies, mostly foreign, we might fairly make guesses about
our own lost antiquities; but we should have to get more exact
information as to the legend of the *Bee-wolf* (pp. 369, 673) and
the mythic relationship of the woodpecker (Lith. melleta) to the
bee (see Suppl.).

CHAPTER XXII.

SKY AND STARS.

The visible heavens have in many ways left their mark on the heathen faith. Not only do gods, and the spirits who stand next them, have their dwelling in the sky, and get mixt up with the stars, but earthly beings too, after their dissolution, are transported thither, and distinguished heroes and giants shine as constellations. From the sky the gods descend to earth, along the sky they make their journeys, and through the sky they survey unseen the doings of men. And as all plants turn to the light of heaven, as all souls look up to heaven, so do the smoke of sacrifice and the prayers of mankind mount upwards.

Heaven covers earth, and our word 'himmel' comes from the root hima (tego, involvo, vestio, Gramm. 2, 55; conf. Lith. dangus coelum, from dengiu tego; OHG. himilezi laquear). The Goths and Old Norsemen agree in preferring the form *himins*, *himinn*, and most other Teutons *himil*; even Swed. Norw. Dan. have *himmel*. The Saxon race has moreover two terms peculiar to itself: one is OS. *hëbhan*, *hëvan*, AS. *hëofon*, Engl. *heaven*, and still in Lower Saxony and Westphalia, *heben*, *heven*, *häven*, *häwen*. I have endeavoured to make out the area over which this name extends (Gramm. I, xiv.). The Frisians did not use it, for the N. and W. Fris. patois of to-day owns to nothing but 'himmel.'[1] Nor does the Netherl. dialect know it; but it is found in Westphalia, in L. Saxony as far as Holstein, and beyond the Elbe in Mecklenburg and Pomerania. The AS. and Engl. are wholly destitute of the word himel; OS., like the present LS. and Westph., employs both terms alike, yet apparently so as to designate by *hëvan* more the visible heaven, and by *himil* the supersensual. Alb. of Halberstadt (ed. 1545, 145ᵇ) uses

---

[1] *Himel*, Lapekoer fen Gabe scroar, Dimter 1834, p. 101. 108. *hemmel*, Hansens Geixhals, Sonderbg. 1833. p. 148. *himel*, Friesche wetten 348. *himul*, As. 274.

hëben (rhym. *nëben*) of the place. Reinolt von der Lippe couples the two words: '*himel* und *hëben* von vreuden muz irkrachen,' burst with joy. People say: 'de *heven* steit nümmer to'; 'wenn de *heven* fallt, ligg wi der all unner;' 'de sterren an dem *häven*;' in Westphalia *hebenscheer* means a sky overcast without rain, and even *heben* alone can signify cloud.[1] In *hävenhüne* (p. 156), in kukuk vam *häven* (p. 676), the physical sense preponderates, whereas one would hardly speak otherwise than of 'going to *himel*,' or *himelrik*. Yet this distinction seems to be comparatively recent: as the AS. hëofon can be used in a purely spiritual sense, so the poet of our Heliand alternates between *himilriki* 149, 8 and *hëbanriki* 143, 24, *himilfader* 145, 12 and *hëbancuning* 143, 20. And of course *himil* had originally, and has everywhere in HG., the physical meaning too; hence *uphimil* in Hel. 88, 15, just like *upheofon* in Cædm. 270, 24. The root of hëbhan, hëvan, hëofon, is probably a lost Gothic, 'hiba, haf,' cognate with Lat. capio, so that it is the all-capacious, ON. *viðfeðmir*, wide-fathoming or encompassing sky.[2]

The other Saxon term may be placed on a level with the Gr. αἰθήρ (thin upper air), whilst himil and hëvan answer to οὐρανός; it is OS. *radur*, AS. *rodor*. In Cædmon we find *rodor* 183, 19. 207, 8. *uprodor* 179, 10. 182, 15. 205. 2. *rodortungol* (star), 100, 21. *rodorbeorht* 239, 10. Its root RAD lies buried as yet in obscurity; it has disappeared from all modern dialects [except as Rother in proper names?]. I am inclined to connect with it the ON. *röðull* (sol), which has nothing to do with rauðr (ruber). From the AS. poets using indifferently '*wuldres* gim' and '*heofones* gim' (Beow. 4142. Andr. 1269); heofonbeorht, rodorbeorht, *wuldor*beorht; heofontorht, *swegl*torht, *wuldor*torht; we might almost infer that *wuldor* (glory) originally meant coelum, which would throw light on the OHG. name *Woldar*hilt. And the same with *swegel* (aether, coelum): conf. *swegles* begong,

---

[1] Sanskr. nabas, Slav. nébo (coelum), pl. nebesá, Gr. νέφος, Lat. nubes, nebula; Ir. neamh, Wel. nêv, Armor. nef, Lett. debbes (coelum), debbess (nubes); conf. Lith. dangus above [and sky, welkin, with ON. ský, Germ. wolke, cloud].

[2] 'Hills of heaven' are high ones, reaching into the clouds, often used as proper names: *himinfjöll*, Sæm. 148ᵃ. Yngl. saga cap. 39; *Himinbiörg*, Sæm. 41, 92ᵇ is an abode of gods; spirits haunt the *Himilinberg* (mons coelius, Pertz 2, 10); *Himilesberg* in Hesse (Kuchenbecker's Anal. 11, 137. Arnsb. urk. 118); a *Himmelsberg* in Vestgötland, and one in Halland (said to be Heimðall's); *Himelberc*, Frauendienst 199, 10.

Beow. 1713; under *swegle* (sub coelo), Beow. 2149; *sweglrâd* (coeli currus), Cod. exon. 355, 47; OS. *suigli*.

I call attention to the AS. *sceldbyrig*, Cædm. 283, 23, which has no business to be translated refugium or sheltering city; it is distinctly our schildburg (aula clypeis tecta), a bit of heathenism the poet let fall inadvertently; so the Edda speaks of Valhöll as ':skiöldum þökt, lagt *gyltum skiöldum*, svâ sem spânþak,' Sn. 2, thatched with golden shields as with shingle-roof (p. 702 and Suppl.).

Eddic names in Sæm. 49ᵇ. Sn. 177; all masculine, some obviously founded on personification.   Heaven is pictured as a husband, embracing the female earth; he is not however admitted into the circle of the gods, like Οὐρανός, whereas Earth does stand among the goddesses.   To us heaven signifies simply a certain space, the residence of gods.   Two poetic names for it have reference to that enigmatical being Mîmir (p. 379): *hreggmîmir*, rain-shedder, from hregg imber; and *vetmîmir*, moistener? conf. væta humor.

To express star, constellation (sidus), our older speech, in addition to *stairnô, stërno, stëorra, stiarna* (Gramm. 3, 392) and OHG. *himilzeichan* (Hymn. 4, 2), has a symbolical term, OHG. *himilzungâ*, Diut. 1, 526ᵇ and Gl. Doc. 249; OS. *himiltungal*, Hel. 18, 2; AS. *heofontungol, rodortungol*; ON. *himintûngl*. Even the simple *tungol* has the same sense in AS., and a Gothic gloss on Gal. 4, 3, gives '*tuggl* astrum,' whilst in ON. *tûngl* means the moon.   This neuter noun tungal, tungol, tûngl, is no doubt from tunga (lingua), which word itself appears in OHG. himilzungâ (Graff 5, 682): the moon and some of the planets, when partially illuminated, do present the appearance of a tongue or a sickle, and very likely some cosmogonic belief[1] was engrafted on that; I know of nothing like it in other languages.

All the heavenly bodies have particular spots, seats, *chairs* assigned them, which they make their abode and resting-place; they have their lodges and stages (sterrôno *girusti*, O. i. 17, 10). This holds especially of the sun, who daily sinks into his seat

---

[1] A translation of the tongue to heaven.   Or was the twinkling of the stars likened to a *tingling* [züngeln, a quivering flickering motion like that of the tongue]?   The moon's steady light does not bear that out, nor the OHG. form without the *l*.

or settle (see Chap. XXIII); but similar chairs (KM. 25), and a seat-going (sedelgang) are attributed to all the stars. N. Bth. 210. 223 says, Boötes 'trâgo ze *sedele* gange,' and 'tiu zeichen ne gânt nicht in *sedel*.' As chair and table are things closely connected, the stars may have had tables of their own, or, what comes to the same thing, may have been regarded as *tables* of the sky; in saying which, I am not thinking of the Egyptian sun-table, but more immediately of the '*bioðum* yppa,' sidera extollere, of the Völuspâ (Sæm. 1b), the three creative 'Börs synir' having set up as it were the tables of the firmament: bioðr is the Goth. biuds, OHG. piot (pp. 38. 68). As the stationary stars had *chairs* and *tables*, the planetary ones, like other gods, had *steeds* and *cars* ascribed to them (see Suppl.).[1]

The two principal stars are the *sun* and *moon*, whose gender and appellations I have discussed in Gramm. 3, 349..350: a MHG. poet calls the sun '*daz mêrere lieht*,' the greater light, Fundgr. 2, 12. It is worth mentioning that some of the Eddic names for the moon are still preserved in patois dialects of Up. Germany. As the dwarfs named the moon *skin* (jubar), the East Franks call her *schein* (Reinwald's Henneb. id. 2, 159).[2] In the under-world the moon bore the name of *hverfandi hvel*, whirling wheel, and in Styria (esp. the Bruck distr.) she is *gmoa-rat* (Sartori's Styria, p. 82), if I may translate that by rota communis, though it may perhaps mean gemeiner rath (vorrath), a common pro-vision at the service of all men. That the sun was likened to a *wheel of fire*, and the element blazing out of him was represented in the shape of a wheel, has been fully shewn, p. 620. Tit. 2983 speaks of the *sun's wheel*. The Edda expressly calls the sun *fagrahvel*, fair wheel, Sæm. 50a Sn. 177. 223. The Norse rune for S is named *sôl* sun, the AS. and OHG. *sigil, sugil*, for which I have proposed (Andr. p. 96) the readings *segil, sagil, sahil*, and may now bring in support the Goth. *sáuil* and Gr. ἥλιος. But the Gothic letter ☉ (= HV) is the very symbol of the sun, and plainly shews the shape of a wheel; we must

---

[1] *Wagen* waggon belongs to *weg* way, as carpentum does to carpere (viam); the *car of heaven* is also that of the highest god. Otfr. i. 5, 5. says of the herald angel: 'floug er sunnûn pad, sterrôno strâza, wega wolkôno.' The Indians also call the sky *path of clouds*, Somadeva 1, 17. 2, 157.

[2] So in Mod. Gr. φεγγάρι brilliance, a name whose surprising identity with the ON. *fengari* (Sn. 177) I have already noticed elsewhere.

therefore suppose it to have been the initial of a Goth. *hvil* = AS. *hweol*, ON. *hvël*. From 'hvel' was developed the Icel. *hiol*, Swed. Dan. *hjul*, O. Swed. *hiughl*; and from 'hweol, hweohl' the Engl. *wheel*, Nethl. *wiel*, and Fris. *fial* (Richth. 737). In view of all these variations, some have even ventured to bring in the ON. *jol*, Swed. Dan. *jul* (yule), the name of the winter solstice, and fasten upon it also the meaning of the wheel; on that hypothesis the two forms must have parted company very early, supposing the Gothic name of November *jiuleis* to be cognate.[1] The word *wheel* seems to be of the same root as *while*, Goth. *hveila*, OHG. *huila*, i.e. revolving time; conf. Goth. hveila-hvairbs, OHG. huîl-huerbîc, volubilis.

Another symbolic epithet of the sun seems to be of great age: the warlike sentiment of olden times saw in him a gleaming circular *shield*, and we noticed above (p. 700) that the sky itself formed a sceldbyrig. Notker cap. 71, finding in his text the words 'sinistra clypeum coruscantem praeferebat (Apollo),' translates: 'an dero winsterûn truog er einen *rôten skilt*,' then adds a remark of his own: 'wanda selbiu diu sunna einemo *skilte* gelîh ist.' In German law and German poetry we catch the glimmer of these 'red shields.' Even Opitz 2, 286 calls the sun 'the beauteous *shield of heaven.*'

The very oldest and most universal image connected with the sun and other luminaries seems after all to be that of the *eye*. Ancient cosmogonies represent them as created out of eyes. To Persians the sun was the eye of Ahurômazdâo (Ormuzd), to Egyptians the right eye of the Demiurge, to the Greeks the eye of Zeus, to our forefathers that of Wuotan; and a fable in the Edda says Oðinn had to leave one of his eyes in pledge with Mîmir, or hide it in his fountain, and therefore he is pictured as one-eyed. In the one-eyed Cyclop's mouth Ovid puts the words (Met. 13, 851):

> Unum est in media lumen mihi fronte, sed instar
> *ingentis clypei*; quid, non haec omnia magno
> sol videt e coelo?　soli tamen *unicus orbis.*

---

[1] The Norse initial H is occasionally dropt: in Icel. both hiula and jula stand for the babbling of infants. The dialect of the Saterland Frisians has an actual jule, jole (rota). It is worthy of notice, that in some parts of Schleswig they used at Christmas-time to roll a *wheel* into the village, and this was called 'at *trille juul i by*,' trundling yule into town; Outzen sub. v. jôl, p. 145.

Like the giant, the god (Wuotan, the sky) has but one eye, which is a wheel and a shield. In Beow. 1135 '*beácen* Godes' is the sun, the great celestial sign.[1] With this eye the divinity surveys the world, and nothing can escape its peering all-piercing glance[2]; all the stars *look* down upon men.[3] But the ON. poets, not content with treating sun, moon and stars as eyes of heaven, invert the macrocosm, and call the human eye the sun, moon, or star of the skull, forehead, brows and eyelashes; they even call the eye the *shield* of the forehead: a confirmation of the similar name for the sun. Another title they bestow on the sun is '*gimsteinn* himins' (gemma coeli); so in AS. 'heofones *gim*,' Beow. 4142 and 'wuldres *gim*,' Andr. 1289 (see Suppl.).

And not only is the sun represented as the god's eye looking down, but as his full *face* and *countenance*; and that is how we draw his picture still. Otfried says of the sun being darkened at the Saviour's death, iv. 33, 5:

> In ni liaz si nuzzi thaz scônaz *annuzzi*,
> ni liaz in scînan thuruh thaz ira *gisiuni* blîdaz.

The Edda speaks of the *sun* and *moon* as brother and sister, children of a mythic *Mundilföri*. Several nations beside the Lithuanians and Arabs (Gramm. 3, 351) agree with us in imagining the moon masculine and the sun feminine. The Mexican *Meztli* (luna) is a man; the Greenlanders think of *Anningat*, the moon, as pursuing his sister *Mallina*, the sun. An Ital. story (Pentam. 5, 5) makes *Sole* and *Luna* children of *Talia* (in Perrault they are named Jour and Aurore). The Slavs make the moon masc., a star fem., the sun neut.; thus in a Servian lay (Vuk 1, 134), God calls the sun (suntse, Russ. solntse, -tse dim. suff.) his child (chedo), the moon (mesets) being its brother, and the star (zvezda) its sister. To think of the stars as children or young suns is nothing out of the way. Wolfram says in Wh. 254, 5: 'jungiu *sünnelîn* möhten wahsen.'

---

[1] The Servians call the deepest part of a lake *oko* (eye), Vuk's Montenegro 62.
[2] When the Iliad 14, 344 says:

> οὐδ ἂν νῶϊ διαδράκοι Ἠέλιὸς περ,
> οὔτε καὶ ὀξύτατον πέλεται φάος εἰσοράασθαι,

it resembles the lay of Wolfram 8, 26:

> Obe der sunnen drî mit blicke wæren (if there were 3 suns looking),
> sin möhten zwischen si gelihten (they could not shine in between).

[3] Πρέσβιστον ἄστρων νυκτὸς ὀφθαλμός, Aesch. Sept. c. Th. 390.

Down to recent times, our people were fond of calling the sun and moon *frau sonne* and *herr mond*.[1] Aventin 19[b] : '*frauw Sonne geht zu rast und gnaden*.' In the country between the Inn and Salzach they say ' der *hêr Mân*,' meaning no more than simply moon, Schm. 2, 230. 582. Gesner in Mithrid., Tur. 1555, p. 28 : ' audio veteres Germanos Lunam quoque deum coluisse et appellasse *hermon*, id est dominum Lunum, quod forte parum animadvertentes aliqui ad Hermann, i.e. Mercurium transtulerunt;' this last guess has missed the mark. Hulderic. Eyben de titulo nobilis, Helmst. 1677. 4, p. 136 : ' qua etiam ratione in veteri idololatrico luna non domina, *dominus* appellatur :

> bis gottwillkommen, *neuer mon, holder herr,*
> mach mir meines geldes mehr ![2]

Also in Nicolaus Magni de Gawe (Superst. E, 10) : ' vetulam novi, quae credidit *solem esse deam,* vocans eam *sanctam dominam;*' and earlier still in Eligius (Sup. A) : 'nullus *dominos solem* aut *lunam* vocet.'[3]

In these invocations lingers the last vestige of a heathen worship; perhaps also in the *sonnenlehn*, sun-fief (RA. 278) ? I have spoken on *bowing* to the sun, p. 31, and *cursing* by him, ' der sunnen haz varn,' p. 19, where he is made equal to a deity.[4] In the same way the *knees were bent* and the head bared to the *new moon* (Sup. E, 11). In taking an oath the fingers were extended *toward the sun* (Weisth. 3, 349); and even Tacitus in Ann. 13, 55 relates of Bojocalus : ' *solem respiciens* et cetera sidera vocans, quasi coram interrogabat, vellentne intueri inane solum ' (see Suppl.).

That to our remote ancestry the heavenly bodies, especially the sun and moon, were divine beings, will not admit of any doubt. Not only do such symbolic expressions as ' face, eye, tongue, wheel, shield, table, car ' bring us face to face with a vivid personification; we have also seen how significantly Caesar

---

[1] *Frau Sunne* (Görres Meisterl. 184). Hence in O.Fr. *Solaus,* without the article, Bekker on Ferabras p. 168.

[2] His authority is Dynkelspuhl tract. 1, praec. 1, p. 59. Is this the Nicolaus Dinkelspuel in Jöcher ?

[3] Conf. the wind addressed as *lord*, p. 631; and *dobropan*, p. 130 note.

[4] Some would trace the name of Salzwedel, Soltwedel in the Altmark to heathen sun-worship, (Ledebur's Allg. arch. 14, 370. Temme's Altmark p. 29), though the first syll. plainly means salt; ' wedel ' will be explained when we come to the moon.

couples together *Sol*, *Vulcanus* and *Luna*, p. 103. conf. p. 602.
As *Sól* is reckoned among ásins in the Edda (Sn. 39), and is
sister to *Máni* (Sn. 12), this last has claims to an equal rank.
Yet Sæm. 1ᵇ calls Sôl '*sinni* Mâna,' companion of the moon,
sinni being the Goth. gasinþja, OHG. kasindeo, sindo; and it is
remarkable that the Merseburg Lay gives the divine *Sunná* not
a companion brother, but a sister *Sindgund* (supra p. 308), whose
name however still expresses attendance, escort; [1] may she have
been a morning or evening star? We should have to know first,
what distinction a dim remote antiquity made between *sáuil* and
sunnô in respect of gender and mythical use; if 'sáuil, sagil,' like
sol and ἥλιος, was masc., then Sunná and Sindgund might be
imagined as female moons like Luna and Σελήνη, yet sôl is always
fem. in ON., and our sunne so late as in MHG. strangely wavers
between the two sexes, Gramm. 3, 350 (see Suppl.).

Be that as it may, we have a right to add in support of the
sun's divinity, that 'she' is described like other gods (pp. 17. 26.
324), as *blithe*, *sweet* and *gracious*. O. iv. 33, 6 speaks of her
'gisiuni *blídas*, thes sih ioh worolt frewita,' whereof the world
had aye rejoiced; and a 13th cent. poem (Zeitschr. f. d. alt. 1,
493-4) thus describes the greetings addressed to her:

Wol dir *frouwe Sunne!*	'Hail to thee, Lady Sun!
du bist al der werlt wunne!	Art all the world's delight.'
sô ir die Sunnen *vrô* sehet,	When ye see the sun glad,
schœnes tages ir ir jehet,	The fair day to her ye ascribe,
der êren ir der Sunnen jehet,	To her ye give the honour,
swenn ir si in liehtem schîne sehet.	Whenever ye see, etc.

Other passages in point are reserved for next chapter.

The personality of the sun and moon shews itself moreover in
a fiction that has wellnigh gone the round of the world. These
two, in their unceasing unflagging career through the void of
heaven, appear to be in flight, avoiding some pursuer. A pair of
wolves are on their track, *Sköll* dogging the steps of the sun,
Hati of the moon; they come of a giant race, the mightiest of
whom, *Mánagarmr* (moon-dog), apparently but another name for
Hati, is sure some day to *overtake and swallow the moon*. How

---

[1] Conf. *sunnagahts*, *sungiht* (solis iter), p. 617 n., and sunnan *stôfet* (iter),
Cædm. 182, 25.

extensively this tradition prevailed, has already been shewn (pp. 244-5).[1] A parhelion or mock-sun (vädersol) is in Swed. called *solvarg*, *solulf*, sun-wolf, Ihre's Dial. lex. 165.

One of the most terrific phenomena to heathens was an *eclipse* of the sun or moon, which they associated with a destruction of all things and the end of the world; they fancied the monster had already got a part of the shining orb between his jaws, and they tried to scare him away by loud cries. This is what Eligius denounces (Superst. A): 'nullus, si quando *luna obscuratur*, *vociferare* praesumat;' it is the cry of 'vince luna!'[2] that the Indicul. paganiar. means in cap. 21 de defectione lunae, and Burchard (Sup. C, 193[b]) by his '*clamoribus* aut auxilio *splendorem* lunae deficientis *restaurare*.' The Norse writings, while minutely describing the threatened deglutition, make no allusion to the shouting: it may have been more customary with Celts and Romans than with Teutons. A 5th cent. father, St. Maximus of Turin, in a Homilia de defectu lunae, preaches thus: 'Cum ante dies plerosque de vestrae avaritiae cupiditate pulsaverim, ipsa die circa vesperam tanta vociferatio populi exstitit, ut irreligiositas ejus penetraret ad coelum. Quod quum requirerem, quid sibi clamor hic velit, dixerunt mihi, quod *laboranti lunae* vestra *vociferatio subveniret*, et *defectum ejus suis clamoribus adjuvaret*.'[3] The same 'laborans' (in distress) is used by Juvenal 6, 442:

> Jam nemo tubas, nemo aera fatiget;
> una *laboranti* poterit *succurrere lunae*.[4]

I may safely assume that the same superstitious notions and practices attend eclipses among nations ancient and modern.[5] The Indian belief is, that a serpent eats up the sun and moon when they are eclipsed (Bopp's Gloss. 148[a]), or a demon (râhus) devours them (Bopp's Nalas, pp. 153. 272.   Somadeva 2, 15. 187).

---

[1] I add from Fischart's Garg. 180[b]: 'sah den *wolf des mons*.' Rabelais 1, 11 has: *la lune des loups*. In old calendars, eclipses are represented by two dragons holding the sun and moon in their mouths, Mone's Untersuch. p. 183.

[2] This would be in OHG. 'Karih mâno!' in Goth. 'jiukâi mêna!' but we find nothing of the kind even later.

[3] Ducange 6, 1618 quotes the passage sub v. vinceluna; but the reprint of the Hom. Maximi taurin. 'De defectu lunae' (in Mabillon's Mus. Ital., tom. i. pars 2, pp. 19. 20) has it not.

[4] Conr. Tac. Annal. 1, 28 and Boeth. de consol. 4 metr. 5: 'lassant crebris pulsibus aëra.'

[5] It is only among Greeks and Slavs that I have not come across them.

To this day the Hindus consider that a giant lays hold of the luminaries, and tries to swallow them (Broughton's Pop. poetry of Hind: p. 131). .The Chinese call the solar eclipse zhishi (solis devoratio), the lunar yueshi (lunae devoratio), and ascribe them both to the machinations of a dragon. Nearly all the populations of Northern Asia hold the same opinion: the Tchuvashes use the phrase 'vubur siat,' daemon comedit (Guil. Schott de lingua Tschuw, p. 5); the Finns of Europe have a similar belief, the Esthonians say the sun or moon 'is being eaten,' and formerly they sought to hinder it by conjuring spells (Thom. Hiärn, Mitau 1794 p. 39). The Lithuanians think a demon (Tiknis or Tiklis) attacks the chariot of the sun, then darkness arises, and all creatures are in fear lest the dear sun be worsted; it has been staved off for a long time, but it must come to that at the end of the world (Narbutt 1, 127. 142). In eclipses of the moon, the Greenlanders carry boxes and kettles to the roofs of their houses, and beat on them as hard as they can (Cranz's Grönland 3, 294). An English traveller says of the Moors in Africa: When the sun's eclipse was at its height, we saw the people running about as if mad, and firing their rifles at the sun, *to frighten the monster* who they supposed was wishing to *devour the orb of day*. The plains and heights of Tripoli resounded with the death-dirge (the cry 'wulliali wu!'), and the same all along the coast. The women *banged copper vessels* together, making such a *din* that it was heard leagues away (see Suppl.).[1]

A Mongolian myth makes out that the gods determined to punish Arakho for his misdeeds, but he hid so effectually, that no one could find out his lurkingplace. They therefore asked the *sun*, who gave an unsatisfactory answer; but when they asked the *moon*, she disclosed his whereabouts. So Arakho was dragged forth and chastised; in revenge of which, he *pursues both sun and moon*, and whenever he comes to hand-grips with one of them, an *eclipse occurs*. To help the lights of heaven in their sad plight, a *tremendous uproar* is made with musical and other instruments, till Arakho is scared away.[2] Here a noticeable

---

[1] Morgenblatt 1817 p. 159ª; conf. Niebuhr's Beschr. Arab. 119. 120.
[2] Benj. Bergmann's Nomad. streifereien 3, 41. Acc. to Georgii Alphab. tibetan. p. 189, it is monsters called Tracehn, with their upper parts shaped like men, and the lower like snakes, that lie in wait for the sun and moon. [South of L. Baikal it is the king of hell that tries to swallow the moon.—TRANS.]

feature is the *inquiry* made *of the sun and moon*, who overlook
the world and know all secrets (Castrén's Myth. 62). So in our
fairytales the seeker asks of the *sun, moon* and *stars* (Kinderm.
no. 25. 88; conf. 3, 218-9), some of whom are found helpful and
sympathizing, others cruel and cannibal (Vuk no. 10). In Servian songs the *moon* and the *morningstar* (danitsa) hold a colloquy
on the affairs of men (Vuk 3, 3). During an eclipse of the sun
(I don't know whether of the moon also) our people cover the
wells up, else their water would turn impure, Superst. I, 589.

Is there a trace of moon-worship to be found in the fact that
people had an image of the moon carved on rocks and stones that
marked a boundary? In RA. 542 an Alamannic doc. of 1155 is
given, which traces the custom all the way up to king Dagobert.
In Westphalian docs. as late as the 17th cent. I find *halfmonds-
schnad-stones*,[1] unless the word halfmoon here means something
else.

In Bavaria there is a Mondsee, OHG. *Máninséo* (lunae lacus),
in Austria a *Mânhart* (lunae silva, ἡ Λοῦνα ὕλη in Ptolemy);[2] we
may safely credit both with mythic associations.

As time is more easily reckoned by the changes of the moon,
which visibly mark off the week (p. 126-7), than by the sun, our
ancestors seem to have had, beside the solar year, a lunar one
for common use, whose thirteen months answered to the twelve
of the solar year. The recurring period of from 29 to 30 days
was therefore called *mênôps, mânôd*, from *mêna, mâno*. Hence
also it was natural to count by *nights*, not days: 'nec dierum
numerum sed *noctium* computant, sic constituunt, sic condicunt,
nox ducere diem videtur,' Tac. Germ. c. 11. And much in the
same way, the year was named by its *winter*, which holds the
same relation to summer as night to day. A section of time was
measured by the number of se'ennights, fortnights, months or
winters it contained.

And that is also the reason why the phases of the moon had
such a commanding influence on important undertakings. They
are what Jornandes cap. 11 calls *lunae commoda incommodaque*.
It is true, the performance of any kind of work was governed by

---

[1] Defence of Wulften castle, Vienna 1766. suppl. p. 71-2. 162.
[2] Can Manhart have come from Maginhart? Helbl. 13, 190 has *Meinharts-
berc*.

the day and solar time, whether of warriors (RA. 297), or of
servants (353), or of tribunals especially (814–6). If, on the
other hand, some new and weighty matter was to be taken in
hand, they consulted the moon; which does not mean that the
consultation was held or the action begun in the night, but on
those days whose nights had an auspicious phase of the moon:
'coeunt, nisi quid fortuitum et subitum inciderit, certis *diebus,
quum aut inchoatur luna aut impletur;* nam agendis rebus hoc
auspicatissimum initium credunt,' Tac. Germ. 11. So in Tac.
Ann. 1, 50 a *nox illunis* is chosen for a festival.

Now the moon presents two distinct appearances, one each
fortnight, which are indicated in the passage just quoted : either
she is beginning her course, or she has attained her full orb of
light. From the one point she steadily increases, from the other
she declines. The shapes she assumes between are not so sharply
defined to the sense.

Her invisibility lasts only the one night between the disappear-
ance of her last quarter and the appearance of her first, at new-
moon (conjunction of sun and moon) ; in like manner, full-moon
lasts from the moment she attains perfect sphericity till she loses
it again. But in common parlance that 'nox illunis' is included
in the new-moon, and similarly the decline is made to begin
simultaneously with the full.

The Gothic for πανσέληνον was *fulliþs* m., or *fulliþ* n. (gen. pl.
fulliþê), from which we may also infer a *niujiþs* for νουμηνία.
Curiously, this last is rendered fulliþ in Col. 2, 16, which to my
mind is a mere oversight, and not to be explained by the supposition that the Goths looked upon full-moon as the grander festival.
The AS. too must have called full-moon *fylleð*, to judge by the
name of the month 'winterfyllið,' which, says Beda (de temp.
rat. 13), was so named 'ab hieme et plenilunio'; but the later
writers have only *niwe môna* and *full môna*. So there may have
been an OHG. niuwid and fullid, though we can only lay our
finger on the neuters *niumâni* and *folmâni*,[1] to which Graff 2, 222
adds a niwilune; MHG. daz *niumœne* and *volmœne*, the last in
Trist. 9464. 11086. 11513 (see Suppl.).

---

[1] Also niuwer mâno, N. ps. 80, 4. foller mâno, ps. 88, 38. In Cap. 107-8 he
uses *vol* and *wan* (empty), and in Cap. 147 *hornaht, halbscaftig* and *fol;* conf. Hel.
111, 8 *wanod* ohtho *wahsid.*

In ON. the two periods are named by the neuters '*ný* ok *nið*,' habitually alliterating; *ný* answers to novilunium, it signifies the new light, and *nið* the declining, dwindling, from the lost root nið́a nað, from which also come the adv. niðr (deorsum) and the noun nåð (quies, OHG. ginåda). So that ný lasts from the beginning of the first quarter to the full, and nið from the decrease of the full to the extinction of light in the last quarter. The two touch one another at the border-line between the faintest streaks of waxing and of waning brightness. But nið meant especially the absence of moonlight (interlunium), and niðamyrkr total darkness (luna silens). Kind gods created these for men of old to tell the year by : '*ný* ok *nið* skôpo nýt regin öldum at år-tali,'[1] Sæm. 34ª. '*Mâni* stýrir göngu tûngls, oc ræðr *nýjum* oc *niðum*,' Sn. 12, Mâni steers the going of the moon, and rules new moons and full. Probably even here personification comes into play, for in Völuspá 11 (Sæm. 2ᵇ) *Nýji* and *Niði* are dwarfs, *i.e.* spirits of the sky, who are connected, we do not exactly know how, with those lunar phases ný ok nið.[2] Of changeful things it is said '*þat gengr eptir nýum ok niðum*,' res alternatur et subit lunae vices. O. Swed. laws have the formula '*ny oc niðar*,' for ' at all times, under any phase,' Gutalagh p. 108. So 'i *ny* ok *niða*,' Sudh. bygn. 32. Upl. vidh. 28, 1. Vestg. thiuv. 22, 1; but here the second word seems to have given up its neut. form, and passed into a personal and masc. Mod. Swed. has '*ny* och *nedan*'; Dan. '*ny* og *næ*,' ' det gaaer efter *nye* og *næe*,' 'hverken i *nye* eller *næ*,' *i.e.* never, 'naar *nyet* tändes,' quando nova luna incenditur; this næ was in O. Dan. *ned*, *need*. To the niðamyrkr above answers a Swed. *nedmörk*, pitchdark. The Norse terminology differs in so far from the H. Germ., that it expresses the total obscuration by nið, while we designate it by neumond (*i.e.* ný); with us new-moon is opposed to full-moon, with the Scandinavians nið to ný, each of them standing for one half of the moon's course. Since a mention of the first and last quarters has come into use, full-moon and new-moon signify simply the points of fullness and vacancy that lie between; and now the Swedes and Danes have equally adopted a fullmåne, fuldmaane, as counter-

---

[1] Acc. to Alvismál, the âlfar call the moon *ártali* (OHG. jârzalo ?), Sæm. 49ᵇ.
[2] Comp. with ' nið ok ný ' the Gr. ἕνη καὶ νέα.

part to nymâne, nymaane, whereby the old 'ned, næ' has become
superfluous, and the meaning of 'ny' somewhat modified.[1]

Though the OHG. remains do not offer us a neuter *niuwi*,[2] such
a form may have existed, to match the Norse *nӯ*, seeing that the
Mülhausen statute of the 13th cent. (Grasshof p. 252), in granting
the stranger that would settle in the town a month's time for the
attempt, says 'ein *nuwe* und ein wedil, daʒ sint vier wochin;'
that Martin von Amberg's Beichtspiegel has 'das *vol* und das
neu,' Dasypodius still later 'das *newe*, interlunium,' and Tobler
331[b] 'das *neu*, der wachsende mond.' For the waning moon,
Tobler 404[b] gives '*nid* si gehender (going down),' which reminds
one of *niðˀ*; otherwise 'der *schwined* mo,' OHG. 'diu *suinenta*
mânin,' N. ps. 88, 38, its opposite being 'diu folla' (see Suppl.).

I have yet to bring forward another expression of wide range
and presumably old, which is used by turns for one and another
phase of the moon's light, oftenest for plenilunium, but sometimes also for interlunium: MHG. *wedel*: 'im was unkunt des
mânen *wedel*,' Martina 181[c]; NHG. *wadel, wädel*, but more among
the common folk and in the chase than in written speech. Pic-
torius 480, Stald. 2, 456, Tobler 441[b] have *wedel, wädel* full-moon,
wädeln to become full-moon, when her horns meet, *i.e.*, when she
completes her circle. Keisersperg's Postille 138[b]: 'ietz so ist er
nüw, ietz fol, ietz alt, ietz die erst qvart, ietz die ander qvart,
ietz *ist es wedel*'; here full-moon and wedel are not so clearly
defined as in another passage of Keisersperg (Oberlin 1957)
on March: 'wan es ist sein *wedel*, sein volmon.' In Dasypodius: 'plenilunium, der volmon, *wädel*.'[5] The Germans in
Bohemia commonly use *wädel* for full-moon, and Schm. 4, 22
produces other notable authorities. But the word is known in
Lower Germany too; Böhmer's Kantzow p. 266 spells it *wadel*,[4]

---

[1] Modern Icel. names are: *blâný* (black new, interlunium); *prím* (nova luna),
also *nӯqveikt* tûngl; *hâlfvaxid tûngl* (first quarter); *fullt tûngl* (plenilunium);
hâlfþrotid tûngl (last quarter). Here too the old names have gone out of use,
'blâný' replaces nið, and 'prím' nӯ.

[2] Notker's Capella 100 has 'mânen niwi' fem.

[3] Yet under luna he has 'plenilunium vollmon oder *bruch*,' and the same under
bruch (=abbruch) a breaking off, falling off, defectus; which confirms my view,
that we reckon the wane from full-moon itself (Wtb. 2, 408). Acc. to Muchar's
Noricum 2, 36 the waxing and waning moon are called the *gesunde* and the *kranke*
man (well and ill).

[4] Following Tacitus, he says, the Germani always chose either new or full-moon,
for *after the wadel* they thought it unlucky. Wadel then comprehends the two phases
of new and full moon, but seems to exclude those of the first and last quarter.

the Brem. wtb. 5, 166 'waal, vollmond' (like aal for adel, a swamp), and Kilian 'waedel, senium lunae.' From the phraseology of Superst. I, 973 one would take wädel to be a general name for the moon, whether waxing or waning, for 'the bad wädel' [new-moon] surely implies a good wädel favourable to the operation. Now wadel, wedel means that which wags to and fro, and is used of an animal's tail, flabrum, flabellum, cauda; it must either, like zungâ and tûngl, refer to the tip or streak of light in the crescent moon, or imply that the moon cruises about in the sky.[1] The latter explanation fits a passage in the AS. poem on Finnesburg fight, line 14 : ' nû scîneð þes môna waðol under wolcnum,' i.e., the moon walking [wading] among the clouds, waðol being taken for the adj. vagus, vagabundus. Probably even the OHG. wadal was applied to the moon, as an adj. vagus (Graff 1, 776), or as a subst. flabellum (1, 662). But, as this subst. not only signifies flabellum [whisk], but fasciculus [wisp], the name may ultimately be connected with the bundle of brushwood that a myth (to be presently noticed) puts in the spots of the full-moon (see Suppl.).

Lith. jáunas menû novilunium, pilnatis plenilunium, puspilis first quarter, pusdylis last qu., delczia luna decrescens, lit. trunca, worn away, tarpijos interlunium (from tarp, inter); puspilis means half-full, pusdylis half-worn, from the same root as delczia truncation, decrease. There is also a 'menû tusczias,' vacant moon; and the sickle-shaped half-moon is called dalgakynos. Lettic: jauns mehnes novilun., pilna mehnes plenilun., mehnes punte luna accrescens, wezza mehnes[2] luna senescens.——Finnic: uusikuu novil., täysikuu plenil., ylikuu luna accr., alakuu decr., formed with uusi novus, täysi plenus, yli superus, ala inferus, which supports our explanation of the ON. nið.——The Servians divide thus: miyena novil., mladina luna accr., lit. young, puna plenil., ushtap luna decr. Slovèn mlay, mlad novil., polna plenil., ship plenil., but no doubt also luna decr., from shipati to nip, impair. Pol. now and Boh. nowy novil., Pol. pelnia and Boh.

---

[1] The Engl. waddle, which is the same word, would graphically express the oscillation of the (visible) moon from side to side of her path; and if wedel meant that oscillation, it would apply equally to new and to full moon.—TRANS.

[2] Wezza mehnes, the old moon. In a Scotch ballad : ' I saw the new moon late yestreen wi' he auld moon in her arm.' Jamieson 1, 159. Percy 1, 78. Halliwell pp. 167-8.

auplnek plenil. Here we see another instance of the ruder races having more various and picturesque names for natural phenomena, which among the more cultivated are replaced by abstract and uniform ones. No doubt Teutonic speech in its various branches once possessed other names beside *niđ* and *wadel*.

Tacitus merely tells us that the Germani held their assemblies at new moon or full moon, not that the two periods were thought equally favourable to all enterprises without distinction. We may guess that some matters were more suitable to new moon, others to full; the one would inspire by its freshness, the other by its fulness.[1]

Caesar 1, 50 reports to us the declaration of wise women in the camp of Ariovistus: 'non esse fas Germanos superare, si *ante novam lunam* proelio contendissent.' A happy issue to the battle was expected, at all events in this particular instance, only if it were fought at new moon.

As far as I can make out from later remnants of German superstition, with which that of Scotland should be compared (Chambers 35[b]. 36[a]), *new-moon*, addressed by way of distinction as 'gracious lord' p. 704, is an auspicious time for commencements properly speaking. Marriages are to be concluded in it, houses to be built: 'novam lunam observasti pro domo facienda aut conjugiis sociandis' (Sup. C, 198[b]), the latter just the same in Esth. Sup. no. 1. Into a new house you must move at new moon (Sup. I, 429), not at the wane (498); count money by the new moon (223), she will increase your store (conf. p. 704); on the other hand, she loves not to look into an empty purse (107). All through, the notion is that money, married bliss and house stores will thrive and grow with the growing light. So the hair and nails are cut at new-moon (French Sup. 5. Schütze's Holst. id. 3, 68), to give them a good chance of growing; cattle are weaned in the waxing light (I, 757), in the waning they would get lean; Lith. Sup. 11 says, let girls be weaned at the wane,

---

[1] New-moon was peculiarly holy to ancient peoples, thus to the Greeks the ἕνη καὶ νέα, which was also expressed by ἕνη alone = Sanskr. amâ (new moon). The return of Odysseus was expected at that season, Od. 14, 162:

τοῦ μὲν φθίνοντος μηνός, τοῦ δ' ἱσταμένοιο.

Râmâ's birth is fixed for the new-moon after vernal equinox (Schlegel on Râmây. i. 19, 2). Probably bealtaine were lighted at this new-moon of spring.

boys at the full, probably to give the one a slim elegant figure, and the other a stout and strong. Healing herbs and pure dew are to be gathered at new-moon (tou an *des mânen niwi* gelesen, N. Cap. 100, conf. 25), for then they are fresh and unalloyed. When it says in I, 764 that weddings should take place at full-moon, and in 238 that a new dwelling should be entered with the waxing or full moon, this full-moon seems to denote simply the utmost .of the growing light, without the accessory notion of incipient decline. If our ancestors as a rule fought their battles at new-moon, they must have had in their eye the springing up of victory to themselves, not the defeat and downfall of the enemy.[1]

At *full-moon* (as opposed to new), i.e. by a waning light, you were to perform operations involving severance or dissolution, cutting down or levelling. Thus, if I understand it rightly, a marriage would have to be annulled, a house pulled down, a pestilence stamped out, when the moon is on the wane. Under this head comes in the rule to cut wood in the forest when it is wadel, apparently that the timber felled may dry. In a Calendar printed by Hupfuff, Strasb. 1511 : 'with the moon's wedel 'tis good to begin the hewing of wood.' The same precept is still given in many modern forest-books, and full-moon is therefore called *holz-wadel*: 'in the bad wädel (crescent moon) fell no timber,' Sup. I, 973. In Keisersperg's Menschl. baum, Strasb. 1521, 19 : 'Alway in wedel are trees to be hewn, and game to be shot.'[2] Grass is not to be mown at new, but at full moon (Lith. Sup. 7); that the hay may dry quickly? and treasures must be lifted at full-moon. If a bed be stuffed when the moon is growing, the feathers will not lie (I, 372. 914); this operation too requires a waning light, as if to kill the new-plucked feathers completely, and bring them to rest. If you open trenches by a waxing moon, they will soon grow together again; if by a waning, they keep on getting deeper and wider. To open a vein with the moon declining, makes the blood press downwards and

---

[1] The Esthonians say to the new-moon : 'Hail, moon! may you grow old, and I keep young!' Thom. Hiärne p. 40.
[2] In Demerara grows a tree like the mahogany, called walala ; if cut down at new-moon, the wood is tough and hard to split, if at full, it is soft and splits easily. Bamboo planks cut at new-moon last ten years, those cut at full-moon rot within the year.

load the legs (Tobler 404[b]); set about it therefore by the mounting moonlight. Vuk sub v. miyena says, the Servian women will wash never a shirt at new-moon, they declare all the linen would get mooned (omiyeniti) in the water, i.e. bulge and pucker, and soon tear; one might find another reason too for washing by the waning moon, that stains and dirt should disappear with the dwindling light (see Suppl.).

Behind superstitious practices I have tried to discover a meaning, which may possibly come near their original signification. Such symbolical coupling of means and end was at all events not foreign to antiquity anywhere: the holy water floats all misfortune away with it (p. 589), the spray from the millwheel scatters all sickness (p. 593). So the sufferer stands with his face to the waning moon, and prays: 'as thou decreasest, let my pains diminish' (I, 245); he can also go on the other tack, and cry to the new moon: 'may what I see increase, and what I suffer cease' (492). Turning the face toward the luminary I take to be a relic of heathen moon-worship.[1]

Superstitions of this kind have long been banished to the narrower limits of agriculture and cattle-breeding; we should arrive at a clearer knowledge of them, had their bearing on public life been described for us in early times. Observation of the lunar changes must in many ways have influenced sacrifices, the casting of lots and the conduct of war. Some things now appear bewildering, because we cannot review all the circumstances, and some no doubt were different in different nations. German superstition (I, 856) thinks it a calamity for the master of the house to die during the moon's decline, for then the whole family will fall away; the Esthonian view (41) is, that a death at new-moon is unlucky, perhaps because more will follow? Fruits that grow *above ground* are to be sown at the waxing, those *under ground* at the waning (Jul. Schmidt p. 122); not so Westendorp p. 129: 'dat *boven den grond* wast, by *afnemende* maan, dat *onder den grond* wast, by *toenemende* maan te zaaien.' Gutslaf (Wöhhanda p. 49, conf. errata) remarks, that winter-crops are not to be sown while the moon stands at the idle quarter (third,

---

[1] Whoever at play turns his back to the moon, has bad luck (I, 801). But the seaman in his hammock takes care not to face the full-moon, lest he be struck with blindness.

kus se kuh mäal). In the sermon of Eligius (Sup. A), the
sentence ' nec luna nova quisquam timeat aliquid operis arripere '
is unintelligible so long as we do not know what sort of operation
is meant.

The *spots* or shady depressions *on the full-moon's disc* have
given rise to grotesque but similar myths in several nations. To
the common people in India they look like a *hare*, i.e. Chandras
the god of the moon *carries a hare* (sasa), hence the moon is
called sasin or sasânka, hare mark or spot.[1] The Mongolian
doctrine also sees in these shadows the figure of a *hare*.[2] Bogdo
Jagjamuni or Shigemuni [the Buddha Sakyâ-muni], supreme
ruler of the sky, once changed himself into a *hare*, simply to
serve as food to a starving traveller; in honour of which meritorious deed Khormusta, whom the Mongols revere as chief of
the tenggri [genii], placed the figure of a hare in the moon.
The people of Ceylon relate as follows : While Buddha the great
god sojourned upon earth as a hermit, he one day lost his way
in a wood. He had wandered long, when a *hare* accosted him :
' Cannot I help thee ? strike into the path on thy right, I will
guide thee out of the wilderness.' Buddha replied : ' Thank
thee, but I am poor and hungry, and unable to repay thy kindness.' ' If thou art hungry,' said the hare, ' light a fire, and kill,
roast and eat me.' Buddha made a fire, and the hare immediately
jumped in. Then did Buddha manifest his divine power, he
snatched the beast out of the flames, and set him in the moon,
where he may be seen to this day.[3] To the Greenlander's fancy
these spots are the marks of Malina's fingers, with which she
touched the fine reindeer pelisse of Anninga (Majer's Myth.
taschenb. 1811. p. 15).

An ON. fable tells us, that Mâni (the moon) took two children,
Bil and Hiuki, away from the earth, just as they were drawing
water from the well Byrgir, and carrying the pail Sægr on the
pole Simul between their shoulders. These children walk behind

---

[1] Schlegel's Ind. bibl. 1, 217. Acc. to Bopp's Gloss. 346ᵃ, a Sanskrit name for
the moon means *lepore praeditus, leporem gerens.*
[2] Bergmann's Streifer. 3, 40. 204. Majer's Myth. wtb. 1, 540.
[3] Douce's Illustr. of Shaksp. 1, 16 from the lips of a French traveller, whose
telescope the Cingalese had often borrowed, to have a good look at the hare in the
moon.

Máni, as one may see from the earth (svá sem siá má af iörðu), Sn. 12. That not the moon's phases but her spots are here meant, is plain enough from the figure itself. No change of the moon could suggest the image of *two children* with a *pail slung on their shoulders*. Moreover, to this day the Swedish people see in the spots of the moon two persons carrying a big *bucket on a pole*.[1] *Bil* was probably a girl, and *Hiuki* a boy, the former apparently the same as the Ásynja named together with *Sól* in Sn. 39; there it is spelt *Bil*, but without sufficient reason; the neuter 'bil' signifies momentum, interstitium, a meaning that would suit any appearance of the moon (conf. p. 874 on OHG. pil). What is most important for us, out of this heathen fancy of a *kidnapping man of the moon*, which, apart from Scandinavia, was doubtless in vogue all over Teutondom, if not farther, there has evolved itself since a christian adaptation. They say the man in the moon is a *wood-stealer*, who during church time on the holy sabbath committed a trespass in the wood, and was then transported to the moon as a punishment; there he may be seen with the *axe on his back* and the *bundle of brushwood* (dornwelle) *in his hand*. Plainly enough the water-pole of the heathen story has been transformed into the axe's shaft, and the carried pail into the thornbush; the general idea of theft was retained, but special stress laid on the keeping of the christian holiday; the man suffers punishment not so much for cutting firewood, as because he did it on a Sunday.[2] The interpolation is founded on Numb. 15, 32–6, where we are told of a man that gathered sticks on the sabbath, and was stoned to death by the congregation of Israel, but no mention is made of the moon and her spots. As to when this story first appeared in Germany I have no means of telling, it is almost universally prevalent now;[3] in case the full-moon's name of *wadel, wedel* in the sense of a *bunch of twigs*[4]

---

[1] Dalin 1, 158: men ännu fins den meningen bland vår almoge. Ling's Eddornas sinnebildslära 1, 78: ännu säger allmänheten i Södraswerge, att månens fläckar äro tvenne varelser, som bära en bryggså (bridge-bucket, slung pail).

[2] A Westphalian story says, the man dressed the church with thorns on Sunday, and was therefore put, bundle and all, into the moon.

[3] Hebel has made a pretty song about it, pp. 86-9: 'me het em gsait der *Dieterle*,' on which Schm. 2, 583 asks: is this Dietrich of Bern, translated in classic fashion to the sky? We must first make sure that the poet found the name already in the tradition.

[4] In the Henneberg distr. *wadel* means brushwood, twigs tied up in a bundle, esp. fir-twigs, *wadeln* to tie up brushwood (Reinwald 2, 137); this may however come from the practice of cutting wood at full-moon.

has itself arisen out of the story (p. 712), it must be of pretty high antiquity. In Tobler's Appenzell sprachsch. 20[b] we are told: An arma ma (a poor man) het alawil am sonnti holz ufg'lesa (picked up wood). Do hed em der liebe Gott d'wahl g'loh (let him choose), öb er lieber wött i' der sonn verbrenna, oder im mo' verfrüra (burn in sun, or freeze in moon. Var.: in'n kalta mo' ihi, oder i' d' höll abi). Do will' er lieber in'n mo' ihi. Dromm sied ma' no' ietz *an' ma' im mo'* inna, wenn's wedel ist. Er hed a' *püscheli* uff 'em rogga (bush on his back). Kuhn's Märk. sagen nos. 27. 104. 130 give us three different accounts: in one a broom-maker has bound twigs (or a woman has spun) on a Sunday, in another a man has spread manure, in the third he has stolen cabbage-stumps; and the figure with the bunch of twigs (or the spindle), with the dungfork, with the cabbage-stalk, is supposed to form the spots in the moon. The earliest authority I know of is Fischart's Garg. 130[b]: 'sah im mon ein *männlin, das holz gestohlen hett;*' Praetorius says more definitely, Welt-beschr. 1, 447: the superstitious folk declared the dark spots on the moon to be the man that gathered sticks on the sabbath and was stoned therefor. The Dutch account makes the man steal vegetables, so he appears in the moon with the 'bundel *moes*' on his shoulders (Westendorp p. 129). The English tradition seems pretty old. Chaucer in his Testament of Creseide 260–4 de-scribes the moon as lady Cynthia:

> Her gite (gown) was gray and ful of spottis blake,
> and on her brest a *chorl* paintid ful even
> *bering a bush of thornis on his bake,*
> which for his *theft* might clime no ner the heven.

In Ritson's Anc. songs (Lond. 1790), p. 35 is a 'song upon the man in the moon,' beginning thus:

> Mon in the mone stond and strit (standeth and strideth),
> *on his bot forke is burthen he bereth;*
> hit is muche wonder that he na doun slyt (slideth),
> for doutelesse he valle, he shoddreth and shereth,
> when the forst freseth much chele he byd (chill he bideth);
> the *thornes* beth kene, *is hattren to-tereth.*

Shivering with cold, he lugs on his fork a load of thorns, which tear his coat, he had cut them down and been impounded by the forester; the difficult and often unintelligible song represents

him as a lazy old man, who walks a bit and stands a bit, and
is drunk as well; not a word about desecration of the sabbath.
Shakspeare alludes more than once to the man in the moon;
Tempest ii. 2 : ' I was the man i' th' moon, when time was ' . . .
' I have seen thee in her, and I do adore thee : my mistress shewed
me thee and thy *dog* and thy *bush.*' Mids. N. Dr. iii. 1 : ' One
must come in with a *bush of thorns* and a lanthorn, and say he
comes to present the person of Moonshine.' In Gryphius too
the player who acts the moon ties a bush round his body (conf.
Ir. elfenm. no. 20).

Two more, and those conflicting, interpretations of the moon's
spots are likewise drawn from the Bible. Either it is Isaac *bearing a burthen of wood* for the sacrifice of himself on Mount Moriah
(Praetor. Weltbeschr. 1, 447) ; or it is Cain carrying a *bundle of
thorns on his shoulders,* and offering to the Lord the cheapest gift
from his field.[1] This we find as far back as Dante, Parad. 2, 50.

> che sono i *segni bui*
> di questo corpo, che laggiuso in terra
> fan di *Caïn* favoleggiare altrui ?

And Inferno 20, 126 : *Caino e le spine.* On this passage Landino
remarks : ' cioè la luna, nella quale i volgare vedendo una certa
ombra, credono che sia Caino, o' habbia *in spalla una forcata di
pruni.*' And another commentator : ' accommodandosi alla favola
del volgo, che sieno quelle macchie Caino, che *inalzi una forcata
di spine.*'

Nearly all these explanations agree in one thing : they suppose
the spots to be a human figure carrying something on its shoulder,
whether a hare, a pole and bucket, an axe and thorns, or the load
of thorns alone.[2] A wood-stealer or fratricide accounts for the
spots of the moon, as a chaff-stealer (p. 357) does for the streaks
in the milky way.

There must have been yet more traditions. A Netherl. poet
of the 14th century speaks of the dark stripes that stand

---

[1] The story of the first fratricide seems to have made a peculiarly deep impression on the new converts from heathenism ; they fancy him a wicked giant,
conf. Beow. 213 seq., and supra p. 525.

[2] Water, an essential part of the Norse myth, is wanting in the story of the
man with the thornbush, but it re-appears in the Carniolan story (for kramerisch
read krainerisch) cited in Brentano's Libussa p. 421 : the man in the moon is called
Kotar, he makes her grow by pouring water.

> recht int midden van der mane,
> dat men in duitsche heet *ludergheer;*

in another passage it is *lendegher*[1] (for leudegher?); and Willems
in Messager de Gand, 1, 195, following a MS. of 1351, reads, ' dat
men in dietsch heet *lodegeer;*' but none of these forms is intelligible to me. Perhaps the proper name Ludgêr, Leodegarius,
OHG. Liutkêr, has to do with it, and some forgotten legend of
the Mid. Ages. A touching religious interpretation is handed
down by Berthold 145, surely not invented by himself, that the
moon is Mary Magdalene, and the spots her tears of repentance
(see Suppl.).

The *Sun* has had a slighter influence than the moon on superstitious notions and observances. Magical herbs must be
gathered, if not by moonlight, at least *before sunrise* (p. 621),
and healing waters be drawn *before sunrise* (p. 586). The
mounting sun dispels all magic, and bids the spirits back to their
subterranean abode.

Twice in the year the sun changes his course, in summer to
sink, in winter to rise. These *turning-points* of the sun were
celebrated with great pomp in ancient times, and our St. John's
or Midsummer fires are a relic of the summer festival (p. 617
seq.). The higher North, the stronger must have been the impression produced by either solstice, for at the time of the summer one there reigns almost perpetual day, and at the winter one
perpetual night. Even Procopius (ed. Bonn. 2, 206) describes
how the men of Thule, after their 35 days' night, climb the
mountain-tops to catch sight of the *nearing sun.* Then they
celebrate their holiest feast (see Suppl.).

Tacitus tells us (cap. 45), that the sun after setting shoots up
such a radiance over the Suiones, that it pales the stars till
morning. ' *Sonum* insuper *audiri, formas deorum et radios capitis
aspici,* persuasio adjicit.' I would have turned this passage to
account in Chap. VI., as proving the existence of Germanic gods,

---

[1] Van Wyn's Avondstonden 1, 306. Bilderdijk's Verklarende gestachtlijst der
naamworden 2, 198 has *ludegeer, ludegaar,* and explains it, no doubt wrongly, as
luikenaar (leodiensis). However, he tells the old story: ' 't mannetjen in de maan,
dat gezegd werd een doornbosch op zijn rug te heben, en om dat hy 't gestolen had,
niet hooger ten hemel te mogen opklimmen, maar daar ingebannen te zijn.' Exactly
as in Chaucer.

had it not seemed credible that such accounts may not have reached the Romans from Germany itself, but been spread among them by miscellaneous travellers' tales.   Strabo 3, 1 (Tsch. 1, 368) quotes from Posidonius a very similar story of the *noise* made by the *setting sun* in the sea between Spain and Africa: μείζω δύνειν τὸν ἥλιον ἐν τῇ παρωκεανίτιδι μετὰ ψόφου παραπλησίως, ὡσανεὶ σίζοντος τοῦ πελάγους κατὰ σβέσιν αὐτοῦ διὰ τὸ ἐμπίπτειν εἰς τὸν βυθόν.   But the belief may even then have prevailed among Germans too ; the *radiant heads*, like a saint's glory, were discussed at p. 323, and I will speak of this marvellous music of the rising and setting sun in the next chapter. Meanwhile the explanation given of the red of morning and evening, in the old AS. dialogue between Saturn and Solomon (Thorpe's Anal. p. 100), is curious : ' Saga me, forhwan byð seo sunne reád on æfen ? '   ' Ic þe secge, forþon heo lôcað on helle.' ' Saga me, hwî scîneð heo swâ *reáde on morgene* ? '   ' Ic þe secge, forþon hyre twynað hwæðer heo mæg oðe [orig. þe] ne mæg þisne middaneard eondiscînan swâ hyre beboden is.'   The sun is red at even, for that she looketh on hell ; and at morn, for that she doubteth whether she may complete her course as she is bidden.

Not only about the sun and moon, but about the other *stars*, our heathen antiquity had plenty of lore and legend.   It is a very remarkable statement of Jornandes cap. 11, that in Sulla's time the Goths under Dicenaeus, exclusive of planets and signs of the zodiac, were acquainted with 344 stars that ran from east to west. How many could we quote now by their Teutonic names ?

The vulgar opinion imagines the *stars* related to each individual man as *friend* or *foe*.[1]   The constellation that shone upon his birth takes him under its protection all his life through ; this is called being born under a good or lucky star.   From this guidance, this secret sympathy of dominant constellations, fate can be foretold. Conversely, though hardly from native sources, it is said in the Renner 10984 that every star has an angel who directs it to the place whither it should go.

---

[1] Swem die sternen werdent gram,
   dem wirt der mâne lîhte alsam.   Frid. 108, 3.

There is a pious custom of saluting the celestial luminaries
before going to bed at night (Sup. I, 112), and among the Mod.
Greeks, of offering a prayer when the evening star is on the rise.

According to the Edda, all the stars were sparks of fire from
Muspells-heim, that flew about the air at random, till the gods
assigned them seats and orbits, Sn. 9. Sæm. 1.

Ignited vapours, which under a starry sky fall swiftly through
the air like fiery threads—Lat. trajectio stellae, stella transvolans,
Ital. stella cadente, Fr. étoile filante, Span. estrella vaga, Swed.
stjernfall, Dan. stiernskud (star-shoot), what the Greeks call
διάγειν trajicere—are by our people ascribed to a trimming of
the stars' light; they are like the sparks we let fall in snuffing a
candle. We find this notion already in Wolfram's Wh. 322, 18:

| Dehein sterne ist sô lieht, | No star so bright |
| ern *fürbe sich* etswenne.[1] | but trims itself somewhen. |

Hence our phrase of ' the stars snuffing themselves,' and our
subst. *sternputze, sternschnuppe.* These falling stars are ominous,[2]
and whoever sees them should say a prayer (Sup. I, 595): to the
generous girl who has given away her all, they bring down with
them [or turn into] gold-pieces (Kinderm. 153); nay, whatever
wish you form while the snuff is falling, is fulfilled (Tobler 408[b]).
The Lithuanians beautifully weave shooting stars into the fate-
mythus: the *verpeya* (spinneress) begins to spin the thread of the
new-born on the sky, and each thread ends in a star; when a man
is dying, his thread snaps, and the star turns pale and drops
(Narbutt, 1, 71).

A comet is called *tail-star, hair-star* in Aventin 74[b]. 119[b],
peacock-tail (Schm. 1, 327); and its tail in Detmar 1, 242 *schin-
schove,* from schof a bundle of straw. Its appearing betokens
events fraught with peril, especially the death of a king (Greg.
tur. 4, 9): ' man siht an der zît einen sterren, sam einen *pfawen
zagel* wît (wide as a peacock's tail), sô müezen siben sachen in
der werlt ergân,' MsH. 3, 468[h] (see Suppl.).

Our old heathen fancies about the fixed stars have for the most
part faded away, their very names are almost all supplanted by

---

[1] MS. n. reads ' sûbere sich.' Even OHG. has furban (mundare, expiare).
[2] So with the Greeks (Reinh. fuchs p. lxxii.). In a poem of Béranger: ' mon
enfant, un mortel expire, son étoile tombe à l'instant.'

learned astronomic appellations; only a few have managed to save themselves in ON. legend or among the common people.

Whether the planets were named after the great gods, we cannot tell: there is no trace of it to be found even in the North. Planet-names for days of the week seem to have been imported, though very early, from abroad (p. 126 seq.) Other reasons apart, it is hardly conceivable that the heathen, who honoured certain fixed stars with names of their own, should not have distinguished and named the travelling stars, whose appearances and changes are so much more striking. The evening and morning Venus is called *eveningstar, morningstar*, OHG. *âpant-sterno, tagasterno*, like the Lat. vesper and lucifer.[1] The *tunkel-sterne* in Ms. 1, 38^b seems to be vesperugo, the eveningstar beginning to blaze in the twilight, conf. Gramm. 2, 526. An OHG. *uhtosterno* morningstar, N. Bth. 223, is from uhtâ, Goth. uhtvô crepusculum. Gl. Trev. 22^b have *stelbóm* hesperus; can this be stellbaum, the bird-catcher's pole? But in Rol. 240, 27 'die urmâren *stalboume*' stands for stars in general, and as every star was provided with stool or stand (p. 700–1), we may connect stel-boum, stalboum with this general meaning. There is perhaps more of a mythic meaning in the name *nahtfare* for eveningstar (Heumanni opusc. 453. 460), as the same word is used of the witch or wise-woman out on her midnight jaunt. The Anglo-Saxons called the eveningstar *swâna steorra* (bubulcorum stella), because the swains drove their herd home when it appeared. Again, in O. iv. 9, 24 Christ is compared to the sun, and the apostles to the eleven daystars, 'dagasterron' here meaning not so much luciferi as the signs of the zodiac. There are no native names for the polar star (see Suppl.).

Twice the Edda relates the origin of particular stars, but no one knows now what constellations are meant. The legend of *Orvandils-tâ* and the AS. *Earendel*, OHG. *Orentil*, has been cited, p. 374; this bright luminary may have meant the morningstar. Then the âses, having slain the giant Thiassi, had to atone for it to his daughter Skaði. Oðinn took Thiassi's eyes and threw them against the sky, where they formed two stars, Sn. 82-3. These *augu Thiassa* are most likely two stars that stand near

---

[1] In an old church-hymn Lucifer is provided with a chariot: currus jam poscit phosphorus (reita giu fergôt tagastern), Hymn. 2, 8.

each other, of equal size and brightness, perhaps the Twins ?
This is another instance of the connexion we found between stars
and *eyes ;* and the *toe* translated to heaven is quite of a piece
with the 'tongues' and the correspondence of the parts of the
body to the macrocosm, p. 568 (see Suppl.).

The *milky-way* and its relation to *Irmin* I have dealt with,
pp. 356–8.

Amongst all the constellations in our sky, three stand prominent to the popular eye: Ursa major, Orion and the Pleiades.
And all of them are still known by native names; to which I
shall add those in use among the Slavs, Lithuanians and Finns,
who give them the same place of honour as we do.

The Great Bear was doubtless known to our ancestors, even
before their conversion, as *waggon, wain ;* which name, un-
borrowed, they had in common with kindred [Aryan] nations,
and therefore it is the common people's name for it to this
day: they say, at dead of night the heavenly wain turns round
with a great noise, conf. p. 745. So the Swiss (Tobler 264ᵃ):
when the *herra-waga* stands low, bread is cheap, when high, it is
dear. O. v. 17, 29 uses the pl. '*waganô* gistelli,' meaning at
once the greater waggon and the less ; which last (Ursa minor)
Berthold calls the *wegelin*.[1] So 'des *wagenes* gerihte,' Wackern.
lb. 772, 26. It comes of a lively way of looking at the group,
which circling round the polar star always presents the appearance of four wheels and a long slanting pole, *deichsel* (temo), on
the strength of which the AS. sometimes has *þisl* alone: *wænes
þisla* (thill), Boeth. Rawlins. 192ᵇ. References are given at
p. 151, also the reasons for my conjecture that the waggon meant
is that of Wuotan the highest god. True, an O. Swed. chronicle
connects the Swed. name *karlwagen* with Thôrr, who stepping
into his chariot holds the seven stars in his hand (Thor statt
naken som ett barn, siu stjernor i handen och Karlewagn), which
I will not absolutely deny; but it is Wôden stories in particular
that are transferred to the Frankish Charles (p. 153). When
in Gl. Jun. 188 'Arturus' is rendered *wagan* (though Gl. Hrab.

---

[1] Ich hân den glanzen *himelwagen* und daz gestirne besehen, Troj. 19062.
There may for that matter be several himelwagens, as there were many gods with
cars. Cervantes too, in a song of the gitanilla (p. m. 11), says: Si en el cielo hay
estrellas, que *lucientes carros* forman.

951[b] has 'arctus' the bear = *wagan in himile*), that is explained by the proximity of the star to the Great Bear's tail, as the very name ἀρκτοῦρος shews.[1] I have to add, that Netherland cities (Antwerp, Gröningen) have the stars of the Great or the Lesser Bear on their seals (Messager de Gand 3, 339), and in England the Charles-wain is painted on the signboards of taverns.

The Greeks have both names in use, ἄρκτος bear, and ἅμαξα waggon, the Romans both *ursa* and *plaustrum*, as well as a *septentrio* or *septentriones* from trio, plough-ox. Fr. *char*, *charriot*, Ital. Span. *carro*. Pol. *woz* (plaustrum), woz niebieski (heavenly wain), Boh. *wos*, and at the same time *ogka* (thill, sometimes og, wog) for Boötes; the Illyrian Slavs *kola*, pl. of kolo wheel, therefore wheels, *i.e.* wain, but in their *kola rodina* and *rodokola*[2] I cannot explain the adjuncts rodo, rodina. Lith. *gryžulio rats*, *gryždo rats*, from ratas (rota), while the first word, unexplained by Mielcke, must contain the notion of waggon or heaven;[3] Lett. *ratti* (rotae). Esth. *wankri tähhed*, waggon-stars, from wanker (currus); Hung. *göntzöl szekere*, from szeker (currus), the first word being explained in 'Hungaria in parabolis' p. 48 by a mythic Göntzöl, their first waggoner. Prominent in the Finnish epos are *päiwä* the sun, *kuu* the moon, and *otawa*, which Castrén translates karla-vagnen, they are imagined as persons and divine, and often named together; the Pleiades are named *seulainen*.

Never, either in our OHG. remains, or among Slavs, Lithuanians and Finns,[4] do we find the name borrowed from the animal (ursa), though these nations make so much of the bear both in legend and perhaps in worship (p. 668).

The carro menor is called by Spanish shepherds *bocina*, bugle;[5] by Icelanders *fiosakonur á lopti*, milkmaids of the sky, Biörn sub v. F. Magnusen's Dag. tid. 104-5 (see Suppl.).

---

[1] [From οὖρος keeper, not οὐρά tail]. Ἀρκτοφύλαξ [bear-ward, or as we might say] Waggoner, is Boötes, of whom Greek fable has much to tell. Arcturus stands in Boötes, and sometimes for Boötes. An OHG. gloss, Diut. 1. 167ᵃ, seems curiously to render Boötes by *stuffala*, Graff 6, 662. Is this stuphila, stipula, stubble?

[2] Bosnian Bible, Ofen 1831. 3, 154. 223. In Vuk roda is stork, whence the adj. *rodin*, but what of that? This roda seems to be rota, rad, wheel over again.

[3] Lith. Bible, Königsb. 1816, has in Job 9, 9 *gryžo wezimmas; gryzdas*, grizulas is thill, and wezimmas waggon.

[4] Can this be reconciled with the statement, p. 729, that Finn. otawa = bear? The Mongol. for bear is ütögö.—TRANS.

[5] Don Quixote 1, 20 (ed. Ideler 1, 232; conf. 5, 261).

The small, almost invisible star just above the middle one in the waggon's thill has a story to itself. It is called *waggoner, hind*, in Lower Germany *dümeke*, thumbkin, dwarf, Osnabr. *dümke*, Meckl. *duming*, in Holstein '*Hans Dümken, Hans Dümkl* sitt opm wagn.' They say that once a waggoner, having given our Saviour a lift, was offered the kingdom of heaven for his reward; but he said he would sooner be driving from east to west to all eternity (as the wild hunter wished for evermore to hunt). His desire was granted, there stands his waggon in the sky, and the highest of the three thill-stars, the 'rider' so-called, is that waggoner. Another version in Müllenhoff's Schles. Holst. sagen no. 484. I daresay the heathen had a similar fiction about Wôdan's charioteer. Joh. Praetorius De suspecta poli declinatione, Lips. 1675, p. 35: 'qui hanc stellam non praeteriissent, etiamsi minor quam *Alcor*, das *knechtgen*, der *dümeke*, das *reuterlein, knechtfink* fuisset;' and again on the thief's thumb, p. 140: '*fabula de pollicari auriga, dümeke, fuhrman.*' That the same fancy of the waggoner to this constellation prevails in the East, appears from Niebuhr's Arabia, and the Hungarian *Göntzöl* seems closely related to him; in Greek legend likewise Zeus places the waggon's driver ($\eta\nu\iota\omicron\chi\omicron\varsigma$) or inventor *Erichthonius* among the stars, though not in the Great Bear, but between Perseus and the Twins in the galaxy. The Bohemian *formánek, wozataŷ* (auriga) or *bowozny* signify Arcturus, Boötes and Erichthonius (Jungm. 1, 550. 3, 401), and *palečky u wozu* thumblings on waggon. But in Slovènic, it seems, *hervor* (Murko 85. Jarnik 229[b]) and *burovzh* mean the waggoner and the Polar Star.

The cluster of brilliant stars in which the Greeks recognised the figure of *Orion*[1] had various Teutonic names, the reasons of which are not always clear to us now. First, the three stars in a line that form Orion's belt are called in Scandinavia *Friggjarrockr, Friggerok* (pp. 270. 302-3), and also by transfer to Mary *Mariärok, Marirok* (Peter Syv in the Danske digtek. middelald. 1, 102), *Mariteen;* here is plain connecting of a star-group with the system of heathen gods. The same three stars are to this day called by the common folk in Up. Germany the *three mowers*, because they stand in a row like mowers in a meadow: a homely

---

[1] Our MHG. poets adopt *Orîôn* without translating it, MS. 1, 87[a]. The Romans, acc. to Varro and Festus, called it *Jugula*, it is not known why.

designation, like that of waggon, which arose in the childlike
fancy of a pastoral people. OHG. glosses name Orion *pfluoc*
(aratrum), and in districts on the Rhine he is called the *rake*
(rastrum) : he is a tool of the husbandman or the mower. The
Scotch *pleuch*, Engl. *plough*, is said of Charles's wain. Some
AS. (perhaps more OS.) glosses translate Orion by *eburðring*,
eburðrung, *ebirdring*, *ebirthíring* (Gl. Jun. 369. 371),[1] which in
pure AS. would have been eoforðryng, eforðring; it can mean
nothing but boar-throng, since þryng, as well as þrang, Mid.
Lat. drungus, is turba. How any one came to see a herd of wild
boars in the group, or which stars of Orion it included, I do not
know : the wild huntsman of the Greek legend may have nothing
to do with it, as neither that legend nor the group as seen by
Greek eyes includes any hunted animal ; the boars of the Teutonic
constellation have seemingly quite a different connexion, and
perhaps are founded on mere comparison. OHG. glosses give
us no *epurdrunc*, but its relation to Iuwaring and Iring was
pointed out, p. 359 note. In the latter part of the Mid. Ages
our ' three mowers ' or the Scandinavian ' Mary's distaff ' is called
Jacobs-stab, Boh. *Jahubahûl;* the heathenish spindle, like the
heathenish Irmin-street (p. 357 note), is handed over to the
holy apostle, who now staff in hand, paces the same old heavenly
path ; in some parts *Peter's staff* is preferred. The Esthonians
call Orion *warda tähhed*, spear stars, from ' wardas ' spear, and
perhaps staff, like St. James's staff. The Lithuanians *szenpjuwis*,
hay-star? from ' szen ' foenum (Nesselmann 515), as August is
called szenpjutis ; because the constellation rises at hay-harvest ?
perhaps also with reference to the ' three-mowers ' ? for in the
same way several Slav nations have the name *kosi* scythes, Boh.
kosy (Jungm. 2, 136), Pol. *kosy* (Linde 1092ª), Slovèn. *koszi*
(Murko 142) mowers. Other Slavic names of Orion are *shtupka*
(Bosn. Bible, 3, 154), for which we ought to read *shtapka*, in Vuk
shtaka crutch, crosier, from our stäbchen, Carniol. *pálize* staves,
in Stulli *babini sctapi* old wives' staves ; and *kružilice*,[2] wheelers,
rovers ? from ' kružiti ' vagari (see Suppl.).

---

[1] The second passage has ' eburdnung,' an error, but an evidence of the MS.'s
age, for in the 8-9th cent. the second stroke of r was made as long as that of n.

[2] Dobrowsky's Slavin p. 425 ; the Pol. *kružlic* is crocklet, mug. Hanka's
Altböhm. glossen have 66, 857 kruzlyk circulea, 99, 164 kruszlyk lix, which I do
not understand. Can it be crutch ?

Between the shoulders of the Bull is a space thickly sown with
stars, but in which seven (really six) larger ones are recognis-
able; hence it is called *sieben-gestirn*, OHG. thaz *sibunstirri*,
O. v. 17, 29. Diut. i. 520ᵃ. Gl. Jun. 188 (where it is confounded
with the Hyades not far off, in the Bull's head). Beside this
purely arithmetical denomination, there are others more living:
Gr. Πλειάδες, Ion. Πληϊάδες, seven daughters of Atlas and
Pleïone, whom Zeus raised to the sky, Il. 18, 486. Od. 5, 272,
and who, like the Norse Thiassi and Örvandill, are of giant kin;
but some explain these Pleiads from πελειάς wild dove, which
is usually πέλεια.[1] Lat. *Vergiliae*, of which Festus gives a lame
explanation. A German poet writes *virîlie*, Amgb. 42ᵇ.

The picture of the Pleiades that finds most favour among the
people in Germany and almost all over Europe is that of a *hen
and seven chickens*, which at once reminds us of the Greek *seven
doves*.[2] Mod. Gr. πούλια (Fauriel 2, 277). Our *klucke, kluckerin,
kluckhenne, brut-henne mit den hünlein*; Dan. *aften-höns*, even-
ing-hen (-*hönne*, Dansk. digtek. middelald. 1, 102); Engl. *hen with
her chickens*; Fr. la *poussinière*, in Lorraine *poucherosse, covrosse*
(couveuse, brood-hen, qui conduit des poussins)[3]; Gris. *cluotschas*
or *cluschas* the cluck-hens; Ital. *gallinelle*; Boh. *slepice s kuřátky*
hen with chickens; Hung. *fiastik, fiastyuk* from tik, tyuk gallina,
and fiazom pario. The sign of the *cluck-hen* seems to me intergrown with our antiquity. Nursery tales bring in a peculiar
feature, viz. that three nuts or eggs having been given as a present, out of them come a golden dress, a silver dress, and a *cluckie
with seven* (or twelve) *chickies*, the three gifts representing sun,
moon and seven-stars. Kinderm. no. 88 (2, 13). So in the
Introd. to the Pentamerone, out of the miraculous nut comes a
voccola co dudece polecine. Now the Hungarian tale in Gaal p. 381
has '*golden hen and six chickens*,' meaning the Pleiades; and the
maiden, seeking her lost lover, has to obtain access to him by the
valuables contained in three nuts; these were three dresses, on
which severally were worked the sun, the moon, and the seven-
stars (conf. Wigal. 812), being gifts of Sun, Moon, and Seven-

---

[1] The Suppl. adds: 'the Pleiades, like doves, carry ambrosia to Zeus, but *one
always gets lost* in passing the Planctae rocks, and Zeus fills up their number again,
Athen. 4, 325-6.'—Homer tells the story simply of doves, πέλαιαι, Od. 12, 61.—Tʀᴀɴs.
[2] Conf. Pentam. 4, 8 'li sette palommielle,' seven children transformed.
[3] Mém. des antiq. 4, 376. 6, 121-9.

stars, bestowed upon her in her wanderings. The third dress
tradition at last converted into the cluckie herself. Treasure-
hunters dig for the costly cluckie with her chicks; conf. the
sunken hoard, Chap. XXXII. A 'hen and twelve hünkeln' was
also an earthly fine, Weisth. 1, 465. 499. I am not sure that we
are entitled to connect the nut with 'Iduns huot'; but what is
'sun, moon and cluckie' with us, is with the Finns far more
plainly 'päiwä, kuu, otawa,' *i.e.* sun, moon, bear. The Span. name
is 'las *siete cabrillas*' seven kids.[1] Pol. *baby* old wives, Russ.
baba old wife [and *nasédka* sitting hen], Linde 1, 38ᵃ; Serv.
vlashitsi (Vuk 78), *vlashnitsi*, (Bosn. Bible 3, 154, 223), Slovèn.
vlastovtse swallows? but Jarnik 229ᵇ explains it 'ramstäbe,' which
I do not understand. The O. Boh. name too is obscure, *scsyet-
nycze* pleiades (Hanka's Glossen 58ᵇ) = štĕtnice, bristly ones, from
štĕtina seta? Slovèn. *gostosévtsi*, *gostozhirtsi* the thick-sown?
The last name agrees with the Lith. and Finn. view, viz. the constellation is a *sieve* having a great many holes, or sifting out a
heap of flour : Lith. *sĕtas* Lett. *setinsh*, Esth. *sööl* or *söggel*, Finn.
seula, seulainen. Why does Suchenwirt 4, 326 say, ' daz her daz
tailt sich in daz lant gleich recht als ain *sibenstirn*' ? because the
army is so thickly spread over the land ? (see Suppl.).

The origin of the Pleiades is thus related : Christ was passing
a baker's shop, when He smelt the new bread, and sent his dis-
ciples to ask for a loaf. The baker refused, but the baker's wife
and her six daughters were standing apart, and secretly gave it.
For this they were set in the sky as the *Seven-stars*, while the
baker became the cuckoo (p. 676 baker's man), and so long as
he sings in spring, from St. Tiburtius's day to St. John's, the
Seven-stars are visible in heaven. Compare with this the Norwegian tale of Gertrude's bird (p. 673).

There may be a few more stars for which popular names still
exist.[2] In Lith. the Kids are *artojis su jáuczeis* plougher with
oxen, and Capella *neszeja walgio* food-bearer (f.). Hanka's O.
Boh. gl. 58ᵇ gives *hrusa* for Aldebaran, *przyczek* for Arcturus.
We might also expect to find names for the Hyades and Cas-

---

[1] Don Quixote 2, 41 (Idel. 4, 83 ; conf. 6, 242).
[2] Cymric and Gaelic Bibles (Job 9, 9), retain the Latin names from the Vulgate;
from which it does not follow that these languages lack native names for stars.
Armstrong cites Gael. *crannarain*, baker's peel, for the Pleiades, and *dragblod*, fire-
tail, for the Lesser Bear.

siopeia. But many stars are habitually confounded, as the Pleiades with the Hyades or Orion, and even with the Wain and Arcturus;[1] what is vouched for by glosses alone, is not to be relied on. Thus I do not consider it proved as yet that the names *plough* and *eburdrung* really belong to Orion. By 'plough' the Irish Fairy-tales 2, 123 mean the Wain rather than Orion, and who knows but the 'throng of boars' may really stand for the 'Τάδες (from ὖς)[2] and the Lat. *Suculae*? (see Suppl.).

Still more unsafe and slippery is the attempt to identify the constellations of the East, founded as they are on such a different way of looking at the heavens. Three are named in Job 9, 9: עָשׁ âsh, כִּימָה kîmeh, כְּסִיל ksîl;[3] which the Septuagint renders πλειάδες, ἕσπερος, ἀρκτοῦρος, the Vulgate 'Arcturus, Orion, Hyades,' and Luther 'the Wain, Orion, the Glucke (hen).' In Job 38, 31 kîmeh and ksîl are given in the LXX as πλειάδες, Ὠρίων, in Vulg. as 'Pleiades, Arcturus,' in Diut. 1, 520 as 'Siebenstirni, Wagan,' and in Luther as 'Siebenstern, Orion.' For ksîl in Isaiah 13, 10 the LXX has Ὠρίων, Vulg. merely 'splendor,' Luther 'Orion.' In Amos 5, 8 kîmeh and ksîl are avoided in LXX, but rendered in Vulg. 'Arcturus, Orion,' and by Luther 'the Glucke, Orion.' Michaelis drew up his 86 questions on the meaning of these stars, and Niebuhr received the most conflicting answers from Arabian Jews;[4] on the whole it seemed likeliest, that (1) âsh was the Arabian constellation *om en nâsh*, (2) kimeh or chima the Arab. *toriye*, (3) ksîl the Arab. *sheil* (sihhêl); the three corresponding to Ursa major,

---

[1] Keisersperg's Postil 206: 'the sea-star or the Wain, or *die henn mit den hünlin* as ye call it.' Grobianus 1572 fol. 93ᵇ: 'wo der wagen steht, und wo die *gluck mit künkeln* geht.' Several writers incorrectly describe the 'dümke, düming' as 'siebengestirn'; even Tobler, when he says 370ᵇ 'three stars of the siebeng. are called the *horses*, near which stands a tiny star, the *waggoner*,' is evidently thinking of the Wain's thill [Germans often take the 'seven-stars' for Ursa instead of Pleiades].

[2] It has long been thought a settled point, that *Suculae* (little sows) was a blundering imitation of Τάδες, as if that came from ὖς a sow, whereas it means 'the rainers' from ὕω to rain ('ab imbribus,' Cicero; 'pluvio nomine,' Pliny). Does the author mean to reopen the question? Did the later Greeks and Romans, ashamed of having these 'little sows' in the sky, invent the 'rainers' theory? May not *Suculae* at all events be a genuine old Roman name, taken from some meritorious mythical pigs?—TRANS.

[3] In Hebr. the three words stand in the order 'âsh, k'sîl, kîmâh; and their transposition here does some injustice to the Vulg. and Luther. As a fact, two out of the four times that k'sîl occurs, it is Ὠρίων in LXX, and the other two times it is Orion in Vulgate. Luther and the Engl. version are consistent throughout.—TRANS.

[4] Beschr. von Arabien p. 114; some more Arabian names of stars, pp. 112—6.

Pleiades and Sirius. If we look to the verbal meanings, *nâsh*, which some Arabs do change into *ash*, is feretrum, bier or barrow,[1] a thing not very different from a 'wain'; *kimeh, kima* seems to signify a thick cluster of stars, much the same sense as in that name of 'sieve': *ksîl*, means foolish, ungodly, a lawless giant, hence Orion.

Constellations can be divided into two kinds, according to their origin. One kind requires *several* stars, to make up the shape of some object, a man, beast, etc.; the stars then serve as ground or skeleton, round which is drawn the full figure as imagination sees it. Thus, three stars in a row form St. James's staff, distaff, a belt; seven group themselves into the outline of a bear, others into that of a giant Orion. The other kind is, to my thinking, simpler, bolder, and older: a whole man is seen in a *single* star, without regard to his particular shape, which would disappear from sheer distance; if the tiny speck drew nearer to us, it might develop itself again. So the same three stars as before are three men mowing; the seven Pleiads are a hen and her chickens; two stars, standing at the same distance on each side of a faintly visible cluster, were to the ancient Greeks two asses feeding at a crib. Here fancy is left comparatively free and unfettered, while those outline-figures call for some effort of abstraction; yet let them also have the benefit of Buttmann's apt remark,[2] that people did not begin with tracing the complete figure in the sky, it was quite enough to have made out a portion of it; the rest remained undefined, or was filled up afterwards according to fancy. On this plan perhaps the Bear was first found in the three stars of the tail, and then the other four supplied the body. Our Wain shews a combination of both methods: the thill arose, like the Bear's tail, by outline, but the four wheels consist each of a single star. One point of agreement is important, that the Greek gods put men among the stars, the same as Thôrr and Oðinn do (pp. 375. 723; see Suppl.).

The appearance of the *rainbow* in the sky has given rise to a number of mythic notions. Of its rounded arch the Edda makes a heavenly *bridge* over which the deities walk; hence it is called

---

[1] Bocharti hierorz., ed. Rosenmüller 2, 680.
[2] Origin of the Grk constell. (in Abh. der Berl. acad. 1826, p. 19–63).

Asbrú (Sæm. 44ᵃ), more commonly *Bif-röst* (OHG. would be pipa-rasta) the quivering tract, for röst, Goth. and OHG. rasta, means a definite distance, like mile or league. It is the best of all bridges (Sæm. 46ᵃ), strongly built out of three colours; yet the day cometh when it shall break down, at the end of the world, when the sons of Muspell shall pass over it, Sn. 14. 72. The tail of this bridge [1] extends to Himinbiörg, Heimdall's dwelling (Sn. 21), and Heimdallr is the appointed keeper of the bridge; he guards it against hrîmthurses and mountain-giants,[2] lest they make their way over the bridge into heaven, Sn. 18. 30. The whole conception is in keeping with the cars in which the gods journey through heaven, and the roads that stretch across it (conf. p. 361). It was Christianity that first introduced the O. Test. notion of the celestial *bow* being a sign of the covenant which God made with men after the *rain* of the Deluge: OHG. *reganpogo*, AS. *scúrboga*, shower-bow, Cædm. 93, 5. Meanwhile some ancient superstitions linger still. The simple folk imagine, that on the spot where the rainbow springs out of the ground, there is a *golden dish*, or a treasure lies buried; that gold coins or pennies drop out of the rainbow. When gold-pieces are picked up, they are called *regenbogen-schüsselein* (-dishes), patellae Iridis, which the sun squanders in the rainbow. In Bavaria they call the rainbow *himmelring, sonnenring*, and those coins *himmelring-schüsseln* (Schm. 2, 196. 3, 109: conf. supra p. 359 note). The Romans thought the bow in rising drank water out of the ground: ' bibit arcus, pluet hodie,' Plaut. Curcul. 1, 2 ; ' purpureus pluvias cur bibit arcus aquas ? ' Propert. iii. 5, 32. Tibull. i. 4, 44. Virg. Georg. 1, 380. Ov. Met. 1, 271. One must *not point with fingers* at the rainbow, any more than at stars, Braunschw. anz. 1754, p. 1063. *Building on the rainbow* means a bootless enterprise (note on Freidank p. 319. 320, and Nib. Lament 1095. Spiegel, 161, 6); and setting on the rainbow (Bit. 2016) apparently

---

[1] *Brúar-spordr* (we still speak of a bridge's *head*, tête de pont), as if an animal had laid itself across the river, with head and tail resting on either bank. But we must not omit to notice the word *spordr* (prop. cauda piscis); as röst, rasta denote a certain stadium, so do the Goth. *spaúrds* OHG. *spurt* a recurring interval, in the sense of our '(so many) times': thus, in Fragm. theot. 15, 19, dhrim spurtim (tribus vicibus), where rastôm would do as well. Do the ' rûnar â *brúarspordi*,' Sæm. 196ᵃ mean the rainbow?

[2] Giants are often made bridge-keepers (p. 556 n.): the maiden Môðguðr guards giallarbrû, Sn. 67.

exposing to great danger? Is 'behûsen unebene ûf regenbogen' (Tit. Hahn 4061) to be unequally seated? In H. Sachs ii. 287 a man gets pushed off the rainbow. The Finns have a song in which a maiden sits on the rainbow, weaving a golden garment. Might not our heathen ancestors think and say the like of their piparasta? There is a remarkable point of agreement on the part of the Chinese: 'tunc et etiamnum viget superstitio, qua *iridem* orientalem *digito monstrare nefas* esse credunt; qui hanc monstraverit, huic subito ulcus in manu futurum. Iridem habent Sinae pro signo libidinis effrenatae quae regnat.'[1]

The Slavic name for the rainbow is O. Sl. *duga*, Serv. and Russ. *duga*, *duga nebeskia*, Boh. *duha*, prop. a stave (tabula, of a cask), hence bow; the Servians say, any male creature that passes under the rainbow turns into a female, and a female into a male (Vuk sub v.).[2] Two Slovènic names we find in Murko: *mávra*, *mávritsa*, which usually means a blackish-brindled cow; and *bozhyi stolets*, god's stool, just as the rainbow is a *chair* of the Welsh goddess *Ceridwen* (Dav. Brit. myth. 204); conf. 'God's chair,' supra p. 136. Lett. *warrawihksne*, liter. the mighty beech? Lith. *Laumés yosta*, Lauma's or Laima's girdle (sup. p. 416); also *dangaus yosta* heaven's girdle, *kilpinnis dangaus* heaven's bow, *ûrorykszte* weather-rod; more significant is the legend from Polish Lithuania, noticed p. 580, which introduces the rainbow as messenger after the flood, and as counsellor. Finn. *taiwancaari*, arcus coelestis. In some parts of Lorraine *courroie de S. Lienard*, *couronne de S. Bernard*. In Superst. Esth. no. 65 it is the thunder-god's sickle, an uncommonly striking conception.

To the Greeks the Ἶρις was, as in the O. Test., a token of the gods, Il. 11, 27; but at the same time a half-goddess Ἶρις, who is sent out as a messenger from heaven. The Indians assigned the painted bow of heaven to their god *Indras*. In our own popular belief the souls of the just are led by their guardian-angels into heaven over the rainbow, Ziska's Oestr. volksm. 49. 110.

As for that doctrine of the Edda, that *before the end of the*

---

[1] Chi-king ex lat. P. Lacharme, interpr. Jul. Mohl, p. 242.
[2] Like the contrary effects of the planet Venus on the two sexes in Superst. I, 167.

world Bifröst will break, I find it again in the German belief
during the Mid. Ages that for a number of years before the
Judgment-day the rainbow will no longer be seen: 'ouch hôrt
ich sagen, daz man sîn (the regenpogen) nieht ensehe *drîzich jâr*
(30 years) vor deme suontage,' Diut. 3, 61.　Hugo von Trimberg makes it 40 years (Renner 19837):

> Sô man den regenbogen siht,
> sô enzaget diu werlt niht
> dan darnâch über *vierzec jâr ;*

so the rainbow appear, the world hath no fear, until thereafter 40
year.　Among the signs the Church enumerates of the approach
of the Last Day, this is not to be found (see Suppl.).

CHAPTER XXIII.

DAY AND NIGHT.

All the liveliest fancies of antiquity respecting day and night are intertwined with those about the sun, moon and stars : day and night are holy godlike beings, near akin to the gods. The Edda makes Day the child of Night.

Nörvi, a iötunn, had a daughter named *Nôtt*, black and dingy like the stock she came of (svört oc döck sem hon átti ætt til) ;[1] several husbands fell to her share, first Naglfari, then Anar (Onar)[2] a dwarf, by whom she had a daughter Iörð, who afterwards became Oðin's wife and Thôr's mother. Her last husband was of the fair race of the áses, he was called Dellíngr, and to him she bore a son *Dagr*, light and beautiful as his paternal ancestry. Then All-father took *Night* and her son *Day*, set them in the sky, and gave to each of them a horse and a car, wherewith to journey round the earth in measured time. The steeds were named the rimy-maned and the shiny-maned (p. 655-6).

The name Dellíngr, the assimilated form of *Deglíngr*, includes that of the son *Dagr*, and as -líng if it mean anything means descent, we must either suppose a progenitor *Dagr* before him, or that the order of succession has been reversed, as it often is in old genealogies.

For the word 'dags, dagr, dæg, tac' I have tried to find a root (Gramm. 2, 44), and must adhere to my rejection of Lat. 'dies' as a congener, because there is no consonant-change, and the Teutonic word develops a *g*, and resolves its *a* into *o* (uo); yet conf. my Kleinere schriften 3, 117.[3] On the other hand, in 'dies' and all that is like it in other languages, there plainly appeared

---

[1] This passage was not taken into account, p. 528; that Night and Helle should be black, stands to reason, but no conclusion can be drawn from that about giants as a body. Notice too the combination 'svört ok döck,' conf. p. 445. Here giant and dwarf genealogies have evidently overlapped.

[2] Conf. Haupt's Zeitschr. 3, 144.

[3] [Sanskr. *dah* urere, ardere (Bopp's Gl. 165) does seems the root both of dies and Goth. dags, which has exceptionally kept prim. *d* unchanged. MHG. tac still retained the sense of heat : 'für der heizen sunnen *tac*,' MS. 2, 84ª.—SUPPL.]

an interlacing of the notions 'day, sky, god,' p. 193. As Day
and Donar are both descended from Night, so Dies and Deus
(Zeus) fall under one root; one is even tempted to identify Donar,
Thunor with the Etruscan Tina (dies), for the notion day, as we
shall see, carries along with it that of din: in that case Tina
need not stand for Dina, but would go with Lat. tonus and toni-
trus. Deus is our Tiw, Ziu, for the same name sometimes gets
attached to different gods; and it is an additional proof how
little 'dies' has to do with our 'dæg, tag'; likewise for
coelum itself we have none but unrelated words, p. 698-9. From
the root *div* the Ind. and Lat. tongues have obtained a number
of words expressing all three notions, gods, day and sky; the
Greek only for gods and sky, not for day, the Lith. for god and
day, not sky, the Slav. for day alone, neither god nor sky, and
lastly our own tongue for one god only, and neither sky nor day.
Here also we perceive a special affinity between Sanskrit and
Latin, whose wealth the remaining languages divided amongst
them in as many different ways. The Greek ἦμαρ, ἡμέρα I do
regard as near of kin to the Teut. himins, himil; there is also
Ἡμέρα a goddess of day.

The languages compared are equally unanimous in their name
for night: Goth. *nahts*, OHG. *naht*, AS. *niht*, ON. *nôtt* (for nâtt),
Lat. *nox noctis*, Gr. νύξ νυκτός, Lith. *naktis*, Lett. *nakts*, O. Sl.
noshti, Pol. and Boh. *noc* (pron. nots), Slovèn. *nozh*, Serv. *notj*,
Sanskr. *nakta* chiefly in compounds, the usual word being *niš*,
nišâ (both fem.). Various etymologies have been proposed, but
none satisfactory.[1] As day was named the shining, should not
the opposite meaning of 'dark' lurk in the word night? Yet it
is only night unillumined by the moon that is lightless. There is
a very old anomalous verb 'nahan' proper to our language, from
whose pret. nahta[2] the noun nahts seems to come, just as from
magan mahta, lisan lista come the nouns mahts, lists. Now

---

[1] [Bopp 196b and Pott 1, 160 explain nišâ as 'lying down' from sî to lie; and
naktam as 'while lying.' Benfey assumes two roots, nakta 'not-waking,' 2, 869
and niš conn. with Lat. niger 2, 57.—Suppl.]

[2] The plurals of Goth. ganah, binah are lost to us; I first assumed ganahum,
binahum, but afterwards ganaúhum, because binaúht = ἔξεστι in 1 Cor. 10, 23, and
ganaúha ἀπρέπεια occurs several times. The u (aú before an h) is the same as in
skal skulum, man munum, OHG. mac mugum, in spite of which the noun is maht.
But the Goth. mag magum proves the superior claim of a, so that nahts (nox)
would presuppose an older nah nahum, nahta, even though Ulphilas had written
nah naúhum, naúhta.

Goth. *ganahan*, OHG. *kinahan*, means sufficere, so that nahts
would be the sufficing, pacifying, restful, quiet, at the same time
efficient, strong, ἄρκια, which seems to hit the sense exactly.
Add to this, that the OHG. *duruh-naht* is not only pernox, totam
noctem durans, but more commonly perfectus, consummatus,
'fullsummed in power,' MHG. durnehte, durnehtec, where there
is no thought of night at all. Where did Stieler 1322 find his
'*durchnacht*, nox illunis'? = the Scand. niŏ (p. 710), and meaning
the height of night (see Suppl.).

Both day and night are exalted beings. Day is called the
holy, like the Greek ἱερὸν ἦμαρ: 'sam mir der *heilic tac!*'
Ls. 2, 311. 'sâ mir daz *heilige lieht!*' Roth. 11ᵇ. 'die *lieben
tage*,' Ms. 1, 165ᵃ. 'der *liebe tag*,' Simplic. 1, 5. Hence both
are addressed with greetings: 'heill *Dagr*, heilir *Dags synir*,
heil *Nótt* ok nipt! ŏreiŏom augom lítit ockr þinnig, ok gefit
sitjondom sigur!' they are asked to look with gracious eyes
on men, and give victory, Sæm. 194ᵃ; and the adoration of day
occurs as late as in Mart. von Amberg's Beichtspiegel. 'diu *edele
naht*, Ms. 2, 196ᵇ. 'diu *heilige naht*,' Gerh. 3541. 'sam mir diu
heilic naht hînt!' so (help) me Holy Night to-night, Helbl. 2,
1384. 8, 606. '*frau Naht*, Ms H. 3,428ᵃ (see Suppl.).

Norse poetry, as we saw, provided both Night and Day with
cars, like other gods; but then the sun also has his chariot, while
the moon, as far as I know, has none ascribed to her. Night
and Day are drawn by one horse each, the Sun has two; consequently day was thought of as a thing independent of the sun,
as the moon also has to light up the dark night. Probably the
car of Day was supposed to run before that of the Sun,[1] and
the Moon to follow Night. The alternation of sexes seems not
without significance, the masculine Day being accompanied by
the feminine Sun, the fem. Night by the masc. Moon. The
Greek myth gives chariots to Helios and Selene, none to the
deities of day and night; yet Aeschylus in Persae 386 speaks
of day as λευκόπωλος ἡμέρα, the *white-horsed*. The riddle in
Reinmar von Zweter, Ms. 2, 136, lets the chariot of the year be
drawn by seven white and seven black steeds (the days and
nights of the week). Here also the old heathen notion of riding

---

[1] *i.e.* day or morning is there *before the sun*, who backs them up, so to speak:
unz daz diu sunne ir liehtez schînen bôt dem morgen über berge, Nib. 1564, 2.

or driving deities peeps out. Again, a spell quoted in Mone's
Anz. 6, 459 begins with 'God greet thee, *holy Sunday!* I see
thee there come *riding*.' This is no doubt the heathen god *Tag*
riding along on *Scinfahso* with his shiny mane (ON. Skinfaxi,
Sn. 11); but if we took it for the white god *Paltar* on his foal
(p. 222-4), we should not be altogether wrong. We shall have
more to say presently on the personification of Day; but that
spell is well worthy of consideration (see Suppl.).

Nevertheless our poets express the break of day by the sun's
uprising, and more especially the fall of night by his setting;
but neither the beginning nor end of night by the moon, whose
rising and setting are seldom simultaneous with them. I will
now give the oldest set phrases that express these phenomena.

The sun rises, climbs: Goth. sunna *ur-rinniþ*, Mk. 4, 6. 16, 2.
OHG. *ar-rinnit*; daranâh *ir-ran* diu sunna, N. ps. 103, 22; MHG.
si was ûf *er-runnen*, Mar. 189. ON. þâ *rann* dagr upp, Ol. helg.
cap. 220. *Rinnan* is properly to run, to flow, and here we see
a strict analogy to the O. Rom. idiom, which in like manner uses
manare of the rising day: 'diei principium *māne*, quod tum
mānat dies ab oriente,' Varro 6, 4 (O. Müller p. 74); '*manar
solem* dicebant antiqui, cum solis orientis radii splendorem jacere
coepissent' (Festus sub v.). Ulphilas never applies ur-reisan
(surgere) to the sun. The Span. language attributes to the
rising sun a pricking (apuntar): 'yxie el sol, dios, que fermoso
apuntaba,' Cid 461; 'quando viniere la mañana, que *apuntare*
el sol,' Cid 2190. After rising the sun is *awake*, 'with the sun
awake' means in broad daylight (Weisth. 2, 169. 173. 183),
'when sunshine *is up*' (2, 250). AS. 'hâdor heofonleoma com
blícan,' Andr. 838 (see Suppl.).

The sun sinks, falls: Goth. *sagq* sunnô (pron. sank), Lu. 4, 40.
gasagq sáuil, Mk. 1, 32. *dissigqái* (occïdat), Eph. 4, 26. OHG.
sunnâ *pifeal* (ruit), *pisluac* (occïdit),[1] Gl. Ker. 254. Diut. 1, 274ᵃ.
MHG. *siget*: diu sunne·sîget hin, Trist. 2402. diu sunne was ze
tal gesigen, Wh. 447, 8. nu begund diu sunne sîgen, Aw. 1, 41.
ON. both sôlar*fall* and sôl*setr*, Engl. sun*set*; so OHG. 'denne
sunnâ *kisaz*,' cum sol occumberet, Diut. 1, 492ᵃ, implying that he
sits down, and that there is a *seat* or *chair* for him to drop into

---

[1] Intrans., as we still say niederschlagen, zu boden schlagen.

at the end of his journey. His setting is called OHG. *sedalkanc*,
Hym. 18, 1; *sedal* ira kât (goeth) 14, 2. AS. *setelgong*,[1] *setlrâd*,
Cædm. 184, 19. oÐÐæt sunne *gewât tô sete glîdan*, Andr. 1305.
oÐÐæt beorht *gewât* sunne swegeltorht *tô sete glîdan* 1248. OS.
sêg sunne tô *sedle*, Hel. 86, 12. sunne ward an *sedle* 89, 10.
geng thar âband tuo, sunna ti *sedle* 105, 6. scrêd *wester* dag,
sunne te *sedle* 137, 20. sô thuo gisêgid warth *sedle* nâhor hêdra
sunna mid hebantunglon 170, 1. Dan. *for vesten* gaaer solen til
säde, DV. 1, 90, in contrast to '*sôl er î austri* (east),' Vilk.
saga p. 58-9. The *West* (occasus) stands opposed to the *East*
(oriens), and as OHG. *kibil* means pole, and Nordkibel, Sunt-
kibel the north and south poles (N. Bth. 208), a set phrase in
our Weisthümer may claim a high antiquity : ' bis (until) die
sonne *unter den Westergibel* geht' (1, 836) ; ' bis die sonne *an
den Wg.* schint' (2, 195) ; ' so lange dat die sonne *in den Wes-
tergevel* schint' (2, 159). The first of these three passages
has the curious explanation added : ' till 12 o'clock.'[2] Ovid's
' *axe* sub *hesperio* ' Met. 4, 214 is thus given by Albrecht :
in den liehten *westernangen*. The similar expression in ON.
seems to me important, Grâgâs 1, 26 : ' fara til lögbergs, at sôl
sê â *gidhamri enum vestra*,' giâhamarr being chasmatis rupes
occidentalis. I shall have more to say about that in another
connexion ; conf. however Landnâma bôk 215 : sôl î *austri* ok
vestri. MHG. diu sunne gie ze *sedele*, Diut. 3, 57. als diu
sunne in ir *gesedel* solde gân, Morolt 38ᵃ; but what place on
earth can that be, whose very name is told us in 14ᵇ, ' ze *Geilât*,
dâ diu sunne ir *gesedel* hât' ? the capital of India ? (see p. 743
note.) I suppose *kadam*, MHG. *gaden* (cubiculum), Mor. 15ᵃ is
equivalent to sedal, unless the true reading be ' ze gnâden.' The
sun gets way-worn, and longs for rest : dô hete diu *müede* sunne

---

[1] ON. and AS. distinguish between two periods of the evening, an earlier *aptan*
æfen=vespera, and a later *qveld*, *cwild*=conticinium : ' at qveldi,' Sæm. 20ᵃ. 73ᵇ,
means at full evening, when night has fallen and its stillness has set in. I derive
cwild, *qveld* from cwellan, qvelja to quell or kill, as in many passages it means liter.
interitus, occisio, nex ; so we may explain it by the falling or felling of the day
(cadere, whence caedere), or still better by the deathlike hush of night ; conf. Engl.
' dead of night, deadtime of n.', the conticinium, AS. cwildtîd. If ' chuiltiwerch '
in a doc. of 817 means cwildweorc, work in the late evening, which is not to be put
upon maidservants, then OHG. too had a *chuilt* corresp. to cwild and qveld, qvöld.
In Cædm. 188, 11 I propose to read : ' cwildrôfu eodon on lâÐra lâst,' *i.e.* (belluae)
vesperi famosae ibant in vestigia malorum.

[2] In fixing boundary-lines *Westergibel* is even used topographically, Weisth. 1,
464-5. 485. 498. 550-6.

ir liehten blic hinz ir gelesen, Parz. 32, 24. He goes to his
bed, his bedchamber : Dan. 'solen ganger til *senge*,' DV. 1, 107.
'solen gik til *hvile*,' 1, 170. MHG. diu sunne gerte lâzen sich
zuo *reste*, Ernst 1326. diu sunne dô ze *reste* gie, Ecke (Hag.)
110. nu wolte diu sunne ze *reste* und ouch ze *gemache* nider gân,
Dietr. 14ᵈ; so M. Opitz 2, 286 : 'muss doch zu *rüste* gehen, so
oft es abend wird, der schöne himmels-schild.' OE. the sun
was gon to *rest*, Iwan 3612. Our *gnade* (favour), MHG. genâde,
OHG. kinâda, properly means inclining, drooping, repose
(p. 710), which accounts for the phrase 'diu sunne gienc ze
gnâden' (dat. pl.), Mor. 37ᵃ. Wolfdietr. 1402. Even Agricola no
longer understood it quite, for he says in Sprichw. 737 : 'it
lasted till the sun was about to *go to gnaden*, i.e, to set, and deny(!)
the world his gnade and light by going to rest.' Aventin (ed.
1580 p. 19ᵇ) would trace it back to our earliest heathenism and
a worship of the sun as queen of heaven : 'never might ye say
she set, but alway that she went to *röst* and *gnaden*, as the silly
simple folk doth even yet believe.' The last words alone are
worth noticing; the superstition may be of very old standing,
that it is more pious, in this as in other cases, to avoid straight-
forward speech, and use an old half-intelligible euphemism. On
this point Vuk 775 has something worthy of note : you must say
'*smirilo se* suntse' (the sun is gone to rest, conquievit), and not
zadye (is gone) nor *syede* (sits) ; if you say zadye, he answers
'*zashao pa ne izishao*' (gone, not come out) ;[1] if you say syede,
he tells you '*syeo pa ne ustao*' (sat down, not risen) ; but to
'*smiri se*' the answer is '*smiryó se i ti*' (rest thee also thou).[2]
And with this I connect the Eddic saw on the peculiar sacredness
of the setting sun : 'engi skal gumna í gögn vega *eiðskinandi*
systor Mana,' Saem. 184ᵇ, none shall fight in the face of the
late-shining sister of the Moon (see Suppl.)

Lye quotes an AS. phrase 'ær sun go to glade,' which he
translates ' priusquam sol vergat ad occasum, lapsum.' The
noun formed from glîdan (labi) would be glâd, and glîdan is

---

[1] Kopitar tells me, 'zashao etc.' is rather an imprecation : mayst thou go in (perhaps, lose thy way) and never get out ! So 'syeo etc.', mayst thou sit down and
never get up !

[2] Mod. Greek songs say, ὁ ἥλιος ἐβασίλευε, ἐβασίλεψε (Fauriel 1, 56. 2, 300. 432),
i.e. has reigned, reigns no more in the sky, is set; and the same of the setting
moon (2, 176).

actually used of the sun's motion : heofones gim glâd ofer grundas, Beow. 4140 [and 'tô sete glîdan' twice in Andreas]. But 'gongan tô glâde' seems nonsense ; perhaps we ought to suppose a noun glæde with the double meaning of splendor and gaudium. Both the ON. glaðr and OHG. klat signify first splendidus, then hilaris, two notions that run into one another (as in our heiter = serenus and hilaris) ; klat is said of stars, eyes, rays (Graff 4, 288), and the sun, O. ii. 1, 13 : êr wurti sunna sô glat (ere he grew so bright). The MHG. poet quoted on p. 705 says (Warnung 2037) :

sô ir die sunnen *vrô* sehet,	When ye see the sun glad,
schœnes tages ir ir jehet,	Ye own the fine day is hers,
des dankt ir ir, und Gote niht.	Ye thank her, not God.

In Switzerland I find the remarkable proper name *Sunnenfroh* (Anshelm 3, 89. 286). But now further, the notions of bliss, repose, chamber, lie next door to each other, and of course brightness and bliss. The setting sun beams forth in heightened splendour, he is entering into his bliss : this is what 'gongan tô glæde' may have meant. In ON. I have only once fallen in with *sôlarglaðan* (occasus), Fornald. sög. 1, 518. We learn from Ihre's Dialectlex. p. 57[a] 165[a], that in Vestgötland 'gladas' is said of the sun when setting: solen *gladas* or *glaas* (occïdit), *sole- glanding, solglädjen* (occasus), which may mean that the setting sun is glad or glitters. That is how I explain the idiom quoted by Stald. 1, 463. 2, 520: the sun *goes gilded* = sets, i.e. glitters for joy. So in Kinderm. no. 165 : sunne *z'gold gange* ; in a song (Eschenburg's Denkm. 240) : de sunne ging *to golde*; and often in the Weisthümer: so die sun *für gold* gat (1, 197), als die sonne *in golt* get (1, 501). Again, as the *rising* sun presents a like appearance of splendour, we can now understand better why the vulgar say he *leaps for joy* or *dances* on great festivals (p. 291) ; he is called 'the paschal piper,' Haupt's Zeitschr. 1, 547. Nor would I stop even there, I would also account for that *noise*, that *clang* once ascribed to the *rising* and *setting* sun (p. 720-1) by a deep affinity between the notions of light and sound, of colours and tones, Gramm. 2, 86-7. A strophe in Albrecht's Titurel describes more minutely the music of sunrise :

Darnâch kund sich diu sunne
wol an ir zirkel rîden (writhe):
der süeze ein überwunne,
ich wæn die süeze nieman möht erlîden.
mit dône dô diu zirkel ruorte;
seitenklanc und vogelsanc
ist alsam glîch der golt gên kupfer fuorte.

(Then in his orb the sun to whirling took, I ween such glut of sweetness none might brook; with dulcet din his orb he rolled, that clang of strings or bird that sings were like as copper beside gold.)   Who can help thinking of the time-honoured tradition of *Memnon's statue*, which at sunrise sent forth a sound like the clang of a harpstring, some say a joyful tone at the rising and a sad at the setting of the sun.[1]   Further on we shall be able to trace some other fancies about the break of day and the fall of night, to light and sound (see Suppl.).

But whither does the evening sun betake himself to rest, and where is his chamber situated?   The oldest way of putting it is, that he dives into the sea, to quench his glow in the cool wave. The AS. Bth. (Rawl. 193ᵃ): 'and þeáh monnum þynceð þæt hio *on mere* gange, *under sǽ swîfe*, þonne hio on setl glîdeð.'   So the ancients said δῦναι and *mergere* of the sun and stars, 'occasus, interitus, vel solis *in oceanum mersio*' (Festus).[2]   Boëth. 4 (metr. 5) says of Boötes: cur *mergat* seras *aequore* flammas; and metr. 6: nec, cetera cernens sidera *mergi*, cupit *oceano tingere flammas*; which N. 223 translates: alliu zeichen sehende in sedel gân, niomer sih ne gerôt *kebadôn* (bathe) *in demo merewazere*.   So, 'sol petit *oceanum*,' Rudlieb 4, 9.   But the expression comes so naturally to all who dwell on the seacoast, that it need not be a borrowed one; we find it in ON. 'sôl gengr *i œgi*,' Fornm. sög. 2, 302, and in MHG. 'der sê, dâ diu sunne ûf gêt *ze reste*,' MS. 2, 66ᵇ.   And, as other goddesses after making the round of the country are bathed in the lake, it is an additional proof of the Sun's divinity that 'she' *takes a bath*, a notion universally preva-

---

[1] Pausan. 1, 42.   Philostr. Vita Apoll. 6, 4.   Heroic. 4.   Pliny 86, 11.   Tac. Ann. 2, 61.   Juven. 15, 5.

[2] Setting in the lake is at the same time depositing the divine eye as a pledge in the fountain.   I will add a neat phrase from Wolfram, Parz. 32, 24: dô hete diu müede sunne ir liehten blic hinz ir gelesen.

lent among the Slavs also: at eve she sinks into her bath to
cleanse herself, at morn she emerges clean with renewed grandeur.
The sea was thought to be the Sun's mother, into whose arms
she sank at night.[1]

To inhabitants of the inland, the horizon was blocked by a
wood, hence the phrases: sôl gengr *til viðar* (Biörn sub v. vidr);
solen går *under vide* (Ihre sub v.).[2] But the AS. word in:
'hâdor sægl wuldortorht gewât *under wâðu* scrîðan,' Andr. 1456,
seems to be a different thing, the OHG. weidi (p. 132 n.). We
say the sun goes behind *the hills*, to which corresponds the AS.
'sunne gewât *under niflan næs*,' sub terræ crepidinem, Andr.
1306 (conf. under neolum næsse, El. 831); a Dan. folksong:
solen gik *til iorde*, down to earth, DV. 1, 170; Ecke (Hagen) 129:
diu sunne *ûz dem himel* gie. Or, the sun is *down*, MHG. 'der
sunne (here masc.) *hinder* gegât,' MS. 2, 192[b] (see Suppl.).[3]

We will now examine other formulas, which express *daybreak*
and *nightfall* without any reference to the sun.

What is most remarkable is, that day was imagined in the
shape of an animal, which towards morning advances in the sky.
Wolfram begins a beautiful watchman's song with the words:
'*sîne klâwen durch die wolken sint geslagen* (his claws through the
clouds are struck), er stîget ûf mit grôzer kraft, ih sih ihn grâwen,
den tac;' and in part third of Wh. (Cass. 317ᵃ) we read: 'daz
diu wolken wâren grâ, und der tac *sîne clâ hete geslagen durch die
naht*.[4] Is it a bird or a beast that is meant? for our language
gives claws to both. In AS. there is a proper name *Dæg-hrefn*,
Beow. 4998, which in OHG. would be Taka-hraban; and Beow.
3599 describes daybreak in the words: 'hræfn blâca heofones
wynne blîð-heort bodôde,' niger corvus coeli gaudium laeto corde
nuntiavit.[5] That piercing with the claw to raise a storm (p. 633)
makes one think of an *eagle*, while an Oriental picture, surprisingly

---

[1] Hanusch, Slav. myth. p. 231, who connects with it the splashing with water
at the Kupalo feast, and derives that name from kupel, kąpiel.
[2] Esth. pääw katsub metsa ladwa, the sun walks on the tips of the wood.
[3] Gudr. 116, 2: 'der sunne schîn gelac verborgen hinter den wolken ze
Gustrâte verre' I understand no better than *Geilâte* (p. 739); but both seem to
mean the same thing.
[4] So in a Weisthum (3, 90): 'de sunne uppe dem hogesten gewest *clawendich*.'
[5] Conf. *volucris* dies, Hor. Od. iii. 28, 6. iv. 13, 16.

similar, suggests rather the king of beasts, who to us is the bear.[1]
Ali Jelebi in his Humayun-nameh (Diez p. 153) describes the
beginning of day in language bombastic it may be, yet doubtless
a faithful reflex of ancient imagery : ' When the falcon of the
nest of the firmament had scattered the nightbirds of the flickering stars from the meadow of heaven, and at sight of the *claws
of the lion of day* the roe of musk-scented night had fled from
the field of being into the desert of non-existence.' The night,
a timid roe, retires before the mighty beast of day : a beautiful
image, and full of life. Wolfram again in another song makes
day press forward with resistless force (see Suppl.).

But the dawn is also pictured in human guise, that of a beautiful
youth, sent like Wuotan's raven as *harbinger* of day : ' dæg byð
Dryhtnes *sond*' says the Lay of Runes. And in this connexion
we ought to consider the formation of such names as Bældæg,
Swip*dæg*, etc., for gods and heroes. This messenger of the gods
stations himself on the mountain's top, and that *on tiptoe*, like the
beast on his claws, that he may the sooner get a glimpse of the
land : ' jocund day *stands tiptoe* on the misty mountain tops,'
Rom. and J. 3, 5 ; a popular image, I have little doubt, and one
that Hebel also uses about Sunday morning : ' und *lisli uf de
zeche goht* und heiter uf de berge stoht de sunntig.' He climbs
and pushes on swiftly, irrepressibly : der tac *stîgende* wart, Trist.
8942. der tac begund *herdringen*, Wolfd. 124. In AS. ' þâ wæs
morgen leoht *scofen* and *scynded*' (praecipitatus et festinatus,
shoved and shindied), Beow. 1828. Hence our poets call him
der rîche, the mighty, as they do God (p. 20) : *rîche* alsô der tac,
MS. 1, 163ª. *rîche muotes* alsam der tac, Wigal. 5222. der tac
wil *gerîchen* (prevail, prosper), MS. 1, 27ᵇ. 2, 28ᵇ ; he is not to be
checked, he chases night away. Put impersonally : thô iz zi dage
want (turned), Otfr. iii. 8, 21 ; but also : der tac wil *niht erwinden*
(turn aside, give it up), MS. 1, 147ᵇ. morge fruo, als der tac
erstarket (gathers strength), Eracl. 587. dô die naht der tac
vertreip, Frauend. 47. 58. He hurls her from her throne, and
occupies it himself : ez taget, diu naht muoz *ab ir trône*, den sie
ze Kriechen hielt mit ganzer vrône, der tac *wil in besitzen*, MS.
1, 2ᵇ ; conf. βασιλεύειν said of the sun (see Suppl.).

[1] The Arabs call the first glimmer of dawn *the wolf's tail*, Rückert's Hariri 1, 215.

Sometimes it appears as if the day, whether pictured as man or as beast, were *tethered*, and delayed in dawning : *ligata, fune ligata* dies, Reinh. lxiv ; he approaches slowly, hindered by the bands : ein *nacht* doch nicht *gepunden* ist *an einen stekchen*, hoer ich sagen, Suchenw. 22, 30. Has that in Fergût 1534, ' quam die dach *ghestrict* in die sale,' anything to do with this ? In a Hungarian fairy-tale (Mailath 1, 137), midnight and dawn are so *tied up*, that they cannot get forward, and do not arrive among men. Stier's Volksm. pp. 3. 5. One MHG. poem represents day as *on sale* and *to be had for money*, Zeitschr. f. d. a. 1, 27 ; like a slave bound by a cord ?

The Romance tongues (not the Teut.) often signify the break of day by a word meaning to prick : Fr. *poindre*, Sp. *puntar, apuntar* (said of the sun also, p. 788), It. *spuntare ;* thus, à la *pointe* du jour, at daybreak. This may indeed be understood of the day's first advance, as though it presented a sharp point, but also it may refer to day as a *rider* who *spurs* his steed, or to the tramping and trotting of a beast, which is also poindre, Reinh. p. xxxix (see Suppl.).

But more significant and impressive are the phrases that connect with daybreak (as well as with sunrise) the idea of a *flutter* and *rustle*, which might be referred to the pinions of the harbinger of day, but which carries us right up to the highest god, whose sovereign sway it is that shakes the air. Wuotan, when spoken of as Wuomo, Wôma, is a thrill of nature (p. 144), such as we actually experience at dawn, when a cool breeze sweeps through the clouds. Expressions in point are the AS. *dæg-wóma* Cædm. 199, 26. Cod. exon. 175, 4. *dægréd-wóma,* Andr. 125, 8. Cod. exon. 179, 24. *morgen-swég,* Beow. 257. *dyne* on dægrêd, Cædm. 289, 27. ær dægrêde þæt se *dyne* becom, Cædm. 294, 4; conf. Introd. to Andr. and El. xxx. xxxi, and the allusion to Donar, p. 736. To this I would trace the ' clang' sent forth by the light of sunrise and sunset. And I venture to put the same sense on an O. Fr. formula, which occurs only in Carolingian poems : Gerard De Viane 1241, ' lou matin *par son l'aube* esclarcie.' Cod. reg. 7183, 3ª, ' un matin *par son l'aube*, quant el fu aparue '; ibid. 5ª, ' un matin *par son l'aube*, quant li jor esclaira ' ; ibid. 161°, ' au matin *par son l'aube*, si con chante li gaus (gallus).' Cod. 7535, 69°, ' a matin *par son l'aube*. I add a few instances from the Charlemagne, ed. Michel 239, 'al matin *sun* la (?) *lalbe*'; 248. 468. 727, 'al matin *par sun lalbe*'; 564, 'le matin *par sun lalbe.*' Was it not originally *per sonum* (sonitum) *albae?* Later they seem to have taken it in a different sense, viz. son=summum, summitas, Fr. sommet; Michel in Gloss. to Charlem. 133 gives a passage which spells 'par *som* laube,' and elsewhere we find ' par son leve,' on the top of the water, 'en sun cel pin,' up on this pine, Charlem. 594. 760, 'en son,' on the top, Renart 2617. In Provençal, Ferabras 182, 'lo mati *sus* en lalba'; 3484, 'lo matinet *sus* lalba.' In It., Buovo p. m. 84. 99. 155, una mattina *su* l' alba, i.e. sur l'aube, which gives only a forced meaning, as though it meant to say 'when the alba stood over the mountain top.'

The English use the expression '*peep* of day': 'the sun began to *peep*' says a Scotch song, Minstr. 2, 430; so the Danes have *pipe frem*: 'hist *piper* solen *frem*, giv Gud en lyksom dag!' says Thom. Kingo, a 17th cent. poet (Nyerup's Danske digtek. middelalder 1, 235). Both languages now make it a separate word from 'to pipe,' Dan. 'pibe.' But, just as in the Fr. 'par son' the sound became a coming in sight, so the old meaning of 'piping' seems to have got obliterated, and a new distinction to have arisen between peep and pipe, Dan. pipe and pibe. Our Gryphius therefore is right in saying (p. m. 740), 'the moon *pipes* up her light.' It is the simultaneous breaking forth of light and noise in the natural phenomenon. We have the same thing in '*skreik* of day' (Hunter's Hallamsh. gloss. p. 81), which can mean nothing but 'shriek'; and in the Nethl. '*kriek*, *krieken* van den dag,' Plattd. 'de *krik* vam dage' for the morning twilight, the chirking (so to speak) of day, as the chirping insect is called cricket, kriek, krikel, krekel (cicada). A remarkable instance of the two meanings meeting in one word is found in the Goth. *svigla* (αὐλός), OHG. *suëkala* (fistula), by the side of the AS. *swegel* (lux, æther), OS. *suigli* (lux).

Our own word *anbrechen* (on-break) implies a crash and a shaking, MHG. så dô der ander tac ûf brach (Frauend. 53. 109);[1]

---

[1] Conf. Bon. 48, 68; and I must quote Ls. 3, 259: 'dô *brach* der tac dâ *herfür*, diu naht von dem tac wart *kinent* (became yawning, was split? conf. supra p. 558), diu sunne wart wol schînent.' The Gute Frau has twice (1539. 2451): 'dô der tac *durch das tach* (thatch) *lûhte* unde *brach.*' We might perh. derive ' ûf brach ' from *brehen*, but we now say anbrechen, anbruch.

Engl. *break* (as well as *rush, blush*) of day. Span. 'el alva
rompe.' O. Sp. 'apriessa cantan los gallos, e quieren *quebrar*
albores,' Cid 235. 'ya *quiebran* los albores, e vinie la mañana'
460. 'trocida es la noche, ya *quiebran* los albores' 3558. O. Fr.
'l'aube *crieve*,' Ren. 1186. 'ja estoit l'aube *crevee*' 1175. 'tantost
con l'aube se *creva*' 16057. Prov. 'can lalba fo *crevada*,' Ferabr.
3977. This romper, quebrar, crevar (Lat. crepare) is the quivering and quaking of the air that precedes sunrise, accompanied
by a perceptible chill; and *crepusculum* contains the same idea.
The Spaniard says also 'el alva se *rie*,' laughs; and the Arab
'the morning *sneezes*' (see Suppl.).[1]

But here the notion of Twilight, and the oldest words by which
it is expressed, have to be examined more minutely.

The very first glimmer of dawn, or strictly that which precedes
it, the latter end of night, is expressed by the Goth. *uhtvô*
(ἔννυχον), Mk. 1, 35, OHG. *uhtâ*, or as N. spells it *uohta*, OS.
uhta, AS. *uhte* (most freq. 'on uhtan,' Cædm. 20, 26. 289, 31.
294, 2. Cod. exon. 443, 24. 459, 17. 460, 14. 'on uhtan mid
ærdæge,' Beow. 251), ON. *ôtta* (Biörn says, from 3 to 6 a.m.).
The root has never been explained; probably the Swiss Uchtland
and ·Westphalian Uchte may be named from uhtâ. Closely
bordering on it is the AS. *œrdæg* (primum tempus), Beow. 251.
2623. 5880; ON. *ârdagi* (conf. árdegis, mane); an OHG. êrtac or
êrtago is unknown to me. Next comes the notion of diluculum,
ON. *dagsbrûn, dagsbiarmi, dagsbirta*, from brûn = ora, margo, as
if supercilium, and biarmi, birta = lux: but OHG. *tagaród, tagarôt*
(Graff 2, 486-7); AS. *dægréd*, Cædm. 289, 27. 294, 4; MLG.
dagerât, En. 1408; M. Nethl. *dagherœt* (Huyd. op. St. 2, 496):
a compound whose last syllable is not distinctly traceable to rôt
(ruber), but is perhaps allied to the rodur, röðull (coelum) on
p. 699. The gender also wavers between masc. and fem.[2] We
catch glimpses of a mythic personality behind, for N. in Cap.
102 translates Leucothea (the white bright goddess, a Perahta)
by 'der *tagerod*,' and carries out the personification: 'ube der

---

[1] Rückert's Hariri 1, 375. In the Novelas of Maria de Zayas 1, 3 is a song
oeginning: 'si se *ríe* el alva,' elsewhere she has 'quando el alva muestra *su alegre
risa*;' conf. p. 502 on laughter that shakes one. The Ital. 'fare *ridere* una botta'
is an expressive phrase for shaking a cask so that it runs over.
[2] Yet conf. OHG. morgan-rôt, -rôto, and -rôtâ (Graff 2, 486); MHG. ûfgânder
morgenrôt (is it morgen rôt?), Walth. 4, 6; but *das* morgenrôt, Trist. 8285. 9462.

tagerod sina facchelun inzundet habe,' have kindled his torches.
And in urkunden we meet with a man's name *Dagharot* (Falke's
Trad. corb. p. 5), also a place named *Wirin-tagaroth* (Höfer's
Zeitschr. 2, 170). When OHG. glosses put tagaród for crepusculum, it comes of unacquaintance with the Latin idiom; it can
be nothing but diluculum, aurora. In O.Fr. there is a woman's
name *Brunmatin* = dawn, Ren. 15666. 15712. 16441 [conn. with
dagsbrûn, SUPPL.]. The ON. has no dagsrod, but it has *sólarrod*
aurora, Fornm. sög. 8, 346. [SUPPL. adds 'með *dagræðom*,'
Sæm. 24ª]. The M. Nethl. has a second term *dachgrake*,
dagherake (fem.), *graken* for the night's blackness brightening
into *gray*; so MHG. der *grâwe* tac, daz *grâwe* licht, MS. 2, 49ª,
der tac wil *grâwen*, Wolfr. 4, 11; 'si kôs den alten jungen
grâwen grîsen (tac)'; '*junc* unde *grâ* der morgen ûf gât,' MsH. 3,
427ᵇ (see Suppl.).

After aurora follows the full morning, Goth. *maúrgins*, OHG.
morkan, OS. *morgan*, ON. *morgun*, strictly αὔριον. I suspect it
has a sense allied to the day's 'breaking or bursting,' for the
Goth. gamaúrgjan means to cut and shorten, like ginnen, secare
(see Suppl.).

To names for the rising day stand opposed those for the sinking. For ὀψέ, ὀψία Ulphilas puts *andanahti*, the times towards
night, but also *seiþu* (serum), as the Mod. Greeks call evening
the slow, late, τὸ βράδυ, and morning the swift, early, τὸ ταχύ,
therefore also the short (conf. gamaúrgjan). The OHG. *âpant*,
OS. *âband*, AS. *œfen*, ON. *uptan* is of one root with aba, aftar,
aptr, which expresses a falling off, a retrograde movement. The
OHG. *dëmar*, our *dämmerung*, stands especially for crepusculum,
and is connected with AS. dim, Lith. tamsus, Slav. temni [dark,
from tma, tenebræ]. AS. *œfenrim*, *œfenglom* crepusculum. What
has peculiar interest for us, the Tagaród above is supported by
an undoubtedly personal *Apantród*, a giant of our heroic legend:
Abentrôt is the brother of Ecke and Fasolt, in both of whom we
recognised phenomena of the sea and air (pp. 239. 636). If day
was a godlike youth, morning and evening twilight may have
been conceived as the giants *Tagaród* and *Apantród* (see
Suppl.).[1]

---

[1] MHG. der *âbentrôt*, Walth. 80, 15; but 'dô diu âbentrôt (f.) uften ir lieht der
erden bôt,' Uolrich 1488.

To the Greeks and Romans Ἠώς, *Aurora*, was a goddess, and she is painted in the liveliest colours. She rises from the *couch* (ἐκ λεχέων, as our sun goes to bed, p. 740) of her husband Tithonos, Od. 5, 1; she is the early-born (ἠριγένεια), the rosy-fingered (ῥοδοδάκτυλος, Il. 1, 477); she digs her ruddy fingers into the clouds as day does his claws, p. 743; she is also called χρυσόθρονος golden-throned, like Hera and Artemis. The Slavs, instead of a goddess of dawn, appear to have had a god, *Yutri-bogh* (see Suppl.).

There is another belief of the Slavs and Hungarians, which, having strayed over to us, must not be passed over in silence. In Hungary dawn is called *hajnal* (Esth. haggo), and the watch-men there cry to one another: '*hajnal* vagyon szep piros, *hajnal*, *hajnal* vagyon!' aurora est (erumpit) pulcra purpurea, aurora, aurora est. The same word *heynal*, *eynal* is in use among the Poles, who cry: '*heynal* świta!' aurora lucet (Linde 1, 623). Now Dietmar of Merseburg tells us under the year 1017 (7, 50 p. 858): 'Audivi de quodam baculo, in cujus summitate manus erat, unum in se ferreum tenens circulum, quod cum pastore illius villae Silivellun (Selben near Merseb.), in quo (l. qua) is fuerat, per omnes domos has singulariter ductus, in primo introitu a portitore suo sic salutaretur: vigila *Hennil*, vigila! sic enim rustica vocabatur lingua, et epulantes ibi delicate de ejusdem se tueri custodia stulti autumabant.' And, coming to our own times, I quote from Ad. Kuhn's Märk. sagen p. 330: 'An old forester of Seeben by Salzwedel used to say, it was once the custom in these parts, on a certain day of the year, to fetch a tree out of the common-wood, and having set it up in the village, to dance round it, crying: *Hennil, Hennil* wache!' Can this have come out of Dietmar? and can this 'Hennil, wake!' and 'Hennil vigila!' so far back as the 11th cent. have arisen through misunderstanding the Hung. vagyon (which means 'est,' not 'vigilat')? Anyhow, the village watchman or shepherd, who went round to all the houses, probably on a certain day of the year, carrying the staff on which was a hand holding an iron ring, and who called out those words, seems to have meant by them some divine being. A Slovak song in Kollar (Zpievanky p. 247, conf. 447) runs thus:

Hainal svitá, giž den biely,   H. shines, now day is white,
stavayte velky i maly!   arise ye great and small!
dosti sme giž dluho spali.   long enough have we now slept.

Bohemian writers try to identify this *Hajnal, Heynal, Hennil* with a Servian or Bohemian god of herdsmen *Honidlo ;*[1] I know not how it may be about this god, but honidlo is neuter in form, and the name of a tool, it must have been gonidlo in Polish, and totally unconnected with eynal, heynal (see Suppl.).

We saw that the rising sun uttered a *joyful* sound, p. 741-2 that the rustling dawn *laughed,* p. 747 ; this agrees with the oft-repeated sentiment, that the day brings *bliss,* the night *sorrow.* We say, ' happy as the day,' and Shaksp. '*jocund* day '; Reinolt von der Lippe ' er *verblide* als der dag '; MS. 2, 192 of departing day, ' der tac *sin wunne* verlât.' Especially do birds express their joy at the approach of day : ' gæst inne swæf oþþæt hræfn blâca *heofenes wynne bliđ-heort* bodôde,' Beow. 3598 ; the heaven's bliss that the raven blithe-hearted announces is the breaking day. ' I am as glad as the hawks that dewy-faced behold the dawn (dögglitir *dagsbrûn sið*),' Sæm. 167[b]; ' nu verðr hann svá feginn, *sem fugl degi*,' Vilk. saga, cap. 39, p. 94; ' Horn was as fain o' fight as is the *foule of the light* when it ginneth dawe,' Horn and Rimen. 64, p. 307; ' ich warte der frouwen mîn, reht als *des tages* diu kleinen *vogellîn,*' MS. 1, 51[a]; ' fröit sich mîn gemüete, sam diu kleinen *vogellîn,* sô si *sehent den morgenschin,*' MS. 2, 102[b]. Hence the multitude of poetic set-phrases that typify the break of day by the song of cocks (han-krât) or nightingales. Biarkamâl near the beginning : ' dagr er upp kominn, dynja hana fiaðrar,' cocks' feathers make a din. ' à la mañana, quando los gallos cantaran,' Cid 317. ' li coo cantoient, pres fu del esclairier.' ' l'aube est percie, sesclere la jornee, cil oisellon chantent en la ramee.' ' biz des morgens vruo, daz diu nahtigal rief,' En. 12545 (see Suppl.).

Night is represented as swift, overtaking, taking unawares, θοὴ νύξ, Il. 10, 394, for does not she drive a chariot ? She *falls* or sinks from heaven, ' la nuit *tombe,* nuit *tombante,* à la *tombée* de la nuit ; ' she *bricht ein* (breaks or bursts *in,* down), whereas day *bricht an* (on, forth) ; she gathers all at once, she surprises. In

---

[1] Jungmann 1, 670. 724. Hanusch pp. 369-70.

Matth. 14, 15, where the Vulg. has 'hora jam praeteriit,' Luther Germanizes it into 'die nacht *fällt daher*' (on, apace); and O. Germ. already used the verbs *ana gân, fallan* in this sense: âband unsih *ana geit*, ther dag ist sînes sindes, O. v. 10, 8. in *ane gâenda* naht, N. Bth. 31. der âbent begunde *ane gân*, Mar. 171. schiere *viel* dô diu naht *an*, Roth. 2653. dô diu naht *ane gie*, Er. 3108. unz daz der âbent *ane gie*, Flore 3468. Ls. 1, 314. Wigal. 1927. 6693. als der âbent *ane gêt*, Wigal. 4763. biz daz der âbent *ane lac*, Ls. 1, 243. diu naht diu *gât* mich an, Wolfd. 1174. diu naht *gêt* uns vaste *zuo*, Livl. chron. 5078. In the same way *sigen* (sink): dô der âbent *zuo seic*, Diut. 3, 68. alsô iz zuo deme âbande *seic* 3, 70. nû *seig* ouch der âbent *zuo*, Frauend. 95, 20. diu naht begunde *zuo sigen*, Rab. 102. begunde *sigen an*, 367. dô diu naht *zuo seic*, Dietr. 62ᵇ. diu naht *siget an*, Ecke 106. der âbent *seic* ie nâher, Gudr. 878, 1. ze tal diu sunne was genigen, und der âbent *zuo gesigen*, Diut. 351, diu naht begunde *sigen an*, Mor. 1620. 3963.[1] diu tageweide diu wil hin (the day's delight it will away), der âbent *siget* vaste *zuo*, Amgb. 2ᵃ. der tach is ouch an uns gewant, uns *siget* der âvent *in die hant*, Ssp. pref. 193. in der *sinkenden* naht, Cornel. releg., Magd. 1605, F. 5ᵃ. in *sinklichter* nacht, Schoch stud. D. 4ᵃ. And we still say 'till sinking night.'[2] Much the same are: nû der âbent, diu naht *zuo geflôz* (came flowing up), Troj. 13676. 10499. A.S. 'æfen com sigeltorht *swungen*,' Andr. 1246.—But this setting in, gathering, falling can also come softly, secretly, like a thief: diu naht begunde *slichen an* (creep on), Dietr. 68ᵇ. nû was diu naht *geslichen* gar über daz gevilde (fields), Christoph. 413. do nû diu naht *her sleich*, und diu vinster in *begreif* (darkness caught him) 376: sô thiu naht *bifêng*, Hel. 129, 16. dô *begreif* in die nacht, Flörsheim chron. in Münch 3, 188. wie mich die nacht *begrif*, Simplic. 1, 18. hett mich die nacht schon *begriffen*, Götz v. Berl. p. m. 164. In MHG. we find predicated of night 'ez benemen,' to carry off (the light? the victory?): unz inz diu naht *benam*, Gudr. 879, 1. ne hete *iz* in diu naht *benomen*, Diut. 3, 81 (conf. Gramm. 4, 334). Hroswitha says, in Fides et spes: 'dies abiit, nox *incumbit*.'

[1] Both times 'segen' in text; if *sigen an* (vincere) were meant, we should expect the word day in the dative.
[2] Goethe says sweetly: For Evening now the earth was rocking, And on the mountains hung the Night.

Clearly in many of these expressions Night is regarded as a *hostile, evil power*, in contrast to the kindly character of Day, who in tranquil ease climbs slowly up above the mountains; hence night is as leisurely about ending, as she is quick in setting in: 'diu naht *gemechlich* ende nam,' slowly the night took ending, Frauend. 206, 21. 'Night is no man's friend' says the proverb, as though she were a demon (see Suppl.).

Between Day and Night there is perennial strife. Night does not rule till day has given up the contest: 'unz der tac *liez sînen strît,*' Parz. 423, 15. 'der tac nam ein ende, diu naht den sige gewan,' the victory won, Wolfd. 2025. 'dô der tac *verquam*, und diu naht daz lieht nam,' En. 7866. 'Nû begunde ouch *strûchen* der tac, daz sîn schîn vil nâch *gelac*, unt daz man durch diu wolken sach, des man der naht ze boten jach, manegen stern der balde gienc, wand er der naht herberge vienc. Nâch der naht baniere kom sie selbe schiere.'[1] In this pleasing description the stars of evening precede the Night herself, as pioneers and standard-bearing *heralds*, just as the morning star was *messenger* of Day.[2]

On p. 742 we had a sunrise taken from the Titurel; a description of failing day, which immediately precedes, deserves to stand here too:

> Dô diu naht *zuo slîchen*
> durch nieman wolte lâzen,
> und ir der tac entwîchen
> muoste, er fuor sâ *wester hin die strâzen,*
> alsô daz man die erd in sach *verslinden,*
> unz er ir möht empfliehen,
> dô kund' er sich von ôrient ûf winden.[3]

Earth devours the departing day (see Suppl.).

I find the older poets dwelling more on the sense of *gloominess*:

[1] The Day 'gan founder then and fall, and much was shent his wonted sheen, till thro' the clouds might they be seen, whom couriers of the Night we call, full many a star that fleetly fares, and harbourage for her prepares. Next her banners, soon Night herself came on.

[2] Lucifer interea praeco scandebat Olympo, Walthar. 1188. Lucifer ducebat diem, Aen. 2, 801. Evening is called in Sanskr.*rajanimukha*, night's mouth, which reminds one of 'Hella's mouth:' so is morning *ahamukha*, day's mouth. Bopp's gloss. 27ᵃ. 284ᵇ.

[3] Then Night came creeping on, for no man would she stay, and Day must needs be gone, retreating down the western way; the earth devouring him thou see'st, until that he might from her flee, then could he hoist him up from east.

νὺξ ὀρφναίη the dusky, in Homer. ' thô warth âband cuman, *naht mid neflu*,' Hel. 170, 25. 'die *finstere ragende* nacht,' gloomy low-ring (jutting), Schreckensgast, Ingolst. 1590, p. 114. 'die *eitele und finstere* nacht,' Kornmann's Mons Ven. 829. '*nipende* niht,' Beow. 1088. 1291, conf. genip (caligo). '*scaduhelm*,' Beow. 1293. '*nihthelm* geswearc deorc ofer dryhtguman' 3576. '*nihthelm* tô glâd,' Andr. 123. El. 78: to her, as a goddess, is ascribed, quite in the spirit of our olden time, a terrible and fearful *helmet*, like a cloak-of-darkness, '*niht helmade*' (put on her helmet) we are told in Andr. 1306. Still finer perhaps is that '*eye* of *black* night,' κελαινῆς νυκτὸς ὄμμα in Aeschylus (Pers. 428) for thick dark-ness as opposed to the bright eye of night, the moon, p. 702 (see Suppl.).[1]

The poetic images I have here collected remove all doubt as to Day and Night having been in the remotest antiquity both alive and divine. But the sentiment must very early have lost some of its hold over the Teutons, from the time they laid aside that name for day, which of itself bespoke his kinship with the gods.

Reckoning by nights instead of days does indeed rest on the observance of lunar time (p. 708), but may have another reason too, the same that prompted men to count winters and not sum-mers. The heathens used to fix their holy festivals for, or prolong them into, the night, especially those of the summer and winter solstices, as we see by the Midsummer and Christmas fires; the fires of Easter and May also bear witness to festal nights. The Anglo-Saxons kept a *hærfestniht* (ON. haustnôtt, haustgrîma), the Scandinavians a *hökunôtt* (F. Magn. Lex. 1021). Beda in his De temp. rat. cap. 13 has preserved a notable piece of informa-tion, though its full meaning is beyond our ken: 'Incipiebant annum (antiqui Anglorum populi) ab octavo cal. Jan. die, ubi nunc natale Domini celebramus; et ipsam noctem, nunc nobis sacro-sanctam, tunc gentili vocabulo *modranecht* (môdra niht),[2] i.e. *ma-trum noctem* appellabant ob causam, ut suspicamur, ceremoniarum quas in ea pervigiles agebant.' Who were these mothers?

---

[1] Images now familiar to us, about quenching the lamps of day, I have not met with in the old poets; but the night burns her tapers too. Shaksp. describes the end of night by 'night's candles are burnt,' Rom. & J. 3, 5.

[2] Afzelius 1, 4. 13 has no right to speak of a *modernatt*, which is not founded on Norse docs., but simply borrowed from Beda. [Can 'môdre niht' have meant 'muntere nacht,' wakeful night? conf. 'pervigiles.']

CHAPTER XXIV.

SUMMER AND WINTER.

The Seasons, which, like day and night, depended on the nearness or distance of the sun, have maintained their personality a great deal more vigorously and distinctly. Their slow revolution goes on with a measured stateliness, while the frequent change of day and night soon effaced the recollection of their having once been gods.

Day and night resemble summer and winter in another point, viz. that the break of day and the arrival of summer are greeted with joyful songs by the birds, who mourn in silence during night and winter. Hence the Eddic kenningar of *gleði fugla* (laetitia volucrum) for summer, and *sút ok stríð fugla* (dolor et angor avium) for winter. This sympathy of nature finds utterance no end of times in the lays of our minnesingers (see Suppl.).

The olden time seems at first to have recognised only two seasons in the year, afterwards three, and lastly four. To this the very names bear witness. Our jahr, Goth. *jêr*, OHG. *jâr*, M. Nethl. *jaer*, OS. *gêr*, AS. *gear*, Engl. *year*, ON. *âr*, is plainly the Pol. *iar, iaro*, Boh. *gar, garo*, which signify spring.[1] In the same way the Slavic *lèto, lieto, liato*, strictly summer, and seemingly akin to our *lenz*, OHG. *lenzo, lengiz*, MHG. *lenze, lengez*, AS. *lencten, lengten* (lent, spring) has come by degrees to cover the whole year. Thus both jâr and lèto mean the warmer season (spring or summer); and southern nations reckoned by them, as the northern did by winters.

Ulphilas renders ἔτος by *jêr*, and ἐνιαυτός either by *aþn*, Gal. 4, 10, or *ataþni*, John 18, 13, a word that has died out of our language everywhere else, but still lingers in the Gothic names Athanagildus, Athanaricus (Aþnagilds, Aþnareiks); it seems

---

[1] The Pol. iar looks like ἔαρ, but this is understood to be for Ϝέαρ, Ϝέσαρ, Lat. vër for verer, veser, closely conn. with Lith. wasara (aestas) and Sanskr. vasanta, Benfey 1, 309. Of the same root seems the Slav. vesna, wiosna (spring), but hardly the ON. vásaðr, which means sharp winter.

akin to ἔτος, perhaps to the Slavic gód, godína, which in Russ.
and Serv. mean a year, while in O.Sl. they stood, as the Pol.
gód, Boh. hód, hodine still stand, for time in general.   The
relation between ἔτος and ἐνιαυτός remains uncertain, for in Od.
1, 16 (ἔτος ἦλθε περιπλομένων ἐνιαυτῶν, a year went past with
circling seasons) ἐνιαυτοί are sections of a year, while other
accounts make an ἐνιαυτός contain three ἔτη.   This comp.
ἐνιαυτός holds in it the simple ἔνος, Lat. annus [1] (see Suppl.).

The year was supposed to make a circle, a ring (orbis, circulus):
jâres umbi-hring, jâr-hring, umbi-huurft; MHG. jâres umbe-ganc,
-ring, -vart, -trit; and the completion and recommencement of
this ring was from a very early period the occasion of solemn
festivities.   Eligius preaches: 'nullus in kal. Jan. nefanda aut
ridiculosa, vetulos aut cervulos aut joticos faciat, neque mensas
super noctem componat, neque strenas aut bibitiones superfluas
exerceat.'   This was apparently a Celtic and Roman custom,
'strenae ineunte anno' are mentioned by Suetonius (Cal. 42. Aug.
57), and the holy mistletoe was plucked amid joyful cries of
'a-gui-lan-neuf!' [Michelet 2, 17: guy-na-né, maguillanneu,
gui-gne-leu. Suppl.].   Nothing of the kind seems to have been
known in Germany; but it is worth while to notice the New-
year's hymns and wishes in Clara Hätzlerin's book as late as the
14th cent. (57ᵇ. 77ᵃ, espec. 196—201 in Haltaus's ed.) where the
year is pictured as a newborn babe, a newborn god, who will grant
the wishes of mortals.   Immediately, no doubt, this referred to
Christmas and the Saviour's birth, in places where the new year
began with that day; yet some heathen practices seem to have
got mixed up with it too, and I cannot overlook the use in these
hymns of the bare adj. new, without the addition of 'year' or
'child' (just as in naming the new-moon, p. 710, nŷ, niuwi):
['des günn dir alles der newgeborn!' this the Newborn grant
thee all, Hätzl. 196ᵇ.   So in other new-year's wishes: 'wunsch
ich dir ain vil gůt jâr zů disem new,' Wolkenst. p. 167.   'gen
disem saeligen guoten newen,' Ad. Keller's Altd. ged. p. 10.—
Suppl.].

Otherwise I hardly find the year as a whole (conf. the riddle,
p. 737) exalted into a person, except in adjurations, spells and

---

[1] For amnus, says Bopp's Gloss. Skr. 16ᵇ; Benfey 1, 310 explains ἐνιαυτός by
Skr. amâvat, ἔνη being amâ, new-moon.

curses: 'sam mir daz *heilec jâr !*' so (help) me holy year, Ls. 1,
287. Haupt's Zeitschr. 7, 104. The two following refer to the
year's commencement only: 'ein *sœlec jâr* gang dich an!' a
blessed year betide thee, Ls. 3, 111; and '*daz dich ein veiges jâr*
müez ane komen!' a doomed (fey) year be thy dole, Ls. 1, 317.
In AS. 'oð þæt oðer com *gear* in geardas,' Beow. 2260 (see
Suppl.).

But even in the earliest times the year had fallen into *halves*,
to which AS. and ON. give the curious name of *missere, misseri*,
and the AS. poems seem to reckon chiefly by these. We find
'missera worn,' store of m., Cædm. 71, 10; 'fela missera' 180,
23. Beow. 306; 'hund missera,' Beow. 2996. 3536 = the 50
winters in 4413; 'misserum frôd, missarum frôd,' Cædm. 104,
30. 141, 16 (wise with age, like 'gearum, dægrîme, fyrndagum
frôd,' Gramm. 1, 750). In the Edda I find only 212ᵃˑᵇ, 'ein
misseri' (per unum annum), and 'sams misseris' (eodem anno);
but the Grâgâs has also misseri (semestrium). The etymology of
the word is not easy: one would expect to find in it the words
half (medius, dimidius) and year, but the short vowel of the
penult conflicts with the ON. âr and AS. gear, and it appears
to be masc. besides (einn misseri, not eitt m.); the ON. misæri
(bad year, annonæ caritas, neut.) is quite another thing. Again,
why should the *d* of the AS. midde (Goth. midja, OHG. mitti)
have passed into *ss*? It must be admitted however, that in
the relation of Lat. medius to Goth. midja we already observe a
disturbance in the law of change; misseri may have come down
and continued from so remote an antiquity that, while in appearance denying its kindred, it will have to own them after all, and
the 'miss' is in the same predicament as the Gr. μέσος, μέσσος
compared with Sanskr. madhyas, or βυσσός = βυθός. No 'misseri, missiri' meets us in the OHG. remains, but the lost hero-
lays may have known it, as even later usages retain the reckoning
by half-years; when the Hildebr.-lied says 'ih wallôta *sumaro*
enti *wintro* sehstic ur lante,' it means only 60 misseri (30 sum-
mers and 30 winters), which agrees with the '30 years' of the
more modern folk-song; and we might even guess that the
'thirteen years' and 'seven years' in Nib. 1082 and 1327, 2,
which make Chriemhild somewhat old for a beauteous bride, were
at an older stage of the epos understood of half-years. In the

North, where winter preponderates, so many winters stood for
so many years, and 'tôlf *vetra* gamall' means a twelve-year-old.
That in OHG. and even MHG. summer and winter represent the
essential division of the year, I infer even from the commonly
used adverbs sumerlanc, winterlanc, while we never hear of a
lengezlanc or herbestlanc; the ON. sumarlângr, vetrlângr, are
supplemented by a haustlângr (the whole autumn).

The Greek year has only *three* seasons, ἔαρ, θέρος, χειμών,
autumn is left out. Our two great anniversaries, the summer
and winter solstices, marked off *two* seasons; the harvest-feast
at the end of Sept. and the fetching-in of summer are perhaps
sufficient proof of a third or fourth. The twofold division is
further supported by the AS. terms *midsumor* and *midwinter*,
ON. *miðsumar, miðvetr*, which marked the same crises of solstice,
and had no midhearfest to compete with them; an AS. *midlencten*
(Engl. *midlent*) does occur, and is about equivalent to our *mit-
fasten*. Now in what relation did the *missere* stand to midsumor
and midwinter? The day (of 24 hours) likewise fell into two
halves of 12 hours each, the AS. *dôgor*, ON. *dægr*; and dôgor
bears the same relation to dæg as missere to gear. Our ancient
remains have no tuogar attending upon tac, but a Gothic *dôgr* by
the side of dags may be inferred from fidurdôgs and ahtáudôgs
in Ulphilas (see Suppl.).

Tacitus, after saying that the Germans cultivate grain only,
and neither enclose meadows nor plant orchards, adds: 'unde
annum quoque ipsum non in totidem digerunt species: *hiems* et
ver et *aestas* intellectum ac vocabula habent; *auctumni* perinde
nomen ac bona ignorantur.' Here auctumnus evidently refers to
garden-fruit and aftermath, while the reaping of corn is placed
in summer, and the sowing in spring. But when we consider,
that North Germany even now, with a milder climate, does not
get the grain in till August and September, when the sun is
lower down in the sky; and that while August is strictly the
ernte-month[1] and Sept. the herbst-month, yet sometimes Sept.
is called the augstin and October the herbst-month; the Tacitean
view cannot have been universally true even in the earliest times.
Neither does the OHG. *herpist, herbist*, AS. *hearfest*, seem at

[1] OHG. aranmânôt, from aran (messis), Goth. *asans*; the O. Saxons said
bewôd or *beo*, Hel. 78, 14. 79, 14; Nethl. *bouw, bouwd.*

all younger than other very old words. More correct surely is the statement we made before, that as we go further north in Europe, there appear but two seasons in all, *summer* and *winter ;* and as we go south, we can distinguish three, four, or even five.[1] Then also for mythical purposes the *two* seasons are alone available, though sometimes they are called spring and winter, or spring and autumn[2] (see Suppl.).

With the Goth. *vintrus* (hiems) we have a right to assume a masc. *sumrus* exactly like it, though Ulph. in Mk 13, 28 (and prob. in Matth. 24, 32 and Lu. 21, 30) rendered θέρος by asans (harvest-time). The declension follows from OHG. *sumar*= sumaru (for a Goth. sumrs of 1 decl. would bring in its train an OHG. somar) ; also from AS. *sumor* with dat. sumera, not sumere. The ON. *sumar* being neut. in the face of a masc. *vetr*, OHG. *wintar*, AS. *winter*, seems inorganic ; it must have been masc. once. The root assumed in my Gramm. 2, 55 runs upon sowing and reaping of crops.

The Edda takes us at once into the genealogy of these two worthies. *Sumar* is the son of *Svásuðr* (Sæm. 34ᵇ. Sn. 23. 127), a name derived from svás (carus, proprius, domesticus), Goth. svês, OHG. suás, for he is one that blesses and is blest, and after him is named all that is sweet and blithe (sváslegt, blítt). But the father of *Vetr* is named *Vindlóni* or *Vindsvalr* (windbringer, windcool), whose father again was *Vásaðr* (ibid.) the dank and moist : a grim coldhearted kindred. But both sets, as we should anticipate, come before us as *giants*, Svásuðr and Sumar of a good friendly sort, Vásaðr, Vindsvalr and Vetr of a malignant ;

---

[1] Spaniards divide spring into *primaverà* and *verano* (great spring), see Don Quix. 2, 53 and Ideler 6, 805. After verano comes *estio*, Fr. été, both masc., while Ital. esta, estate remains fem, like aestas.

[2] The Slavs too, as a race, hold with two principal seasons: summer and year are both *lěto*, i.e. the old year ends with winter, and with summer the new begins ; lěto, like our jahr, is neut., and of course impersonal. Winter they call *zimà* (fem.). When intermediate seasons have to be named, they say *podlěti* (subaestas) for spring, *podzim* (subhiems) for autumn. But other names have also come into vogue, beside the *garo*, *iaro* above : Russ. and Boh. vesnà, Pol. wiosna ; Slověn. *vy-gred* (e-grediens, in Germ. Carinthia auswärt), *mlado lěto* (young summer), *mladlětie, po-mland, s-pomlad, s-prot-lětie* (fr. s-prot, against), all denoting spring; the South Slavs espec. felt the need of parting spring from summer. Autumn is in Serv. *yésen*, Slověn. *yézen* or *predzima* (prae-hiems), Russ. *ósen*. Zimà must be very old, Lith. *žiema*, Gr. χειμών, Lat. *hiems*, Skr. *hêmanta*. Our *frühling, frühjahr* (early year) is neither O. nor MHG., but formed during the last few cents. on the model of printemps or primavera ; *spätling, spätjahr* (late year) is also used for autumn. On *auswärts* and *einwärts* conf. Schm. 1, 117. 4, 161.

so that here again the twofold nature of giants (p. 528-9) is set
in a clear light. The Skáldskaparmál puts them down among the
ancient iötnar : 209ᵇ *Somr* (al. Sômir) ok *Svásuðr*, 210ᵃ *Vindsvalr*
ok *Viðarr* (l. Vetr). Even now *Summer* and *Winter* are much
used as proper names, and we may suppose them to have been
such from the beginning, if only because [as names of seasons]
they do not agree with any in the Non-Teutonic tongues. An
urkunde in Neugart no. 373 (as early as A.D. 958) introduces us
to two brothers named *Wintar* and *Sumar*. Graff 1, 631 has the
proper name *Wintarolf* in the augmentative form (see p. 762 n.)

Now I will produce plain marks of their personality, which
have long maintained themselves in popular phrases and poetic
turns of speech. We say every day : *Summer, Winter* is at the
door, comes in, sets in. H. Sachs iv. 3, 21ᵃ : ' till Summer step
this way.'[1] In MHG. the one is commonly called lieb (lief,
dear), the other leid (loathly, sad) : ' der *liebe Sumer* urloup
genam,' took leave, Ben. 344. ' urloup nam der *Winder*,' 362.
Both are provided with a retinue : ' *Sumer*, dîne *holden* (retainers)
von den huoben sint gevarn,' 304. ' *Suiner*, dîn *gesinde*,' 406.
' mîn sanc süle des *Winters wâpen* tragen,' my song should W.'s
livery wear, MS. 1, 178ᵇ. ' *Winder* ist mit sînen *vriunden* komen,'
Ben. 414. Evidently they have marched up with their men, each
with intent to war upon and chase away his foe : ' der *leide
Winder* hât den *Sumer* hin verjaget,' 381. ' er (der *Winter*) ist dir
gehaz, er en-weiz niht umbe waz, selten er des ie vergaz, swenne
er *dînen stuol besaz*, er en-ructe in vür baz, sîn gewalt wol tûsend
ellen vür den dînen gât,' he hateth thee, he wot not why; he
seldom forgat, when thy chair he besat, but he pushed it further;
his power passeth thine, etc. MsH. 3, 258. Ben. 303. ' *Winter*[2]
hât ez hie gerûmet' cleared out, Ben. 437.—Again, as summer
begins with *May*, we have that month acting as its representative,
and just as full of life and personality. (All three receive the
title of lord : ' mîn *herre* Winter !' MsH. 3, 267ᵃ. ' *her* Meie !'
3, 443ᵇ. ' *her* Meige !' Walth. 46, 30). May makes his entry :
' sô der Meige *in gât*,' Meist. Alex. 144ᵇ. ' sô der vil süeze
Meige *in gât*,' Trist. 537. ' Meige ist komen in diu lant,' Ms. 1,

---

[1] Alse die *Somer* quam int lant, Reinaert 2451. alse de *Sommer* quême iut
lant, Reineke 2311. dô here de *Summer* trat, Wiggert 2, 48.
[2] Without article, therefore not com. noun; conf. p. 704 note, Solaus.

13^b. Ben. 364. 'der Meie sîn *ingesinde* hât,' has his retinue 1,
14^b. 'des Meien *tür* ist *ûf getân*, MsH. 3, 296^a. 'der Mei ist in
den landen hie' 3, 230^a. 'sô der Meie sînen *krâme* schouwen
lât (his store displays), unde *in gât* mit vil manigem liehten
mâle' 30, 30^b. 'vil manager hande varwe (full many a hue)
hât in sînem *krâme* der Meige,' MS. 1, 59^a. 'der Meie hât
brieve für gesant, daz sie künden in diu lant sîne kunft den
vruoten,' Ben. 433; like a king who after a long absence
returns victorious, he sends letters on before, to announce his
coming. 'da ist der Meie und al sîn kraft, er und sîn geselle-
schaft diu (sic l.) ringent manige swære (lighten many a
burden); Meie hât im angesiget' overcome him (winter), Ben.
449. 'ich lobe dich, *Meie*, dîner kraft, du tuost *Sumer* sigehaft,'
thou makest S. victorious (both prop. n.), MS. 2, 57^a. 'ob der
Meige ze velde lac,' Ls. 1, 199. 'sô der Meige alrêrst *in gât*.'
Frauend. 14. 'der Mei hât sîn *gezelt* bestelt,' set up his tents,
camp, MsH. 3, 303^b. 'des Meien *schilt*,' 3, 307^a. 'Sumer der
hât sîn *gezelt* nu gerihtet überal,' Ms. 2, 57^a. 'des Meien
waldenære kündet an die sumerzît,' May's forester announces
summertide, MsH. 3, 230^b. 'die (waldes ougenweide, forest's
eye-feast) hât der Meie für gesant, daz si künden in diu lant sîn
kunft' 3, 227^b. 'der Meie vüeret den walt *an siner hende*,' leads
the wood by the hand, MS. 2, 81^b; he is provided with hands
(like Wish, p. 142). Men worship him with thanks and bowing,
like a king or god making his progress (p. 213, Freyr); like
them he has his *strete* (highway): 'des Meigen *strâze*,' Ben. 42.
'ûf des Meien *strâzen*,' MS. 23^a. 'Meie, ich wil dir *nîgen*,' bow
to, Ben. 398. '*êrent* den Meien,' Ben. 184. MsH. 1, 147^{a. b}.
'der Meie habe des *danc* !' thanks thereof,[1] Ben. 434. May and
Summer put on their *verdant attire*: 'der Meie ist ûf sîn *grüenez
zwî* gesezzen,' MS. 2, 75^a. May hears complaints, he commands
his flowers, 1, 3^b. 'des Meigen vriunt (attendant), der grüene
wase (sward), der het ûz bluomen angeleit (laid on) sô wüneclîche
sumerkleit,' Trist. 562. 'der Sumer sneit sîn kleit,' Ben. 159.
'der Meie sendet dem walde kleider' 436. 'der *Sumer* gab diu

---

[1] In Gramm. 4, 725 is a coll. of the oft-recurring phrases 'des Meigen *êre*
(honour), d. M. *güete*, des Sumers *güete* (goodness),' which seem to imply an ancient
worship (p. 29, êra). I add a few more references: MsH. 1, 52^a. 60^a. 61^a. 194^a.
305^a. 348^b. 3, 222^b. Notice: 'Got gebe daz der *herbest* sîn *êre* volbringe !' that
autumn his worship fulfil, MS. 2, 180^a.

selben kleit, *Abrelle* maz, der *Meie* sneit,' April measured, May cut out, MS. 2, 94ᵇ. 'diu (kleider) het gegeben in (to them) der Meie z'einer niuwen wât (weeds, clothing),' MsH. 3, 286ᵇ. 'Mei hât enprozzen berg und tal' 3, 188ᵇ. 'Sumer hât gesendet ûz sîn wunne, der Meie spreit ûf diu lant sîn wât' (2, 291).[1] 'der blüenden *heide voget* (heath's controller) ist mit gewalt ûf uns gezoget (has rushed), hœrt wi er mit winde broget (blusters) ûf walt und im gevilde,' MsH. 1, 193ᵃ (see Suppl.).

But more especially does the antithesis demand attention. In *Winter's* train come *Rime* and *Snow*, still personifications, and giants from of old (p. 532). They declare war against Summer: 'dir hât widerseit beidiu *Rîf* and *Snê*,' Ben. 398. 'der Meie lôste bluomen ûz *Rîfen bande*' 437. 'manegen tac stark in sînen *banden* lac diu heide (the heath lay fast in Winter's bonds); uns was verirt der *wunne hirt* von des argen Winter's nît,' long did we miss our shepherd of bliss by wicked W.'s envy, MsH. 1, 192ᵃ. 'der W. und *sîne knechte* (his men), daz ist der *Rîfe* und der *Wind*,' Hartm. erst. büchl. 834. MsH. 3, 232ᵃ. What Summer clothed, Winter strips bare: '*über diu ôren*[2] er dem *wald* sîn kleider brach,' tore the wood's clothes over his ears (ibid.). 'dâ daz niuwe loup (leafage) ê was entsprungen, des hâstu nu *gevüllet dînen sac*' 2, 386ᵇ; like an enemy or robber, he fills his sack with booty (saccage). 'bluomen unde loup was des *Rîfen* êrster roup (first plunder), den er *in die secke schoup* (shoved into his sacks), er enspielt in noch enkloup,' Ben. 304. Yet, 'sunder *Rîfen* danc, allez grüenez in fröiden lît,' no thanks to Jack Frost, all green things are in glee, MS. 1, 34ᵇ. 'unbesungen ist der walt, daz ist allez von des *Rîfen* ungenâden (illwill) komen,' Ben. 275. Wizlau in one song exclaims: '*Winder*, dich vorhôte (take heed)! der *Sumer* komt ze môte,' to meet thee, Amgb. 29ᵃ; and Walther 39, 9: 'weizgot, er lât ouch dem Meien den strît,' Winter gives up the battle; conversely, 'der *Sumer* sînen strît dem *Winder* lât,' Warnung 2386. And, what is more than all, one poem[3] has preserved even the mythic name

---

[1] So that 'des Meigen *wât, kleit*' MS. 2, 105-6-7 is a metaphor for foliage, and 'boten (messengers) des Sumeres' 1, 97ᵇ for flowers.

[2] 'Walt hât ôren, velt hât gesiht,' wood has ears, field has sight, MS. 2, 131ᵃ; 'velt hât ôren, walt hât ougen,' eyes, 135ᵇ.

[3] Nîthart's, Ben. 384. To this poet we owe the liveliest images of Summer and Winter.

of the Rime-giant: it is *Aucholf*, formed just with the suffix *-olf*, which like *-olt* is characteristic of monstrous ghostly beings;[1] the root áuka, OHG. ouhhu, means augeo, so that Oucholf may contain the notion of enormous, gigantic[2] (see Suppl.).

Summer and *Winter* are at war with one another, exactly like Day and Night (p. 752); Day and Summer gladden, as Night and Winter vex the world.[3]

Now the arrival of Summer, of May, or as we now say, of Spring, was kept as a holiday from of old. In the Mid. Ages this was called *die zît empfâhen*, welcoming the season, MS. 1, 200ª. 2, 78ᵇ. Ben. 453; *die zît mit sange begên* (keep), Misc. 2, 198; den Sumer *empfâhen*, MsH. 3, 207ª. 211ª. 232ª. 'Sumer, wis (be) *empfangen* von mir hundert tûsent stunt (times)!' Ben. 328. 'vrouwen und man *empfiengen* den Meien,' MsH. 3, 185ᵇ. 'dâ wart der Mei *empfangen* wol' 3, 218ᵇ. 219ª. 'den Meigen *enpfâhen* und tanzen' 1, 47ᵇ. 'nû wolûf *grüezen* (greet) wir den süezen!' 1, 60ᵇ. 'ich wil den Sumer *grüezen*' 3, 446ᵇ. 'helfent *grüezen* mir den Meien,' MS. 1, 202ᵇ. 'si (diu vogellîn, small fowl) wellent alle *grüezen* nû den Meien' 2, 84ᵇ. '*willekome* her Meige!' 1, 57ᵇ. 'sît *willekome* her Meie!' 1, 59ª. 'sô *wol dir*, lieber Sumer, daz dû komen bist!' MsH. 2, 316ᵇ. A song in Eschenburg's Denkm. 458 has the burden 'willkommen Maie!' (see Suppl.).

But the coming in of Summer did not happen on any fixed day of the year, it was determined by accidental signs, the opening of flowers, the arrival of birds. This was called finding Summer: 'ich hân *den Sumer vunden*,' MsH. 3, 202ᵇ.

Whoever had spied 'den *êrsten viol*'[4] made it known; the whole village ran to the spot, the peasants stuck the flower on a pole, and danced around it. On this subject also Nîthart has some spirited songs, MsH. 3, 298-9; conf. 202ª (den êrsten vîol

---

[1] Gramm. 2, 334—40; conf. Nahtolf, Biterolf, Egisgrîmolt (p. 238), Fasolt (p. 529), Mîmerolt (p. 379), Kobolt (p. 414).

[2] A MHG. poet paints the battle between May and Autumn, in a pretty story (Fragm. 29), but it does not come within the mythic province, conf. MS. 2, 105. More to the point is H. Sachs's poem 1, 420-1. A M. Nethl. 'spel van den winter ende sommer' is printed in Hoffm. hor. belg. 6, 125—146. Notker in Cap. 27 calls 'herbest unde lenzo, zwêne genôza,' fellows twain.

[3] The Fris. Laws too couple night with winter: 'si illa tenebrosa nebula et frigidissima hiems in hortos et sepes descendit,' Richth. 46 (huersâ thiu thiustera nacht and thi nêdkalda winter ur tha tûner hleth).

[4] Florum prima ver nuntiantium viola alba, Pliny 21, 11 (38).

schonwen). H. Sachs iv. 3, 49 seq. describes the same festival; round the *first summer flower* they dance and sing. ' den *ersten bluomen vlehten*,' MS. 1, 41ᵇ (see Suppl.).

That the *first cockchafer* also was fetched in with ceremonies, we saw on p. 693-4; to this day the passion for hunting these chafers and playing with them is indestructibly rooted among boys.

In like manner the *first swallow*, the *first stork* was hailed as *messenger of spring* (ἄγγελος ἔαρος). The swallow's return was celebrated even by the Greeks and Romans: Athenaeus 8, 15 p. 360 gives a χελιδόνισμα,[1] chanted by children at Rhodes, who carried a *swallow* about and collected eatables. The custom still survives in Greece; the young people assemble on March 1, and traverse all the streets, singing a sweet spring-song; the singers carry a *swallow carved out of wood*, which stands on a cylinder, and keeps turning round.[2] ' *Hirundine prima*,' says Horace Epist. i..7, 13. That in Germany also the *first swallow* was taken notice of in the Mid. Ages, is shewn by the superstitious observance (Sup. G, and I, 217) of digging a coal out of the ground on her appearance. In Sweden the country folk welcome her with a thrice repeated shout of joy (Westerdahl p. 55). Both swallow and stork are accounted sacred inviolable creatures. He that first announced the return of the stork to the Greeks, received messenger's pay. As late as last century the warders of many German towns were required to blow-in the approaching *herald of spring*,[3] and a drink of honour was served out to them from the town-cellar. An epigram by Joach. Olearius begins :

> Ver laetum rediit, rediitque *ciconia grata*,
> aspera dum pulso frigore cessat hiems.[4]

The cuckoo may also be regarded as the announcer of spring, and an O.Engl. song appeals to him : ' sumer is icumen in, *lhude sing cucu !* ' Hone's Daybook 1, 739 (see Suppl.).

The *proclaiming of summer* by songs of the younger folk still

---

[1] Ilgen. opusc. philol. 1, 165. Zell's Ferienschr. 1, 53. 88. Schneidewin's Delectus 2, 465-6.
[2] Fauriel 2, 256. Disc. prélim. xxviii. More fully in Theod. Kind p. 12.
[3] Alpenrosen (Bern 1817) p. 49 ; conf. Hebel's song Der storch.
[4] Rostock 1610 ; conf. Joh. Praetorius's ' Storchs und schwalben-winterquartier,' Francf. 1676, p. 185.

prevails, or did prevail in recent centuries, almost everywhere in
German and Slav countries, and bespeaks a very ancient origin.
What the minnesingers, with their elegant phrases about the old
'chair, entry, highway, grace and glory of Summer' as a king
or god, may have led us to guess, is supplemented and illustrated by abiding customs of the people, which in rude artless
fashion drive at the main point. The modes of celebration and
the songs vary greatly.[1] Often there is only a wreath, a doll, an
animal carried about in a basket, and gifts demanded from house
to house.[2] Here it is a *cock*, there a *crow* or a *fox*,[3] that the
children take round, as in Poland at the time of coleda (new-
year) they go about with a stuffed *wolf*, collecting gifts (Linde
sub v. koleda). These animals do not migrate, and I leave it
undetermined, what right they can have to represent the stork
or swallow, or whether they mean something altogether different.
The approach of Summer is only mentioned in a few words and
phrases, or not at all.

In many places however the collecting of gifts is only the
sequel to a previous performance full of meaning, in which youths
and maidens take part. Two disguised as *Summer* and *Winter*
make their appearance, the one clothed with *ivy* or *singrün*, the
other with *straw* or *moss*, and they fight one another till *Summer
wins*. Winter is thrown on the ground, his wrappages stripped
off and scattered, and a summer's wreath or branch is carried
about. Here we have once more the ancient idea of a quarrel or
war between the two powers of the year, in which *Summer* comes
off victorious, and *Winter* is defeated; the people supply, as it
were, the chorus of spectators, and break out into praises of the
conqueror.

[1] The most diligent collector of them, though in a scattered disorderly way, is
Chr. Heinr. Schmid of Giessen, both in the 'Journal von und für D.' for 1787. 1,
186-98. 480-5; for 1788. 1, 566-71. 2, 409-11; for 1790. 1, 310-4; for 1791. 1002;
and in the 'Deutsche monatschrift' for 1798. 2, 58-67; he gives references to a
great many authors old and new. A still earlier article in 'Journal v. u. f. D.' for
1784. 1, 282 is worth consulting. Isolated facts in Krünitz's Encyclop. 58, 681
seq., Gräter's Idunna 1812 p. 41, Büsching's Wöch. nachr. 1, 183-6. 3, 166 and
other places to be cited as they are wanted. The two earliest treatises are by Paul
Chr. Hilscher ' de ritu Dominicae Laetare, quem vulgo appellant den tod austreiben,'
Lips. 1690 (in Germ. 1710), and Joh. Casp. Zeumer 'de Dominica Laetare,' Jena
1706.

[2] Let the *summer-children sell you a summer*, and your cows will give plenty
of milk, Sup. I, 1097.

[3] Reinhart, Introd. p. ccxix. Athen. also, ubi supra, speaks of a *crow* being
carried about, instead of the swallow.

The custom just described belongs chiefly to districts on the middle Rhine, beyond it in the Palatinate, this side of it in the Odenwald betwixt Main and Neckar. Of the songs that are sung I give merely the passages in point:

Trarira! der *Sommer* der *ist da;*
wir wollen hinaus in garten
und wollen des *Sommers warten* (attend).
wir wollen hinter die hecken (behind the hedges)
und wollen den *Sommer wecken* (wake).
der *Winter hats verloren* (has lost),
der *Winter liegt gefangen* (lies a prisoner);
und wer nicht dazu kommt (who won't agree),
den-schlagen wir mit stangen (we'll beat with staves).

Elsewhere : Jajaja! der *Sommertag* [1] ist da,
er *kratzt dem Winter die augen aus* (scratch W.'s eyes out),
und jagt die bauern zur stube hinaus (drive the boors out of doors).

Or : Stab aus! [2] dem *Winter gehn die augen aus* (W.'s eyes come out);
veilchen, rosenblumen (violets and roses),
holen wir den Sommer (we fetch),
schicken den *Winter über 'n Rhein* (send W. over Rhine),
bringt uns guten kühlen wein.

Also: *Violen* und die *blumen*
bringen uns den *Sommer,*
der *Sommer* ist so keck (cheeky, bold),
und *wirft den Winter in den dreck* (flings W. in the dirt).

Or : Stab aus, stab aus,
blas dem Winter die augen aus (blow W.'s eyes out)!

Songs like this must have come down through many centuries; and what I have quoted above from poets of the 13th cent. pre-

---

[1] For Sommer? conf. Bældæg for Bealdor, p. 222-9, and Day, p. 788.
[2] Also 'stam aus' or 'sta maus,' and 'heib aus, treib aus, dem W. ist ein aug' aus.' Stabaus may be for *staubaus* = up and away, Schm. 3, 602; conf. Zingerle 2, 147.

supposes their existence, or that of songs substantially the same. The conception and setting of the whole are quite heathenish : valiant Summer found, fetched, wakened from his sleep; vanquished Winter rolled in the dust, thrown into chains, beaten with staves, blinded, banished; these are demigods or giants of antiquity. *Violets* are mentioned with evident reference to the welcoming of Summer. In some parts the children march out with *white peeled rods*, either for the purpose of helping Summer to belabour the foe, or perhaps to represent the retinue of Winter, for it was the old custom for the conquered and captive to be let go, carrying white staves (RA. 134). One of the band of boys, marching at their head *wrapt in straw*, stands for Winter, another *decked with ivy* for Summer. First the two fence with their poles, presently they close and wrestle, till Winter is thrown and his *straw garment stript off* him. During the duel, the rest keep singing :

> stab aus, stab aus,
> *stecht dem Winter die augen aus !*

This is completely the 'rauba birahanen, hrusti giwinnan, caesos spoliare armis' of the heroic age; the barbarous punching out of eyes goes back to a still remoter antiquity.[1] The *wakening* of Summer is like the wakening of Sælde.

In some places, when the fight is over, and Winter put to flight, they sing :

> So *treiben* wir den *Winter aus*
> durch unsre stadt zum thor hinaus (out at the gate) ;

here and there the whole action is compressed into the shout : ' *Sommer* 'rein (come in), *Winter* 'naus (go out) ! '

As we come back through the Odenwald toward inner Franconia, the Spessart and the Rhön Mts, the words begin to change, and run as follows :

> Stab aus, stab aus,
> stecht dem *Tod* (death) die augen aus !

---

[1] The MHG. songs keep pace : ' der Meie hât sînen *schaft* ûf den Winter verstochen,' dug his shaft into, MsH. 3, 195ᵇ. ' Mai hat den W. *erslagen*', slain, Hätzl. 131, 58. ' *vehten* wil der W. kalt gegen dem lieben Sumer,' MsH. 3, 423ᵃ.

Then :   Wir haben den *Tod* hinausgetrieben (driven out),
        den lieben *Sommer* bringen wir wieder (again),
        den Sommer und den *Meien*
        mit blümlein mancherleien (of many a sort).

So *Death* has stept into *Winter's* place; we might say, because
in winter nature slumbers and seems dead; but it may also be,
that at an early time some heathenish name for Winter had to
give place to the christian conception of Death.

When we get to the heart of Franconia, e.g. Nürnberg, the
songs drop all mention of Summer, and dwell the more emphatically on the *expulsion of Death*.[1] There country lasses of
seventeen or eighteen, arrayed in all their finery, parade the
streets of the whole town and suburbs; on or under their left
arm they carry a little open coffin, with a shroud hanging over
the sides, and a *puppet* lying under that. Poor children carry
nothing but an open box, in which lies a green bough of beech
with a stalk sticking up, on which an *apple* is fixed instead of
the head. Their monotone song begins : ' To-day is Midlent,
we *bear Death into the water*, and that is well.' Amongst other
things :

> *Wir tragen den Tod in's wasser,*
>   tragen ihn 'nein, und *wieder 'raus*[2] (in, and out again),

---

[1] Seb. Frank's Weltbuch 51ᵃ thus describes the Shrovetide custom in Franconia : ' Four of them hold a sheet by his 4 corners, whereon is laid a *straw
puppet* in hose, jerkin and mask, like a *dead man*, the which they *toss up by the
4 corners*, and catch him again in the sheet. This they do the whole town through.
At Midlent they make in some places a *straw man* or *imp*, arrayed as a *death*, him
the assembled youth *bear into the nigh lying villages*. And by some they be well
received, eased and fed with dried pears, milk and peas ; by others, which hold it
a presage of coming death, evil entreated and driven from their homesteads with
foul words and oftentimes with buffets.'

[2] This seems to indicate, that the deity of Death is not to be annihilated by
the ducking, but only made sensible of the people's *dissatisfaction*. Cruel Death
has during the year snatched many a victim, and men wish, as it were, to be
revenged on him. This is of a piece with the idea brought out on p. 20 : when
a god has not answered your expectations, you bully him, you plunge his image
into water. So by the Franconians, on a failure of the wine-crop, St. Urban's
image, who had neglected to procure them wine (Fischart's Garg. 11) was *flung into
the brook*, or *the mud* (Seb. Frank 51ᵇ), or *the water-trough*, even in the mere anticipation of a poor vintage (Agricola's Sprichw. 498. Gräter's Idunna 1812, p. 87).
So the Bavarians, during St. Leonhard's solemn procession, would occasionally
drop him *in the river* (Schm. 2, 473). We know how the Naples people to this day
go to work with their San Gennaro, how seamen in a storm ill-use St. James's
image, not to speak of other instances.

tragen ihn vor des biedermanns haus (up to the goodman's
house).

Wollt ihr uns kein schmalz nicht geben (won't give us no
lard),

lassen wir euch den *Tod* nicht sehen (won't let you see D.).

Der *Tod* der *hat ein panzer an* (wears a coat of mail).

Similar customs and songs prevailed all over Franconia, and in
Thuringia, Meissen, Vogtland, Lausitz and Silesia. The beginning of the song varies :

Nun treiben wir den *Tod* aus [1] (drive D. out),

den *alten weibern* in das haus (into the old women's house).

Or : hinter's alte hirtenhaus [2] (behind the old shepherd's house).
Further on :

hätten wir den *Tod* nicht ausgetrieben (not driven D. out),

wär er das jahr noch inne geblieben [3] (he'd have staid all the
year).

Usually a *puppet*, a figure of *straw* or *wood*, was carried about,
and thrown *into water*, into a *bog*, or else *burnt;* if the figure
was female, it was carried by a boy, if male, by a girl. They
disputed as to where it should be made and tied together ; whatever house it was brought out of, there nobody died that year.
Those who had thrown Death away, fled in haste, lest he should
start up and give them chase; if they met cattle on their way
home, they beat them with staves, believing that that would
make them fruitful. In Silesia they often dragged about a bare
fir-tree with chains of straw, as though it were a prisoner. Here
and there a strong man, in the midst of children, carried a *may-*

---

[1] Luther parodied this song in his Driving of the Pope out, Journ. von u. für
D. 1787. 2, 192-8.

[2] 'Dem alten *Juden* in seinen bauch, etc.', into the old Jew's belly, on to the
young Jew's back, the worse for him ; over hill and dale, so he may never come
back ; over the heath, to spite the shepherds ; we went through the greenwood,
there sang birds young and old. Finn Magnusen (Edda 2, 185) would have us take
the old 'Juden' for a *iötunn.*

[3] J. F. Herrl, on certain antiquities found in the Erfurt country 1787, p. 28,
has the line : 'wir tragen den *Krodo* in's wasser,' but confesses afterwards (Journ.
v. u. f. D. 1787. 483-4) that he dragged the dubious name into the text on pure conjecture. The more suspicious becomes the following strophe in Hellbach's Suppl.
to the Archiv v. u. f. Schwarzburg, Hildburgh. 1789. p. 52 : 'wir tragen den alten
thor (fool) hinaus, hinter's alte hirtenhaus, wir haben nun den sommer gewonnen,
und *Krodes* macht ist weggekommen,' K'.s power is at an end. The expressions
in the last line smack of recent invention.

pole.[1] In the Altmark, the Wendish villages about Salzwedel, especially Seeben (where we saw Hennil still in use, p. 749), have preserved the following custom: at Whitsuntide men-servants and maids tie *fir-branches*, *straw* and *hay* into a large *figure*, giving it as much as possible a human shape. Profusely garlanded with field-flowers, the image is fastened, sitting up-right, on the brindled cow (of which more hereafter), and lastly a pipe cut out of alder wood stuck in its mouth. So they conduct it into the village, where all the houses are barred and bolted, and every one chases the cow out of his yard, till the figure falls off, or goes to pieces (Ad. Kuhn's Märk. sagen, p. 316-7).

From Switzerland, Tobler 425-6 gives us a popular play in rhymes, which betray a Swabian origin, and contain a song of battle between Summer and Winter. Summer is acted by a man in his bare shirt, holding in one hand a tree decorated with ribbons and fruit, in the other a cudgel with the end much split. *Winter* is warmly clad, but has a similar cudgel; they lay on to one another's shoulders with loud thwacks, each renowning him-self and running down his neighbour. At length Winter falls back, and owns himself beaten. Schm. 3, 248 tells of the like combat in Bavaria: *Winter* is wrapt in fur, *Summer* carries a green bough in his hand, and the strife ends with Summer thrusting Winter out of doors. I do not find the custom reported of Austria proper; it seems to be known in Styria and the adjoining mountains of Carinthia: the young fellows divide into two bands, one equipt with winter clothes and snowballs, the other with green summer hats, forks and scythes. After fighting a while in front of the houses, they end with singing jointly the praises of victorious Summer.[2] It takes place in March or at St. Mary's Candlemas (see Suppl.).

Some of the districts named have within the last hundred years discontinued this old festival of announcing Summer by the defeat of Winter, others retain it to this day. Bygone centuries may well have seen it in other German regions, where it has not left even a historical trace; there may however be some

---

[1] At Leipzig in the 17th cent. the festival had become so discredited, that they had the straw puppet carried about and immersed by women of ill fame.

[2] Sartori's Neueste Reise d. Oestr., Vienna 1811. 2, 848. The Styrian battle-song is printed in Büsching's Wöch. nachr. 1, 226-8.

accounts that have escaped my notice. In S. Germany, Swabia, Switzerland, Bavaria, Austria, Styria, the ditties are longer and more formal, but the ceremony itself not so artless and racy. In Lower Hesse, Lower Saxony, Westphalia, Friesland, and the Netherlands, that is to say, where Easter-fires remained in vogue, I can hardly anywhere detect this annunciation of Summer; in lieu of it we shall find in N. Germany a far more imposing development of May-riding and the Maigraf feast. Whether the announcing of Summer extended beyond the Palatinate into Treves, Lorraine, and so into France, I cannot say for certain.[1] Clearly it was not Protestant or Catholic religion that determined the longer duration or speedier extinction of the custom. It is rather striking that it should be rifest just in Middle Germany, and lean on Slav countries behind, which likewise do it homage; but that is no reason for concluding that it is of Slav origin, or that Slavs could have imported it up to and beyond the Rhine. We must first consider more closely these Slav customs.

In Bohemia, children march, with a *straw man* representing Death, to the end of the village, and there burn him while they sing:

Giž nesem *Smrt* ze wsy,	Now bear we D. from the village,
nowe *Lèto* do wsy;	new Summer to the village;
witey *Lèto* libèzne,	welcome Summer sweet,
obiljóko zelene!	little grain so green.

---

[1] C. H. Schmid has indeed drawn up (Journ. v. u. f. D. 1790, 814-5) a list of the lands and spots where Winter or Death is carried out, and it includes parts of L. Saxony, Mecklenburg, even Friesland. But no authorities are given; and other customs, similar, but without any of the distinctive features of the subject in hand, are mixed up with it. Aug. Pfeiffer (b. Lauenstein 1640, d. Lübeck '98) in Evang. Erquickungstunden, Leipz. 1698 mentions a 'battle of Sum. and Win.', but names no places, and he had lived long in Silesia and Leipzig. H. Lubbert (preacher at Bohlendorf by Lübeck, b. 1640, d. 1703) in his Fastnachtsteufel p. 6 describes a March (not May) procession, but does not sufficiently bring out the essential features. I extract the passage (from J. P. Schmidt's Fastelab. p. 132), because it illustrates the far from ineffectual zeal of the clergy against popular amusements, almost as strikingly as the diatribe, 560 years older, quoted on pp. 259 seq.: 'The last year, on Dominica Quinquag. (4 weeks bef. Laetare), I again publicly prayed every man to put away, once for all, these pagan doings. Alas, I was doomed to see the wicked worldlings do it worse than before. Not alone did *children carrying long sticks wrapt in green leaves* go about within doors, and sing all manner of lewd jests, but specially the *men-servants*, one of them having a *green petticoat tied about him*, went *in two parties* through the village from house to house with a bag-pipe, singing, swilling, rioting like madmen in the houses; afterward they joined together, drank, danced, and kept such pother several nights through, that one scarce could sleep for it. At the said ungodly night-dances were even some lightminded maids, that took part in the accursed business.'

Elsewhere:

Smrt plyne po wodĕ,	D. floats down the water,
nowe *Lèto* k nám gede.[1]	new Summer to us rides.

Or:

Smrt gsme wám zanesly,	D. we've from you taken,
nowe *Lèto* přinesly.	new Summer to you brought.

In Moravia:

Nesem, nesem *Mařenu.*	We bear, we bear Marena.

Other Slavs:

Wyneseme, wyneseme *Ma-*	
muriendu.	Remove we Mamurienda.

Or:

wynesli sme *Murienu* se wsi,	we've taken Muriena out, and
přinesli sme *May nowy* do wsi.[2]	brought new May to the town.

At Bielsk in Podlachia, on Dead Sunday they carry an *idol of plaited hemp* or *straw* through the town, then drown it in a marsh or pond outside, singing to a mournful strain:

Smierć wieie się po plotu,	D. blows through the wattle,
szukaiąc klopotu.	seeking the whirlpool.

They run home as fast as they can : if any one falls down, he dies within the year.[3] The Sorbs in Upper Lausitz make the figure *of straw* and *rags;* she who had the last corpse must supply the shirt, and the latest bride the veil and all the rags ;[4] the scarecrow is stuck on a long pole, and carried away by the biggest strongest lass at the top of her speed, while the rest sing:

Lecž hore, lecž hore!	Fly high, fly high,
jatabate woko,	twist thyself round,
pan dele, pan dele !	fall down, fall down.

---

[1] Celakowsky's Slowanské narodni pisnĕ, Prague 1822. p. 209. He quotes other rhymes as well.

[2] J. Kollár's Zpiewanky 1, 4. 400.

[3] Hanusch Slav. myth. 413. Jungmann sub v. Marana, who puts the Polish rhyme into Bohem. thus: Smrt wĕge po plotu, šukagjc klopotu. Conf. a Morav. song (Kulda in d'Elv 107-8-9).

[4] Indicul. superst. 27-8 : ' de *simulacris de pannis factis,* quae per campos portant.' The Esthonians on New year's day make an idol of straw in the shape of a man, to which they concede the name of *metziko* and the power of protecting their cattle from wild beasts and defending their frontier. All the people of the village accompany, and set him on the nearest tree, Thom. Hiärn, p. 40.

They all throw sticks and stones at it: whoèver hits Death will not die that year. So the figure is borne out of the village to a piece of water, and drowned in it. But they often carry Death to the *boundary* of the next village, and *pitch him over it;* each picks for himself a green twig, and carries it homeward in high glee, but on arriving at his village throws it away again. Sometimes the youth of the village within whose bounds they have brought Death will run after them, and *throw him back,* for no one likes to keep him; and they easily come to words and blows about it.[1] At other places in Lausitz women alone take part in this Driving-out of Death, and suffer no men to meddle. They all go in black veils that day, and having tied up a *puppet of straw,* put a white shirt on it, and give it a broom in one hand, and a scythe in the other. This puppet they carry singing, and pursued by boys throwing stones, to the *border* of the next town, where they *tear it up.* Then they hew down a handsome *tree* in the wood, hang the shirt upon it, and carry it home with songs.[2] This tree is undoubtedly a symbol of Summer introduced in the place of Death driven out. Such decorated trees are also carried about the village by boys collecting gifts, after they have rid themselves of Death. In other cases they demand the contributions while taking the puppet round. Here and there they make the straw man *peep into* people's *windows* (as Berhta looks in at the window, p. 274): in that case Death will carry off some one in the house that year, but by paying a money ransom in time, you can avert the omen. At Königshain by Görlitz the whole village, young and old, wended their way with torches of straw to a neighbouring height called the Todtenstein, where formerly a god's image is said to have stood; they lit their torches on the top, and turned home singing, with constant repetition of the words: 'we have driven out Death, we bring back Summer.' [3]

So it is not everywhere that the banished idol represented Winter or Death in the abstract; in some cases it is still the *heathen divinity* giving way to Christianity, whom the people thrust out half in sorrow, and uttering songs of sadness.

[1] Lausitz. Mag. for 1770, p. 84-5, from a MS. of Abraham Frencel.
[2] Chr. Arnold's Append. to Alex. Rossen's Unterschiedn. gottesdienst, Heidelb. 1674. p. 185.
[3] Anton's first Versuch über die alten Slaven, p. 78-4.

Dlugosz,[1] and others after him, report that by order of king Miecislaus all the idols in the land were broken up and burnt; in remembrance of which the people in some parts of Poland, once a year, singing mournful songs, conduct in solemn procession *images of Marzana and Ziewonia,* fixed on poles or drawn on drags, to a *marsh or river,* and there *drown* them;[2] paying them so to speak, their last homage. Dlugosz's explanation of *Marzana* as 'harvest-goddess' seems erroneous; Frencel's and Schaffarik's 'death-goddess' is more acceptable : I derive the name from the Pol. marznąć, Boh. mrznauti, Russ. merznut', to freeze, and in opposition to her as winter-goddess I set the summer-goddess *Wiosna,* Boh. *Wesna.* The Königenhof MS. p. 72 has a remarkable declaration : 'i iedinu družu nám imiét' po puti z *Wesny* po *Moranu,'* one wife (only) may we have on our way from Wesna to Morana, from spring to winter, i.e. ever. Yet the throwing or dipping of the divine image in a stream need not have been done by the Christians in mere contempt, it may have formed a part of the pagan rite itself ; for an antithesis between summer and winter, and an exalting of the former, necessarily implied a lowering of the latter.[3]

The day for carrying Death out was the quarta dominica quadragesimae, i.e. *Laetare Sunday* or *Midlent,* on which very day it also falls in Poland (w niezielę środopostną), Bohemia, Silesia and Lausitz. The Bohemians call it *smrtedlna,* samrtná nedĕle, the Sorbs *smerdnitsa,* death Sunday ; coming three weeks before Easter, it will almost always occur in March. Some have it a week earlier, on Oculi Sunday, others (espec. in Bohemia) a week later, on Judica Sunday ; one Boh. song even brings in ' Mag nowy,' new May. But in the Rhine and Main country, as

---

[1] Hist. Polon. lib. 2, ad a. 965. Matth. de Mechovia chron. Polon. ii. 1, 22. Mart. Cromer lib. 3, ad a. 965. Mart. Hanke de Silesior. nominibus, p. 122-3.

[2] So the Russian Vladimir, after his conversion, orders the image of Perun to be tied to a horse's tail, beaten, and *thrown into the Dnieper.* Afterwards, when the Novgorod Perun was in like manner thrown *into the Volkhov,* he set up, while in the river, a loud lament over the people's ingratitude.

[3] The Indian Káli, on the 7th day after the March new-moon, was solemnly carried about, and then thrown into the Ganges ; on May 13 the Roman vestals bore *puppets plaited of rushes* to the Pons Sublicius, and dropt them in the Tiber, Ov. Fast. 5, 620:

Tum quoque priscorum virgo simulacra virorum
mittere roboreo scirpea ponte solet.

in most places, Laetare is the festive day, and is there called *Summerday*.

There is no getting over this unanimity as to the time of the festival. To the ancient Slavs, whose new year began in March, it marked the commencement of the year, and likewise of the summer half-year, i.e. of their lèto; to Germans the arrival of summer or spring, for in March their stork and swallow come home, and the first violet blows. But then the impersonal ' lèto ' of the Slavs fights no battle with their *Smrt :* this departing driven-out god has the play nearly all to himself. To our ancestors the contest between the two giants was the essential thing in the festival; vanquished *Winter* has indeed his parallel in *Smrt*, but with victorious *Summer* there is no living personality to compare. And, beside this considerable difference between the Slav ceremony and our own, as performed on the Rhine or Neckar, it is also difficult to conceive how a native Slav custom should have pushed itself all the way to the Odenwald and the Palatinate beyond Rhine, accountable as it might be on the upper Main, in the Fulda country, Meissen or Thuringia. What is still more decisive, we observe that the custom is known, not to all the Slavs, but just to those in Silesia, Lausitz, Bohemia and, with a marked difference, in Poland; not to the South Slavs at all, nor apparently to those settled in Pomerania, Mecklenburg and Lüneburg. Like our Bavarians and Tyrolese, the Carniolans, Styrians and Slovaks have it not; neither have the Pomeranians and Low Saxons.[1] Only a central belt of territory has preserved it, alike among Slavs and Germans, and doubtless from a like cause. I do not deny that in very early times it may have been common to *all* Slav and *all* Teutonic races, indeed for Germany I consider it scarcely doubtful, because for one thing the old songs of Nîthart and others are sufficient proof for Austria, and secondly because in Scandinavia, England, and here and there in N. Germany, appears the custom of *May-riding*, which is quite the same thing as the Rhenish ' summer-day ' in March.

Olaus Magnus 15, 4 says: ' The Swedes and Goths have a custom, that on the *first day of May* the magistrates in every

---

[1] The Holstein custom of going round (omgaan) with the fox, p. 764, took place in summer (says Schütze 8, 165), therefore not on Laetare; and the words they sing have no explicit reference to summer and winter.

'city make two troops of horse, of tall youths and men, to assemble, as tho' they would go forth to a mighty battle. One
troop hath a captain, that under the name of *Winter* is arrayed
in much *fur* and *wadded garments*, and is armed with a winter-
spear: he rideth arrogantly to and fro, showering snowballs and
iceflakes, as he would fain prolong the cold, and much he vaunteth
him in speech. The other troop hath contrariwise a captain, that
is named the *Blumengrave*, he is clad in *green boughs, leaves and
flowers*, and other summer raiment, and not right fencible; he
rides into town the same time with the winter-captain, yet each
in his several place and order, then hold a public tilting and
tourney, wherein *Summer* hath the mastery, bearing *Winter* to
the ground. Winter and his company scatter ashes and sparks
about them, the other fend them with birchen boughs and young
lime-twigs; finally, by the multitude around, the victory is
awarded to Summer.'

Here Death is not once alluded to; in true Teutonic fashion,
the whole business is made to lie between *Summer* and *Winter*;
only, the simple procession of our peasant-folk has turned more
into a chivalry pageant of opulent town-life. At the same time
this induction of May into the city ('hisset kommer Sivard
Snarensvend [p. 372n.], han *förer os sommer*,' or 'och *bär os
sommer i by*,' DV. 1, 14. Sv. forns. 1, 44. '*bära maj i by*,'
Dybeck runa 2, 67; in Schonen '*före somma i by*') cuts a neater
statelier figure than the miserable array of mendicant children,
and is in truth a highly poetic and impressive spectacle. These
Mayday sports are mentioned more than once in old Swedish
and Danish chronicles, town regulations and records. Lords
and kings not seldom took a part in them, they were a great
and general national entertainment. Crowned with flowers, the
majgrefve fared with a powerful escort over highway and thorp;
banquet and round-dance followed. In Denmark the jaunting
began on Walburgis day (May 1), and was called '*at ride Som-
uer i bye*,' riding S. into the land: the young men ride in front,
then the *May-grave* (floriger) with two garlands, one on each
shoulder, the rest with only one; songs are sung in the town,
all the maidens make a ring round the *may-grave*, who picks out
one of them to be his *majinde*, by dropping a wreath on her
head. Winter and his conflict with May are no longer mentioned

in the Schonish and Danish festival. Many towns had regularly organized *majgreve gilde*.[1] But as the May-fire in Denmark was called 'gadeild,' gate (street) fire, so was the leader of the May-feast a *gadebasse* (gate bear), and his maiden partner *gadelam* (gate lamb) or *gadinde*; gadebasse and gadinde therefore mean the same as maigreve and maigrevinde.[2] There is a remarkable description in Mundelstrup's Spec. gentilismi etiamnum superstitis, Hafn. 1684 : 'Qui ex junioribus rusticis contum stipulis accensis flammatum efficacius versus sidera tollere potuerit, praeses (gadebasse) incondito omnium clamore declaratur, nec non eodem tempore sua *cuique* ex rusticis puellis, quae tunc temporis vernacula appellantur *gadelam*, distribuitur, et quae *praesidi* adjicitur titulum hunc *gadinde* merebitur.[3] Hinc excipiunt convivia per universum illud temporis, quod inter arationem et foenisecium intercedit, quavis die dominica celebrari sueta, *gadelams-gilder* dicta, in quibus proceriorem circum arborem in antecessum humo immissam variisque corollis ac signis ornatam, corybantum more ad tympanorum stridentes sonitus bene poti saliunt.'

Now this *May-riding*, these *May-graves*, were an old tradition of Lower Germany also ; and that apparently is the very reason why the Mid-German custom of welcoming summer at Laetare was not in vogue there. How could spring, which does not reappear in the North till the beginning of May, have been celebrated there in March ? Besides, this May-festival may in early times have been more general in Germany ; or does the distinction reach back to the rivalry between March and May as the month of the folkmote ?[4] The *maigreve* at Greifswald, May 1, 1528, is incidentally mentioned by Sastrow in his Lebensbeschr. 1, 65-6 ; a license to the scholars at Pasewalk to hold a *maigraf*

[1] Ihre sub v. majgrefve. Skråordning for Knutsgillet i Lund an. 1586, § 123-7 in Bring's Monum. scânensia, p. 207-10 ; the same for Malmö, p. 211. Er. Tegel's Hist. Gustavi i. 1, 119. Nyerup's Danske digtek. 1, 246. 2, 136. 143. Thiele 1, 145-58 ; conf. 200. For the Zealand custom see Molbech's Hist. tidskrift 1840. 1, 203. The maigreves in Ribe are mentioned by Terpager in Ripae cimbricae, p. 723 ; the Aalburg maigreve in Wilda's Gildewesen p. 285, from a statute of the 15th century ; conf. Molb. dial. lex. p. 533.
[2] Molb. dial. lex. pp. 150-1-2, where doubt is thrown on the derivation of gade from ON. gata (gate, road). He has also a *midsommers-lam*, p. 359.
[3] The italics here are mine. Each man has a *gadelam*, but only the leader a *gadinde*.—TRANS.
[4] Conf. RA. 821-6 on the time of assizes.

jaunt, in a Church-visitation ordinance of 1563 (Baltische studien 6, 137) ; and more precise information has lately been collected on the survival of May-riding at Hildesheim, where the beautiful custom only died out in the 18th century.[1] Towards Whitsun-tide the maigreve was elected, and the forest commoners in the Ilse had to hew timber from seven villages to build the *May-waggon;* all loppings must be loaded thereon, and only four horses allowed to draw it in the forest. A grand expedition from the town fetches away the waggon, the burgomaster and council receive a *May-wreath* from the commoners, and hand it over to the maigreve. The waggon holds 60 or 70 bundles of may (birch), which are delivered to the maigreve to be further dis-tributed. Monasteries and churches get large bundles, every steeple is adorned with it, and the floor of the church strown with clippings of boxwood and field-flowers. The maigreve entertains the commoners, and is strictly bound to serve up a dish of crabs. But in all this we have only a fetching-in of the *May-waggon* from the wood under formal escort of the *May-grave;* not a word now about the battle he had to fight with winter. Is it conceivable that earlier ages should have done without this battle? Assuredly they had it, and it was only by degrees that custom left it out. By and by it became content with even less. In some parishes of Holstein they keep the commence-ment of May by crowning a young fellow and a girl with leaves and flowers, conducting them with music to a tavern, and there drinking and dancing ; the pair are called *maigrev* and *maigrön,* i.e. maigräfin (Schütze 3, 72). The Schleswig maygrave-feast (festum frondicomans) is described in Ulr. Petersen's treatise already quoted (p. 694 n.).[2] In Swabia the children at sunrise go into the wood, the boys carrying silk handkerchiefs on staves, the girls ribbons on boughs ; their leader, the *May-king,* has a right to choose his *queen.* In Gelders they used on Mayday-eve to set up trees decorated and hung with tapers like a Christmas-tree ; then came a song and ring-dance.[3] All over Germany, to this day,

---

[1] Koken and Lüntzel's Mittheilungen 2, 45–61.

[2] He says : 'the memory of this ancient but useless May-feast *finally passed by inheritance to the town-cattle,* which, even since 1670, had every Mayday a gar-land of beech-leaves thrown about the neck, and so bedizened were driven home ; for which service the cowherd could count upon his fee.'

[3] Geldersche Volksalmanak voor 1835, pp. 10–28. The song is given in Hoffm.

we have *may-bushes* brought into our houses at Whitsuntide : we do not fetch them in ourselves, nor go out to meet them.[1]

England too had *May-games* or *Mayings* down to the 16-17th century. On Mayday morning the lads and lasses set out soon after midnight, with horns and other music, to a neighbouring wood, broke boughs off the trees, and decked them out with wreaths and posies ; then turned homeward, and at sunrise set these May-bushes in the doors and windows of their houses. Above all, they brought with them a tall birch tree which had been cut down; it was named *maiepole, maipoll*, and was *drawn by 20 to 40 yoke of oxen*, each with a nosegay betwixt his horns ; this tree was set up in the village, and the people danced round it. The whole festival was presided over by a *lord of the May* elected for the purpose, and with him was associated a *lady of the May*.[2] In England also a *fight between Summer and Winter* was exhibited (Hone's Daybook 1, 359) ; the Maypole exactly answers to the May-waggon of L. Saxony, and the lord of the May to the May-grave.[3] And here and there a district in France too has undoubtedly similar May-sports. Champollion (Rech. sur les patois, p. 183) reports of the Isère Dept. : '*maïe*, fête que les enfans célèbrent aux premiers jours du mois de mai, en parant un d'entre eux et lui donnant le titre de *roi*.' A lawsuit on the 'jus eundi prima die mensis maji ad *majum colligendum* in nemora' is preserved in a record of 1262, Guérard cart. de N.D. 2, 117 (see Suppl.). In narrative poems of the Mid. Ages, both French and German, the grand occasions on which kings hold their court are Whitsuntide and the blooming Maytime, Rein. 41 seq. Iw. 33 seq., and Wolfram calls King Arthur ' der *meienbære* man,' Parz. 281, 16; conf. ' pfingestlîcher (pentecostal) küniges name,' MS. 2, 128ᵃ.

On the whole then, there are four different ways of welcoming

---

Horae belg. 2, 178–180. Conf. ' ic wil den mei gaen houwen voor mijns liefs vein-sterkyn,' go hew before my love's window, Uhland's Volksl. 178.

[1] Has the *May-drink* still made in the Lower Rhine and Westphalia, of wine and certain (sacred?) herbs, any connexion with an old sacrificial rite? On no account must woodroof (asperula) be omitted in preparing it.

[2] Fuller descript. in J. Strutt, ed. Lond. 1830, p. 351–6. Haupt's Zeitschr. 5, 477.

[3] The AS. poems have no passage turning on the battle of S. and W. In Beow. 2266 ' þâ wæs winter scacen' only means winter was past, ' el ibierno es exido,' Cid 1627.

Summer, that we have learnt to know. In Sweden and Gothland a battle of Winter and Summer, a triumphal entry of the latter. In Schonen, Denmark, L. Saxony and England simply May-riding, or fetching of the May-waggon. On the Rhine merely a battle of Winter and Summer, without immersion,[1] without the pomp of an entry. In Franconia, Thuringia, Meissen, Silesia and Bohemia only the carrying-out of wintry Death; no battle, no formal introduction of Summer.[2] Of these festivals the first and second fall in May, the third and fourth in March. In the first two, the whole population takes part with unabated enthusiasm; in the last two, only the lower poorer class. It is however the first and third modes that have retained the full idea of the performance, the struggle between the two powers of the year, whilst in the second and fourth the antithesis is wanting. The May-riding has no Winter in it, the farewell to Death no Summer; one is all joy, the other all sadness. But in all the first three modes, the higher being to whom honour is done is represented by living persons, in the fourth by a puppet, yet both the one and the other are fantastically dressed up.

Now we can take a look in one or two other directions.

On the battle between *Vetr* and *Sumar* ON. tradition is silent,[3] as on much else, that nevertheless lived on among the people. The oldest vestige known to me of a duel between the seasons amongst us is that ' Conflictus hiemis et veris' over the cuckoo (p. 675-6). The idea of a *Summer-god marching in*, bringing blessings, putting new life into everything, is quite in the spirit of our earliest ages: it is just how Nerthus comes *into the land* (p. 251) ; also Freyr (p. 213), Isis (p. 258), Hulda (p. 268), Berhta

---

[1] It was a different thing therefore when in olden times the Frankfort boys and girls, every year at Candlemas (Febr. 2), *threw a stuffed garment* into the *Main*, and sang : ' Reuker Uder schlug sein mutter, schlug ihr arm und bein entzwei, dass sie mordio schrei,' Lersner's Chron. p. 492. I leave the song unexplained.

[2] Yet Summer as a contrast does occasionally come out plainly in songs or customs of Bohemia and Lausitz.

[3] Finn Magnusen, always prone to see some natural phenomenon underlying a myth, finds the contrast of summer and winter lurking in more than one place in the Edda: in Fiöllsvinnsmål and Harbardsliod (th. 2, 135. 3, 44 of his Edda), in Saxo's Oller and Othin saga (th. 1, 196. Lex. 765), in that of Thiassi (Lex. 887), because Oðinn sets the eye of the slain giant in the sky (p.   ), and Winter is also to have his eyes punched out (p. 765) ; to me Uhland (Ueber Thor p. 117. 120) seems more profound, in regarding Thiassi as the storm-eagle, and kidnapped Iðunn as the green of summer (ingrün, so to speak) ; but the nature of this goddess remains a secret to us.

(p. 273), Fricg (p. 304), and other deities besides, whose car or ship an exulting people goes forth to meet, as they do the waggon of May, who, over and above mere personification, has from of old his *êre* and *strâze* (p. 670 n.): in heathen times he must have had an actual worship of his own. All these gods and goddesses appeared at their appointed times in the year, bestowing their several boons; deified *Summer* or *May* can fairly claim identity with one of the highest divinities to whom the gift of fertility belonged, with *Frô, Wuotan, Nerthus*. But if we admit goddesses, then, in addition to Nerthus, *Ostara* has the strongest claim to consideration. To what was said on p. 290 I can add some significant facts. The heathen Easter had much in common with the May-feast and the reception of spring, particularly in the matter of bonfires. Then, through long ages there seem to have lingered among the people *Easter-games* so-called, which the church itself had to tolerate: I allude especially to the custom of *Easter eggs*, and to the *Easter tale* which preachers told from the pulpit for the people's amusement, connecting it with Christian reminiscences. In the MHG. poets, 'mînes herzen *ôsterspil, ôstertac*,' my heart's Easter play or day, is a complimentary phrase for lady love, expressing the height of bliss (MS. 2, 52b. 37b. Iw. 8120. Frib. Trist. 804); Conr. Troj. 19802 makes the 'ôsterlîchen tac mit lebender wunne spiln' out of the fair one's eye. Later still, there were dramatic shows named *ôsterspile*, Wackern. lb. 1014, 30. One of the strongest proofs is the summer and dance song of lord Goeli, MS. 2, 57a (Haupt's Neidh. xxv): at the season when ea and eyot are grown green, Fridebolt and his companions enter with long swords, and offer to play the *ôsterspil*, which seems to have been a sword-dance for twelve performers, one of whom apparently was leader, and represented Summer beating Winter out of the land:

Fridebolt setze ûf den huot	F., put on thy hat,
wolgefriunt, und gang ez vor,	well backed, and go before,
bint daz *ôstersahs* zer linken sîten	bind o. to thy left side,
bis dur Künzen hôchgemuot,	be for K.'s sake merry,
leite uns vür daz Tinkûftor,	lead us outside the T. gate,
lâ den tanz al ûf den wasen rîten !	let dance on turf be rid.

This binding on of the 'Easter seax,' or sword-knife, leads us to infer that a sword of peculiar antique shape was retained; as the Easter scones, ôsterstuopha (RA. 298) and moonshaped ôstermâne (Brem. wtb.) indicate pastry of heathenish form. The sword may have been brandished in honour of Ostara, as it was for Fricka (p. 304). Or is Ôstersahs to be understood like Beiersahs (Haupt's Neidh. xxv. 17, note) ?

May we then identify Ostara with the Slav goddess of spring Vesna, the Lith. vasara (aestas), Lett. vassara, and with ver and ἔαρ in the forms ascribed to them on p. 754? True, there is no counterpart, no goddess answering to Marzana; but with our ancestors the notion of a conflict between two male antagonists, the giants Summer and Winter, must have carried the day at a very early time [to the exclusion of the goddesses].

The subject was no stranger to the Greeks and Romans : in one of Aesop's fables (Cor. 422. Fur. 380) χειμών and ἔαρ have a quarrel.[1] The Roman ver began on Feb. 7, the first swallow came in about Feb. 26, though she does not reach us till near the end of March, nor Sweden till the beginning of May (Tiedemann's Zool. 3, 624). The Florealia were kept from Apr. 28 till May 1 : there were songs, dances and games, they wore flowers and garlands on their heads, but the contrast, Winter, seems not to have been represented. I am not informed what spring customs have lasted to this day in Italy. Polydore Vergil, of Urbino in Umbria, tells us (de invent. rer. 5, 2) : ' Est consuetudinis, ut juventus promiscui sexus laetabunda Cal. Maji exeat in agros, et cantitans inde virides reportet arborum ramos, eosque ante domorum fores ponat, et denique unusquisque eo die aliquid viridis ramusculi vel herbae ferat; quod non fecisse poena est, praesertim apud Italos, ut madefiat.' Here then is a ducking too; this May-feast cannot have meant there a fetching-in of spring, for that comes earlier, in March (see Suppl.).

Much more remarkable is the Italian and Spanish custom of tying together at Mid Lent, on that very Dominica Lætare, a puppet to represent the oldest woman in the village, which is carried out by the people, especially children, and sawn through the middle. This is called segare la vecchia. At Barcelona the boys on that day, in thirties and forties, run through all the

---

[1] Creuzer's Symb. 2, 429. 494, following Hermann's interpret. of names, makes of the giant Briareus a fighting winter-demon.

streets, some with saws, some with billets of wood, and some
with napkins in which people deposit their gifts. They declare
in a song, that they are looking for the *very oldest woman in the
town*, to *saw her* through the body; at last they pretend they
have found her, and begin sawing something, and afterwards
burn it.[1] But the same custom is also found among the South
Slavs. In Lent time the Croats tell their children, that at the
hour of noon *an old woman is sawn in pieces* outside the gates;[2]
in Carniola it is at Mid Lent again that the old wife is led out of
the village and *sawn through* the middle.[3] The North Slavs call
it *bábu rézati*, sawing old granny, i.e. keeping Mid Lent (Jungm.
1, 56). Now this sawing up and burning of the old wife (as of
the devil, p. 606) seems identical with the carrying out and
drowning of Death, and if this represented Winter, a giant, may
not the Romance and South Slav nations have pictured their
hiems, their zima, as a goddess or old woman (Sl. bába)?[4] Add
to this, that in villages even of Meissen and Silesia the straw
figure that is borne out is sometimes in the shape of an *old woman*
(p. 768), which may perhaps have meant Marzana (p. 773)? I
should not be surprised if some districts of Bavaria, Tyrol and
Switzerland were yet to reveal a similar sawing of the old wife.[5]
The Scotch Highlanders throw the auld wife into the fire at
Christmas (Stewart's Pop. superst. p. 236 seq.).

But Lower Germany itself presents an approximation no less
worthy of attention. On p. 190 we mentioned that it was the
custom at Hildesheim, on the Saturday after Laetare, to set forth
the triumph of christianity over the heathen gods by *knocking
down logs of wood*. The agreement in point of time would of
itself invite a comparison of this solemnity with that Old-Polish
one, and further with the carrying-out of Death; one need not
even connect the expulsion of the old gods with the banishment

---

[1] Alex. Laborde's Itinéraire de l'Espagne 1, 57-8; conf. Doblados briep.
Hone's Dayb. 1, 369.
[2] Anton's Versuch über die Slaven 2, 66.
[3] Linhart's Geschichte von Krain 2, 274.
[4] The Ital. inverno, Span. invierno, is however masc.
[5] In Swabia and Switz., frônfasten (Lord's fast = Ember days, Scheffer's
Haltaus p. 53) has been corrupted into a *frau Faste*, as if it were the fast-time
personified (Stald. 1, 394. Hebel sub v.). Can cutting Mid Lent in two have signified a break in the fast? I think not. What means the phrase and the act of
'*breaking the neck of the fast*,' in an essay on Cath. superst. in the 16th cent.? see
Förstemann's Records of Augsburg Diet, Halle 1833, d. 101 (see Suppl.).

of Winter at all. In Geo. Torquatus's (unpublished) Annal. Magdeb. et Halberst. part 3 lib. 1 cap. 9 we are told that at Halberstadt (as at Hildesheim above) they used once a year to set up a *log* in the marketplace, and *throw* at it till its *head came off*. The log has not a name of its own, like Jupiter at Hildesheim; it is not unlikely that the same practice prevailed at other places in the direction of these two cities. At Halberstadt it lasted till markgraf Johan Albrecht's time; the oldest account of it is by the so-called 'monk of Pirna,' Joh. Lindner (Tilianus, d. ab. 1530) in his Onomasticon: 'In the stead of the idol's temple pulled in pieces at Halberstadt, there was a dome-church (cathedral) edified in honour of God and St. Stephen; in memory thereof the dome-lords (dean and chapter) young and old shall on Letare Monday every year set up a *wooden skittle* in the idol's stead, and throw thereat, every one; moreover the dome-provost shall in public procession and lordly state let lead a *bear* (barz, l. baren) beside him, else shall his [customary dues be denied him; likewise a *boy* beareth after him a sheathed *sword* under his arm.' Leading a *bear* about and delivering a *bear's loaf* was a custom prevalent in the Mid. Ages, *e.g.* at Mainz (Weisth. 1, 533) and Strassburg (Schilter's Gloss. 102).

This Low Saxon rejection, and that Polish dismissal, of the ancient gods has therefore no necessary connexion with a bringing in of summer, however apt the comparison of the new religion to summer's genial warmth. In the Polish custom at all events I find no such connexion hinted at. At the same time, the notion of bringing summer in was not unknown to the Poles. A Cracow legend speaks of *Lel* and *Po-lel* (after-lel), two divine beings of heathen times, *chasing each other round the field, and bringing Summer*; they are the cause of 'flying summer,' i.e. *gossamer*.[1] Until we know the whole tradition more exactly, we cannot assign it its right place. Lel and Polel are usually likened to Castor and Pollux (Linde i. 2, 1250^b), to whom they bear at least this resemblance, that their names, even in old folk-songs, make a simple interjection,[2] as the Romans used the twin

---

[1] Hall. allg. lz. 1807. no. 256, p. 807.

[2] Pol. lelum, polelum; Serv. lele, leljo, lelja (Vuk sub v.); Walach. lerum (conf. lirumlarum, verba effutitia). It seems to me hazardous to suppose them sons of Lada as C. and P. were of Leda. Conf. supra p. 366.

demigods to swear by. *Fliegender sommer, flugsommer, sommer-flug, graswebe,* are our names for the white threads that cover the fields at the beginning of spring, and still more of autumn; the spring tissue is also called *maidensummer,* Mary's yarn, Mary's thread (p. 471), that of autumn aftersummer, autumn yarn, *old-wives' summer;* but generally both kinds are covered by the one name or the other. Nethl. *slammetje* (draggletail? Brem. wtb. 4, 799); Engl. *gossamer* (God's train, trailing garment), also *samar, simar* (train); Swed. *dvärgsnät* (dwarf's net), p. 471. Boh. *wlačka* (harrow, because the threads rake the ground?); Pol. *lato święto marcinskie,* Mary's holy summer. Here again the Virgin's name seems to have been chosen as a substitute or antidote for heathen notions: the ancient Slavs might easily believe the gauzy web to have been spread over the earth by one of their gods. But the autumn gossamer has another Slavic name: Pol. *babie lato,* old wives' summer, Boh. *babské lèto,* or simply *babj,* which puts us in mind once more of that antithesis between summer and the old wife (p. 782). She rules in winter, and the god in summer (see Suppl.). Can the words of the Wendish ditty, quoted p. 771, be possibly interpreted of the film as it floats in the air?

I hope I have proved the antiquity and significance of the conceptions of Summer and Winter; but there is one point I wish to dwell upon more minutely. The *dressing-up* of the two champions in *foliage and flowers,* in *straw and moss,* the dialogue that probably passed between them, the accompanying chorus of spectators, all exhibit the first rude shifts of dramatic art, and a history of the German stage ought to begin with such performances. The *wrappage of leaves* represents the stage-dress and masks of a later time. Once before (p. 594), in the solemn procession for rain, we saw such leafy garb. Popular custom exhibits a number of variations, having preserved one fragment here, and another there, of the original whole. Near Willings-hausen, county Ziegenhain, Lower Hesse, a boy is *covered over and over with leaves,* green branches are fastened to his body: other boys lead him by a rope, and make him dance as a *bear,* for doing which a present is bestowed; the girls carry a hoop decked out with flowers and ribbons. Take note, that at the knocking down of logs at Halberstadt (p. 783), there was also a *bear* and a boy with a sword (conf. supra p. 304 n.) in the procession ; that Vïldifer, a hero disguised in a *bearskin*, is led about by a musician, and dances to the harp.[1] Doubtless a dramatic performance of ancient date, which we could have judged better, had the M. Nethl. poem of *bere Wislau*[2] been preserved ; but the name Vildifer seems to be founded on an OS. Wild-efor, which originated in a misapprehension of the OHG. Wildpero ('pero' ursus being confounded with 'pêr' aper), as only a dancing bear can be meant here, not a boar. Now this bear fits well with the *gadebasse* of the Danish May feast (p. 776). Schmid's Schwäb. wtb. 518ᵇ mentions the Augsburg *waterbird* : at Whitsuntide a lad *wrapt* from head to foot *in reeds* is led through the town by two others holding *birch-boughs* in their hands : once more a festival in May, not March. The name of this 'waterfowl' shews he is meant to be ducked in the brook or river ; but whether Summer here is a mistake for Winter, whether the boy in reeds represents Winter, while perhaps another boy in leaves played Summer, or the mummery was a device to bring on rain, I leave undetermined. Thuringian customs also point to Whitsuntide : the villagers there on Whit-Tuesday choose their *green man* or *lettuce-king* ; a young peasant is escorted into the woods, is there *enveloped in green bushes and boughs*, set on a horse, and conducted home in triumph. In the village the community stands assembled : the bailiff is allowed three guesses to find who is hidden in the green disguise ; if he fails, he must pay ransom in beer.[3] In other places it is on Whit-Sunday itself that the man who was the last to drive his cattle to pasture, is *wrapt in fir and birch boughs*, and whipt through the village amidst loud cries of '*Whitsun-sleeper!*' At night comes beer-drinking and dancing. In the Erzgebirge the shepherd who drives out earliest on Whit-Sunday may crack his whip, the last comer is laughed at and saluted *Whitsun-looby*: so with the latest riser in every house. The *sleeping away* of sacred festive

---

[1] Vilk. saga, cap. 120-1 ; mark, that the minstrel gives him the name of *Vitrleo* (wise lion), which should of course have been *Vitrbiörn ;* for a bear has the sense of 12 men (Reinh. p. 445). The people's 'king of beasts' has been confounded with that of scholars.

[2] Horae belg. 1, 51. Mone's Niederl. volkslit. p. 35-6. Conf. Wenezlan, Altd bl. 1, 333. Wislau is the Slav. Weslav, Waslav (Wenceslaus).

[3] Reichsanz. 1796. no. 90, p. 947. The herdsman that drives earliest to the Alpine pastures on May 1, earns a privilege for the whole year.

hours (conf. p. 590 n.), and the penalty attached to it, of acting the butze and being ducked, I look upon as mere accessories, kept alive long after the substance of the festival had perished (see Suppl.).

Kuhn (pp. 314–29) has lately furnished us with accurate accounts of Whitsun customs in the Marks. In the Mittelmark the houses are decorated with 'mai,' in the Altmark the farm-servants, horse-keepers and ox-boys go round the farms, and carry May-crowns made of flowers and birch twigs to the farmers, who used to hang them up on their houses, and leave them hanging till the next year. On Whitsun morning the cows and horses are driven for the first time to the fallow pasture, and it is a great thing to be the first there. The animal that arrives first has a bunch of 'mai' tied to its tail, which bunch is called *dau-sleips* (dew-sweep),[1] while the last comer is dressed up in fir-twigs, all sorts of green stuff and field flowers, and called the *motley cow* or *motley horse*, and the boy belonging to it the *pingst-kääm* or *pingst-käärel*. At Havelberg the cow that came home first at night used to be adorned with the crown of flowers, and the last got the *thau-schleife*; now this latter practice is alone kept up.[2] In some of the Altmark villages, the lad whose horse gets to the pasture first is named *thau-schlepper*, and he who drives the hindmost is made *motley boy*, viz. they *clothe him from head to foot in wild flowers*, and at noon lead him from farm to farm, the *dew-sweeper* pronouncing the rhymes. In other places a pole decked with flowers and ribbons is carried round, and called the *bammel* (dangle) or *pings-kääm*, though, as a rule, this last name is reserved for the boy shrouded in leaves and flowers, who accompanies. He is sometimes led by two others called *hunde-brösel*. In some parts of the Mittelmark the muffled boy is called the *kaudernest*. On the Drömling the boys go round with the *pingst-kääm*, and the girls with the *may-bride*, collecting gifts. Some villages south of the Drömling have a more elaborate

---

[1] So named, because it has to touch the dewy grass: which confirms my interpretation of the Alamannic *tau-dragil* (R.A. 94, 680), supra p. 887 note.

[2] In some places a winning horse has a stick cleft in three fixed on his head and richly encircled with the finest flowers; the boy who rides him, beside many garlands, receives a *cap woven of rushes*, and must preserve a serious countenance while the procession slowly advances: if he can be provoked to laughter, he loses, Kuhn, p. 328.

ceremonial. On 'White Sunday,' a fortnight before Easter, the herdboys march to the pasture with *white sticks* (supra p. 766), and with these they mark off a spot, to which no one may drive his cattle till Whitsuntide.[1] This being done, the smaller boys *name their brides*[2] to the bigger ones, and no one must reveal the name till Whitsunday, when the railed-off pasture is thrown open, and any one may tell the *brides' names*. On Whitmonday one of the boys is *disguised* by having two petticoats put on him, and one of them pulled over his head and tied up; then they *swathe him in may*, hang flower-wreaths about his neck, and set a flower-crown on his head. They call him the *füstge mai* (well-appointed, armed), and lead him round to all the houses; at the same time the girls go round with their *may-bride*, who is completely covered with ribbons, her bridal band hanging to the ground behind; she wears a large nosegay on her head, and keeps on singing her ditties till some gift is handed to her.

Other villages have horse-races on Whitmonday for a wreath which is hung out. Whoever snatches it down both times is crowned, and led in triumph to the village as *May-king*.

A work composed in the 13th cent. by Aegidius aureae vallis religiosus reports the Netherland custom of electing a *Whitsun queen* in the time of bp. Albero of Lüttich (d. 1155): 'Sacerdotes ceteraeque ecclesiasticae personae cum universo populo, in solemnitatibus *paschae* et *pentecostes*, aliquam ex sacerdotum concubinis, purpuratam ac diademate renitentem in eminentiori solio constitutam et cortinis velatam, *reginam creabant*, et coram ea assistentes in choreis tympanis et aliis musicalibus instrumentis tota die psallebant, et quasi idolatrae effecti ipsam *tanquam idolum colebant*,' Chapeaville 2, 98. To this day poor women in Holland at Whitsuntide carry about a girl sitting *in a little*

---

[1] While this fallow pasture is being railed off, the new lads (those who are tending for the first time) have to procure *bones* to *cover the branches of a fir-tree which is erected*. The tree is called the *gibbet of bones*, and its top adorned with *a horse's skull* (Kuhn 323-4): plainly a relic of some heathen sacrificial rite, conf. the elevation of animals on trees, pp. 53, 75, esp. of horses' heads, p. 47; the good Lubbe's hill of bones is also in point, p. 526.

[2] This *naming of brides* resembles the *crying of flefs* on Walburgis eve in Hesse, on the L. Rhine, the Ahr and the Eifel, Zeitschr. f. Hess. gesch. 2, 272-7. Dieffenbach's Wetterau p. 234. Ernst Weyden's Ahrthal, Bonn 1839, p. 216. And who can help remembering the ON. *heit strengja* at Yule-tide? when the heroes likewise chose their loved ones, *e.g.* in Sæm. 146ª: 'Heðinn strengdi heit til Svavo.'

carriage, and beg for money. This girl, decked with flowers and ribbons, and named *pinxterbloem,* reminds us of the ancient goddess on her travels. The same *pinxterbloem* is a name for the iris pseudacorus, which blossoms at that very season; and the sword-lily is named after other deities beside Iris (perunika, p. 183-4). On the Zaterdag before Pentecost, the boys go out early in the morning, and with great shouting and din awake the lazy sleepers, and tie a bundle of nettles at their door. Both the day and the late sleeper are called *luilap* or *luilak* (sluggard). Summer also had to be *wakened,* p. 765.

Everything goes to prove, that the approach of summer was to our forefathers a holy tide, welcomed by sacrifice, feast and dance, and largely governing and brightening the people's life. Of Easter fires, so closely connected with May fires, an account has been given; the festive gatherings of May-day night will be described more minutely in the Chap. on Witches. At this season brides were chosen and proclaimed, servants changed, and houses taken possession of by new tenants.

With this I conclude my treatment of Summer and Winter; i.e. óf the mythic meanings mixed up with the two halves of the year. An examination of the twelve *solar* and thirteen *lunar* months[1] is more than I can undertake here, for want of space; I promise to make good the deficiency elsewhere. This much I will say, that a fair proportion of our names of months also is referable to heathen gods, as we now see by the identification of *May* with summer, and have already seen in the case of *Hrede* (March) and *Eastre* (April), p. 289. *Phol,* who had his Phol-day (p. 614), seems also to have ruled over a *Phol-mânôt* (May and Sept.), conf. Diut. i. 409, 432, and Scheffer's Haltaus 36. The days of our week may have been arranged and named on the model of the Roman (p. 127); the names of the three months aforesaid are independent of any Latin influence.[2] A remarkable feature among Slavs and Germans is the using of one name for two successive months, as when the Anglo-Saxons

---

[1] That there were *lunar years* is indicated by the moon's being given 'at ártali,' for year's tale, p. 710.

[2] Martius rests on Mars, Aprilis must contain a spring-goddess answering to Ostara, Majus belongs to Maja, a mother of gods. The same three consecutive months are linked in the Latin calendar, as in ours, with divinities.

speak of an ærra and æftera Geola, ærra and æftera Líða, and
we of a great and little Horn (Jan. and Feb.), nay, Ougest is
followed up by an Ougstin, the god by a goddess; I even see
a mythical substratum in popular saws on certain months, thus
of February they say: 'the Spörkelsin has seven smocks on,
of different lengths every one, and them she shakes,' i.e. raises
wind with them. 'Sporkel,' we know, is traced to the Roman
spurcalia.

CHAPTER XXV.

TIME AND WORLD.

In the last chapter we examined myths having reference to the alternation of seasons, to phenomena of the year. Our language affords several instances of transition from the notion of time to that of space.

Ulphilas translates χρόνος, καιρός, ὥρα alternately by *mêl*, *hveila*, *þeihs*, yet so that 'mêl' usually stands for χρόνος or καιρός, rarely for ὥρα, and 'hveila' mostly for ὥρα, seldomer for χρόνος and καιρός; the former expressing rather the longer section of time, and the latter the shorter. *Mêl*, OHG. *mâl*, AS. *mœl*, ON. *mâl*, lit. mark or measure, is applied to measured speech or writing as well as to a portion of time; on the contrary, *hveila*, OHG. *huila*, MHG. *wîle*, AS. *hwîl* (p. 702), denotes rest, and is purely a notion of time, whereas mêl was transferred from space to time. We come across *þeihs* (neut. gen. þeihsis) only twice, viz. Rom. 13, 11 : 'vitandans þata þeihs, þatei mêl ist,' εἰδότες τὸν καιρὸν, ὅτι ὥρα, and 1 Thess. 5, 1 : ' bi þô þeihsa jah mêla,' περὶ τῶν χρόνων καὶ τῶν καιρῶν. Each passage contains both þeihs and mêl, but the choice of the former for χρόνος and the latter for καιρός shews that þeihs is even better adapted than mêl for the larger fuller notion, and the most complete arrangement would be : þeihs χρόνος, mêl καιρός, hveila ὥρα. I derive *þeihs* from þeihan (crescere, proficere, succedere), as veihs gen. veihsis (propugnaculum) from veihan (pugnare); so that it expresses profectus, successus, the forward movement of time, and is near of kin to OHG. dîhsmo, dêhsmo (profectus), probably also to dîhsila (temo), our deichsel, AS. þîsl, thill, for which we may assume a Goth. þeihslo, þeihsla, the apparatus by which the waggon is moved on. Schmeller 4, 294 cleverly connects têmo itself with tempus : the celestial waggon-thill (p. 724) marks the movement of nocturnal time (Varro 7, 72–5), and þeihsla becomes a measure like the more general þeihs. Even if the connexion of the two Latin words be as yet doubtful, that of the two Gothic ones can hardly be so. But now, as the Goth. *þeihs* has no representative in the other Teutonic tongues, and in return the OHG. *zît*, AS. *tîd*, ON. *tíð* seems foreign to Gothic, it is natural, considering the identity of meaning, to suppose that the latter form arose from mixing up *þeihan* (crescere) with teihan (nuntiare), and therefore that the AS. *tîd* stands for *þîd*, and OHG. *zît* for *dît*; besides, the OHG. *zît* is mostly neut., like *þeihs*, whereas the fem. *zît*, *tîd* would have demanded a Goth. *þeihaþs*. Of course a Goth. *þeihs* ought to have produced an OHG. *dîhs* or *dîh* (as veihs did *wîh*) ; but, that derivation here branched in two or three directions is plain from the ON. *tími*, AS. *tíme* (tempus, hora), which I refer to the OHG. *dîhsmo*[1] above, and a Goth. *þeihsma*, with both of which the Lat. tempus (and têmo?) would perfectly agree (see Suppl.).

Like hveila, the OHG. *stulla*, and *stunt*, *stunta*, AS. ON. *stund* (moment, hour), contain the notion of rest, and are conn. with stilli (quietus), standan (stare), while conversely the Lat. mōmentum (movi-mentum) is borrowed from motion.[2] We express the briefest interval of time by *augenblick*, eye-glance; Ulph. renders Luke 4, 5 ἐν στιγμῇ χρόνου 'in *stika* mêlis,' in a prick of time, in ictu temporis ; 1 Cor. 15, 52 ἐν ῥιπῇ ὀφθαλμοῦ, ' in *brahva* áugins,' brahv being glance, flash, micatus, AS. twincel, and traceable to braíhvan (micare, lucere), OHG. prëhan, MHG. brëhen ;[3] AS. ' on *beorhtm-hwíle*' from bearhtm ictus oculi, ' on eágan *beorhtm*,' Beda 2, 13 ; ON. 'í *augabragði*,' conf. Sæm. 11[b]. 14[a]. 19[b]. OHG. 'in *slago dero bráwo*,' N. ps. 2, 12, in a movement of the eyelid (conf. *slegipráwa* palpebra, Graff 3, 316) ; 'ante-

---

[1] In dîhan, dîhsmo the *d* remained, in *zît* it degenerated. Just so the Goth. þvahan first became regularly OHG. duahan, then irregularly tuahan, now zwagen ; the OS. thuingan first OHG. duingan, then tuingan, now zwingen. Less anomalous by one degree are OHG. zi for Goth. du (to), and our zwerg for ON. dvergr (dwarf), MHG. twero.

[2] Numeral adverbs of repetition our language forms with *stunt* as well as *mâl*, but also by some words borrowed from space, Gramm. 3, 230.

[3] Beside the inf. *brëhen* (MS. 1, 47[a]. 185[a]. Gudr. 1856, 2) we are only sure of the pres. part.: ouge-*brehender* klê, MS. 1, 8[b]. brehender schîn 2, 231[a] ; for the pret. *brach*, MS. 2, 52[a]. Bon. 48. 68, could be referred to brechen, conf. ' break of day,' p. 747, yet the two verbs themselves may be congeners. In OHG. the perf. part. appears in *prëhan*-ougi (lippus), a compound formed like zoran-ougi, Gramm. 2, 693. The Goth. *brahv* assures us of the princ. parts in full, braíhva, brahv, brêhvum (like saíhva, sahv, sêhvum). But instead of an adj. braíhts (bright), even the Gothic has only a transposed form baírhts, OHG. peraht, AS. beorht, ON. biartr ; yet our Perahta is afterwards also called Prehta, Brehte (pp. 277–9), and other proper names waver between the two forms, as Albrecht Albert, Ruprecht Robert.

quam supercilium superius inferiori jungi possit,' Caesar. heisterb.
12, 5. ' minre wîlen (in less time) dan ein oucbrâ zuo der andern muge geslahen,' Grieshaber p. 274. 'als ein oucbrâ mac
ûf und zuo gegên,' can open and shut, Berth. 239. ' ê ich die
hant umbkêrte, oder zuo geslüege die (or better, diu) brâ,' Er.
5172. 'alsô schier sô (as fast as) ein brâwe den andern slahen
mac,' Fundgr. 1, 199 (see Suppl.).[1]

A great length of time is also expressed by several different
words : Goth. *áivs* (m.), OHG. *êwa* (f.), Gr. *αἰών*, Lat. *aevum*
shading off into the sense of seculum, O. Fr. *aé* (p. 678); the
OS. *eo* (m.) means only statutum, lex, as the Goth. *mêl* was
scriptura as well as tempus. Then Goth. *alþs* (f.), by turns *αἰών*
(Eph. 2, 2. 1 Tim. 1, 17. 2 Tim. 4, 10), and *βίος* or *γενεά*;
ON. *öld;* OHG. with suffix *altar* (aevum, aetas), though the
simple word also survives in the compound *wëralt* (assimil.
worolt), MHG. *werlt*, our *welt*, AS. *wërold*, Engl. *world*, Fris.
wrald, ON. *vërald*, *vëröld*, Swed. *world*, Dan. *verd :* constant use
accounts for the numerous distortions of the word.[2] Its Gothic
form, wanting in Ulph., would have been *vair-alþs* or ' vaírê
alþs,' virorum (hominum) aetas, aetas (lifetime) passing into the
local sense of mundus (world), just as seculum, siècle, has come
to mean mundus, monde. We saw on p. 575 that Greek mythology supposes four ages of the world, *golden*, *silver*, *brazen*
and *iron :* a fancy that has travelled far,[3] and was apparently
no stranger in Scandinavia itself. Snorri 15 gives the name of

---

[1] Can brâwe, OHG. prâwa, ON. brâ, be derived from brëhen ? Perhaps the
set phrases in the text reveal the reason for it. In that case the OHG. prâwa must
be for prâha, and we might expect a Goth. brêhva ? Then the Sanskr. bhrû, Gr.
ὀφρύς, would be left without the vivid meaning of the Teut. word.

[2] Its true meaning was so obscured, that other explanations were tried.
Maerlant at the beginn. of his Sp. Hist. : ' die de *werelt* êrst *werrelt* hiet, hine was
al in dole niet. Adam die *werelt* al *verwerrede*.' This deriv. from werren (impedire,
intricare) was, if I mistake not, also hit upon by MHG. poets, *e.g.* Renner 2293.
Equally wrong are those from wern to last, and werlen to whirl. It is quite possible, that werô alt (virorum aetas) was intended as an antithesis to a risônô alt
(gigantum aetas) which preceded it.

[3] In our Mid. Ages the *World* was personified, like Death, and the various ages
were combined in a *statue* with a head of gold, arms of silver, a breast of brass and
iron, and feet of earth, MS. 2, 175ᵇ ; another representation gave the figure a
golden head, silver breast and arms, brazen belly, steel thighs, iron legs, earthen
feet, MS. 2, 225ᵃ ; a third, a golden head, silver arms, brazen breast, copper belly,
steel thighs, earthen feet, Amgb. 27ᵇ. This medley, though borrowed from Daniel
2, 31–43, reminds us of ancient idols formed out of various metals, and also of
Hrûngnir with the stone heart, and Möckrkâlfi who was made of loam, and had a
mare's heart put into him, Sn. 109. Hugo in his Renner 13754 speaks of a steel,
diamond, copper, wood, and straw world.

gull-aldr to the period when the gods had all their utensils made of gold, which was only cut short by the coming of giantesses out of Iötunheim. Had he merely borrowed this golden age from the classics, he would have taken the trouble to discover the other metals too in Norse legend.[1] But in the Völuspá (Sæm. 8ᵃ) we see that other ages are spoken of, *skegg-öld* (see p. 421), *skâlm-öld, vind-öld* and *varg-öld*, which are to precede the destruction of the world.

To translate κόσμος, Ulph. takes by turns, and often one immediately after the other, the two words *fairhvus* and *manasêþs*; both must have been in common use among the Goths. *Manasêþs* [2] means virorum satus (seed of men), and is used at once for λαός and for κόσμος, thus fully coinciding with the above developed sense of weralt. *Fairhvus* I take to be near of kin to OHG. ferah, AS. feorh, MHG. vërch, so that it expressed lifetime again, like aevum; it is also connected with OHG. firahî (homines), and would mean first 'coetus hominum viventium,' then the space in which they live. It has nothing to do with fairguni, earth, mountain (see Suppl.).

As κόσμος properly means the ordered, symmetrical (world), *mundus* the clean, well-trimmed, bright, and as the Frisian laws 126, 26 speak of 'thi *skêne* wrald'; so the Slavic *sviet, svèt, swiat* is, first of all, light and brightness, then world, the open, public,[3] all that the sun illumines, whatsoever is 'under the sun.' [4] So the Wallach. *lume*, the Hung. *világ*, signify both light and world. The Lith. *swietas*, O. Pruss. *switai*, world, is borowed from Slavic. Like mundus, the Slav. sviet passes into the time-sense of seculum, vièk (Dobrowsky's Inst. 149). The older Slavs called the world *mir* and *ves'mir*, Dobr. 24. 149; *mir* is also the word for peace, quietness, and seems akin to mira or mèra, measure (order?). The Finnic for world is *maa' ilma*, the Esth. *ma ilm* (from ilma, the expanse of air, and maa, earth), the Lapp. *ilbme.*

---

[1] We may connect the golden age with Frôði, whose mill ground *gold* and *peace*. The Finns say, in Ukko's time gold was ground in the mills, honey trickled from the oaks, and milk flowed in the rivers (conf. p. 697), Ganander 98.

[2] Always with single *n*, as in mana-maúrþrja, mana-riggvs, manags (many), manáuli, and as in OHG. mana-houpit, mana-luomi, manao, conf. MHG. sunewende, p. 617 n. The reason of this peculiarity grammar must determine.

[3] To bring to light, impart to the world, is in Serv. 'na svièt izdáti.'

[4] The Lett. word *pasaule* seems to have been modelled on this 'sub sole' in Eccles. 1, 3. 2, 22. So ' unter disem wolken,' Rol. 9, 31.

The ON. *heimr* is mundus, domus, and akin to himinn, himil
(p. 698), as mundus also is applied both to world and sky ;
heimskringla, orbis terrarum. Ulphilas renders οἰκουμένη, Luke
2, 1. 4, 5. Rom. 10, 18, by *midjungards ;* to this correspond the
AS. *middangeard,* Cædm. 9, 3. 177, 29. Beow. 150. 1496; the
OHG. *mittingart,* Is. 340. 385-6. 408. Fragm. theot. 17, 6.
mittigart, Fragm. th. 17, 3. 20, 20. 25, 9. *mittiligart,* Gl. Jun.
216. T. 16, 1. *mittilgart,* T. 155, 1. 178, 2. 179, 1 ; the OS.
middilgard; the ON. *miðgarðr,* Sæm. 1ᵇ. 45ᵇ. 77ᵇ. 90ª. 114ᵇ. 115ᵇ.
Sn. 9. 10. 13. 45. 61; and even a Swed. folksong 1, 140 has
retained *medjegârd.* O. Engl. *middilerd, mediløarth,* like the Gr.
μεσογαία. Fischart's Garg. 66ª has *mittelkreiss,* mid-circle. We
saw (p 560) that *miðgarðr* was, to the Norse way of thinking,
created out of Ymir's eyebrows, and appointed to men for their
habitation. The whole compound, doubtless very ancient, is of
prime importance, because it is native to our oldest memorials,
and at the same time strictly Eddic. Nor is that all : in similar
harmony, the world is called in ON. *Oegisheimr,* Sæm. 124ᵇ. 125ª,
and in MHG. *mergarte,* Annolied 444. Rol. 106, 14. Kaiserchr.
501. 6633. Karl. 38ᵇ; *i.e.* the sea-girt world, conf. Goth.
marisâivs (ocean), and OHG. *merikerti* (aetherium),[1] Diut. 1, 250.
Lastly, OHG. *woroltring,* O. ii. 2, 13. iii. 26, 87. iv. 7, 11. v. 1,
33. 19, 1. *erdring,* O. i. 11, 47. MHG. *erdrinc,* Mar. 198-9, orbis
terrarum, Graff 4, 1163.

According to the Edda, a huge *serpent,* the *miðgarðs ormr,* lies
coiled round the earth's circumference, 'umgiörð allra landa' :
evidently the ocean. When Alexander in the legend was carried
up in the air by griffins, the sea appeared to him to twine like a
snake round the earth. But that 'world-serpent,' hateful to all
the gods (sû er goð fîa, Sæm. 55ª) was the child of Loki, and
brother to the Fenris-ûlfr and Hel ; he was called *Iörmungandr*
(Sn. 32), the great, the godlike (conf. p. 351), and like Hel he
opens wide his jaws, Sn. 63 (see Suppl.).

Everything shews that the notions of time, age, world, globe,
earth, light, air and water ran very much into one another ; in
'earth-ring,' ring indicates the globular shape of the earth and

---

[1] The Finnic *ilma ?* Festus says *mundus* meant coelum as well as terra, mare,
aër.

its planetary revolution. *Manasêþs, faírhvus,* and *wëralt* point to spaces and periods filled by men.[1]

' So far as ' world' contains the notion of seculum and life, it is significantly called, even by the OS. poet, a dream: *liudio drôm,* Hel. 17, 17. 104, 7. 109, 20. *manno drôm* 23, 7. 103, 4. AS. *gumdreám,* Beow. 4933; 'la vida es sueño.' Its perishableness and painfulness have suggested yet other designations: 'diz ellende *wuoftal* (weep-dale),' Tod. gehugde 933, as we say 'this vale of tears, house of sorrow' (see Suppl.).

From its enormous superficial extent is borrowed the phrase 'thius *brêde werold,*' Hel. 50, 1. 131, 21; MHG. 'diu *breite werlt,*' Mar. 161; our *weite breite welt.* Also: 'thiz lant *breitâ,*' O. ii. 2, 18. daz *breite* gevilde, Mar. 34. Wigal. 2269. diu *breite* erde, Roth. 4857. Wh. 60, 29. Geo. 4770, εὐρεῖα χθών. This reminds one of the name of Balder's dwelling spoken of on p. 222-3, *breiða blik,* which seems to include the two notions of breadth and brightness. An expression used by miners is remarkable in this connexion: 'blickgold, blicksilber' is said of the clear molten metal gleaming on the fining-hearth, and 'der *breite blick*' when there is a plentiful yield of it.[2] The beautiful bright world is, as it were, a wide glance.

When 'world' or 'heimr' is merely used in the general sense of dwelling place, we can think of several worlds. The Völuspâ, Sæm. 1ᵃ, supposes *nine worlds* and *nine firmaments* (íviðir), conf. Sæm. 36ᵇ. 49ᵃ, just as Sn. 222ᵇ speaks of *nine heavens* (see Suppl.).[3]

Of these worlds, not abodes of the living human race, those that demand a close investigation are: the Flame-world, the Dead-world, and Paradise; but all are connected more or less

---

[1] As we often use ' world' and ' earth' indifferently, so did the MHG. poets. The beginning of time is expressed at option either thus: ' von anegenges zît, daz sich *diu werlt* erhuop (up-hove), und muoter ir kint getruoc (bore),' Rol. 285, 12. ' sît (since) *diu werlt* êrste wart,' Ulr. Trist. 3699; or thus: ' sît *disiu erde* geleget wart,' Rol. 187, 7. ' sît *diu erde* alrêrst begunde bern (to bear),' Karl 70ᵇ.

[2] In Matthesius's Sermons 84ᵃ: ' Now this Cyrus hath a silver kingdom, wherein the word of God, as silver refined in the fire, is preached *zu breitem plick.*' 91ᵇ : ' He hath sent his apostles into all the world, that they may preach the gospel *zu breitem plick,* as ye mining folk say.' 101ᵃ : ' Elsewhere lead appeareth in blocks, as at Goslar, where the Rammelsberg is *zu breitem plick* almost all lead.'

[3] *Nine* choirs of angels, Fundgr. 1, 101. Pass. 539. 341. ' niu fylkîrigar engla,' Fornald. sög. 3, 663 ; conf. the *nine* punishments of hell, Wackernagel's Basel MSS. 24ᵇ [Buddhist books describe 18 hells, some hot, some cold].

with the upper world, that inhabited by man, and passages exist
from the one to the other.

The ON. system supposes a world-tree, *askr Yggdrasils*, which
links heaven, earth and hell together, of all trees the greatest
and holiest. It is an ash (askr), whose branches shoot through
all the world, and reach beyond heaven. Three roots spread out
in three directions, one striking toward the âses into heaven,
another to the hrîmþurses, the third to the under world. From
under each root gushes a miraculous spring, namely, by the
heaven root *Urðarbrunnr* (p. 407), by the giants' root *Mîmis-
brunnr*, by the hell root *Hvergelmir*, i.e. the roaring (or the old)
cauldron, olla stridens (p. 563). All these wellsprings are holy:
at the Urðar-well the âses and norns hold their council, the
giants' well is watched by a wise man Mîmir (p. 379), I know
not whether a sage old giant himself or a hero, anyhow a semi-
divine being, or nearly so. Every day the norns draw water
from their well, to water the boughs of the ash: so *holy* is this
water, that it imparts to anything that gets into the well the
colour of the white of an egg; from the tree there trickles a
bee-nourishing dew, named *hunângsfall* (fall of honey). On
its boughs, at its roots, animals sit or dart about: an eagle,
a squirrel, four stags, and some snakes; and all have proper
names. Those of the stags are elsewhere names of dwarfs,
notably *Dâinn* and *Dvalinn*. The snake *Niðhöggr* (male pun-
gens, caedens) lies below, by Hvergelmir, gnawing at the root.
The squirrel *Ratatöskr*[1] runs up and down, trying to sow discord
between the snake and the eagle who is perched aloft. The
eagle's name is not given, he is a bird of great knowledge and
sagacity; betwixt his eyes sits a hawk *Veðrfölnir*.[2]

The whole conception bears a primitive stamp, but seems
very imperfectly unfolded to us. We get some inkling of a feud
between snake and eagle, which is kept alive by Ratatöskr; not
a word as to the purpose and functions of hawk or stags.
Attempts at explaining Yggdrasil I have nothing to do with; at

---

[1] The word contains *rata* (elabi, permeare), Goth. *vratôn*, and perh. *taska*, pl.
töskur, pera: peram permeans? Wolfram in Parz. 651, 13 has 'wenken als ein
eichorn,' dodging like a squirrel. The *squirrel* is still an essential feature in the
popular notion of a forest, conf. RA. 497 and the catching of squirrels at Easter
(supra p. 616), perhaps for old heathen uses.
[2] The eagle's friend, for *haukr î horni* (hawk in the corner) means a hidden
counsellor.

present, before giving my own opinion, I must point out two coincidences very unlike each other. This tree of the Edda has suggested to others before me the tree of the Cross, which in the Mid. Ages gave birth to many speculations and legends. Well, a song in the 'Wartburg War,' MsH. 3, 181 sets the following riddle:

> Ein edel boum gewahsen ist
> in eime garten, der ist gemacht mit hôher liat;
> *sin wurzel kan der helle grunt erlangen,*
> *sin tolde* (for 'zol der') *rüeret an den trôn*
> dâ der süeze Got bescheidet vriunde lôn,
> *sin este breit hânt al die werlt bevangen :*
> der boum an ganzer zierde stât und ist geloubet schœne,
> dar ûfe *sitzent vogelin*
> süezes sanges wîse nâch ir stimme fîn,
> nâch maniger kunst sô haltents ir gedœne.

(A noble tree in a garden grows, and high the skill its making shews; its roots the floor of hell are grasping, its summit to the throne extends where bounteous God requiteth friends, its branches broad the wide world clasping: thereon sit birds that know sweet song, etc.) This is very aptly interpreted of the Cross and the descent into hell. Before this, O. v. 1, 19 had already written:

> Thes *krûzes horn* thar obana *zeigôt ûf in himila,*
> thie *arma* joh thio *henti* thie *zeigônt worolt-enti,*
> ther selbo *mittilo boum* ther scowôt thesan *woralt-floum,*
> . . . . theiz *innan erdu stentit,*
> mit thiu ist thar bizeinit, theiz imo ist al gimeinit
> in *erdu* joh im *himile* inti in *abgrunte* ouh hiar nidare.

(The cross's top points to heaven, the arms and hands to the world's ends, the stem looks to this earthly plain, . . . stands in the ground, thereby is signified, that for it is designed all in earth and heaven and the abyss beneath.) It matters little if the parallel passage quoted by Schilter from cap. 18 de divinis officiis comes not from Alcuin, but some later author: Otfried may have picked up his notion from it all the same.[1] It says: 'Nam ipsa crux magnum in se mysterium continet, cujus positio

---

[1] I do not know if Lafontaine had Virgil's verses in his mind, or followed his own prompting, when he says of an oak:

> Celui, de qui la tête au ciel était voisine,
> et dont les pieds touchaient à l'empire des morts.

talis est, ut superior pars *coelos petat*, inferior *terrae inhaereat*, fixa *infernorum ima contingat*, latitudo autem ejus *partes mundi* appetat.' I can never believe that the myth of Yggdrasil in its complete and richer form sprang out of this christian conception of the Cross; it were a far likelier theory, that floating heathen traditions of the world-tree, soon after the conversion in Germany, France or England, attached themselves to an object of christian faith, just as heathen temples and holy places were converted into christian ones. The theory would break down, if the same exposition of the several pieces of the cross could be found in any early Father, African or Oriental; but this I doubt. As for the birds with which the 13th cent. poem provides the tree, and which correspond to the Norse eagle and squirrel, I will lay no stress on them. But one thing is rather surprising: it is precisely to the ash that Virgil ascribes as high an elevation in the air as its depth of root in the ground, Georg. 2, 291:

> Aesculus in primis, quae quantum *vortice ad auras*
> *aetherias*, tantum *radice in tartara tendit;*

upon which Pliny 16, 31 (56) remarks: 'si Virgilio credimus, esculus quantum corpore eminet tantum radice descendit.' [1] So that the Norse fable is deeply grounded in nature; conf. what was said, p. 696, of the bees on this ash-tree.

Another and still more singular coincidence carries us to Oriental traditions. In the Arabian 'Calila and Dimna' the human race is compared to a man who, chased by an elephant, takes refuge in a deep well: with his hand he holds on to the branch of a shrub over his head, and his feet he plants on a narrow piece of turf below. In this uneasy posture he sees two *mice*, a black and a white one, gnawing the root of the shrub; far beneath his feet a horrible *dragon* with its jaws wide open; the elephant still waiting on the brink above, and four worms' heads projecting from the side of the well, undermining the turf he stands on; at the same time there trickles *liquid honey from a branch* of the bush, and this he eagerly catches in his mouth. [2]

---

[1] Perhaps Hrabanus Maurus's Carmen in laudem sanctae crucis, which I have not at hand now, contains the same kind of thing.

[2] Calila et Dimna, ed. Silvestre de Sacy. Mém. hist. p. 28-9, ed. Knatchbull, p. 80-1; conf. the somewhat different version in the Exempeln der alten weisen, p.m. 22.

Hereupon is founded a rebuke of man's levity, who in the utmost stress of danger cannot withstand the temptation of a small enjoyment. Well, this fable not only was early and extensively circulated by Hebrew, Latin and Greek translations of the entire book,[1] but also found its way into other channels. John Damascenus (circ. 740) inserted it in his Βαρλάαμ καὶ 'Ιωάσαφ,[2] which soon became universally known through a Latin reproduction.[3] On the model of it our Rudolf composed his Barlaam and Josaphat, where the illustration is to be found, p. 116-7; in a detached form, Stricker (Ls. 1, 253). No doubt a parable so popular might also reach Scandinavia very early in the Mid. Ages, if only the similarity itself were stronger, so as to justify the inference of an immediate connexion between the two myths. To me the *faint* resemblance of the two seems just the main point; a *close* one has never existed. The ON. fable is far more significant and profound; that from the East is a fragment, probably distorted, of a whole now lost to us. Even the main idea of the world-tree is all but wanting to it; the only startling thing is the agreement in sundry accessories, the trickling honey (conf. p. 793 n.), the gnawed root, the four species of animals.

But if there be any truth in these concords of the Eddic myth with old Eastern tenets, as well as with the way the Christians tried to add portions of their heathen faith to the doctrine of the Cross; then I take a further step. It seems to me that the notion, so deeply rooted in Teutonic antiquity, of the *Irminsûl*, that 'altissima, universalis *columna*, quasi sustinens omnia' (p. 115-7), is likewise nearly allied to the world-tree Yggdrasil. As this extended its roots and boughs in three directions (standa á þria vega), so did three or four great highways branch out from the Irminsûl (pp. 356. 361); and the farther we explore, the richer in results will the connexion of these heathen ideas prove. The pillars of Hercules (p. 364), of Bavo in Hainault, and the Thor and Roland pillars (p. 394) may have had no other purpose than to mark out from them as centre the celestial and terrestrial direction of the regions of the world; and the sacred Yggdrasil

---

[1] Also in the East, conf. Jelaleddin's Divan in Hammer's Pers. redek. p. 183.
[2] First publ. in Boissonade's Anecd. Graeca, tom. 4, Paris 1832, pp. 1—365.
[3] Hist. duorum Christi militum (Opera, Basil. 1575. pp. 815—902); also printed separately, Antv. s.a. (the illustration at p. 107); another version in Surius 7, 858 seq., the parable at p. 889.

subserved a very similar partition of the world. The thing might
even have to do with ancient land-surveying, and answer to the
Roman cardo, intersected at right angles by the decumanus. To
the ashtree we must also concede some connexion with Asciburg
(p. 350) and the tribal progenitor Askr (p. 571-2). Another
legend of an ashtree is reserved for chap. XXXII (see Suppl.).

Niflheimr, where *Niðhöggr* and other serpents (named in Sæm.
44ᵇ. Sn. 22) have their haunt round the spring Hvergelmir, is
the dread dwelling-place of the death-goddess *Hel* (p. 312), Goth.
Halja ('or heljo,' Sæm. 94ª, 'í heljo' 49. 50. 51, is clearly
spoken of a place, not a person), it is gloomy and black, like her;
hence a *Nebelheim*, cold land of shadows, abode of the departed,[1]
but not a place of torment or punishment as in the christian view,
and even that was only developed gradually (p. 313). When Ulphilas uses *halja*, it is always for ᾅδης (Matt. 11, 23. Luke 10, 15.
16, 23. 1 Cor. 15, 55), the *infernus* of the Vulg.; whenever the
text has γέεννα, Vulg. gehenna, it remains gaíaínna in Gothic
(Matt. 5, 29. 30. 10, 28),it was an idea for which the Gothic had
no word. The OHG. translator T. renders 'infernus' by *hella*
(Matt. 11, 23), 'gehenna'[2] by *hellafiur* (5, 29. 30) or *hellawizi*
(-torment 10, 28), and only 'filium gehennae' by *hella sun* (23,
15), where the older version recently discovered is more exact:
quâlu sunu, son of torment. When the Creed says that Christ
'niðar steig zi *helliu*' (descendit ad inferna), it never meant the
abode of souls in torment. In the Heliand 72, 4 a sick man is
said to be 'fûsid an *helsîd*', near dying, equipped for his journey
to Hades, without any by-thought of pain or punishment. That
AS. poetry still remembered the original (personal) conception of
Hel, was proved on p. 314, but I will add one more passage from
Beow. 357: '*Helle* gemundon, Metoð ne cuðon,' Helam venera-
bantur, Deum verum ignorabant (pagani). So then, from the
4th cent. to the 10th, *halja*, *hella* was simply Hades or the death-
kingdom, the notion of torment being expressed by another word
or at any rate a compound; and with this agrees the probability

---

[1] A dead man is called *nifl-farinn*, Sæm. 249ª. The progenitor of the Nibelungs
was prob. *Nebel* (Fornald. sög. 2, 9. 11, Næfill for Nefill): a race of heroes doomed
to Hades and early death.   'Nibelunge: spirits of the death-kingdom,' Lachmann
on Nib. 342.

[2] From gehenna comes, we know, the Fr. gehene, gêne, *i.e.* supplice, though in
a very mitigated sense now.

that as late as Widekind of Corvei (1, 23) Saxon poets, chanting
a victory of Saxons over Franks, used this very word *hella* for
the dwelling-place of the dead: 'ut a mimis declamaretur, ubi
tantus ille *infernus* esset, qui tantam *multitudinem caesorum* capere
posset?'[1] A Latin poem on Bp. Heriger of Mentz, of perhaps
the 10th cent.,[2] describes how one that had been spirited away
to the underworld declared 'totum esse *infernum* accinctum densis
ndique silvis,' meaning evidently the abode of the dead, not the
place of punishment. Even in a poem of the 12th cent. (Diut. 3,
104) Jacob says: 'sô muoz ich iemer cholen, unze ich sô *vare ze
der helle*,' until I fare to hell, i.e. die. The 13th cent. saw the
present meaning of helle already established, the abode of the
damned; e.g. in Iw. 1472: 'God bar thee out of *helle!*' take
thee to heaven, not guard thee from death, for the words are
addressed to a dead man (see Suppl.).

Hell is represented as a *lodging*, an *inn*, as *Valhöll*, where those
who die put up the same evening (p. 145): 'ver skulum â *Valhöll
gista i qveld*,' Fornald. sög. 1, 106; 'við munum *i aptan Oðin
gista*' 1, 423; singularly Abbo 1, 555 (Pertz 2, 789), 'plebs
inimica Deo *pransura Plutonis in urna.*' No doubt, people used
to say: 'we shall put up at Nobis-haus to-night!' The Saviour's
words, σήμερον μετ' ἐμοῦ ἔσῃ ἐν τῷ παραδείσῳ, Luke 23, 43 have
'this day,' but not 'to-night'(see Suppl.).

Here and there in country districts, among the common people,
helle has retained its old meaning. In Westphalia there are
still plenty of common carriage-roads that go by the name of
hellweg, now meaning highway, but originally death-way, the
broad road travelled by the corpse. My oldest example I draw
from a Record of 890, Ritz 1, 19: '*helvius* sive strata publica.'
Later instances occur in Weisth. 3, 87. 106, in Tross's Rec. of
the feme p. 61, and in John of Soest (Fichard's Arch. 1, 89).[3]

---

[1] Trad. Corbeiens. pp. 465. 604 makes a regular hexameter of it: 'tantus ubi
infernus, caesos qui devoret omnes?' This overcrowding of Hades with the dead
reminds one of Calderon's fanatic fear, lest heaven stand empty, with all the world
running to the other house after Luther:
    Que vive Dios, que ha de tener en cielo
    pocos que aposentar, si considero
    que estan ya aposentado con Lutero.
                    (Sitio de Breda, jorn. primera).

[2] Lat. gedichte des X. XI. jh. p. 335, conf. 344.

[3] Also in Lower Hesse: *hellweg* by Wettesingen and Oberlistingen (Wochenbl.
for 1833, 952. 984. 1023. 1138), *hölleweg* by Calden (951. 982. 1022), *höllepfad* by
Nothfelden (923).

In the plains of Up. Germany we sometimes find it called *todten-weg* (Mone's Anz. 1838. pp. 225. 316). The ON. poetry makes the dead *ride* or *drive* to the underworld, '*fara til heljar*' or '*til Heljar*,' to the death-goddess: Brynhildr, after she is burnt, travels to Hel in an ornamental car, ' ôk meŏ reiŏinni â *helveg*,' and the poem bears the title *Helreiŏ*, Sæm. 227. In our Freidank 105, 9. 151, 12 it is the christian notion that is expressed by ' zer helle varn' and ' drî strâze zer helle gânt.' For the rest, a hellweg would necessarily bring with it a *hellwagen* (p. 314), just as we meet with a Wôdan's way and waggon both (p. 151). Nay, the Great Bear is not only called himelwagen and herren-wagen, but in the Netherlands *hellewagen* (Wolf's Wodana i. iii. iv.) ; see a 'Wolframus dictus *hellewagen*,' MB. 25, 123 A.D. 1314 (see Suppl.).

The O. Saxons at first, while their own hellia still sounded too heathenish, preferred to take from the Latin Bible *infern*, gen. infernes, e.g. Hel. 44, 21, and even shortened it down to *fern*, Hel. 27, 7. 103, 16. 104, 15. 164, 12 ; so that the poet cited by Widekind may actually have said *infern* instead of hellia.[1]

The heathen hellia lay *low down toward the North;* when Hermôŏr was sent after Baldr, he rode for nine nights through valleys dark and deep (dökva dala ok diupa), the regions peopled by the dark elves (p. 445) ; he arrived at the river *Giöll* (strepens), over which goes a bridge covered with shining gold ; a maiden named Môŏguŏr guards the bridge, and she told him that five fylki of dead men[2] had come over it the day before, and that from this bridge the 'hellway' ran ever lower and northwarder: ' niŏr ok norŏr liggr *helvegr*.' This I understand of the proper hall and residence of the goddess, where she is to be met with, for all the country he had been crossing was part of her kingdom. This palace is surrounded by lofty railings (hel-grindr), Sn. 33. 67. The hall is named *Eliuŏnir* (al. Elvîŏnir), the threshold *fallanda forad* (al. the palisade is fallanda forad, the threshold þolmôŏnir), the curtain *blikjandi böl*, Sn. 33. It is probably a door of this underworld (not of Valhöll, which has 540 huge

---

[1] A place *Infernisi* (Erhard p. 140, A.D. 1113) ; Gael. *ifrinn*, Ir. *ifearn*, Wel. *yfern, uffern.*
[2] A fylki contains 50 (RA. 207), so that Baldr rode down with an escort of 250, though one MS. doubles the number : ' reiŏ Baldr hèr meŏ 500 manna.'

gates) that is meant in Sæm. 226ᵃ and Fornald. sög. 1, 204, where Brynhildr wishes to follow Sigurð in death, lest the door fall upon his heel: a formula often used on entering a closed cavern.[1] But Hel's kingdom bears the name of *Niflheimr* or *Niflhel*, mist-world, mist-hell,[2] it is the *ninth world* (as to position), and was created many ages before the earth (p. 558); in the middle of it is that fountain *Hvergelmir*, out of which twelve rivers flow, *Giöll* being the one that comes nearest the dwelling of the goddess, Sn. 4. From this follows plainly what I have said: if Hvergelmir forms the centre of Niflheimr, if Giöll and the other streams pertain exclusively to hell, the goddess Hel's dominion cannot begin at the 'hel-grindr,' but must extend to those 'dank dales and deep,' the 'dense forests' of the Latin poem. Yet I have nothing to say against putting it in this way: that the dark valleys, like the murky Erebos of the Greeks, are an intermediate tract, which one must cross to reach the abode of Aïdes, of Halja. Out of our Halja the goddess, as out of the personal Hades, the Roman Orcus (orig. uragus, urgus, and in the Mid. Ages still regarded as a monster and alive, pp. 314, 486) there was gradually evolved the local notion of a dwelling-place of the dead. The departed were first imagined living with her, and afterwards in her (it). In the approaches dwelt or hovered the dark elves (see Suppl.).

Niflheimr then, the mist-world, was a cold underground region covered with eternal night, traversed by twelve roaring waters, and feebly lighted here and there by shining gold, i.e. fire. The rivers, especially *Giöll*, remind us of *Lethe*, and of *Styx*, whose holy water gods and men swore by. With Hvergelmir we may

---

[1] The O. Fr. poem on the 'quatre fils Aïmon' (Cod. 7183 fol. 126ᵇ) makes Richart, when about to be hung, offer a prayer, in which we are told that the Saviour brought back all the souls out of hell except one woman, who would stop at the door to give hell a piece of her mind, and is therefore doomed to stay there till the Judgment-day: all were released,

> Ne mes que une dame, qui dist une raison :
> 'hai enfer' dist ele, 'con vos remanez solz,
> noirs, hisdoz et obscurs, et laiz et tenebrox!'
> *a l'entrer de la porte*, si con lisant trovon.
> jusquau terme i sera, que jugerois le mont.

The source of this strange legend is unknown to me.

[2] 'Diu *inre helle*, wo *nebel* und *finster*.' The Lucidarius gives ten names of hell : stagnum ignis, *terra tenebrosa*, terra oblivionis, *swarziu ginunge*, etc. Mone's Anz. for 1834, 313; conf. expressions in the OS. poet : hêt endi *thiustri, suart sinnahti*, Hel. 65, 12; an *dalon thiustron*, an themo alloro ferrosten *ferne* 65, 9; under *ferndalu* 33, 16; *diap* dôdes *dalu* 157, 22.

connect *Helleborne* in Brabant, the source of *Hellebeke;* several places are named *Helleput* (Wolf's Wodana 1, v. and 35). *Helvoetsluis* was cited, p. 315 note; the name *Helle-voet* (-foot) is, we are told, still to be seen on signboards (uithangborden) in the Netherlands (see Suppl.).

Gloomy and joyless as we must imagine Niflheimr,[1] there is no mention anywhere of its denizens being punished and tormented; neither is it the wicked especially that are transported thither at the end of their life, but all and sundry, even the noblest and worthiest, as the examples of Brynhildr and Baldr may shew.[2] The only exceptions seem to be the heroes that fall in battle, whom Oðinn takes to himself into Valhöll.

In contradiction with this view stands another and, I think, a later one, that presented in Sn. 4: Allfather the highest god has given to all men an immortal soul, though their body rot in the ground or burn to ashes; all good men (rétt siðaðir) go to him in Gimill or Vingólf, *all the wicked* (vándir) to Niflheimr or *hell* (conf. Sn. 21 and 75, of which more hereafter). This is already the christian idea, or one extremely like it.

For the old heathen hell, pale and dim, the Christian substituted a pool filled with flames and pitch, in which the souls of the damned burn for ever, at once pitch-black and illumined with a glow. Gehenna is interpreted *hellafiuri*, MHG. *hellefiwer* Parz. 116. 18; the poet of the Heliand, when he wants to picture vividly this black and burning hell, turns the old fem. form into a masc.: 'an thene *hêtan hel*' 76, 22. 'an thene *suartan hel*' 103, 9. Erebi *fornax*, Walther 867. Nay, O. and other OHG. writers make the simple *bëh* (pix) stand for hell[3]: 'in dem *beche*,'

---

[1] Cædmon still pictures the wítehûs (house of torment) as 'deop, dreáma leás, sinnihte beseald.' Striking images occur in a doc. of the 11th cent. (Zeitschr. f. d. a. 3 445): swevilstank, *genibele, tôdes scategruobe,* wallente stredema, etc.

[2] So all the Greek heroes sink into *Hades'* house under the earth. But it is hard to distinguish from it *Tartarus,* which lies lower down the abyss, and where the subjugated giants sit imprisoned. This denoted therefore, at least in the later times, a part of the underworld where the wicked dwell *for their punishment,* which answers to the christian hell. But that the 'roots of earth and sea from above grow down' into Tartarus (Hes. Theog. 728) suggests our Norse ashtree, whose root reaches down to Niflheim. Conf. also Ovid's description of the underworld (Met. 4, 432 seq.), where 'Styx *nebulas exhalat iners*' fits in with the conception of Niflheim.

[3] Quotations in my ed. of the Hymns p. 51. Add Muspilli 5, on which Schm. quotes a line from Walafrid: 'At secum infelix *piceo* spatiatur *averno.*' Eugenius in Dracont. p. m. 30: 'Ut possim *picei* poenam vitare *barathri.*'

Warnung 547 and Wernher v. Niederrh. 40, 10; 'die *pechwelle*,'
Anegenge 28, 19. It is a fancy widely scattered over Europe;
the Mod. Greeks still say πίσσα for hell, as in a proverb of Alex.
Negri: ἔχει πίσσαν καὶ παράδεισον, putting hell and heaven side
by side. This pitchy hell the Greeks seem to have borrowed
from the Slavs, the O. Sl. *péklo* meant both pitch and hell (Dobr.
instit. 294), so the Boh. *peklo*, hell, Pol. *pieklo*, Serv. *pakao*,
Sloven. *pekel*, some masc., some neuter; Lith. *péklà* (fem.), O.
Pruss. *pickullis* (pickullien in the Catechism p. 10 is Acc.), the
devil himself is in Lith. *pyculas*, O. Pruss. *pickuls*, conf. Rausch
p. 484. The Hungarians took their *pokol*, hell, from the Slavic,
as our ancestors did 'gaíaínna' and 'infern' from Greek and
Latin. And the *smela*, hell, of the Lüneburg Wends seems
allied to the Boh. smola, smûla, resin or pitch. With the heat
of boiling pitch was also combined an intolerable stench; Reineke
5918: 'it stank dâr alse dat *helsche pek*.' Conf. generally En.
2845. 3130 (see Suppl.).

Since the conversion to Christianity therefore, there has clung
to the notion of hell the additional one of punishment and pain:
kvöllheimr, mundus supplicii, in Sôlarl. 53 (Sæm. 127ª) is unmistakably the christian idea. The OHG. *hellawizi*, OS. *helliwiti*,
Hel. 44, 17, AS. *hellewíte*, expresses supplicium inferni, conf.
Graff 1, 1117 on *wizi*, MHG. *wize*, MsH. 2, 105ᵇ; upon it are
modelled the Icel. *helvíti*, Swed. *helvete*, Dan. *helvede*, which
mean simply our hell; from the Swedes the converted Finns
received their *helwetti* (orcus), the Lapps their *helvete*, and from
the Bavarians the Slovèns in Carniola and Styria got their *vize*
(purgatorium), for the Church had distinguished between two
fires, the one punitive, the other purgative, and hanging midway
betwixt hell and heaven.[1]

But the christians did not alter the position of hell, it still was
down *in the depths of the earth*, with the human world spread out
above it. It is therefore called *abyssus* (Ducange sub v.), and
forms the counterpart to heaven: 'a coelo usque in abyssum.'
From *abyssus*, Span. *abismo*, Fr. *abîme*, is to be explained the
MHG. *âbîs* (Altd. bl. 1, 295; in âbisses grunde, MsH. 3, 167),
later *obis*, *nobis* (en âbis, en obis, in abyssum). OS. *helligrund*,

---

[1] Of one in purgatory the Esthonians say: ta on kahha ilma wahhel, he is between two worlds.

Hel. 44, 22; in *afgrunde* gân, Roth. 2334; ir verdienet daz *af-grunde*, 1970; 'varen ter helle in den *donkren kelre*,' dark cellar, Florîs 1257.[1] AS. se *neowla grund* (imus abyssus), Cædm. 267, 1. 270, 16; þæt *neowle genip* (profunda caligo) 271, 7. 275, 31. This *neowel, niwel* (profundus) may explain an expression in the Frisian Asega-bok (Richth. 130, 10), 'thiu *niuent* hille,' where a M. Nethl. text has 'de grundlose helle,' bottomless hell. Hell sinking downwards is contrasted with heaven mounting upwards: 'der himel allez ûf gêt, *diu helle siget allez ze tal*,' Warnung 3375-81 (see Suppl.).

It appears that men imagined, as lying at the bottom of our earth, like a ceiling or grating of the underworld, a *stone*, called in MHG. poems *dille-stein* (fr. dille, diele, deal = tabula, pluteus, OHG. dil, dili, ON. þil, þili): 'grüebe ich ûf den *dille-stein*,' if I dug down to the d., Schmiede (smithy, forge) 33; 'des hœhe vür der himele dach und durch der *helle bodem* vert,' its height passes over heaven's roof and through hell's floor, ibid. 1252; 'vür der himele dach dû blickest, u. durch der *helle dillestein* [is not this *floor* rather than ceiling?],' MS. 2, 199[b]; 'wan ez kumt des tiuvels schrei, dâ von wir sîn erschrecket: der *dillestein* der ist enzwei (in-two, burst), die tôten sint ûf gewecket,' Dietr. drachenk. cod. pal. 226[a]. This makes me think of the ὀμφαλός at Delphi, a conical stone wrapt in net (Gerhard's Metroon p. 29), still more of the *lapis manalis* (Festus sub v.) which closed the mouth of the Etruscan *mundus*, and was lifted off on three holy days every year, so that the souls could mount into the upper world (Festus sub v. mundus) Not only this pit in the earth, but heaven also was called mundus,[2] just as Niflheimr is still a heimr, i.e. a world. And that hell-door (p. 802) is paralleled by the '*descensus Averni*,' the '*fauces* grave olentis *Averni*,' the 'atri *janua* Ditis' in Virgil's description, Aen. 6, 126. 201 (conf. helle înfart,' Veldeck's En. 2878. 2907); fairytales of the Slavs too speak of an entrance to the lower world by a *deep pit*, Hanusch p. 412 (see Suppl.).

The mouth or jaws of hell were spoken of, p. 314; Hel yawns

---

[1] Does 'eggrunt' stand for eck-grunt? 'Das iuwer sêle komen ûzer *eggrunde*.' Cod. pal. 349, 19[d].

[2] Conf. O. Müller's Etrusker 2, 96-7. The Finn. *manala* is 'locus subterraneus, ubi versantur mortui,' sepulcrum, orcus, but derived from maa (terra, mundus), and only accidentally resembling 'manalis.'

like her brother Fenrir, and every abyss gapes:[1] *os gehennae* in Beda 363, 17 is the name of a fire-spouting *well* (puteus);[2] in an AS. gloss (Mone 887) *mið* (os) means orcus. The same Coll. of glosses 742 puts down *seáð* (puteus, barathrum) for hell, and 2180 *cwis* for tartarus, 1284 *cwis-husle*, where undoubtedly we must read *cwis-susle*. To *cwis* I can find no clue but the ON. *qvis* calumnia [quiz, tease? queror, questus?]; *susl* is apparently tormentum, supplicium, the dictionaries having no ground for giving it the sense of sulphur (AS. swefel); 'susle ge-innod,' Cædm. 3, 28, I take to be supplicio clausum. The notion of the *well* agrees remarkably with the fable in the Reinhart, where the hero having fallen into a well wheedles the wolf into the bucket; he pretends he is sitting in *paradis* down there, only there is no getting to it but by taking ' einen tuk (plunge) in die *helle.*' The well easily leads to the notion of bathing: ' ze helle *baden,*' MsH. 2, 254[a]; for you can bathe in fire and brimstone too (see Suppl.).

Christian and heathen notions on the punishments of the lost are found mixed in the Sôlarlióð of the Edda, Sæm. 128-9. Snakes, adders, dragons dwell in the christian hell (Cædm. 270-1), as at the Hvergelmir root (p. 796). It is striking how the poem of Oswald (Haupt's Zeitschr. 2, 125) represents a dead heathen woman as a *she-wolf*, with the devils pouring pitch and brimstone down her throat. Dante in his Purgatorio and Inferno mixes up what he finds handed down by the Mid. Ages and classical literature. Read also the conclusion of Cædmon (Fundgr. 202); and in the Barlaam 310, Rudolf's brief but poetic picture of hell [3] (see Suppl.).

That the heathen Mist-world lying far to the *north* was not filled with fire, comes out most clearly from its opposite, a Flame-world in the *south* (p. 558), which the Edda calls *Muspell* or *Muspells-heimr.* This is bright and hot, glowing and burning,[4]

---

[1] Wallach. *iad* (hiatus), *iadul* hell.

[2] As evening is the 'mouth of night.'

[3] Here we may sum up what living men have reached Hades and come back: of the Greeks, Orpheus in search of Eurydice; Odysseus; Aeneas. Of Norsemen, Her-móðr when dispatched after Baldr, and Hadding (Saxo Gram. p. 16). Medieval legends of Brandanus and Tundalus; that of Tanhäuser and others like it shall come in the next chap. Monkish dreams, visions of princes who see their ancestors in hell, are coll. in D.S. nos. 461. 527. 530. 554; of the same kind is the vision of the vacant chair in the Annolied 724, conf. Tundalus 65, 7.

[4] Muspellsheimr is not heaven, nor are the sons of Muspell the same as the *light elves* that live in heaven (p. 445); when Surtr has burnt up heaven and earth,

natives alone can exist in it, hence human beings from our world
never pass into it, as into the cold one of the north. It is guarded
by a god (?) named *Surtr*, bearer of the blazing sword.

In the word Muspell we find another striking proof of the
prevalence of ON. conceptions all over Teutondom. Not only
has the Saxon Heliand a *mudspelli* 79, 24, *mutspelli* 133, 4, but
a High German poem, probably composed in Bavaria, has at line
62 *muspilli* (dat. muspille). Besides, what a welcome support
to the age and real basis of the Edda, coming from Saxon and
Bavarian manuscripts of the 9th cent. and the 8th! Everywhere else the term is extinct : neither Icelanders nor other
Scandinavians understand it, in Anglo-Saxon writings it has
never shewn itself yet, and later specimens of German, High
and Low, have lost all knowledge of it. Assuredly a primitive,
a heathenish word.[1]

On its general meaning I have already pronounced, p. 601 :
it can scarcely be other than fire, flame. The Heliand passages
tell us : ' *mudspelles* megin obar man ferid,' the force of fire
fareth over men ; ' *mutspelli* cumit an thiustrea naht, al sô thiof
ferid darno mid is dâdiun,' fire cometh in dark night, as thief
fareth secret and sudden with his deeds (Matth. 24, 43.   2 Pet.
3, 10) ; and the OHG. poet says : ' dâr ni mac denne mâk andremo helfan vora demo *muspille*, denna daz preitâ wasal (Graff
1, 1063) allaz varprennit,[2] enti viur enti luft allaz arfurpit,' then
no friend can help another for the fire, when the broad shower
of glowing embers (?) burns up all, and fire and air purge
(furbish) everything.

It must be a compound, whose latter half *spilli*, *spelli*, *spell*
we might connect with the ON. spiöll (corruptio), spilla (corrum-
pere), AS. spillan (perdere), Engl. spill, OHG. spildan, OS.
spildian (perdere) ;[3] ON. mannspiöll is clades hominum, læspiöll
(Nialss. c. 158) perhaps bellum. But we are left to guess what

---

there lies above this heaven a second, named *Andlângr*, and above that a third
named *Viðblâinn*, and there it is that *light elves* alone live now, says Snorri 22.
    [1] In Nemnich, among the many names given for the bittern (OHG. horotumbil,
onocrotalus, ardea stellaris), there is also *muspel*, which probably has to do with
moss and moor, not with our word.
    [2] So I read (trans.) for ' varprinnit' (intrans.), as ' wasal ' cannot otherwise be
explained.
    [3] OHG. ld = ON. ll ; conf. ' wildi, kold ' with ' villr, gull.' But then why is it
not muspildi in the OHG. and OS. poems ?

mud, mu (mû?) can be, whether earth, land, or else wood, tree. In the latter case, *mudspelli* is a descriptive epithet of fire, an element aptly named the wood-destroying, tree-consuming, as elsewhere in the Edda it is *bani viðar* (percussor, inimicus ligni), *grand viðar* (perditio ligni), Sn. 126; the Lex Alam. 96, 1 has *medela, medula* in the sense of lancwitu, lancwit (Gramm. 3, 455), the Lex Rothar. 305 *modula*, apparently for quercus, robur (Graff 2, 707), and the ON. *meiðr*. (perh. for meyðr, as seiðr for seyðr) is arbor, Lith. *medis* [Mongol. *modo*] arbor, lignum. The other supposition would make it land-destroying, world-wasting; but still less do I know of any Teutonic word for land or earth that is anything like *mud* or *mu*. We may fairly regard it as a much obscured and distorted form; Finn. maa is terra, solum (see Suppl.).[1]

Surtr (gen. Surtar, dat. Surti, Sæm. 9ᵃ) is the swart, swarthy, browned by heat, conn. with svartr (niger), yet distinct from it;[2] it occurs elsewhere too as a proper name, Fornald. sög. 2, 114. Islend. sög. 1, 66. 88. 106. 151. 206; and curiously 'Surtr enn hvíti,' ibid. 1, 212. But there must have been another form *Surti*, gen. Surta, for in both Eddas we meet with the compound *Surtalogi*, Sæm. 37ᵇ. Sn. 22. 76. 90. A certain resinous charred earth is in the North still called *Surtarbrandr* (Surti titio, Biörn sub v., F. Magn. lex. 730), a mode of naming indicative of a superior being, as when plants are named after gods. Volcanic rock-caves in Iceland are called *Surtarhellir* (F. Magn. lex. 729); the Landnámabók 3, 10 (Isl. sög. 1, 151) tells how one Thórvaldr brought to the cave of the iötunn Surtr a song composed about him: 'þá fór hann upp til *hellisins Surts*, oc fœrði þar drápu þá, er hann hafði ort um *iötuninn í hellinum*'; and Sn. 209ᵇ 210ᵃ includes *Surtr* and *Svartr* among the names of giants. Nowhere in the two Eddas does *Surtr* appear as a

---

[1] Should any one reject these explanations, and take *e.g.* OS. mudspelli for 'muth-spelli,' oris eloquium, or 'mût-sp.,' mutationis nuntius (as I proposed in Gramm. 2, 525), he is at once met by the objection, that the Bav. poet writes neither 'mund-sp.' nor 'mûz-sp.,' any more than the ON. has munn-spiall' or 'mût-sp.'; and then how are these meanings to be reconciled with that of 'heimr'? let alone the fact that there is no later (christian) term for the world's end or the judgment-day pointing at all that way.

[2] Surtr might stand related to svartr, as the Goth. name Svartus to the adj. svarts. Procopius de bello Goth. 2, 15. 4, 25 has a Herulian name Σουοϱουας, Svartva? The AS. geneal. of Deira has Swearta and Swerting, conf. Beow. 2406, and 'sweart racu' below.

god, but always, like other giants, as an enemy and assailant of the gods. In Völuspâ 48 (Sæm. 8ª) fire is called 'Surta sefi,' Surti amicus; and in 52 (Sæm. 8ᵇ) we read:

> Surtr fer sunnan með sviga leifi,
> skîn af sverði sôl valtîva,

i.e. Surtus tendit ab austro cum vimine gigas, splendet e gladio (ejus) sol deorum: 'leifi' is plainly another word for giant, Sn. 209ª; 'valtîva' can only be a gen. pl. (conf. Sæm. 10ª 52ª) and dependent on sôl, not gen. sing. of valtîvi (which never occurs, p. 194) dep. on sverði; what can be the meaning here of 'svigi' (usually twisted band, wisp?) I cannot say, one would think it also referred to the brandished sword. Surtr then is expressly called a giant, not a god. Sn. 5 says: 'så er *Surtr* nefndr, er þar sitr å landzenda til landvarnar, hann hefir *loganda sverð*', Surtus vocatur, qui sedet in fine regionis (*i.e.* Muspellsheims) ad eam tuendam, ensemque gestat ardentem (see Suppl.).

The authors of the Heliand and the OHG. poem, both christian, but still somewhat versed in heathen poetry, alike introduce *muspilli* at the end of the world, at the approach of the Judgment-day, when the earth and all it contains will be consumed by fire. And that is exactly how the Edda describes the same event: Surtr arises with the sons of muspell, makes war upon all the gods and overcomes them, the whole world perishes by his fire, Sn. 5. 73. When he with his blazing brand comes on from the South, the rocks in the mountains reel, the giantesses flee, men go the way of the dead, heaven cracks asunder, Sæm. 8ᵇ; the Ases do battle with Surtr and his host on a holm called Oskopnir (supra p. 144), they are all slain, and the world comes to an end (see Suppl.).

It is only the Edda that brings in the name of Surtr; but our OHG. poetry seems to have interwoven features of him into the church doctrine about *Antichrist*, OHG. Antichristo (p. 173-4), which, originally founded on the 11th chap. of Revelation, was afterwards worked out further on Jewish-christian lines of thought. The name occurs in two epistles (1 John 2, 18. 4, 3. 2 John 7), not in the Apocalypse, where he is meant by the many-headed *beast*. In his time *two* prophetic *witnesses* are to be sent from heaven to earth, but to be conquered and slain by him.

Their names are not given either; that they are *Enoch* and *Elias*
follows from the power given them to shut heaven that it rain
not, and is expressly acknowledged by the Fathers.[1] Their
bodies lie unburied in the street: after this victory the power of
Antichrist attains its greatest height, until he gets upon the
Mount of Olives, to ascend into heaven; then the angel *Michael*
appears, and cleaves his skull.[2]

With this narrative our O. Bavarian poet had become acquainted
through learned men (weroltrehtwîsê), but still the old heathen
pictures of the world's destruction come floating before him as
' muspilli' draws nigh: he makes much of the *flames*, he sees
the mountains *set on fire* by the blood of the mortally wounded
Elias dropping on the earth; no such circumstance is found in
any christian tradition. The *sky swelters in a blaze* (suilizôt
lougiû), the *earth burns* (prinnit mittilagart), and his already
quoted ' dar ni mac denne mâk andremo helfan vora demo *muspilli* ', supported as it may be by Mark 13, 12. Luke 21, 16,
sounds very like the Eddic

> brœðr muno berjaz ok at bönom verða,
> muno systrûngar sifjum spilla,
> man ecki maðr öðrum þyrma (Sæm. 7ᵇ 8ᵃ).

He has ' *mâno* fallit,' as Sæmund has ' *sôl* tekr sortna, hverfa
af himni heiðar *stiörnur*.' Again Sn. 71: ' þâ drepaz brœðr fyrir
âgirni sakar, oc engi þyrmir föðr eða syn î manndrâpum oc
sifjasliti.'[3] So even a MHG. poet of the 12th cent. (Fundgr.
194): ' sô ist danne niht triuwe diu frowe der diuwe (maid), noch
der man dem wîbe; si lebent alle mit nîde; sô hazzet der vater
den sun,' etc. One would like to know what heathen figure

[1] Justin Martyr's Dial. cum Tryph. ed. Sylb. p. 208; Tertull. de anima cap. 50,
de resurr. carnis cap. 58; Hippolytus in Λόγος περί τῆς συντελείας τοῦ κόσμου καὶ περὶ
τοῦ ἀντιχρίστου; Dorotheus Tyr. de vita prophet. cap. 18; Ambrose on Apocal. cap.
11; Aug. de civ. Dei 20, 29; Greg. Magn. in moral. 15, 18. And see authors
quoted in Hoffm. Fundgr. 2, 102 seq. and Kausler's Anl. denkm. 1, 486. For later
times, conf. N. ps. 58, 7. 73, 10; Burcard. Wormat. 20, 93–7; Otto Frising. 8, 1–8;
Discip. de tempore, serm. 10.
[2] 12-13th cent. accounts of Antichrist in the Hortus delici. of Herrat of Lands-
berg (Engelhard p. 48); in Cod. vind. 653, 121-2; Fundgr. 1, 195-6. 2, 106—134;
Martina 191 seq.; Wackernag. Basle MSS. 22ᵃ; and conf. Introd. to Freidank
lxxi. lxxii.
[3] No stronger argument do I know for the theory that Völuspâ is an echo of
our Scriptures, than the agreement of the Edda and the Bible in this particular; if
only the rest would correspond!

Antichristo took the place of to Bavarians and Alamanns, it must have been one similar to the Norse *Surtr*. Antichristo plays the fiendish hypocrite, Surtr is painted as the adversary of the Ases, as a giant, and his fire consumes the world. The muspells-synir are all drawn up in squadrons of light, they and Surtr by their fighting bring about a higher order of things, while Antichrist is but transiently victorious, and is finally overthrown by a mightier power (see Suppl.).

What adds new weight to the whole comparison is the affinity between *Donar* and *Elias*, which was made out on p. 173-4 and is clear on other grounds. To the 8th cent. Elias might well seem something more than the Hebrew prophet, viz. a divine hero, a divinity. The Edda makes all the Ases, *Oðinn, Thôrr, Freyr,* and *Týr,* unite their powers to do battle with the sons of fire and their confederates, yet they are beaten like Enoch and Elias : Elias bears a marked resemblance to Thôrr (or Donar), Michael to the queller of Garmr or Fenris-úlfr ; I do not say that Enoch is equally to be identified with any particular god, but he might. Surtr with the flaming sword may remind us of the angel that guards Paradise, but he also finds his counterpart in the story of Enoch and Elias, for these two, at least in the legend of Brandan (in Bruns p. 187), have an angel *with a fiery sword* standing by their side.[1]——An AS. homily De temporibus Antichristi quoted by Wheloc on Beda p. 495 (supra p. 161n.) contains remarkable statements. Arrogant *Antecrist*, it says, not only strives against God and his servants, but sets himself up above all heathen gods: ' He âhefð hine silfne ofer ealle þâ þe hæþene men cwædon þæt godas beon sceoldon, on hæþene wîsan. Swylc swâ wæs *Erculus* se ent, and *Apollinis,* þe hî mærne god lêton, *Dhôr* eác and *Eowðen,* þe hæþene men heriað swîðe. Ofer ealle þæs he hine ænne up âhefð, forðam he læt *þæt he âna si strengra þonne hi ealle.'* Why does the preacher say all this ? Had Saxon songs also identified the advent of Antichrist with heathen traditions, and recognised his victory, like that of Surtr, over *Wôden* and *Thunor* ? The un-Saxon forms Eowðen and Dhôr indicate Norse or Danish influence.——But a decisive connexion is established by the AS. Salomon and Saturn (Kemble p. 148) : in the great battle

---

[1] M. Nethl. poems in Blommaert 1, 105ª. 2, 12ª have simply an 'out man' in Enoch's place, but they mention the cherubin *med enen swerde vierin.*

between God and Antichrist, we are told, *Thunder* was threshing with his *fiery axe*, ' se *Thunor* hit þrysceð mid þære *fýrenan œcœe*,' by which is unmistakably meant Thôr's Miölnir, the torrida chalybs (p. 180), and the confluence of heathen beliefs with those about Antichrist is placed beyond the reach of doubt. The devil too is called malleus, hammer, chap. XXXIII.

Whoever is inclined to refer the characteristics of our antiquity as a whole to Roman and christian tradition, could easily take advantage of this harmony between the two pictures of the world's destruction, to maintain that the Eddic doctrine itself sprang out of those traditions of Antichrist. This I should consider a gross perversion. The Norse narrative is simple, and of one piece with all the rest of the Edda ; the myth of Antichrist is a jumble, nay artificially pieced together. The two leading personages, Surtr and Antichrist, have totally different characters. How should the Scandinavians have foisted-in a number of significant accessories, notably this of muspell, and again a H. German poet unconnected in time and place have tacked on the very same ?

What the Edda tells of Surtr and his combat with the Ases is the winding-up of a fuller representation of the end of the world,[1] whose advent is named *aldar rök* (Sæm. 36ᵃ), *aldar lag, aldar rof* (37ᵇ. 167ᵃ),[2] but more commonly *ragna rök* (7ᵃ. 38ᵇ. 96ᵇ. 166ᵇ) or *ragna rökr* (65ᵃ. Sn. 30. 36. 70. 88. 165), i.e. twilight, darkening, of time and the sovran gods (supra p. 26). *Rök* and *rökr* both mean darkness, *rök rökra* in Sæm. 113ᵃ is an intensified expression for utter darkness ; Biörn renders *röckur* (neut.) crepusculum, *röckva* vesperascere. It is akin to the Goth. *riqis* σκότος, *riqizeins* σκοτεινός, *riqizjan* σκοτίζεσθαι, only that is increased by a suffix -is, and has its radical vowel alien from the Norse *ö*, which must be a modified *a*, so that rök stands for *raku*. This is confirmed by the Jutish *rag* nebula, still more by the AS. *racu* : ' þonne *sweart racu* stîgan onginneð,' Cædm. 81, 34 must be rendered ' cum atra caligo surgere incipit.' *Rökstólar* (Sæm. 1ᵇ, conf. supra p. 136) are the chairs of mist whereon the gods sit up in the clouds. To this rök, racu I refer the expression quoted

---

[1] It is worth noting, that it is proclaimed by *prophetesses*, *Vala*, *Hyndla* ; and later, *Thiota* (p. 96) announced consummationis seculi diem.

[2] *Rof* ruptura ; as they said ' regin *riufaz*,' dii rumpuntur, the world is going to pieces.

on p. 753, 'die finstre *ragende* nacht,' which can hardly be explained from our ragen (rigere) stick out.[1] *Ragnarök* then is
the night of the gods, which comes over all beings, even the
highest, p. 316 (see Suppl.).

Then the evil beings, long held in check and under spell, break
loose and war against the gods: a wolf swallows the sun, another
the moon (p. 705-6), the stars fall from heaven, the earth quakes,
the monstrous world-snake Iörmungandr, seized with giant fury
(iötunmôðr, p. 530), rises out of the waters on to the land,
Fenrisûlfr is set free (p. 244), and *Naglfar* afloat, a ship constructed out of dead men's nails.[2] Loki brings up the hrîmthurses
and the retinue of Hel (Heljar sinnar), all the hellish, wolfish kindred have mustered together.   But it is from the flame-world
that the gods have most danger to dread: Surtr and his glittering host come riding over Bifröst the rainbow (p. 732) in such
strength that they break it down.   The single combatants are
disposed thus : Oðinn fights with Fenrisûlfr, Thôrr with Iörmungandr, Freyr with Surtr, Týr with Garmr,[3] Heimdall with Loki;
in every case the old gods go down, though Garmr and Loki fall
too, and Fenrisûlfr is slain by Víðar.[4]   That Loki and all his kin
should come out as allies to the sons of flame, follows from his

---

[1] Pers. rache is said to mean vapour; may the Sanskr. rajanî (nox) be also
brought in? The Slav. *rok* tempus, annus, terminus, fatum, Lith. *rakus*, is worth
considering ; its abstract meaning may have sprung out of a material one, and fits
in perfectly with the notions of time and world developed on p. 790 [*rok*, fate, is
from reku, I speak]. Neither rök, rökr, nor riqis has anything to do with our
rauch, reek, ON. reykr. It is not correct for Danish writers to use the form ragna-
rok; ON. rök must in their dialect be rag (as sök is sag) ; the OHG. form of ragnarök would be regino-rahha, or -rah, -rahhu, according as it were fem. or neuter.
In Swed. and Dan. the term is extinct, but they both have a word for crepusculum,
Swed. *thysmörker*, Dan. *tusmörke*, which may be from þuss, þurs, implying an ON.
þursmyrkr, giant's murk, and that would tally with the giant nature of Surtr.

[2] This is intended to express the enormous distance and tardy arrival of the
world's end: before such a vessel can be built of the tiny nail-parings of dead bodies
a longish time must elapse, which is still further protracted by the wholesome precept, always to pare the nails of the dead before burying or burning them ; conf. F.
Magnusen's Lex. 520. 820. Not unlike is the image of the mountain of eternity, to
which a bird adds one grain of sand every hundred years.

[3] *Garmr*, the hugest of all *hounds* (Sæm. 46ᵃ), no doubt, like Κέρβερος, only
a metamorphosed giant, seems like him also to be a native of the under-world;
when Oðinn journeys to Niflhel, ' mœtti hann hvalpi þeim er or heljo kom,' met he
the whelp that came out of hell (94ᵃ) ; he barks long, he lies chained and barks 'for
Gnípahellir ' (7ᵃ. 8ᵃ).   The hell-hound of christian legend comes nearer the Norse
wolf (see next note).

[4] Víðar's victory over the *wolf*, in whose jaws he plants a foot mythically shod
(Sn. 73), resembles the description in christian traditions of how the *hell-hound* was
assailed ; conf. Fundgr. 1, 178-9.

very nature, he being a god of fire (p. 241). After the *world-conflagration* or *Surtalogi*, a new and happier earth rises out of the sea, with gods made young again, but still called *Aesir*, Sæm. 10 : a finale bearing an indisputable likeness to the Last Judgment [1] and New Jerusalem of the christians. Strophe 65 of the Völuspâ, which expressly mentions the *regindómr*, has been pronounced an interpolation, because it is wanting in some MSS.; but interpolation is not a thing to be gauged by the contents alone, it must be incontrovertibly established by explicit proofs. Even if it did take place, neither the heathen character of the myth nor the age of the poem as a whole is thereby brought under suspicion. For, as the heathen faith among early converted races was not demolished at a blow,[2] so here and there a christian dogma may also have penetrated even to nations that were still heathen; conversely some heathen ways of thinking lingered on among christians. Consider how the author of the Heliand (131-2-3), while following the Gospels in describing the approach of the Last Day, yet admits such rank heathenisms as ' Gebanes strôm ' and ' Mudspelli.' In the very personifying of the Judgment day (' *verit* stuatago in lant,' like ' muspelli *kumit* ') there is a flavour of heathenism.

There seem to have existed some other traditions about the world's destruction, which have not come down to us in their fulness. Among these I reckon the folk-tale mentioned on p. 429, of the ring which the swan will drop from his mouth : it sounds altogether antique, and possibly harks back to the notion of the world-ring, p. 794.

To the destruction of the world *by fire*, which heathens and christians[3] look forward to as *future*, stands opposed that *by water*, which the histories of both represent as *past*. The Burning, like the Deluge (pp. 576—81), is not to destroy for ever, but to purify, and bring in its wake a new and better order of things (see Suppl.).

---

[1] OHG. *antitago, suonotac, suonotago, tuomistac, tuomtac, stuatago* (Goth. stáuadags?) ; MHG. *endetac, stienetac, tuomtac;* OS. 'the *lasto dag*,' *dômdag, dômesdag*, AS. *dômdæg*, Engl. *dooms-day*, ON. *dômsdagr*.

[2] In Leyden's Complaynt p. 98 is actually mentioned a story, 'the tayl of the wolfe and the warldis end,' which was current in Scotland and elsewhere (supra p. 245) as late as the 15th cent. Worth reading is an Icel. free adaptation of the Vaticinium Merlini, said to have been composed towards the end of the 12th cent., in which are mixed ON. ideas of the world's end, F. Magn. lex. 658-9.

[3] 2 Pet. 8, 12 ; conf. Freidank 179, 4.

The church tradition of the Mid. Ages (based on Matth. 24,
Mark 13, Luke 21) accepts fifteen signs as premonitions of the
Judgment-day;[1] these do not include the unearthly winter, *fim-
bulvëtr*, that wind-age (vindöld, p. 793, Haupt's Zeitschr. 7,
309), which according to both Eddas (Sæm. 36ᵇ. Sn. 71) precedes the ragnarökr, and is doubtless a truly Teutonic fancy;[2]
but we have a *darkening of the sun and moon* described (p. 244),
and an *earthquake*, which equally precedes the twilight of the
gods: ' griotbiörg *gnata*, himinn klofnar, *gnýr* allr Iötunheimr,'
Sæm. 8ᵇ; the ordinary term in ON. is *land-skiâlfti*, Sn. 50, or
' iörd *skâlf*;' ' landit skâlf, sem â þræði lêki,' Fornald. sög. 1,
424. 503.[3]   For σεισμός Ulphilas gives the fem. *reirô*, he says
' aírþa *reiráida*;' OS. ' ertha *bivôda*,' Hel. 168, 23; OHG. ' erda
bibinôta,' O. iv. 34, 1, and the subst. erdpipa, erdbibunga, erd-
girnornessi.   Reinardus 1, 780 puts in juxtaposition: 'nec *tremor
est terrae, judiciive dies*;' and Servian songs: ' ili *grmi*, il se
zemlia trese?' does it thunder, or does the earth shake? (Vuk 2,
1. 105).   But the earth's quaking, like the Deluge, is oftener
represented as a past event, and is ascribed to various causes.
The Greek fable accounts for it by imprisoned cyclops or titans
(Ov. Met. 12, 521); the Norse by the struggles of chained Loki
when drops of poison fall upon his face (Sæm. 69. Sn. 70), or by
Fâfnir's journey to the water (Fornald. sög. 1, 159. 160).   The
earth also quakes at the death of certain heroes, as Heimir (Fornald. sög. 1, 232), and of the giant (Vilk. saga cap. 176).   At
Roland's death there is lightning, thunder and earthquake, Rol.
240, 22.   To the Indians the earth quakes every time one of the
eight elephants supporting the globe is tired of his burden, and
gives his head a shake.[4]   The Japanese say of an earthquake:
' there is another whale crept away from under our country;' the

---

[1] Thom. Aquinas (d. 1274) in Librum 4 sententiar. Petri Lomb. dist. 48. qu. 1.
art. 4 (Thomae opp. Venet. 13, 442).   Asegabôk (Richth. 130-1).   Haupt's Zeitschr.
1, 117. 3, 523.   Hoffm. Fundgr. 1, 196-7: 2, 127.   Amgb. 39.   Wackernagel's Basle
MSS. 22ᵇ.   Massm. denkm. 6.   Berceo (d. 1268) de los signos que aparecerán ante
del Juicio, in Sanchez coleccion 2, 273.   Thomas, Asegabôk and Berceo all refer to
Jerome, but no such enumeration of the 15 signs is to be found in his works.   Rol.
289-90 and Karl 89ᵃ have similar signs at Roland's death (see Suppl.).
[2] Notice Sæm. 119ᵃ: 'þaðan koma *sniofar* ok *snarir vindar*,' and the poetic descriptions of *winter* in AS. writers: Andr. 1256-63.   Beow. 2258.
[3] ' Lönd öll *skulfu*,' Sn. 66; ' fold för *skiâlfandi*,' 148.
[4] Schlegel's Ind. bibl. no. 2.

Tahitians: 'God shakes the earth;'[1] the Lettons: 'Drebkuls beats the earth, and makes her tremble,' just as the Greeks call their Poseidon (Neptune) Ἐννοσίγαιος, Ἐννοσίδας (see Suppl.).

Our forefathers thought of the sky not only as a roof to the earth (p. 698), but as a heavenly kingdom, the dwelling-place of gods and of blessed men whom they had taken up. The bridge of the heavenly bow leads into it (p. 732), so does the milky way (p. 356).

We must first suppose all that to have happened which was told in chap. XIX about the creation of the world according to ON. views. After the gods had set in order heaven and earth, created Ask and Embla, and appointed Miðgarð to be the habitation of man, they fitted up for themselves in the centre of the world a dwelling-place named Asgurðr, in whose vast extent however a number of particular spots are specified.

None of these separate mansions is more celebrated than the Odinic Valhöll (OHG. Walahalla?), whose name has an obvious reference to the god's own appellation of Valföðr and to the valkyrs (p. 417).[2] Into this abode, sometimes known as Oðins salir (Sæm. 148[b]), the war-maidens have conducted to him all the heroes that from the beginning of the world have fallen in valr, on the battle-field (the vâpn-bitnir, weapon-bitten, Yngl. saga c. 10); these he adopts as children, they are óskasynir, sons by wishing, ad-option,[3] and likewise sons of the god Wish (p. 143). Their usual name is einherjar, egregii, divi, as Oðinn himself is called Herjan and Herjaföðr, and heri means the fighting hero (p. 342-3). It must not be overlooked, that Thôrr himself is called an einheri, Sæm. 68[a], as if a partaker of Valhöll. From the existence of a proper name Einheri in OHG. (e.g. Meichelbeck no. 241. 476. Schannat 137), I argue the former prevalence of the mythical term amongst us also; yet not with certainty, as it may be a contracted form of Eginheri, Aganheri, like Einhart for Eginhart, Reinhart for Reginhart. Valhöll is covered with shields

---

[1] Zimmerm. Taschenb. f. reisen, jahrg. 9 abth. 2. Adelung's Mithrid. 1, 634.
[2] Prob. also to Valaskiálf, the hall covered with silver, Sæm. 41[a]. Sn. 21; conf. Hliðskiálf, p. 185. Skiálf expresses the quivering motion of the airy mansion, like bif in Bifröst. Our OHG. 'walaëht des êwigen lîbes,' Is. 73, 4 seems not merely possessio vitæ æternæ, but an emphatic term purposely chosen.
[3] 'Got setzet si in sîne schôz,' in his bosom, Ls. 3, 92.

(Sn. 2) and numbers 540 doors, each affording passage to 800
einheries at once, or 432,000 in all, Sæm. 43ª. In the midst of
it stands a mighty tree *Ljeraðr*, *Læráðr*, whose foliage is cropt by
the she-goat *Heiðrûn;* the goat's udder yields (as Amalthea's
horn did nectar) a barrelful of mead a day, enough to nourish all
the einheries. The stag *Eikþyrnir* gnaws the branches of the
tree, and out of his horns water trickles down into Hvergelmir
continually, to feed the rivers of the underworld (pp. 558. 561).

This mansion of bliss all valiant men aspired to, and attained
after death; to the evildoer, the coward, it was closed [1]: 'mun
sâ maôr braut rekinn ur *Valhöllu*, ok þâr aldrei koma,' Nialss.
cap. 89. To wage a life-and-death conflict with a hero was
called shewing him to Walhalla (vîsa til Valhallar), Fornald.
sög. 1, 424. Sagas and panegyric poems paint the reception of
departed heroes in Walhalla: when Helgi arrives, Oðinn offers
to let him reign with him, Sæm. 166ᵇ; the moment Helgi has
acquired the joint sovereignty, he exercises it by imposing menial
service on Hundîngr, whom he had slain. Thus the distinctions
of rank were supposed to be perpetuated in the future life. On
the approach of Eyrîkr, Oðinn has the benches arranged, the
goblets prepared, and wine brought up (Fragm. of song, Sn. 97);
Sigmund and Sinfiötli are sent to meet him (Müller's Sagabibl.
2, 375). The Hâkonarmâl is a celebrated poem on Hâkon's welcome in Valhöll. Bnt even the hall of a king on earth, where
heroes carouse as in the heavenly one, bears the same name
Valhöll (Sæm. 244ª. 246ª anent Atli). The abodes and pleasures
of the gods and those of men are necessarily mirrored in each
other; conf. pp. 336. 393 (see Suppl.).

Indian mythology has a *heaven for heroes*, and that of Greece
assigns them an elysium in the far West, on the happy isles of
Okeanos; we may with perfect confidence assert, that a belief in
Walhalla was not confined to our North, but was common to all
Teutonic nations. A 'vita Idae' in Pertz 2, 571 uses the ex-
pression 'coelorum *palatinae sedes*,' implying that a court is
maintained like the king's palatium, where the departed dwell.
Still more to the point is the A.S. poet's calling heaven a *shield-*

---

[1] A 13th cent. poem, to be presently quoted, has already an unmistakable reference to our tale of the *spielmann* or *spielhansel* (Jack player), who is turned out of
heaven, because he has led a bad life, and performed no deeds.

burg, which, like Valhöll, was covered with golden shields (p. 700). In the 'vita Wulframi' there is shewn to the Frisian king Radbot a *house glittering with gold,* prepared for him when he dies (D.S. no. 447. V. d. Bergh's Overlev. 93) ; like that described in MS. 2, 229ᵦ :

> In himelrîch ein hûs stât,
> ein guldîn wec darîn gât,
> die siule die sint mermelîn,
> die zieret unser trehtîn
> mit edelem gesteine.

A poem of the 13th cent. (Warnung 2706—98) declares that the kingdom of heaven is to be won by heroes only, who have fought and bear upon them scars from stress of war (nâch urliuges nôt), not by a useless fiddler :

> Die herren vermezzen
> ze gemache sint gesezzen,
> unt ruowent immer mêre
> nâch verendetem sêre.
> Versperret ist ir burctor,
> belîben müezen dâ vor
> die den strît niht en-vâhten
> unt der flühte gedâhten.—
> Swâ sô helde suln belîben
> ir herren ir müezet vehten,
> welt ir mit guoten knehten
> den selben gmach niezen (see Suppl.).

(There men high-mettled to repose are settled, they rest evermore from ended sore. Barred is their borough-gate ; and they without must wait who the fight ne'er fought, but of flight took thought, etc.)

But another thing must have been inseparable from the heathen conception, viz. that in Walhalla the goblet goes round, and the joyous carouse of heroes lasts for ever.[1] Several expressions may

---

[1] The same thought is strongly expressed in a well-known epitaph :
Wiek, düvel, wiek ! wiek wit van mi (get away from me) !
ik scher mi nig (I care not) en har um di,
ik ben en meklenburgsch edelman :
wat geit di düvel min sûpen an (to do with my quaffing) ?

be accepted as proofs of this. *Glaðs-heimr* is the name of the spot on which Valhöll is reared, Sæm. 41ª; in *Glaðsheim* stands the high seat of Allfather, Sn. 14. A house by the side of it, built for goddesses, bears the name of *Vin-gólf*, but it seems also to be used synonymously with Valhöll, as one poet sings : ' vildac glaðr í *Vingólf* fylgja ok með einherjum öl drecka.' Vingólf is literally amica aula, and it is by the almost identical words *win-burg, winsele*, as well as *goldburg, goldsele*, that AS. poets name the place where a king and his heroes drink (Pref. to Andr. and El. xxxvii.-viii.). Glaðsheimr or glaðheimr may mean either glad, or bright, home; even now it is common to call heaven a *hall of joy, vale of joy*, in contrast to this vale of tears (p. 795). I do not know if the ancient term *mons gaudii, mendelberc* (p. 170 n.) had any reference to heaven ; but much later on, a joyful blissful abode was entitled sældenbero (Diut. 2, 35), wonnenberg, freudenberg: ' to ride to the *freudenberg* at night ' says a Rec. of 1445 (Arnoldi's Misc. 102); ' thou my heart's *freudensal* ' is addressed to one's lady love (Fundgr. 1, 335), like the more usual ' thou my heaven '; and in thieves' slang freudenberg and wonnenberg = doxy. *Freuden-thal, -berg, -garten* often occur as names of places (see Suppl.).[1]

Let us see how much of these heathen fancies has survived among christian ones, or found its counterpart in them. The name Valhöll, Walahalla, seems to have been avoided; *winsele* may indeed have been said of heaven, but I can only find it used of earthly dwellings, Cædm. 270, 21. Beow. 1383. 1536. 1907. On the other hand our later and even religious poets continue without scruple to use the term *freudensal* for heaven, for heavenly

ik sûp mit min herr Jesu Christ,
wenn du, düvel, ewig dörsten müst,
un *drink mit en fort kolle schal*,
wenn du sittst in de höllequal.

This is not mere railing, but the sober earnest of heroes who mean to drink and hunt with Wuotan ; conf. Lisch's Mekl. jahrb. 9, 447.

[1] Such a land of bliss is part of Celtic legend too, the fay Morgan (p. 412 n.) conducts to it ; I read in Parz. 56, 18 : den fuort ein feie, hiez Murgan, in *Ter de la schoye* (joie ; see Suppl.). Remember also the Norse *glêrhiminn* (coelum vitreum), a paradise to which old heroes ride (Iarlmagns saga p.m. 320-2) ; legends and lays have *glass-bergs* and *glass-burgs* as abodes of heroes and wise women, e.g. Brynild's smooth unscalable *glarbjerg* (Dan. V. 1, 182), and the four *glassbergs* in Wolfdiet. (Cod. Dresd. 289), conf. the Lith. and Pol. glass-mountain of the underworld, p. 836 n. A *glass-house in the air* (château en l'air) occurs as early as Tristan, ed. Michel 2, 103, conf. 1, 222

joy is christian too. Also: 'stîgen ze himel ûf der *sœlden berc*,' climb the mount of bliss, Wackern. Basle MSS. p. 5. The christian faith tells of two places of bliss, a past and a future. One is where the departed dwell with God; the other, forfeited by our first parents' sin, is represented as a *garden*, Eden. Both are translated παράδεισος in the LXX, whence *paradisus* in the Vulg.; this is said to be a Persian word, originally denoting garden or park, which is confirmed by the Armenian *bardez* (hortus). The only passage we have the advantage of consulting in Ulph., 2 Cor. 12, 4, has *vaggs*, the OHG. *wanc* (campus amoenus, hortus). Our OHG. translators either retain *paradîsi*, Fragm. theot. 41, 21, or use *wunnigarto*, Gl. Jun. 189. 217. Hymn 21, 6. *wunnogarto*, N. ps. 37, 5; conf. 'thaz *wunnisama* feld,' O. ii. 6, 11. 'after paradîses *wunnen*,' Diut. 3, 51. MHG. 'der *wunne garte*,' Fuozesbr. 126, 27. 'der *wollüste* garte,' MsH. 3, 463ª. OHG. *zartgarto*, N. ps. 95, 10. The name *wunnigarto* may be substantially the same as *vingôlf*, *winsele*, as wunna for wunia, Goth. vinja, lies close to wini (amicus). A strange expression is the AS. *neorzena-wong, neorznawong*, Cædm. 11, 6. 13, 26. 14, 12. 115, 23, of which I have treated in Gramm. 1, 268. 2, 267. 3, 726; it is apparently field of rest,[1] and therefore of bliss, and may be compared to Goth. *vaggs*, OS. *heben-wang*, Hel. 28, 21. 176, 1; the 'norns' are out of the question, especially as heaven is never called norna-vângr in ON. poems. Beside hebenwang, the OS. poet uses *ôdas-hêm* 96, 20 and *úp-ôdas-hêm* 28, 20. 85, 21, domus beatitudinis, the 'hêm' reminding us of heimr in glaðsheimr, as the 'garto' in wunnigarto does of âsgarðr. Up-ôdashêm is formed like ûphimil, and equally heathen. All the Slavs call paradise *rai*, Serv. *raj*, Pol. *ray*, Boh. *rag*, to which add Lith. *rojus*, sometimes called *rojaus sôdas* (garden of par.), or simply *daržas* (garden). Rai as a contraction of paradise (Span. parayso) is almost too violent; Anton (Essay on Slavs 1, 35) says the Arabic *arai* means paradise.[2]

Like Valhöll, the Greek Elysium too, ἠλύσιον πεδίον (Plutarch 4, 1156. Lucian de luctu 7) was not a general abode of all the

---

[1] The ῥητότη βιοτή, Od. 4, 565.

[2] To me the connexion of *rai* (and perh. of *râd* glad, willing) with ῥᾶϊς, ῥᾴ, ῥᾴδιος (ῥαΐδιος) easy, and ῥεῖα easily, seems obvious. Homer's gods are ῥεῖα ῥώοντες living in *ease*.—TRANS.

dead, but of picked heroes: the Greeks too made the highest blessedness wait upon the warrior's valour. Neither were all heroes even admitted there, Menelaos was as son-in-law of Zeus, Od. 4, 569; others even more renowned were housed with Aïdes, in Hades. Achilles paces the *flowery mead*, the ἀσφοδελὸς λειμών of the underworld, whither Hermes conducts the souls of the slain suitors, Od. 11, 539. 24, 13. Lucian de luctu 5. philops. 24.

This 'ea' of the blest is no less known to our native song and story. Children falling into wells pass through *green meadows* to the house of friendly Holla. Flore 24, 22 : 'swer im selber den tôt tuot, den geriuwet diu vart, und ist im ouch verspart *diu wise*, dâr dû komen wilt, an der Blancheflûr spilt (plays) mit andern genuogen (enow), die sich niht ersluogen;' who slays himself will rue such journey, to him is eke denied that mead, etc. Floris 1107 : 'int *ghebloide velt* (flowery field), ten paradise.' 1248 : 'waenstu dan comen int *ghebloide velt*, daer int paradîs ?' 1205 : 'ic sal varen int *ghebloide velt*, daer Blancefloeren siele jeghen die mine gadert, ende leset bloemekine.' The French Flores in the corresponding passages has *camp flori* (Altd. bl. 1, 373),[1] in Bekker's ed. of Flore 786. 931. 1026. But our older poets, probably even those of heathen times, imagined heaven, like the earth, as a *green plain* : 'teglîdid *grôni wang*' (the earth), Hel. 131, 1; 'himilrîki, *grôni Godes wang*' 94, 24. '*grôni wang* paradîse gelîc' 96, 15. 'the *grôneo wang*' 23, 4 is said of Egypt. Cædm. 32, 29 : 'brâde sind on worulde *grêne geardas*.' Hâkonarmâl 13 : 'rîða ver nu sculom *grœna heima* goða,' i.e. to heaven. In many parts of Germany *paradis* and *goldne aue* are names of places to this day. So *viretum* in Virgil has the sense of paradise, Aen. 6, 638 :

> Devenere locos laetos et amoena vireta
> fortunatorum nemorum sedesque beatas.

Paradise then is twofold, a lost one, and a future one of the earth emerging newly green out of the wave: to *Iðavöllr*, in whose grass the gods pick up plates of gold (for play), Sæm. 9^b 10^a, corresponds that older *Iðavöllr* where the âses founded As-

---

[1] The M. Nethl. poem Beatris 1087 places the Last Judgment 'int *soete dal*, daer God die werelt doemen sal.'

garð, to the renovated realm of the future a vanished golden age that flowed with milk and honey (see Suppl.).[1]

The younger heaven has in the Edda another name, one peculiar to itself, and occurring only in the dative 'å gimli,' Sæm. 10.[b] Sn. 4, 75 [but 21 gimli as nom.?], for which I propose a nom. *gimill* (not gimlir) standing for *himill*, a form otherwise wanting in ON., and = OHG. OS. *himil* by the same consonant-change as Gýmir for Hýmir; and this is confirmed by the juxta-position 'å gimli, å himni,' Sn. 75. Now this *Gimill* is clearly distinct from the Odinic Valhöll: it does not make its appearance till ragnarökr has set in and the åses have fallen in fight with the sons of muspell. Then it is that a portion of the åses appear to revive or become young again. *Baldr* and *Höðr*, who had gone their way to the underworld long before the twilight of the gods, *Hœnir* who had been given as a hostage to the Vanir, are named in Völuspå (Sæm. 10[b]), as gods emerging anew; they three were not involved in the struggle with Surtr. Then again Sn. 76 gives us *Viðar* and *Vali*, who unhurt by Surtalogi revive the old Asgarð on Iðavöllr, and with them are associated *Móði* and *Magni*, beside Baldr and Höðr from the underworld; Hœnir is here passed over in silence. Viðar and Vali are *the two avengers*, one having avenged Oðin's death on Fenrisúlf, the other Baldr's death on Höðr (hefniåss Baldrs dólgr Haðar, Sn. 106). They two, and Baldr the pure blameless god of light, are sons of Oðinn, while Móði and Magni appear as sons of Thôrr by a gýgr, and from that time they bear the emblem of his might, the all-crushing Miölnir. Unquestionably this means, that Oðinn and Thôrr, the arch-gods of old Asgarð, come into sight no more, but are only renewed in their sons. Baldr signifies the beginning of a mild spring time, p. 614 (see Suppl.).

[1] It is natural that this paradise, past or to come, should have given birth to various tales of an earthly paradise, lying in regions far away, which has been reached by here and there a traveller : thus Alexander in his Indian campaign is said to have arrived at paradise. Not the Eddas themselves, but later Icel. sagas tell of *Odáins-akr* (immortalitatis ager) ; a land where no one sickens or dies, conf. dáinn mortuus, morti obnoxius (p. 458) ; the Hervararsaga (Fornald. sög. 1, 411. 513) places it in the kingdom of a deified king *Goðmundr* (conf. Goðormr p. 161); acc. to the Saga Ereks viðförla (Fornald. sög. 3, 519. 661-6. 670) it lay in the east, not far from India. Can this ' Erekr hinn viðförli ' be the hero of the lost MHG. poem Erek der wallære (pilgrim)? The name Odáinsakr may however be an adaptation of an older and heathen Oðinsakr = Vallhöll, conf. the Oden såker in Sweden, p. 158, last line.

Again, as Valhöll had only received men who died by weapons (vâpn-dauða vera), whilst other dead men were gathered in Fôlk-vângr with Freyja (p. 304), and virgins with Gefjon (Sn. 36); from this time forward *Gimill* takes in without distinction all the just, the good, and *Hel* all the bad, the criminal; whereas the former Hel, as a contrast to Valhöll, used to harbour all the residue of men who had not fallen in fight, without its being implied that they were sinners deserving punishment.

The most difficult point to determine is, how matters exactly stand with regard to *Surtr*, to whom I must now return. That he is represented, not as a god, but as a giant of the fire-world, has been shown, p. 809; nor is he named among the renovated gods 'â gimli' in Sæm. 10ª or Sn. 76, which would have been the place for it. In one MS. alone (Sn. 75, var. 3) is apparently interpolated 'â Gimli *meðr Surti*;' and it is mainly on this that Finn Magnusen rests his hypothesis, that *Surtr* is an exalted god of light, under whose rule, as opposed to that of Oðinn, the new and universal empire stands. He takes him to be that *mightier* one from whose power in the first creation days the warmth proceeded (p. 562), the *strong* (öflugr) or *rich* one revealed by the vala, who shall direct all things (sâ er öllu ræðr, Sæm. 10ᵇ), likewise the *mighty* one foreseen by Hyndla, whose name she dare not pronounce (þâ kemr annar enn mâttkari, þô þori ec eigi þann at nefna, Sæm. 119ª); conf. the *strengra* of the A.S. homily (p. 812). But why should she have shrunk from naming Surtr, of whom no secret is made in Sæm. 8ᵃˑᵇ. 9ª. 33ª, the last passage positively contrasting him with the mild merciful gods (in svâso goð)? The invasion of Surtr in company with the liberated Loki must anyhow be understood as a hostile one (of giant's or devil's kin); his very name of the swart one points that way.

The unuttered god may be likened to the ἄγνωστος θεός (Acts 17, 23), still more to the word that Oðinn whispered in the ear of his son Baldr's corpse, as it ascended the funeral pile: a secret which is twice alluded to, in Sæm. 38ª and Hervarars. p. 487; so an Etruscan nymph speaks the name of the highest god in the ear of a bull.[1] It has already been suggested (p. 815) that presentiments of a mightier god to come may have floated before

---

[1] O. Müller's Etr. 2, 88, with which must be conn. the medieval legend of Silvester (Conrad's poem, pref. p. xx).

the heathen imagination, like the promise of the Messiah to the Jews.[1]

The world's destruction and its renewal succeed each other in rotation; and the interpenetration of the notions of time and space, world and creation, with which I started, has been proved. Further, as the time-phenomena of the day and the year were conceived of as persons, so were the space-phenomena of the world and its end (Halja, Hades, Surtr).

---

[1] Martin Hammerich om Ragnaroks-mythen, Copenh. 1836, argues plausibly that the twilight of the gods and the new kingdom of heaven are the expression of a spiritual monotheism opposed, though as yet imperfectly, to the prevailing Odinic paganism. But then there are renovated *gods* brought on the scene ' á gimli ' too, though fewer than in Asgarð, and there is nothing to shew their subordination to the mighty One. Still less do I think the author entitled to name this new god *fimbultýr*, a term that in the whole of the Edda occurs but once (Sæm. 9b), and then seems to refer to Oðinn. Others have ventured to identify the word fimbul- (which like the prefix irman-, heightens the meaning of a word, as in fimbulfambi, fimbul-þulr, fimbulvetr, fimbullioð, as well as fimbultýr) with the AS. fifel (p. 239); to this also I cannot assent, as fifill itself occurs in ON., and is cited by Biörn as the name of a plant.

CHAPTER XXVI.

SOULS.

Languages treat the living life-giving *soul* as a delicate feminine essence: Goth. *sáivala*, akin to *sáivs* the sea, an undulating fluid force, OHG. *séola, séla*, MHG. *séle*, NHG. *seele*, AS. *sáwl*, ON. *sál*, Swed. Dan. *själ*, and hence Finn. *sielu*; Gr. ψυχή; Lat. Ital. *anima*, Fr. *âme*, O. Fr. sometimes *arme*, Span. *alma*; Russ. Serv. *dusha*, Slov. *duzha*, Boh. *duše*, Pol. *dusza*, Lith. *duszia*, Lett. *dwehsele*. They all distinguish it from the masc. breath and spirit, ἄνεμος, which goes in and out more palpably; often the two names are next door to each other, as Lat. *animus* and *anima*, Slav. *dukh* and *dusha*.[1]

And this intimate connexion may be recognised in the myths too. The soul freed from the fetters of the body is made to resemble those airy spirit forms of chap. XVII (conf. pp. 439. 630). It hovers with the same buoyancy, appears and vanishes, often it assumes some definite shape in which it is condemned to linger for a time (see Suppl.).

It is a graceful fancy which makes the departing soul either break into blossom as a flower, or fly up as a bird. Both these notions are connected with metamorphosis into plants and animals in general, and are founded on the doctrine of metempsychosis so prevalent in early antiquity. Immortality was admitted in this sense, that the soul still existed, but had to put up with a new body.

Its passing into a flower I can only infer. A child carries home a bud, which the angel had given him in the wood; when the rose blooms, the child is dead (Kinder-leg. no. 3). In Rhesas dainos p. 307, a rosebud is the soul of the dead youth. The Lay of Runzifal makes a *blackthorn* shoot up out of the bodies of slain heathens, a *white flower* by the heads of fallen christians, Karl

---

[1] Where soul stands for life, vitality, a neuter word is used, OHG. *ferah*, MHG. *verch*, AS. *feorh*, ON. *fiör*; but we saw (p. 798), how from *vita* and βίος there arose the sum total of all that lives, the world, Goth. *fairhvus*.

118^b. When the innocent are put to death, *white lilies* grow out of their graves, *three lilies* on that of a maiden (Uhland's Volksl. 241), which no one but her lover may pluck ; from the mounds of buried lovers flowering shrubs spring up, whose branches intertwine. In Swedish songs *lilies* and *limes* grow out of graves, Sv. vis. 1, 101. 118. In the ballad of 'fair Margaret and sweet William' :

> Out of her brest there sprang a *rose*,
> And out of his a *briar* ;
> They grew till they grew unto the church-top,
> And there they tyed in a true lovers knot.[1]

In Tristan and Isote I believe it to be a later alteration, that the *rose* and *vine*, which twine together over their graves, have first to be planted. In a Servian folksong there grows out of the youth's body a *green fir* (zelén bor, m.), out of the maiden's a *red rose* (rumena ruzhitsa, f.), Vuk 1, no. 137, so that the sex is kept up even in the plants :[2] the rose twines round the fir, as the silk round the nosegay. All these examples treat the flower as a mere symbol, or as an after-product of the dead man's intrinsic character : the rose coming up resembles the ascending spirit of the child ; the body must first lie buried, before the earth sends up a new growth as out of a seed, conf. chap. XXXVII. But originally there might lie at the bottom of this the idea of an immediate instantaneous passage of the soul into the shape of a flower, for out of mere drops of blood, containing but a small part of the life, a flower is made to spring : the soul has her seat in the blood, and as that ebbs away, she escapes with it. Greek fables tell us how the bodies of the persecuted and slain, especially women, assumed forthwith the figure of a flower, a bush, a tree (p. 653), without leaving any matter behind to decay or be burnt ; nay, life and even speech may last while the transformation is taking place. Thus Daphne and Syrinx, when they cannot elude the pursuit of Apollo or Pan, change themselves into a laurel and a reed ; the nymph undergoing transformation speaks on so long as the encrusting bark has not crept up to

---

[1] Percy 8, 123 ; variant in Rob. Jamieson 1, 33-4.
[2] Therefore *der rebe* (vine) belongs to Tristan's grave, *diu rôse* to Isote's, as in Eilhart and the chap-book ; Ulrich and Heinrich made the plants change places.

her mouth. Vintler tells us, the *wege-warte* (OHG. wegawartâ, wegapreitâ), plantago, was once a woman, who by the wayside waited (wartete) for her lover; he suggests no reason for the transformation, conf. Kinderm. no. 160 (see Suppl.).

In the same way popular imagination, childlike, pictures the soul as a *bird*, which comes flying out of the dying person's mouth. That is why old tombstones often have *doves* carved on them, and these the christian faith brings into still closer proximity to spirit.[1] A ship founders: the people on shore observe the souls of those who have sunk ascending from the wave toward heaven in the shape of *white doves*.[2] The Romance legend of the tortured Eulalia says: 'in figure de *colomb* volat a ciel.' As a *bird* the little brother, when killed, flies out of the juniper-tree (machandelbom, Kinderm. 47). To the enigma of the green tree and the dry, each with a little bird sitting on it, the interpretation is added: 'ir *sêle* zen *vogelen* sî gezalt!' their (the christians') soul be numbered among birds, MS. 2, 248[b]. In the underworld there fly scorched *birds* who were souls (sviðnir fuglar er sâlir voro), like swarms of flies, Sæm. 127[a]. The heathen Bohemians thought the soul came out of the dying lips as a bird, and hovered among the trees, not knowing where to go till the body was buried; then it found rest. Finns and Lithuanians call the Milky-way the *path of birds* (p. 357n.), i.e. of souls.

The Arabs till the time of Mahomet believed that the blood of a murdered man turns into an accusing bird, that flits about the grave till vengeance be taken for the dead.

According to a Polish folk-tale every member of the Herburt family turns into an *eagle* as soon as he dies. The first-born daughters of the house of Pileck were changed into *doves* if they died unmarried, but the married ones into *owls*, and to each member of the family they foretold his death by their bite (Woycicki's Klechdy 1, 16). When the robber Madej was confessing under an appletree, and getting quit of his sins, apple after apple flew up into the air, converted into a *white dove*: they were the souls of those he had murdered. One apple still remained, the

---

[1] Servati Lupi vita S. Wigberhti, cap. 11: Verum hora exitus ejus . . . circumstantibus fratribus, visa est *avis* quaedam specie pulcherrima supra ejus corpusculum *ter advolasse*, nusquamque postea comparuisse. Not so much the soul itself, as a spirit who escorts it.

[2] Maerlant 2, 217, from a Latin source.

soul of his father, whose murder he had suppressed; when at length he owned that heinous crime, the last apple changed into a *gray dove*, and flew after the rest (ibid. 1, 180). This agrees with the unresting birds of the Boh. legend. In a Podolian folk-song, on the grave-mound there shoots up a little oak, and on it sits a snow-white dove (ibid. 1, 209).[1]

Instances of transformation into *birds* were given above, (pp. 673-6. 680), under *woodpecker* and *cuckoo*. Greek mythology has plenty of others (see Suppl.).

The popular opinion of Greece also regarded the soul as a winged being (ψυχὴ πνεῦμα καὶ ζωΰφιον πτηνόν[2] says Hesy-chius), not bird, but *butterfly*, which is even more apt, for the insect is developed out of the chrysalis, as the soul is out of the body; hence ψυχή is also the word for butterfly. A Roman epitaph found in Spain has the words: M. Porcius M. haeredibus mando etiam cinere ut meo *volitet* ebrius *papilio*.[3] In Basque, 'arima' is soul (conf. arme, alma, p. 826), and 'astoaren arima' (ass's soul) butterfly. We shall come across these butterflies again as will o' the wisps (ziebold, vezha), and in the Chap. on Witches as elvish beings (see Suppl.).

When men are in a trance, or asleep, the *soul* runs out of them in the shape of a *snake, weasel* or *mouse* (chap. XXXIV and Suppl.).

Of *will o' the wisps* a subsequent chapter will treat; synony-mous with them I find *wiesenhüpfer, wiesenhüpferin*, meadow-hopper, e.g. in the Mägdelob (printed 1683) p. 46; its explana-tion, from their dancing on marshy meadows, is right enough, but perhaps too limited. Hans Sachs is not thinking of ignes fatui, when he more than once employs the set phrase : ' mit im schirmen, dass die *seel in dem gras umbhupfen*,' fence with him till their souls hop about in the grass iii. 3, 13ᵃ. iv. 3, 28ᵃ. ' und schmitz ihn in ein fiderling, dass sein *seel* muss *im gras umbhupfen*' iv. 3, 51ᵇ; he simply means that the soul flies out of him, he dies. Therefore the same superstition again, that the soul of the dying flutters (as bird or butterfly) in the *meadow*, i.e. the

---

[1] Na tój mogile wyróśt ci dąbeczek,
  na niéj bieluchny siada gołąbeczek.

[2] ψυχὴ δ' ἐκ σώματος ἔκτη, *flew* out of the body, Batrach. 207. ψυχὴ δὲ μελέων ἐξέπτη 211. ἐκ μελέων θυμὸς πτάτο, Il. 23, 880.

[3] First in Ambr. de Morales's Antiguidades de las ciudades de España, Alcala 1575, fol. 31ᵇ; thence in Gruter, and in Spon's Miscell. erud. antiq. p. 8.

meadow of the underworld spoken of in p. 822.[1] Just so the Bohemians make the soul *fly about in trees*, Königinh. hs. p. 88. 106; hence both souls and elves dance to and fro in the meadows at night. Strange, that a minnesänger already makes the soul of a drunken (as if entranced) man *jump*: ' mîn sêle ûf eime rippe stât, wâfen! diu von dem wîne darûf *gehüppet hât* ' (MS. 2, 105ᵇ).[2] So the souls of the drowned keep jumping up out of the jars, p. 496 (see Suppl.). Shooting stars are supposed to be the souls of dying men (p. 722); not only heroes and other men, but separate limbs of their bodies were fixed in the sky as *stars*, chap. XXII.

These are the simplest (if you will, rudest) notions as to the nature of the soul, and to them I ascribe a high antiquity.

More polished, more deeply rooted in ancient myths, is the opinion of the soul's *passage* into the domain of the underworld *across a water* which divides the realm of living men from that of the dead.

The Norse narrative of the death of Baldr has the remarkable incident, that the âses placed his body *on board a vessel*, in which they erected the funeral pile, set it on fire, and so *committed it to the sea at high water* (Sn. 66).[3] In the same way the corpse of the deified hero Scild (p. 369) is adorned and *carried into a ship*, which *drifts away on the sea*, nobody knows whither, Beow. 55— 105. Sigmundr bears the body of his beloved son Sinfiötli to the seashore, where a stranger waits with a skiff, and offers

---

[1] Those who are neither saved nor damned come into the *green meadow*, Heinse's Ardinghello 1, 96.

[2] Conf. Helbl. 1, 354: ' *vrou Sêle*, tretet *ûf ein rippe*.' Renart in his bucket at the bottom of the well (p. 807), to humbug Ysengrin, pretends he is living in paradise there, and that every soul, on parting from the body, has to sit on the bucket-pole till it is penitent, then it may climb down, and leave all its ills behind, Renart 6804-13.

[3] What deep root this custom had taken in the North, may be gathered from the fact that bodies were also *buried in a boat* [on land], doubtless so that on their journey to the underworld, when they came to a water, they might have their ferry at hand. ' Hâkon konûngr tôk þar *skip öll* et âtt höfðo Eiríks synir, ok lét draga á land upp; þar lét Hâkon *leggja* Egil Ullserk *í skip*, oc með hânom alla þá menn er af þeirra liði höfðo fallit, lét bera þar at törð oc griot. Hâkon konûngr lét oc *fleiri skip* uppsetja, oc bera á valinn,' Saga H. góða, cap. 27. ' Unnr var *lögð í skip í hauginum*,' Laxd. p. 16. ' Asmundr var *heygðr ok í skip lagðr*, þræll hans lagðr *í annan stafn skipsins*,' Islend. sög. 1, 66. ' Geirmundr *heygðr ok lagðr í skip* þar útí skóginn frá garði,' ibid. 1, 97. Probably the bodies of the great were first laid in a coffin, and this put in the boat, which was then buried in the hill. Gudrun says: ' *knör* mun ek kaupa ok kisto steinða,' Sæm. 264ᵇ. No boats have been found, that I know of, in ancient barrows of Continental Germany.

a passage; Sigmundr *lays the dead in the boat*, which has then its full freight, the unknown pushes off and sails away with the corpse, Sæm. 170-1. Fornald. sög. 1, 142. Frotho's Law p. 87 lays down distinctions of rank: 'Centurionis vel satrapae corpus rogo *propria nave* constructo funerandum constituit; *dena* autem gubernatorum corpora *unius puppis* igne consumi praecepit; ducem quempiam aut regem interfectum *proprio* injectum *navigio* concremari.' The dead Iarlmâgus is conveyed *in a ship* by his widow to a holy land, Iarlm. saga cap. 45. A Swedish folk-tale (Afzelius 1, 4) speaks of a *golden ship* lying sunk near the schlüsselberg at Runemad; in that ship Odin is said to have carried *the slain* from Brâvalla *to Valhall.* In the O. Fr. romance of Lancelot du lac, ed. 1591, p. 147 the demoiselle d'Escalot arranges what is to be done with her body: 'le pria, que *son corps fût mis en une nef* richement equippée, *que l'on laisseroit aller au gré du vent sans ·conduite.*' [1] And in the romance of Gawan a swan tows a boat in which lies a dead knight (Keller's Romvart 670). Was it believed that the corpse, abandoned to the sacred sea and the winds, would of itself arrive at the land of death that was not to be reached under human guidance?

Here it is the corpse that is transported, in other legends merely the soul when released from the body: it is over again the distinction we noticed above, p. 827. In the Nialss. cap. 160, old Flosi, weary of life, is even said to have taken a battered boat, and thrown himself on the mercy of the sea-waves: 'bar â skip ok lêt î haf, ok hefir til þess skips aldri spurt sîðan,' never heard of since.

The Greeks believed that Charon ferried the souls in a narrow two-oared boat over the Styx, Acheron or Cocytus to the kingdom of Hades. For this he charged a ·*fare*, τὰ πορθμία, therefore they placed an obolos (the danaka) *in the mouth* of the dead.[2] This custom of putting a small *coin in the mouth* of a corpse occurs among Germans too, Superst. I, 207 where a modern and

---

[1] Cento novelle antiche 81: La damigella di Scalot; the 'navicella sanza vela, sanza remi e sanza neuno sopra sagliente' is carried down to Camalot, to the court of Re Artu.

[2] Diodor. 1, 90. Eurip. Alc. 253. 441. Aen. 6, 298. At Hermione in Argolis, supposed to be no great distance from the underworld, no money was given to the dead, Strabo 8, 373. These coins are often found in ancient tombs, K. Fr. Hermann's Antiq. 198.

mistaken reason is alleged for it [lest they come back to visit buried hoards]: originally the money could be no other than that same naulum.

One stormy night a monkish figure wakes a boatman who lies buried in sleep, puts *passage-money in his hand*, and demands to be taken across the river. At first six monks step into the boat, but no sooner is it fairly launched, than suddenly it is filled by a throng of friars black and white, and the ferryman has scarcely room left for himself. With difficulty he rows across, the passengers alight, and a hurricane hurls the ferryboat back to the place of starting, where another set of travellers wait and take possession of the boat, the foremost of whom with fingers cold as ice presses the *fare-penny* into the boatman's *hand*. The return voyage is made in the same violent way as before.[1] The like is told, but less completely, of monks crossing the Rhine at Spire.[2] In neither story can we detect the purpose of the voyage; they seem to be early heathen reminiscences, which, not to perish entirely, had changed their form (see Suppl.).

Procopius de bello Goth. 4, 20 (ed. Bonn. 2, 567), speaking of the island of Brittia, imparts a legend which he had often heard from the lips of the inhabitants. They imagine that the souls of the dead are *transported to that island*. On the coast of the continent there dwell under Frankish sovereignty, but hitherto exempt from all taxation, fishers and farmers, whose duty it is to *ferry the souls over*.[3] This duty they take in turn. Those to

---

[1] Neue volksmärchen der Deutschen, Leipz. 1792. 3, 45–7.
[2] D.S. no. 275 ; earliest auth. an account by Geo. Sabinus (b. 1508 d. 1560). Melander's Joc. no. 664.
[3] Τὰ μὲν ἄλλα Φράγγων κατήκοοι ὄντες, φόρου μέντοι ἀπαγωγὴν οὐδεπώποτε παρασχόμενοι, ὑφειμένου αὐτοῖς ἐκ παλαιοῦ τοῦδε τοῦ ἄχθους, ὑπουργίας τινός, ὥς φασιν, ἕνεκα. λέγουσι οἱ ταύτῃ ἄνθρωποι ἐκ περιτροπῆς ἐπικεῖσθαι τὰς τῶν ψυχῶν παρακομιδὰς σφίσι. On this passage and one in Tzetzes, consult Welcker in Rhein. mus. 1, 288 seq. Conf. Plutarch de defectu oracul. cap. 18 (ed. Reiske 7, 652) : Ὁ δὲ Δημήτριος ἔφη τῶν περὶ τὴν Βρεταννίαν νήσων εἶναι πολλὰς ἐρήμους σποράδας, ὧν ἐνίας δαιμόνων καὶ ἡρώων ὀνομάζεσθαι, πλεῦσαι δὲ αὐτὸς ἱστορίας καὶ θέας ἕνεκα, πομπῇ τοῦ βασιλέως, εἰς τὴν ἐγγιστα κειμένην τῶν ἐρήμων, ἔχουσαν οὐ πολλοὺς ἐποικοῦντας, ἱεροὺς δὲ καὶ ἀσύλους πάντας ὑπὸ τῶν Βρεταννῶν ὄντας. ἀφικομένου δ' αὐτοῦ νεωστί, σύγχυσιν μεγάλην περὶ τὸν ἀέρα καὶ διοσημείας πολλὰς γενέσθαι, καὶ πνεύματα καταρραγῆναι καὶ πεσεῖν πρηστῆρας. ἐπεὶ δ' ἐλώφησε, λέγειν τοὺς νησιώτας, ὅτι τῶν κρεισσόνων τινὸς ἔκλειψις γέγονεν. ὡς γὰρ λύχνος ἀναπτόμενος φάναι δεινὸν οὐδὲν ἔχει, σβεννύμενος δὲ πολλοῖς λυπηρός ἐστιν, οὕτως αἱ μεγάλαι ψυχαὶ τὰς μὲν ἀναλάμψεις εὐμενεῖς καὶ ἀλύπους ἔχουσιν, αἱ δὲ σβέσεις αὐτῶν καὶ φθοραὶ πολλάκις μέν, ὡς νυνί, πνεύματα καὶ ζάλας τρέφουσι, πολλάκις δὲ λοιμικοῖς πάθεσιν ἀέρα φαρμάττουσιν. ἐκεῖ μέντοι μίαν εἶναι νῆσον, ἐν ᾗ τὸν Κρόνον κατείρχθαι φρουρούμενον ὑπὸ τοῦ Βριάρεω καθεύδοντα. δεσμὸν γὰρ αὐτῷ τὸν ὕπνον μεμηχανῆσθαι, πολλοὺς δὲ περὶ αὐτὸν εἶναι δαίμονας ὀπαδοὺς καὶ θεράποντας. This

whom it falls on any night, go to bed at dusk; at midnight they hear a knocking at their door, and muffled voices calling. Immediately they rise, go to the shore, and there see *empty boats*, not their own but strange ones, they go on board and seize the oars. When the boat is under way, they perceive that she is *laden choke-full*, with. her gunwales hardly a finger's breadth above water. Yet they see no one, and in an hour's time they touch land, which one of their own craft would take a day and a night to do. Arrived at Brittia, the boat speedily unloads, and becomes so light that she only dips her keel in the wave. Neither on the voyage nor at landing do they see any one, but they hear a voice loudly asking each one his name and country. Women that have crossed give their husbands' names.

Procopius's Brittia lies no farther than 200 stadia (25 miles) from the mainland, between Britannia and Thule, opposite the Rhine mouth, and three nations live in it, Angles, Frisians and Britons. By Britannia he means the NW. coast of Gaul, one end of which is still called Bretagne, but in the 6th century the name included the subsequent Norman and Flemish-Frisian country up to the mouths of Scheldt and Rhine; his Brittia is Great Britain, his Thule Scandinavia.

Whereabouts the passage was made, whether along the whole of the Gallic coast, I leave undetermined. Villemarqué (Barzas breiz 1, 136) places it near Raz, at the farthest point of Armorica, where we find a bay of souls (baie des âmes, boé ann anavo). On the R. Treguier in Bretagne, commune Plouguel, it is said to be the custom to this day, to convey the dead to the church-yard *in a boat*, over a small arm of the sea called *passage de l'enfer*, instead of taking the shorter way by land; besides, the people all over Armorica believe that souls at the moment of parting repair to the parson of Braspar, whose dog escorts them to Britain: up *in the air* you hear the *creaking wheels of a waggon overloaded with souls*, it is covered with a white pall, and is called *carr an ancou, carrikel an. ancou*, soul's car (Mém. de l'acad. celt. 8, 141). Purely adaptations to suit the views of the people. As christians, they could no longer ferry their dead

Kronos asleep on the holy island far away, with his retinue of servants, is like a Wuotan enchanted in a mountain, conf. Humboldt in Herm. Müller p. 440-1. Welcker's Kl. schr. 2, 177.

to the island: well, they will take them to the churchyard by
water anyhow; and in their tradition they make the voyage
be performed no longer by ship, but through the air (as in the
case of the Furious Host), and by waggon.   Closer investigation
must determine whether similar legends do not live in Normandy,
Flanders and Friesland.   Here I am reminded once more of old
Helium and Hel-voet, pp. 315 n. 804.

Procopius's account is re-affirmed by Tzetzes (to Lycoph. 1204)
in the 12th century; but long before that, Claudian at the beginning of the 5th (in Rufinum 1, 123—133) had heard of those
Gallic shores as a trysting-place of flitting ghosts:

> Est locus, extremum qua pandit Gallia littus,
> oceani praetentus aquis, ubi fertur Ulixes
> sanguine libato populum movisse silentem.
> Illic *umbrarum tenui stridore volantum*
> *flebilis auditur questus : simulacra* coloni
> *pallida, defunctasque vident migrare figuras ;*

and not far from that region are Britain, the land of the Senones,
and the Rhine.   This faint murmur of the fleeting shades is
much the same thing as the airy waggon of the Bretons.   The
British bards make out that souls, to reach the underworld, must
sail over the *pool of dread* and of *dead bones*, across the *vale of
death,* into the sea on whose shore stands open the mouth of
hell's abyss[1] (see Suppl.).   A North English song, that used to
be sung at lykewakes, names ' the *bridge of dread, no brader
than a thread,*' over which the soul has to pass in the underworld (J. Thoms' Anecd. and trad. pp. 89. 90).   The same
bridge is mentioned in the legend of Tundalus (Hahn's ed. pp.
49. 50) : the soul must drive a stolen cow over it.[2]

The same meaning as in the voyage of souls over the gulf or

---

[1] Owen's Dict. 2, 214. Villemarqué 1, 135.
[2] The narrow bridge is between purgatory and paradise, even Owain the hero
had to cross it (Scott's Minstr. 2, 360-1).   In striking harmony with it (as supra
p. 574) is a Mahom. tradition given in Sale's Koran (ed. 1801, introd. 120) : in
the middle of hell all souls must walk over a bridge thinner than a hair, sharper
than the edge of a sword, and bordered on both sides by thorns and prickly shrubs.
The Jews also speak of the hell-bridge narrow as a thread, but only unbelievers
have to cross it (Eisenmenger 2, 258) ; conf. Thoms p. 91.   Acc. to Herbelot, the
Mahometans believe that before the judgment-day they shall pass over a redhot
iron rod, that spans a bottomless deep ; then the good works of each believer will
put themselves under his feet.

river of the underworld appears to lie in their *walking the bridge that spans the river.* The bridge-keeper's words to (the living) Hermôðr are remarkable: 'my bridge groans more beneath thy single tread, *than under the five troops of dead men* who yesterday rode over it,' Sn. 67. I see in this a very strong resemblance to the *soft patter of the dwarfs' feet on the bridge when quitting the country,* as also their *ferrying over* by night (pp. 275. 459); and the affinity of souls with elvish beings comes out very plainly. When the dwarfs moved out of Voigtland, they were *a whole night crossing the Elster* (Jul. Schmidt p. 143-8). At their departure from the Harz, it was agreed that they should pass over a narrow bridge at Neuhof, each dropping his toll-money in a vessel fixed upon it, but none of the country folk were to be present. Prying people hid under the bridge, and heard *for hours their pit-a-pat,* as though a flock of sheep were going over (Deut. sagen no. 152-3). The *bridge-toll* brings to mind the *ferry-money* of souls. With all this compare the story of the *elf making his passage* in a boat by night (D.S. no. 80). Then again 'the bridge of dread no brader than a thread' is a kindred notion, which moreover connects itself with the iron sword-bridge crossed by the soul that has crept out of a sleeping man (see Suppl.).

A minute examination of the various funeral ceremonies of European nations, which is no part of my purpose here, would throw some more light on the old heathen views as to the nature of the soul and its destiny after death. Thus the dead, beside the passage-money and the boat, had a particular shoe called *todtenschuh,* ON. *hel-skó,* given them for setting out on their journey, and tied on their feet. The Gisla Surssonarsaga says: 'þat er tïðska at binda mönnum helskô, sem menn skulo á gánga til Valhallar, ok mun ek Vesteini þat giöra' (conf. Müller's Sagabibl. 1, 171). Sir W. Scott in Minstr. 2, 357 quotes a Yorkshire superstition: 'They are of beliefe, that once in their lives it is good to give *a pair of new shoes* to a poor man, forasmuch as after this life they are to *pass barefoote through a great launde full of thornes and furzen,* except by the meryte of the almes aforesaid they have redeemed the forfeyte; for at the edge of the launde an *oulde man* shall meet them with the *same shoes* that were given by the partie when he was lyving, and after he hath shodde them, dismisseth them to go through thick and thin, without scratch or scalle.' The land to be traversed by the soul is also called *whinny moor*, i.e. furzy bog (Thoms 89). In Henneberg, and perhaps other places, the last honours paid to the dead are still named *todtenschuh* (Reinwald 1, 165), though the practice itself is discontinued; even the funeral feast is so denominated. Utterly pagan in character, and suited to the warlike temper of old times, is what Burkard of Worms reports p. 195ᶜ: Quod quidam faciunt homini occiso, cum sepelitur : dant ei in manum *unguentum* quoddam, quasi illo unguento *post mortem vulnus sanari* possit, et sic cum unguento sepeliunt.[1] For a similar purpose, *slaves, horses, dogs* were burnt with a dead man, that he might use them in the next world. King Ring had king Harald buried in a great barrow, his horse killed that he had ridden in Brâvalla fight, and his *saddle* buried with him, so that he could ride to Walhalla. It was thought that to convey the corpse by any road but the traditional one (the hellweg, p. 801) was bad for the soul of the deceased, Ledebur's Archiv 5, 369 (see Suppl.).

The poems of the Mid. Ages occasionally describe a *conflict of angels and devils* round the parting soul, each trying to take possession of it. At the head of the angels is an archangel, usually Michael, who, as we shall see in chap. XXVIII, has also the task of weighing souls; sometimes he is called *Cherubim* : ' vor dem tievel nam der sêle war der erzengel *Kerubin*,' he saw the soul first, Wh. 49, 10.

> Lâzâ lâzâ tengeln !
> dâ wart von den engeln

---

[1] The Lithuanians bury or burn with the dead the *claws* of a *lynx or bear*, in the belief that the soul has to climb up a steep mountain, on which the divine judge (Kriwe Kriwaito) sits : the rich will find it harder to scale than the poor, who are unburdened with property, unless their sins weigh them down. A wind wafts the poor sinners up as lightly as a feather, the rich have their limbs mangled by a dragon Wizunas, who dwells beneath the mountain, and are then carried up by tempests (Woycicki's Klechdy 2, 184-5. Narbutt 1, 284). The steep hill is called *Anafielas* by the Lithuanians, and *szklanna gora* (glass mountain) by the Poles, who think the lost souls must climb it as a punishment, and when they have set foot on the summit, they slide off and tumble down. This *glass mountain is* still known to our German songs and fairytales, but no longer distinctly as an abode of the deceased, though the little maid who carries a huckle-bone to insert (like the bear's claw) into the glass mountain, and ends with cutting her little finger off that she may scale or unlock it at last, may be looked upon as seeking her lost brothers in the underworld (Kinderm. no. 25).

> manec sêle empfangen
> ê der strît was zegangen.
> Daz weinete manec amie :
> von wolken wart nie snîe
> alsô dicke sunder zal
> beidiu ûf bergen und ze tal,
> als engel unde tievel flugen,
> die dô ze widerstrîte zugen
> die sêle her und widere,
> d' einen ûf, die ander nidere.　　Geo. 1234.
> Der engelfürste *Michahêl*
> empfienc des marcgrâven sêl,
> und maneo engel liehtgevar
> die kâmen mit gesange dar
> und fuorten in vrœlîche
> inz schœne himelrîche.

Geo. 6082, conf. Diut. 1, 470. In the Brandan (Bruns p. 192-3)
we read : ‘ de duvele streden umme de sêle mit sunte *Michaêle* ’;
conf. Fundgr. 1, 92.

> Gebt mir eine gâbe,
> daz des küniges sêle
> von sante *Michahêle*
> hiate gecondwieret sî.　　Gute frau 2674 ;

Michael having taken upon him the office of Mercury or the
Walchure. A record of the 13th cent. (MB. 7, 371) calls him
‘ praepositus paradisi et princeps animarum.’ A still more important passage, already noticed at p. 446, occurs in Morolt 28[a,b],
where three troops are introduced, the *black*, *white* and *pale* :
‘ den *strît* mahtu gerne schouwen, dens *umb die sêle* suln hân.’
For similar descriptions in the elder French poets, conf. Méon 1,
239. 4, 114-5. 3, 284.

And even so early as the 8-9th cent. we find quite at the
beginning of the Muspilli fragment :

> Wanta sâr sô sih diu sêla in den sind arhevit (rises)
> enti sî den lîhhamun likkan lâzit (leaves the body lying),
> sô quimit ein heri (comes one host) fona himilzungalon,
> daz andar fona pehhe (pitch, hell) ; *dar pâgant siu umpi.*

I have questioned (p. 420) whether this ‘ pâc umpi dia sêla ’ (tussle for the soul) between the hosts of heaven and hell be traceable to christian tradition. The Ep. of Jude v. 9 does tell of archangel Michael and the devils striving for the body of Moses,[1] and the champion Michael at all events seems borrowed thence. But jealousy and strife over the partition of souls may be supposed an idea already present to the heathen mind, as the Norse Oðinn, Thôrr and Freyja appropriated their several portions of the slain. At pp. 60 and 305 we identified *Freyja* with *Gertrude* : 'some say the soul, on quitting the body, is the first night with *St. Gerdraut*, the next with *St. Michael*, the third in such place as it has earned,' Superst. F, 24. Now as Antichrist in the great world-fight is slain by Michael (p. 811), while Surtr has for adversaries Oðinn and Thôrr: 'Gêrdrût and Michael' may fairly be translated back into 'Frôwa and Wuotan (or Donar)'. So at p. 198 a 'mons sancti Michaelis' was found applicable to Wuotan or Zio (see Suppl.).

An Irish fairytale makes the spirits of the Silent Folk maintain a violent contest for three nights at the cross-roads, as to which churchyard a human corpse shall be buried in, Ir. elfenm. p. 68. So that elves and dwarfs, as they steal live children and maidens, (p. 386–8), would seem also to have a hankering for our bodies and souls. The souls of the drowned the water-nix keeps in his house (p. 496).

All this leads up to a more exact study of the notions about Death.

---

[1] The passage is supposed to be founded on a lost book named ''Ἀνάβασις Moyses', conf. Grotius ad S. Judae ep. 9, and Fabricii Cod. pseudepigr. V. T. p. 839.

CHAPTER XXVII.

DEATH.

To the olden time Death was not a being that killed, but simply one that fetched away and escorted to the underworld. Sword or sickness killed; Death came in as *messenger of a deity*, to whom he conducted the parting soul. Dying is announced, not caused, by his arrival. So to that child in the fairytale the angel of death had given a flower-bud: when it blossomed, he would come again.

And the Jewish notion, which Christianity retained, is in harmony with this. The soul of the beggar is *fetched away* by angels of God, and carried into Abraham's bosom, Luke 16, 22; or, as the Heliand 103, 5 expresses it: ' Godes engilôs *andfengon* is ferh, endi *lêddon* ine an Abrahâmes barm';[1] and it completes the picture of the rich man's fate by adding the counterpart. (103, 9): ' lêtha wihti bisenkidun is sêola an thene suarton hel,' loathly wights (devils) sank his soul into swart hell. A sermon in Leyser 126 has: ' wane ir ne wizzit niht, zu welicher zît der *bote* (messenger) unsers herren Gotis zu ture clopfe (may knock at the door). Welich ist der *bote* ? daz ist der Tôt (death)'; and 161: ' nu quam ouch der *gemeine bote* (general messenger), der nieman ledic lât (lets alone), wie lange im maniger vorgât, daz ist der gewisse tôt.' ' Dô der Tôt im sîn zuokunft enbôt (announced), sô daz er in *geleite,*' he might escort him, Greg. 20.

There is no substantial difference between this and the older heathen view. *Halja, Hel,* the death-goddess, does not destroy, she receives the dead man in her house, and will on no account give him up. To kill a man is called sending him to her. Hel

---

[1] It is a beautiful image, that the dying return to God's *bosom,* children to that of their father, whence they had issued at birth. But the same thing was known to our heathenism, which called newborn and adopted children ' bosom-children, wish-children,' RA. 455. 464, and interpreted *dying* as departing to Wuotan, to Wish (p. 145). To heathens then, as well as christians, to die was to fare to God, to enter into God's rest and peace, ' Metod seon,' Beow. 2360, ' fêran on Freán wære,' the Lord's peace 52. So, to be buried is to fall into the mother's bosom (p. 642); mother and father take their children into their keeping again.

neither comes to fetch the souls fallen due to her,[1] nor sends messengers after them. The dead are left alone to commence the long and gloomy journey; shoes, ship and ferry-money, servants, horses, clothes, they take with them from home for the hell-way. Some ride, others sail, whole companies of souls troop together: no conductor comes to meet them.

There were other gods besides, who took possession of souls. The sea-goddess Rân draws to herself *with a net* all the bodies drowned within her province (p. 311). Water-sprites in general seem fond of detaining souls: dame Holle herself, at whose dwelling arrive those who fall into the well (pp. 268. 822), has a certain resemblance to Hel (see Suppl.).

It is another matter with the souls destined for Valhöll. Oðinn *sends out* the *valkyrs* to *take up* all heroes that have fallen in fight, and *conduct* them to his heaven (p. 418): wish-maidens fetch his wish-sons, ' þær kiósa feigð å menn,' Sn. 39. Their attendance and the heroes' reception are splendidly set forth in the Hâkonarmâl. But these *messengers* also take charge of heroes while alive, and protect them until death: they are *guardian-angels* and *death-angels*. How beautiful, that the gracious god, before he summons them, has provided his elect with an attendant spirit to glorify their earthly path!

I can see a connexion between valkyrs and *Hermes*, who is wielder of the wishing-rod (p. 419) and conductor of souls to the underworld, ψυχαγωγός, ψυχοπομπός, νεκροπομπός. These maids are Oðin's messengers, as Hermes is herald of the gods, nay *Hermes is Oðinn* himself, to whom the souls belong. Thus the god's relation to the dead is an additional proof of the identity between *Wuotan* and *Mercury*. A distinction appears in the fact that Hermes, like the Etruscan *Oharun* (O. Müller 2, 100), conducts to Hades, but not, as far as I know, to Elysium; valkyrs, on the contrary, to Valhöll, and not to Hel. Further, the function of guardian-spirit is wanting to Hermes.

This idea of a protecting spirit finds expression more in the personified *Thanatos* (death) of the Greek people's faith. He is pictured as a genius, with hand on cheek in deep thought, or

---

[1] It is only in a dream-vision that she appears: ' postera nocte eidem *Proserpina* per quietem adstare aspecta postridie ejus complexu usuram denunciat. nec inane somnii praesagium fuit.' Saxo Gram. p. 48.

setting his foot on the psyche (soul) as if taking possession of her; often his hands are crossed over the extinguished torch. At times he appears *black* (like Hel, p. 313) or *black-winged* (atris alis) : τὸν δὲ πεσόντα εἷλε μέλας θάνατος, ψυχὴ δ᾽ ἔκ σώματος ἔπτη (Batrach. 207)[1], and ἀλεύατο κῆρα μέλαιναν (ibid. 85). But usually the departing dead is represented riding a *horse, which a genius leads :* an *open door* betokens the departure, as we still throw open a *door* or *window* when any one dies (Superst. I, 664). As a symbol, the *door* alone, the *horse's head* alone, may express the removal of the soul.[2] The Roman genius of death seems to announce his approach or the hour of parting by *knocking at the door ;*[3] a knocking and poking at night is ghostly and ominous of death (see Suppl.).

Roman works of art never give Death the shape of a female like Halja, though we should have expected it from the gender of *mors*, and originally the people can scarcely have conceived it otherwise ; the Slavic *smrt, smert* (the same word) is invariably fem., the Lith. *smertis* is of either gender, the Lett. *nahwe* fem. alone. And the Slav. *Morena, Marana* (Morena, Marzana), described p. 771, seems to border closely on smrt and mors.

These words find an echo in Teutonic ones. *Schmerz, smart*, we now have only in the sense of pain, originally it must have been the pains of death, as our qual (torment) has to do with quellan, AS. cwellan, Eng. kill:[4] the OHG. MHG. and AS. have alone retained the strong verb smërzan, smërzen, smeortan (dolere). OHG. *smerza* is fem., MHG. *smerze* masc., but never personified. *Nahwe* answers to the Goth. masc. *náus*, pl. naveis, funus (conf. ON. *nâr, nâinn* p. 453), as θάνατος too can mean a corpse.[5] But this Grk. word has the same root as the Goth. *dáuþus*, OHG. *tôd*

---

[1] One would suppose from this passage, that Death took only the corpse of the fallen to himself, that the soul flew away to Hades, for it is said of her in v. 235 ἀΐδὸς δε βεβήκει.

[2] O. Müller's Archäol., ed. 2, pp. 604. 696. For the horse's head, conf. Boeckh's Corp. inscr. no. 800. Marm. Oxon. p. 2, no. 63-7. R. Rochette's Monum. inéd. 1, 126. Pausan. vii. 25, 7. Gerhard's Antike bildw. p. 407.

[3] Hor. Od. i. 4, 13 : *pallida mors* aequo pulsat pede pauperum tabernas regumque turres.

[4] Constant use will soften down the meaning of the harshest terms ; we had an instance in the Fr. gêne, p. 800m.

[5] Goth. *leik* (corpus, caro), our *leiche, leichnam,* Eng. *lich* (cadaver) ; the OHG. *hrêo*, AS. *hræw*, MHG. *rê* (cadaver, funus), and Goth. *hráiv* (whence hráiva-dubô, mourner-dove) are the Lat. *corpus.*

(orig. tôdu) masc., OS. *dôd, dôđ*, AS. *deáđ*, ON. *dauđi*, all masc.,
the M. Nethl. *dôt* having alone preserved the fem. gender, which
is however compatible with the Gothic form. The verb in Gothic
is diva, dáu (morior), standing in the same relation to θνῄσκω,
ἔθανον, θάνατος as the Gothic Tiv to the Slavic dan (day, p. 195).
The ON. dauđi I find used only of the condition, not of the
person, while the Goth. *dáuþus* does express the latter in 1 Cor.
15, 55 (see Suppl.).

To this affinity of words corresponds a similarity of sentiments. The most prominent of these in our old poets seem to
be the following.

As all spirits *appear suddenly*,[1] so does Death; no sooner
named or called, than he comes: 'hie *nâhet* der Tôt manigem
manne,' Roth. 277[b]. 'daz in *nâhet* der Tôt,' Nib. 2106, 4. 'dô
nâhte im der Tôt' 2002, 3. 'Mors *praesens*,' Walthar. 191. 'der
Tôt gêt dir vaste zuo,' Karl 69[b]. He lurks in the background
as it were, waiting for *call* or *beck* (Freidank 177, 17. 'dem Tôde
winken,' beckon to D., Renn. 9540). Like fate, like Wurt, he is
nigh and *at hand* (p. 406). Like the haunting homesprite or will
o' wisp, he rides on people's necks: 'der Tôt mir *sitzet ûf dem
kragen*,' Kolocz. 174. '*stêt vor der tür*,' Diut. 2, 153. A story in
Reusch (no. 36) makes Death sit *outside the door*, waiting for it
to open; he therefore catches the soul as it goes out.

Luckless life-weary men call him to their side, complain of his
delay: '*Tôt*, nu nim dîn teil an mir!' now take thy share of me,
Wh. 61, 2. '*Tôt*, daz du mich nu kanst sparn!' 61, 12. '*wâ nú
Tôt*, du nim mich hin!' Ecke 145.[3] '*Mort*, qar me pren, si me
delivre!' Ren. 9995. '*Mors*, cur tam sera venis?' Rudl. 7, 58.
'ô wê *Tôt*, dazt' ie sô lange mîn verbære!' shouldst forbear,
shun me, MsH. 1, 89[a]. 'por ce requier à Dieu la mort,' Méon
nouv. rec. 2, 241. We know the Aesopic fable of the old man
and Thanatos. To wish for death is also called *seeking Death*,[3]
sending for Death, having him fetched: 'jâ wænet des der degen,

---

[1] Supra p. 325. Reinhart p. liii. cxxx.; like Night, Winter, and the Judgment-
day, Death 'breaks in.'
[2] So beasts of prey are invited, Er. 5832: 'wâ nú hungerigiu tier, bêde wolf
und ber, iwer eines (one of you) kume her und ezze uns beide!'
[3] Straparola 4, 5 tells of a young man who from curiosity started off to hunt
up Death.

ich habe gesant nách Tóde (he fancies I have sent for D.): ich
wil's noch lenger pflegen,' Nib. 486, 5. Of a slothful servant it is
said *he is a good one to send after Death,* i.e. he goes so slow, you
may expect to live a good while longer. This saying must have
been widely diffused : ' en lui avon bon mesagier por querre *la
Mort* et cerchier, que il revendroit moult à tart,' Ren. 5885. ' du
werst ein bot gar guot zuo schicken nach dem Todt, du kommst
nit bald,' H. Sachs 1, 478°. 'werst gut nach dem Tod zu schicken'
iv. 3, 43ᵈ. Fischart geschichtkl. 84ᵃ. 'du är god att skicka
efter Döden,' Hallman p. 94. 'bon à aller chercher la mort,'
Pluquet contes p. 2. In Boh. : 'to dobré gest pro Smrt posjlati,'
Jungmann 4, 193ᵃ. Can this lazy servant be connected with
Gânglati and *Gânglöt,* the man and maid servant of the ancient
Hel ? Sn. 33.

Death takes the soul and carries it away : ' *hina fuartanan*
Tôd,' O. i. 21, 1. 'dô quam der Tôt und *nam in hin,*' Lohengr.
186. ' er *begrîfet,*' Gregor. 413. Diut. 3, 53. *ergreif,* gript,
Greg. 19, an expression used also of Sleep, the brother of Death,
when he falls upon and overpowers : 'der Slâf in *begreif,*' Pf.
Chuonr. 7076. He presses men into his house, the door of which
stands open : ' gegen im het der Tôt *sînes hûses tür entlochen*
(unlocked),' Bit. 12053. ' der Tôt weiz manige sâze (trick), swâ
er wil dem menschen schaden und in *heim ze hûs laden* (entice),'
Türh. Wh. 2281. 'dô in der Tôt *heim nam in sîn gezimmer*
(building),' ' brâht *heim in sîn gemiure* (walls),' Lohengr. 143.
150. These are deviations from the original idea, which did not
provide him with a dwelling of his own ; or is he here an equivalent for Hel ?

Probably, like all messengers (RA. 135), like Hermes the conductor of souls, he carries a *staff,* the symbol of a journey, or
of delegated authority. With this wand, this rod (of wish), he
touches whatever has fallen due to him : ' la Mort *de sa verge le
toucha,*' Méon 4, 107.[1]

To Death is ascribed a *highway,* levelled smooth and kept in
repair, on which the dead travel with him : ' des Tôdes *pfat* wart
g'ebenet,' Turl. Wh. 22ᵃ. 23ᵇ. ' dâ moht *erbouwen* der Tôt sîn
strâze,' Bit. 10654. ' nu seht, wie der Tôt umbe sich mit kreften

---

[1] In Danse Macabre p. m. 55, *trois verges* are wielded by Death.

hât *gebouwen*,' Kl. 829. Like a shifty active servant, he *greases the boots* of the man he comes to fetch, in preparation for the great journey; in Burgundy his arrival is expressed in the phrase: 'quan la Mor venré *graisse no bote*,' quand la Mort viendra graisser nos bottes; Noei Borguignon p. 249 (see Suppl.).

A thoroughly heathen feature it is, to my thinking, that he appears *mounted*, like the valkyrs; on horseback he fetches away, he *sets the dead on his own horse*. In a folksong of wide circulation the lover, dead and buried far away, comes at midnight and rides off with his bride.[1] Possibly that *horse's head* at p. 841 stands more for Death's horse than for the dead man's. Both Hel and her messenger, like other gods, had doubtless a horse at their service; this is confirmed by certain phrases and fancies that linger here and there among the people. One who has got over a serious illness will say: 'jeg *gav Döden en skiäppe havre*' (Thiele 1, 138), he has appeased Death by sacrificing to him a bushel of oats for his horse. So the heathen fed the horse of Wuotan (p. 154), of dame Gaue (p. 252); the Slavs did the same for their Svantevit and Radegast (p. 661). Of one who blunders in noisily they say, in Denmark as above: 'han gaaer *som en helhest*,' he goes like a hel-horse, Dansk ordb. 2, 545ª. There are more things told of this *hel-hest*: he goes round the churchyard on his three legs, he fetches Death. One folktale has it, that in every churchyard, before it receives human bodies, a live horse is buried, and this is what becomes the walking dead-horse (Thiele 1, 137); originally it was no other than the Deathgoddess riding round. Arnkiel quotes 1, 55 the Schleswig superstition, that in time of plague 'die Hell[2] *rides about on a three-legged horse*, destroying men'; if at such a time the .dogs bark and howl in the night (for dogs are spirit-seers), they say 'Hell is at the dogs'; when the plague ceases, 'Hell is driven away'; if a man on the brink of death recovers, 'he has *come*

---

[1] 'The moon shines bright, *the dead rids fast*,' Bürger's life p. 87. Wh. 2, 20. ''t maantje schijnt zo hel, mijn paardtjes lope zo snel,' Kinderm. 3, 77. 'mânan skiner, *dôdmon rider*,' Sv. vis. 1, liii. and even in the Edda: '*rida* menn *dauðir*,' Saem. 166ᵇ. 167ª. Norw. 'manen skjine, *dôman* grine, värte du ikkje räd?' Conf. the Mod. Grk. song in Wh. Müller 2, 64, and Vuk 1, no. 404.

[2] He writes '*der* Hell,' masc.; but the Plattdeutsch, when they attempt H. Germ, often misuse the article, *e.g.* '*der* Pest' for '*die* Pest.'

to terms with Hell.' Here, as in other cases, the notion of Death
has run into one with the personified plague. In our own
medieval poems we never read of Death riding about, but we do
of his *loading his horse* with souls. Thus, in describing a battle :
'seht, ob der Tôt dâ iht *sin soumer lüede* (loaded his sumpter
at all) ? jâ er was unmüezec gar (high busy),' Lohengr. 71. 'daz
ich des *Tôdes vuoder* mit in *lüed* und *vazzet !'* Ottocar 448ᵃ.
The Mod. Greeks have converted old ferryman Χάρων into a
death's-messenger Χάρος; you see him crossing the mountains
with his dusky throng, himself *riding*, the young men walking
before him, the old following behind, and the tender babes
ranged on his saddle.[1] The Lübeck Dance of Death makes him
ride *on a lion*, and he is so represented in a picture also, Douce
p. 160. 'Mortis *habenae*,' Abbo de bellis Paris. 1, 187. 322 (see
Suppl.).

The dead march like captives *in Death's bonds;* to the Indian
imagination likewise he *leads* them away *bound.*[2] 'ei, waz nû
dem Tôde geschicket wart *an sin seil* (to his rope) !' Lohengr.
115. 'maneger quam an des Tôdes *seil'* 123. 'in Tôdes *sil
stigen*,' Ls. 3, 440. ' zuo dem Tôde wart *geseilet*,' Geo. 2585. 'wê
dir Tôt ! dîn *slôz* und dîn *gebende bindet* und *besliuzet*,' Wigal.
7793. ' der Tôt hât mich *gevangen*,' Karl 81ᵇ. Greg. 50.

As the old divinity of the lower world fell into the background,
and Death came forward acting for himself, there could not but
ensue a harsher reading of his character, or a confounding of
him with other gods. From the silent messenger who did no
more than punctually discharge his duty, he becomes a grasping
greedy foe, who will have his bond, who sets traps for mortals.
Already O. v. 23, 260 imputes to him crafty *besuichan* (decipere),
and Conrad *strik* (meshes) and *netzegarn*, Troj. 12178, which
reminds of the goddess Rân with her net (pp. 311. 840). We
think of him still under the familiar figure of a fowler or fisher,
spreading his toils or baiting his hook for man : ' dô kam der
Tôt als ein *diep* (thief), und *stal* dem reinen wîbe daz leben ûz
ir lîbe (the life out of her body),' Wigal. 8033.[3] But he uses

---

[1] Τὰ τρυφερὰ παιδόπουλα 'ς τὴν σελλ' ἀρραδιασμένα, Fauriel 2, 228. Wh. Müller
2, 8; conf. Kind 1849, p. 14.
[2] Bopp's Sündflut, pp. 37. 50. In Buhez santez Nonn p. 205, Death says
' j'attire tout dans mes liens à mon gîte.'
[3] *Life-stealer, man-slayer*, names for Death.

open violence too, he *routs out*, pursues and *plunders*, Nib. 2161,
3. 2163, 1; he '*bifalta* sie,' felled them, O. iii. 18, 34; 'mich
hat der Tôt *gevangen*,' clutched, Greg. 50; he *juget*, hunts, Roth.
2750, *bekrellet* (claws?), Fundgr. 196, 20; and the Bible has the
same thing: in Ps. 91, 3—6 he comes out as a hunter with *snares*
and *arrows*. His messenger-staff has turned into a *spear* which
he hurls, an *arrow* which he discharges from the bow. Worth
noting are the Renn. 24508: 'wirt dem des Tôdes *sper* gesandt;'
and Freid. 177, 24: 'der Tôt gât her, der widerseit uns *an dem*
sper,' defies us at point of lance; a reading which I prefer to the
accepted one '*âne sper*,' without spear. Oðinn has a spear
Gûngnir (p. 147) whose thrust or throw was fatal. The Lith.
Smertis comes as a warrior with *sword* and *pike*, riding in a
chariot, i.e. in the form of a god. All this carries with it the
idea of Death having a regular *fight* and *wrestle* with man, whom
he overpowers and brings to the ground: 'mit dem Tôde *vehten*,'
fence with D., MS. 2, 82ᵇ. 'der Tôt wil mit mir *ringen* (wrestle),'
Stoufenb. 1126. 'dô *ranc* er mit dem Tôde,' Nib. 939, 2. 'alsô
der Tôt hie mit ime *rank*,' Ecke 184; and we still speak of the
death agony, though without any thought of a personality. In
a Mod. Grk song a daring youth *wrestles* with Charos on smooth
marble from morn till midday; at the hour of eve Death flings
him down. In another case Charos takes the shape of a *black*
swallow, and shoots his arrow into a maiden's heart.[1] A doubtful passage in Beow. 3484 we ought perhaps to refer to Death,
who is there called a destroyer that shoots with arrow-bow of
fire: '*bona*, se þe of *flânbogan fŷrenum* sceoteð;' conf. the Serv.
krvnik, bloodshedder p. 21. Brun von Schonebeke makes Death
wield a *scourge of four strings;* and our MHG. poets lend him an
arrow and *battle-axe:* 'des Tôdes *strâle* het si gar versniten,'
cut them up, Tit. 3770. 'wâ snîdet des Tôdes *barte*,' Wh. 3,
220 (Cod. cass.). The '*isernporte*' in a Meister-song of the
14th cent. (Hagen's Mus. 2, 188) means surely *isernbarte?*
Here Death promises a *thousand years' grace*, should his adversary
gain the victory (see Suppl.).[2]

---

[1] Wh. Müller 2, 4. 6; conf. Tommaseo's Canti popolari 3, 301 seq.
[2] Our poets too are no strangers to the idea of Death *prosecuting at law* his
claim upon a man: 'do begunde der Tôt einen grâven *beclagen* und mit *gewalte*
twingen ze nôtigen dingen,' accuse a count and drive him to straits, Iw. 5625 seq.

In such a conflict, however, Death must appear as the leader of a *large* and ever increasing *army*. There is a following, a retinue assigned him : ' der Tôt suochte sêre dâ sîn *gesinde* was,' Nib. 2161, 3. The Greeks set us the fashion of calling the dead οἱ πλέονες the majority, and ἐς πλεόνων ἱκέσθαι meant the same as ἐς Ἀιδου ἰκ., to reach the abode of the great multitude, join the great host, as we still say. In the ' Bohemian Ploughman,' Death is styled *captain of the mountain ;* because, as in the Greek song (p. 845), the march of his army covers the mountains ? ' In des Tôdes *schar varn,*' fare to D.'s host, Wh. v. Orl. 2113. ' ist *an die vart,*' gone his way (obiit), Walth. 108, 6. Though taking no part in the fight, the dead seem to *bear a badge* (flag or lance), which, so to speak, he fastens on the dying, with which he touches them, enrolls them in his band.[1] That is how I understand ' des Tôdes *zeichen tragen,*' Nib. 928, 3. 2006, 1, though it may include the collateral sense of having received a death-wound, which now serves as his badge and cognisance. Hence in Nib. 939, 3 : ' des Tôdes *zeichen* ie ·ze sêre sneit,' D.'s token aye too sore he cut ; where one MS. reads *wâfen* (arms), and elsewhere we find ' eines *wâfen tragen,*' carry some one's arms, Parz. 130, 4. Freidank 74, 18. Wigal. 7797, and even ' des tôdes *wâpen* (coat of arms) tragen,' Wh. 17, 16. ' Tristandes *zeichen vüeren,*' Heinr. Trist. 2972, is to be wounded like him. So far back as Ælfred's Boeth. p. 16 (Rawl.) we have ' Deáðes *tácnung* '; even Zio's or Tiwes *tácen* p. 200, and Oðin's *spear* p. 147 are worth considering (see Suppl.).[2]

With the idea of messengership and that of the great company were associated some others, which probably reach a long way

the count is called ' der verlorne, wand' er muose im ze suone (satisfaction) geben beide sîn gesunt und sîn leben.' So Iw. 7161 speaks of having to ' *gelten* (pay) vür des Tôdes *schelten* '; and the same perhaps is meant by ' der Tôt hât ûf si *gesworn,*' Nib. 2017, 5. In the ' Ackermann aus Böhmen ' on the contrary, Death is the defendant, and a man whose wife he has carried off is prosecutor. Similar law-suits are brought by the *Devil.* ' Nu kume vil grimmeclîcher Tôt, und rihte Gote von uns beiden ! ' MS. 1, 17. Observe too ' mit des Tôdes *hantveste über-sigelet,*' sealed with D.'s sign manual, Wh. 391, 27. The Indian god of death, Yama, is a lord of law.

[1] Conf. ' einem des Tôdes *muoder* (mieder) snîden,' Titur. ; to cut D.'s coat on (or for) a man.

[2] It is worthy of note, that in the Meister-song already quoted (Mus. 2, 187) Death says : ' be ready, when I send thee my messengers (the infirmities) to *give thee the signs,*' to mark thee for my own. Death, orig. a messenger himself, sends out under-messengers. Conf. Kinderm. no. 177. Even the O. Fr. Chanson des Saxons 2, 134 has : ' la Mors le *semont* sovent et menu,' viz. by fainting-fits.

back. *Messengers* in ancient times were often fiddlers and pipers:
it was nothing out of the way, to make Death and his meny
perform a *reihen* (rig, round dance); with fife and fiddle he seeks
to win recruits. Really a pleasant fancy, tending to mitigate
the harshness of dying: the souls of the dead enter at once
upon dancing and revelry. To the ancient Romans there were
songs and dances in the Elysian fields;[1] and it accords with the
resemblance of departed spirits to elves, who also love music and
dancing (p. 470). Yet our poets of the 13th cent. never once
allude to the *Dance of Death*, which from the 15-16th became
such a favourite subject. The oft-recurring phrase ' er hât *den
Tôt an der hant*,' by the hand (Nib. 1480, 4. 1920, 4. 1958, 4.
Wigal. 2453. 4700. Alph. 286. 345. 359) seems to mean, not
catching hold for the purpose of dancing, but of leading away
(like ' dôd is *at hendi*,' p. 406).

Holy Scripture having already likened our fleeting life to grass,
it was not difficult to see in Death a *mower* or *reaper*, who
cuts men down like flowers and corn-stalks. *Knife, sickle,* or
scythe is found him in this connexion: 'There's a reaper they call
Death, Power from God most high he hath, He whets his knife
to-day, Keener it cuts the hay; Look to thyself, O flowret fair!'
Pop. Hymn. The older poets never give him these implements,
but the figure of 'Death carried out' is sometimes furnished with
a *scythe* (p. 772). In later times the *harpé* (sickle) of the Greek
Kronos (O. Müller's Archäol. p. 599) may have had an influence
too, conf. *falcitenens* in Radevicus 2, 11. To 'match men with
flowers, make them bite the grass,' Lohengr. 138, is said equally
of other conquerors beside Death. But he weeds out the plants:
'in lebens garten der Tôt nu *jat*,' Turl. Wh. 23ᵇ. Conversely
Death, like the devil, is called a *sower*, who disseminates weeds
among men; ' dô der Tôt sînen *sâmen* under si gesæte,' Wh.
361, 16. ' er *ier* durch in *des Tôdes furch*,' he eared through him
D.'s furrow, Ulr. Trist. 3270, simply means: he planted in him
a mortal wound (see Suppl.).

Before explaining certain other conceptions, I have to enumer-
ate the names and epithets of Death in our old poetry.

---

[1] Virg. Aen. 6, 644: pars pedibus plaudunt *choreas* et *carmina* dicunt. Tibull.
. 3, 59: hic *choreae cantusque* vigent.

Very commonly he is called 'der *grimme*,' furious, Roth. 2750. Nib. 1360, 4. 1553, 3. Mar. 218. Flore 1931. Troj. 2317-25. 10885. Ls. 3, 124; [1]—'der *ferchgrimme*,' Morolt 4059, a felicitous compound, as Death has designs upon the life or soul (ferch); —der *grimmige*,' Roth. 517. Reinh. 360. 1248. Berthold 303; —'der *bittere*' (πικρὸς θάνατος) and '*amara* Mors,'[2] Rudl. 1, 110. Unibos 117, 4. Diut. 3, 89. Mar. 206. Alex. (Lampr.) 820. 1097. 3999. 4782. Gr. Ruod. C[b] 15. Wh. 253, 28. Wigal. 1113;—der *bitterliche*, Troj. 3521. 22637;—'der *süre*,' sour, Parz. 643, 24;—der *scharfe*': ein *scharpher* bote, Freid. 21, 6;— 'der *irre*,' Amgb. 29ᵃ in Wizlau neighbhd. therefore prob. for *ërre*, ireful;—'der *gemeine*,' common (qui omnes manet), En. 2081. All, so far, epithets taken from his unavoidableness, cruelty, bitterness; not a hint about his personal presence. Nowhere is he the black, the pale, after the Latin 'mors atra, pallida.' Otto II was called '*pallida mors* Saracenorum,' Cod. lauresh. 1, 132; and in Renner 23978. 80 I find 'der *gelwe* tôt,' yellow d.; in both cases the aspect of the dead, not of Death, is meant. So when Walth. 124, 38 says of the world, that it is 'innân *swarzer* varwe, *vinster* sam der tôt,' inwardly black of hue, dark as death, he means the abode of the dead, hell, not the figure of Death. In one song he is addressed as '*lieber* Tôt!' dear D. (Hagen's Mus. 2, 187), and H. Sachs i. 5, 528ᵈ speaks of him as 'der *heilig* Tod,' holy D.; '*her Tôt!*' Sir D., again in voc. case only, Apollonius 295 and often in the Ackermann aus Böhmen (see Suppl.).

It is more important to our inquiry, that in the Reinardus 3, 2162 a bone fiddle is said to be '*ossea* ut *dominus Blicero*,' by which nothing but Death can have been meant, whether the word signify the pale (bleich), or the grinning (bleckend), or be, as I rather think, the proper name *Blidger, Blicker* with a mere suggestion of those meanings. A *bony horse's head* is here handed in mockery to the wolf as a skilful player (joculandi gnarus) by way of fiddle, 'bony as a *skeleton*.' And now that unexplained *caput caballinum* at p. 661n. may be interpreted as in fact a sym-

---

[1] Der *grimme tôt*, the name of a knife (Wolfd. 1313), is remarkable, as Hel's knife was called *sultr* (p. 313) from *svelta* esurire, which in the Goth. *sviltan* takes the meaning of mori.

[2] Isidore even says, 'mors dicta quod sit *amara*.'

bol of Death (p. 844) and the dead-man's steed (p. 841). As
the convent clergy set up human death's-heads in their cells for
a memento mori, may not they also have nailed up *horse's skulls*
inside their walls? did an older heathen custom, here as in so
many instances, have a christian thought breathed into it? If
this holds good, we can see why the horse's head should have set
the Flemish poet thinking of Death; it may even be, that fanatic
sculptors used to fashion Death as playing on it instead of a
fiddle or fife.[1]

In any case *dominus Blicero* proves that in the middle of the
12th cent. it was the practice to represent Death as a *skeleton*.
.I do not know of any earlier evidence, but think it very possible
that such may be hunted up. We know that to the ancient
Romans fleshless shrivelled-up masks or *skeletons* served to
indicate Death.[2] On tombs of the Mid. Ages, no doubt from an
early time, corpses were sculptured as whole or half *skeletons* (see
Suppl.). Poets of the 13th cent. paint the *World* (p. 792n.) as
a beautifully formed woman in front, whose back is covered with
snakes and adders:[3] the notion itself may be of much higher
antiquity; it is closely related to the story of three live and three
dead kings.[4]

This mode of representing Death, which soon became universal,
stands in sharp contrast with the ancient portraitures and the
old heathen conceptions of him. The engaging form of the
genius, akin to Sleep, the childlike Angel of death, is now
supplanted by a ghastly figure copied from the grim reality of
corruption in the grave. Yet even here poetry steps in with her
all-embracing, all-mellowing influence. The older conceptions
of Death as *leading away*, as *attacking*, as *dancing*, applied to this
new and hideous figure, have called forth a host of truly popular,
naïve and humorous art-productions; nay, their wealth is not
nearly exhausted by the artists yet. Without this *bag of bones*

---

[1] *Todenpfeife* is a place in Lower Hesse, Rommel 5, 375. Remigius demonol.
145 says, at witches' gatherings they played on a dead *horse's head* instead of a
cithern: a coincidence almost decisive. Philand. von Sittew. (p. m. 174) has also
a Death with his lyre.

[2] O. Müller's Archäol. 696-7. Lessing 8, 251-2.

[3] The poem was printed before the Wigalois.

[4] Staphorst i. 4, 263. Bragur 1, 869. O. Fr. 'les trois mors et les trois vis,'
Roquefort 2, 780. Catal. de la Vallière p. 285-6; conf. Douce p. 31 seq. and Catal.
of MSS. in Brit. Mus. (1834) 1, 22 (Cod. Arund. no. 83 sec. xiv), also plate 7.

aping the garb and gestures of the living,[1] and his startling
incongruity with the warm life around, all the charm and quaint-
ness of those compositions would be gone. Less enjoyable must
have been the processions and plays in which these spectacles
were exhibited in France during the 15th cent. and perhaps
earlier; there and then originated that peculiar name for the
Dance of Death: *chorea Machabaeorum*, Fr. *la danse Macabre*.[2]

Another name of Death, much later seemingly than Blicker,
but now universally known, is *Freund Hein* or *Hain*; I cannot
even trace it up to the middle of last century.[3] 'In itself it looks
old and fitting enough, and is susceptible of more than one
explanation. Considering that Death has so many points of
contact with giants and other spirits, the name *Heine* (p. 503)
might be borrowed from the homesprite for one, and the addition
of *Friend* would answer to the 'fellow, neighbour, goodfellow'
of those elvish beings whom we meet with under the name of
Heimchen, Heinchen (pp. 275. 459n.), and who border closely on
the idea of departed spirits. Add the L. Germ. term for a
winding-sheet, *heinenkleed* (p. 446). But it is also spelt *hünen-
kleed*, which brings us to 'heun, hüne,' giant (p. 523); and
Hein itself might be explained as *Heimo* (p. 387), or *Hagano*
(p. 371). A Voigtland story of the god *Hain* (Jul. Schmidt,
p. 150), or the Thuringian one about an ancient *haingott*, grove-
god (Rosencranz's Neue zeitschr. i. 3, 27), being themselves very
doubtful, I am not inclined to fasten on our still doubtful Friend
Hein. Still less attention is due to a name for mortuarium,
'hainrecht,'[4] coming as it probably does from heimrecht, *i.e.*
heimfall, lapse of property.

---

[1] As the beasts in a fable ape those of men.

[2] Latest writings on the Dance of Death: Peignot, 'Recherches sur les danses
des morts' (1826). F. Douce, 'The Dance of Death' (1833). The latter derives
Macabre from St. *Macarius*, to whom three skeletons appeared in a vision. I do
not see how 'chorea Machabaeorum,' as the oldest authorities have it, could have
come from that; conf. Carpentier sub v. (a. 1424-53). It ought to appear by the
old paintings, that the 7 heroes of the O.T. martyred in one day [2 Maccabees 7]
were incorporated as leading characters in the dance. Perhaps it is more correct
to explain 'macabre' from the Arabic magabir, magabaragh (dead-yard, cimeterium).
On the French performances conf. Michelet's Hist. de France 4, 409—412 (Paris
1840).

[3] It is used by Musäus (Volksm. 1, 16), Claudius and Gotter. J. R. Schellen-
berg in Pref. to Freund Heins erscheinungen (Winterthur 1785) thinks Claudius in
his Asmus (after 1775) invented the name, which I very much doubt; he has given
it currency.

[4] Mittermaier's Privatrecht § 77, no. 27.

Kaisersberg calls Death *holz-meier*, wood-mower. He wrote a book, De arbore humana (Strasb. 1521 fol.), 'wherein easily and to the glory of God ye may learn to await blithely the *woodcutter Death.*' Then, p. 118[b]: 'So is death called a *village-mower* or *wood-mower*, and justly hath he the name, for he hath in him the properties of a *wood-cutter*, as, please God, ye shall hear. The first property of the *village-mower* is communitas, he being possessed in common by all such as be in the village, and being to serve them all alike. So is the *wood-cutter* likewise common to all the trees, he overlooketh no tree, but heweth them down all.'[1] Here Death is regarded as a forester, a ranger, who has a right to fell any of the forest-trees. It is said that in some places the gravedigger is called *holzmeier*.

In the Deutsche Schlemmer, a drama of the 16th cent., Death is called the pale *Streckefuss* or *Streckebein* (leg-stretcher), as Gryphius too (Kirchhofsged. 36) names him *Streckfuss*, because he stretches out the limbs of the dying, loosens them (λυσιμελής); and before that, the twice quoted Meister-song of the 14th cent. has: 'er hat kein ru, er hab *gestrecket mir das fell* (my skin),' Hag. mus. 2, 188. In Chr. Weise's Drei erzn. 314 I find *Streckebein* and *Bleckezahn*, bleak (*i.e.* bared) teeth; and elsewhere *Dürrbein*, *Klapperbein*, names for a skeleton. The allusion in *kupferbickel* (Ackerm. aus B. p. 34) remains obscure (see Suppl.).

It remains for me to mention certain more fully developed myths respecting Death, which have survived from assuredly a remote antiquity.

H. Sachs (1, 102[b]), speaking of Death's arrival, says he *twitches* or *jerks the stool* from under man, tips it over, so that he tumbles to the ground. He takes from him his seat and standing among the living: I suspect there was a fuller story at the back of this. More commonly the same thing is expressed by 'Death has *blown* the man's *candle out*' (as Berhta blew out the lights of the eyes, p. 277), for the notions of light, life and sojourn among the living, run into one another.[2] The living principle was linked

---

[1] The earlier editions in Latin (1514, 115[b,c], and 1519, 105[b,c]) have in parentheses 'der dorfmeyger' and 'der holzmeyger.'

[2] Wh. 416, 14: 'bî liehter sunnen dâ *verlasch* (went out) manegem Sarrazin sîn *lieht*.' Lohengr. 133: 'er sluoc in, daz im muose *das lieht erlischen*.'

to a light, a taper, a brand: when these were wasted, death
ensued (pp. 409. 415). Here then the idea of Death is intimately
connected with that of fate. The genius *lowers his torch*, re-
verses it, and the light of life is quenched. For the child as
soon as born, the norn has *kindled a light*, to which his thread of
life is fastened; possibly even our lighting of tapers in connexion with birthday gifts has reference to this.[1] We have a
capitally contrived story of *Gossip Death* (gevatter Tod, Kinderm.
no. 44), the conclusion of which represents a subterranean
cavern, with thousands of lights burning in endless rows. These
are the lives of men, some still blazing as long tapers, others
burnt down to tiny candle-ends; but even a tall taper may topple
or be tipt over. The preceding part relates, how Death has
stood gossip[2] to a poor man, and has endowed his godson with
the gift of beholding him bodily when he approaches the sick,
and of judging by his position whether the patient will recover
or not.[3] The godson becomes a physician, and attains to wealth
and honours: if Death stands at the sick man's head, it is all
over with him; if at his feet, he will escape. Occasionally the
doctor turns the patient round, and circumvents Death; but in
the end Death has his revenge, he catches his godson napping,
and knocks his candle over.[4] Throughout this fable Death shews
himself friendly, good-natured and indulgent, only in case of
absolute need does he fulfil his function; hence too his *gossiphood*[5] with man, which evidently corresponds to that ancient
visit of the norns to the newborn child, and their bestowing
gifts on him (pp. 408—12), as in some nursery-tales the fays are
invited to stand *godmothers*.[6] The extinguished light resembles
the taper and the brand, to which are linked the lives of Norna-
gestr and Meleager (pp. 409. 415). It is then a primitive myth

---

[1] In the child's game 'If the fox dies I get the skin' (Kinderm. 2, xviii.), a
piece of *burning wood* is passed round, and its extinction decides.
[2] *God-sib* expresses the kinship of god-parents to each other or to the parents.
—TRANS.
[3] So the bird charadrius, by looking at or away from you, decides your life or
death, Freid. introd. lxxxvi., where a couplet in Titurel 5154-5 and the O.Fr. Bes-
tiaire (Roquef. sub v. caladrio) are left unnoticed.
[4] May not that 'stool' also, when upset, have knocked the candle over?
[5] Is Death likewise called the *brother* of man, as he is of Sleep? The
'bruoder tôt' in Ben. 262 means *fratris* mors.
[6] The semi-divine norns and fays protect and bestow gifts like christian
sponsors.

of heathen Germany; in telling which, Death was pictured, even till recent times, not as a skeleton, but in the shape of a living man or god. We cannot wonder that the story is found with a great many variations, which are collected, though still incompletely, in Kinderm. 3, 72 : in some of them Death presents his godson with a ring, by which he can judge of diseases.[1] Old Hugo von Trimberg at the close of his work had told a tale ' von dem *Tôde, wie er ein kint huop* (took up),' but there is not much in it (Bamb. ed. 23665—722) : Death promises to *send* his gossip some *messengers* before he comes to fetch him (as in the Meister-song p. 847n.) ; these are, ringing in the ears, running at the eyes, toothache, wrinkled skin, and grizzled beard. The gossiphood is the only guarantee of any connexion with the later märchen.——The resemblance of the OHG. *toto*, godfather, MHG. *tote* (Parz. 461, 10. Wh. 7, 21) to *tôt*, death, is striking, though strictly the quantity of the vowel keeps the two words apart, and to harmonize them some derivative process must be presupposed. The story never grew out of a play on the words (see Suppl.).[2]

Equally celebrated, but gayer in tone, is the tale of *Death* and Player Jack (Spielhansel, no. 82 ; conf. 3, 135—148), who by a spell binds Death to a tree, so that nobody dies in the world for seven years. Welcker (Append. to Schwenk p. 323-4) has pointed out a parallel story in Pherekydes, how *Death* is set on by Zeus to attack Sisyphos, who binds him in strong chains, and then no one can die; *Hades* himself comes and sets Death free, and delivers Sisyphos into his hands. Our German fable interweaves the *Devil* into the plot. Once the *Devil* was put in possession of hell, he had to take his place beside Death, as the alliteration ' death and devil ! ' couples them together. So *Welnas, Wels*, originally the death-god of the Lithuanians and Lettons, got converted into the Devil. According to the christian view, *angels* received the souls of the just, *devils* those of the wicked (p. 836) ; therefore Death in coming for souls was divided into a double power, according as he resembled the angel or the devil. As angelic messenger, he comes nearest the christian *Michael*, whose office it was to receive souls (Morolt

---

[1] Ettner's Unwürd. doctor p. 290.
[2] Conf. p. 14 on the affinity between *gŏd* and *gŏde*.

2660. 2715), conf. p. 836. Of very aged people, who still live on, we say 'Death has *forgotten* to fetch them.' The Nib. Lament 122 has: 'der Tôt *het* ir *minne*, die dâ sterben solden,' D. bore those *in mind* that there should die, or, as Lachmann interprets it, *desired* them for his band (conf. p. 848).

These investigations will hardly have left it doubtful, that the heathen 'Death' is one of a secondary order of gods; hence too he coincides more especially with the semi-divine valkyrs and norns, he is dependent on Oðinn and Hel; of the Grecian gods, it is Hermes and Hades, Persephone and the ferryman Charon that come nearest to him. But his nature is also not unrelated to that of elves, homesprites and genii.

Chap. XXIV. has explained how he got mixed up with one of the time-gods, Winter; no wonder therefore that he now and then reminds us of Kronos.

In our Heldenbuch, *Death* figures as a *false god*, whom the heathen Belligan serves above all other gods, and whose image is demolished by Wolfdietrich. I do not know exactly how to account for this: it must be a diabolic being that is meant.

In the Finnish lays, *Manala* and *Tuonela* are often named together, but as separate beings. One is the underworld, from 'maa,' earth; the other the kingdom of the dead, as *Tuon* (θάνατος) is Death, Halja. In Kalewala, runes 6—9, Tuonela seems to be a river of the underworld, with sacred swans swimming on it (see Suppl.).

CHAPTER XXVIII.

DESTINY AND WELL-BEING.

This is the place to insert a more exact survey of ancient opinions on fortune and destiny, than it was possible to take in chap. XVI, where the semi-divine directresses of human fate were spoken of. Fate in the proper sense has so much to do with men's notions about birth, and more especially those about death, and these have only just been expounded. Thus, a man over whom there impends a speedy and inevitable death is said to be *fey*.[1]

Our ancestors, like other heathens, appear to have made a distinction between destiny and fortune. Their gods bestow prosperity and bliss: above all, Wuotan is the giver of all good, the maker and author of life and victory (pp. 133-7). But neither he nor any other god was at the beginning of creation, he has himself sprung out of it (p. 559), and can do nothing against a higher constitution of the world, which exempts neither him nor victory-lending Zeus[2] from a general destruction (pp. 316-8). Some things turn out contrary to his will: Oðinn and all the âses cannot prevent the misfortune of Balder; another instance of overruling destiny at p. 425. Ragnarök, the world's destruction, far overtops the power of the gods.

This predetermined and necessary character of all that comes into being and exists and perishes, was expressed by a plural

---

[1] OHG. *feigi*, MHG. *veige*; OS. *fêgi*, Hel. 72, 4; AS. *fæge*, Beow. 5946; ON. *feigr*. The old meaning of the word has been preserved longest in Lower Saxony [and Scotland]: 'dar is en *veege* in'n huse'; 'en *veegminsche*, dat balde sterven werd (will die soon)'; per contra, 'he is nau nig *veege* (not fey yet)' of a man who comes in when you are talking of him. Also Nethl. 'een *veeg* man (with one foot in the grave), een *veege* teken (sign of death)', hence also *veeg* = debilis, periculis expositus. Our own *feig* has acquired the sense of fainthearted, cowardly, pitiable, as the Lat. fatalis has, in the Fr. fatal, that of unlucky, disagreeable. So the Lith. *paíkas*, bad (see Suppl.).

[2] Τρώεσσι βούλεται νίκην (Il. 7, 21. 16, 121), as βουλή will, counsel, is usually attributed to Zeus (ἡμῖν βούλεται 17, 331); and sometimes νόος (17, 176) or νόημα, purpose (17, 409). His great power is illustrated by the gold chain (σειρά, Il. 8, 19—28), but passages presently to be cited shew that he had to leave destiny to be decided by the balance.

noun, ON. *scöp*, OS. *giscapu*, AS. *gesceapu; I have not found an OHG. *scaf*, *kiscaf* in the same sense, though the sing. is forthcoming, and, like the sing. *skap* in ON., signifies indoles, consilium, Graff 6, 450. The later Icelandic uses a masc. *skapnaðr*, and the Dan. *skiebne* (ON. skepna = forma, indoles). The OS. intensifies its *giscapu* by prefixes: *wurdigiscapu*, Hel. 103, 7. *reganogiscapu* (supra p. 26), decreta fati, superorum, where the old heathen notions of *wurd* and *regin* plainly assert themselves. In ON. the neut. pl. *lög* (statuta) is never used of destiny, except when joined to the particle *ör* (for or), *örlög*, which in all the other dialects becomes a sing., OHG. *urlac* (neut. ? Graff's quotations 2, 96-7 leave it doubtful, Notker uses urlag as masc., pl. urlaga), OS. *orlag*, AS. *orlæg*, all denoting a 'fixing from the first;' but as the most momentous issue of fate was to the heathen that of war, it early deviated into the sense of bellum, and in Hel. 132, 3 *urlagi* bellum seems distinct from *orlag*, *orleg* fatum, but in reality both are one. So the OHG. *urteil*, *urteili*, AS. *ordæl*, from being the award of a judge, came to mean that of battle. The OS. compound *aldarlagu* (vitae decretum), Hel. 125, 15 retains the old plural form. Now *aldr*, *aldar* is strictly aevum (p. 792), and *hveila*, OHG. *huila* tempus, but also vitae tempus; hence these words also run into the sense of fatum, conf. AS. *gesceap-hwil*, *orleg-hwil*, Beow. 52. 4849. 5817, OS. *orlag-huila*, Hel. 103, 8, and OHG. *huilsâlida*.[1] Then there is an ON. *auðna*, Swed. *öde*, destiny, and 'auðinn' fato concessus: '*auðna* ræðr hvörs manns lífi,' rules every man's life, Fornald. sög. 1, 95. Our modern words, not introduced till late, *schicksal* (fr. schicken aptare, conf. geschickt aptus), *verhängnis*, *fügung*, do not come up to the old ones in simplicity or strength.

To the nouns 'scapu, lagu,' correspond the verbs to *shape*, to *lay*, which are used in a special sense of the decrees of fate (pp. 407. 410): 'ist tha kindee *skepen* (is it shaped for the child)' says the O. Fris. Law 49, 10. But we also meet with an ON. *œlla* (destinare, to intend for some one), OHG. *ahtôn* and perhaps ahtilôn, MHG. *ahten*, and *beslahten*, as ahte and slahte are akin to one another (see Suppl.).

[1] *Wilsâlda* (fortuna), N. Cap. 20-3-5. 53. 77. MHG. *wilsælde*, Kaiserchr. 1757. Massmann 3, 669. Geo. 61ᵃ. 'diu *wile* mîn und ich müez Got bevolhen sîn,' must be committed to God, Bit. 3ᵇ.

Destiny has principally to do with the beginning and the end of human life. The Wurd visits the newborn and the dying, and it is for one or the other of these events that the above-mentioned names of destiny are mostly used by the poets; thus Beow. 51 speaks of dying 'tô gesceaphwîle,' at the appointed time: Hel. 103, 7: 'tho quâmun wurdegiscapu themu ôdagan man, orlaghuîle, that he thit licht farlêt.' The hour of birth too settles much as to the course and outcome of one's life: 'qualem *Nascentia* attulit, talis erit,' and '*Parcae, dum aliquis nascitur,* valent eum designare ad hoc quod volunt,' Superst. A, and C 198°. The infant's whole course of life shall be conformable to what the norns or fays in their *visitation* have *bestowed*, have *shaped.* [1]

It is a deviation from this *oldest* way of thinking, to put the settlement of destiny into the hands of the gods; yet it is a very old one. Undoubtedly the faith of many men began early to place the Highest God *at the very head* of the world's manage-ment, leaving those weird-women merely to make known his mandates. The future lies on the lap of the gods, θεῶν ἐν γούνασι κεῖται, and with this agrees that 'laying on the lap,' that 'taking to the bosom,' which is performed by the paternal or maternal deity (pp. 642. 839). If above the gods themselves there could be conceived a still higher power, of the beginning and end of all things, yet their authority and influence was regarded by men as boundless and immeasurable, all human concerns were undoubtedly under their control (see Suppl.).

The Gautrekssaga tells us (Fornald. sög. 3, 32), that at mid-night *Hrosshârsgrani* [2] awoke his foster-son Starkaðr, and carried him in his boat to an island. There, in a wood, eleven men sat in council; the twelfth chair stood vacant, but Hrosshârsgrani took it, and all saluted him as Oðinn. And Oðinn said, the demsters should deem the *doom* of Starkaðr (dômendr skyldi dœma örlug St.). Then spake Thôrr, who was wroth with the mother of the lad: I *shape* for him, that he have neither son nor

---

[1] We still say: 'born in *happy hour*.' OHG. '*mit heilu* er giboran ward,' O. Sal. 44. Freq. in the O. Span. Cid: 'el que en *buen ora* nascio, el que en *buen punto* nascio.' From this notion of a good hour of beginning (à la bonne heure) has sprung the Fr. word bonheur (masc.) for good hap in general. Similarly, about receiving knighthood, the O. Span. has 'el que en *buen ora* cinxo espada.'

[2] That is, Grani, Stögrani, the bearded, a by-name of Oðinn (p. 147).

daughter, but be the last of his race. Oðinn said: I *shape* him, that he live three men's lifetimes (conf. Saxo Gram. p. 103). Thôrr: in each lifetime he shall do a ' nîðîngs-verk.' Oðinn: I *shape* him, that he have the best of weapons and raiment. Thôrr: he shall have neither land nor soil. Oðinn: I *give* him, that he have store of money and chattels. Thôrr: I *lay* unto him, that he take in every battle grievous wounds. Oðinn: I *give* him the gift of poetry. Thôrr: what he composes he shall not be able to remember. Oðinn: this I *shape* him, that he be prized by the best and noblest men. Thôrr: by the people he shall be hated. Then the demsters awarded to Starkaðr all the doom that was deemed, the council broke up, and Hrosshârsgrani and his pupil went to their boat.

Thôrr plays here exactly the part of the ungracious fay (pp. 411-2), he tries to lessen each gift by a noxious ingredient. And it is not for an infant, but a well-grown boy, and in his presence, that the destiny is shaped.

According to Greek legend, Zeus did not always decide directly, but made use of two *scales*, in which he *weighed* the fates of men, e.g. of the Trojans and Achæans, of Achilles and Hector:

> Καὶ τότε δὴ χρύσεια πατὴρ ἐπίταινε τάλαντα·
> ἐν δ' ἐτίθει δύο κῆρε τανηλεγέος θανάτοιο,
> Τρώων θ' ἱπποδάμων καὶ Ἀχαιῶν χαλκοχιτώνων.
> ἕλκε δὲ μέσσα λαβών· ῥέπε δ' αἴσιμον ἦμαρ Ἀχαιῶν.

Il. 8, 69. 22, 209; conf. 16, ʋ58. 19, 223. The same of Aeneas and Turnus, Aen. 12, 723 :

> Jupiter ipse, *duas* aequato examine *lances*
> sustinet, et *fata* imponit diversa *duorum*,
> quem damnet labor, et quo *vergat* pondere letum.

I am the more particular in quoting these, as the christian legend also provides the archangel Michael, the conductor of souls, with *scales*, in which the good and evil deeds of them that die are weighed against one another, and the destinies of souls determined by the outcome [1] (see Suppl.). The application of a balance to actions, to sins, is very natural; the (apocryphal) 2 Esdras 3, 34

---

[1] Conf. Deut. S. no. 479; a coll. of authorities in Zappert's Vita Acotanti (Vienna 1839), pp. 79, 88.

has: 'nunc ergo pondera *in statera* nostras iniquitates,' and 4, 36: 'quoniam *in statera* ponderavit seculum.'[1] The Jomsvîkînga-saga cap. 42 (Fornm. sög. 11, 128-9) describes the magical luck-scales or wishing-scales of Hâkon iarl: 'Sîðan tekr iarl *skâlir góðar* þær er hann átti, þær voro gervar af brendu silfri ok gylldar allar, en þar fylgðo 2 *met*, annat af gulli en annat af silfri; â hvârotveggja metino var gert sem væri lîkneskja, ok hêto þat hlotar, en þat voro reyndar hlutir, sem mönnum var títt at hafa, ok fylgði þesso náttûra mikil, ok til þess alls, er iarli þótti skipta, þá hafði hann þessa hluti. Iarl var þvî vanr at leggja hluti þessa î skâlirnar, ok kvað á hvat hvâr skyldi merkja fyrir honum, ok âvalt er vel gêngo hlutir, ok sâ kom upp, er hann vildi, þá var sâ ôkyrr hlutrinn î skâlinni, er þat merkði at hann vildi at yrði, ok breysti sâ hlutrinn nokkot svâ î skâlinni, at glam varð af.'

I do not find that in our earlier heathen time the fates of men were calculated from the *stars* at their birth. This kind of soothsaying (p. 721) seems to have become known till the latter part of the Mid. Ages. Radulphus Ardens (an Aquitanian priest of the 11th cent.) says in his Homilies (Antverp. 1576, p. 41[b]): Cavete, fratres, ab eis qui mentiuntur, quod quando quisque nascitur, *stella sua secum nascitur, qua fatum ejus constituitur*, sumentes in erroris sui argumentum, quod hic in scriptura sacra (on the star of the Magi) dicitur 'stella ejus.' One instance we find in Klinsor's star-gazing on the Wartburg; another in the wishing-wife who *looks into the stars*, Altd. bl. 1, 129 (see Suppl.).

For individuals then, as well as for whole families and nations, length of days and happiness were ordained beforehand.[2] But the decrees of norns and gods lay shrouded in an obscurity that disclosed its secrets only to the glances of wise men and women (p. 400).[3] The people believed in a predetermining of fates, as they did in the certainty of death.

---

[1] We need not go to 2 Esdras to find plenty of similar passages in the O. T., e.g. 1 Sam. 2, 3. Job 31, 6. Prov. 16, 2. Isa. 26, 7. Dan. 5, 27.—TRANS.

[2] Not unfrequently depending on their possession of certain things: a *hoard* drags the whole kindred of the Nibelungs to ruin; the gift, the *jewel*, of the dwarfs (p. 457) insures the prosperity of particular families.

[3] It is worthy of remark, that, acc. to the ON. view, not all the gods, but only the highest ones possessed a *knowledge of destiny*; so to the Greeks, none but Zeus and those whom he made his confidants knew of it. Of Frigg it is said, Sæm. 65[b]: 'at öll örlög viti, þótt hun sialfgi segi,' all fates she knows, but tells not. And

The Old Norse *fatalism* is proved by the following passages:
'*lagt* er alt *for*,' predestined is all; and 'era me*ð* löstom *lögð*
æfi þer,' Sæm. 175ᵇ. '*siâ* mun gipt *lagið* â grams æfi,' and
'*munat skōpom* vinna,' 179ᵇ. '*eino dœgri mer var aldr um
skapaðr* oc allt *líf um lagit*,' 83ᵃ. '*var þer þar skapat*,' 164ᵇ. 'þat
verðr hverr at vinna, er *ætlat* er'; 'þat man verða fram atkoma,
sem *ætlat* er'; 'ecki man mer þat stoða, ef mer er *dauðinn
ætlaðr*'; '*koma man til mîn feigðin*, hvar sem ek em staddr, ef
mer verðr þess *auðit*', Nialss. pp. 10. 23. 62. 103. So in Swed.
and Dan. folksongs: '*detta var mig spâdt uti min barndom*,'
Arvidss. 2, 271. '*hver skal nyde skiebnen sin*,' Danske V. 1,
193.

The same with our MHG. poets: '*swaz sich sol füegen*, wer
mac daz understên (what is to happen, who can hinder)?' Nib.
1618, 1. '*swaz geschehen sol*, daz füeget sich,' what shall be,
will be, Frauend. '*dâ sterbent wan die veigen*,' there die (none)
but the fey, Nib. 149, 2. '*ez sterbent niuwan die veigen*, die
lægen doch dâ heime tôt,' would lie dead though at home,
Wigal. 10201. '*di veigen fielen dar nider*,' Lampr. 2031. 'hin-
nerstirbet niman wan di *veigen*,' Pf. Chuonr. 8403. 'then *veigen*
mac nieman behuoten, thiu erthe ne mag in niht ûf gehaven
(hold up), scol er tha werthen geslagen, er sturve (would die)
thoh thaheime,' Fr. belli 42ᵇ. '*swie ringe er ist, der veige man,
in mac ros noch enkan niht vürbaz getragen*,' the fey man, however light, no horse can carry farther, Karl 72ᵇ. Rol. 207, 24.
'*die veigen muosen ligen tôt*,' Livl. chron. 59ᵇ. '*der veigen* mac
keiner genesen,' none recover, ib. 78ᵃ. '*ich ensterbe niht vor
minem tac* (day),' Herb. 53ᵈ. '*nieman sterben sol wan zu sînem
gesatten zil* (goal),' Ulr. Trist. 2308. '*daz aver* (whatever) scol
werden, daz *nemac nieman erwenden* (avert),' Diut. 3, 71. 'ge-
mach erwenden niht enkan swaz dem man *geschehen sol*,' Troj.
58ᶜ. '*daz muose wesen* (what had to be), daz geschach,' Orl.
11167. '*swaz geschehen sol*, daz geschiht.' Freid. 132ᵇ. MS. 1,
66ᵃ. 71ᵇ. '*daz solt elit sin*, nu ist ez geschehen,' MS. 74ᵃ. 80ᵃ.
'*ez geschiht niht wan daz sol geschehen*,' Lanz. 6934. '*ez

Oðinn says (62ᵇ), that Gefjon knows the world's destiny (aldar örlög) equally with
himself. Among men, particular heroes and priests spy out the secrets of the
future, preëminently Grípir (p. 94); to women, to priestesses, belonged the gift of
divination.

ergât doch niht, wan *als ez sol,*' Trist. 6776. 'tot avenra qan-
que *doit avenir,*' Ogier 7805. ' bin ich *genislich,* sô genise ich,'
if I was made to live thro' it, I shall, A. Heinr. 190. 'swaz ich
getuon (do), bin ich *genislich,* ich genise wol; bin ich dem valle
ergeben (doomed to fall), so n' hilfet mich mîn woltuon nicht ein
hâr,' MS. 2, 129ª. 'ez *muose sin,* und ez was mir *beschaffen,*' it
was to be, was shaped for me (134ᵇ). ' diu maget was in *beschaffen,*' that girl was cut out for you, Wigal. 1002. 'ez was im
beslaht (destined),' Eracl. 2394. 'swaz ist *geschaffen* (shapen),
daz muoz geschehen,' MsH. 3, 434ᵇ. 'nu mir daz was *in teile,*'
well, that was in my lot (portion), En. 11231. ' ez was *enteile* uns
getän,' Herb. 18418. 'ez ist mich *angeborn,*' I was born to it,
Herb. 6ᵉ.—The words *geschaffen, beschaffen* and *beslaht* are identical with the ON. *skapat* and *œtlat,* and this sameness of the
words testifies to their original connexion with the heathen doctrine. Even at the present day the fatalist view prevails largely
among the common people (Jul. Schmidt pp. 91. 163). 'ez müste
mir sein *gemacht* gewesen,' must have been made for me, Sieben
ehen eines weibes, p. 211. 'fatum in vulgari dicitur "'tis *allotted*
unto me (*bescheert,* my share)"; ego autem addo "allotting and
deserving run alway side by side."' Sermones disc. de tempore,
sermo 21. ' was *bescheert* ist, entläuft nicht,' Schweinichen 3,
249 (see Suppl.).[1]

Now, in themselves, the gifts of destiny would include every
earthly blessing. But gradually men began ascribing whatever
in human life seemed bane or blessing (excepting birth and
death) to a separate being: thus the Greeks and Romans, in
addition to μοῖρα and fatum, held by an independent Τύχη and
Fortuna.

Müllenhoff in the Nordalbingia p. 11 (conf. Schlesw. holst.
sagen xliv) infers from the name of a place *Welanao,* occurring
in Ansgar (Pertz 2, 687-99), an OS. god *Welo,* AS. *Wela,* the
very thing I had had in my mind (p. 163): an older god of *weal*
in the place of the later goddess Sâlida, Sælde. But instead of
his interpretation Welanaha, I should prefer Welan-owa, which
is supported by the more modern Welnau, a place that stood on

---

[1] The same belief is held by the Lithuanians and Lettons, fate they call *likkimas
liktens,* from lik-t to lay down, arrange: ' tai buwo jo likkims,' ' tas jau bija win-
nam liktz,' that was destined for him.

the right bank of the Elbe near Itzehoe, the river Stör having
apparently formed the 'aue, ea'; Welan-owa would then be
uniform with Wunschesouwa and Pholesouwa (p. 600). The
great thing is, first to establish from other sources the personality
of *Welo*, which the quotations from the Heliand fail to do, for
welanowa taken simply as isle of luck (Atterbom's lycksalighetens
ö) is quite compatible with the old ways of thinking: Reichenau
(augia dives) has much the same meaning, and in the vicinity of
Welnau has arisen Glückstadt. In the AS. '*welan* bewunden'
(Gramm. 4, 752), wela is used, though mythically, yet not of a
person but a thing: God himself sits 'welan bewunden,' Adam
and Eve stand 'mid welan bewunden,' wrapt in splendour, in
bliss, Cædm. 42, 2. 27, 19. But the 'gold *welan* bewunden'
forms a contrast to the 'gold *galdre* bewunden,' a holy divine
power is imagined confronting that of sorcery; and this *wela*
does seem to lead up to *Wela*, as the kindred notion of *wunsch*
to *Wunsch*.

The ON. distinguishes its fem. heill (felicitas) from a neut. heil
(omen), so does the AS. its hælu f. (salus) from hæl n. (omen),
and the OHG. its heilî f. (salus) from heil n. (omen). Both
meanings are combined in MHG. heil n. Personifications of
this I scarcely know, unless such be intended by a passage
obscure to me, Ottoc. 683[b], which gives out as a common proverb: 'chum *hail* hauenstain!' In MS. 2, 130[b]: 'waz ob iuwer
heil eime andern kumet an sîn seil,' what if your hap prove
another's hanging? And so early as O. ii. 18, 7: 'thaz *heil* ni
gifâhit iuwih,' luck comes not your way (see Suppl.).

On the other hand, it is the commonest thing with our 13th
cent. poets to treat *sælde* (fortuna) as a female person, and that
apparently not in imitation of the Romance writings: even the
OHG. *sâlida* occurs with the like import, and the compound
huilsâlida (supra p. 857) was a stronger expression of the same
thing. O. i. 26, 4 speaking of the baptism of Christ in the
water, uses a remarkable phrase, to which no church writer could
have prompted him: 'sîd *wachêta* allên mannon thiu *Sâlida* in
thên undon.' Waking presupposes life. The personification
comes out still more clearly in poets four centuries after him:
'unser *Sælde wachet*,' Parz. 550, 10. 'mîn sorge slâfet, sô dîn
Sælde wachet,' Tit. 31, 3. 'z'aller zît des *S. wachet*,' MS. 1, 16[b].

'unser *S.* diu wil *wachen*,' Trist. 9430. 'des noch sîn *S. wachet*,' Ernst. 5114. 'ir *S. wachet*,' Amgb. 35ᵃ. 'daz mir *S. wache*,' ib. 43ᵃ. 'ich wæn sîn *S. slâfe*,' ib. 44ᵃ. 'sô ist im al diu *S. ertaget* (dawned),' Trist. 9792. 'diu S. ist dir *betaget*,' Wartb. kr. jen. 21. 'diu S. was mit im *betaget*,' Dietr. 5ᵃ. 27ᵃ. 'iuwer *S.* wirt *erwecket*,' Lohengr. 19. Observe in these MHG. quotations the frequent poss. pron.[1] or gen. case : the Sælde dedicates herself to certain men, protects and prospers them, *wakes for them while they sleep*, as we say 'luck came to me in my sleep.' A mode of speech so common need not always be felt to personify : 'daz im sîn heil niht slief,' Troj. 9478. 'dâ wachet schande, und slæft daz heil,' Zauberbecher (magic bowl) 1113. 'Tristans gelücke dâ niht slief,' Heinr. Tr. 2396. It was even extended to other notions of the same kind : 'wachet sîn êre und ouch sîn lop,' honour, praise, Amgb. 47ᵃ. 'ir milte wachet,' ib. 12ᵇ. 'ir genâde (kindness) mir muoz wachen,' MS. 1, 33ᵃ. 'ich wæne an ir ist genâde entslâfen (asleep), daz ich ir leider niht erwecken kan,' MS. 1, 48ᵃ. 'du (minne) bist gegen mir hart entslâfen,' MS. 1, 60ᵃ. 'mîn schade wachet,' Ben. 121. 'dîn kraft mit ellen dô niht slief,' Parz. 85, 24. We still say, 'treason sleeps not'; and some phrases of this sort can have a personal sense. The heathen colouring of Sælde's *waking* and *being waked* I infer chiefly from the analogous 'vekja Hildi' noticed on p. 422, who not only was awaked, but herself awoke the heroes (Sn. 164). And 'vilbiörg scal vaka,' Sæm. 46ᵃ, may bear the same meaning : we can translate it 'jucunda salus,' or suppose it a proper noun. Frôði makes Fenja and Menja (p. 531) grind gold, peace and happiness (gull, frið oc sælu), allowing them but scanty rest at night : they *wake* to grind *prosperity* for him, and afterwards misfortune (salt) for Mýsîngr, Sn. 146-7 (see Suppl.).

And this is far from being the only way personification is applied to her. Sælde is called *frau*, she appears, meets, bends her face toward her favourites, hearkens to them (as a god hears prayer), smiles on them, greets them, is kind and obliging, but can be cross ; those whom she dislikes, she forgets, shuns, flees, runs away from,[2] turns her back upon ; she has a door and a

---

[1] So : 'des sî mîn *S.* gein iu bote,' Parz. 416, 4. 'des sol mîn *S.* pfant sîn,' be pledge thereof, Frauend. 23. 'lât dir'z dîn *S.* wol gezemen,' MS. 2, 252ᵃ.
[2] This *escaping* is the same thing as the ON. hverfa (evanescere): *heillir*

road. Here again old Otfrid leads the way (ii. 7, 20): 'thiu
Sálida in thar *gaganta*' (eis occurrit). Walther sings 55, 35:
'*frô Sœlde* teilet umbe sich (scatters gifts around), und *kêret mir
den rügge zuo* (turns her back), sie stêt ungerne *gegen mir*, si n'
ruochet (recks) mich *niht an gesehen*'; and 43, 5: 'mîn *frou S.*,
wie si mîn *vergaz !*' '*vrô S.* hât in an sich genomen, wil dîn
pflegen (cherish),' Ecke 10, 160. 'ob *vrouwe S.* mînes heiles
welle ruochen,' Ben. 425. 'die wîle es *mîn S.* ruochte,' Parz.
689, 20. 'hæte mir diu *S. ir ôre baz geneiget,*' inclined her ear,
MS. 2, 220ᵇ. 'dô was mir *S. entrunnen,*' Parz. 689, 8. '*S.* was
sîn *geleite,*' conductress, Wigal. 8389. '*frou S. ir* was *bereit,*'
ready to help, Er. 3459; and perhaps we ought to add what
follows: 'diu Gotes *hövescheit* ob mîner frowen *swebte,*' God's
kindness over my lady hovered; for so hover the valkyrs over
the heroes they befriend. 'Got wîse mich der *Sœlden wege,*'
guide me on Fortune's way, Parz. 8, 16. 'den vuoz (foot) setzen
in der *S. pfat,*' Ben. 306. '*frowe S.* muoz in ûf ir *strâze* wîsen,'
Tit. 5218. 'der *Sœlden stîc,*' path, Karl 19ᵇ. 'über *frô S. stec*
gân,' Fragm. 46ᵃ. 'tuo mir ûf (open) der *S. tür !*' MS. 1, 36ᵃ.
'der *S. porte,*' A. Heinr. 243, 33. 'der *S. tür* besliezen,' shut,
MsH. 3, 336ᵃ. 'setzen zuo der *S. tür,*' Zauberb. 1150. 'den
begiuzet *S. vluot,*' flood, MsH. 3, 205ᵃ. '*Sœlde* und ir *gesinde*
(household) walt ir,' MS. 1, 88ᵇ. 'diu *Sálde folget* sînen vanen,'
follows his banners, Lampr. 2089. 'mir enwil diu *S.* ninder
folgen einen fuoz,' Ben. 367. 'mir ist diu *S. gram,*' unfriendly,
Gregor 2390. 'diu *S.* was ime *gram,*' Diut. 1, 10. Athis D. 84.
'diu *S. vliuhet* (flees) von mir,' Greg. 1526. 'diu *S.* hât mich
verlân,' Karl 95ᵃ. 'diu *S.* hât si *besezzen,*' possessed her, Wigal.
884. 'diu *S.* het ir *gesworn*' 941. 'diu *S.* het zuo im *gesworn*
zeim stæten ingesinde,' to be his steadfast follower, Lanz. 1561.
'der *Sœlden spil,*' game, Wigal. 8761. 9271. 9386. 'diu *gespil*
der *S.,*' playmate 10532. 'swes diu *S. ze gesellen* gert,' desires
as companion 945. 'im gab diu *S. ir hantgift,*' Silv. 534. 'diu
S. vlôz im in den munt' 1024. 'ez rîse (drop) ûf dich der *S.
tuft*' 1389. 'so grüenet *dîner S. rîs,*' spray, MsH. 2, 258ᵃ.
'*frouwe S. lachet mir,*' laughs, Ernst 4334. 'daz dir *frô S. lache,*
und al dîn heil *bewache,*' Silv. 2565. '*Fortûne* wolt im dô niht

horfnar (felicitates evanitae), Sæm. 98ᵃ. 'swi ime di Sâlden *volgen,* werdent si ime
verbolgen, si ne *kêren sornliche wider,*' once offended, they come not back, Al. 6189.

mê genædeclîchen (graciously) *lachen*,' Troj. 5754. 'sô decket
uns der *S. huot*,' hood, hat, Winsbekin 45, 7: a wishing-cap.
'daz inch *frouwe S.* müeze *behüllen*' (fovere), Lohengr. 101:
behüllen prob. in its literal sense, to wrap, to clothe, as Walther
43, 1 and 7 makes frô Sælde *kleiden* (clothe) people, and *schrôten*
(cut out) for them ; she cuts out sorrow and high courage. And
so, no doubt, under many more aspects, which we can guess from
our present figures of speech: 'fortune favours, visits, pursues
him,' etc. etc. And here again we find, even in old poets, the
more vague neuter: 'gelücke hât den nuwen gegen mir gekêrt,'
turned its back toward me, LS. 1, 238; 'hât den nuwen noch
gegen mir endecket; enblecket gên mir sînen zan (bared its
teeth, gnashed); het zer rechten hende griffen' 3, 539. 'dô
kêrte von im unde vlôch gelücke,' Troj. 5750. We say 'my
fortune blooms, grows,' as though it were attached to a tree
or herb: 'mein glücke das blühete mir,' Schweinichen 1, 170.
'gelücke wahset mit genuht,' Troj. 5686. 'uns ist niht wol
erschozen gelücke' 12438. 'Got wil uns sælde lâzen wahsen,'
Lohengr. 66. The proverb ' das glück kommt von ungefähr wol
über neunzig stauden her,' Simplic. 2, 158, well expresses the
suddenness and surprise, the windfall nature of luck, to which
are owing the very names of $\tau\acute{u}\chi\eta$ (from $\tau\upsilon\chi\epsilon\hat{\imath}\nu$, $\tau\upsilon\gamma\chi\acute{a}\nu\epsilon\iota\nu$) and
fortuna (from fors). Very likely some of the phrases quoted
above have come to us from the ancients, or they had them in
common with us (see Suppl.).

The tale of the Wunderer (wonder-worker, Etzels hofh. 208),
makes *frau Sœlde* a *king's daughter* with three miraculous gifts,
(1) that of knowing a man's thoughts, (2) of blessing warriors
against wounds in battle, (3) of transporting herself whither she
will (24—26). Who can fail to detect in this the echo of an old
heathen valkyr ?

The now universally familiar image of Fortune riding *on a
rolling wheel* ($\kappa\acute{u}\lambda\iota\nu\delta\rho\sigma$),[1] which was attributed to Fors, Tyche
and Nemesis (O. Müller's Archäol. 607), is, I consider, an im-
portation. ' Versatur celeri *Fors* levis *orbe rotae*,' Tibull. i. 5, 70.
' *stans in orbe dea*,' Ov. ep. ex Ponto ii. 3, 56. '*Fortunae rotam*
pertimescebat,' Cic. in Pison. 10. '*rota Fortunae*,' Tac. de orat.

---

[1] A different thing therefore from the wheel that Krodo and Vishnu *carry in
the hand* (p. 248-9).

23. 'assumptus in amplissimum Fortunae fastigium, *versabiles* ejus *motus* expertus est, qui ludunt mortalitatem, nunc *evehentes* quosdam in sidera, nunc ad Cocyti profunda *mergentes*,' Amm. Marc. 14, 11 : '*Fortunae volucris rota* adversa prosperis semper alternans' 31, 1. '*Fortunae* te regendum dedisti, dominae moribus oportet obtemperes, tu vero *volventis rotae* impetum retinere conaris ? Si manere incipit, *Fors* esse desistit,' Boëth. de consol. ii. pr. 1. Notker cap. 25. '*rotam volubili orbe* versamus (says Fortuna of herself), infima summis, summa infimis mutare gaudemus. *ascende* si placet, sed ea lege uti ne, cum ludicri mei ratio poscet, *descendere* injuriam putes,' ib. ii. pr. 2.—There seem to be two separate images here : one, that of the goddess herself standing or sitting[1] on the revolving wheel,[2] and so whirling by in breathless haste; the other, that she makes the favoured ones ascend the wheel, and the unlucky ones descend, those soar aloft, these hang below. Our poems of the Mid. Ages often speak in general terms of the *rat* (wheel) or *schîbe* (disc, orb) of Fortune, of luck, of Sælde : '*orbita Fortunae* ducit utroque rotam (a better reading : utramque viam),' Reinh. 1, 1494. '*volubilis Fortunae rota*,' Rodulfus chron. Trudonis, p. 381. '*rota Fortunae*,' Radevicus 1, 40. 'swaz ie geschiht, daz stât an *glückes rade*,' whatever happens rests on fortune's wheel, Freid. 110, 17. 'daz im der *sælekeit rat* mit willen umbe lief,' Troj. 9471 ; 'jâ walzet ir *gelückes rat* vil stæteclich ûf und nider, her und hin, dan und wider loufet ez,' her (i.e. Sælde's) wheel of luck rolls right steadfastly,[3] etc. 2349. 'im dienet daz *gelückes rat*, daz im nâch êren umbe lief' 7229. '*gelückes rat* louft uns die sumer und die winder,' Lohengr. 119. '*min schibe* gât ze wunsche,' Ben. 353 ; 'dem gêt *sin schibe* enzelt,' 360. 'wol gie (or, gie für sich) *ir schibe*,' Lohengr. 146. 189. 'si vuoren (they rode) ûf *gelückes rade*,' Flore 844. '*Sælde* diu ist sinewel (sphe-

---

[1] Pentam. 5, 9 has also a 'vecchia *seduta ncoppa na rota*' as Fortuna.

[2] The mere turning of a wheel (daz *sueibônta rad*, N. Boëth. 47) may, quite apart from the goddess, suggest the mutability of fate. When Cyrus saw a captive king attentively watch the rising and falling spokes of wheels, and inquired the reason, the latter replied, that they put him in mind of the instability of life, πῶς τὰ κάτω ἄνω γίνονται, καὶ τὰ ἄνω κάτω (Cedrenus, ed. Paris, 142).

[3] This is contrary to James I. of Scotl.'s idea : 'the *sudden* sweltering of that ilk wheel .... so *tolter* whilom did she it to-wry (twist about).' But it seems the prevailing one here, unless 'sin schîbe gêt *en-zelt*' (3 lines lower) mean 'goes tolter,' tolutans, ambling, as zelter is an ambler. Further on, 'mich hin verdrücke,' push me off, need not imply a waddling movement.—TRANS.

rical), und walzet umb als ein *rat*,' Uebel wîp 241. ' der *Sœlden
schiben* trîben,' Amis 2053. '*entschiben*,' Ulr. Trist. 708. Yet
that ascending and descending is often mentioned too : ' sô stîge
ich ûf, und ninder abe,' never down, Parz. 9, 22. ' gelücke ist
rehte als ein *bal*, swer stîget der sol vürhten val,' who climbs
must fear a fall, Freid. 115, 27. ' sô hangen ich an dem *rades*
teile (limb), dâ maneger hanget âne trôst (without hope),' Ben.
88 ; ' ê daz der *Sœlden schibe* mich hin verdrücke gar zuo der
verzalten schar ' 91. ' si waren hôhe gar gestigen (mounted
high) ûf des . . . *gelückes rat*, nû müezens leider von der stat aber
nider rücken (move down again),' Flore 6148. ' swer hiute sitzet
ûf dem rade, der sîget morgen drunder (sinks under it to-morrow),'
Troj. 18395. ' er ist komen *ûf gelückes rat*, daz muoz im immer
stille stân,' Geo. 193. ' *gelückes rat*, wenne sol ich mîne stat ûf
dir vinden ? ' Ben. 306. ' swebe oben an der *Sœlichkeit rade*,'
Zauberb. 1860. ' Got werfe in von (hurl him from) *gelückes rat* !'
Kolocz. 74. ' *gelückes rait* geit up ind neder, ein velt (one falls),
der ander stiget weder,' Hagen's Cöln. chr. 1770. ' *gelückes rat*
nu rîde in ûf die hœhe,' turn (writhe) him up aloft, Tit. 5218 ;
' *gelücke, dîn rat* nu rîde ! ' 5275. ' *Fortûna* diu ist sô getân, ir
schibe lâzet si umbe gân, umbe loufet ir *rat*, dicke vellet der da
vaste saz,' oft falleth he that sat there fast, Lampr. Alex. 3066.[1]
This notion carried into detail shews us four (or twelve) men at
once standing on fortune's wheel in ceaseless revolution : ' *gelückes rat* treit vier man, der eine stîget ûf, der ander stîget abe,
der dritte ist obe, der vierde der ist under,' MS. 2, 221ª; and
Wigal. p. 41 tells us of one who had in his house such a *wheel*
cast *of gold*, and who was always happy (like Frode with his mill
of luck, which also went round): ' ein rat enmitten ûf dem sal,
daz gie ûf und ze tal (down) ; da wâren bilde gegozzen an (molten
images thereon), iegelîchez geschaffen als ein man. hie sigen diu
(sank these) mit dem rade nider, sô stigen (mounted) diu ander
ûf wider. daz was des *gelückes rat*.' [2] In Renart le nouvel 7941
—8011, Fortune lifts the fox on to her wheel, and promises not
to turn it. Hence too the story of the twelve landsknechts or

---

[1] Conf. the passage on *la roe de la Fortune* in the Jeu d'Adan (Théâtre français au moyen âge p. 82).
[2] From this wheel, which Wigalois wore on his helmet (1862—6), came the
name of *Ritter mit dem rad* (already in Gildas of Banchor ' miles quadrigae '), not
from the adventure he had to brook with a brazen wheel (pp. 252—4 of the poem).

Johanneses on *fortune's wheel*, Deut. sag. nos. 209. 337. Our Sælde is never painted *blind* or blindfolded [1] (see Suppl.).

What seems to me to be far more significant than this wheel, which probably the Sâlida of our heathen forefathers never had (a whole carriage to herself would be more in their way), is the circumstance of her *adopting children*, owning her favourites for her sons : 'ich bin ouch in *frô Sælden schôz geleit*,' laid in her lap. Fragm. 45ᵇ. To be a *darling of fortune*, a *child of luck*, to *sit in fortune's lap*, implies previous adoption (Goth. frasti-sibja, Rom. 9, 4), conf. RA. 160. 463-4. A select being like this is called ' der *Sælden barn*,' Barl. 37, 36. 191, 38. Engelh. 5070. ' Artûs der *S. kint*,' Zauberb. 1433. ' *S. kint* hât S. stift ' 1038. ' Maria der *S. kint*,' Wartb. kr. jen. 56. 'ir sît gezelt gelücke ze *ingesinde* (as inmate), dem heile ze *liebem kinde*,' Warnung 2596. ' Si ist *S. sundertriutel* (fondling), in der würzegarten kan si brechen ir rôsen,' MS. 1, 88ᵃ. Now, as Wuotan can take the place of the gifting norn (p. 858), so he can that of Sælde; he is himself the bestower of all bliss, he takes up children to his bosom. Altogether identical therefore with Sælden barn must be ' des *Wunsches barn*, an dem der *Wunsch* was volle varn,' on whom Wish had perfectly succeeded, Orl. 3767. A child of luck has ' des *Wunsches segen*,' Lanz. 5504. For more references, see pp. 138—144.[2] Accordingly *Sâlida* can be regarded as a mere emanation of Wuotan (see Suppl.).

Such a child of luck was Fortunatus, to whom *Fortuna* (conf. Felicia, MsH. 2, 10ᵇ and infra ch. XXXII.) appears in a forest of Bretagne, and gives a fairy purse : and who also wins the *wishing-cap* (souhaitant chapeau), the tarn-cap, which one has only to put on, to be in a twinkling at some distant place. Evidently a hat of *Wish* or *Wuotan* (p. 463), a πέτασος or winged cap of *Hermes* the giver of all good, of all sælde. And ' Sælde's hat' is expressly mentioned : ' sô *decket* uns der *Sælden huot*, daz uns dehein weter selwen mac,' no weather can befoul us, MsH. 3, 466ᵃ. The never empty purse I connect with the goddess's horn of plenty : ' mundanam *cornucopiam* Fortuna gestans,' Amm.

---

[1] Nor is she called *glesin*, like the Lat. Fortuna *vitrea;* Gottfrid of Strassburg alone (MS. 2, 45ᵇ) has ' daz *glesin glücke*,' and we have now the proverb ' luck and crock are easy broke.'

[2] I find also a proper name Seldenbot = Sælde's messenger, Weisth. 3, 277-8.

Marc. 22, 9. 'formatum Fortunae habitum cum *divite cornu*,' Prudent. lib. 1 contra Symm.; also with Amalthea's horn or Svantovit's (p. 591), nay with the κέρας σωτηρίας, Luke 1, 69. Of the wishing-rod we are reminded by the synonymous expressions: 'alles heiles ein *wünschel-ris*,' -twig, -wand, Troj. 2216, and 'des *Wunsches* bluome,' Barl. 274, 25.

The belief in *fairy things* [wünscheldinge, lit. wishing-gear] is deeply rooted in our mythology: let us examine it minutely. There are things, belonging to gods, but also lent to men, which can bestow a plenitude of bliss, the best that heart can *wish*; so that our old vernacular word seems quite appropriate. The Sanskrit for wish is significant: *mano-ratha*, wheel of the mind; does this open to us a new aspect of the divine wish? *Wish* turns the wheel of our thoughts. In the Edda the wishing-gear is the cunning workmanship of dwarfs, and is distributed among the gods. Oðinn possessed the spear *Gúngnir*, the hurling of which brings victory, Thôrr the hammer *Miölnir*, which comes crashing down as thunderbolt, which also consecrates, and *of itself comes back* into his hand. Freyr had a *sword* of similar nature, that *swung itself* (er siâlft vegiz), Saem. 82ᵃ. Sn. 40; its name is unrecorded. The 'cudgel jump out o' your sack!' in our fairy-tale is the same story vulgarized; in Œgi's hall the pitchers or beakers of ale *brought themselves* (siâlft barsc þar öl), Saem. 48; Wolfdieterich (Cod. dresd. 296-7) fell in with goddesses, to whose table the wheaten *loaf came walking*, and the *wine poured itself out*: such gear the Greeks called αὐτόματον (self-taught), Il. 18, 376. *Œgis-hialmr* must originally have been Œgi's own (and Œgir is at times undistinguishable from Oðinn), as Aegis is wielded by the two highest deities Zeus and Athena: afterwards the helmet came into the hand of heroes. Out of the magic helm sprang *helot-helm, grim-helm, tarn-kappe, wunsch-mantel* (Kinderm. no. 122), *wunsch-hut*, which bestow on dwarfs, heroes and fortune's favourites the power to walk unseen, to sail swiftly through the sky. To the goddesses Freyja and Frigg belonged *Brîsinga men*, which, like the ἱμάς of Venus and Juno, awakened longing (ἵμερος), and matches the sword, spear and hammer of the gods (p. 885). On the veil or hood of the goddess Sif grew golden hair, as corn does on the earth: its proper name is not given. *Skiðblaðnir* is described,

now as a ship, now as a hat, both of which could either be folded
up or expanded, for sailing in or for raising a storm; *wishing-
ships* occur in Norske eventyr 1, 18. 142 and Sv. folkv. 1, 142-3.
Not unlike this are our *winged sandals* and *league boots*. *Gullin-
bursti*, too, Frey's boar, carries him through air and water.
From Oðin's ring *Draupnir* dropped other rings as heavy; the
miraculous power of Fulla's ring (Fullo fîngrgull, Sn. 68) is not
specified, perhaps it made one invisible, like that of Aventiure
(p. 911). Draupnir suggests the *broodpenny* (Deut. sag. no. 86)
or *hatching dollar* of later times: whoever ate the bird's heart,
would find a gold-piece under his pillow every morning. With
this are connected the *wishing-purse*, and the *wishing-rod*, which
unlocks the hoard, but apparently feeds it as well (ch. XXXI);
also the *wunderblume* and the *springwurzel* [root which springs
open the door of a treasure]; a *bird's nest* makes invisible (Deut.
s. no. 85. Haupt's Zeitschr. 3, 361. Mone's Anz. 8, 539).
Fróði's *wishing-mill* Grôtti would grind anything the grinder
wished for aloud (Sn. 146), gold, salt, etc.; this we can match
with the *wheel of fortune*, an image that may be an importation
to us (p. 866), yet not have been strange to our remote ancestry;
of manoratha I have spoken before. British legend too had
its own version of fortune's wheel (p. 869). Such a mill, such
a wheel ought above all to grind food for gods. The gods
possess the *drink of immortality*, which inspires man with song,
and keeps a god young. Iðun's *apples* restore youth, as *apples*
in Völsûngasaga make pregnant, in Sneewitchen send sleep, and
in Fortunatus give horns and take them away. But the wishing-
cloak becomes a *wishing-cloth*, which when spread brings up any
dish one may desire: in Danish and Swedish songs such a cloth
is woven of field wool (*ageruld*, D. vis. 1, 265. 300. *åkerull*, Sv.
vis. 2, 199), a sort of grass with a woolly flower (eriophorum
polystachium); the same wishing-cloth occurs in Norske ev. 1,
44. 274, it is pulled *out of a mare's ear*, p. 112. Other *wishing-
cloths* have to be spun in silence, or the hemp for them must be
picked, baked, braked, hatchelled, spun and woven all in one
day. The Servians tell of a *miraculous cow, out of whose ear*
yarn is spun, she is then killed and buried, and miracles are
wrought on her grave. A wishing-cow *Kâmaduh* or *Kâmadhenu*
is mentioned in Indian myth (Pott 2, 421. Somadeva 1, 198);

a *wishing-goat*, who procures money, in the Norw. tales 1, 45;
an *ass* in Pentam. 1, 1. The machandelbom (juniper) in our
fairy-tale is a *wishing-tree*, so is that from which Cinderella
shakes down all her splendid dresses; the Indians call it *kalpa
vriksha* (tree of wishes) or *Manoratha-dayaka* (wish-giving),
Somadeva 2, 84. Beside the dresses of sun and moon, the
gold-hen and seven chickens (p. 728) are contained in the nut.
Fortuna carries a *horn of plenty* (p. 870). The goat Amaltheia's
horn supplied the nymphs who had nursed Zeus with all they
wished for; another legend makes the nymph Amaltheia possess
a bull's horn, which gave in abundance all manner of *meat* and
drink that one could wish. A Scottish tradition has it, that
if any one can approach a banquet of the fairies, take away their
drinking-bowl or *horn*, and carry it across a running stream
without spilling, it will be to him a cornucopia of good fortune;
if he break it, his good days are done (R. Chambers pp. 32-3).
We know that wise-women and elfins offer *drinking-horns* to men
(p. 420); that jewels of the elves (like those of the smith dwarfs)
ensure luck to human families, viz. their *sword, ring* and *goblet*
(p. 457); that the swan left in Loherangrîn's family a *sword,
horn* and *fingerling* (ring, Parz. 826. 19). Oberon's *horn*, and
he is of elf kind, was a *wishing-horn*, and excited magic dancing.
Other wonders are wrought by the *harps* of gods and heroes
(p. 907). The elves, beside the horn, have in their gift a *bread*
of grace that blesses. By the side of this may stand the beautiful myths of the *cruse of oil* that never runs dry, the savoury
pottage that brims over, the *yarn* that has never done winding.
Jemshid's goblet too was a miraculous one, so was the far-famed
Grail (greal, Ducange sub v. gradalus, graletus, grasala, grassale,
grassellus), that nourished and healed, which Romance legend took
up and interwined with christian, as indeed the spear of Longinus
and the bleeding lance are very like a heathen wishing-spear;
nails of the true cross are worked up into bridles that bring
victory (El. xxii), wood of the cross and a thousand relics are
applied to thaumaturgic uses (ch. XXXVI), rings and precious
stones were held against a relic, that its virtue might pass into
them; precious stones themselves are in a sense *wishing-stones,*
such to the Indians was *Divyaratna* (Pott 2, 421), which fulfilled
all the wishes of its owner. And the Grail cannot be more

CPSIA information can be obtained
at www.ICGtesting.com
Printed in the USA
BVHW091045080222
628387BV00001B/55